A History of
Presbyterian Missions

A History of
Presbyterian Missions
1944–2007

EDITED BY

Scott W. Sunquist
and
Caroline N. Becker

A Project of the World Mission Initiative
of Pittsburgh Theological Seminary

Geneva Press
Louisville, Kentucky

Scripture quotations from the New Revised Standard Version of the Bible are copyright © 1989 by the Division of Christian Education of the National Council of the Churches of Christ in the U.S.A. and are used by permission.

Book design by Sharon Adams
Cover design by Night & Day Design
Cover art: The Glory of the Cross, *Sawai Chinnawong. This painting by an ethnic Mon artist from northern Thailand at the McGilvary College of Divinity represents a major theme of this book: the transition of Christian leadership to local leadership, while show-ing respect for the past missionaries.*

First edition
Published by Geneva Press
Louisville, Kentucky

This book is printed on acid-free paper that meets the American National Standards Insti-tute Z39.48 standard. ∞

PRINTED IN THE UNITED STATES OF AMERICA

08 09 10 11 12 13 14 15 16—10 9 8 7 6 5 4 3 2 1

Library of Congress Cataloging-in-Publication Data

A history of Presbyterian missions : 1944–2007 / edited by Scott W. Sunquist and Caroline N. Becker.—1st ed.
     p. cm.
  Includes bibliographical references and index.
  ISBN 978-0-664-50300-0 (alk. paper)
  1. Presbyterian Church (U.S.A.)—Missions—History—20th century.
2. Presbyterian Church (U.S.A.)—Missions—History—21st century. I. Sunquist, Scott W., 1953–   II. Caroline Becker.
  BV2570.H57   2008
  266'.5109—dc22

                                                    2007046196

This book is dedicated to Lois Anderson,
wife of William Anderson, and their daughter,
Zelda White, who were both shot and killed in a carjacking
near Nairobi, Kenya, January 27, 2007.

It is hard to imagine that God has created a person who had
more joy in the Lord, trust in other people, and love
for the people of Africa than Lois Anderson.

To the memory of Lois, her daughter, Zelda, and all the other missionaries
and missionary families who have laid down their lives for their friends,
we dedicate this volume.

Precious in the sight of the LORD is the death of his saints.
Psalm 116:15 RSV

Contents

Foreword

You are about to read a Christian love story. American Presbyterians have been caught up in God's love for the world, and so we have formed enduring relationships that witness to that love in scores of countries.

Our relationships and witness have been tested, and this book's review of a sixty-year period provides a breathtaking summary of the tests. Our.mission relationships have gone through decolonization and nationalism, the rise of the United States to superpower status, official repression of Christ's disciples in many lands, widespread movements for equality and social justice, declines in U.S. mainline church membership, denominational unions, and experiments in organizational and funding systems, to name some major examples.

Through it all, one constant that emerges clearly in these pages is the steadfastness of a love that has repeatedly moved U.S. Presbyterians, sometimes in considerable anguish, to a new level of creativity and adaptability. This was true of their mission workers as well as the people who sent them, and true also of many of the other dimensions that make up a denomination. Perhaps the most dramatic example of a loving willingness to change for the sake of witness was the move so many mission workers made in this period from a decision-making role as a missionary to a more servant-like role as a fraternal worker or mission coworker. They embraced this challenging life change, and for that they deserved more affirmation than they often received back in their U.S. context. There are many other examples of bold adaptability for the sake of God's love in mission, including the development of new patterns of mission service such as binational service and bringing people in mission to the United States; the founding of new mission-support organizations, mission networks, and grassroots international mission partnerships to mobilize grassroots church involvement; the creation of new offerings and programs to mobilize support; and generous and strategic responses to the opening up of large unevangelized territories, especially after the Cold War.

It is good to consider how best to approach reading this Christian love story. Because it is a collective story, I recommend that you find others with whom to read it. Look for other persons, ideally in your own congregation, who care about the church of Jesus Christ and its manner of participating in God's ministry of reconciliation and redemption in the whole world. Since the book is long, you might divide up the geographic chapters among you, each choosing regions of the world about which you have special feelings. Pose for yourselves the same kinds of questions that led to the creativity and commitment about which you will read: "In what ways will we as Christ's church witness to all nations in light of the major dynamics in the world today?" "In what specific ways can my congregation and denomination improve ourselves and our manner of involvement?" You have in your hands not only a book, but also a way to begin a dialogue with the written and human resources available today concerning these two questions.

Everything you will read about here happened because people like yourself wanted their church to be part of God's gracious gathering of all things in creation (Eph. 1:10), and did not take that participation for granted. Please remember that the commitments to which this book leads you and your fellow believers will provide part of the Christian love story that will eventually be written about the first half of the twenty-first century!

—(The Reverend) Marian McClure, PhD, Director of the PC(USA)'s World-wide Ministries Division 1997–2006.

Acknowledgments

All projects have an inspiration and a genesis. The inspiration that led to this volume came from the committee introduced on the following pages. The first prodding came from Rev. David Dawson and Dr. Kenneth Bailey, and so we deeply acknowledge that we never would have picked up the baton had it not be thrown (actually thrust) into our hands by these two concerned gentlemen. Second, we must acknowledge the inspiration and faithfulness of the many "retired" missionaries who kept feeding us information and who in the end made this project possible by making $100 donations to be used to complete the project. The names of these people are given at the end of this section. We thank them for their faithfulness and commitment to mission and to the Presbyterian Church (U.S.A.).

We also give thanks to Dr. Don Dawson and the World Mission Initiative of Pittsburgh Theological Seminary. Funding and administration for this project came through WMI, and Don's sound leadership and helpful advice were always a much-appreciated counsel. Holly McKelvey, faculty secretary at Pittsburgh Theological Seminary, could probably now give a good critical reading of this volume since she helped with all of the surveys, worked for many days typing up the transcripts of the missionary interviews, and has been involved in most of the communications for the past three years. We greatly appreciate her faithful labors.

We thank all of these people and the hundreds of missionaries who filled out surveys, sent in writings and pictures, and participated in interview sessions. This project has come about because of the work of these people. The editors take full responsibility for the shortcomings and pray that this volume might be a stimulus to future discussion in the PC(USA) and among our ecumenical partners around the world, concerning how best to move forward in mission in positive, creative, and theologically responsible ways.

DONORS TO THE PRESBYTERIAN
MISSION HISTORY PROJECT

Griffith Theological Research
  Foundation
Rev. Priscilla Abbott
Dr. and Mrs. Paul and Lucy
  Alexander
Rev. and Mrs. Robert and Ellen Alter
Miss Lois R. Anderson
Rev. and Mrs. Frank and Hope
  Arnold
Rev. Dr. Evelyn Birkel Thompson
  Aye
Dr. and Mrs. Kenneth and Ethel
  Bailey
Rev. and Mrs. Gayle and Joy
  Beanland
Ms. Mary Anna Bode
Rev. and Mrs. Robert and Mary
  Boehlke
Mrs. Faith Bradley
Miss Patricia Coombs
Mrs. Marjorie Christy
Dr. and Mrs. Norval and Dorothy
  Christy
Miss Virginia Deter
Rev. and Mrs. Robert and Rebecca
  Dodson
Mr. and Mrs. Richard and Alma
  Gordon Dole
Dr. Forrest Eggleston
Mr. and Mrs. John and Jo Ann
  Ellington
Mr. and Mrs. Robert and Mary
  Etheridge
Mrs. Carol Fong
Miss Dorothy Gilbert
Mr. and Mrs. Eugene and Jane
  Glassman
Mr. and Mrs. Farris and Thelma
  Goodrum
Dr. and Mrs. Alan and Alma Gordon
Dr. and Mrs. John and Betsy Guyer

Rev. Dr. John Hamlin
Mr. and Mrs. Edwin and Arpine
  Hanna
Drs. J. Harold and Harriet Hanson
Ms. Virginia Henderlite
Rev. Harriet A. Johnson
Mr. Charles A. Jordan
Mrs. Merilyn Kraftenberg
Ms. Lois Kroehler
Mr. Lewis Lancaster
Rev. and Mrs. Eugene and Jeanne
  Marie Lee
Rev. Dr. and Mrs. John and Mary
  Lorimer
Ms. Susan Lorimer
Mr. and Mrs. Lee and Connie
  Lybarger
Rev. and Mrs. James and Dorothy
  McKaughan
Ms. Dorothy Miller
Mrs. Aurie Montgomery Miller
Rev. Dr. and Mrs. Robert and Pauline
  Montgomery
Mr. and Mrs. Ralph and Jane Myhre
Drs. Henry and Kathryn Nelson
Ms. Clara Olivas
Mr. and Mrs. Rodger and Josephine
  Perkins
Mr. and Mrs. James and Rachel
  Pollock
Revs. Taylor and Elizabeth Potter
Mr. and Mrs. John and Helen
  Pritchard
Ms. Agnes (Nancy) Ramer
Rev. and Mrs. Robert and Edith
  Rasmussen
Mr. and Mrs. Wade (Hap) and Doris
  Reeves
Rev. and Mrs. Homer and Natalie
  Rickabaugh
Rev. Charles Riddle

Dr. and Mrs. Jefferson and Megan
  Ritchie
Ms. Genevieve Roberts
Mr. and Mrs. John and Maxine
  Rollins
Rev. and Mrs. Charles and Nancy
  Ross
Mr. and Mrs. J. Otis and Wilma
  Rowe
Dr. and Mrs. Kenneth Scott
Mr. Robert Seel
Dr. and Mrs. Scott and Nancy
  Sunquist

Rev. and Mrs. Robert and Rowena
  Tebbe
Ms. Alberta Tedford
Drs. Stanley and Ane Marie
  Topple
Mr. and Mrs. Malcolm and Martha
  Vandevort
Ms. Laura Weaver
Dr. and Mrs. Marshall Welles
Mr. and Mrs. John and Dorothy
  Wilder
Rev. and Mrs. Bill and Judi
  Young

Abbreviations

AACC	All-Africa Conference of Churches
ABCFM	American Board of Commissioners for Foreign Missions
ACBC	Association of Costa Rican Bible Churches
ACMC	Advancing Churches in Mission Commitment
ACT	Action by Churches Together
ANC	African National Congress
AP	American Presbyterian
APCCM	Association of Presbyterians for Cross-Cultural Mission
APCM	American Presbyterian Congo Mission
APMP	Association of Presbyterian Mission Pastors
APRCLA	Alliance of Presbyterian Reformed Churches in Latin America
ASHA	American Schools and Hospitals Abroad
AUC	American University in Cairo
BFM	Board of Foreign Missions—UPCNA, UPCUSA, PCUSA
BNM	Board of National Missions
BNS	Bi-National Service
BWM	Board of World Missions—PCUS
CANACOM	Caribbean and North American Council for Mission
CAREE	Christians Associated for Relationships in Eastern Europe
CASA	Center for Arabic Study Abroad
CCAP	Church of Central Africa Presbyterian
CCC	China Christian Council
CCD	Christian Commission for Development
CCT	Church of Christ in Thailand
CELEP	Latin American Evangelical Center for Pastoral Studies
CEOSS	Coptic Evangelical Organization for Social Services
CFK	Christian Friends of Korea
CIMADE	Comité Inter-Mouvements auprès de Evacués
CIP	Inter-Presbyterian Council
CLAI	Latin American Council of Churches
CMS	Church Missionary Society
COCAR	Council on Church and Race
COEMAR	Commission on Ecumenical Mission and Relations

CORAT	Christian Organizations Research Advisory Trust
DCM	Division of Corporate and Social Mission—PCUS
DCS	Division of Central Support Services—PCUS
DCW	Division of Cooperative Work
DIM	Division of International Mission—PCUS
DMS	Directed Mission Support
DNM	Division of National Mission—PCUS
DPD	Division of Professional Development—PCUS
ECO	Extra Commitment Opportunities
ECZ	Church of Christ in Zaire
EEC	Emerging Economies Corporation
EPC	Evangelical Presbyterian Church
EPCC	Evangelical Presbyterian Church in Chile
FCEC	Fraternity of Costa Rican Evangelical Churches
FIM	Frontier Internship in Mission
FTPY	Facultée de Théologie Protestante de Yaounde
GA	General Assembly
GAMB	General Assembly Mission Board
GMU	Global Mission Ministry Unit
IMC	International Missionary Council
IMCK	Institut Médical Chrétien du Kasai
IPB	Presbyterian Church of Brazil
IPC	Inter-Presbyterian Council
IPIB	Independent Presbyterian Church of Brazil
IPRC	Presbyterian Reformed Church in Cuba
IRD	Institute on Religion and Democracy
ISEDET	University Institute of Higher Theological Studies
LEI	Literary and Evangelism International
LINKS	International Short-Term Volunteer Program of the PC(USA)
MBF	Medical Benevolence Foundation
MECC	Middle East Council of Churches
MRTI	Mission Responsibility through Investment
MUSA	Mission to the U.S.A.
NCC	National Council of Churches in the USA
NECC	Near East Council of Churches
NEPCG	National Evangelical Presbyterian Church of Guatemala
NGO	Nongovernmental Organization
NPCM	National Presbyterian Church of Mexico
NSCC	National Sudan Council of Churches
NTC	Nile Theological College
NWMC	New Wilmington Missionary Conference
OAU	Organization of African Unity
ORE	Office of Review and Evaluation—PCUS
PCA	Presbyterian Church in America

PCC	Presbyterian Church of Colombia
PCEA	Presbyterian Church of East Africa
PCI	Presbyterian Church in Ireland
PCIR	Permanent Committee on Interchurch Relations—PCUSA
PCK	Presbyterian Church in Korea
PCMS	Presbyterian Center for Mission Studies
PCOS	Presbyterian Church of Sudan
PCPC	Permanent Commission of Presbyterian Cooperation
PCR	Program to Combat Racism
PCUS	Presbyterian Church in the United States; Southern
PCUSA	Presbyterian Church in the United States of America
PC(USA)	Presbyterian Church (U.S.A.)
PECGA	Project for Evangelism and Church Growth in Africa
PFF	Presbyterian Frontier Fellowship
PGF	Presbyterian Global Fellowship
PIMM	People in Mutual Mission
PMHP	Presbyterian Mission History Project
PMMF	Presbyterian Medical Mission Fund
POP	Program of Progress
POWE	Presbyterian Order for World Evangelization
PROK	Presbyterian Church in the Republic of Korea
PSCE	Presbyterian School of Christian Education
PUMA	Presbyterians United for Mission Advancement
R&M	Reconciliation and Mission
RCA	Reformed Church in America
REO	Regional Ecumenical Organization
SDP	Self-Development of People
SOS	Special Opportunities for Support
SPEC	Sudan Presbyterian Evangelical Church
SPLA	Sudan People's Liberation Army
TEF	Theological Education Fund
TOF	The Outreach Foundation
TSPM	Three-Self Patriotic Movement (China)
UAIM	United Andean Indian Mission
UCCP	United Church of Christ of the Philippines
UCJCI	United Church of Jamaica and the Cayman Islands
UCNI	United Church of Northern India
UECE	United Evangelical Church of Ecuador
UN	United Nations
UP	United Presbyterian
UPC	Union des Populations de Cameroun
UPCUSA	United Presbyterian Church in the United States of America
UPCNA	United Presbyterian Church of North America
VIM	Volunteers in Mission

VMSG	Validated Mission Support Groups
WARC	World Alliance of Reformed Churches
WCC	World Council of Churches
WECRP	Waldensian Evangelical Church of the River Plate
WGMS	Women's General Missionary Society
WMD	Worldwide Ministries Division
YAV	Young Adult Volunteer
YMCA	Young Men's Christian Association

Introduction

SCOTT W. SUNQUIST
AND CAROLINE N. BECKER

In the last two generations Christianity and Christian mission went through the greatest transformation since the time of Constantine. When Christians went from persecuted sect to favored faith in the early fourth century, Christians and especially priests and bishops went through ecclesial whiplash. One day they were hiding and carrying on what others often interpreted as secret or Gnostic religious practices. Within a generation they were being called together by the emperor to his palace in Nicaea (present-day Turkey) to discuss theology. It was like the collapse of the Berlin Wall, the slow decay of the bamboo curtain, and the end of Western colonialism all at once. There has been no such sudden change in the place of Christianity globally[1] until the second half of the twentieth century.

Our recent transformation of Christianity was no less dramatic, but probably less well-known. We begin this volume with the end of World War II (War of Japanese Aggression, East Asians call it) and the rather sudden dismantling of Western and Asian colonialisms. The ecumenical church was reeling from two world wars, the territorial loss of the largest Christian nation in the world (Russia), and the rise of atheistic communism in both Eastern Europe and Asia. Many of the former colonial regions in Africa and Asia took on precolonial religious identities. The new state of Pakistan was intentionally Muslim, Burma was intentionally

Buddhist, Malaysia was Muslim, and Nepal, Hindu. Over 95 percent of the colonial nations gained their independence between 1945 and 1969, in what Ralph Winter has called the *Twenty-Five Unbelievable Years*.[2] Those years were unbelievable for the political reconfigurations of the countries of the world, but of greater importance and almost more unbelievable is what happened regarding the development of Christianity from 1944 to the turn of the century. Until quite recently—but still in many universities in the West—it was assumed that the "extension" of Christianity in countries like China, Ghana, Kenya, and India was the result of Christian missions riding on the coattails of Western colonialism. Christianity only spread, so the story goes, because it was protected and promoted by Western European imperial countries like Great Britain, the Netherlands, and Germany. Lamin Sanneh[3] of Yale and many others have now proved this to be blatantly false, for in fact Christianity grew much more rapidly *after* colonialism was dismantled. Growth can be measured in terms of numbers of adherents, percent of Christians in a country, number of new movements and institutions, or in terms of the many new Latin American, African, and Asian missionary societies. The postcolonial growth has involved all of these. It seems that Western imperialism had been a great hindrance to Christian development in the non-Western world. This volume covers that very period when colonialism was being dismantled, Western churches were in decline, and, paradoxically, Christianity grew more in the non-Western world than it had in 1,900 years.

HISTORY OF THE HISTORY

Early in 2003 a number of concerned Presbyterian mission advocates recognized the fact that nothing had been written and nothing was being written about Presbyterian missions[4] since World War II, during this time of great transition. The people who have firsthand information about this story are getting much older and many have already passed on. Recognizing the need to act quickly, a group was informally called together at Pittsburgh Theological Seminary, under the auspices of the World Mission Initiative. Present at that first meeting on March 25–26 of 2003 were Scott Sunquist (moderator), Harold Kurtz (Ethiopia, now with the Presbyterian Frontier Fellowship), Paul Pierson (Brazil, now at Fuller Theological Seminary), Tommy Brown (Korea and China, now retired from Columbia Theological Seminary), Kenneth Bailey (Cyprus, Egypt, and Lebanon, now in New Wilmington, Pennsylvania), Don Dawson (Director of the World Mission Initiative and the New Wilmington Mission Conference), and David Dawson (Presbytery Executive from Shenango Presbytery). At the last minute Sam and Eileen Moffett (Korea) had to cancel out, but they participated throughout the planning stages. This was our Presbyterian Mission History Project committee that guided the project from that first formative meeting until publication. During this meeting much of the mission history was rehearsed, and later we realized that some of our writing would have been much easier if we had only taped these two days of reminiscing, celebrations, mourning, frustrations, joy, and hope. It is not often that missionaries working on different continents get together to share common experiences and to contrast political and religious contexts of church ministry. The overwhelming impression that I (Scott) remember from this meeting is the resolute commitment and love that all of these missionaries have for the people in Brazil, Lebanon, China, Korea, and Ethiopia. Institutions may enhance or detract from that loyalty, but missionaries, at least these missionaries at this time and place, were unambiguous.in their purpose. Later, after we had interviewed retired missionaries, we found this to be true as a general rule.

This meeting resulted in a commitment to find a way to gather as much information as possible, study the results, write it up, and make it available to as many as possible. We owe it to the ecumenical church to write up what has happened in Presbyterian mission from the United States since World War II. We owe it also to our own denomination to reflect on our recent past in global mission. Five years later we have this volume.

METHOD AND PURPOSE

From the beginning the purpose of the project was to give as accurate a picture as we could of the Presbyterian missions during the turbulent years after World War II up to the opening years of the twenty-first century. We desired to pull together information that would be available for scholars in future years, as well as produce a single volume that would be of help in the present as Christians consider and reconsider what it means to be responsibly involved in God's mission. We hoped that simply raising the issue of "what happened" and asking people for pictures, writings, and other materials to be placed in an archive—all this would help to preserve important materials. This is happening. Many missionaries sent us their life stories and other printed material regarding their missionary work. Again, we were concerned both to produce a volume for today and to provide materials for future scholars.

Our methodology actually involved five stages; this was much more than just a project to write a book. First, it was decided by the PMHP Committee that the missionaries who lived through this turbulent period needed to be surveyed. We wanted to gather as much information as quickly as possible from those still alive. A survey instrument was drawn up (see appendix 2), names were gathered from the Worldwide Ministries Division (World Mission) in Louisville, Kentucky, and we asked (on the survey) for suggestions of other names. Then, after gathering all the names, 830 surveys were sent out between 2003 and 2005 by me (Caroline) and 332 surveys were filled out and returned.[5] One of the most common comments on the surveys was something like this: "These questions are awfully long and involved." Many of the people filling out the surveys were in their eighties and even their nineties, so it was difficult for them to write long answers. A number of the surveys were returned with just the basic information, but quite a few had very detailed responses. One can only assume that being a missionary makes you very exacting and careful, or it could be that only people who are very exacting and careful become missionaries. Some people attached essays as a way of answering the questions, and others sent us copies of books that they had written and published—books that described their missionary work, with helpful reflections on how they viewed their work. When looking over these surveys, we realized that we had touched the pulse of something very special. It was then decided that we needed to be intentional about listening to the missionaries, by interviewing some of them personally.

Our second stage in this project involved a series of interviews. As much as possible we wanted the missionaries to have a voice in what was their work, their lives, on behalf of the Presbyterian Church. Many times on these trips we heard something like this: "I am so glad that someone is going to listen to us. Is this going to be published?" Listening was a necessary step in remembering, and so we worked to listen carefully. But listening carefully also meant reading all of the surveys and summarizing them, and it meant videotaping interviews and then putting them into transcript form. In past interviews, both in Asia and in the United States, we had learned that it is often better to have two or more people together in an interview to help in the "remembering." People remember different things, and they remember different things in different ways. Thus, our interviews were never done with a single person (although one couple was interviewed alone). Instead, we generally interviewed between five and ten people at a time, and usually people who had worked in different regions of the world. Therefore, when we asked questions about the impact of world events or church decisions upon the work in the various mission lands, we would gather a broader picture. Some issues were very localized in their impact on missionary work (communist insurgency in Ethiopia, partition of India, and the civil wars in Korea or China), and other issues seemed to have had an impact upon all missionaries (restructuring, funding crises, and so forth).

Interviews were done in Scott Sunquist's office, at the New Wilmington Missionary Conference,[6] at Westminster Gardens in Duarte, California, and at the Lodge in Montreat, North Carolina. It would have been wonderful to have had more centers to bring in more people, but these interviews did begin to paint a thematic picture of the period and the people. Missionaries were generally given a series of questions to be thinking about before the session, and the sessions varied from one-and-a-half to three hours each. After the interviews were done, the videotapes were transcribed, and some corrections were made with feedback from missionaries, which we believe has given a more-accurate rendition of the interviews. This was quite helpful since some of the missionaries had comments attributed to them that were spoken by someone else, and some of the missionaries had time to reflect and sharpen their responses.

A note of appreciation is in order. All of the interviews were done by the coeditors, and we cannot thank the missionaries enough for their grace, wisdom, and attention to detail in these interviews. A number of the missionaries provided hospitality for us, and many came with notecards and paper to make sure they did not forget important issues. Some came skeptical ("Now who exactly are you, and why are you doing this?"), but virtually all thanked us for listening. We did not plan it this way, but we believe our listening performed a pastoral function for many of these wonderful people.

Listening to the stories was an experience we will never forget. It was truly sacred time and space as we listened to mothers tell about children who died because of poor medical facilities, or other parents who talked about adopting local children who were abandoned. We heard people talk about being imprisoned by the Japanese, taken to court, and exiled; our favorite opening line was, "We lived through four major regional wars." Were the missionaries bitter or upset about changes in the world, or about the perceived failures of their work or of governments? It would be hard to detect any bitterness. In fact, the overwhelming impression we got from our time with all of these missionaries is that they are an uplifting group of people to be around. Even those whose work was "lost" or destroyed by governments or wars—we found them to be gentle, kind, forgiving, and gracious. It would be hard to design a better job for overcoming melancholy than sitting down and talking to retired missionaries. We believe that the most overwhelming impression we have, even taking these previous impressions into account, is their love for the people with whom they worked. Most, but not all, of the people we interviewed had been long-term missionaries who learned the local language(s) and who saw their children raised with local children. When these people would talk about their work "on the field," they would talk about specific people who had become good friends, and many had tears in their eyes as they began to remember their Japanese, Brazilian, Pakistani, Lebanese, or Ethiopian friends. We are thankful for this precious part of an academic project.

The third stage of the project was deciding upon and assigning chapters related to important themes in Presbyterian mission. The themes (part 1 of this volume) were suggested by the editors and then refined by the committee. We do believe that the more ways you slice the history, the more accurate the picture will be. We were fortunate to gather an excellent team of writers who know the period well and who are experts on the areas about which they write. In this section, as you will see, we have missionaries, former missionaries, academics, former mission board personnel, and one person at the World Council of Churches. Perspective is not everything, but it is important. Looking at Presbyterian mission from the perspectives of these different writers and from the various perspectives of the chapters will, we believe, fill in a lot of the blanks regarding our past sixty years of missionary work.

The fourth stage of the history project was to produce the histories by geographic region. This was probably the most frustrating for the authors, since all of our authors know the material and the history quite well. If given the time and space, each could write a book this size just on their region of the world. These chapters have to be considered an outline of the Presbyterian work in each region. All of the authors were given access to the interviews and surveys to help fill in more personal reflections on what happened during the time period.

The final stage of this project is harvested in the last chapter: "An Epilogue and a Prologue." It is a brief reflection on some of the themes that have emerged, but it is also a prologue to future missional involvement of the PC(USA), as well as for others who may be listening in. Before writing this last chapter, we sent most of the previous chapters to ecumenical partners from other churches and from other countries and asked them for comments. Some of these observations have been incorporated into this final chapter. There are no dramatic conclusions, but most of the observations and conclusions will not surprise the reader who has worked through the previous chapters. We believe that this is a valuable chapter for all those involved in mission leadership today.

AUTHORS AND CHAPTERS

The authors in this volume come from a variety of backgrounds, experiences in mission, and educational preparation for this task. The first chapter on the changing context for mission is written by Theo Gill. Theo serves in Geneva as the senior editor working for the World Council of Churches. He comes from a family of Presbyterian leaders and previously did editorial and reporting work for the PC(USA) in Louisville, Kentucky. He is very well situated and prepared to write this chapter on the ecumenical changes that took place during our sixty-year period. Presbyterians were carrying out missionary work not in a vacuum but in the midst of global shifts and changes that were also having an impact on other churches. Chapter 2 is written by David Dawson, the Executive for the Shenango Presbytery in Western Pennsylvania. David has been studying Presbyterian mission and money since he did his STM degree at Yale on this very topic in 1987. In this chapter he traces not only the money problem, but he also looks at other statistical trends and has some creative insights and conclusions about Presbyterians in mission. Chapter 3, on the changing structures, is written by two "insiders," T. Donald Black and G. Thompson (Tommy) Brown. Donald Black's name comes up a number of times in this volume since he held several important leadership positions: Executive Secretary—Board of Foreign Missions (UPCNA), General Secretary—Commission on Ecumenical Mission and Relations (UPCUSA), Associate General Director—Program Agency (UPCUSA), Executive Director—General Assembly Council (PCUSA), and interim staff positions with the National Council of Churches and the WCC. Tommy Brown was born of missionary parents in China, served twenty years in Korea, returned to the United States, served as Asia Secretary for the Board of World Missions, was elected to the position of Director of Division of International Mission (PCUS), and then became a faculty member at Columbia Theological Seminary. We were very fortunate to have these two work together on the chapter since the story of structural changes with three different denominations is quite complex.

Chapter 4, on the changing ideas and practices of mission in the period, is written by a Presbyterian missionary to Brazil, Sherron George. Sherron has studied and taught this subject matter for over three decades, so she brings a varied perspective from both North and South Americas. Chapter 5 helps to explain some of the shifting movements in Presbyterian mission that are mentioned in other chapters. Rob Weingartner, Executive Director of the Outreach Foundation, brings to this chapter personal involvement both on the General Assembly Council and as a board member and now staff with the type of "mission within a mission" about which he writes. One of the themes of the whole volume, which is central to Rob's chapter (as you will soon see), is keeping together the diversity of Presbyterian mission around a core of commitments in an increasingly distrustful milieu. Chapter 6, where we give the missionaries a chance to speak, concludes the thematic section of the book. After looking at structures and ideas, it seems only fitting that we look at people. Caroline organized and oversaw the surveys and organized the personal interviews, so she brings with her a good feel for the material. Hundreds of hours of "listening" were involved in this chapter, and we pray that all who read will have a better understanding of the thoughts, joys, disappointments, and idiosyncrasies of Presbyterians working through a period of tremendous transition. We believe this is a unique chapter in missionary history writing: giving voice to the people on the front line.

Part 2 looks at Presbyterian mission geographically. We begin with the chapter by Frank Arnold on Presbyterians in Latin America. Frank worked over thirty years in Brazil and was also, for two years, Area Secretary for Latin America and the Caribbean for the Division of International Mission of the former PCUS. Again, it is helpful to have someone write who, on both sides of the water, has been participating in Presbyterian Mission. Chapter 8, on mission to the United States of America, is written by Patricia Lloyd-Sidle. Tricia has served as a coworker in Uruguay, and from 1993 to 2001 she was the coordinator of the Global Awareness and Involvement unit of the Worldwide Ministries Division in Louisville. At present, she serves as the Regional Liaison for the Caribbean, with special attention to Cuba and the Caribbean–North American Council for Mission (CANACOM). Chapter 9 is one of four chapters that either covers or touches on Asia. Presbyterians have focused on Muslim regions of West Asia, on India and Pakistan, and on the Confucian and Buddhist countries of South and Southeast Asia. This chapter on East Asia is written by Scott Sunquist, now at Pittsburgh Theological Seminary, but who previously served for eight years in Singapore, teaching Asian Church History at Trinity Theological College. Chapter 10, on the Middle East, is written by Stan Skreslet of Union-PSCE in Richmond, Virginia. Previously Stan taught at the Evangelical Theological Seminary in Cairo, Egypt, for ten years. Chapter 11, on Presbyterian mission work in Africa, is written by William (Bill) Anderson, African historian and missionary, who worked for nearly half a century in Africa. Chapter 12, on Europe, was written by Duncan Hanson with the help of Art Beals. Duncan Hanson has been the PCUSA area coordinator for Western Europe and is currently the supervisor of Reformed Church in America mission programs in Europe and Russia. Art Beals presently serves as the Regional Liaison for the Presbyterian Church (U.S.A.) in Turkey, Azerbaijan, and the

Balkans. Formerly Art was the Mission Pastor at University Presbyterian Church, Seattle, Washington. Chapter 13 is written by John Webster, well-known scholar of Indian Christianity, but especially of Dalit Church history and theology. John has served over twenty-two years in India.

WHAT TYPE OF HISTORY IS THIS?

History of Christian missions used to be the cornerstone of mission studies. Many of the great mission scholars, like Kenneth Scott Latourette, Stephen Neill, and others, were really historians of Western missions and missionaries. This book is not a mission history. If it were, you would have before you a chrono-logical description of the story of Presbyterians going out into different lands, planting churches, building schools, and developing hospitals. Mission history is really the intercultural dimension or foreign relations department of church his-tory. Much of this type of history focuses upon institutional development and the "extension" of the church in foreign lands. Some of this volume partakes of history of missions, but there are other angles and concerns—other questions—that moved this project forward.

In this project we were concerned about two issues: making a record of what happened, and doing this in such a way that it would serve the church. It is pos-sible to simply record history as one sterile fact after another. That is not what you have in your hands now. In service to the church, we designed this history so that it tries to uncover motives, responses to social change, and contextual vari-ables. Still there is much missing. If we had the time and space, we could easily write a "volume 2" made up of biographies of twenty or thirty missionaries and executives. History is, after all, really about people, their thoughts, relationships, and decisions. In this history, we have decided that future generations need to have different angles of vision to better understand what has happened in, to, and through the various Presbyterian missions. For those more attuned to historical studies today, we have sipped from the pools of sociological studies, postcolonial studies, and postmodern critique to give some definition and heightened aware-ness of some of the issues before us. In editing this volume, we have become aware of the limits of such a grand design, but also the benefits. One of the benefits is that certain themes begin to present themselves, and these themes have more integrity when they come from a variety of approaches, people, and disciplines.

These themes emerged as we saw that many of the topics discussed in this vol-ume were taken up in different chapters, giving the reader a sense of repetition. What this actually reveals is that there are a number of themes, issues, events, and writings that have had a broad impact on Presbyterian mission, and this volume looks at these items from different perspectives. Four examples will make this clear. First, the 1956–61 period of mission study that culminated with the pub-lication of *An Advisory Study* was a critical moment in Presbyterian mission. This study is mentioned in the first chapter on the larger ecumenical context, in the chapter on changing structures of the Presbyterian Church (U.S.A.) (chapter 3) and in chapter 4, on Presbyterian theology during this period. The initiative of Charles Leber and the forward-looking concept of listening to and following the advice of overseas partners set a major new direction, with deep and lasting consequences. Presbyterian missionary activity, priorities, funding, and deployment and recalling of missionaries were all decisions that were made in light of the new pattern of mission outlined in *An Advisory Study.*

A second issue that comes up a number of times is the issue of funding. Even in talking about Presbyterian theology of mission, Sherron George mentions methods of funding and the decrease in funding for missionaries. Funding issues also came up quite often in our interviews of missionaries, and in addition, these issues are mentioned in the Annual Reports beginning in the mid-1950s. Dave Dawson sorts through some of the funding issues in all three streams of the Presbyterian Church to show similar patterns, which produced chronic results in the late 1960s. As early as the 1951 Report of the Board of World Missions (PCUS) to the General Assembly, we hear the concern expressed as a warning:[7] in 1920 the church gave 12 cents of every dollar to foreign mission; in 1930—8 cents; in 1945—5 cents; and in 1950 only 3 cents.

A third theme that resurfaces a number of times is the relationship between "ecumenical partnerships" and "mission." Renaming the "Board of Foreign Missions" as the "Commission on Ecumenical Mission and Relations" expressed a theological and ideological turn toward the newly formed national churches. No longer were we imposing our will upon these self-governing churches; instead, we now worked as ecumenical partners, as requested by national churches overseas. However, it soon became clear that when it came to ecumenical partners, one size did not fit all. Some of the national churches, although self-governing, were far from ready to assume responsibility for the large institutions that Presbyterian missions had established. Some of the partners were more than ready, and the transfer was quite late indeed. However, a quick read of the General Assembly Minutes reveals the radical nature of the change. The reports of the General Assembly through the 1950s always speak of the national churches *and* the work of missionaries. In the index we find "missions" and "missionaries," and we also find information on missionary work in the Report. By 1964, the Minutes no longer list "mission," "missionaries," or even the new term "fraternal workers" in the index. In fact, the COEMAR report for 1964 is an extensive analysis of the global situation and social shifts, with nothing on the work of our missionaries. "The changes which are taking place in our world are not normal phases in the familiar process of change which is always at work in history, but the most radical revolution that has taken place since the dawn of civilization."[8] The word "revolution" is used six times in the first two paragraphs. The report discusses meetings, consultations, and ecumenical gatherings in which the church is engaged, but nothing is said of missionary work. It was remarked by a number of missionaries that their work was not appreciated as it had been, and COEMAR had become, so it seemed, dominated by ecumenical relations. Other missionaries, however, said the changes did not touch their work at all.

Closely related to the shift toward ecumenical relations, as we see in this volume, is the repeated theme of missionary presence: the size, purpose, and duration. It is clear that there has been a decline in global Presbyterian mission presence, and David Dawson in chapter 2 describes that neatly for us. However, is a moratorium, "reduction of force," or relocation and repositioning the proper response to the contemporary context? Don Snow, Presbyterian teaching in Nanjing, has argued that with the political and religious tensions in the world today, Christians need to be present, even as English teachers, as "preemptive peacemakers." Most all Presbyterians agreed that a different set of skills and training are required today than during the heyday of colonialism, but how does that translate into missional presence? We have found no disagreement that the missionary is commissioned to prepare a church, its leaders, and its institutions to be under local church authority, but the timing and method, we have found, are most difficult to work out. By the end of the volume, there may be some answers to these questions, or at least some better questions.

The advantage of having these themes and issues treated in different chapters and from different contexts is that we begin to have a better understanding of what really happened in and through Presbyterian mission(s) in this critical sixty-year period. We hear some from the executives, from missionaries, from official reports, and then from the global church. History is best told from different perspectives, listening to a variety of sources, and turning over more rather than less evidence. We think the reader will find this true in the present volume.

And so the hundreds of Presbyterian missionaries, scholars, and church leaders also offer this volume as a gift to the global church, with the prayer that it will bring about greater faithfulness to God's mission as together we pray, "Thy kingdom come on earth." We end with an appropriate quotation from the Minutes of the 1953 General Assembly of the PCUS: just as the Korean War was coming to a close, the last missionaries were being released by Communist China, and just a year before the important 1954 Evanston Assembly of the World Council of Churches, whose theme was, "Jesus Christ—Hope for the World."

> There is no participation in Christ without participation in His mission to the world. That by which the church receives her existence is that by which she is also given her world mission.[9]

PART I
HISTORICAL SETTING AND THEMES

Chapter 1

Historical Context
for Mission, 1944–2007

THEODORE A. GILL JR.

*Culture after culture with which the faith has been intimately associated
has passed into history, seemingly to carry it also into oblivion. Yet the faith
spreads ever more widely and moulds more and more peoples.*

*To many who have been counted wise by their fellows and in their own
eyes, the story of the cross has seemed foolishness. Yet never has Jesus been as
widely potent in shaping history as in A.D. 1944, when in many ways he
and what he stood for have appeared the most obviously defeated.*

Kenneth Scott Latourette,
A History of the Expansion of Christianity[1]

SIGNS OF THE TIME

Perhaps each moment in human history is both the best and worst of times. Yale
professor Kenneth Latourette, concluding his magisterial seven-volume account
of the spread of Christianity through nineteen centuries, saw divine providence
at work in the world of 1944 despite the evidence that principalities and powers
were doing their utmost to thwart Christ's love. Our consideration of sixty years
in Presbyterian mission history begins at that beginning, with events unfolding
around Dr. Latourette as he contemplated the world.

In May 1944, Mahatma Gandhi was released from British custody; whatever
its significance for the British Empire, the Quit India movement was no longer
reckoned a threat to the war effort. The following August, Anne Frank and her
family were taken into custody in Amsterdam. Dietrich Bonhoeffer spent the full
year in German captivity. Aleksandr Solzhenitsyn, a decorated Soviet soldier who
included criticism of the Kremlin in letters home from the front, by year's end
was just weeks away from deportation to the Siberian gulag. Hundreds of millions

languished due to war and repression, under occupation, under siege, in camps or prisons, and in fear.

In 1944 a Chinese-born child of YMCA missionaries, John S. Service, undertook the first U.S. diplomatic mission to Mao Zedong. Elsewhere in China an Indian-born child of Southern Baptist missionaries, the passionately anticommunist John Birch, served with distinction as an officer of the Flying Tigers seconded to OSS operations. At the same time, an envoy was sent from Washington to Chiang Kai-shek, seeking a temporary alliance with Mao to defeat the common enemy. The nationalist leader was also persuaded to release Ho Chi Minh from a Chinese prison to command guerrillas resisting the Japanese occupation of Indochina. Imperial Japan dominated East Asia, from Indonesia and the Philippines to Korea and Manchuria.

In El Salvador and Guatemala, national strikes drove dictatorial presidents from power. The president of Argentina, a general in office since the preceding year's military coup, appointed Colonel Juan Perón as vice president and secretary of war.

For many people from the global south, colonialism and paternalism set life's pattern. In 1944 Jomo Kenyatta, who would become the first prime minister and president of an independent Kenya, was laboring as a farm worker in England to avoid conscription into the armed forces. In South Africa, young activists impatient with moderate policies of the African National Congress organized the more radical ANC Youth League; the rising leadership included Nelson Mandela, Walter Sisulu, and Oliver Tambo.

In Syria, the Muslim Brotherhood, expanding across the Middle East since its founding by Hassan al-Banna in 1928, relocated its central offices from Aleppo to Damascus. In Palestine, the British commissioned a Jewish Brigade of three infantry battalions and related support units, authorizing use of the Zionist flag as the brigade's standard.

Allied authorities began to show optimism that the war was in its closing stages. In Bretton Woods, New Hampshire, a July conference of statesmen, economists, and bankers laid plans for a postwar international bank for reconstruction and development, and for an international monetary fund. The following month at a Washington, D.C., mansion called Dumbarton Oaks, diplomats drafted a framework for the future United Nations.

Harvard University installed the Mark 1, the first automatic digital computer put into daily use. Scientists and technicians of the Manhattan Project in Los Alamos, New Mexico, received the first shipments of reactor-bred plutonium from colleagues in Oak Ridge, Tennessee. Meanwhile, aircraft with jet engines were introduced into service by both the Luftwaffe and the Royal Air Force.

Germany's long-range missiles were in production at last, and the V-2's frightening success established rocket science as a potent technology. Nevertheless, there were decisive events throughout 1944 that threatened the Axis dominion: the successful invasion of Normandy; the liberation of Rome, Paris, and Warsaw; the defeat of the Japanese navy in the Philippine Sea with repercussions across the Pacific; failure in late December of Germany's counteroffensive in the Ardennes.

The year was bracketed by meetings of the "Big Three"—Stalin, Roosevelt, and Churchill—at Tehran in late 1943 and Yalta in early 1945. Media coverage of these conferences emphasized the immediate impact of decisions on the war, with limited speculation concerning long-term consequences. The term "Cold War" had no currency in the searing heat of World War II. Nor did any real optimism survive from an earlier conflict that this might be "the war to end war." It was called the "Second" World War, with no guarantee that the count was complete.

Among the natural deaths that fell in 1944 was that of William Temple, for two and a half years the archbishop of Canterbury and since 1938 chair of the provisional committee of the "World Council of Churches in process of formation." Temple was widely known and well regarded as a priest, social activist, scholar, author, advocate of Christian mission near and far, former bishop of Manchester and archbishop of York, and Anglican representative to international gatherings since his youthful service as an usher at the Edinburgh World Missionary Conference of 1910.[2] In his 1942 enthronement sermon the archbishop had surveyed the global situation, noting a significant development within Christianity despite the nations' tumult: "Almost incidentally the great world-fellowship has arisen; it is the great new fact of our era." While this assertion came to be associated with the World Council of Churches (WCC), William Temple's intent was to describe the emergent fellowship among all Christians rendered possible by advances in transport and communication.

With the expansion of rail services and shipping, and the beginnings of passenger air travel, prewar Christian convocations had welcomed an ever-broader cross section of people from churches and mission agencies spread across the inhabited continents and islands. Now newspapers and magazines linked to foreign correspondents by cable- and radio-telegraphy reported recent news from locations around the globe, among other things serving as a compelling resource for intercessory prayer. Maps and photos from war-torn regions were staples of print journalism, and newsreels conveyed, with audio-video impact, up-to-date information to mass audiences. Developments in radio broadcasting since the First World War made it possible to hear voices, music, or the sounds of battle on another continent with only a slight lag in transmission. Contacts between churches, too, were being maintained even across enemy lines. The unprecedented immediacy of far-flung believers and communities led Christians from many traditions and cultures to recognize a "great world fellowship" maintained through a relatively informal network of relations rather than by any one institution. A concomitant secular appreciation of the world's many cultures bred the tentative hope that a postwar United Nations could avoid the fate of the League of Nations.

Delay in founding a global council to direct the ecumenical impulse inspired a sense of déjà vu among church veterans. Following the Edinburgh conference of 1910, churches and mission agencies intended to move with dispatch toward a council through which the evangelistic, educational, medical, and diaconal work of foreign missions could be coordinated. The First World War had intervened in 1914, so the International Missionary Council (IMC) finally came into being in 1921. Now proposals of the late 1930s for an assembly inaugurating a World Council of Churches, intended to provide leadership in the quest for Christian unity in faith and service, had been postponed in 1939, following yet another outbreak of hostilities in Europe. As the political and economic spheres were planning a U.N. and World Bank, the churches looked forward to new possibilities for cooperation and reconciliation in a world at peace. But the past was prelude to succeeding decades, and the germ of events in the remainder of the century was evident in the realities of 1944.

MISSION IN PARTNERSHIP AND OBEDIENCE

Three Presbyterian churches from the United States were members of the IMC and would be among the founders of the WCC in 1948. They were the Presbyterian Church in the USA (PCUSA), the Presbyterian Church in the U.S. (PCUS, or the "southern church," dating from separation at the outbreak of the American Civil War), and the United Presbyterian Church of North America (UPCNA). Cooperation among the three foreign mission boards was not unknown, but it was not routine before the 1950s. In 1958 the PCUSA and UPCNA formed the United Presbyterian Church in the U.S.A. (UPCUSA). In the spring of 1983 the denominations would evolve through further negotiation and reunion into one church, the Presbyterian Church (U.S.A.), or PC(USA).

International mission, from the end of the war to the end of the century and beyond, was to be conducted in an interactive mode. A postwar model put forward by the International Missionary Council was partnership, building on the theme of "partnership in obedience" at the 1947 mission conference in Whitby, Ontario. Christians in each place were claiming responsibility for taking the gospel to their neighbors, according to Lesslie Newbigin, and discussion of mission within the IMC, the WCC, and their member institutions was "about evangelism in six continents, rather than about mission to six continents."[3] This concept of partnership inspired such program titles as "interchurch aid" and "joint action in mission."

After the Allied victory, many overseas ministries of the American Presbyterian churches put an emphasis on the reconstruction of devastated lands and communities, a concern for refugees, rebuilding, infrastructure, and finances that would contribute to Christian involvement in later economic and social development worldwide. Veteran service agencies of the historic peace churches like the American Friends Service Committee (founded 1917) and Mennonite Central Committee (1920) were now joined by such U.S.-based diaconal organizations as Catholic Relief Services (1943), Church World Service and Lutheran World Relief (1946), and World Vision International (1950).[4] With U.S. mission workers returning in significant numbers to Europe and Asia, such ministries to refugees and ruined communities became unavoidable preoccupations. Suffering and recovery from war and occupation called for a compassionate Christian response, and this continued to be true during the death throes of colonialism, the East-West conflict between ideologies, and later clashes of civilizations. The call to rebuilding and relief efforts involved mission workers from many churches, including the American Presbyterian denominations, often under the coordination of the International Missionary Council (IMC). The IMC was chaired from 1947 to 1958 by Presbyterian John A. Mackay, president of Princeton Theological Seminary.

As North American Protestants of the postwar period found themselves working alongside members of European churches, and as others experienced ancient Asian cultures awakening from alien captivity, many from the United States began to call themselves "fraternal workers" in ecumenical mission, rather than "missionaries," vocabulary that would become official by the late 1950s as union negotiations between the PCUSA and the UPCNA created the UPCUSA and its Commission on Ecumenical Mission and Relations (COEMAR).[5] At this time John Mackay could report that cooperation in mission had come to include full partnership with newly independent churches on every continent, transforming "the Protestant Christian mission from a unilateral Western sending operation into a missionary enterprise with a world-wide base and a world-wide field of operation."[6]

The fraternal approach drew on Whitby's theme of partnership and later on mission theory emerging from the 1952 IMC conference in Willingen, Germany, best remembered for its affirmation of Christian mission as *missio Dei*; that is, *God's* mission rather than the churches' mission—or even the church's mission. According to the concept of *missio Dei*, God is the "sending agent," all mission is God's alone, and all churches together cooperate in carrying out this mission in obedience to God. The field is the world, the whole world, "developed" as well as underdeveloped.[7] This was mission theory for a postcolonial age. Henceforth, it was said, a missionary going "to a country other than his own knows that he is going as a servant."[8] Global mission partnerships envisioned at this time were not with people of other faiths but between one Christian group and other Christians elsewhere, to be carried out in a spirit of equality and interdependence, for the proclamation of the gospel of Jesus Christ "as the crucified and living One, as Savior and Lord."[9]

In the years between Willingen and the founding of COEMAR, the interactive approach to mission was hailed by PCUSA mission planners as a "new day dawning."[10] In the spring of 1956 that church's board of foreign missions, with the participation of the UPCNA mission leadership, invited twenty-two representatives of newly independent churches in the developing world to a consultation at Lake Mohonk, New York. The gist of the invitation has been summarized in the words "We want you to tell us what to do."[11] Through listening to overseas representatives,

> the Mohonk Consultation witnessed the process of growing independence and achieving maturity on the part of the younger churches coming to fruition. The Consultation took decisive action concerning the integration of missionary work with that of indigenous churches around the world, so that these churches might increasingly determine policy and administer work within their borders.[12]

Two years later, the creation of COEMAR combined the ecumenical relations commissions of the two predecessor churches with their boards of foreign mission. Lake Mohonk's participatory style of making strategy carried over into the new body, resulting in the 1961 publication of *An Advisory Study* pointing the way for the UPCUSA's mission on the basis of input offered by consultants from churches on other continents.[13] An addendum to the study was titled "The Ecumenical Movement as a Factor Conditioning the United Presbyterian Church's Fulfillment of Mission Overseas."

Not all American Presbyterians had been ecumenically conditioned. In the PCUS, resistance to ecumenical mission theory appeared frequently in the pages of the influential *Presbyterian Journal*. A new journalistic voice, *Christianity Today* magazine, cautioned against excessive novelty in the field of evangelism. On the other hand, the equally independent *Presbyterian Outlook* offered generally positive coverage of developments in the IMC and the WCC. The executive secretary of the PCUS Board of World Missions, C. Darby Fulton, favored the older system of evangelization from a "sending" church to "receiving" missions. Even the General Assembly's ad interim committee on the future of PCUS mission—appointed in 1952 and producing recommendations that there be greater cooperation with local leadership and integration of work into the life of national churches—failed to achieve immediate change.[14] But when Fulton retired in 1960, the PCUS called as his successor T. Watson Street, professor of missiology and church history at Austin Theological Seminary, a committed proponent of the conciliar ecumenical movement. Street convened a consultation on mission culminating at Montreat, North Carolina, in 1962. The report from Montreat called for mutuality in international mission, the need to evangelize through actions as well as words, and the courage to experiment in response to changing times and social situations. Lake Mohonk and Montreat set the tone for the two churches' mission policies through the 1960s.

Change in policy at the level of a Presbyterian mission board does not signal a change in every Presbyterian heart. There were and are Presbyterians who personally or collectively have chosen to support independent and parachurch organizations in preference to efforts by their own church's mission board. Some individuals and congregations, convinced that older methods are proved and remain faithful to the gospel, have favored agencies and missionaries that continue sending-receiving models of evangelism and use traditional categories and language. Many have insisted upon evangelistic preaching and a call to conversion as the leading pattern in any mission program they support. A denomination's more traditional missionaries who have solid support from congregations seldom are required to alter the philosophy of mission assumed in their letters and itineration, although other longtime missionaries have lobbied for and endorsed new policies.

Many Presbyterian donors and participants in mission have balanced the partnership model with proclamation aimed at conversion of populations. The Billy Graham organization has been deliberately interdenominational in its structure and appeal, inviting congregations of many Christian traditions to join its crusades, and some members of the Graham family maintain the Presbyterian heritage of Ruth Bell Graham, the Chinese-born daughter of famed PCUS missionary L. Nelson Bell. World Vision International has also been successful in its appeals for support of an evangelistic approach to relief services and has shown willingness to interact with both evangelical and ecumenical alliances as well as denominational mission offices. Some other organizations not directed by the PC(USA) have negotiated mutually beneficial "covenant relationships" with church structures. Such arrangements address a waning enthusiasm for church-based approaches to mission:

> In the USA, ecumenical churches with the admirable goal of involving the whole church in mission have included mission activity in unified budgetary, planning and administrative procedures. Yet many lay people and missionaries believe this has stifled flexibility, initiative, and close personal relations between missionaries, congregations, and the areas of missionary engagement.[15]

Whatever Presbyterians' official policies, a variety of mission theories have come into operation across Presbyterian churches. Hans Küng has observed that theological paradigms abandoned by some Christians remain the standards of others, so that patristic Hellenism remains the confessional norm in Eastern Orthodoxy, medieval scholasticism forms the basis for contemporary Catholic traditionalism, Reformation and seventeenth-century canons shape Protestant confessionalism, and Enlightenment thought exercises considerable influence on theological modernism.[16] David Bosch added that theologians on the cusp of change, like Erasmus, Luther, and Barth, may incorporate ideas from worldviews old and new. According to Bosch, mission strategists of the late twentieth century found themselves caught between paradigms, influenced by biblical and confessional models, inescapably molded by Enlightenment assumptions, and open to the voices of oppressed people with whom Western churches have been in partnership and conversation. This leaves Christians in mission with "a kind of theological schizophrenia, which we just have to put up with while at the same time groping our way toward greater clarity."[17]

A paradigm shift at the highest level of the Roman Catholic Church came with the papacy of John XXIII and Vatican II, the council he convened in Rome. This in turn affected the network of relationships among Christian world communions as well as joint operations of the churches. Meeting from October 1962 into the reign of Paul VI (pope, 1963–78) in December 1965, the Second Vatican Council signified a renewal of Catholic thinking on theology, ecumenical relations, modern culture, and the role of the church in the world. Orthodox and Protestant theologians were among the experts (*periti*) who participated in discussion and in the drafting of conciliar documents. The 1965 General Assembly of the UPCUSA hailed the new ecumenical situation in which "doors have been opened for conversation and cooperation between Protestant and Roman

Catholic, and for ventures in ecumenical trust and faith."[18] Soon joint projects in the areas of research, theology, education, service, and outreach were flourishing from the local to the international levels of the churches. In 1970 a joint working group of the WCC and the Roman Catholic Church began to issue a series of study documents on common witness, described as "a demand of the very gospel we proclaim" and calling on Christians in all churches to "look beyond our own and see the millions of people who do not know the gospel of Jesus Christ."[19] Catholic participation grew on joint commissions dedicated to faith and order, mission and evangelism, and Christian medical work. Following progressive social teachings in such Vatican II documents as *Mater et magistra* (1961) and *Pacem in terris* (1963), and the Latin American bishops' Medellín endorsement of "God's preferential option for the poor" in 1968, ecumenical work on justice was accentuated; from 1968 to 1983, many of these ministries were coordinated through a joint WCC and Vatican committee on society, development, and peace.[20] Together, the people of God approached Christian unity through service.

Mission theology became well integrated at the level of formal dialogues and in academic circles. By 1976 missiologist R. Pierce Beaver would note that younger participants in a symposium on American missions had come to lump the history of Catholic and Protestant missionary efforts into one undifferentiated "history of Christian mission," failing to recognize that until recently the two traditions were prone not to identify each other as truly Christian, having "completely identified the gospel with their own particular varieties of Christianity."[21] That so great a change in thinking had been taken for granted in so short a time is testimony to the radical shift in self-understanding brought about by Vatican II.

In this period the Catholic Church also opened bilateral dialogues with particular confessional families, represented by communions like the World Alliance of Reformed Churches (WARC), "for thorough and detailed study of specific issues which separate two traditions," while also surfacing "the elements they have in common and which have been preserved in both traditions, despite their separation." In this way, Presbyterian and Reformed churches with membership in WARC but not in the WCC became engaged in dialogue with Catholics on such issues as "the problem of mixed marriages" or "the presence of Christ in church and world."[22] By the 1980s, the Roman Catholic Church would also be in formal dialogues with representatives of the Evangelical and Pentecostal movements.[23]

The World Alliance of Reformed Churches, too, welcomed bilateral and multilateral dialogues with their fellow Christian world communions, from Lutherans and Disciples of Christ to Orthodox churches. Like the Roman Catholics, world communions including WARC have sought out dialogues with Evangelical and Pentecostal associations. Many international sister churches of the American Presbyterians, in places like Canada, the United Kingdom, India, China, Japan, and Australia, have become united and uniting churches—either by choice or of necessity—holding membership in WARC and one or more other Christian world communions. WARC has devoted decades to exploring the relationship between

Christian mission and church unity, with the terminology shifting from "mission and unity" in the 1980s to "mission in unity" by the end of the 1990s.[24]

REGIONALISM, FRAGMENTATION, AND SECULARIZATION

From the late 1950s, the creation of regional ecumenical organizations (REOs) and the proliferation of national councils of churches provided additional connections within the ecumenical network. The earliest REOs, the Christian Conference of Asia and the Conference of European Churches, have been joined by equivalent bodies in Africa, the Caribbean, Latin America, the Middle East, and the Pacific. The only major inhabited region not formally represented in an REO by the start of the twenty-first century was North America; the functional substitute was found in cordial relations between the Canadian Council of Churches and the National Council of the Churches of Christ in the U.S.A. The growth of regional and national expressions of interconfessional activity "demonstrates that the goals of the global ecumenical movement cannot be attained unless churches are able to apply them in the milieu where they live and witness"; in addition, the formation of such councils in the global South may be seen as a deliberate attempt to find a voice "over against the Northern powers dominating the world scene."[25]

Decolonization, national independence, and the autonomy of churches, conferences, and councils have manifested a degree of cultural fragmentation, beginning with awareness of the East-West political and ideological division during the Cold War and a North-South divide in global economics. The modernist, "ecumenical" ideal of one world, or one household of God, came into conflict with the particularities of those Christians, viewed from the West and North as "younger churches," who were in search of a clear self-identity within their own national and cultural contexts. Contextual theologies began to clash with "ecumenical" theologies.

The sociological theory of secularization, based on arguments advanced by Max Weber early in the twentieth century, describes an Enlightenment and post-Enlightenment process of rationalization in Western culture that gradually drives religion from the public sphere until it becomes a largely private set of beliefs.[26] Western civilization, in turn, moves steadily from the assumption of an established Christendom with religious values at its moral core to the disestablishment of any church and to moral relativism. Christianity is no longer the insider's faith but must approach all aspects of culture from outside the circle of temporal authority. Secularization was seen as an especially important facet of urban, as opposed to rural, life, and adoption of the theory held important consequences for mission in an age of rapid urbanization. In the late 1950s and early 1960s, youth and mission conferences began to focus on the consequences of what seemed a rising tide of secularization.[27] Publication of the prison correspondence of Dietrich Bonhoeffer invited Christian communities to develop a theological theory of secularization that contemplates a faith appropriate to "a world come of age," a renewed, "reli-gionless" Christianity. "Before God and with him we live without God," Bon-hoeffer wrote on July 16, 1944. "God allows himself to be edged out of the world and onto a cross. God is weak and powerless in the world, and that is exactly the way, the only way, in which he can be with us and help us."[28]

For many thinkers in newly liberated churches, the way of mission was no longer the way of empire, or crusades, or "Christian soldiers marching as to war": the way of the gospel was, as Bonhoeffer wrote just months before his execution, the way of servanthood and the cross. If this were accepted, then more marginal Christian communities had at least as much to contribute to theology and prac-tice as the churches of traditional Christendom. Who was in the best position to teach the lessons learned from poverty, suffering, marginalization—and who had the need to learn them? Methodist bishop Federico Pagura of Latin America warned missionaries that attitudes must change if the mission workers were to remain a part of Southern societies:

> If your allegiance and fidelity to your nation of origin are stronger than loy-alty and obedience to Jesus Christ, who came "to put down the mighty and lift up the lowly" (Luke 1:52): Missionary, go home. If you are not able to love and respect as equals those whom you once came to evangelize as "the lost": Missionary, go home. If you are not able to rejoice at the entry of new peoples and churches upon a new stage of maturity, independence, and responsibility, even at the price of committing errors like those which you and your compatriots committed also in the past: Missionary, go home.[29]

Doubts about Christian entanglement with culture were not exactly new. On the eve of the Edinburgh conference in 1910, John R. Mott had asked a colleague, "Do you now consider that we have on the home field a type of Christianity that should be propagated all over the world?"[30] Ecumenical theologian H. Richard Niebuhr had grappled with the same subject in his 1951 book *Christ and Culture*.[31]

Now it was in regional circles that the call for a "moratorium" on foreign mis-sionaries began to arise. In 1971 the concept of "partnership" between north and south was challenged by Emerito P. Nacpil, then president of Union Seminary in Manila, who argued that "cooperation between Asian and western Christians can only be a partnership between the weak and the strong. And that means the con-tinued dependence of the weak upon the strong and the continued dominance of the strong. . . . In other words, the most *missionary* service a missionary under the present system can do today in Asia is to go home." Similar sentiments were being expressed in other regions, notably by Paul Verghese in India, José Míguez-Bonino in Argentina, and Presbyterian theologian John Gatu in Kenya. Vergh-ese, who would later come to be known as Syrian Orthodox Metropolitan Paulos Mar Gregorios, claimed at this time that "the mission of the church is the great-est enemy of the gospel."[32] In 1972, the National Presbyterian Church in Mex-ico celebrated its centennial with a request that the PCUS and UPCUSA withdraw all their missionaries for a period of at least five years; full relations were not reestablished until 1979.[33] Such calls for a moratorium on missionaries, and a pattern for mission that led beyond unequal partnerships to a broader *koinōnia,* or fellowship, set the stage for the great debates on inculturation and contextualization of the mid-1970s and 1980s. But the dynamics of North-South church relations in this period cannot be fully understood apart from the East-West tensions of the Cold War.

THE GEOPOLITICS OF MISSION

As the printing press had brought the Bible to vast new audiences in the sixteenth century, news and entertainment media of the twentieth century gave consumers vivid images of the world. Some observed with appreciation or trepidation, while others were motivated to action. After mushroom clouds over Hiroshima and Nagasaki hastened the surrender of Japan, the attention of a generation was riveted upon the potentials and dangers of science and technology in "the atomic age." Optimistic reports on the peaceful use of nuclear energy ran alongside sobering stories on the testing of ever more sophisticated weapons. World War II–era allies of East and West now vied for dominance in Europe, Asia, Africa, and Latin America, while border wars, civil wars, and revolutions proliferated around the globe. India and Pakistan were born amid bloodshed and ancient religious hatreds, as was the modern state of Israel. Indonesia refused to be reoccupied by colonial forces, winning its own independence from the recently liberated Netherlands. Chiang Kai-shek's forces retreated to Taiwan as Mao took command in Mainland China. Confrontation in Korea led to the withdrawal of communist delegates from the United Nations and of Chinese churches from the WCC. Any sign of an uprising in Eastern Europe was thwarted by Soviet force. The United States and members of its military alliances rushed support to governments threatened by leftists. Reporters and broadcasters hastened to bring all this into people's homes.

At the end of the Second World War, Christian leaders and institutions occupied high-profile positions. John R. Mott, the grand old man of the student volunteer movement, YMCA, and nascent WCC, shared the 1946 Nobel Prize for Peace with American social activist Emily G. Balch. The following year, the prize went to the Religious Society of Friends' service committees of the United States and Great Britain. In 1952, the Nobel peace laureate would be awarded to Protestant medical missionary Albert Schweitzer. Representatives of churches, most of them from the West, played key roles in the shaping of postwar institutions. Reinhold Niebuhr, a professor of social ethics at Union Seminary in New York and counselor to leading U.S. political thinkers, was the subject of a cover story in *Time* magazine. International lawyer, diplomat, and PCUSA member John Foster Dulles, later President Eisenhower's secretary of state, had been a longtime chair of the Federal Council of Churches' commission on a just and durable peace. At war's end, Dulles was instrumental in persuading the IMC and WCC to form the Churches' Commission on International Affairs, and this body in turn became a "principal player" in helping to formulate the U.N.'s universal declaration on human rights and structures by which it was to be upheld.[34]

While the intentions of these and other Christian founders of the new world order were oriented primarily toward the ideals of freedom and justice, some observers from other regions of the world perceived many such churchmen as servants of the Western power elite. Ancient Eastern churches harbored mistrust of the value that Westerners placed on religious freedom. It seemed to them a cover for the practice of proselytism by Protestant missionaries and evangelists in traditionally Orthodox lands. This was denounced as sheep-stealing, and worse: its consumer-oriented approach embodied elements of the worst in Western culture. Indeed, this became the deal breaker when Orthodox churches of Eastern Europe were invited to participate in the WCC from its founding in 1948. The Russian Orthodox Church declined in these words:

> The direction of the efforts of the ecumenical movement into the channels of social and political life, and towards the creation of an "Ecumenical Church" as an influential international force, appears to us to be a falling into the temptation rejected by Christ in the wilderness. For the Church to accept it would involve departure from its own true path through attempting to catch souls for Christ by using non-Christian means.[35]

Although the Russian Orthodox and other Orthodox churches of Eastern Europe would decide to join the WCC in 1961, the issues of Enlightenment culture, the manner of participation in politics, and especially proselytism remain sore points in the Council's internal dialogue.[36]

When the United Nations began in 1945, its members numbered 51 states. By 2004, membership had grown to 191. The WCC's first assembly in 1948 welcomed 147 member churches; for the most part, they were traditional "sending" churches based in Europe and North America. As we have seen, the three American Presbyterian founders had united into one church by 1983, and a similar diminution of denominations through church union (see below) was experienced in other united and uniting denominations; however, the total number of WCC members in 2004 had increased to 347.[37]

The IMC merged with the WCC at the Council's 1961 assembly in New Delhi, at the same time that a significant number of Orthodox and newly independent churches came into membership. The character of the Council was obviously changing, and questions arose concerning the effect a church body of such diversity might have on the mission activities that it encouraged and reviewed. John Coventry Smith of COEMAR, one of the architects of the IMC's incorporation into the WCC, argued vigorously that "the church is the instrument that God founded for witness and it should be trusted."[38] It was in the setting of this merger that two influential and widely studied books were written by American Presbyterian leaders: *Ecumenics: The Science of the Church Universal*, a textbook by John A. Mackay, and T. Watson Street's adult education text *The Church and the Churches*. These books introduced Presbyterian pastors and people in the pews to the modern ecumenical movement, in theory and practice.[39] Both works on ecumenics were grounded in the Protestant missionary enterprise. Church unity, wrote Mackay, "is never so real or so Christian as when it is fulfilled in mission. For it is in mission, and only in mission, that individual members of the community achieve true stature, when each discovers his place within the whole and becomes equipped to play his part worthily."[40] But not everyone agreed on the nature of "mission." During the 1960s many Presbyterians were involved in the civil rights movement, viewing it as an essential part of God's mission at that time. In the summer of 1963, Eugene Carson Blake, stated clerk of the UPCUSA General Assembly, marched on Washington with Martin Luther King Jr. and was arrested while protesting the segregation of an amusement park near Baltimore. Presbyterian congregations in the South and North provided resources for civil rights projects. Two hundred fifty PCUS missionaries signed a 1964 statement on race relations, decrying "the effect that the existence of various forms of racial segregation in the church has on the work of Christ in other lands."[41] While some evangelical leaders distanced themselves from civil rights demonstrations, others like Donald McGavran lent support, if "only as a kind of parenthesis, a temporary diversion from evangelism and church growth," which they saw as the ultimate route to a just society.[42] Nevertheless, there also were Protestants who saw civil disobedience and attempts to change society as an attack on the American system. Similarly, criticism of U.S. policy overseas was taken by some Presbyterians as a form of defeatism. It was an age of activism but also an age of controversy, and the struggle to uphold one's ideals transcended national borders.

War and rumors of war sounded a constant undertone throughout the twentieth century. The departure of the French from Indochina was followed by a simmering civil war that came to a boil as the great powers supplied and supported the combatants. The revolutionary government of Cuba formed an alliance with the USSR, building toward the 1962 missile crisis with the United States. Images of violence and devastation were transmitted from the Middle East, the Dominican Republic, Brazil, Korea, the borders of India and Pakistan, Congo, Nigeria, Angola, Rhodesia, Namibia, South Africa, Chile, Argentina, Nicaragua, El Salvador—the list goes on. In dialogue with church leaders throughout the world, mission officials of the American Presbyterian churches heard their partners' expressions of discontent with U.S. policy and tactics on many fronts.

Responding to entreaties from partners and reports from fraternal workers, many in Protestant leadership felt compelled to play an advocacy role. In 1965, a deputation from COEMAR met with Secretary of State Dean Rusk and Defense Secretary Robert MacNamara (both Presbyterians) and Rusk's deputy George Ball to explain their misgivings about the American presence in the Dominican Republic and Vietnam. When challenged why leaders of an American church felt compelled to speak about foreign policy, John Coventry Smith replied, "We are not just American Christians. We belong to a wider Christian community which is disturbed, and we cannot keep quiet."[43]

In 1966, Eugene Carson Blake was elected general secretary of the WCC. His arrival coincided with the 1966 Church and Society Conference in Geneva, focusing on rapid social and technological change. For the first time, a global ecumenical conference hosted as many representatives from the developing world as from the North Atlantic nations, in addition to a significant representation from Orthodox churches based in Eastern Europe. Radical change was embraced by many speakers, one of the most widely quoted of whom was mission professor Richard Shaull of Princeton Seminary. In an early evocation of Latin American liberation theology, the former UPCUSA fraternal worker in Brazil called for Christians to support "guerilla units with a clear sense of self-identity, a vision of a new social order and a commitment to constant struggle for change, inside or outside the social structures."[44] Less revolutionary statements from Geneva nonetheless leveled criticism at U.S. foreign policy, especially in Vietnam, and supported civil disobedience in defense of human rights. In the following months, themes of social change were taken up by WCC member churches, national and regional councils of churches, congregations, and mission agencies. The struggle for justice in Latin America was to be a project in which churches and councils confronted dictatorial governments for decades, often finding themselves running afoul of U.S. foreign policy in the region and risking charges of being soft on communism.[45]

Opposition to the official line on mission and ecumenics crystallized in conservative publications, and notably in the UPCUSA with the organization of the Presbyterian Lay Committee. The first edition of its newspaper, *The Presbyterian Layman,* appeared in early 1968, and from its inception the *Layman* opposed Presbyterian involvement in the WCC and the National Council of the Churches of Christ in the U.S.A. Editorials held that the policies of these ecumenical bodies were "not in the best interests of the United States."[46]

Social activism has been an easier target than theology for opponents of ecumenical councils. There is no official "ecumenical theology" since the doctrines of churches in membership of ecumenical councils run the gamut from Orthodox patristic thought through the fundamentalism of nineteenth-century missionary church planters to liberationist statements of recent decades. This theological pluralism in itself may be cause for criticism, and it is the subject of continuing discussion at several levels through faith-and-order commissions. But it is difficult to pin a particular heresy on the movement as a whole.

Ecumenical social activists and their critics opened a new chapter of mutual antagonism at the end of the 1960s when the World Council of Churches under the leadership of Eugene Carson Blake took on the policy of apartheid in South Africa and the white minority government in Rhodesia. A key theme at the WCC's 1968 assembly in Uppsala (Sweden) was "white racism." Following the assembly, Blake organized a conference at Notting Hill in London under the chairmanship of U.S. senator and future presidential candidate George McGovern, who had been a United Methodist delegate to the Uppsala assembly. The conference's purpose was to formulate concrete proposals, eventually resulting in the WCC's Program to Combat Racism (PCR) and the Special Fund to Combat Racism. Baldwin Sjollema, the first director of PCR, later observed that, after Uppsala,

> Christians could no longer live between the fortified walls of their churches, but had to cooperate with the much wider *oikoumenē* of the whole inhabited earth. In the case of the PCR this meant that its partners were not only the churches and their agencies, but also the many secular groups constituting the worldwide anti-apartheid movement and all those struggling against racism in many parts of the world. Most importantly, the debate about racial justice had to take place in the presence and with the participation of the victims themselves.[47]

Blake was instrumental in the formulation of the WCC's program and special fund against racism, and in seeing it through to adoption by the central committee during a stormy meeting at Canterbury late in 1969. The program and fund, once created, began to supply money to meet the humanitarian needs of refugees and other victims of racially separatist regimes, including those of Rhodesia and South Africa. Contributions were administered through agents recommended by churches in Africa; among these agents were auxiliaries of banned organizations like the African National Congress. As might be expected, most of the money was used for its intended purposes, but accurate accounting and accountability were difficult in wartime conditions, and it is this ambiguity that critics seized upon. The WCC, however, was joined in its condemnation of apartheid by bodies like the Lutheran World Federation and WARC, which declared apartheid theologically incompatible with Lutheran and Reformed traditions of the Christian faith.

Before Archbishop Desmond Tutu and Nelson Mandela were awarded the Nobel Peace Prize in 1984 and 1993 respectively, the antiapartheid movement was frequently depicted in Western media as a front for world communism, brutal, and intent on destruction of Western democracies. Many church members believed that ecumenical organizations and their supporting churches had become more political than religious, and that ecumenical politics tended to favor the forces of socialism.

The ecumenical campaign against apartheid would make the WCC and member churches targets of criticism into the 1990s, but the dangers were apparent from early on. In 1971 Eugene Carson Blake addressed the joint commission on Faith and Order at Louvain,[48] defending the struggle for justice and peace in the world as an intrinsic part of the churches' quest for unity. Despite his conviction that the World Council's path was correct, Blake warned: "Unless it becomes clearer to our whole constituency than it now is that all that the World Council is and does arises out of the gospel, the revelation of God in Jesus Christ, an increasing and destructive polarization of the church may be expected."[49] A generation later another WCC general secretary, Konrad Raiser of Germany, recognized "that the destructive polarization of which Gene Blake spoke in 1971 did indeed occur and that it became a serious threat to the ecumenical movement."[50]

CLASHES OF CULTURES AND CIVILIZATIONS

The impact of secularization theory on ecumenical mission played out dramatically at a teaching conference of the World Student Christian Federation at Strasbourg, France, in 1960. Johannes C. Hoekendijk deplored the ecclesiological assumptions of fellow lecturers Karl Barth and W. A. Visser 't Hooft, calling for "high worldmanship" among Christian students in place of "high churchmanship."[51] He issued this challenge: "Are there no revolutionaries here? People who do not want to improve or to modify the structures and institutions of our Christian life but who are ready to break out of these prisons?"[52]

Adopting Bonhoeffer's description of Jesus as "the man for others," Hoekendijk argued that Christians in the world must live and act for others, and not for the sake of the churches and their institutions. The themes of the world as the arena for Christian mission and "the church for others" were key elements in the development of ecumenical approaches to mission, from the WCC's assembly at New Delhi in 1961, through the 1966 Geneva Conference on Church and Society and the emphasis on "humanization" at the Uppsala assembly of 1968, to the WCC's Mission and Evangelism Conference at Bangkok in 1973. Ecumenical studies concerning mission increasingly focused on social, economic, and cultural factors.[53]

While the 1973 conference on world mission and evangelism at Bangkok did produce statements endorsing church growth and personal evangelism, it was most famous—many would say notorious—for its explication of cultural dimensions of its theme "Salvation Today." The conference's definitions of salvation were mostly this-worldly, including liberation from economic injustice, political oppression, social alienation, discrimination on the basis of one's sex, and personal despair. In the first section of its final report on "Culture and Identity," the conference voiced approval of theological inculturation of the gospel, citing black theology as an example of the translation of Christian teaching into the life experience of a community.[54] In the field of Christian social ethics, the unified theory of "responsible society" that had provided a conceptual framework for approaching a limited number of economic contexts[55] gave way to case-by-case encounters with particular situations through action followed by reflection. From Bangkok onward, contextualized theology including instances of liberation and feminist theology would become a regular feature of ecumenical discussions, where these new schools of thought would vie with traditional orthodoxies. The scattered diversity of world Christianity led some "to encourage these many self-confident social theologies to undertake a more incisive dialogue with each other."[56]

In parts of the world a mission focus on cultures encouraged dialogue both with some Christians unrelated to the World Council of Churches and with peoples of other faiths and ideologies. A Catholic theologian from Africa described the broad approach to inculturation:

> Inculturation asserts the right of all peoples to enjoy and develop their own
> culture, the right to be different and to live as authentic Christians while

remaining truly themselves at the same time. It makes Christianity feel truly at home in the culture of each people, thus reflecting its universality. . . . The scope of inculturation extends to the totality of Christian life and doctrine, the central ministry of Christ and all other ministries which derive from it, the manner of witnessing to Christ, to proclaiming his message, worship, organization of church, study of the Bible, and theology and pastoral methods.[57]

Latin American liberation theologian Gustavo Gutiérrez described the "rise of ecumenical groups, often marginal to their ecclesiastical authorities, in which Christians shared their faith and struggled to create a more just society. The common struggle made the traditional ecumenical programs seem obsolete ('a marriage between senior citizens,' as someone has said) and impelled them to look for new paths towards unity."[58] Subsequent proposals for a new, universal paradigm to serve as a framework for ecumenical theology were liberation thought, the equality of men and women in church and society, justice, peace, and creation—or several of these in combination.

For evangelicals like Arthur F. Glasser, the WCC's sponsorship of contextual theology as an approach to mission at Bangkok (1973), the Nairobi assembly (1975), and the Melbourne mission conference (1980) resulted in discussions "so deeply committed to listening to voices from Latin America that great contemporary missiological issues were hardly given serious attention."[59] In approaching people of other faiths and ideologies, he denounced the apparent ecumenical "obligation" to "'dialogue' of the sort that stops short of gospel proclamation and the essentiality of the call to conversion."[60] Within WCC circles, too, there were those who worried over what they perceived as "the 'loss of nerve' in Christian mission that has accompanied the decline of western imperialism."[61]

A new international mission body came into existence following the July 1974 Congress on World Evangelism held in Lausanne, Switzerland. John R. W. Stott provided leadership, with principal funding from the Billy Graham organization. In a keynote address, Stott affirmed that humanization, liberation, and justice are desirable goals, but "these things do not constitute the 'salvation' that God is offering the world in and through Christ. They could be included in the 'mission of God,' insofar as Christians are giving themselves to serve in these fields. But to call socio-political liberation 'salvation' is to be guilty of a gross theological confusion."[62] The congress culminated in adoption of the fifteen-article "Lausanne covenant," a document "reflecting the spirit and stance of the evangelical community in the late twentieth century."[63] Although it was not the intention of organizers of the congress to found an ongoing missionary body, the covenant became the platform used several months later by enthusiastic evangelicals who became founders of the Lausanne Committee for World Evangelization.[64]

Not without reason, the "Lausanne movement" and the conciliar "ecumenical movement" were depicted in succeeding years as competitors or even opponents, the former majoring in old-style evangelism and the latter frequently portrayed as blown about by trends of doctrine.[65] The truth was more complex.

There was an overlap in the two circles of mission activity and support.[66] Among other concerns, evangelical leaders insisted on Christians' obligations to the poor and to social justice. In the 1980s, reconciliation between East and West became an important theme of Billy Graham's preaching and media interviews. The WCC leaders responded to the challenge of Lausanne with a reexamination of their policies and rhetoric, deliberating in the WCC's Nairobi assembly of 1975 and the Melbourne mission conference of 1980, finally issuing the report *Mission and Evangelism: An Ecumenical Affirmation.*[67]

The network of dialogues on mission that included Catholics, Orthodox, ecumenical and evangelical Protestants, Pentecostals, and others marked out common ground on which Christians could stand together, evidencing a "movement toward convergence" on mission and evangelism through "a basis of trust" that made honest dialogue possible.[68] The shared concerns for conversion of hearts and for justice came into focus as complementary aspects of Christian mission.[69] Common projects in mission and advocacy multiplied, among them programs addressing hunger, malaria, tuberculosis, and the new scourge of HIV and AIDS. In retirement, Eugene Carson Blake became the first chairperson of the citizen's lobby Bread for the World. World Vision International opened new channels of communication and cooperation with conciliar agencies.

There continued to be moments when theologies of inculturation tested the limits of a wider community, as when Korean theologian Chung Hyun-Kyung combined aboriginal spirituality and ancestor worship with elements of minjung and feminist theologies in her keynote address at the WCC's 1991 assembly in Canberra. Another high-profile moment came in 1993–94, when a "Re-Imagining Conference" highlighting feminist theology was held in Minneapolis (November 1993), with partial funding from an office of the World Council and from the women's unit of the PC(USA). Less-than-flattering reports of the event circulated in publications ranging from *Christianity Today* to *The Presbyterian Layman*, and unit director Mary Ann Lundy was asked to resign from her PC(USA) leadership position. Subsequently, she was called as deputy general secretary to the WCC's newly installed Konrad Raiser. In these cases and others, Orthodox and more traditional Protestant members of the WCC—many from the global South—were as uncomfortable as was anyone in the Lausanne movement.[70]

One issue raised throughout debates on inculturation and a missionary moratorium was the question of the ability of indigenous minority communities of Christians to prosper if cut off from outside aid. A stunning reply came following the Cultural Revolution (1966–76) in the People's Republic of China. For decades, Westerners had mourned the "loss" of China and its churches to communism after Mao's conquest (or what the Chinese call the Liberation) of China in 1949. But with the reopening of church buildings and renewed permission for the public practice of religion, it became apparent that the Chinese church had been multiplying far beyond Western imagining. A Presbyterian "old mission hand" put it this way:

In the early 1950s the missionary movement had come to an end. . . . Yet in spite of the limitations of the missionaries—their foreignness and their connection with the colonial system—the seed of the Christian gospel had been buried deep in the soil of China. And when springtime finally came, new shoots full of vitality and life began to emerge. But it was not the same as what had been planted. Christianity had taken a form and shape which the missionary could not have planned or predicted or understood. What finally came up . . . was distinctively and thoroughly Chinese![71]

Chinese church leaders saw the next decade as a period of recovery, followed by rapid expansion in the 1990s. In a 2003 study sponsored by the Lutheran World Federation, seminary president Feng Gao reported on officially recognized congregations:

> It is estimated that there are now fifteen million [Protestant] Christians, more than a twenty-fold increase compared with the 700,000 disciples in 1949. In the last twenty years, sixteen thousand churches have been opened, seventy percent of which are newly constructed; and there are over three thousand meeting points. The church has reclaimed from government and private sources an average of six church buildings a day.[72]

The news from China contrasted strikingly with church statistics in the United States and both Western and Eastern Europe. By the late 1970s it was common to speak of the "decline" of "mainline" Protestant churches, a trend perceived by more than a few as "the blaring alarm of a denominational meltdown."[73] Total memberships in the PCUS and UPCUSA had peaked in the early 1960s, and the combined membership dropped steadily from the PC(USA)'s 1983 reunion through the period covered by this book.[74] The number of postwar, full-time missionaries peaked at 1,284 in the UPCUSA during 1959, and at 567 in the PCUS during 1965.[75] Although lower numbers of U.S. mission workers had much to do with new strategies of mission through partnership, and although giving to Presbyterian causes in general actually rose, raw membership figures fed the sense of "decline" and inferiority to conservative religious organizations that had ongoing numerical growth. It was easy to move from a conviction of church decline to the belief that Christianity itself was in retreat. Early in the twenty-first century, WCC general secretary Samuel Kobia of Kenya reminded a North American audience that theirs was not the only perspective to be considered:

> In the world context, Christianity is growing—not shrinking. Its growth is most prodigious in the global South, and particularly on my own continent of Africa. Statisticians now locate Christianity's demographic center of gravity near Timbuktu in the Sahara desert, and it continues to shift southward year by year. In addition, traditional forms of Christianity that were shaped in Europe, from Constantinople and Rome to Wittenberg and Geneva, are less and less normative. African-initiated churches proliferate, and in all the regions of the globe Pentecostalism expands even as the U.S. mainline churches contract. It is all part of the interplay, the ebb and flow, of the

church's life. Within this exciting and nerve-racking pattern of global change, each member has its role to play within the unity of the one body. And within the providence of God, prosperity may come again to the North American mainline through the Spirit's action among Christians of Indonesia or Nigeria or Brazil.

Perhaps this poses the greatest of the contemporary challenges to North American Christians and their churches: the need to adjust to a new position within the wider church of Jesus Christ, the need to give up total control of the missionary enterprise, the need—as has been said—to "let go, and let God."[76]

A number of initiatives developed over the years that encouraged multidirectional patterns of aid, evangelism, and renewal, including the Frontier Internship Program, Mission to the U.S.A., and international exchanges of Christians through the Presbyterian Peacemaking Program and governing body partnerships. Support for mission in and to the West came from Lesslie Newbigin's drive to reconceptualize the "first world" in post-Enlightenment times as a mission field in need of cross-cultural encounter with authentic Christianity from other shores.[77] While he approved of conciliar statements in favor of joint action with more conservative evangelicals, he doubted "that the desire here expressed will be fulfilled unless the WCC gives much more evidence of being filled with a longing to bring the Gospel to all peoples."[78] Nevertheless, ensuing years brought interaction on "gospel and culture" involving participants from diverse theological perspectives.

The acceptance of cultural pluralism and the broad internationalism of ecumenical mission came into conflict with a rising tide of neoconservatism in the era of Margaret Thatcher, Ronald Reagan, and a new pope from Communist Poland suspicious of liberationist thought and activities. Neoconservative philosophy stepped away from the geopolitical "realism" and the superpowers' "spheres of influence" that had been accepted by strategists ranging from Reinhold Niebuhr to Henry Kissinger. Neoconservatives demanded an unyielding mission to eradicate Marxist ideology. Princeton political scientist Stephen Kotkin categorizes neoconservatism as a continuation of "the missionary impulse" of U.S. triumphalism earlier embodied by William McKinley and Woodrow Wilson: the world was to be "converted" to Western democratic ideals and remade in the image of America.[79] Neoconservatism reinforced themes that had long been found in critiques of the WCC and the National Council of Churches (NCC) like those of *The Presbyterian Layman*. Erskine Clarke has offered a sympathetic explanation of why such criticism of ecumenical mission sways readers:

> Behind many of these attacks are opposing views of the American experience and the role of the United States in the world. The *Layman* expresses the older view, long held by the Protestant establishment, that the United States has been a great source of hope for the world and a defender of justice and democracy. An alternative view, often found in the pronouncements of the NCC and WCC, is that the United States is the source of most serious problems because of its racism, consumerism, militarism, and impe-

rialism. Such an alternative view of the American experience and the United States' place in the contemporary world has contributed ironically to the decline of the ecumenical movement in the United States.[80]

One expression of the neoconservative political movement is the Institute on Religion and Democracy (IRD), which from its founding in the early 1980s has opposed the policies of the WCC and NCC. The IRD particularly objected to ecumenical ties with opponents of the "dirty wars" in Latin America and apartheid in southern Africa, to the sanctuary movement and antinuclear campaigning at the close of the Cold War. The IRD proved effective in attracting media attention to their charges of churchly anti-Americanism. Paul Crow, former ecumenical officer of the Christian Church (Disciples of Christ), has described the prime examples of conservative and neoconservative criticism of ecumenical internationalism:

> The severest attacks on both councils came in three articles in *The Reader's Digest* in 1973, 1983, and 1993. Also in 1983 the CBS television show "60 Minutes" did a television version of these attacks—claiming the councils misused funds and lost the trust of the churches by supporting liberation armies in Africa and elsewhere and by involvement in similar political activities around the world. . . . Research at the time brought forth evidence that assistance to those who made these erroneous attacks was given in the form of funds by the Institute on Religion and Democracy, a neo-conservative research institute in Washington that received a large percentage of its funds from right-wing foundations. After considerable time, the churches have proved that these critiques were gross distortions, but unfortunately the correct impression did not always reach the pews and pulpits.[81]

With the end of the Cold War, neoconservative Francis Fukuyama foresaw "the end of history," or a least an end to worldwide ideological conflict. He wrote that he observed the coming peace "with ambivalence," since it seemed to be the end of a struggle "that called forth daring, courage, imagination, and idealism."[82] There was an unprecedented opening of trade and dialogue between East and West. Representatives of Eastern and Western churches began gingerly to reassess their relationships.[83] In postapartheid South Africa, ecumenist and Anglican Archbishop Desmond Tutu was put in charge of the nation's Truth and Reconciliation Commission, an attempt to find healing that was embraced by peace activists in many parts of the world.

On the other hand, the historian Samuel P. Huntington prophesied "that the fundamental source of conflict in this new world will not be primarily ideological or primarily economic. The great divisions among humankind and the dominating source of conflict will be cultural. Nation states will remain the most powerful actors in world affairs, but the principal conflicts of global politics will occur between nations and groups of different civilizations. The clash of civilizations will dominate global politics. The fault lines between civilizations will be the battle lines of the future."[84] He noted that militant expressions of religion were an engine of bellicosity among competing cultures.

After September 11, 2001, the date of al-Qaeda's attacks on the World Trade Center and the Pentagon, "the clash of civilizations" seemed a fair summary of the framework within which the U.S. administration viewed the world and promoted its policy of "preemptive war" in the face of terrorism. Following Western-led invasions of Afghanistan and Iraq, and the incarceration without trial as well as rendition for torture of suspected terrorists, the WCC and NCC found themselves once again in opposition to central policies of the U.S. government, while the IRD and others renewed their critique of the councils.[85] Ecumenical leadership was unapologetic, emphasizing again their responsibility to Christians in all countries. Samuel Kobia, in his challenge to North Americans, explained what he was hearing as he visited Christians in each of the world's regions:

> Many people in the world—east and west, north and south, regardless of political or economic conviction—mistrust or openly fear the United States. . . . People in many nations ask themselves where the doctrine of preemptive war may next be employed, and for what stated reason, . . . if any.
> The U.S. is seen as the bulwark of economic globalization that forces poorer nations to live according to the dictates of wealthy corporate interests and financial institutions controlled by those interests. In recent years, we have seen a gathering backlash to these policies in Latin America—but this is not the only region in which the United States has suffered a loss of respect and support. . . . Among educated people, the U.S. is feared for its willful disregard of global warming as a threat to the future of our planet.[86]

As civilizations clashed, the churches and their councils sought new means toward dialogue and cooperation. The WCC spoke of the post-9/11 period as "a critical moment" for interreligious dialogue, inviting representatives of Islam, Judaism, and many other world faiths to consultations and conferences.[87] At the same time, the conciliar movement was seeking a wider network of national and regional "churches together" and a "global forum" that could attract Catholics, Pentecostals, and conservative evangelicals in addition to the traditional membership of the WCC.[88] Unfortunately, simultaneous attempts at intra-Christian and interreligious dialogue provoked disagreement, since varying traditions could agree neither on basic guidelines nor on theological assumptions. This was also an obstacle to some joint mission projects.

Michael Kinnamon, reflecting on preparations for the 2005 Athens conference on mission and evangelism, noted that this WCC event was attracting unprecedented numbers of Catholics, Pentecostals, and evangelicals not affiliated with the council. But he also remarked that in the first decade of the twenty-first century,

> the great question for us is that of inter-religious dialogue, yet the interfaith dimension of mission is noticeable by its absence from the agenda of this conference. . . . [So,] expanding participation on the part of Christian traditions may also make some issues more difficult to deal with. As an ecumenist, I want to say an emphatic Yes! to expanding participation in the movement. But we should recognize that it does complicate things. For the moment, we continue to accept the two main assertions on interfaith rela-

tions formulated in the San Antonio mission conference in 1989: We know that we can place no limits on the extent of God's grace, but at the same time we know that we are called as Christians to proclaim Jesus Christ as Lord and Savior.

Kinnamon expressed hope that, "as the relationship matures" among traditions represented at the Athens conference, a new conversation may begin on "the place of faiths other than Christianity in God's plan for salvation."[89] But this remains one of many mission projects for the future.

Prophecy is a dangerous business, and as our little journey through ecumenical mission history and theology has shown us, no one in 1944 could have predicted such global and seismic shifts among the world's churches from the end of World War II to the present. We can see immediately before us the need to focus on theologies of religion, witness in partnership, the growth of mission from the non-West, and the ongoing struggle to find full and visible expressions of Christian unity. But what major changes will develop in Christianity in the next ten or twenty years? No one knows.

Now, as in the past, the great world fellowship struggles to be obedient in each place, in each year. As ever, principalities and powers conspire together. And Presbyterians, by the grace of God and in communion with the church militant and triumphant, press on in faith and action, seeking to follow wherever Christ leads.

Chapter 2

Counting the Cost

Statistics and What They May Tell Us

DAVID DAWSON

Global and ecumenical changes that were taking place were also reflected in the Presbyterian Church. Although numbers and statistics can easily be used to conceal as well as to reveal, some careful quantification of Presbyterian mission is helpful to better understand the last half century of Presbyterian mission. As we noted in the introduction, the second half of the twentieth century saw the most dramatic changes in mission, particularly in mission sending structures, that the Presbyterian Church (U.S.A.) and its predecessor denominations had ever experienced. The chart on the next page outlines the changes in mission-sending structures during this time period.[1]

For over 120 years (1837–1959) the basic agent for international mission in the northern Presbyterian Church remained the same: the Board of Foreign Missions. Over the next forty-eight years the name changed seven times in the three denominations that merged (1958) and then reunited (1983).

Even within the history of a particular board, the annual reports have changed their overall format and nomenclature for reporting and classifying data. Consequently it is difficult to precisely track the numbers involved so that accurate comparisons can be drawn. Although this chapter revolves around statistics, its

	PCUSA/UPCNA	UPCUSA	PCUS
1949	Board of Foreign Missions		Board of World Missions[2]
1958[3]		Commission on Ecumenical Mission and Relations	
1972		Program Agency	
1974			Division of International Mission[4]
1983		**PC(USA)**	
1988		Global Mission Ministry Unit	
1993		Worldwide Ministries Division	
2007		World Mission	

purpose is not to provide finely researched numbers, but rather to use basic and reliable statistics related to the number of missionaries serving, where they served, and their funding to draw conclusions about the trends in Presbyterian mission during this period.[5]

MISSIONARIES UNDER APPOINTMENT

First, let us turn to the overall numbers of missionaries serving through the various boards. A few basic numbers will help to frame the discussion:

	1944	1957[6]	1959[7]	1970	1981	1990[8]	2007
PCUSA[9]	1,160[10]	1,031					
UPCNA	246[11]	259					
UPCUSA			1,356	841	347		
PCUS	398	483	493	409[12]	344		
PC(USA)						458	250
Totals	1,804	1,773	1,849	1,250	691	458	200[13]

Especially after the early 1960s, these numbers do not strictly represent the total number of long-term missionaries. Although this was the historical trend of mission work up until World War II, in the post–World War II era numerous other categories of "missionary" became common, yet the published total number of missionaries remained wholly undifferentiated.[14]

CATEGORIES OF MISSIONARY SERVICE

When the Presbyterian Church began sending foreign missionaries in the first half of the nineteenth century, they were always understood to be lifetime commitments. Missionaries often took their caskets with them, expecting to serve overseas until their death. At the beginning of our period, all mission personnel were considered fully funded "career" missionaries with five-year initial appointments before any furlough home. As early as the late 1940s short-term missionaries and volunteers emerged as new and regular patterns of service.[15] The main difference between the career and short-term missionaries, besides duration of service, was the extensive language and cultural study the career missionaries were required to complete before moving to their mission fields.[16]

In 1961 the UPCUSA established the Frontier Intern program as a way to engage Christian young adults and laity in the evolving mission work of their age. Twelve young men and women were commissioned "to witness on new frontiers."[17] These frontiers were not understood geographically, but rather in relation to human problems.[18]

By the 1970s there were a variety of other categories of missionaries being recorded. In the UPCUSA, Volunteers in Mission (VIMs) were added into the overall missionary count, often reaching up to 250.[19] Sometimes a VIM served for several years, but frequently VIMs were actually individuals participating in an "overseas summer experience."[20] Additional noncareer missionary categories in the UPCUSA reached a total of almost 200 persons by the late 1970s and included the following: Binational servants,[21] International Subsistence Service,[22] Overseas Associates,[23] Special Ecumenical Personnel,[24] Mission to the U.S.A.,[25] and Three-way Mission partners.[26]

Over the years, many board reports appear to be guilty of what might be termed "missionary inflation": they would include all types of mission workers (paid and volunteer) in their total count of supported mission personnel. For example, the 1993 General Assembly (GA) joint worship commissioning service included a worship bulletin listing all mission personnel in the United States and internationally:

Mission to the U.S.A.	58
Mission Personnel Retiring	37
Mission Personnel Completing Service	64
Mission Personnel Appointments	60
Several categories of volunteers	266
	485

While these 485 names made for an impressive list, in reality the total number of long-term Presbyterian-appointed "missionaries" continued to decline.[27] This practice of listing volunteers in the commissioning service continued through 2004, when there were 17 Mission Coworkers and 180 volunteers in several categories.[28]

COUNTRIES OF SERVICE

In 1944 the three Presbyterian denominations had missionaries serving in their historical mission stations. The 1,160 active PCUSA missionaries in 1944 served in sixteen countries with the largest being: 330 in China, 209 in India, 99 in Korea, and 85 in Cameroon.[29] The 246 UPCNA missionaries were concentrated in four countries: 91 in India-Pakistan, 113 in Egypt, 28 in Sudan, and 14 in Ethiopia. In 1944 the PCUS had 398 missionaries serving in six countries: 138 in China, 75 in Congo, 71 in Korea, 48 in Brazil, 40 in Japan, and 26 in Mexico.

Just before the 1958 merger with the UPCNA, the PCUSA had 1,245 missionaries serving in twenty-one countries with the largest being: 227 in India, 148 in Cameroon, 114 in Iran, 85 in Brazil, 85 in Thailand, 80 in Syria-Lebanon, 75 in Korea, and 73 in Japan.[30] The most obvious change that took place between 1944 and 1958 was the displacement of all the missionaries from China after the communist takeover in 1949.[31] At this same juncture the UPCNA had 259 missionaries in its same four countries: 87 in India-Pakistan, 78 in Egypt, 59 in Sudan, and 35 in Ethiopia. After the 1958 merger, the combined UPCUSA had 1,555 missionaries serving in twenty-two countries, with the largest missionary presence as follows: 201 in India, 150 in Cameroon, 133 in Pakistan, and 121 in Iran. By 1958 the PCUS had 483 missionaries serving in seven countries: 164 in Congo, 128 in Brazil, 67 in Japan, 59 in Korea, 34 in Formosa/Taiwan, 29 in Mexico, and 2 in Ecuador. The decline in missionary presence, it can be clearly proved, was both "accidental" and intentional. It was accidental in that funding became more and more of a problem. General Assembly reports alone prove the preoccupation with finding the money to support full-time missionaries. The decline was also accidental in that wars, changes in government, and changes in social policy of "receiving" nations made missionary work difficult and nearly impossible in many of the Presbyterian Churches' strongest fields. The decline was also intentional, and this will be discussed later.[32] By 1973 there were a total of 531 full-time missionaries with the UPCUSA and 401 PCUS, making a total of 932 missionaries. In 1983 there were 278 and 226 respectively for a total of 504 full-time missionaries. In 2007, according to the PC(USA) Web site, a total of 497 "missionaries" or "missionary workers" are listed working in 71 nations.[33] However, on the Web site only 151 missionaries working in 61 nations are listed as sending out letters. To complicate matters further, of the 497 missionaries, 298 are listed as "long-term compensated personnel." The World Mission office confirmed for us that there are actually 250 compensated mission personnel.[34] In a number of countries, mostly in Eastern Europe and Western Asia, the number of mission personnel is increasing.

NUMBERS OF STAFF

Another way to look at personnel during this period is to look at the mission coworker to staff ratio. How did this ratio change over the years? Staff for the international programs of the Presbyterian denominations were located in New York, Philadelphia, Nashville, Atlanta, and Louisville during the period under consideration. The board reports and minutes usually do not include the number of staff members. When they do include national staff, it is often not clear if support staff are included, but we can assume that they are not, unless otherwise indicated. During the era of the Program Agency in the UPCUSA (1972–1983), it is difficult to determine how many staff were involved in raising funds for international mission (the Support Agency's role) and recruitment of missionaries (the Vocation Agency's role). Even with these disclaimers, we can still make some general observations.

The PCUSA (New York) recorded 30 staff supervising the work of its 1,160 overseas missionaries in 1944 (ratio of 39/1), and 34 in 1955 working with about 1,050 missionaries (ratio of 31/1).[35] In 1944 the UPCNA (Philadelphia) listed 246 missionaries and 3 staff (ratio of 82/1).[36] The year before the merger (1957) the PCUSA listed 36 staff and the UPCNA listed 5 (combined ratio of 37/1).[37] When COEMAR was formed and field staff were distributed in four locations across the United States, the joint staff of the combined denominations quickly grew to 65 in just two years (missionary to staff ratio of 20/1).[38] The number of staff peaked during the COEMAR era at 71 (1,088 missionaries and a ratio of 15/1) in 1967 before slipping back to 50 (604 missionaries; but a ratio of 12/1) just before the formation of the Program Agency.

After the new UPCUSA structures were up and running in the mid-1970s, we find that the Program Agency listed 116 executive staff and 113 clerical staff. The Support Agency had 211 staff, although this probably includes both.[39] It is impossible to identify how many of these (plus the Vocation Agency) were related to international work since this period was an aberration, with international work covered in all three agencies. However, even a cursory observer would note that these are quite large numbers of administrative and support staff during a period of rapid decline in funding and missionaries.

Following the 1983 reunion of the UPCUSA and the PCUS, the Global Mission Ministry Unit (GMU) was formed in 1987 with an executive staff of 30 (assuming there were additional support staff) for 505 missionaries (ratio of 17/1).[40] The staff numbers are not reported in subsequent years, but by 2000 there were over 100 executive and support positions in the Worldwide Ministries Division (WMD), in a year with less than 300 mission personnel. Severe cuts came over the next few years, especially in May 2006. Before May the total number of executive and support staff was still 89, with less than 250 missionaries (ratio of 3/1). After May the total was 64.[41]

NUMBER OF MISSIONARIES AND EFFORTS
TO REVERSE THE DECLINE

On several occasions the denominations lamented their continued decline in the overall number of missionaries. Several General Assemblies (GA) even made commitments to end the decline, searching year after year for a way to recover mission funding and to increase the number of mission personnel. During this post–World War II zeal to integrate all missions into the local churches, the Presbyterian Church was both wary of keeping too many missionaries on the field and thereby being too paternalistic, and concerned with listening to its overseas church partners' requests for help. With the decline in mission personnel, the Presbyterian Church continued to receive from overseas partners far more requests for missionaries than it could provide.[42] Between 1955 and 1957, the PCUS put forth a special effort to increase mission personnel through the campaign called "Forward with Christ." Its goal was to add another 168 missionaries.[43] The PCUS also had requests for 175 more missionaries in 1977. There were fewer than 300 missionaries in the field at the time.[44]

In 1972 the UPCUSA General Assembly addressed the decline in mission personnel. Referring to the position paper "Role and Style of the UPC in Mission and Relations through COEMAR," the GA said that the paper "provides a perspective in which judicatories and congregations can clarify their expectations concerning the work of our denomination as we move from one era of history to another."[45] But given the funding problems, even in 1972, the GA proposed to congregations and presbyteries that their funding priorities be first established in light of needs around the world. This appears to be an encouragement to send more money to the GA for mission work. Second, the GA proposed that "each synod, presbytery, and congregation be requested to establish a committee that will serve as an advocate for the mission of the Church on six continents."[46] In other words this would provide for local advocates, at each of these governing levels, for giving to the GA. Third, it proposed that presbyteries and synods provide funding for overseas work comparative to what they provide for local projects. This was a response to the increasing percentage of designated giving, which made it difficult to procure proper support for administrative costs and less-popular projects.

In that same year, the 1972 PCUS GA Board of World Missions commissioned 73 missionaries (the most ever), bringing the total to 401. It further pledged never to drop below 400 again, but by 1978 the total was 289.[47] Then the 1976 UPCUSA GA noted the declining real dollars available and called for a 20 percent increase from congregations.[48] Thus both denominations were struggling to find a way to respond to declining support for global mission through the 1970s.

In the early 1980s a major new initiative was introduced to help build on the UPCUSA Major Mission Fund and reverse the declining giving to Presbyterian mission.[49] In 1984 increases of 16.36 percent for the GA were noted, but the Consumer Price Index for that period was 25.7 percent, and invested funds produced 26.8 percent, which is indicative of high interest and inflation during that period.[50] Five "directions" were established as the basis for this growth in giving initiative. Even though the 1984 budget included $250,000 for newly appointed personnel, the decline in mission personnel was not reversed. Church leaders continued to look for ways to reverse the downward trends in terms of missionaries and money. The 1986 PC(USA) GA received an overture from Pee Dee Presbytery calling for recruitment of 80 new missionary units, including personnel for frontier mission, and calling for a new "Mission Challenge" to fund these new missionaries. Instead, GA adopted a substitute motion and referred it to the Global Mission Ministry Unit for further study.[51]

Along a similar vein, the 1987 PC(USA) GA instructed the GA Council to maintain the level of mission personnel and "to devise a method to insure continuing adequate funding for global mission as one of its highest priorities for expenditure of any funds available to it." This was in response to the 1986 action, which continued to be under consideration by the new GMU.[52] But the 1988 GA revealed the dilemma: simply mandating more funding was not the answer. Then the 1988 GA approved the response of the GMU that essentially said: due to budget restraints and a lack of funds, even with $800,000 of special funding, and request for personnel and qualified people to go, the GMU would maintain the present level of mission personnel and increase as able, but increases would depend upon having more money available. No response was made to the proposal for a new funding initiative to meet the need, and mission personnel numbers continued to decline.[53]

In 1989 the Global Mission Ministry Unit produced an important policy paper, "A Witness among the Nations," which set a goal of having at least 550 missionaries in place by 1992. At that time there were 460.[54] This was the main response of the GMU to the 1986 overture from Pee Dee Presbytery. This plan was mentioned only one more time, in 1990, but by then the number of missionaries had dropped to 458. Two years later the total number of missionaries was not listed, and three years later the numbers were quite imprecise. Finally, the first report of the WMD (1994) began by quoting Matthew 28 and the statement: "Our vision is to enable the Presbyterian Church (U.S.A.) to be a Great Commission Church." Among the programmatic commitments was one "to recruit, maintain, and support a growing number of people in mission around the world in both short- and long-term service."[55] By that time, the number of mission personnel had dropped below 350.

In spite of these regular and numerous calls to reverse the decline, the trend for the number of missionaries continued downward. In fact, in spite of the 1989 GA's commitment to increase from 460 to 530 by 1992, the next year's report showed an actual decline of 2. The next sixteen years of reports in the GA Minutes did not give specific or comparable numbers to the 458 missionaries that were in place at the end of 1989.[56] On a number of occasions there are indications in the Minutes that congregations did not understand the changes in mission and how they affect missionary personnel. The change in terminology from "missionary" to "fraternal worker" and then to "mission coworker" was one such attempt to bring greater clarity.[57]

This era was in constant flux with respect to the understanding of missionary vocations and missiology. One snapshot from the middle of the period (1974) from the UPCUSA Program Agency is instructive of the dramatic and sometimes confused changes afoot:

A major focus of this year's work has been the rethinking of how the UPC resources mission through persons. The constantly changing issues, needs, and opportunities for witness to the claim of the Gospel require evaluation of old patterns and development of new styles to use and enable people in mission. This means building on historic commitments and concepts, but going farther to fulfill past missionary experiences in ways appropriate to today. . . . It isn't the length of term . . . that distinguishes who is considered the "real missioner." . . . [What is needed is] a major review and reformulation of mission personnel policy appropriate to present and future relationships with overseas churches and a more accurate description of what it means to be in mission on six continents today.[58]

CHANGES IN PRESBYTERIAN UNDERSTANDINGS OF "MISSIONARY VOCATIONS"

As other chapters in this volume will make clear, the postwar and postcolonial era resulted in many changes and adjustments in how Presbyterians did mission overseas. The UPCNA-PCUSA merger (1958), in the context of Lake Mohonk (1956), was the occasion for the formation of the Commission on Ecumenical Mission and Relations (COEMAR). The very first GA of the new church (1958) approved the formation of COEMAR. As the name implies, the emphasis was reoriented toward relationships with emerging independent churches in the postcolonial era. Mission would now be much more about ecumenical relationships.

All of this was under the COEMAR period; the Program Agency era (1972–88) actually involved the most dramatic rethinking of the missionary role and purpose during all of Presbyterian mission history.[59] A review of some of the UPCUSA Program Agency (as well as parallel developments in the PCUS) statements and the events surrounding those statements will give us a sense of the dramatic developments that had been emerging since the end of World War II.[60] In 1971 the mission boards were confronted with a call by the Reverend John Gatu (Presbyterian Church of East Africa) for a moratorium on missionaries and money from the West to the churches of the Third World (as it was called then). Gatu gave a talk at the Reformed Church in America Mission Festival that year with the provocative title, "Missionary, Go Home!" But even Gatu admitted that not everyone around the world agreed with him.[61] However, this challenge to missionary-sending assumptions contributed to a less-confident position by all mission boards, Presbyterians included.

In 1974 the PCUS GA made a significant statement on the subject of international mission: "The Presbyterian Church U.S. throughout its history has emphasized the primacy of people in overseas mission in two respects: (1) priority has been given to sending people rather than programs and funds, and (2) priority has been given to serving people in each field."[62] This statement appeared to contrast the general movement of the time, but the statement itself could be interpreted as either deemphasizing big capital projects (institutions), or focusing upon interchurch relations rather than missionary outreach. The 1974 GA

Minutes of the UPCUSA (working out the reorganization of 1972) identified three new themes from the Program Agency:[63]

1. Internationalization of mission—Rather than separating overseas and US mission work, "All missionaries and fraternal workers have been assigned for program oversight to the unit related to their type of work." One purpose was to "minimize the old 'sending and receiving' split among churches of the world."[64]
2. Ecumenism—Rather than bilateral relations in international mission, the Program Agency was committed to "forming working coalitions of . . . persons doing the same kind of work" through U.S. and international agencies. There would be shared training, programs and funding: the more ecumenical the better. The ecumenical movement was really an extension of the missionary movement, having been started by missionaries. At this time there were proposals to send all missionaries through the National and World Council of Churches, but it was an ideal that never happened, and we might guess, it would have distanced the supporting churches even further from the missionary work.[65]
3. Shifting roles—"The focus now is on providing resources—money, materials, and people—in response to requests from appropriate judicatories, related churches, ecumenical bodies, and constituency groups." There would be no unilateral initiatives, for obvious reasons, since the UPCUSA was moving for full integration. However, this also meant that the missionary and the missions would consequently be defined by one party (our overseas partners), and the UPCUSA would be forced into a passive role.[66] In retrospect and from discussion with many missionaries, we can now see that all other potential partners were precluded; the vision of the one partner became the vision of Presbyterian mission. What many missionaries found out was that often the partner was the party least interested in work among neighboring people groups with whom they had been at enmity for centuries.[67] Submitting completely to the mission partner at times meant submitting to their own personal injustices and prejudices.

The 1974 GA produced some mixed signals regarding mission: mission was being worked out among the churches and in the Program Agency. The report in the Minutes stated, "Until some of these responsibilities are transferred, a great deal of the Program Agency's staff time and budget are locked into these institutions [referring here to hospitals and schools], instead of being available for new forms of ministry and response to emerging needs."[68] This was a strong statement about turning over all mission institutions to the national churches. But, at the same GA (1974), there was a directive "to develop bold strategies for . . . some two billion people who are without the gospel."[69] This directive came from the churches, not from the Program Agency. The next year there was a Program Agency response, which said in part:

> In response to a referral . . . on "unevangelized people," the staff has been exploring the need and opportunity in order to recommend new strategies for evangelization that do not violate the principle of "mutuality in mission." . . . In countries where we work, evangelization and church development is done by established churches, and our contributions undergird their efforts.[70]

This was going to be hard to do in countries where we had no partner church, and where our partner church or institutions were small, highly ethnic, or very young. The ad interim committee of approximately twenty-five people that made this report consisted of a diverse constituency, most of whom, however, were not conversant with the missiological discussions of this issue. The cautious statement seems to preclude even a dialogue on such an issue being initiated by the UPCUSA. Mutuality in mission was not mutual in initiatives. The issue and mission of reaching the "unreached" was restarted outside of the Program Agency.

SUMMARY COMMENT ON THE NUMBERS OF MISSIONARIES

Clearly the decline in long-term PCUSA mission personnel has been dramatic during this period. The number today is only slightly more than 10 percent of what it was at the highest point. At the same time the supporting staff in the UPCUSA and PCUSA home offices grew and then stayed quite large. But there is another angle or view that we would like to suggest, another way of viewing this history. From a different perspective we can say that the number of "Presbyterian missionaries" is probably more than ever today. First, the schisms in the Presbyterian family has created the Evangelical Presbyterian Church (1981) and the Presbyterian Church in America (1974). At present the PCA has 519 career missionaries and the EPC has 61.[71] We need to count those missionaries to have a comparative figure to 1944. Furthermore, we believe that there is a much larger number to be included, and those are the Presbyterian missionaries who serve overseas through other sending agencies. We get a glimpse of how large that number might be when we note that the largest single group of attendees at the triennial Urbana mission conference is PC(USA) members. Most of those "Urbana Presbyterians" who go into full-time missionary service do so through parachurch groups like World Vision, Habitat for Humanity, Frontiers, Heifer Project, SIM International, World Harvest, and countless others. Furthermore, our estimates of Presbyterian giving to mission need to expand greatly for a large portion of these (and those from many other denominations) who are substantially supported by PC(USA) congregations.[72] Thus, when we look at "Presbyterian" involvement in mission, we need to keep this perspective as a large footnote to our conclusions.

FINANCIAL SUPPORT

Jesus said, "Where your treasure is, there will your heart be also" (Matt. 6:21), and we believe that this also applies to mission support.[73] A more secular way of saying the same thing would be "Follow the money if you want to know where the church's heart really is." Nevertheless, it is nearly impossible to follow the money in any precise way. Hundreds of hours of archival research would not be sufficient to determine anything close to precise numbers. That kind of research is beyond the scope of this historical narrative. Fortunately, having precise figures is not essential to this account. Rather, it is important for the reader to understand that this discussion of financial trends is based on broad strokes from data provided in GA Minutes and annual board reports. Therefore the conclusions drawn are modest and understated.

INCOME REPORTED BY THE DENOMINATIONS
FOR INTERNATIONAL WORK

	1944	1957	1981	2005
PCUSA	$3,193,037[74]	$12,517,866[75]	$23,958,209	
UPCNA	$678,449[76]			
PCUS	$1,844,544	$7,253,877	$16,358,010[77]	
PC(USA)				$41,921,122
	$5,716,030	$19,771,743	$40,316,219	$41,921,122[78]

These are very bottom-line statistics that do not allow for the rise of inflation. One important dimension missing from the above chart is the role of women in supporting Presbyterian missions. This support was most dramatic in the years before 1944, but it still remained quite significant beyond the middle of the twentieth century. The Presbyterian Women were significant in terms of financial support well into the second half of the century, but in recent years giving has declined dramatically through that channel. In 2005 it was projected to be $237,000 or 2.27 percent of the Worldwide Ministries Division budget.[79]

Total support for foreign missions in 1944 was $5,716,030 (see above). In the PCUSA, women's organizations contributed almost a third of this amount. In the UPCNA, women supported their own board (included in the total) with almost half of the total UPCNA giving. In the PCUS, women gave a total of $1,772,788 to Benevolence in 1944, their largest contribution ever.[80] The Executive Committee for Foreign Mission reports $229,621 as coming from the Woman's Committee, but the figures are difficult to reconcile in the reports. In any case, in the middle of the twentieth century, a substantial amount of support for foreign missions came through the women's organizations. This dramatic change in funding through women's organizations is a tale in itself.[81]

TRENDS AND ISSUES IN MISSION GIVING

What do we make of these numbers and the rapid decline in women's support for mission? First, we must make sure that we are comparing the same dollar figures, so we must make adjustment for inflation by using the Consumer Price Index. The CPI has increased a remarkable 944 percent from 1944 until 2003. Expenditures for international mission in 2003 were $42,820,103, compared to $5,716,030 in 1944. Considering inflation, there was an actual decline of 20.6 percent in comparative dollars for international mission during that period. Another way to measure this is by using per-member giving to international mission. In 1944 it was $1.99 per annum. This means that Presbyterians are giving 5.2 percent less in real dollars now than they did in 1944. However, incomes have grown much faster than inflation over the past sixty years. During this same period of time, the Presbyterian predecessors of the PC(USA) have actually enjoyed an increase in incomes (on average) greater than most Americans' incomes. Thus, Presbyterians could have been giving far more in 2003 because of their relative increase in income. Presbyterian giving did not keep up with the growth in incomes.[82] Another angle of analysis shows us international mission as a percent of total congregational expenditures. Mission giving was 7.35 percent of total congregational giving in 1944, but it dropped to only 1.5 percent in 2003.[83] Congregations are spending more money on local mission and other mission than in 1944, but even if all of the giving listed as "other mission" were international, it would still be only 4.8 percent.[84] Any way one measures it, Presbyterian giving has dropped significantly.

There has been regular consternation about this long and sustained decline in funding for international mission and especially for personnel. We have seen some of the efforts to reclaim Presbyterian mission dollars, but there were other more-direct statements that show how the funding issue was always before the church. The 1971 PCUS GA Minutes lamented, "The Presbyterian dollar for the overseas missionary outreach of our Church has declined from 11 cents in 1928 to 3.3 cents in 1970."[85] Then, the 1976 UPCUSA GA Finance Committee observed the continued decline in "real dollars" and called on the congregations to increase their giving by 20 percent in 1977.[86] A year later, the 1977 PCUS Task Force on Mission Funding called for a fresh commitment to mission, noting significant cuts in missionaries and the Atlanta staff. This has been the ongoing concern expressed throughout the past three or four decades.

These sixty years, as we have seen, represent an almost uninterrupted decline in giving for international mission. Missionaries were quite aware of the threat of cutbacks because of declining funds, and in our interviews with missionaries, these financial concerns came up again and again. One missionary put it this way:

> One of the things that bothered me was the many cutbacks. For example, when I was on furlough and I was asked to be the representative that year, I felt the people were willing to cut mission without putting out much effort to raise the funds that were necessary; the mission folk at one time even gave up 10 percent of their income to keep another missionary in the field.[87]

Another agreed, "I was on furlough at that time in rural Minnesota, and I was welcomed when I heard that a new chandelier was dedicated that cost $50,000, and I stood up and spoke, saying that the money they had spent on the church could support missionaries."

Missionaries also had firsthand experience with churches that would not continue to give through the UPCUSA GA because of controversial issues or controversial General Assemblies. One missionary mentioned that when their family returned for home assignment, they were asked at nearly every church, "What do you think of the (1990) human sexuality report?" Churches were very conscious of controversial issues, and many decided to vote with their dollars. Many churches, according to missionaries, began to question their support at the time of the "Angela Davis affair," when the Presbyterian Church gave $10,000 toward Davis's defense fund in 1971. When released, Davis, a member of the Communist Party, migrated to Cuba temporarily. It was very hard for missionaries to raise extra dollars with all of the publicity around the UPCUSA's support of Davis; in fact some missionaries were terminated because of the sudden decline in giving.

UNIFIED AND DESIGNATED GIVING

Designated mission giving has always been common in the Presbyterian Church. In fact, it was the norm except for the few decades that encompass the first portion of our period of study (1944–ca. 1980s). But even during those postwar decades, when most of the giving was "unified," there was still a tremendous amount of designated giving. The official bias of the denomination's elected and staff leadership has favored unified giving throughout this period and even to the present day.[88]

The unified or centralized funding system actually began with the reorganization that occurred in the 1920s in many denominations. It is often forgotten that previously there were a number of mission boards in the PCUSA, so reorganization was initiated, resulting in one "Board of Foreign Missions" (BFM). As we noted, the women's mission boards were eventually forced into those denominational boards. Even though funding specifically designated for the BFM continued for many years, eventually the "One Mission" concept (UPCUSA) of the last third of the century meant that there was one preferred way to fund mission: one large pot. Money was to be sent by churches to presbytery, synod, and GA according to a percentage distribution, and it was to be undesignated. The elected commissioners and their committees would make the distribution decisions. Despite this trend, designated giving still continued to grow throughout this period. As early as 1949 the PCUS, even as it tried to centralize giving, established an "Equalization Fund" that allowed for designated giving.[89]

The 1970s controversy over the Angela Davis affair resulted in both more designations, often through the UPCUSA's Personnel Interest Program, and more cancellations of support.[90] The Personnel Interest Program involved relating to a particular missionary or project. There were 4,200 churches involved, and some of these specifically designated their giving to missionaries. The 1975 GA Minutes reported on the situation:

> Churches which care to designate moneys through the GA approved program of Specific Mission Support are kept informed as to what projects are available for designation. . . . In 1974 slightly more than 1,000 churches provided nearly 20 percent of congregational receipts designated to mission programs in the United States and abroad.[91]

In the late 1970s the Extra Commitment Opportunity (ECO) channel for funding outside the budget (but approved) was allowed, and by 1985 the annual total was $819,000, with another $2,194,698 listed for "projects outside the budget." This money was received from congregations, individuals, and United Presbyterian Women for projects outside the budget.[92] In the UPCUSA, by the early 1980s, churches were designating $4 million each year, mostly for missionary support within the budget.[93] The 1982 expenditures of the PCUS on international mission from basic funds (undesignated) was $4,104,613, whereas expenditures from other (designated) funds was $4,570,346.[94] By 1987 those numbers were $4,519,129 and $7,144,178, indicating that a growing percentage of income for international mission was coming from designated gifts. Also in 1987 the UPCUSA stream reported $5,254,012 unrestricted and $2,949,451 restricted giving.[95] Clearly there was a strong interest among churches and their members in having some say as to where mission dollars were to be spent.

In both of the churches, "restricted" funds included income from endowments and other sources that required it to be used in specific ways. Increasingly, churches' regular giving was also designated. The 1975 PCUS GA Report indicated that there was an effort to raise designated support for missionaries and listed $2,330,000 as coming from 953 churches. In 1976 there were 242 missionaries assigned to 203 churches and three presbyteries for partial financial support.[96]

While designated giving was on the rise, missionaries were instructed to be advocates for unified giving during their itineration when on home assignment. They were given information about the whole spectrum of the "One Mission" so that they would not be seen as exclusively supporting international mission or their personal missionary work. Some missionaries were frustrated that giving continued to decline, and many wondered if "unified giving is just something from an earlier generation."[97] Although many missionaries lamented the demise of the unified system, which meant they were increasingly required to raise their own support, they had many conflicted thoughts about the transition that they were living through.

> It is complicated, but we did not [really] have a unified budget, . . . but now they have put it all together [and] people who wanted to designate and couldn't, just stop giving. [There] ought to be some type of opportunity for people to designate what they want to give to, to give more generously to what they want to support. . . . *That was the beginning of the end when they established the unified budget in giving to the church.* It ruined the whole picture of giving to the missions. In the division, the money would go in the top and be taken out of the bottom to balance out.[98]

Many missionaries had mixed feelings about designated and undesignated giving and its impact on authentic partnership with churches around the world. An indication of this is found in one missionary's comment.

> I still question the concept of partnership as it is expressed; that it is creating an illusion of a partnership that really does not exist. I like the idea, but I really don't see it happening. In the PC(USA) now there is much emphasis on congregations becoming little mission bodies, but it does create a new type of paternalism; and this can revert to an older type of view of what mission is all about. A congregation working in partnership can become very dominating and especially since they are sending money; and they don't have the experience to know what this means and what can and should be done. I am always a little worried when I hear this. Even though it is our money, we may have to go about it in a different way.[99]

Early in the twenty-first century, missionaries started being asked to raise their own personal support before they could go to the field. This was considered to be quite unusual and not really acceptable to most in the Presbyterian funding culture. However, there were examples of missionaries who had to raise their own support in the 1950s:

> I had to raise my own funds the first time; appointed outside of the budget; and raised the money in L.A., most of it from Mrs. G., a member who inherited money; . . . she was a friend of my mother. B.G. was the same way; appointed without funding. So we went out and raised money on the side while in Meadville.[100]

This drastic shift in funding can clearly be seen in that only 13.2 percent of the budget came as undesignated to the Worldwide Ministries Division in 2005.[101] Interviews and anecdotal evidence indicate several reasons for the growth in designated giving: People distrusted denominational leadership (elected and staff) over controversial issues. Unified giving was a historic aberration that "worked" for only a few decades. Cultural shifts in giving were experienced by all philanthropies, such as the United Way. And direct involvement in mission was easier and expected in local churches.

SPECIAL OFFERINGS AND APPEALS

Although undesignated giving was promoted as the preferred way to give, there were really many other "official" examples of designated giving. These included "special offerings" and "special appeals." Each year special offerings were received at a particular season. Usually there were three or four such offerings. In the PCUS a major offering designated for international mission was the Witness Season Offering. It was usually received in February. Offerings in the UPCUSA were designated partially to support international mission, including the One Great Hour of Sharing (also in the PCUS), which was received at Easter for relief, resettlement, and self-development work. The Peacemaking Offering addressed international peace issues, including bringing international peacemakers to the United States, much like the Mission to the U.S.A. program.[102]

During the second half of the twentieth century, special appeals were used on a number of occasions to assist in international mission during attempts to reverse the financial decline. In fact, the Fifty Million Fund was initiated because Harold Kurtz, a missionary in Ethiopia, was a missionary advisory delegate to the UPCUSA GA in 1959. He made a plea to the Assembly to raise funds for a new initiative in frontier evangelism work in southwestern Ethiopia. The "Macedonian Call" offering was approved, but by the time it was launched as the Fifty Million Fund in 1963, it had become something quite different from its original purpose.[103]

Among the many special ("designated") appeals were the following:

- Fifty Million Fund (1963–72) as a UPCUSA offering received almost $17 million for international work, and 87 percent of that was designated by 444 churches.[104] This was probably the only truly successful campaign of its sort in the period under study.
- Mission Plus[105] (1977–78) was a UPCUSA effort to reverse the decline in mission giving.
- The PCUS annually observed the Season of Study, Prayer, and Self-Denial in January–February for special financial support of world mission. This later became the World Mission Season and later the Witness Season.
- In 1971 the PCUS also authorized a World Hunger Offering at Easter.[106]
- Major Mission Fund (1979–85) was a broadly conceived effort for a variety of mission needs in the UPCUSA.
- Second Mile Missionary Support was a source of funding in the PCUS going into reunion (1983) through 1988.[107] This period also included the Northern stream SOS giving category and the emergence of the Extra Commitment Opportunity (ECO).
- The Bicentennial Fund (1988–93) actually continued until 1998, at which time the Comprehensive Mission Funding Task Force Report was made in the PC(USA).[108]

- Mission Initiative (2002–7) was originally designed to address international mission personnel, but a second element was added: new church development and redevelopment in the United States, especially among racial ethnic and immigrant persons. The goal is $40 million, and $26 million had been received or pledged as of 2006, but the program became broadly defined and struggled to meet its goals, with international mission getting far less than projected.

These special appeals actually bailed out the international mission effort of the denominations on a number of occasions of fiscal crisis.[109]

THE PROBLEM WITH EQUALIZATION

Designated giving also raises the issue of "equalization," a practice hardly known or understood even by very knowledgeable leaders at the presbytery and GA level. Both the UPCUSA, the PCUS, and now the PC(USA) have utilized this policy. Essentially the policy is designed to get the money where the leadership decides that it is needed.

To simplify, we can say that if a project is budgeted for $100 and a donor designates $50 toward that project, it does not receive $150. The $50 designated gift plus $50 from undesignated sources cover the $100 needed for the project. The remaining $50 undesignated, which is no longer needed, is shifted to another area of the budget. The following excerpt from the PCUS Board of World Missions 1970 report identifies some of the frustration that the Board felt:

> [The Board] fully supports and abides by the Benevolence Program of the denomination. However, the Board has sought greater flexibility in the policy and practice of equalization. Contributions for "Home Mission" endeavors or "Christian Education" work can be made at every level of the Church's life, and many of these contributions are not counted against the budget approved for the Assembly agency. However, World Missions operates only at the Assembly level, and its receipts, including Special Askings receipts of $100,000 in the budget, are counted against its budget quota and are equalized.[110]

Another indication of equalization is found in the same year when the 1972 budget showed that the Board of World Missions got 51.2284 percent of the budget. Equalization was used to hit that very precise distribution target.[111] Although those figures were from 1970, equalization was nothing new. In 1951 the PCUSA Benevolence Budget was prepared by the Joint Budget Conference, which set percentages for each board. It stated that only individual gifts would not be included in the equalization.[112] Among the negotiated percentages were National Missions, 37.778 percent; Foreign Missions, 31.371 percent; Christian Education, 15.947 percent. The 1977 PCUS GA Minutes mention the

> constraints placed on designated gifts [indicating that] . . . there was a feeling by many Presbyterians that their designated gifts were used in mission work not directly related to the donor's wishes. . . . The most vexing problem with which the task force has grappled is the matter of so-called "equalization." . . . There should be more opportunity for donors to give to GA causes without the effect of their gifts being set-off by equalization. On the other hand, testing of preliminary recommendations dealing with this matter indicate that there is also considerable resistance to any change in our present plan of equalization.[113]

The report goes on to propose making the process clear, which would allow for giving without equalization, but at the same time, discouraging donors from doing just that. Yet it seems unlikely that most donors knew to give with the stipulation that their gift not be equalized.

The very next year (1978) Clinton Marsh led a series of UPCUSA meetings across the United States and recommended that the systemic bias for unified giving based on equalization needed to be changed and "not just grudgingly yielded a step at a time."[114] Over twenty years later the director of the Worldwide Ministries Division, Marian McClure, made a presentation at the 1999 meeting of the Association of Presbyterian Mission Pastors in which she stated that the only way to increase the numbers of mission personnel was to give "extra-commitment" money for that purpose.[115] She indicated to the group that if their churches simply designated to missionaries within the budget, the contributions would be equalized with the whole GA budget, and no increase would be realized in the total budget to fund missionaries.

As noted earlier, equalization was (and continues to be) an issue for presbyteries. Typically a presbytery approves a percentage distribution for money that it receives undesignated/unified. For example, the dollar might be divided as follows: presbytery, 60 percent; synod, 10 percent; GA, 30 percent. The problem arises when churches send their contributions as designated to projects in the budget. If the total undesignated (known as "shared" in the present parlance) and designated within the budget (called "selected") giving from the churches of a presbytery were $500,000, then $150,000 (30 percent) would go to the GA. But if fifteen churches each designate $10,000 to a missionary's support, a presbytery that equalizes will count those fifteen contributions as accounting for the $150,000, and the remaining churches of the presbytery that give undesignated (shared) will actually have all of their funds distributed between the presbytery and synod. The effect is to meet the predetermined percentages by equalizing the money as it is received.

After the reorganization of the UPCUSA in the early 1970s, the principle of "mission at the lowest possible judicatory" affected giving for the GA. As noted above, presbyteries set the percentage distribution of undesignated giving. They formally did this in official "consultations" with their synod and the GA-elected and staff leadership present, but presbyteries had the final say. Once presbyteries were expected to take responsibility for more mission work, including voting on the distribution of monies at presbytery meetings, the percentages started to shift in favor of the presbyteries. The 1975 Program Agency report made this comment: "Trends in the way some middle judicatories are dividing General Mission giving indicate that without a new and general denomination-wide funding pattern, the GA is continuing to fall behind, even though the general trend of General Mission giving is upward."[116]

This matter of equalization is a clear reminder that the structure of a system will significantly determine what will be funded, what will have a lower priority and, therefore, what will not be funded. The funding assumptions of the PC(USA) and its predecessors have ultimately worked to the detriment of the international work of the PC(USA). The funding system, it seems clear, has been a significant reason for the decline in giving and subsequently the decline in the number of missionaries.

MISSION FUNDING PLANS

Working to turn around the sliding and declining support system for Presbyterian mission, Presbyterians designed specific plans to help the church move forward. The UPCUSA developed a Mission Funding System in the late 1970s that was designed to build on the Major Mission Fund (1979–85), which was just concluding.[117] It incorporated several elements, including Mission Funding Counselors, modeled after the Major Mission Fund Counselors, who provided staff support in presbyteries for that campaign. This effort focused on staff support and advocacy for a program intended to continue the centralized funding system that had been the national priority for many years. Even though the success of the previous Fifty Million Fund and Major Mission Fund had demonstrated that donors preferred a more personalized and designated system for funding, this was never part of the new program. In some locations the General Mission giving grew faster than inflation during this period, but overall the program was top-down in design and brought no real innovation to mission funding. Over the next decade more than thirty counselors were placed, but by 1981 only one of those positions remained in place.

When the new Stewardship and Communication Development Ministry Unit was formed in the 1980s, it embarked on an effort to set goals for mission funding in the 1990s. The PC(USA)'s "Partners in Mission" paper called for a virtual doubling of giving for all governing bodies. It focused attention on undesignated giving, saying it would "continue to promote dollar commitment giving [unified] as the primary form of church-wide mission funding."[118] Giving, however, continued to decline.

In 1995 the GA Council approved the formation of the Comprehensive Mission Funding Strategy Work Group (drawn widely from across the church) "to propose a funding strategy and a plan for support of the whole mission of the whole church." The 1998 GA adopted the resulting document. The report begins, "The funding of our national Presbyterian Church (U.S.A.) mission budgets has reached a crisis level we can no longer afford to ignore."[119] The report further declares, "Presbyterian leaders have preferred the system of unified and unrestricted giving."[120] This bias is challenged, and a serious embrace of designated giving is proposed. The work group acknowledged that since sessions and local churches had become the dominant controllers of mission funding, the future of funding was "beyond" its control. The impact of this alarming report on the funding structures of the GA has been tepid at best.[121] In 2004 the GA Council formed a mission funding task force consisting of some of its own members. Those selected did not bring any particular expertise to the task. A preliminary and provisional draft report was made in December 2005, but it was met with such disappointment that the task force announced that it would not make any further report until 2008.

DISTRIBUTION OF THE GA BUDGET

Historically, there has always been the philosophical question in the unified funding system of how much of the GA budget should be used for international mission and how much should be kept in the United States. This distribution decision has substantially determined the level of PCUSA international involvement. In 1944 the PCUSA GA projected income in the following year to be just over $7 million. It was to be distributed by the Central Receiving Agency by a formula that included 41 percent for the Board of National Missions, 31.5 percent for the Board of Foreign Missions, and 20 percent for the Board of Christian Education. Presbyterian women anticipated raising $2 million of this total, most of it divided evenly between the BFM and BNM. The BFM also received additional direct designated funds.[122] The 1945 report indicated that the BFM 1944 income was well over the goal ($2,815,950). Just over half came from churches as undesignated funds ($1,557,614). Women and youth raised additional funds ($911,745), which were virtually all designated.[123]

During the era of the Program Agency, a period of particular decline for international mission, the overseas work of the UPCUSA received only 10 percent of the Program Agency budget, which meant that only 4.5 percent of the entire GA General Mission budget (including Program Agency, Support Agency, Vocations Agency, etc.) went overseas.[124] The total dollars from 1973 to 1983 for Program Agency grants for international work were close to $20 million, whereas the grants for domestic programs were close to $26 million.[125]

The major disparity is only seen in comparing how much Presbyterians spend on church work in the United States as compared to overseas. As stated earlier in this chapter, the international work now stands at 1.5 percent of the total Living Donors contributions for all Presbyterian churches. This is the lowest figure since the nineteenth century.

SUMMARY OF FINANCIAL ISSUES

So what is the bottom line regarding financial support of mission personnel and other international mission efforts by Presbyterian Churches in the second half of the twentieth century? In a word: a declining number of Presbyterians are giving fewer inflation-adjusted dollars, and a smaller percent of their growing personal income, for the purpose of international mission. Most of the giving is designated and dramatically more of their giving is outside the denominational channels. After World War II, "foreign missions" concerned the work of the Board of Foreign Missions. But by 2006 "worldwide mission" had become the prerogative of congregations, decentralized, personalized, and much harder to track. If one "follows the money," this change is clear.

It seems quite clear that there was much at the GA level that ignored this change, not least of which was the propensity to cling to an archaic funding system.[126] However, some mission directors, such as Clifton Kirkpatrick and Marian McClure, took certain initiatives that indicate their recognition of the changing situation, and specific moves to respond to these changes. But it simply takes a long time from initial recognition to significant change, especially in an institution as large and complex as the PC(USA).

Several significant examples could be mentioned, but one pivotal point, while not explicitly related to the funding, had profound implications for financial support. Moreover, it was probably a critical turning point for a new way of thinking about international mission: the Congregations in Global Mission conference held in St. Louis in November 1997. Attendance exceeded expectations, indicating more interest from the congregational level than anyone had anticipated. A significant change in the understanding of mission was reflected in the following quotations: "The congregation is the basic agency for global mission" (Sherron George). "Congregations do mission and they need partners" (Marian McClure). Here were two statements that clearly articulated what we have seen in this chapter in terms of local congregations (and individuals) taking ownership of missional participation. As an interesting historical note, these statements are consistent with one made by John Holt Rice, a founding mission visionary from the 1830s:

> Instead of the world mission being the function of the Board [of Foreign Missions], actually the only reason for such a Board is that the church considers this the work of its members. The Board has been established by the GA to co-operate with the churches in their foreign missions work. . . . Many think of foreign missions as a work in which the Board asks the local church for its help. But is not the opposite the actual fact?[127]

The institutional disconnect between congregations and mission, along with problematic missiology, were possibly among the most significant internal factors in the decline of PCUSA mission involvement during the period under consideration. The missiological dimension is well defined in a 1987 article by the West

African scholar Lamin Sanneh, who is the D. Willis James Professor of Missions and World Christianity and Professor of History at Yale University. Sanneh writes, "[My purpose is] to confront directly the guilt complex about missions that so often prevails in liberal counsels."[128] I would suggest that the discouraging record in the number of missionaries and the amount of money given in support of Presbyterian international mission for the past sixty years is due in large part to, as Sanneh suggests, missiological confusion about missionary vocations and the refusal to consider any change in the unified, centralized funding system. In this same period, global mission in the world did not recede, even though PCUSA missionary involvement did. In fact, it was a period of great growth and diversification.

Should we still have 1,804 missionaries as we did in 1944? Possibly not, and definitely not in the roles that they played at that time. This is the twenty-first century, and the context has changed very much, but the call and purpose has not. Much has rightly changed in world mission, and Presbyterians have been as thoughtful as any denominational group in addressing those changes. However, the calling to be world Christians has not diminished, and 200 people serving internationally does not begin to honor the legacy of the Presbyterian missionary calling, a calling that has not been rescinded. There is at least as much to be done "from everywhere to everywhere" as there was in 1944. Presbyterian failure to be as engaged through mission personnel and money has greatly diminished us both missiologically and as world Christians.

Linda Valentine was elected Executive Director of the GA Council by the 2006 GA. She has said, "Gone are the days, for example, when a centralized national organization did most of the international mission work on behalf of the church. As past GA moderator Rick Ufford-Chase said: 'People want to get out of the pews and into the world—they don't want to do mission by proxy.'"[129]

These words are hopeful, even if maybe a bit too optimistic about the commitment of Presbyterians and their congregations. But if there is to be any reversal of the international mission efforts of the Presbyterian Church (U.S.A.), whatever that might mean in the twenty-first century, the issues discussed in this chapter are among those that must be carefully addressed.

Chapter 3

Structures for
a Changing Church

G. THOMPSON BROWN AND T. DONALD BLACK

1944–1945 marks the end of World War II and the beginning of this 63-year mission history. Following this history is somewhat like boarding a moving train. In 1837 the PCUSA started its journey. The UPCNA was formed in 1858 from the union of two other Reformed Churches.[1] The division between the PCUS and the PCUSA occurred in 1861 over the issues of slavery, states' rights, and the Civil War. The PCUS was first called the Presbyterian Church in the Confederate States of America until the end of the Civil War. While the UPCNA and PCUSA united to form the UPCUSA in 1958, it took until 1983 for the PCUS and UPCUSA to reunite, forming the PC(USA). Each denomination had its own structure, but the earlier routes they followed were different. This chapter will follow three streams—the Northern stream, the Southern stream, and the combined stream (after 1983)—to help us understand the changing church and mission structures in the United States.

The months immediately following the Second World War were a time of recovery in many areas. Missionaries had been evacuated from China, Japan, Korea, the Philippines, Egypt, and Ethiopia. Some had been imprisoned or confined in internment camps, and soon deputations were sent to assess damage to mission property and to consult with Christian leaders. It was a time of return, reassessment, and restoration. The churches' concern for relief in Europe resulted in new relations with churches in those countries. The Presbyterian Board of Foreign Missions assumed responsibility for administering this relief effort, sending both funds and personnel, opening up a new field, and entering a new experience in church relations: Europe. Since many denominations shared the same concerns, Church World Service was organized, and each of the Presbyterian Churches participated in its work. Each stream followed what might be called the classic model of missionary service. Although it would all change, it is helpful to first give a brief account of what the structure looked like in two streams at the conclusion of the Second World War.

MISSION STRUCTURES

Each church had a "Mission" in the land where they were doing mission, which included all missionaries under appointment who had passed their language examination. The Mission met annually for seven to ten days and made all decisions concerning personnel assignments, annual budgets, policy matters, language study, and relations with the national church. Both women and men had a vote, and each year they elected a chairperson for the Mission. Each Mission had a treasurer and a corresponding secretary responsible for communicating with the mission board in the United States.

The Mission acted somewhat as a semiautonomous body, providing reports concerning decisions that were made and work that was accomplished. Advice and permissions were requested, but most of the decision making took place in the Mission: "on the field." Travel to and from the United States was by steamer (at least two weeks by ship), and airmail letters took at least one week to reach home. Time lapses, obviously, made it difficult to wait for board approval for all but major and long-term decisions. When the country was large or certain areas inaccessible, there might be more than one Mission. The PCUS had two missions in China (North Jiangsu and Mid China), with the boundary between the two being the Yangtze River. The PCUSA had seven missions in China. The PCUS had three missions in Brazil (East Brazil, Central Brazil, and North Brazil). The PCUSA had three Missions in India (Punjab, North India, and Western India, all coordinated by the India Council). Each Mission was semiautonomous because of distances, dialects, and travel time.

The local Mission structure was the "Station" and included all missionaries assigned to the city or region. It generally met once a month and was responsible for the work assignments, maintenance of buildings, finances, pastoral support, and relations with the local Christian community. If there was an institution (school or hospital), the Station was its board of directors and the assigned personnel its executive staff.

THE NATIONAL CHURCH

In each country where these Presbyterian denominations worked, a National Church had developed.[2] Many of them had reached the mission goal of a church that was "self-governing, self-propagating, and self-supporting." Many of them had adopted the Presbyterian form of government; others, as part of the ecumenical movement toward greater unity, had become "united churches." Relations with the sending churches in the United States were through the local Mission. In several countries the separate Presbyterian Missions were working with the same National Church: Brazil, Taiwan, China, Korea, Lebanon, Indonesia, and Portugal. However, in countries where there was only one of the three denominations, the relations with the National Church differed accordingly.

All of these churches were influenced by the rapidly changing and often-violent world scene. The end of colonialism was often achieved through armed conflict, and church people suffered as they were caught in the turmoil. The removal of colonial authority often released tribal enmities and struggles for power; civil war and refugees became a major concern in many areas. The spirit of independence permeated the new nations, and the national churches assumed their role in the world ecclesiastical scene. Some national churches no longer wanted to relate to other churches, even the sending church, through the Mission. The three denominations differed in their approach to these developments, and we will now break the story into the Southern stream and the Northern stream.

THE SOUTHERN STREAM: THE PRESBYTERIAN CHURCH IN THE UNITED STATES (PCUS)

On board the *U.S.S. Missouri,* anchored in Tokyo Bay, the conqueror faced the conquered. On that historic day, September 2, 1945, when the surrender documents were signed, General Douglas MacArthur made an address that would go down in history as a new approach of the victor to the vanquished: "The problem is basically theological and involves a spiritual recrudescence and improvement of human character that will synchronize with our almost matchless advance in science. It must be of the spirit if we are to save the flesh."[3] For missionaries returning to Asia, MacArthur's affirmation that the problem is basically theological made a deep impression. Many responded by sending or being sent as missionaries to help to rebuild, or to build for the first time, things of the "spirit." Before the "Pacific War," the PCUS had missionaries in three East Asian countries: Japan, Korea, and China. During the war years almost all of them had taken refuge in the United States or the Philippines: some had suffered imprisonment by the Japanese. The largest numbers were repatriated on the exchange ship *Gripsholm.* Those confined to the Shantung Compound received a tumultuous welcome when released.

Immediately, survey teams were sent out by the Board to Japan, Korea, and China. Their assignment was to review relations with the national churches, survey property losses, and determine what the first priorities should be. Decisions as to the future of missions in East Asia had to be made quickly, for many of the missionaries were eager to return. In spite of the difficulties of travel in the aftermath of the war, within eighteen months over two hundred missionaries had returned. The PCUSA launched a campaign to raise 23 million dollars for the War Restoration Fund, and the PCUS followed suit with a Program of Progress. The initial return to missionary work was overwhelming: at least a third of the mission schools, hospitals, and mission residences had been destroyed. The survey team for China made three important decisions: (1) they voted to combine two missions (North China and Jiangsu), (2) they appealed to the Board to send as many missionaries as possible, and (3) they decided that church officials would be consulted in the case of former missionaries. One is struck with the speed with which the former PCUS and PCUSA missionaries returned and settled back into the same patterns. With the radical changes sweeping the countryside, it seems a pity that the same old mission structures emerged, but could it have been otherwise? Chinese Christian leadership had been decimated during the Japanese occupation and the war. Many were exhausted from the long years of carrying on alone, and much of the property was in such sorry state to be unusable.

In Korea, finally the half century of occupation and oppression by the Japanese ended with their surrender on August 15, 1945. This event was momentous for the Koreans, for it finally brought an end to the long night of oppression and exploitation.[4] The Presbyterian Church during the early postwar years was in constant transition. The Mission had to adjust to the loss of missionary activity north of the 38th parallel by the occupying Soviet forces, and then the communist invasion, first by North Korea alone, and then aided by the Chinese Communists (1950–53). During the war years the missionaries to Korea served as U.S. Army chaplains for the North Korean and Chinese POWs, in relief work, and in the language school "in exile" in Tokyo. As soon as the armistice was signed in 1954, they returned to their stations. A similar story of evacuation, temporary assignment in other countries, and return describes the PCUSA experience.

In Japan, the devastation was both physical and spiritual. Japan had been shaken to its very foundation. It had lost its army, navy, national pride, and honor. The cities were in ruin. The seminary, schools, a dozen churches, and three residences were gone. During the war years, a number of Presbyterian missionaries suffered terribly in internment camps. Yet once peace had been declared, the attitude of the people changed. There appeared to be no resentment, and orders from the U.S. command were dutifully carried out. How could this be explained? On New Year's Day, 1946, the emperor had spoken: "The ties between us and our people have always stood on mutual trust and affection. They do not depend on mere legends and myths; they are not predicted upon the false conception that the emperor is divine."[5]

The Japan Survey Team faced a difficult decision over which denomination in Japan it would support: the Kyodan (United Protestant Church) or the reconstituted Reformed Church (which had withdrawn from the Kyodan union after the Pacific War)? The result was that the PCUS Mission maintained relations with both the Reformed Church and the much larger Kyodan, whereas the PCUSA Mission only maintained relations with the Kyodan. The Japan Mission focused on education and medicine, establishing a number of strong institutions: the Yodogawa Christian Hospital, the Shikoku Christian College, and the Japan International Christian University.

The PCUS did not have a mission in Taiwan before the war. Pioneer mission work had been done by the English Presbyterians in the south and the Canadian Presbyterians in the north. A strong Taiwanese-speaking church had been established, a church that had strong nationalistic leanings for independence from Mainland China. The Canadian Presbyterians invited the Southern Presbyterians, who had many missionaries with Chinese mission experience, to join in working with them, focusing work on the Chinese Mainlanders who were coming to the island in large numbers. The China missionaries, fluent in Mandarin, would be a big help in relating to the Mainlanders. At first the PCUS Board declined the invitation, still hoping to return to the China they had known. When it became evident that this was impossible, they opened a Taiwan Mission, somewhat under the umbrella of the Canadians. Their work was primarily with the aborigine tribes on the east coast, the Changwha Christian Hospital, and university student work.

ADVANCES

The years 1945–61 were characterized by revolution, wars, civil strife, and chaos in the non-Western world. Yet despite this turmoil, tremendous progress was being made. Note these comparisons of PCUS missionary strength:[6]

Country	1928	1958
Africa (Congo)	77	165
East Brazil	24	46
North Brazil	13	46
West Brazil	15	38
Ecuador	0	2
Japan	56	71
Korea	83	67
Mexico	20	29
Portugal	0	2
Taiwan	0	33
Total	288	499

THE DARBY FULTON YEARS: 1932–61

Dr. C. Darby Fulton was born to missionary parents in Japan and served for a short time as a missionary to Japan.[7] He was elected executive secretary of the Board of World Missions in May 1932 and served until his retirement in 1961, a total of twenty-nine years. The most important characteristic of Darby Fulton's tenure is that he retained the loyalty and support of the missionary community and the home church during these tumultuous years. During the latter years of his tenure, he was criticized for being antiecumenical because of his opposition to the integration of the missions into the national churches, and his concern that our theological standards not be watered down. He defended his ecumenical record in an article in the *Southern Presbyterian Journal:*

> There are no Southern Presbyterian Churches on our foreign fields. In Brazil, Korea, Mexico, Portugal and Taiwan we have joined with other Presbyterian Church bodies in the creation of one National Presbyterian church. In China we are part of the Church of Christ in China, which brought together in one ecclesiastical body the work of fourteen denominational missions. In Congo, where no other Presbyterian bodies were at work, we serve in close collaboration with the Methodists. . . . Of the nine theological colleges our board supports on the foreign field, seven are operated on an interdenominational basis. . . . In the last fifteen years we have helped [to] inaugurate the following major interdenominational ventures: The Presbyterian Committee on Evangelical Cooperation, The United Andean Indian Mission, The United Mission in Iraq, and the Amazon project in Brazil.[8]

THE T. WATSON STREET YEARS: 1961–73

Upon Dr. Fulton's retirement in 1961, the Board elected Dr. T. Watson Street as his successor. Dr. Street had served as a professor at Austin Theological Seminary and was recognized for his scholarship. He had also served for a number of years as a member of the Board of World Missions. After the long years of Dr. Fulton's tenure, it was expected that changes would be made. Almost immediately, Dr. Street began to propose changes in board structure, priorities, and policy. Dr. Street suggested that the Board call a major consultation, which would provide a mandate for change and call the church to a renewal of its mission. This became the first Montreat Consultation.

Two hundred delegates were invited from various overseas national churches and missions. They included ecumenical leaders such as the Church of South India Bishop, Lesslie Newbigin, as well as those from conservative churches. An important feature was that each body chose its own representatives. For example, the Korea Mission and the Presbyterian Church of Korea each sent three representatives of their own choosing.

The consultation met October 13–19, 1962, in North Carolina. A whole range of mission strategies and policies was covered, but the key issue was the integration of the mission into the church. Following the Darby Fulton years, it was bound to be a risky subject. After considerable debate, the following motion was adopted unanimously: "That the structure of relationships of missionaries to a national church should be worked out by the national church in consultation with the Presbyterian Church in the United States."[9]

Though the resolution was innocuous-sounding, the authority had been passed from the Mission to the national church, almost imperceptibly. This set in motion a series of "miniconsultations" with partner churches around the world. The direction of each was toward integration, but each chose the way that this would be worked out. Whenever possible, it included representatives from other churches or nationals. For example, the Korean model included PCUSA, and Australian missionaries established a Division of Cooperative Work (DCW) composed of the same number of nationals and missionaries. The DCW made all decisions on personnel, budgets, and policy. For the next twenty years it functioned smoothly. Three countries, Congo, Brazil, and Mexico, required radical structural changes and will require special attention.

The PCUS operated two missions in the region of the Congo in Africa: The Presbyterian Community in Kinshasa, the nation's capital, and the American Presbyterian Congo Mission (APCM). The Kinshasa Mission enjoyed tremendous growth in an urban setting. Integration of the mission into the church proceeded without too much difficulty except for the transfer of some mission residences to the church. Relationships with the much-larger Church of Christ in Zaire (ECZ), which had two synods and a number of presbyteries, were more complicated.

The Congo Mission was founded in 1806, and by 1960 it was the largest PCUS mission field, with 171 missionaries in the Kasai province in central Africa.[10] It was organized along Presbyterian lines, with a General Assembly, but in 1960 the APCM still exercised paternalistic oversight. The annual meeting of the General Assembly was advisory only, and it was called a "trial" assembly—a term that the Africans disliked. The real authority remained with the APCM and its missionaries. The forces of nationalism, however, were sweeping across Africa. In 1958 the term "trial" was dropped, and the church took its first steps toward independence. Dr. Street's election accelerated the transfer of institutions, committees, and programs from missionary to local control. Sadly, there was not enough time for an orderly transfer of authority.

On June 30, 1960, Belgium declared the independence of the Congolese colony, but with little or no time for preparation. The mission had been operating a number of schools under concession from the Belgians, but all this now had to change. In July the country broke out in tribal warfare, followed by an ongoing frenzy of hate and bloodshed between these two prominent tribes. All missionaries were evacuated from the Congo to neighboring countries. In late 1960 a delegation of missionaries returned to the newly independent Republic of the Congo and met with national church leaders. What should they do? The church leaders pled with them to return, and most of them did. Unfortunately, the warfare and civil strife has continued to this day with millions dying in the last years of the twentieth century and the first years of the twenty-first century.

The other two countries that require a special discussion are Brazil and Mexico. Relations between the Presbyterian Church of Brazil (IPB) and the two North American churches differed sharply from that of other countries. Before 1954 the relationship was known as the Modus Operandi or simply the "Brazil Plan." The PCUSA and PCUS missionaries did pioneer evangelism in the interior, while the IPB worked mostly in the large urban areas. This plan, which the church and the missionaries welcomed, freed up missionaries for pioneer work and also "protected" the IPB from possible North American church interference. When churches in a mission field reached a certain level of growth and maturity, they were organized as a presbytery and transferred to the jurisdiction of the IPB.

The Brazil Plan worked well in some areas, but it had its share of problems. For one, it tended to isolate the Brazilian church from its North American partners. Also, it tended to minimize the importance of the rapidly growing urban areas along the coast. To meet these needs, the Inter-Presbyterian Council (CIP) was formed in 1954 to coordinate the work of the missions and the IPB. Its membership consisted of twelve representatives from the IPB and six representatives each from the PCUS and the PCUSA. The PCUSA's Lake Mohonk Conference[11] was a strong advocate of the missions integrating into national churches. However, the IPB and most of the missionaries of the two churches were strongly opposed to integration, as was the PCUS Board under Dr. Darby Fulton. Instead of integration, they favored the continuation of the Modus Operandi as it had been modified by the CIP, which led to strained relations between the UPCUSA and the IPB.

The issues between the two churches included integration but also control of the educational institutions and a lack of trust between the leaders of the two churches. The UPCUSA drastically reduced the number of missionaries when the IPB declared some of them personae non grata.[12] Several UPCUSA missionaries transferred their membership to the Southern church (PCUS) so they could continue their work. In 1972 there was no exchange of representatives between the two churches, and the IPB broke off the relationship. At a 1973 consultation in Brazil, IPB and PCUS representatives met to see if something could be worked out bilaterally in spite of the IPB/PCUSA collapse. A mutual agreement was adopted, which established a Permanent Commission in Presbyterian Cooperation (PCPC), under which the PCUS missionaries continued to serve for thirteen years. Several mutual conversations were held during these years in Sao Paulo, Montreat, and Camp Calvin.

During the consultation of 1973, what might be called a "time bomb" was planted in church relations. The IPB decided that if either of the partner churches united with another denomination, their cooperation agreement would be terminated. Everyone knew that this clause was directed at the UPCUSA. When the PCUS and the UPCUSA united in 1983, the relationship automatically ended. The Brazil church had no quarrel with PCUS missionaries. They were welcomed by a number of the entities of the IPB, including Campinas Seminary, the Board of National Missions, and surprisingly, the Independent Presbyterian Church of Brazil (IPCB), a denomination that had split from the IPB in 1903 over the issues of Masons and the role of North American missionaries.[13]

In 1972 the National Presbyterian Church of Mexico asked its two partner churches, UPCUSA and PCUS, to suspend their relations. A conservative leadership was concerned about the new attitudes in the Roman Catholic Church following Vatican II and, thus, the new relations between the RCC and the partner churches. Some missionaries were openly relating to the new Catholic mission priests and discussing possible cooperation. Additionally, the Mexican church wanted to develop its own identity and sense of mission. The partner churches agreed, and some missionaries were assigned to other countries; however, relations with ecumenical agencies were not affected. This separation lasted for about six years. Relationships were restored in a consultation of the three churches in 1978. These relationships became more important and meaningful with the genesis of the Border Ministries, in which all three of the churches worked together.

THE RESTRUCTURING OF 1973

By 1969 there was increasing dissatisfaction with the way the General Assembly and its agencies were organized. A committee of the GA was appointed to consider a major restructuring. Here are a few of the reasons given for the need for such a restructure:

- The proliferation of agencies reporting directly to the GA.
- The lack of a strong coordinating committee to monitor the multitudinous agencies, and thus each agency tended to go its own way.
- The tendency for each cause (and its structural unit) to develop a cadre of fierce defenders, to the detriment to the work of the whole church.
- The reality that synods and presbyteries were increasingly performing functions that in previous years had been done at the General Assembly level.

The ad-interim committee made its report to the General Assembly in 1969. It called for sweeping changes in nearly every area of the General Assembly program. An abbreviated outline of the plan from the 1969 GA is as follows:

- Three boards were relocated in Atlanta: the Board of Christian Education from Richmond, the Pension Board from Louisville, and the Board of World Missions from Nashville.
- The General Executive Board and its General Director were given total responsibility for programs.

- Five divisions were created:
    1. Division of National Mission (DNM)
    2. Division of International Mission (DIM)
    3. Division of Corporate and Social Mission (DCM)
    4. Division of Professional Development (DPD)
    5. Division of Central Support Services (DCS)

Three features of this organizational plan were unique: the Office of Review and Evaluation (ORE), the Priority Building System, and the Communication Cabinet. Three professional staff officers formed a small committee, which was assigned to monitor all features of the structure periodically and to report to the General Assembly on how it was working. The ORE determined that placing missionary personnel in one division and mission program in another was dysfunctional and recommended that both be placed in DIM. This was done, with marked improvement in missionary recruitment, care, and support.

The designers of the plan were concerned that the budget-building process would become ingrown as staff followed their own priorities rather than listening to voices coming from the church at large. A Priority Management team was appointed to review, screen, and prioritize requests coming from the various corners of the church. Annually, at the meeting of the General Assembly, these requests would be considered. Those worthy of consideration would be assigned to the proper office or division for implementation. Five percent of the annual budget would be set aside to fund those requests.

Another concern of the designers was the lack of communication between GA staff, synods, and presbyteries on one hand, and the church at large on the other hand. The Communication Cabinet provided a "forum for continuing two-way communication between the constituencies and the central gentry."[14] The cabinet included the General Staff Director, one person from each of the synods, the Washington Communication Director, and three missionaries on home assignment. The functions assigned to the DIM were for the most part those assigned to the Board of World Missions. The five division directors were all new faces. As part of the new restructuring, it was thought that new leadership would enable the staff to start afresh. A collegial style of management was emphasized, with the five directors forming a management team.

T. Watson Street had served twelve years as Executive Secretary of the BWM and would have been eligible for the new position of Director of the Division of International Mission, but he asked that his name not be considered. He made a distinctive contribution to the mission of the PCUS during the transition years of passing from a mission-based approach to a church-based approach. These were difficult changes, which at the time were bitterly opposed by some. But, looking back, the changes had to be made. There was no way that mission could be continued in the Republic of Zaire in the same way that it had been done in the Belgian Congo. The reason that the PCUS was able to get through those years as well as it did was because of Dr. Street's tenacity and devotion to the mission of the church.

THE G. THOMPSON BROWN YEARS: 1973–81

Rev. G. Thompson Brown was elected to be the Director of the Division of International Mission. He had served as a missionary in Korea for twenty years and then as the East Asia Secretary. His task was made considerably easier because of the groundwork that Dr. Street had laid. A second mission consultation, Montreat II, was held in 1978 on the recommendation of the ORE. It involved over two hundred delegates from across the world, and the theme was "One Mission under God." It emphasized the oneness of mission and listed the following priorities for the General Assembly to consider in the next decade: Proclamation, Compassion, Justice, Reconciliation, Partnership, and Education for Mission. The restructure (mentioned above) lasted only sixteen years (1973–88), but some comments, both positive and negative, deserve noting.

The original plan called for a transition year before its initiation, but this was dropped. At the time, a number of the staff thought that this was a serious mistake. If the transition year had been retained, much of the turmoil of the first two years might have been avoided. It was unfortunate that the initiation of the system took place just at the time that there was a downward spiral in the amount of funds available for national and international programs.[15] Also, the new plan was more expensive to operate. Funding had to be provided for the ORE and the Communication Cabinet. Programs had to be curtailed, and some missionaries had to be brought home. The funding of projects through the Priority Building System proved to be too complex and time-consuming.

On the other hand, the placement of all boards and agencies under one roof certainly emphasized the cooperative nature of the enterprise and eliminated some, but not all, areas of competition. Ecumenical commitments were kept intact. Four major programs were started:

1. A new mission was started in Bangladesh in response to desperate appeals for help.
2. A renewal of relations with the churches and Christians in China began.
3. The Hunger Program was adopted as a major priority.
4. The Outreach Foundation[16] was created to enable the PCUS to reach out to areas of need.

THE CLIFTON KIRKPATRICK YEARS: 1981–88

After G. Thompson Brown served the maximum of two four-year terms, Clifton Kirkpatrick was elected as his successor. He had served with the Council of Churches in the Dallas/Fort Worth area, and at the time of his election, he was the Executive Director of the Houston Metropolitan Ministries. With the reunion of the PCUS and the UPCUSA on the horizon, Kirkpatrick spent much time coordinating work with the PCUSA's Program Agency and, during the five-year interim administration period, preparing to enter a new structure and move to a new headquarters.

THE NORTHERN STREAM: THE UNITED PRESBYTERIAN CHURCH OF NORTH AMERICA (UPCNA)

As noted earlier, the UPCNA had Missions in the Punjab area of India, Egypt, the Sudan, and Ethiopia.[17] The churches in India/Pakistan and Egypt/Sudan were synods of the UPCNA. These two "overseas synods" had a special ecclesiastical relationship to the GA. Their statistics were included in the annual denominational records, but they only sent two commissioners to the GA in alternate years. The commissioners were given an opportunity to address the Assembly, but only during "foreign missions night." The people of these synods, who lived in an unfriendly society, saw their relation to a church in America as security. Therefore, suggestions from the U.S. church that it was time to dissolve this ecclesiastical tie were usually met with resistance.

The general theory included in the classic model of mission that was prevalent at this time was that while the local church should grow in strength and responsibility, the Mission's power and control should correspondingly decrease. The church was in control of selecting and training its clergy, establishing new congregations, and financing its own activities. Although primary schools were the responsibility of local congregations, educational institutions above the primary level, social service programs, and medical institutions were still the responsibility of the Mission. The assumption was that these Mission-related institutions would be turned over to the church when the church was prepared to manage and support them on its own. Dr. Glenn Reed, Corresponding Secretary of the Board of Foreign Missions, proposed an intermediate step of joint administrative boards, with representatives of both Synod and Mission. Before this step could be implemented, however, discussions of a Presbyterian Church merger back in the USA became the dominant topic of discussion.

MISSION BOARDS

Under the classic model, mission organization and governance were the responsibility of the Boards of Foreign Missions, which were GA agencies. The Assembly elected the members of the Boards, set their length of terms, and assigned them a portion of the General Mission Budget. The Boards were then responsible for conducting the Foreign Mission Program of their respective denominations. Their assignment included setting mission policy, interpreting the mission programs, recruiting and appointing missionaries, allocating mission funds to the various Missions, and recommending new mission fields to the GA. The UPCNA had two mission boards related to its foreign mission: the Board of Foreign Missions and the Women's Board.

THE MRS. ARTHUR MCBRIDE YEARS: 1930–56

The Women's General Missionary Society (WGMS) was the national organization for United Presbyterian women. It had a Board of Directors known as the Women's Board, which directed its extensive mission work in the United States and in the denomination's foreign fields. The volunteer board members were the administrators of its various programs, assisted by two secretaries and a bookkeeper in the Pittsburgh office. Its funds came from various church, presbytery, and synod women's missionary societies, especially the Thank Offering.[18] The Women's Board Secretary for Foreign Mission, Mrs. Arthur McBride of Sewickley, Pennsylvania, provided outstanding leadership to this facet of the WGMS. The Women's Board appointed all single women missionaries, supported hospitals for women, and related to nursing schools, girls' boarding schools, and Bible training schools for Bible Women.[19] A number of factors related to changes in American society led to the appointment of an Executive Secretary in the early 1950s. Ms. Evelyn Fulton was elected to that post. Further changes led to the merger of the Foreign Mission section of the Women's Board with the Board of Foreign Missions in 1956. This later became an integration of the Women's Board with the denominational Board, a trend common in all denominations during the early to middle part of the twentieth century. We observe that this was a trend with mixed consequences: there was greater streamlining of mission, but also a loss of women's leadership and initiative. Women lost an important avenue of church leadership.

THE GLENN P. REED YEARS: 1938–54

Glenn P. Reed, former missionary to Sudan, was the staff leader of the Board of Foreign Missions until 1954, carrying the official title of Corresponding Secretary. During his tenure he led the Board from its deep Depression debt to financial stability. For a period preceding World War II, no new personnel assignments were made, but Reed helped to increase the number of appointments following the war. After serving as Corresponding Secretary for a number of years, Reed wished to return to missionary service. However, the BFM thought that his wisdom and experience should not be limited to one area, so it created the post of Foreign Secretary with an office in Asmara, Eritrea, for Reed. He was equal to the Executive Secretary in the staff, and yet he was located where he would not be engaged in any one mission: he was within easy travel distance to all of them.

THE T. DONALD BLACK YEARS: 1954–58

During these times of Board transition, the Board also established the office of Executive Secretary, electing T. Donald Black to this post. Previously, he had served two pastorates and was president of the Board when elected in 1954. During the next four years he increased the missionary staff and developed the new Board, so as to include members also selected by the Women's Board.

For fifty years the BFM had sponsored the New Wilmington Missionary Conference, with a board staff member as its director and a separate conference board. Occurring every summer, NWMC drew attendance from several states and was always preceded by one of the BFM's annual meetings. In this way, new and furloughed missionaries could all attend the conference and be together for intermissionary fellowship. As the merger with the PCUSA approached in the mid-1950s, the conference board realized that the structure of the new church would neither have a place for a conference that was not related to a specific synod, nor would its new mission organization be able to give NWMC the same focused attention and support that it had enjoyed under the UPCNA's BFM. Therefore, the conference became an independent corporation and has continued to serve the PC(USA) with a mission emphasis to this day.[20]

By 1957 it was evident that the UPCNA and the PCUSA would merge. A joint committee was appointed by the two BFMs to propose a combined mission-governing structure. It was this committee, in consultation with the two Interchurch Relations Committees, which proposed the new mission-governing body, Commission on Ecumenical Mission and Relations (COEMAR), to the uniting assembly in 1958.

PCUSA: THE CHARLES T. LEBER YEARS: 1936–59

The General Secretary of the PCUSA's BFM was Charles T. Leber. He had joined the staff from a pastorate that had a strong emphasis on mission, and he therefore exercised creative and dynamic leadership during his tenure. For several years his position was Chairman of the Administrative Council, elected annually by the staff. In 1956 the BFM changed its staff structure and elected Dr. Leber as its General Secretary. During his leadership the BFM responded to many of the changes of the post–World War II era. One of his projects was to produce a major film for commercial distribution (*The Mark of the Hawk*), which would show how missions were confronting the changes in Africa. It failed in commercial distribution, but it was shown on television for years.

During Leber's tenure, there was a great sense that the church was experiencing a "new day" in mission.[21] World War II was over, colonialism was ending, and mission-planted churches had become so rooted in certain countries that they had survived, even thrived, during the war-forced absence of missionaries. The Board sought ways to express the new relationships between the missions, missionaries, and developing churches overseas in the changing world. Both its interactions with the ecumenical church and its own reflections moved the Board to emphasize and reflect upon the concept of Ecumenical Mission. There are two related lines to follow in developing this theme, the mission line and the ecumenical relations line. We will continue to address them in that order.

John A. Mackay, former missionary to Latin America, chairman of the Board, and President of Princeton Seminary, greatly influenced the PCUSA's BFM. Mackay was a leading proponent of the ecumenical movement, for he believed that it incorporated both the mission and the unity of the church. He pointed out that the term *oikumenē* (from which "ecumenical" is derived) as used in the New Testament meant "the whole household of God," and that mission belonged to all of the churches in the household. Ecumenical mission was, as he often said, "everything that relates to the whole task of the whole Church to bring the Gospel to the whole world."[22]

As the BFM listened to ecumenists such as Mackay, it also formally interacted with Christians from the ecumenical church. In order to further develop the implications of Ecumenical Mission, the Board invited the churches of its "mission fields" to a consultation at Lake Mohonk in 1956.[23] The overseas attendees of the Lake Mohonk consultation formally called for Missions to be integrated into the indigenous churches within five years. The call was clearly given, but no intermediate step of joint administration between the BFM and overseas churches was implemented. The Board stressed the importance of integration to all of its missionaries and overseas churches. It had decided that part of integration meant a general reduction in the overall number of missionaries in any one country. This meant that overseas churches were often left with the responsibility of determining which missionaries were still "needed" in the field and which should return home after integration.[24] The general policy of integration applied to all, but the method and timing of the integration certainly varied from "field to field."[25]

The PCUSA was beginning to recognize that it was not the possessor of mission, nor the only one responsible for carrying the gospel to the whole world. It learned to understand itself as one of many church bodies, which jointly participated with all other churches in an "ecumenical mission." The BFM desired for its nomenclature and structure to reflect this burgeoning theological understanding of mission. However, in 1956 the PCUSA had already begun to discuss plans for the upcoming merger with the UPCNA in 1958. Realizing that it was not the best time to change its name, only to have it changed a few years later, the Board decided to just change its letterhead and publicity documents to say "The Presbyterian Church in Ecumenical Mission."

Additional changes reflecting this new understanding of ecumenical mission soon followed. The term "missionary" was changed to "fraternal worker" as a way to express equality between those serving overseas and those being served.[26] In order to help mission personnel adjust to the changing world, in 1955 the Board held a Study Fellowship for some people on furlough and some new appointees. The fellowship had a flexible schedule and used visiting lecturers conversant with world changes. After four years of using rented facilities, buildings were erected on property that the Board owned in Stony Point, New York. The Study Fellowship was enlarged by participation of several boards, and the Missionary Orientation Center played a part in missionary orientation for several denominations in the following years.

Ecumenical relations also became a central theme in the BFM as churches around the world expressed their independence and began to participate in various ecumenical organizations. The PCUSA was a member of the National Council of Churches, World Council of Churches, and World Alliance of Reformed Churches. These affiliations were the responsibility of the Permanent Committee on Interchurch Relations (PCIR).[27] The Presbyterian delegates to such ecumenical gatherings, though, were not representatives of the BFM. The PCIR had historically managed PCUSA relationships with churches in Europe and Canada (countries with established churches), serving as the PCUSA representatives to all ecumenical meetings. When churches from current and former PCUSA mission fields (such as Brazil, Egypt, and Korea) began participating in ecumenical gatherings, they interacted with PCIR representatives, as opposed to the BFM representatives with whom they had interacted in a mission context. This situation shed light on a disconnect in the working of the church. The need to bring the BFM and PCIR, and thus ecumenical mission and ecumenical relations, closer was recognized, and the upcoming union with the United Presbyterians gave the opportunity to try a new approach. The result was formation of the Commission on Ecumenical Mission and Relations (COEMAR), which combined the Foreign Boards and the Interchurch relations committees from both northern denominations when the PCUSA and the UPCNA united in 1958.

COEMAR AND THE UNITED PRESBYTERIAN CHURCH IN THE UNITED STATES OF AMERICA (UPCUSA)

The theory behind COEMAR's organization was that since a commission holds the full power of the governing body that creates it, the commission, as opposed to another board, could both develop church-to-church relations and carry on mission work. The commission would report to the Assembly, but it would not require its approval. Theoretically, it was not another board or agency of the Assembly. However, this distinction was never fully recognized, and the Commission went about its work as though it were an agency. Charles T. Leber served as the General Secretary, John Coventry Smith was Associate Secretary for Ecumenical Mission, Margaret Shannon was the Associate Secretary for Ecumenical Relations, and Donald Black was the Associate Secretary for Administration.

Although created to unite the work of mission and ecumenical relations, the new structure immediately created two divisions: Ecumenical Mission and Ecumenical Relations. Margaret Shannon was wisely unwilling to confine Ecumenical Relations to the organized ecumenical bodies (i.e., WCC), so she probed the possibility of directly relating to other churches in Africa and the Middle East. What started as conversations and general acquaintance building often moved into providing help with some new aspect of the church's work. Relations with the Presbyterian Church in Kenya were started in this way, even though it threatened to strain relations with the Church of Scotland Presbyterians, who had been the main mission agency there. New UPCUSA relations with Orthodox Churches also brought tension with our partners in mission in the Middle East, who typically distanced themselves from the Orthodox Church. The idea of these types of outreach into new areas beyond our traditional mission fields was the result of the new emphasis on ecumenical relations.

THE JOHN COVENTRY SMITH YEARS: 1959–70

Charles Leber died unexpectedly in 1959 while attending the Presbyterian Alliance meeting in Brazil. John Coventry Smith was then elected as General Secretary, and Donald Black was elected as Associate Secretary for Ecumenical Mission. John Smith had served as a missionary in Japan and was interned during the early war years. When he was released, he served as a pastor in the UPCNA before being called to the staff of the Presbyterian Board as Secretary for East Asia.

In the first year of the Commission, Leber proposed an Advisory Study Committee that would advise the UPCUSA on implementing this new approach to mission and relations. Although Leber passed away before this committee was formed, his vision was implemented in January 1960, when a special group of fifteen people was selected to form the Advisory Study Committee. The UPCUSA was quite pleased that of the fifteen committee members, ten were church members from outside the United States, two were UPCUSA fraternal workers serving in other countries, and only three were members of the Commission.[28] Although COEMAR was specifically designed to be a group of outsiders who would objectively advise, it ended up controlling the selection of who gave COEMAR advice.[29]

The Advisory Study Committee was assigned the task of discussing "What are the policies which should determine the participation of the UPCUSA, through its Commission on Ecumenical Mission and Relations, in ecumenical mission and relations during the years immediately ahead?"[30] The committee met three times in three different locations over a period of twenty-one months. Although their discussions were directed at being rather practical, they ended up producing a 94-page written pamphlet that began with an extended theology of mission. This section addressed the relation of mission to Jesus Christ, the church, and the present moment in redemptive history. Its sound missiological statements were later said to have been praised by the great mission historian Kenneth Scott Latourette.[31]

The second half of *An Advisory Study* emphasized the role of each church as a missionary community in the new era of mission, whereby mission was from everywhere to everywhere.[32] Churches were to be indigenous, charismatic, evangelistic, and serving, as well as ecumenically working together for the sake of mission. Thus the study continued, emphasizing the importance of mission integration into local churches. Along with integration, it was assumed that the number of missionaries serving in any one place would decrease, so as to prevent unintentional domination.

The study also lifted up the increasingly important role of nonprofessional missionaries, citing a new shift from missionaries to laypeople as the symbols and instruments of Jesus Christ's service in the world. Correspondingly, the study suggested appointing people for a specific number of years of service (ten to twelve) and only extending this number if they were found to have a "special gift" for lifetime service.[33]

Smith worked closely with the Advisory Study Committee during its two years of meetings and study. *An Advisory Study* was to be used in discussions with related churches overseas, as well as in local churches throughout the United States. As originally intended, COEMAR received the report as a document with recommendations to consider, instead of adopting it as policy. The follow-up of the Advisory Study became the process by which COEMAR worked with its various overseas church partners to complete the integration arrangements envisioned at the Lake Mohonk consultation.[34] In some instances, formal partnership agreements were developed with each of the churches to clarify what was expected of COEMAR and what the church would provide for personnel that it invited to work with it. Though the process was different, it was similar to the way in which the PCUS's BWM implemented its position that the structure of the relationship of missionaries to the national church should be worked out by the national church in consultation with the Presbyterian Church U.S. During this period of Smith's leadership, the overseas synods and presbyteries were all granted their independent status.

Back in 1950 the PCUSA's BFM created the posts of Field Representatives. These were staff members who resided in their major mission fields. Having a staff presence in mission and church discussions was expected to strengthen the relation between the Board and field organizations in a time of change. In the new UPCUSA structure, these positions were changed to Commission Representatives. In the consultations regarding the integration of church and mission, these posts came under fire. The church leaders now assumed that they had a direct line to the church in the United States, and so they questioned the practice of having another office between them and the sending church (Commission Representatives). Over a period of time, with retirements and personnel changes, these positions disappeared, which both removed a layer of bureaucratic structure and also moved decision making far away from the national church.

The Division of Relations tried to involve congregations in relating to churches in other nations, and so special delegations of women meeting women and youth meeting youth were developed. The Frontier Intern program was designed to involve recent college graduates in a two-year exploration of new possibilities in mission.[35] Margaret Flory designed the program, which was quite successful in challenging youth to deal with the realities of racial tension, new nationalisms, modern secularism, militant non-Christian faiths, and displaced, uprooted, rejected people. It eventually became an international program related to the World Student Christian Federation.[36]

MISSIONARIES

The central figures in the Foreign Mission movement had always been the missionaries. Honored by congregations as the supreme examples of Christian service, respected and appreciated by the people among whom they worked, ridiculed by novelists as hypocritical egoists, condemned by radical nationalists as subversive political agents, labeled as condescending overlords by discontented churchmen—they responded to God's call and left their home countries to be witnesses for Jesus Christ. Through their commitment, they educated generations, healed the sick, established social service activities, and above all, made disciples of all nations. They were a special group of people, for whom—in spite of all of their weaknesses—the world should be ever grateful.

Chapter 6 in this book is devoted to personnel, but here we are tracking some of the factors related to the changing structures. The integration of the Missions into the churches meant that mission personnel would now be serving under national leadership in schools, hospitals, and church-related programs. It is a fine testimony to the flexibility of missionaries that they willingly accepted these new working relationships. In some institutions they had served as principals or chiefs of staff and later were transferred to another field or a different position in their own field as national personnel were available to replace them.

The missionary support system also changed. The original support system provided a base field salary that was needed to maintain a couple in their country of service. Additional allowances for children, medical treatment, school fees, vacation travel, and other expenses were added on top of the base. Setting the base salary level was not easy since the missionaries in a particular field would have different ideas about what was necessary. In addition, the cost of living varied from country to country and from year to year. Therefore, the Board applied a common base salary related to the average salary of ministers in the denomination. There were still allowances, and the result was a mixture of the support system and a salary. A married couple was only enrolled in the husband's name. Single personnel received a base salary that was slightly more than half of a couple's salary. Missionaries were enrolled in the pension plan, and dues were paid at the base salary level.[37]

The changing role of women brought some other personnel changes. In a world with increasing career opportunities for women, some wives did not wish to be listed as missionaries and wanted to follow careers outside of church activity. In some cities with sizeable American business communities, this option was a possibility. The question of equality for women in the workplace was also raised. If a single woman doctor and a married man doctor were working in the same institution, was the salary to be determined by their professional standing or by the fact that they were under a mission board? A number of adjustments were tried. Couples were each given a specific assignment, and each was paid. Both were enrolled in the pension plan. A variable compensation plan has continued as different categories of service have developed.

Changes in the world brought another basic change: the decline in the number of career missionaries. Appointment and commissioning had been assumed to be for a lifetime, though through the years many people had returned from service before retirement. The serious time investment of learning another language or two and becoming familiar with a foreign culture led to the assumption of career service. But new governments were setting restrictions on foreigners, and new churches were assigning their own personnel to institutional leadership. It was no longer possible to assume that people would have long service in a particular country.[38]

DENOMINATIONAL DEVELOPMENTS

The developments in the world scene also included changes taking place in the United States. The economy was changing, and steadily increasing costs depleted the resources that were available for mission support. The 1950s were a time of church growth and prosperity, but the 1960s and 1970s were a time of social revolution, which suddenly reversed these trends of growth and prosperity for the church.

An important event in the ecumenical organizations influenced COEMAR's response to the turmoil of the times. John Smith had been involved in the merger of the International Missionary Council into the World Council of Churches in 1961. He authored a statement adopted by the Assembly, which reminded the churches that the mission was not only in Asia, Africa, and Latin America, but was also a mission to six continents. COEMAR was justified in becoming involved in helping to shape American churches into effective participants in a truly global mission.

SOCIAL TURMOIL

The social revolution began with the struggle for racial equality. Martin Luther King Jr. symbolized the role of clergy in the effort to end segregation, and denominational leaders supported his efforts. The Foreign Board had often commented that a segregationist church would be suspect in its mission around the world. John Smith became active in the organization of the new Council on Church and Race (COCAR). One of its first efforts was to help church agencies become more inclusive in their staff recruitment. COEMAR used funds to bring both mission personnel and national church leaders to work in various urban crises during the "long hot summer" of 1968. COEMAR staff were given time to participate in voter registration demonstrations in Hattiesburg, Mississippi. Staff leaders and furloughed personnel were encouraged to participate in the March on Washington (August 28, 1963), one of the major events of this period.

Part of the social protest was focused on responsible investing, and so the church formed a committee on Mission Responsibility through Investment. They called on the church agencies to challenge the corporations in which they held stock to become socially responsible in their employment standards and business practices. In the international scene COEMAR challenged corporations operating in South Africa and other African countries. Representatives attended stockholders' meetings and raised their issues.

America's participation in the Vietnam War was also a national target of protest. Students in many major universities demonstrated against authority, disrupted meetings, occupied administrative offices, and skipped classes to hold teach-in sessions about their issues. Church meetings also received similar treatment of protests and interruption.

A Black Economic Development Corporation was formed and demanded "reparations" from the churches for their part in the injustice laid on African Americans through slavery and segregation. For a few weeks, the UPCUSA's denominational offices in the Interchurch Center in New York were occupied by sit-in groups. The church agencies were not prepared to deal with such turmoil. The COCAR tried to help, but its sympathies were clearly with the protesters' concerns, if not their methods.

The turmoil in society was reflected in the churches. Congregations were under pressure to become racially integrated and to become involved in local protests for equality. There was little opportunity to communicate with the congregations about the steps that the denominational officials were taking. Presbyterian churches, with their middle-class orientation, were not anxious to embrace racial equality or antiwar sentiments. A steady drop in mission contributions resulted from the turmoil.

SHIFTS IN GOVERNING BODY AUTHORITY AND RESPONSIBILITY

During these six decades, the church experienced a shift of authority and responsibility away from the General Assembly agencies to more regional and local involvement. One responsibility of each Assembly-related board was to interpret its work to the congregations. For years, each agency went directly to the congregations, sending news, prayer letters, and speakers. Missionaries were assigned to congregations for special relationships—what the congregations called "our missionaries." The congregations corresponded with them and learned much about mission work from these personal contacts.

In the PCUSA the Assembly boards joined in establishing regional offices in New York, Chicago, Kansas City, and San Francisco. Following the merger with the UPCNA in 1958, an additional office was established in Pittsburgh. The staff in these offices interpreted mission to congregations and governing bodies and assisted the Presbyterian Women's organizations with programming. There was little coordination at the General Assembly level in the interpretation programs. The congregations often felt that they were besieged by agencies and institutions of their own church that were competing for the mission dollar. Following World War II, each denomination established a coordinating council that prepared a total mission budget for the denomination. Each agency was assigned a portion of this budget, and the agencies were expected to promote support of the entire budget, not just their portion. As the denomination shifted responsibility away from General Assembly agencies to synods and presbyteries, the regional offices' interpretation responsibility was discontinued, and the agencies worked with the governing bodies.

NEW ORGANIZATIONS FOR MISSION

The struggle for racial equality in society had created the concept of the Self-Development of People (SDP), based on the assumption that people who had been kept out of the economic mainstream had talents that should be used. If given some basic resources, these people could develop income-producing ventures. Churches were challenged to participate. One approach was for COEMAR to use some of the funds normally invested in the American stock market as investments in other countries. These investments were expected to raise the economic level of the country, benefiting the churches by raising the overall economic level of their people. COEMAR gave a grant to fund the formation of the Emerging Economies Corporation (EEC). It funded one successful venture in Korea, but it finally disbanded. Compared to the whole economy of a foreign country, COEMAR's modest investments overseas were unable to make the dramatic impact that was earlier envisioned.

There was a strong effort to have UPCUSA churches work on SDP projects in the US and around the world. During a tense time at the 1968 GA, John Smith and Kenneth Neigh proposed that such a fund be started with a grant of $1.5 million from COEMAR and the Board of National Missions. The fund was developed and continues to receive part of the One Great Hour of Sharing offering, which is a source of help to projects both in the United Sates and in other countries. The changing global economy also brought to prominence the large number of people in our nation who were homeless and hungry. In response, the UPCUSA created the Hunger Fund, which provides special funds for food banks, nutrition programs, and direct feeding both in this country and across the world.

A number of organizations with mission concerns appeared that were related to the United Presbyterian Church but not a part of its structure. The Medical Benevolence Fund was started by the PCUS's BWM under Watson Street and was related to a similar group under COEMAR. The Presbyterian Frontier

Fellowship was concerned for unreached tribes. The Outreach Foundation was formed for special emphasis on evangelism under the PCUS. The Association of Presbyterians for Cross-Cultural Mission was formed to keep world mission concerns before the church.[39]

John Smith provided strong leadership for the Commission and the ecumenical organizations during his tenure. He served as Moderator of the General Assembly and as a president of the World Council of Churches. Upon his retirement in 1970, Donald Black was elected to be his successor, and J. Oscar McCloud was elected to be Associate Secretary for Ecumenical Mission.

THE DONALD BLACK YEARS: 1970–72

The financial crisis of the 1960s had now caught up with the agencies. For several years, COEMAR had been drawing on its reserves. It ultimately reached the point where it could no longer support its staff or the number of missionaries. Missionary personnel who were scheduled for furlough were warned that they probably would not be returned to the field. Consultations with church leaders about missionary personnel prioritization confronted them with decisions that they were not prepared to make. Some churches offered to assume support of personnel in their field. For example, the schools in Japan offered to support missionaries as their regular teaching staff. Congregations made special efforts to continue support of missionaries. Five COEMAR staff members were released, and the number of missionaries was reduced.[40]

During this early 1970s period of declining funding and sending of missionaries, another process of reorganizing the General Assembly agencies was well under way. Much of the final year was spent in developing proposals for the new structure. Donald Black's service was terminated when his position was abolished in 1972. Mission functions formerly served by COEMAR were divided among several departments in the new Program Agency.

THE J. OSCAR MCCLOUD YEARS: 1972–87

The new GA agencies were created by making a horizontal cut across the existing boards and combining certain functions from each of them. All of the endowment funds and investment activities became concentrated in the Presbyterian Foundation. General personnel concerns were placed in the Personnel Agency. Mission interpretation and financial operations were given over to the Support Agency, while mission activities in the United States and around the world—racial-ethnic ministries, Christian education services, work with Presbyterian Women, Presbyterian Men, and youth organizations—were combined into the Program Agency.

J. Oscar McCloud, who had been on the staff of the Board of Christian Education, COCAR, and COEMAR, became the Director of the Program Agency. He was the first African American to head a GA agency. During his tenure, the Program Agency structure developed new relationships and increased staff and programming. World mission concerns were placed within the Program Agency's unit of Ecumenical Relations and Mission. These years saw Lebanon involved in civil conflict, Iraq under severe dictatorship, Iran expelling Americans, and Ethiopia under dictatorship (followed by a return to democratic rule). The Program Agency was called upon to be flexible in adjusting to the many world changes.[41]

One critical occasion was the abduction of Rev. Benjamin Weir, a missionary serving in Beirut. He, along with two other people, was held hostage for sixteen months. Fred Wilson, Associate General Director of the Program Agency, led the church's efforts to gain his release. He worked with the Lebanese Church, the American government, and international agencies. Weir was finally released in good health, reunited with his family in the United States, and later elected to serve as Moderator of the General Assembly.

In 1982, the Program Agency held a major consultation with the theme "Mission in a Global Perspective." One hundred fifty people from churches and ecumenical organizations attended. They urged the Presbyterian Church to develop an approach to mission that was more global and thus less centered on the United States, a theme that echoed the 1956 Lake Mohonk Conference.

THE COMBINED STREAMS:
THE PRESBYTERIAN CHURCH (U.S.A.)

In 1983, adjustments to Presbyterian denominational structures and thus also mission policy once again occurred. After 119 years of separation, the UPCUSA and the PCUS were finally reunited into one denomination, the Presbyterian Church (U.S.A.). This new structure's governing body was the General Assembly Council, whose members were elected for six years with a mandate to provide a new mission structure. They initially tried to operate without staff, but within a year they called some support staff, and in 1985, they called Donald Black to be the first Executive Director.

For several months before the union, Assembly agencies had been participating in joint consultations and projects. The Division of International Mission (PCUS) and the Program Agency (UPCUSA) held joint meetings and joined in bringing the document "Mission and Evangelism: An Ecumenical Affirmation" to the reuniting 1983 GA.

Soon after the union, a Committee on Mission Structure was appointed with a mandate to report in five years. During that period, the existing agencies continued as separate organizations, trying to work together as was possible. The two organizations were not parallel structures, making it difficult to cooperate in many activities. In 1986, Oscar McCloud resigned in order to become the Director of the Fund for Theological Education, and Fred Wilson became the Director of the Program Agency.

A General Assembly special committee was appointed to propose a new head-quarters for the new denomination. The committee reached the conclusion early that neither New York nor Atlanta should be chosen since those were the previous headquarters of the Northern and Southern denominations. It finally made its report to the General Assembly in 1986 that Kansas City should be the locale. Instead, the Assembly chose an alternate proposal of Louisville, where a building was offered, thanks to the efforts of Louisville Presbyterian Theological Seminary President John M. Mulder. The new structure of the PC(USA) was finally implemented in 1988. One of its nine program units was the Global Mission Ministry Unit (GMU). Clifton Kirkpatrick, the director of the PCUS's Division on International Mission at the time of the merger, was elected to be the GMU director.

THE CLIFTON KIRKPATRICK YEARS: 1988–96

The GMU combined the work of the two former mission agencies. It continued to reach out into new areas while also inheriting some supplementary groups. The Medical Benevolence Fund, the Presbyterian Frontier Fellowship, and the Outreach Foundation had raised money from Presbyterians for special mission projects. The GMU entered into a covenant relationship with these three, listing them as Validated Mission Support Groups.

The new denominational structure was to be reviewed after four years. At the four-year mark, it was decided that it was too unwieldy, and therefore it was completely revised and consolidated. All members of the General Assembly Council were assigned to serve on one of three Division Committees: Worldwide Ministries, Congregational Ministries, and National Ministries.

THE WORLDWIDE MINISTRIES DIVISION: 1992–2006

The Worldwide Ministries Division (WMD) was bestowed the responsibility for Ecumenical Partnership, Global Service and Witness, and People in Mutual Mission. Clifton Kirkpatrick was elected as the director. In the early 1990s, it was clear that a significant change was taking place in mission outreach, and so there was a decided shift from traditional Presbyterian Mission fields to relating to churches in many new areas. At the end of World War II, the three churches' foreign mission activities were in twenty-five countries. The movement to new areas started in a small way under COEMAR's Division of Ecumenical Relations and under the leadership of Watson Street in the PCUS's BWM. In a changing world, illustrated by the dissolution of the Soviet Union, many new opportunities to witness to the gospel appeared. Refugees from civil conflicts, ethnic immigrants in Europe, and churches seeking renewal after years of Soviet domination—all welcomed the presence of American Presbyterians. In 2000, the contacts had reached churches in more than eighty nations.

The 1993 GA adopted the paper "Mission in the 1990s," which affirmed the historic purpose of evangelistic witness and opened new ways to witness. Guidelines for working·in the former Soviet countries were established. The possibility of congregational involvement was affirmed. With international travel a ready possibility, congregations and presbyteries developed mission contacts and sent mission teams for short-term involvement.

THE MARIAN MCCLURE YEARS: 1997–2006

When Clifton Kirkpatrick was elected to be the Stated Clerk of the General Assembly in 1997, Dr. Marian McClure was elected to be the Director of the World Ministries Division. She had done research in Haiti and served as a Program Officer for the Ford Foundation in Mexico City.

McClure carried out a program (initiated by Gwen Crawley) in cooperation with the Presbyterian Historical Society on mission history, which involved retired missionaries. Groups were formed in several areas of the country and reviewed current mission policies. They also worked to have missionaries send their letters and papers to the Presbyterian Historical Society for safekeeping and for availability to future historians. A conference of representatives from these groups was held in 1999. Sadly, because of a lack of funding, this project was never able to progress beyond the circulation of conference papers.[42]

During these years, congregational involvement in mission projects continued to grow. Small national churches did not have the organization or the personnel to be arranging some of these "mission invasions," so a new assignment appeared in U.S. mission personnel: Coordinator of Visiting Teams. A church-wide conference to discover the extent of such involvement and to share experiences was held in St. Louis in 1997. It became evident that many such efforts were developing across the denomination, and several were even directed to the same church or country. The WMD developed a networking program that put people relating to the same country in touch with each other. These consultations enabled groups to space their visits, avoid duplication of work, and improve the total mission activity in that area. In 2003, the General Assembly affirmed the WMD's principle that "Presbyterians Do Mission in Partnership," an important guide to groups assuming mission projects in other countries.

Contributions to support the general work of the denomination continued to decline. In 1999, a special fund drive, Joining Hearts and Hands, was begun with the goal of raising $40 million. Of this amount, $20 million were designated for new missionary personnel; but rather than a structural change, this was more of an emergency fund, with the hope that long-term funding would follow. Through all of these changes and struggles with funding, ongoing ministry to the most needy continued. The WMD contained the departments of Self-Development of People, Presbyterian Disaster Assistance, Hunger Fund, International Evangelism, Global Education, and International Health Ministries, and they developed a comprehensive approach to mission, responding to requests from partner churches with the program that best met their needs.

CONCLUSIONS

As we close this portion of the sixty-three-year history, we call to our readers' attention a few long-term developments and themes that have pointed the way ahead: (1) Unity. At the heart of the story is the movement toward the unity of the church of Jesus Christ. This is clearly seen in the union of denominations, but also in the countless ways that missionaries and national staff have demonstrated the essential unity of Christ's church. Unity and mission belong together, and the PC(USA) has kept this as a guiding theological principle. (2) The movement from mission and missionary control to the national church. Sixty years ago, missionaries ran everything in the many mission fields. Today, all of the institutions and church bodies with whom we are engaged are under the control of the body of believers in that country. (3) The shift from General Assembly to congregations and presbyteries. Today, mission is not implemented through GA agencies alone; it is also carried out through lay and youth work camps, presbytery exchanges and partnerships, volunteers, students abroad, and any number of other groups seeking to be part of Presbyterian mission. Mission has now become a people's movement to the ends of the earth. (4) The definition of what constitutes mission has now been expanded. Sixty years ago it was largely limited to preaching, teaching, and medical assistance. Today it continues to stress these three basics, but it has been expanded to include race relations, justice issues, homelessness, peace and reconciliation, AIDS education, and community development, to name a few. Mission includes anything that brings life in all its abundance to humankind. (5) At the heart of the program is Jesus Christ. This has not changed and never will. The Great Commission and Great Commandment are still our guides in mission. We still define our mission by what he brought to the world: good news to the poor, release to the captive, recovery of sight to the blind, and freedom to the oppressed. And his presence goes with us to the end of the age.

Chapter 4

Faithfulness through the Storm

Changing Theology of Mission

SHERRON GEORGE

The changes in North American Presbyterianism from 1944 to 2004 have been so significant and turbulent that they can aptly be called "storms." Through the storms, however, Presbyterians have not abandoned their strong commitment to God's mission. Considering the magnitude of the storms that we have experienced, this can only be explained by the faithfulness of God to use frail Presbyterians as instruments and signs of God's plan and intention for the world.

The nature of mission is revealed in the title of South African missiologist David Bosch's monumental work *Transforming Mission*. Purposefully ambiguous, the title suggests that mission transforms and that mission is being transformed. There have been substantial transformations in our understanding and involvement in mission in the past six decades. Bosch locates mission today in the context of crisis and opportunity. A fitting subtitle for this essay could be "Crises, Challenges, and Opportunities in Mission." I want to reflect theologically and missiologically on some of the major changes and crises that Presbyterians in America have experienced in the past sixty years and the challenges and opportunities that they have offered and continue to offer to us.

Perhaps *pluralism* is the best word to describe one root of the crises. Theological, religious, and cultural pluralism mark our contemporary world. We live with

85

the tensions caused by our globalized and pluralistic church and society. How do we maintain Christian identity and faithfulness in mission without becoming exclusive, intolerant, or irrelevant? Do the limits that we fearfully impose on our theological pluralism and differences rob us of "freedom in Christ" and the plenitude of God's grace? Both the *Book of Confessions* and the *Book of Order* show our shared doctrines and core beliefs about the Trinitarian God, God's mission (*missio Dei*), the church as God's instrument in history, evangelism, discipleship, solidarity with those in need, and commitment to social justice. The theological pluralism in the Presbyterian Church (U.S.A.) that threatens our unity could also be an opportunity for a renewed commitment to God's holistic mission.

However, our Presbyterian predicament is complicated by another storm. The rise of theological pluralism, debates over mission, and the gap between congregations and denominational leadership have resulted in a crisis for our "corporate denomination" model. Coalter, Mulder, and Weeks's book *Vital Signs* describes the "denominational revolution" caused by the failure of the "corporate denomination" that threatens our denominational identity.[1] The authors identify two problems of the "managerial denomination": (1) the conflict between national agendas and congregational concerns and (2) the fragmentation of mission.[2] Consequently, a subtle shift in the denomination's self-definition has occurred. What used to be characterized as "a missionary organization" has shifted into "an organization managing mission."[3] The denominational leaders responsible for our international mission programs rarely lack sound missiological vision that is articulated in theological statements, but they are often forced to spend their energies "managing mission" rather than thinking and acting missiologically.

Our internal storms of theological pluralism and organizational revolution have taken place in the post–World War II global arena. Daniel J. Adams deems 1945 as "the dawning of a new age" in world history and in "the mission of the church."[4] As nations emerged from World War II, churches were challenged to recognize the end of "the view that western civilization would lead humankind steadily upward on the path toward peace, prosperity, and material well-being."[5] In our post–Cold War and post-9/11 world, the disparity of power and U.S. hegemony in an unequal world pose new challenges requiring introspection and paradigm shifts.

PART OF A GLOBAL AND ECUMENICAL
FAITH COMMUNITY

Presbyterians believe that the "one holy catholic and apostolic Church" is by nature *ecumenical*, or covering the whole "inhabited earth" (*oikoumenē*), universal, all-inclusive.[6] International cooperation is not new for U.S. Presbyterians. The Presbyterian Church in the U.S. (PCUS), Presbyterian Church in the U.S.A. (PCUSA), and United Presbyterian Church of North America (UPCNA) were all founding members of the oldest organized confessional family—the Alliance of Reformed Churches throughout the World Holding the Presbyterian System (1877; later called World Alliance of Reformed Churches, WARC). Recognizing that the church had become a worldwide reality, participants in a conference in Oxford, England, in 1937 reclaimed the word "ecumenical," giving it a "new connotation that embraced the mission of the Church and the unity of the Church as integral facets of the 'Ecumenical Movement,'" and recommended the creation of a World Council of Churches (WCC).[7] As the world passed through the divisions, destruction, and losses of World War II, and as Presbyterians engaged in battles over fundamentalism and modernism, the ecumenical vision was not lost.

The first global Christian post–World War II conference, the International Missionary Council (IMC), met in Whitby, Ontario, in 1947. The conference mantra, "Partners in Obedience," became a "dynamic watchword" for "the beginning of a new era" in mission.[8] In spite of their internal theological debates, when the WCC was formally instituted in 1948, the PCUS, PCUSA, and UPCNA were, again, all founding members. So-called younger and older churches from East, West, North, and South all became *equal* members of the WCC. The challenge was, How would these worldwide churches relate to each other in new ways? Though the Cold War represented a new source of international disagreement, the member churches in the 1948 WCC Assembly recognized postwar reconstruction, including that of church structures and relationships and aid to refugees, as "ecumenical" tasks. Presbyterian John Coventry Smith saw the formation of the WCC as "another indication that we must hurry to find the pattern of mission which would follow the end of the present era. We still lived in the old era but we were getting glimpses of the future."[9] Indeed, we have been struggling for sixty years to make this transition and change, to leave the old era of mission behind.

Though Presbyterians have often criticized the WCC and some of its positions, especially in the political arena, we have been active and faithful members. At the 1956 meeting of the WARC, its acting president, John Mackay, spoke of the importance of cooperation between confessional bodies and the ecumenical movement, the WCC. Consequently, at the initiative of the WARC, fourteen world confessional families have met annually since 1957 in Geneva for conversations between themselves and WCC staff.[10]

After a century and a half of foreign mission work and of fruitful responses of national Christians, Presbyterians recognized that the church had become a global ecumenical faith community, doing mission on six continents. This called for certain adjustments. In the emerging ecumenical mission theology, the "s" was dropped from "missions," because it was God's one mission, in which all churches participated. Because of the ubiquity of mission, the word "foreign" was replaced by global, international, worldwide, or ecumenical mission. It is noteworthy that when the UPCNA and PCUSA united in 1958 to become the United Presbyterian Church in the U.S.A. (UPCUSA), they intentionally named the united mission agency the "Commission on Ecumenical Mission and Relations" (COEMAR). In 1962, COEMAR produced *An Advisory Study* with follow-up that encouraged the churches to follow the new ecumenical approach to global mission.

The 1963 WCC Conference of World Mission and Evangelism in Mexico City exemplified this new paradigm.[11] The watchword was "mission on six continents." It affirmed that mission was done on six continents by the church on six continents. Mission frontiers were no longer geographical. The distinction between "sending churches" and "mission fields" no longer existed. Ecumenical mission became multilateral and multidirectional. Every place was deemed a mission field in need of evangelization, including the increasingly pluralistic and secular North America and Western Europe. Today, this emphasis continues, as Darrell Guder states in his book *Missional Church*: "The church of every place . . . is a mission-sending church, and the place of every church is a mission-receiving place."[12]

The change in the collective consciousness in local congregations has been gradual. Moving beyond the idea of unidirectional "foreign" mission in faraway lands has not been easy. Furthermore, not all Presbyterians were comfortable with the social justice involvement of the WCC during the 1960s and 1970s. As the storms of WCC-led ecumenism gained momentum, evangelicals "sought an alternative means of cooperating in a depoliticized style of world evangelization."[13] A new movement was launched at the Billy Graham Organization–sponsored Lausanne International Congress on World Evangelization in 1974. The resulting "Lausanne Covenant" and movement proclaimed "the urgency of offering salvation in the name of Jesus Christ alone . . . and opposed the WCC's method of dialogue with peoples of other living faiths and secular ideologies."[14] Many members of the then UPCUSA participated and continue to participate in this movement. Recently, the WCC has gone through transitions and sought ways to bring evangelicals into their ecumenical circle. Recognizing and respecting the religious and cultural pluralism in the global church; being sensitive to global contextual realities; and promoting human interdependence, dignity, and equality—these are key challenges in all mission endeavors of Presbyterians today.

After many years of unilaterally planning, sending, and controlling Presbyterian mission work around the world, the move to multilateral sending and receiving in a global church has been a revolutionary change. Furthermore, as Philip Jenkins demonstrates in *The Next Christendom: The Coming of Global Christianity*, the demographic center of the global church has shifted to the Southern hemisphere.[15] Slowly, Presbyterians are waking up to the reality that the majority church today is composed of Southern Christians in Latin America, Africa, and Asia, who are the leaders now in shaping mission theology and practice in the global mission movement.

While Presbyterians in mission seek our new role and place in a global ecumenical church, we also struggle over our Reformed and Presbyterian identity. In the 1980s, Robert McAfee Brown declared, "I am a Presbyterian—therefore I am ecumenical."[16] In *The Re-Forming Tradition,* Coalter, Mulder, and Weeks conclude that the "Presbyterian predicament" in the twentieth century is a case of several sets of "dual" or "conflicting allegiances," in which we are challenged to "complementary loyalty." They state that "Ecumenism and Denominational Identity" are a "difficult balance" for Presbyterians.[17]

However, outstanding models—like John Mackay, Clifton Kirkpatrick, and Marian McClure—and official denominational statements have demonstrated our Presbyterian commitment to the global ecumenical faith community.[18] The "Life and Mission Statement" declares: "We are called to be part of a global and ecumenical community. Our world is wider and more diverse than that which our Reformed forebears knew. We live in a multilingual, multiracial, multicultural, and economically diverse world. . . . We are one part of the body of Christ."[19] Both "Mission in the 1990s" and "Gathering for God's Future" emphasize the privilege of being part of a global church, the significance of changing global realities for us, and our commitment to work ecumenically.[20]

BEYOND SUPERIORITY AND DOMINATION TO EQUALITY AND SHARING

The postwar spirit of global interdependence was followed by the dismantling of colonial empires, the independence of nations in the developing world, the civil rights movement and concurrent social changes in the 1960s in the United States, and the devastation of the Vietnam War. For the ecumenical church-in-mission, the last half of the twentieth century was a time of transition and self-criticism, demanding the end of all attitudes of Western superiority, missionary imperialism, and cultural imposition. John Coventry Smith captured the moment in *From Colonialism to World Community: The Church's Pilgrimage*:

> It would be a time of troubles and change for all of us, and we in the United States were part of the problem. Four hundred years of colonialism had deepened Western superiority complexes, mixed them with racial feelings and often left us unable to understand our fellow Christians. . . . We have begun to dig out the roots of centuries of colonial and racial prejudices, but it will take decades longer before we make substantial progress. Some Christians do not yet know that these roots exist.[21]

In *Christianity in Africa,* Kwame Bediako interprets our postcolonial "crisis in mission" as

> the process of adjustment whereby the Western church [is] coming to terms with the emergence of the non-Western church. . . . [This is] part of the dying stages of Western ethnocentrism, with the Western church still largely unaware of the shift in Christianity's centre of gravity to the non-Western world . . . [and of] the impact of the southward shift of the Church upon the theology of mission.[22]

In the storms we have been going through, have we grasped the magnitude of the metamorphosis in mission, or are we clinging to an old mission paradigm that is obsolete?

PARTNERSHIP

The new era in mission, which began to unfold at the 1947 IMC Conference with the challenge to become "Partners in Obedience," started taking shape for Presbyterians at the 1956 Mohonk Consultation of the Presbyterian Board of Foreign Missions of the PCUSA. At this conference, the decision was made to fully integrate the missionary organizations around the world into the indigenous national churches within five years. Two years later, COEMAR was created with the goal of implementing these changes. In 1962, there was a similar consultation of the PCUS with its church partners held at Montreat, which resulted in a commitment to equal partnerships. More steps were taken at the Conference on Mission in Global Perspective sponsored by the Program Agency of the UPCUSA in 1982.[23]

In 1987, G. Thompson Brown wrote *Presbyterians in World Mission,* celebrating 150 years of mission effort since the 1837 founding of the PCUSA's Board of Foreign Missions. He describes four stages of mission, the fourth being "The Era of the CHURCH-BASED MISSION."[24] Then he asks if it is time for a fifth new model. Brown recognizes some of the problems: national churches that did not receive the authority that they expected, missionaries who suffered crises of identity, and the disparity of resources between continents. Currently, a new model is emerging without forgoing the theology of mission in partnership with both the triune God and with partner churches worldwide.

In "Mission in the 1990s," the Presbyterian Church (U.S.A.) expressed a strong commitment to partnership and mutuality as the "way we carry out our mission" as part of "a global Christian community in mission."[25] It is easy to articulate the beautiful theory of mission in partnership, but moving beyond paternalism and colonialism to egalitarianism has been a long slow process. It implies that we not only release control, respect autonomy, listen patiently, wait for invitations, share decisions, exist in solidarity, but we also learn to do two-way mutual mission, namely to be "mutually encouraged by each other's faith."[26] At times, moratoriums have been a part of the maturation of relationships. Mission organizations parallel to national churches have been dissolved. The PC(USA) maintains relationships with some 165 partner churches in 80 countries, some of which have more than 150 years of history. Over 100 presbytery-to-presbytery and synod partnerships have been formed around the world with joint projects and many mutual visits.

The PC(USA)'s present vision statement, "Gathering for God's Future," is the product of two years of listening to global church partners and jointly discern- ·

ing our contemporary contextual realities and priorities. This statement reaffirms the commitment "Joining in Partnership," which is described as a "demanding and rewarding calling" that requires "humility and vulnerability to seek God's will together for the partnership relationship." This commitment has been recorded as "the goal of ecumenical mission practice for at least fifty years."[27] The Worldwide Ministries Division's (WMD) 2003 policy statement, "Presbyterians Do Mission in Partnership," clearly articulated and refined the earlier-stated commitment to ecumenical mission. It claimed that "the practice of partnership guides our whole connectional church" and that in "doing mission in partnership," we seek to adhere to certain biblical and missiological principles:[28]

1. Shared Grace and Thanksgiving.
2. Mutuality and Interdependence.
3. Recognition and Respect.
4. Open Dialogue and Transparency.
5. Sharing of Resources.

The statement provides sound guidelines for the denomination, presbyteries, and congregations. One resource to help Presbyterians implement "Presbyterians Do Mission in Partnership" is the book *Called as Partners in Christ's Service: The Practice of God's Mission.* It challenges us to develop the missional attitudes of respect and humility and to engage in practices based on mutuality—giving *and* receiving, learning *and* teaching, listening *and* speaking.[29]

Ultimately, however, essential missiological questions remain with us as the new century begins: How is our sustained discipline and practice of partnership working? Have we made substantial progress in moving beyond superiority and domination to equality and sharing? What have been the impediments and problems along the way? Where have our mission theology and practice in partnership failed? Have we, as Wickeri asks, been willing to "follow through with the radical demands of what partnership and working together in God's mission requires?"[30] He wisely perceives that "without a critical perspective on existing mission practices, structures, and working styles, any statement on partnership in mission lacks a prophetic cutting edge."[31]

One of the greatest concerns that our global partners have expressed is the impact of the economic globalization and neoliberalism of the 1980s and 1990s. The democratic liberalism of the free market has engendered the growing wealth of nations in the North, the persistent poverty of nations in the South, and the escalating economic inequality between the hemispheres. Trade agreements have not always been fair for the emerging nations. Consequently, our partners have become "increasingly impatient with the unequal power relationships between churches in the North and the South. Despite the many discussions of partnership, the pattern of domination and dependency" continues.[32] Because of the "crisis of inequality," in the 1970s a partial "moratorium" on sending mission personnel from the North to the South was implemented. The greatest obstacle to equal partnerships has perennially been the emphasis on one-way financial support. Is it possible for partners with unequal economic resources to be equal? How do we practice authentic two-way mission of mutual giving and receiving? Does our mission practice today, in the name of partnership, as Wickeri suggests, "hide the stubborn reality of inequality, dependency, domination, and the sense that 'we' are in control of the *missio Dei*?"[33] We are still wrestling with these issues.

To give an example of how strongly our partners feel about this situation, the Latin American Council of Churches, of which nearly all of our partner churches in Latin America are members, published a "public pronouncement to member churches" from a 2003 consultation, "Globalize Fullness of Life [*Globalizar la vida plena*]" held in Buenos Aires. "Seeking Exits . . . Moving On! (Buscando salidas . . . caminando hacia adelante!)" denounces the effects of neoliberal globalization and the "free" market on the poor in Latin America and proposes an alternative way of just globalization for all.[34]

The East-West divide, which diminished with the fall of the Berlin wall, has become a "clash of civilizations" and religions. Our partners in the global South are articulating another concern in relation to the neo-imperialism and unilateralism that has resurfaced in the United States since September 11, 2001. Our partners extended solidarity and hoped for a spirit of global cooperation in the fight against terrorism, but they have been very disappointed and critical of the invasions of Afghanistan and Iraq, asking if it is possible to impose democracy with domination. The fear is that, again with Iran, an exacerbated nationalism will lead to a unilateral preventive invasion. All of this goes against the grain of partnership. How have U.S. foreign policy and military interventions affected our mission partnerships? The storms continue to reveal the damaging depth of our superiority complex and the strength of our cultural tendency to dominate.

RECEIVING AND DEVELOPING GLOBAL LEADERS

Missional practices that have been challenges and growing edges for Presbyterians in mission during the second half of the twentieth century are listening, learning, receiving, following, and empowering. During the Central American unrest in the 1980s, many Presbyterians discovered and accompanied new conversation partners who helped them learn to do what Robert McAfee Brown calls "reading the Bible with third-world eyes."[35] This is not an easy task. As Joerg Rieger notes, it exposes our blind spots and gives us a critical evaluation of much of our Western culture and religion of superiority.[36] A serious problem that still persists is the reticence of Presbyterians to listen, learn, and receive from partners who come from other cultures and speak English with an accent. It is especially hard for us to look at our own church, mission practice, and country through the eyes of others who have a different perspective. We would rather give than receive. It is hard for us to experience dependence and identification with people unlike ourselves.

"Mission in the 1990s" clearly stated that we must learn to see "the U.S.A. as a Mission Field" and to be "receivers" in global mission. Consequently, one important program of the WMD is Mission to the United States. Missionaries are sent from our partner churches to spend time in the United States of America. Many congregations and presbyteries have participated in Mission to the United States and received guests. They perceptively interpret the global context and the signs of the times and share cutting-edge and sometimes disturbing insights with us. The book *A Strange Accent: The Reflections of a Missionary to the United States* contains penetrating sermons preached by Thomas John, a professor and pastor in the Church of South India, while he was a Mission Partner in Residence for the PC(USA).[37]

"Gathering for God's Future" reminds us of the importance of graciously receiving and learning from new immigrants to the USA and also of our commitment to "Developing Leaders."[38] In pioneer educational mission, Presbyterians established schools and seminaries around the world. Those institutions have formed many leaders and are now run by national churches and governments. In 2001, the office of Global Education and International Leadership Development in the WMD coordinated the work of 160 mission coworkers serving in educational ministries in forty-two countries. A current challenge is to cooperate in strengthening centers of excellence and in providing scholarships for postgraduate studies to train leaders of partner churches worldwide. Since 1942, more than 3,500 leadership development scholarships have been awarded.[39] At first, this meant giving scholarships to study in the United States, but now the trend is to encourage South-South exchanges where people study on their own continent. Education is the key to empowerment. "Gathering for God's Future" states: "Through leadership development, the church in each place is empowered . . . to establish equal relationships with the mission-sending church. It often leads to the partner church's ability to be self-supporting, and to send persons from the indigenous church in mission. It is the form of aid most requested by partners."[40]

As we support, respect, and learn from leaders in our partner churches, leadership development becomes mutual, and we are transformed. We are to relate as equals and follow the new global leadership that is transforming mission theology. A 2001 article in *Newsweek*, "The Changing Face of the Church," concludes that "for the first time in its history Christianity has become a religion mainly of the poor, the marginalized, the powerless and—in parts of Asia and the Middle East—the oppressed."[41] What implications will this have for our mission structures and practices?

NEW ROLES, PATTERNS, AND IMAGES
FOR WESTERN MISSION WORKERS

Leadership development obviously prepares nationals to take the place of many foreign missionaries. If we have entered the postcolonial era where strong autonomous denominations on every continent are engaged in God's mission, providing dynamic and empowered leadership for the global church, does this mean that Western missionaries have become obsolete? Has the PC(USA) entered the "postmissionary" era? No, it means that there must be no more missionary paternalism, no more unidirectional mission, no more binary "us" and "them" mentality.

Western missionaries are being reinvented, reimagined, and retooled. In the past sixty years, we have been seeking new images for the changing roles that we are assuming alongside our myriad counterparts from the majority church in the South and the East. Donald Black shows how COEMAR exchanged the term "missionary" for "fraternal worker" during the 1960s, and how the traditional pattern of "career missionaries," who committed a lifetime to mission service, began to change. Later, the PC(USA) adopted the term "mission coworker," which is often shortened to "mission worker" or collectively "mission personnel." The most important thing is that the term "missionary" has such strong connotations with the paternalistic era that it is best to not use it. Slowly, the term "missionary" has been replaced by "mission worker."[42] Black explains that "it was assumed after World War II that the new missionaries would all be specialists, sent to perform a specific task, expected to teach others to do that work. In the new day, missionary service would be in short-term assignments."[43] The new emerging pattern consisted of term assignments, and most people served for more than one term. As with other professions in our globalized world, the idea of "career missionaries" is losing currency. Today, full-time mission coworkers are appointed for renewable terms of three to five years.

The debate between long-term and short-term assignments has been rigorous in these last decades. During the 1970s, many new opportunities for short-term assignments were developed with creativity and sensitivity. The PCUS created a program titled Volunteers in Mission (VIM), which appointed young men and women, as well as some retired adults, to specific assignments for one or two years.[44] The PC(USA) continued programs of long-term and short-term volunteers and initiated a dynamic Young Adult Volunteer (YAV) program, with ecumenical partners in over a dozen sites around the world, which has been extended to include the LINKS program. (In the LINKS program staff work with organizations outside of the General Assembly Council to provide meaningful short-term volunteer mission experiences connected to our larger mission effort.)

As the trend toward short-term personnel has grown, many Presbyterians fear that the balance of needed long-term personnel has been threatened. Obviously, both are important, and the long-term coworkers who anchor and guide our worldwide denominational work should not be entirely replaced by short-term workers. An equilibrium between "compensated" long-term coworkers and short-term "volunteers" is vital. The PC(USA) has maintained more long-term international mission personnel than other mainstream denominations in recent decades have. One recent affirmation of the significance of key long-term personnel with language and cultural skills was the creation of sixteen (now thirty) positions for regional liaisons, who facilitate communications and connections with partner churches and mission personnel on the field and national staff, presbyteries, and local congregations in the United States. While most liaisons live on the field, some are based in the United States.

In the past five decades of changing patterns and roles, as Stephen Knisely reminds us, "Presbyterians have been on the cutting edge in experimenting with new ways of being in mission with partner churches around the world, for example: Mission to the U.S.A, two-way and three-way mission personnel service; international presbytery partnerships; ecumenical partnerships; young adult volunteers; global interns; diaconal workers; and funding of mission personnel from multiple sources."[45] We should add to this list: the Reconciliation and Mission exchange program with partners in Central America, the interfaith listening program, the itineration of international peacemakers, mission personnel assigned to assist congregations taking mission trips, and hosting delegations assigned to accompany human rights workers and displaced people. In addition, Clifton Kirkpatrick includes the mission pastor's network, the "share the good news" program, validated mission support groups, the border ministry on the Mexico-U.S. border, refugee resettlement programs, and ministries in hunger.[46] These innovative programs and patterns demonstrate the growing circle of direct involvement in mission, as well as continued responsiveness to invitations from partner churches to collaborate in specific tasks and projects. When mission coworkers are invited, partners help to define job descriptions and complete evaluations at the end of the term of service, with freedom to request another term or not reappoint.

Therefore, categories of mission personnel today include regional "experts," mission educators, "specialists" (educators and trainers, health consultants, frontier evangelism workers, English teachers, disaster response, community development, enablers of special projects), and volunteers. One important fact is that *people* are the priority in Presbyterian mission work. God's faithfulness in loving the people of God's world is our guide and motivation in mission. The PC(USA) mission personnel work under the human resources office of People in Mutual Mission (PIMM). Through all of the changes in patterns and experiments with programs, people—both partners and mission personnel—come first. The PC(USA) has every reason to be proud of our faithfulness to our partner churches and of our care for and benefits extended to mission personnel.

In the midst of the storms of theological pluralism, organizational restructuring, and funding shortages, the PC(USA) faithfully supports various patterns of mission and seeks new images for people in mutual mission. The 2003 statement "Gathering for God's Future" uses a variety of images of mission: "joining in partnership," "working ecumenically," "developing leaders," and "sharing people and resources."[47] Moreover, it affirms the need to "seek to share in ways that affirm and assist rather than demean or dominate."[48] People are the priority, and thus our partner churches continue to want, invite, and welcome people in mission. This vision statement demonstrates the awareness of new images: "We are sometimes guests, sometimes hosts in the process of sharing people."[49] When we act properly as guests, we can move beyond domination.

In the final analysis, more important than changing patterns of service and funding are the changing images and roles, including role reversals. The leaders in our partner churches have assumed roles that missionaries formerly held, and parallel structures in which missionaries were dominant have been dissolved. In discovering new roles and fresh images for mission work, Presbyterians have experienced "mission in reverse." We have learned that the whole world is a mission field, for even as we receive mission workers in the United States, these sisters and brothers from around the world transform us.

As the global church enters the new postcolonial millennium with a radically changed face and missionary situation, the traditional image of missionaries as "pioneers, explorers, founders, evangelists, teachers, healers, and church leaders" not only has changed but "may well become counterproductive in nurturing different relationships in a changed context in church and mission."[50] Only through discovering new images of cross-cultural mission will Western missionaries be able to continue to engage in such endeavors. Missiologists have offered a number of such new images: partner, disciple, *diakonia*, coworker, companion,[51] treasure hunter, teacher, prophet, guest, stranger, partner, migrant worker, and ghost.[52] The images of servant, coworker, and partner are favorable, and we remember other evocative images that the Bible provides: penitent sinner, beggar, friend, neighbor, follower, disciple, participant-observer, listener, and learner. Such images mark the continuing conversion of the missionary today. These images flow from the triune God's self-emptying, self-giving, other-receiving, and other-empowering mission.[53]

It has been as hard for us to assume these new roles and images as it has been for us to become accustomed to no longer using the word *missionary*. Our attitudes in mission are surely part of the problem. It might be said that one of the greatest challenges before Presbyterians in mission today is to cultivate and demonstrate the missional attitudes of respect and humility. Only then can we truly move beyond attitudes of superiority and domination to attitudes that demonstrate equality and exemplify mutual sharing.

As the PC(USA) adopts new patterns, roles, and attitudes, we are also reinventing missional practices based on the dynamic of mutuality and reciprocity in multilateral and multidirectional mission. In *Called as Partners in Christ's Service,* I present the following dyads of practices: observing and participating, listening and speaking, sharing sufferings and suffering, sharing joys and celebrating, waiting and praying, receiving and giving, learning and teaching, building community and empowering builders, receiving witnesses and witnessing, being healed and healing.[54] Presbyterians in mission have majored in educating, evangelizing, and healing. What has changed? We are learning *new ways* of doing traditional mission practices with respect and humility in partnerships of reciprocal receiving and giving. Sometimes this learning process has been painful because it requires self-criticism, self-emptying, and relearning.

DENOMINATION IN CRISIS

Lamentably, the Presbyterian emphasis on mutuality and partnership in mission has occurred in the context of a major shift that has complicated mission endeavors. In the nineteenth century, mission was the unifying theme in American Protestantism, and evangelism was an unquestioned perspective and primary task. During the twentieth century, due to theological pluralism and organizational changes, the consensus and clarity about the nature and importance of mission and evangelism have been "eroded by a contentious debate over mission priorities."[55] As Presbyterians shifted to corporate programmatic organizational church models, mission and evangelism became programs among many options and priorities, and our understanding of mission and the relationship between mission and evangelism became clouded and confused.

COHERENCE ERODED WITH
THE FRAGMENTATION OF MISSION

Years ago Stephen Neill warned, "If everything is mission, nothing is mission."[56] However, with the proliferation of special-interest groups, often in response to "crises" since the 1960s, and the spilling over of single-issue politics into American Presbyterianism, every cause finds a space under the ambiguous umbrella of mission. Coalter, Mulder, and Weeks explain that "as American culture lost its cohesion and fragmented during the 1960s through the 1980s, so did the sense of a unifying mission for American Presbyterians."[57] They cite a study further concluding that as "the concept of Presbyterian mission became more variegated and unfocused, congregations became uncertain about the direction of the denomination and less likely to support its General Assembly causes."[58] Not only are there polarities and fractious visions of mission among congregations, but the gap between the mission agendas of the national offices of the denomination and of congregations has been steadily widening over the past sixty years.

At the heart of these debates over mission is our cultural and theological pluralism. While partnership, ecumenism, diversity of gifts, and complementary perspectives are inevitable blessings in today's world church, our denominational crisis and confusion over mission is a stark reminder of our need to clarify and remain faithful to our Reformed understanding of the gospel of Jesus Christ. We often struggle to define our common vision, values, and attitudes. How many Presbyterians could succinctly articulate their understanding of the gospel message and of God's mission activity in the world? Our debates over the lordship of Christ intensify our confusion. How do we understand salvation and the new human community in Christ?

In all of these debates, another storm in the Presbyterian conceptualization and practice of mission has been the false dichotomy, bifurcation, and polarity between evangelism and social justice. In the last half of the century, the PC(USA) and its predecessors (re)discovered the importance of social justice, reconciliation, peacemaking, sustainable development, and ecology in God's mission. For many, these aspects of mission supplanted the former emphasis on new church development and evangelism, which were seen as too manipulative, imperialistic, and/or individualistic. Many individuals and local congregations tend to polarize evangelism and social justice, placing themselves at one end of the continuum and the national staff of the denomination at the other end. Socially committed evangelicals and partner churches in the global South (especially Latin America) are helping us restore the wholeness of the gospel and the wholeness of God's cosmic mission.

The WCC offered a major contribution toward coherence in mission in 1982 with the publication of *Mission and Evangelism: An Ecumenical Affirmation*, which the 195th General Assembly of the Presbyterian Church (U.S.A.) adopted in 1983. This document tried to restore evangelism as a vital part of God's mission, alongside social justice. Even though the PC(USA) General Assembly in 1989 adopted *two mission priorities*, evangelism and social justice, Ron White demonstrates that clarifying their relationship and restoring evangelism to its rightful place is still a challenge.[59] On behalf of the Evangelism and Church Development and the Social Justice and Peacemaking Ministry Units, the Presbyterian Peacemaking Program published a helpful study guide titled *Hand in Hand: Doing Evangelism and Doing Justice*.[60] The WMD provided solid mission thinking in "Mission in the 1990s." The opening paragraph of "Gathering for God's Future" is another clear missiological affirmation:

> The Good News of Jesus Christ is to be shared with the whole world. As disciples of Jesus Christ, each of us in the Presbyterian Church (U.S.A.) is sent into the world to join God's mission. As individuals and as a church, we are called to be faithful in this discipleship. Our mission is centered in the triune God. Our mission is God-called, Christ-centered and Spirit-led. Our mission is both proclamation and service; it is the reason the church exists.[61]

Moreover, it ends with a gracious invitation, calling the church "to be one large mission society."[62]

Obviously, these documents do not fully develop a theology of mission as a final definition of God's mission, but they are a start in our search for coherence. The question for us remains: how many congregations are aware of the vision statement "Gathering for God's Future," and have used the study guide to reflect critically on it and the implications for their mission practice?

SHIFTING FUNDING PATTERNS

The fragmentation of mission in the postwar period of the 1950s triggered a trend that has steadily increased every decade and has more recently reached tempestuous proportions. Partly fueled by a mistrust of denominational leadership and programs, local congregations started diminishing their mission support at the General Assembly level. The unified funding system, based on the same theological foundations as ecumenism and connectionalism—the desire for church unity and equality according to Jesus' prayer in John 17—was questioned and came under intense attack.

The problem is not that Presbyterians have been giving less. To the contrary, the practice of giving is one in which Presbyterians excel. Per capita giving continues to increase. The fact is that congregations and presbyteries have become more autonomous and are funding mission differently. More budget spending occurs locally and regionally, both in support of their own infrastructure and programs and in support of local agencies engaged in mission. Consequently, less money goes to General Assembly–sponsored mission endeavors. Furthermore, individuals and congregations maintaining the Presbyterian tradition of strong support for international mission want to be more directly involved in mission activity, choosing to designate their funds for specific programs. Some funds even go to non-Presbyterian causes or Presbyterians serving overseas through mission agencies other than the WMD. Thus, unrestricted giving has steadily declined.

During the 1970s, in response to this trend toward localism and designated giving with more control by congregations, both Presbyterian denominations (PCUS and UPCUSA) made adjustments in the patterns of global mission support and funding. Structurally, they moved toward decentralization. Gradually, as support through general unified or equalized budgets decreased, more support came from designated funds. Currently, funding of mission personnel comes from a variety of sources. Special sources of designated funds include the Second Mile Missionary Support (for salaries of mission workers who otherwise could not be funded), which developed into Directed Mission Support (DMS), designating money from churches and presbyteries for support of overseas mission workers. A steady decline in DMS funds for mission worker support is leading to reductions in the mission force. Appeals are being made to all Presbyterians to be connected with mission personnel and to support them in order to reverse this trend.

The Special Opportunities for Support (SOS), which became Extra Commitment Opportunities (ECO), funds special projects approved by denominational staff in association with mission workers and partners around the globe. Special offerings such as the Witness (Season) Offering and One Great Hour of Sharing have been designated in different ways. Significant designated funds for numerous mission projects now come through three Validated Mission Support Groups (VMSG): the Medical Benevolence Foundation (MBF), the Outreach Foundation (TOF), and Presbyterian Frontier Fellowship (PFF). Designated specialized giving is another growing trend that is also channeled through synod, presbytery, and congregational partnerships. The denomination seeks to match presbyteries that have specific interests with programs identified by WMD. Presbyterian programs addressing hunger, health, disasters, and self-development all mobilize grant support.

While localism, or "congregationalism," and designated giving are signs of the times and produce positive results in building personal relationships and mission partnerships with hands-on involvement, Presbyterians are being challenged to be generous also with general giving to the Shared Mission Support at the General Assembly level. The lack of balance of unified or undesignated giving with designated giving is beginning to undermine much of the historic mission presence of the PC(USA) in over eighty countries around the world. The trend has produced a financial crisis. We entered the new millennium with annual budget shortfalls, which have resulted in an annual agony of cuts in national staff, grants, and programs. The tension and alienation between national structures and local congregations due to mistrust, theological pluralism, and anti-institutionalism has reached the proportions of threatening the calling home of mission personnel from the field. We must be careful not to succumb to our consumer and individualistic culture, which is merely donor-driven. There is no way that we can maintain coherent mission work in the world if designated giving replaces basic support for the mission of the whole connectional denomination through agencies responsible to the General Assembly. Our Reformed identity and polity are at stake.

The present debate over the shape of a new mission funding system for the twenty-first century will enable us to continue our mission in partnership with the ecumenical and global church and is part of an ongoing paradigm shift in giving and mission funding. However, our search for an operative funding system cannot preclude our search for a coherent theological vision of holistic mission. "Gathering for God's Future" states: "Methods of funding the church are shifting. Donors with particular interests bring new resources to bear in international mission. We are called to be faithful to this trend while remaining faithful and creative with our partners."[63] The statement further recognizes that "funding for all ministries is uncertain. . . . Mission committees and church sessions are asked to fund more than they can possibly support."[64] The challenge before the General Assembly Council is to be faithful to our mission history through the storm of financial crisis and open to changes in the quest for new funding systems and mission investors. Financial crises are leading to the launching of special appeals to shore up mission funding.

OPPORTUNITIES AND CHALLENGES
FOR DENOMINATIONAL RENEWAL

The General Assembly in 2004 adopted four goal areas: evangelism and witness, justice and compassion, spirituality and discipleship, leadership and vocation.

Four crucial challenges for worldwide ministry in the twenty-first century were put forth in "Gathering for God's Future":

1. Witnessing and evangelizing worldwide;
2. Equipping the Church for transforming mission;
3. Engaging in ministries of reconciliation, justice, healing, and grace;
4. Living the Good News of Jesus Christ in community with people who are poor.[65]

The Presbyterian predicament of theological pluralism, "conflicting allegiances," fragmented mission, and funding crises reminds me of the thousand-piece jigsaw puzzles that I loved to do with my family as a child. Each family member would choose a certain part of the picture to assemble, but we all constantly looked at the "big picture" on the box to see how each assembled group fit into it. During the past sixty years, Presbyterians have been participating with creativity and zeal in over a thousand pieces of "God's redeeming and reconciling activity in the world" (G-3.0103).[66] Our problem is that we have focused on our differences rather than on the big picture of God's mission, on God's loving intentions for the whole world. We struggle to fit the pieces together into a whole and to accept and value those who are working on other pieces. As a result, we end up competing rather than cooperating. Mission unites us across the theological spectrum when we grasp the fact that the *missio Dei* is the foundation and source of the church's mission and the identity, reason, and purpose of the church's existence. The final goal of all of the pieces of God's mission in which we participate is God's glory and realm of love, peace, and justice.

UNITED IN GOD'S HOLISTIC MISSION

While pluralism and the fragmentation of mission have caused serious storms for ecumenical and evangelical Presbyterians, Latin American missiologists (and others from the church in the global South) urge us toward holistic mission. God wants to gather all things and all people in right relationship with God (Eph. 1:8–10). The reconciling and gathering mission of the triune God is universal and holistic, embracing the whole person and the whole of society in the whole created world with the whole gospel. "Turn to the Living God: A Call to Evangelism in Jesus Christ's Way" encourages the whole church to recognize the wholeness of evangelism.[67] Our present crisis presents an opportunity for the whole denomination to unite in the multiple dimensions of mission as presented in the *Book of Order,* which challenges the PC(USA) "to be a sign in and for the world of the new reality which God has made available to people in Jesus Christ" (G-3.0200) and to be obedient to this integrated and cohesive vision:

a. The Church is called to tell the good news of salvation by the grace of God through faith in Jesus Christ as the only Savior and Lord, proclaiming in Word and Sacrament that

(1) the new age has dawned,

(2) God who creates life, frees those in bondage, forgives sin, reconciles brokenness, makes all things new, is still at work in the world.

b. The Church is called to present the claims of Jesus Christ, leading persons to repentance, acceptance of him as Savior and Lord, and new life as his disciples.

c. The Church is called to be Christ's faithful evangelist

(1) going into the world, making disciples of all nations . . . ,

(2) demonstrating by the love of its members for one another and by the quality of its common life the new reality in Christ . . . ,

(3) participating in God's activity in the world through its life for others by

(a) healing and reconciling and binding up wounds,

(b) ministering to the needs of the poor, the sick, the lonely, and the powerless,

(c) engaging in the struggle to free people from sin, fear, oppression, hunger, and injustice,

(d) giving itself and its substance to the service of those who suffer,

(e) sharing with Christ in the establishing of his just, peaceable, and loving rule in the world. (G-3.0300)

God's holistic mission always includes and often mixes three integral, overlapping, and intertwining aspects, which we must carefully distinguish and also intimately relate (see fig. 1).

1. Evangelism through Witness and Proclamation

"God sends the church in the power of the Holy Spirit to announce the good news that in Christ Jesus the world is reconciled to God . . . [and] to call people everywhere to believe in and follow Jesus Christ as Lord and Savior " (W-7.2001a, e). Every local congregation witnesses by its life and outreach; proclaiming in word and in deeds. The church has a message (kerygma) and therefore is a messenger of hope in a world of much despair. Through worship, sacraments, faith sharing, media, and deeds, we communicate good news with relevance to diverse cultures and generations. By inviting, welcoming, and integrating people, we make disciples and build up the body of Christ. Every church is primarily responsible for evangelism in its country. Presbyterian mission workers are involved in frontier evangelism in a few places today. Many of our partner churches are models of effective evangelism and growth and are teaching us a great deal. When we receive new immigrant fellowships from other countries, we open ourselves to reevangelization and transformation. God's grace offers life in all its fullness and continually

GOD'S MISSION OF RESTORATION, SALVATION, LIBERATION, AND RECONCILIATION

is the foundation and source of the mission of the church.

MISSION, therefore,

is the identity, reason, and purpose of the church;
is the responsibility of every baptized Christian;

is done in partnership with God for God's glory on six continents by the church on six continents;
is local-global and holistic (integral), without compartmentalization, polarization, or dichotomy.

Therefore, God's mission sends the church into the world with at least three roles and always includes and mixes three aspects:

EVANGELISM (church as messenger)	COMPASSIONATE SERVICE (church as servant/diakonia)	SOCIAL JUSTICE (church as prophet)
with bold humility and respect by lifestyle, words, attitudes, and actions:	with mercy by actions, attitudes, dialogue, lifestyle, and words:	by political actions, attitudes, dialogue, lifestyle, and words:
Verbal Proclamation of "Good News"	Emergency Crisis Assistance	Reconciliation and Peace-building
Faithful Witness & Dialogue	Displaced Persons	Human Rights
Faith Commitment & Sharing	Human Need: Dignity, Food, Shelter, Health, Education, Living Wage	Advocacy
Inviting/Calling	Interfaith Dialogue and Cooperation	Solidarity with the Poor
Hospitality—	Formation of Coalitions & Alliances	End to Violence, Terrorism, & War
Welcoming/Receiving	Intention: Serving Human Need	Economic Justice
Initiation/Belonging/Baptismal Calling	Capacity-building/Empowerment	Just Distribution of Power & Systems
Assimilating New Members & Gifts	Healing and Building Sustainable Communities	Ecological Justice
New Church Development	Promoting the Values of God's Reign	Public Policy
Intention: "Life in all its fullness"		Interfaith Dialogue and Cooperation
Conversion/Discipleship/Growth		Intention: Social Transformation
Confessing Jesus as Lord		Promoting the Values of God's Reign
Building the Church		
Self-Propagation		

(continued)

FINAL GOAL OF ALL MISSION: GOD'S GLORY AND REALM OF LOVE, PEACE, AND JUSTICE

"Your kingdom come, your will be done on earth." Is it?

GOD'S WORLD CREATION (Gen. 1–2) FALL (Gen. 3) "Where are you?" God's Mission of Restoration Salvation Liberation	ELECTION OF ISRAEL for Mission to Nations (Gen. 12) Israel misunderstood her identity, turned inward. Psalms & Prophets reminded, envisioned the nations in God's reign.	INCARNATION God **Sends** Savior "Flesh-on" Mission (John 1:14) Jesus inaugurates The Reign of God Evangelizes, meets human needs, and challenges social injustices Forms a Community and **sends** them to "make disciples" "I glorified [worshiped] you on earth by finishing the work [mission] that you gave [sent] me to do" (John 17:4) DEATH RESURRECTION ASCENSION	PENTECOST God **Sends** Spirit To Empower the Church for Mission To All Nations (Acts 2) "As the Father has sent me, so I send you" (John 20:21). The Church is a Body of People Called and Sent into the World on a mission to Represent the Reign of God as Sign, Foretaste, Agent, and Instrument. Has the Church Understood her identity and purpose?	KINGDOM REIGN OF GOD: CONSUMMATION (John 14:27) Shalom Justice Peace Love Celebration

Figure 1. God's Mission

transforms people and societies. The goals of personal, frontier, rural, and urban evangelism are confession of Jesus Christ as Lord, conversion, discipleship, new church development, and congregational transformation. Every Christian and congregation can be a missionary witness through lifestyle and daily missional practices clothed in the attitudes of respect, humility, and compassion.

2. Compassionate Service

"God calls the church in worship to join the mission of Jesus Christ in service to the world" (W-7.1002). "God sends the church in the power of the Holy Spirit to exercise compassion in the world" (W-7.3001). The church is a servant, offering emergency crisis assistance and responding to basic human needs for food, shelter, health, education, and employment with living wages both in its country and in solidarity with partners in other countries. Local, regional, and denominational programs provide local-global service and witness through education, leadership development, health, disaster assistance, self-development of people, and combating hunger. We learn from the ministry of Jesus that compassionate service (*diakonia*) is an end in itself, which seeks to promote life according to the values of God's reign. In many cases, however, these ministries lead us to seek the root causes of the problems and thus to make the necessary step to social justice. Compassion is not a tool of evangelism, although they often go hand in hand. It is offered in loving service to people created in God's image, with no strings attached. It may or may not lead to a verbal witness. In many countries social outcasts find that the majority community denies them opportunities for education, literacy, hospital care, and vocational training, but churches offer such opportunities, together with the self-affirmation that they receive from the gospel. We engage in God's mission of compassion as we practice, model, and promote the values of God's liberating reign.

3. Reconciliation: Justice and Peace

"God sends the church in the power of the Holy Spirit to share with Christ in establishing God's just, peaceable, and loving rule in the world" (W-7.4001). The church has a prophetic voice that must be nourished by grace. A challenge for the PC(USA) today is "living the good news of Jesus Christ in community with people who are poor."[68] As faithful disciples in mission, we join hands in solidarity with local-global partners in political actions against hunger, violence, war, and oppression. One important tool in the processes of reconciliation is dialogue. Presbyterians are engaged in interfaith dialogue on many fronts. God's mission promotes personal and social transformation. Our global partners in mission challenge the U.S. hegemony, domination, and imposition around the world, calling us to seek a just distribution of power and resources in our public policy. We are challenged to be concerned about the practice of human rights by the United States and to advocate international trade agreements that are just and fair for all countries. In some parts of the world where there is no church, Presbyterian mission workers engaged in frontier mission have a great concern for justice. They are help-ing us to see that justice and evangelism can join hands and aid in our under-standing of the individual and corporate dimensions of faith, conversion, and discipleship. In *Faith in Action,* Stephen Knisely shows models of development as compassion, justice, and transformation in which a "holistic, integrated process of development is a lifestyle of good news in all realms of life."[69] In every mission activity that is part of our quest for a more just and peaceful world, we seek to prac-tice and promote the values of God's reign.

LOCAL-GLOBAL MISSION: THE CUTTING EDGE[70]

Our stormy changes in organizational structures and funding patterns and our fractious debates over the nature of denominational mission and theological plu-ralism have led us to become a "new denomination" in which "the congregation is now the locus of power and mission in American Presbyterianism."[71] In our "new denomination," local congregations are the primary agents in local and global mission. This new hands-on involvement is wonderful, but it can threaten our global witness and partnerships unless pastors and members of the PC(USA) remember that they are connected to the greater church in mutual service. The church is both "catholic" (there is one universal global church) and "particular" (there are many local congregations). We join in mission with God and with one another locally and globally.

In 1997, recognizing the growing trend toward localism and decentralization, the Presbyterian Church (U.S.A.) sponsored the Congregations in Global Mis-sion: New Models for a New Century Conference. This was hailed by many as a "watershed event." In the opening plenary session, Clifton Kirkpatrick stated: "There is a renewed understanding that we are a missionary people and that each congregation is called to be in mission locally and globally. . . . In the past, inter-national mission was done by the denomination for the churches. But, as we face a new century, what we know increasingly is that everything is local and every-thing is global and we've got to be working together to form new patterns of mis-sion in the next century to . . . renew our congregations by our encounter with the global Christian community."[72] The paper that I presented at that conference suggests that a frontier for the Presbyterian Church (U.S.A.) today is *local-global mission.* The critical element is in the *hyphen.* How do we become truly mutual partners in local-global mission? How do we encourage and facilitate local con-gregations in mission, maintain support and our connection with the global mis-sion partners, and also support programs at the denominational level? What is the authentic "Presbyterian" way of doing mission in the twenty-first century? "What difference does it make that we in the PC(USA) do mission connection-ally?" was the question Marian McClure posed at the end of the conference. She suggested numerous "advantages of our connectionalism" and challenged us to be "Dichotomy Busters."[73] She spoke of the top five dichotomies that we need to overcome in holistic local-global mission in the new century, which are the storms that we are going through:

1. Evangelism versus Social Justice and Compassion Ministries
2. Long-term versus Short-term Mission Service
3. Serving Our Congregation versus Serving Partners Overseas
4. Seeking Equality versus Conscious Stewardship of Power
5. Local versus Global

Today, localism or decentralized mission is a strong trend, representing a conceptual change as local congregations assume missional responsibility and identity. When Rick Ufford-Chase was asked in an interview for *Presbyterians Today*, "What changes are you seeing in the denomination?" he replied, "Presbyterians want to go out and do mission themselves and get their hands dirty."[74] Through his travels as moderator, he learned "that mission is moving to the congregations and to the pews," which requires "a culture change across the denomination in order to be open to this change that God is trying to put in front of us."[75] He further states that in this new mission model, the national staff and our mission coworkers have a new role, which is "to know the [global] players and enable relationships to take place, to know how to access information and resources both inside and outside the church."[76]

Indeed, in this new local-national-global model, there are new roles for national church staff and for our international mission workers. Our denominational offices provide global awareness and help to equip and guide congregations and presbyteries in cooperative mission and social witness. Utilizing our history of over 170 years in international mission and our theology of mission, the denomination facilitates direct mission involvement of local congregations and offers support through our ecumenical partnerships, programs, projects, and people. The denomination provides opportunities for international connections through presbytery partnerships, mission networks, study trips, and interfaith dialogue. Leaders have the responsibility of equipping the community to live out its baptismal call. Individual Presbyterians look to the denomination to find resources for mission education, prayers, and worship, as well as for information about opportunities, resource allocations, and mission connections.

Theologically, we all agree that the triune God is the source and initiator of all mission. We have seen that mission today is ecumenical, because the church is now a global church, with strong denominations engaged in God's mission on six continents. The global church on each of those continents engages in God's mission near and far. The PC(USA) participates in God's two-way mission of mutual receiving and giving with over 160 partner churches around the world. Churches in the global South are shaping the ecumenical mission agenda. Therefore, *the global church* is a key player in all mission today. However, every *local congregation* is a primary agent in God's mission, but it is never a solitary agent. God's mission is always done in partnerships and with local-global implications (see fig. 2).

LOCAL-GLOBAL MISSION CHALLENGES
IN OUR WORLD

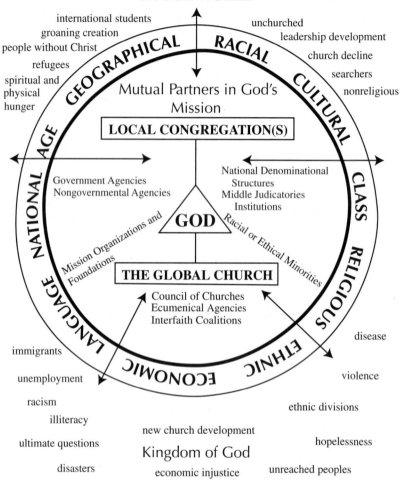

Figure 2. Local-global mission challenges

In her sermon at another mission conference, Marian McClure spoke of the "new mission movement," which includes "a great desire and need for direct involvement."[77] She gave examples of the 118 presbytery and synod international partnerships, Mission to the U.S.A. and Young Adult Volunteer programs, conferences on congregations in global mission, two dozen WMD-related country mission networks that national staff have helped to create, the Joining Hands against Hunger program, which supports eight overseas country networks involving twenty-five PC(USA) congregations and eleven presbyteries, and Presbyterian Disaster Assistance (PDA), which mobilizes two dozen expert volunteers in providing significant immediate and long-term "help without handouts" in response to national and international natural disasters. All of these programs represent creative ways that the PC(USA) offers cutting-edge opportunities in response to the new trend of local congregations and presbyteries in direct mission involvement.

To be a member of the local-global church is to be part of a particular congregation in mission together with the catholic church, which is ecumenical, universal, and connected: a worldwide web of Christians. The burgeoning PC(USA) country networks and Joining Hands against Hunger networks are new strategies for holistic local-global mission. Stanley H. Skreslet explains how the metaphor of "networking" describes a new model of mission that has institutional form mirrored in the "nongovernmental organization" (NGO), and which reflects the trend to "build relationships, expand alliances, and establish networks of groups and individuals committed to values implied by the biblical reign of God."[78] In addition to being flexible and holistic, networking is *essentially egalitarian.* It assumes no fixed center. Networks do not need hierarchies and function most purely without them. Networking is thus rigorously horizontal in approach, rather than vertical, and is founded on the ideal of interdependent relationships."[79]

We live in the age of the network. No person or congregation does mission alone. In local-global mission today, we are networking on a human worldwide web with many kinds of partners (represented inside the circle in fig. 2). Local congregations relate to local and global ecumenical agencies, as well as denominational structures. As congregations join forces with others in their communities and around the world, new and creative mission networks emerge.

In spite of all of our shortcomings, the participation of the PC(USA) in God's local-global mission during the past sixty years has faithfully continued with opportunities, challenges, storms, crises, and changes. The sending of people to serve in mission worldwide and the involvement of local congregations in mission are two constants. Presently, we are "dealing with shifts in patterns of support and connectionalism," as the "authority within churches is shifting from the connectional denomination to other kinds of connections."[80] "Gathering for God's Future" further recognizes other changes in the PC(USA) that affect mission today, including the facts that "international connections have increased," allowing for increased mobility, and that "local mission is often globally connected."[81] The document ends with a renewed call to worldwide mission: "God offers us an urgent call. It is a call to pray and discern. It is a call to study the most crying needs and the ways God would have us address them. It is a call to let God transform us for our role in the world church for the sake of God's intentions for the world."[82]

Chapter 5

Missions within the Mission

New Diversities in the One Family

ROBERT WEINGARTNER

A history of mission through the Presbyterian Church (U.S.A.) and its predecessor denominations during recent decades must take into account the formation of groups organized by Presbyterians to focus passion and resources on
mission in ways that went beyond the work of the denomination's mission offices.
The relationship of these groups to the denominational mission program has
taken different forms, ranging from efforts that simply marked a deeper commitment to existing denominational mission priorities to those that sought to
address some perceived deficiency in the mission program. Although some
viewed the formation of such groups to be a new development, this phenome-
non reflects a recurring pattern in the history of Christian mission.

Ralph Winter, Presbyterian mission strategist and strong promoter of multiple missions within denominations, describes this pattern in terms of God's two
"redemptive structures" that have continuously appeared in the Christian movement and remain essential today.[1] The first structure, the "modality," is a struc-
tured fellowship in which there is no distinction of gender or age. The second
structure, the "sodality," refers to a group of what Winter calls "second decision"
people, who are committed to a specific task beyond modality membership, such
as participating in or supporting mission. Though the forms that these structures

have taken varies, their basic function has remained. In this manner of thinking about the church, both the denomination and the congregation are modalities. Mission agencies and orders are sodalities. Tracing the contours of this construct through the New Testament and Christian history, Winter contends that mission beyond the cultural boundaries of the church (the modality) rarely occurs without a group of people who have come together in common cause to establish clearly focused mission structures (sodalities).

Paul E. Pierson agrees that mission and renewal movements normally appear on the periphery of the broader church, and he points out that they usually exist in some tension with it even as they have often resulted in new streams of life and outreach.[2] During the first years of the church, it was the formation of the Jewish-Gentile and then fully Gentile church that enabled the Christian movement to understand its mission in universal terms. During the Constantinian era, the groups that provided leadership in mission—the Celts, East Syrians (Nestorians), Waldensians, Copts, and historic Catholic mission orders—all functioned beyond the control of the headquarters at Rome, Constantinople, Alexandria, or Seleucia-Ctesiphon, often without official sanction. In the Reformation and early modern periods, the four movements that formed the foundation for later Protestant missions—Puritanism, Pietism, Moravianism, and Methodism—all arose on the periphery of the established ecclesial structures and experienced a great deal of opposition from them.[3]

The Protestant mission societies in late-eighteenth-century Britain, on the continent, and later in the United States, also formed on the periphery. Virtually none of the early Protestant missions were sponsored by an official church body.[4] When William Carey lifted up the Great Commission in the late eighteenth century, he had pragmatic concerns in mind: How could Christians join together in obedience to the word of Christ out of concern for the salvation of all peoples? Thus, the early mission societies that developed did so in response to the real limitations of the existing church structures. As Andrew Walls puts it: "The simple fact was that the Church as then organized, whether Episcopal, Presbyterian, or congregational, could not effectively operate mission overseas."[5] These classical patterns of church government simply lacked the capacity to undertake a task such as the evangelization of the world.

As mission interest and activity grew, it did not take long for most American denominations to establish their own mission boards. The Presbyterian Board of Foreign Mission was established in 1837 out of a desire to exert more denominational influence over mission activities,[6] and in that same year the Old School / New School split was in part due to the desire of Old School leaders to bring mission activities under the umbrella of the denomination.[7] Practically speaking, the Presbyterian Church through the nineteenth century continued to function as a loose confederation of quasi-independent groups and agencies focused on mission. With the shift to conceptualizing the denomination as a corporation in the early twentieth century, the focus became structure and polity more than mission. Beginning around 1960, with declining resources and the need to control funding, the denomination increasingly functioned more like a regulatory agency.[8] Control became a critical concern, and this shaped how denominational leaders related to the special mission organizations that were forming on the periphery of the denominational structures, both within and outside the church.

This concern about control may be seen in how the church made a distinction between official Presbyterian mission and "other" mission activities. In 1960, the Board of World Missions of the Presbyterian Church in the United States (PCUS) adopted a statement on unofficial relief agencies. The statement mentions such groups as CARE, Christian Children's Fund, and World Vision, and it goes on to state, "While it is not our function to evaluate the work of these agencies, it is pointed out that they are not related to our Church and are not recommended as the approved channel for the relief activities of our own people. All members of our Church are urgently requested to send their relief funds through their churches to the Treasurer of the Board of World Missions for administration by the Department of Overseas Relief and Inter-Church Aid. This, we believe, will assure the most effective and economical use of our relief funds, and provide an avenue through which the Church can give a direct Christian witness in its ministry with human need."[9]

A program audit by the PCUS Office of Review and Evaluation for the 1980 General Assembly noted continuing tension within the church concerning overseas mission:

> The recent establishment within PCUS by constituencies with a special interest in overseas mission of a new Outreach Foundation, which has taken its place alongside the already-existent Medical Benevolence Foundation as another internal para-church organization, is a further indication [of concern]. The basic problem is that of a denomination with a strong traditional commitment to overseas mission, facing a radically changed context for mission in the Third World, and reflecting divergent views from a pluralistic constituency as to the appropriate shape of overseas mission.[10]

The report goes on to describe important mission developments, beginning with the increasing autonomy of national churches and the ongoing shift from dependency and paternalism to partnership in interchurch mission relationships. A second major change cited in the audit was a shift from traditional forms of "church-centered" work (evangelism, church development, medical and educational ministries under church auspices) to work that focused on hunger and development issues. Other shifts mentioned include a decided trend toward presbytery overseas projects and a shift of fiscal support, particularly by evangelicals who wished to focus on overseas mission by means of the designation of mission gifts.

The language of the audit report is worth noting. Medical Benevolence Foundation and Outreach Foundation are each described as an "internal para-church organization," a phrase that reflects the historic tension between ecclesial structures and peripheral mission initiatives. Such awkwardness continued to be mirrored in reports to the General Assembly even after reunion. The 200th General Assembly (1988) of the Presbyterian Church (U.S.A.) approved a report titled "Is Christ Divided?"[11] which endorsed centralized denominational structures and raised concern to the proliferation of Chapter 9 organizations and other special-interest groups in the church.[12] Theological discourse, the report claims, has been reduced to competing claims made by competing structures.

Formal constitutional provisions for Presbyterian special organizations go back to the beginning of the twentieth century.[13] While these provisions typically sought to balance the judicatories' right to oversight and direction of the special-purpose groups with the groups' rights and responsibilities, the actions of some General Assemblies emphasized one set of rights over the other. A new relationship was created in 1988, when the General Assembly Council established a Validated Mission Support Group status by which organizations could covenant with the council for the purpose of increasing Presbyterian involvement in and support for Presbyterian mission. Three such groups have had this covenant relationship with the General Assembly Council: Medical Benevolence Foundation, The Outreach Foundation, and Presbyterian Frontier Fellowship. While the mission and vision of each will be described below, it is worth noting that the Stewardship and Communication Development Ministry Unit viewed the primary purpose of the groups as promoting the work of the General Assembly and raising funds for the denomination's mission program.[14]

The 1980 program audit reflects the historically difficult relationship between central church structures and new mission movements. The report also helpfully identifies some of the issues that were behind the formation of new mission groups. The context for Presbyterian involvement in global mission had changed. A new emphasis on partnership and mutuality in mission had affirmed the integrity of global partners in wonderful ways and clarified the need to move beyond paternalism and dependence; however, the practical implementation of this new vision served to disenfranchise missionaries and shift power not so much to partners as to the denominational mission leadership.[15] And, some feared that the new emphasis upon sending missionaries and establishing programs only in response to the mission invitation of partners had reduced mission to a matter of ecumenical relations and shared participation in ministries of compassion and justice.[16] In his book *Merging Mission and Unity*, Donald Black describes how mission in the 1960s came to mean church-to-church relationships.[17] Others feared that the first great end of the church, "the proclamation of the gospel for the salvation of humankind," was being lost as a Presbyterian priority. As the audit reflects, these years involved disagreement about what the church's mission priorities should be. At the same time, presbyteries were beginning to establish their own global partnerships, and donors were increasingly looking for ways to designate their gifts to the church to reflect what they believed should be the church's mission priorities. New groups began to form to focus the church's attention and resources on mission in new ways, and on priorities that many thought were lost.

MEDICAL BENEVOLENCE FOUNDATION

As a validated mission support group of the PC(USA), the Medical Benevolence Foundation (MBF) exists to proclaim and demonstrate the gospel of Jesus Christ through ministries of health and healing. From its inception, the MBF has seen itself as an arm of the international health offices of the Presbyterian Church, interpreting the health concerns of the church and its global partners, raising funds to support international health programs, and recruiting health-care professionals and other volunteers to serve in health-related mission programs outside the United States.

The idea for a group to support Presbyterian medical missions was conceived in 1962 by the Board of World Missions (BWM) of the PCUS, at the suggestion of Dr. Paul Crane, a medical missionary.[18] It had become evident that involving physicians in new ways to advocate for and gain support of medical mission work was needed. The BWM appointed General Joseph B. Fraser from Atlanta as chairman of a committee that reported its investigation and recommended the formation of a foundation to support medical work. The MBF charter was registered in Nashville on July 3, 1963. The first board meeting was held in November of 1963 in Atlanta, and Dr. J. K. Fancher was elected as president. Initially, support was directed primarily to missions in Mexico and Korea. Later, Africa, especially the Congo, became a focus of the MBF's work.

In July of 1964, Dr. Cecil Thompson took a one-year leave of absence from his position at Columbia Theological Seminary in Decatur, Georgia, to become the first executive director, serving also for one year as secretary-treasurer. This position was made possible by a $10,000 grant from the BWM, reflecting the organic relationship between the mission board and the new organization. Dr. Herb Codington, a furloughed missionary from Kwangju, Korea, was the second director. The base of operation was moved to Nashville, the location of the BWM, with a 1965–66 budget of $12,000. Dr. Codington continued the practice of setting up area dinner meetings, corresponding with missionaries, and serving as liaison with the BWM. He also began a quarterly newsletter and oversaw the production of other materials to interpret medical mission to potential donors. In February of 1965, the charter was amended to more clearly state the mission of the MBF, and the number of directors was increased from the original five to twelve.

The first national fund-raising effort in 1967 was led by Mr. James R. Kitchen, former treasurer of the BWM, and raised $166,000. The board had expanded to sixteen trustees, who recognized the need for continuous fund-raising. In January of 1968, Mr. Keith McCaffety was hired as an administrative assistant for that purpose. That fall, McCaffety was made executive director, and under his leadership, the MBF headquarters was moved to Woodville, Texas.

Following approval of the reunion between the PCUS and the UPCUSA in 1983, negotiations began with Presbyterian Medical Mission Fund (PMMF), a similar organization from the Northern stream of the church, based in New York, to join into one medical mission support group. After several years and through a process of difficult negotiation, the organizations voted to unite. The MBF's board of thirty was joined by the PMMF's board of fifteen, to constitute the present number of forty-five trustees. The name of the combined organization remained the Medical Benevolence Foundation. The mission focus of the MBF was greatly expanded by this union and now included India and other Asian countries not previously served by the MBF. Ms. Gwen Crawley of the PC(USA) office, headquartered in Louisville, worked with the MBF to develop a new covenant agreement.

Following Keith McCaffety's tenure, Rev. George Carpenter became interim executive director and served until Mr. Ed Stein was elected as executive director in May of 1992. At Stein's recommendation, the MBF operation was moved to Houston in August of 1992. Rev. Dan Force was hired in April of 1996 to conduct an endowment campaign and had barely begun his new job when Stein resigned in July of 1996. Force was appointed to be the interim director and was elected as permanent executive director in April of 1997.

In 2001, the MBF entered into a partnership with the Denver-headquartered nonprofit humanitarian organization Project C.U.R.E. (Commission on Urgent Relief & Equipment), whose mission it is to identify, solicit, collect, sort, and distribute medical surplus. This partnership greatly enlarged the MBF's ministry, strengthening its ability to respond to the needs of Presbyterian-related medical facilities around the world.

During Rev. Force's tenure, the MBF expanded its funding base by competing for grant awards from American Schools and Hospitals Abroad (ASHA), a division of USAID. These ASHA grants—to build and renovate hospital facilities, purchase furnishings and medical equipment, and provide educational opportunities—required the MBF to raise shared funding as part of the total cost of the project.

Rev. Force retired in September of 2003. The current executive director, Rev. Dr. George F. Pope, was elected in October of 2004 and began his duties on July 1, 2005. The MBF raised $128,940 in 2004 in support of Presbyterian medical missionaries. Overseas shipping of supplies and equipment totaled $2,103,855. Today the MBF supports primary health care in over a hundred hospitals and clinics, provides vaccinations to thousands of children every year and program support for HIV/AIDS orphan-feeding programs, and continues to raise financial support for PC(USA) medical missionaries.

THE OUTREACH FOUNDATION
OF THE PRESBYTERIAN CHURCH, INC.

In the spring of 1977, the moderator, Dr. Jule Spach, a former PCUS missionary to Brazil, called a small group of leaders together to pray and seek the Lord's direction for the Presbyterian Church.[19] They gathered out of concern about the denomination's loss of members, a decline in the number of missionaries, and conflicts that impaired the witness of the church. The group decided to present a resolution on the floor of the next General Assembly, calling for an additional $15,000 in the budget for an evangelism program. The resolution passed, but broad concern about the mission commitments of the church remained.

A few months later, another group was convened by Toddie Lee Wynne Sr. and Dr. B. Clayton Bell Sr. of Highland Park Presbyterian Church in Dallas, Texas. The purpose of the meeting was to discuss further the loss of members and missionaries, to consider problems with the equalization of mission gifts, and to take whatever action seemed wise. Four former moderators of the PCUS attended this meeting: Dr. William M. Elliot, Dr. McDowell Richards, Dr. Jule Spach, and Dr. George Vick. The group decided to present a general outline for a new mission initiative at gatherings in Atlanta and Dallas. Hundreds gathered, and the responses in Atlanta and Dallas were enthusiastic, with both groups drawing the same conclusions: the mandate of the Great Commission is still valid. The proclamation of the gospel will bring a harvest. There are still unreached people groups in the world. Overseas partner churches are calling for our help. Parachurch organizations increasingly find funds and volunteers from within the denomination. Funds are being withheld from the church because of equalization.

A meeting was requested with the General Assembly Council of the PCUS to secure endorsement or recognition by the church at large. The meeting was respectful but concluded with the members of the council informing the group that they did not know how to deal with this new organization. The group informed the council that they would pursue their course, seeking ways to support evangelism and overseas missions within the denomination. They agreed to keep the council apprised of their efforts, and both groups pledged not to criticize each other openly. The work of the Outreach Foundation of the PCUS, a tax-free, charitable organization, would be conducted by a self-perpetuating board, seek financial contributions for the work of evangelism and overseas mission over and above the annual budgets of the local churches, and send financial contributions for the work to the designated causes without equalization.

The Outreach Foundation of the PCUS was incorporated in the state of Georgia on August 20, 1979. The initial Board of Trustees consisted of seven members, with Dr. John William Lancaster, pastor of First Presbyterian Church in Houston, Texas, serving as board chair. The Outreach Foundation adopted the following statement of purpose: "To support the preaching and teaching of the Gospel of Jesus Christ in the United States of America and throughout the world; to initiate and stimulate programs of evangelism in the United States and overseas; to encourage the establishment of new church congregations and the construction of new buildings, both domestic and foreign; and to promote the growth and nurture of the Christian community."

Despite its name, the Outreach Foundation did not become a funded foundation with significant income from investments to be used for mission causes. Instead, Outreach has continued to raise the funds that it disburses in support of mission in the United States and abroad. The work of the Outreach Foundation began modestly, as participating churches made gifts for missionary and project support above their regular mission budget commitments. In 1980, Outreach mission disbursements totaled $52,313. By 2005, disbursements for mission through the foundation had grown to $5,509,357.

A number of executive directors have led the Outreach Foundation. Dr. Howard Chadwick was a founding trustee who left First Presbyterian Church in Orlando, Florida, to become the executive director. During his tenure, the offices were moved to Charlotte, North Carolina. Projects were adopted, a support base of both individuals and churches was developed, and the newssheet called "The Trumpet" was distributed. Mission conferences were organized, and the Outreach Foundation began to grow and added more trustees.

Other executives who would lead Outreach included Dr. David Jenkins and James B. Phillips. During the Jenkins and Phillips years, the foundation initiated broad work in Africa under the umbrella of the Project for Evangelism and Church Growth in Africa (PECGA). Missionary Bill Warlick and Outreach trustee Alex E. Booth Jr. were champions of this major initiative, a program that continues today. The PECGA work of planting churches, equipping evangelists, building schools, and providing leadership training played a major role in the growth of Presbyterian partner churches in Africa.

A significant domestic initiative sought to strengthen Presbyterian seminaries by supporting teaching and research in the field of evangelism. The Outreach Foundation provided initial funds for a Chair of Evangelism at Columbia Theological Seminary. Peachtree Presbyterian Church in Atlanta, under the leadership of Dr. Frank Harrington, gave one million dollars to endow the chair. Other successful efforts were initiated at Pittsburgh, Union (Richmond), Louisville, and Austin Theological Seminaries.

In 1988, when the Global Witness Unit of the General Assembly Council suggested to the trustees of the Outreach Foundation that a new status be created called Validated Mission Support Group, it was seized upon as a new day of cooperation. The basis of the covenant was a working relationship between the denomination and the validated groups. The covenant dealt with communication, finances, and organizational structures. The parties of the covenant committed themselves to be in a mutually supporting relationship, maintaining a focus on mission that was validated by the church. The initial covenant was for three years, and it was ratified by the General Assembly Council. Subsequent covenants have been for five years, with a review required each year.

Outreach's greatest growth took place under the leadership of Dr. William T. Bryant, who had previously served as pastor of First Presbyterian Church in Nashville. Dr. Bryant moved the offices to Franklin, Tennessee, and led the Outreach Foundation from 1994 until 2002. A newsletter, *Reaching Out*, became an important vehicle for communicating with supporting churches. Visits to the Outreach Foundation–sponsored projects by potential contributors, trustees, and church mission leaders became one of the hallmarks of Bryant's tenure. He led groups to Africa, Russia, India, Cuba, and Mexico. These trips expanded mission commitments and support. In 1998, Dr. Jefferson I. Ritchie, the associate director in the PC(USA) Office of International Evangelism, was called to become Outreach's assistant director. As a former missionary and mission staff member, he brought new strengths in mission interpretation, project design, and networking, concentrating on projects in the Middle East, South Asia, East Asia, and new immigrant church development in the United States. In 2002, Dr. Robert J. Weingartner, a pastor who had previously served on the General Assembly Council and the Worldwide Ministries Division committee, was called to succeed Bryant as executive director.

In 2004, in recognition of the growth of the global church and new opportunities for Presbyterian congregations to partner with others around the world in mission, the Board of Trustees approved new mission and vision statements:

> The mission of The Outreach Foundation is to engage Presbyterians in Christ-centered evangelistic mission for the salvation of humankind. Our vision is to be a dynamic catalyst in helping congregations develop relationships and participate with global partners in God's mission, and to focus our resources on programs and projects that build our partners' own capacity for evangelistic mission.

Outreach's programmatic priorities continue to support Presbyterian missionaries, planting and building churches, equipping leaders for the global church, and caring for vulnerable children.

FRONTIER MISSION AND PRESBYTERIAN FRONTIER FELLOWSHIP

Developments around frontier mission work provide a good example of how new Presbyterian mission initiatives arising from outside the denominational structure could shape the church's official mission commitments. In the 1970s, even as Western churches celebrated the new autonomy and initiative of national churches that once had been missions, Christians around the world began to realize that there was much that remained to be done in the proclamation of the gospel. It was out of that realization that Presbyterian Frontier Fellowship was born.[20]

In 1974, Dr. Ralph Winter, a linguist and pioneer in theological education who had served as a Presbyterian missionary and on the faculty of the School of World Mission at Fuller Theological Seminary, challenged the delegates at the Lausanne Conference on World Evangelization to cross a new frontier, to cross cultural barriers to share the gospel with people groups who had not yet heard the good news. Winter and his wife, Roberta, took up the challenge themselves by starting a new missionary society, the Frontier Mission Fellowship. This society, formed in 1976, was committed to awaken and mobilize the church to reach the estimated 17,000 unreached people groups around the world. People were asked to commit to a daily discipline of prayer, study, and giving. Giving was patterned after the Burmese custom of setting aside a handful of rice each day. The rice from the families of the church was collected and sold to support frontier mission. Americans were challenged to empty their pockets of loose change daily and, like the Burmese, collect it and give to the cause of frontier mission.

When Ralph Winter had been sent to Guatemala as a missionary in 1956, the chairman of the Board of Foreign Missions gave a talk to those who were going out; he said that the Presbyterian Church needed what the Roman Catholic Church had: a decentralization of missions so that the church can harvest the passion and gifts of all of the different groups in the church.[21] Upon his return to the United States, Winter became an apologist for mission sodalities, intentional groups of believers who committed themselves to special mission advocacy and service, and he himself was the founder of many such ministries. Winter founded the William Carey Library, a specialized publisher and distributor of mission materials, cofounded the American Society of Missiology, assisted in the founding of Advancing Churches in Mission Commitment (ACMC), inaugurated the Perspectives study program, and shaped other frontier mission-focused initiatives. The Frontier Mission Fellowship would also give birth to the U.S. Center for World Mission and William Carey International University. Yet, long before these events, a vision for reaching the unreached had been brewing within the United Presbyterian Church (U.S.A.). At the 1960 General Assembly in Cleveland, Harold Kurtz, a UPCUSA missionary from Ethiopia, pleaded for increased resources to witness to the unreached peoples in that country. The response to his entreaty was the initiation of the "50 Million Fund."[22]

Winter relates that early board members of the Presbyterian Center for Mission Studies (which he also founded) wanted to criticize strongly the denominational offices for their failings, but the idea came to him that "it would be better than throwing mud to bring bags of money."[23] His strategy was to shape the priorities of the denominational mission program by raising money for mission to the frontiers. Interest in frontier mission continued to grow, and as Presbyterians were inspired to join the Frontier Mission Fellowship movement, Winter organized a board made up of Presbyterians to form a Presbyterian Frontier Fellowship. This new organization was introduced at the 1981 General Assembly and approved as a Chapter 28 organization. John Shindeldecker, who worked at the U.S. Center for World Mission, helped Winter launch PFF. Three years later, Shindeldecker and his family left the center to work as missionaries. By this time, Harold Kurtz had returned from Ethiopia to pastor a church in Portland, Oregon. Winter encouraged Kurtz to lead PFF, and with the blessing of his congregation, he became the part-time executive director. In 1989, he retired from the pastorate to devote all of his time to the goals of PFF as they were articulated at the time: "Our specific task is to help the Presbyterian Church (USA) get actively involved in helping churches to be established among hidden people around the world. For that task of evangelism we believe God has called the Presbyterian Frontier Fellowship into being." The PFF's goal was to have a hundred thousand Presbyterians learning about, praying for, and giving to the work of frontier missions through the PC(USA). Money was to be raised by collecting loose change. Local Frontier Fellowships were encouraged to gather together to pray and study, and at the monthly meetings, they would collect their loose change offerings, to be sent on for the support of frontier mission.

Kurtz worked closely with Morton Taylor in the Office of International Evangelism and began traveling widely across the country, challenging Presbyterians to become part of the movement. Through their efforts, one working within the denominational mission system and the other pushing the system from the outside, frontier mission work grew, and in 1988, PFF became one of three Validated Mission Support Groups of the PC(USA). Although all of the project funds raised by PFF were administered through the PC(USA), the relationship between the organizations was not always easy. Despite the fact that PFF was responsible for raising the funds, for eight years the denominational officials prevented Kurtz from receiving reports about who was making gifts in support of frontier mission.[24]

When Dr. Jeff Ritchie returned to the States after two terms of service in Korea, Taylor asked him to work with Kurtz to develop the denomination's frontier mission program. One concrete result was "Turn to the Living God: A Call to Evangelism in Jesus Christ's Way," a document adopted by the General Assembly in 1991 that set out the denomination's policy on evangelism and clearly states the case for frontier mission. A few years later, with the encouragement of Ritchie, who had become coordinator for the Office of International Evangelism, the 1996 General Assembly adopted the goal of the AD2000 movement, making a commitment to reach two hundred people groups by the year 2000. By this action, the PC(USA) became the only mainline church to commit formally to the AD2000 movement.

Three organizations worked closely together to mobilize Presbyterians for frontier mission: Presbyterian Frontier Fellowship (PFF), the Presbyterian Center for Mission Studies (PCMS), and the PC(USA)'s Office of International Evangelism. The Presbyterian Center for Mission Studies, founded in 1973, worked with the Global Mission Ministry Unit (GMMU), the Evangelism and Church Development Unit, and PFF to develop an Adopt-A-People concept for Presbyterians. The plan invited Presbyterians to choose two unreached peoples, one in the United States and the other overseas. After approval from the GMU, congregations affirmed the "Commitment to Share Good News"[25] and worked to develop a strategy to fulfill that commitment. In the first twenty months of the plan, seven congregations adopted peoples. The PCMS also provided resources and research on unreached peoples to the denomination. A quarterly update kept friends of the PCMS informed about the latest Presbyterian frontier mission news.

As PFF's work continued to expand, more staff were added, and the vision for PFF's work grew. Through a process of discernment and the growing realization that working in partnership was critical to being a catalyst for movement toward Christ among unreached people groups, the board adopted new mission and vision statements in 1999.

We challenge, mobilize, and empower Presbyterian congregations into global partnerships that establish indigenous churches among unreached people groups.

For Every People: An Indigenous Church
For Every Church: A Mission Vision

This focus on partnership and the deepening commitment of the Worldwide Ministries Division (WMD) to the frontier mission movement converged in 2000 when the WMD sponsored the Frontier 2000 conference in San Diego. A celebration of Presbyterian involvement in the AD2000 and Beyond movement, the conference lifted up the challenge of reaching the unreached peoples of the world. PFF led a preconference event on partnership that drew a larger-than-expected number of people. To provide for further training and encouragement, PFF sponsored a conference to nurture and launch global frontier partnerships in March of 2001 at College Hill Presbyterian Church in Cincinnati, Ohio. Those who gathered represented commitments to thirteen different people groups.

Financial support for frontier mission was channeled through the Frontier Mission Fund of the Worldwide Ministries Division, growing from $17,000 in 1982 to nearly $2 million by the end of 2000. By that time, the staff of Presbyterian Frontier Fellowship had grown to eight full-time and seven part-time adjunct volunteers. In the fall of 2000, Harold Kurtz stepped aside from his executive duties to become PFF's senior associate. Under David Hackett's leadership as executive director, PFF's national office moved from the Kurtz basement in Oregon to an office building in Eden Prairie, Minnesota. Hackett directed the organization until 2005, when he moved into ministry with visionSynergy.

In April of 2005, Rev. Bill Young became PFF's new executive director. Bill had been well acquainted with PFF, both from his mission experience in Ghana and in his role as the PC(USA)'s coordinator for International Evangelism. After Young's arrival, several new associate directors were added, including new staff who joined through PFF's assimilation of its sister organization, the Presbyterian Center For Mission Studies, located at the U.S. Center for World Mission in Pasadena.

THE PRESBYTERIAN ORDER
FOR WORLD EVANGELIZATION

Dr. Ralph Winter registered a mission structure called "The Presbyterian Order for World Evangelization" (POWE) as a Chapter 28 organization of the Presbyterian Church in 1974.[26] The POWE incorporated in 1991 and is recognized by the Internal Revenue Service as a Protestant religious order. It identifies two purposes for its work: the evangelization of all the world's people groups, especially those that remain outside any active evangelistic effort, and the cultivation of a "wartime lifestyle,"[27] by which individuals reduce their living costs and free up funds for the priority of world evangelization. By calling people together in a mission "order," the POWE has sought to strengthen personal resolve through a mutual covenant and shared financial discipline. The POWE does not function as a sending agency, and it does not solicit funds for its own work; rather, it seeks to serve as a grassroots call to believers to live on what they need and give the rest that they earn to where it is needed most. Rev. Robert A. Blincoe serves as general director of the POWE.

ASSOCIATION OF PRESBYTERIANS
IN CROSS-CULTURAL MISSION

The formation of the Association of Presbyterians for Cross-Cultural Mission (APCCM) in 1984 was in response to two needs identified by missionaries at the time of the reunion of the Northern and Southern Presbyterian churches.[28] In the first place, with reunion approved and separate mission departments moving toward integration, the two different communities of cross-cultural mission workers realized that they needed an organization that would bring them together. Second, there was a real concern that those who were developing the new mission structures did not value input from the missionaries themselves. The missionaries, who would be among those most affected by the changes, sought a platform from which to try to shape those changes.

Ralph Winter convened an informal group of missionaries, including Harold Kurtz, Walter Shepard Sr., and Roberta Winter, to talk about such an association. G. Thompson (Tommy) Brown joined them as one who knew a great deal about the structures in the PCUS.[29] The proposals for this new group were forwarded to the mission offices in New York and Atlanta, and they were well received.

Enthusiasm for setting up a voluntary organization of missionaries and others in cross-cultural mission spread. In New York, Sarah Scotchmer and John Webster took the lead in organizing a Chapter 9 organization under the provisions of the Plan for Union. John Webster, the first president, states the name and purpose of the organization in the first issue of the APCCM Newsletter:

> An Association of Presbyterians in Cross-Cultural Mission: The name is important. What ties us together is a shared experience of involvement in the cross-cultural mission of the PC(USA). It is this shared experience and whatever wisdom we have derived from it which we wish to share with others as the PC(USA) develops its design for mission. This newsletter is to provide the means by which those with this experience can share their knowledge and their convictions with one another.

Structural concerns dominated the early discussions. At issue was whether to follow the Program Agency model of the UPCUSA, which merged domestic and international mission functions into one larger organization, or to follow the PCUS model, which had separate divisions for national and international missions. At a meeting in Towson, Maryland, in November of 1984, APCCM members adopted what came to be called "the Towson Statement," calling for separate boards of national and international mission. The statement was given widespread publicity and gained the support of many who signed the document, including both John Coventry Smith and T. Watson Street, mission secretaries from the predecessor denominations.

The cross-cultural mission workers had, indeed, found their platform, and the APCCM was invited to send representatives to meet with the General Assembly committee on structure. The significant role that the missionaries played in this conversation was reflected in the decision of the 196th General Assembly (1985) to maintain a separate unit for missionary personnel and program. During twenty years of ministry, the APCCM maintained its advocacy within the PC(USA) on behalf of mission personnel and the need for a strong Presbyterian commitment to long-term cross-cultural missionaries. Seeking to work collaboratively with denominational mission staff, the APCCM has remained steadfast in its commitment to mission through the church. Representatives of the APCCM met with the Worldwide Ministry Division staff at the Simpsonwood Conference Center in Atlanta in December of 1992. A Memo of Understanding was adopted, which outlined the ways in which the APCCM could best be of assistance to the WMD.

Programmatically, the APCCM lobbied for the retention of the missionary correspondence program, worked with the Worldwide Ministries Division to provide assistance to missionaries who were returning from their field of service, established several country-focused mission e-mail groups, and served as an advocate for continuing Presbyterian missionary involvement around the world. A newsletter—edited by Sara Scotchmer, Tommy Brown, and then coedited by Tommy Brown and Glenice Johnson—helped to keep members and others informed about trends and issues in mission, especially regarding the PC(USA). In 2006, the APCCM board voted to discontinue distribution of a printed newsletter, as it seeks to discern the organization's future.

MISSION PARTNERSHIPS

A recent development has been the proliferation of direct relationships between Presbyterian entities and global mission partners. Twenty-five years ago, only a handful of presbyteries had global partnerships, and most of them focused on hunger issues. Between 1988 and 2006, the number of synod and presbytery partnerships grew from about twenty-five to more than a hundred, including nearly two-thirds of the presbyteries. Many of these new partnerships were facilitated by Homer Rickabaugh, a PC(USA) staff member who was charged with the task of multiplying and strengthening middle governing body international partnerships.[30]

The continuing shift away from paternalism toward partnership in mission found articulation in a significant policy statement adopted by the 215th General Assembly (2003).[31] Affirming the participation of the Presbyterian Church (U.S.A.) in the whole body of Christ, "Presbyterians Do Mission in Partnership" recognizes that the church participates in God's mission for the sake of the world that God loves. "Recognizing our human limitations and because of our fundamental unity in Jesus Christ, we believe we are called to mission in the discipline of partnership . . . [which] assumes that mission can best be done by joining hands with those who share a common vision."[32]

The statement describes the character of authentic partnerships in mission: shared grace and thanksgiving, mutuality and interdependence, recognition and respect, open dialogue and transparence, and sharing of resources. Guidelines for international partnerships were approved in November of 2004, incorporating the assembly's policy statement. These principles have informed the growing number of mission partnerships and initiatives such as the Russia Twinning Project, a sister church ministry begun by the Outreach Foundation and now coordinated with the PC(USA). Project materials state: "Twinning represents the spiritual journey together of two congregations. Each congregation gives. Each congregation receives. The relationship is not, nor should it be, a 'one-way street.' . . . Those relationships that thrive are grounded in a long-term, shared vision together."

An example of a vital middle governing body partnership, one that has matured and deepened through its history, is the one between Pittsburgh Presbytery and the Church of Central Africa Presbyterian (CCAP) Blantyre Synod in Malawi. The partnership began in 1991 and quickly became a struggling, project-driven relationship. The U.S. partners often assumed that they understood what the African partners needed, and they sometimes funded projects that the Synod could not sustain or funded projects that resulted in unintended consequences, such as jealousy among parishes in Malawi. Since then, as a result of prayerful and careful consultation, projects must now be approved by leaders of both partners. The partnership has been recast in terms of relationships that are a mutual blessing. Hundreds of people have traveled back and forth, sharing in worship, Bible study, and deepening of Christian friendship. Church leaders have been seconded from each partner to the other.

These partnerships have shaped PC(USA) members and congregations in important ways as they have forged long-term cross-cultural mission relationships. Rev. Mark Plumb, cochair of Pittsburgh Presbytery's Malawi Ministry Team, described how the depth of faith embodied by Presbyterians in Malawi has challenged him. "While in this country we have the gift of material blessings, in many ways our faith is very immature," he says. "When we go to Third World countries like Malawi, they have little in terms of material possessions, but in terms of faith they are far richer than we are. These people rely on faith every single day of their lives."[33]

MISSION NETWORKS

Many partnerships with overseas churches have been established in recent decades by local congregations. Another significant innovation has been the formation of mission networks that bring Presbyterians who are involved with particular countries, partners, or people groups together for information sharing, prayer, encouragement, and mutual cooperation. Drawing upon the experience of partnerships and sister church relationships, and the work of more formally constituted entities such as the Czech Working Group and the Northern Ireland Working Group, mission networks began forming in the mid-1990s, the first being the Sudan Network, which formed in 1996.

The Worldwide Ministries Division's active encouragement and support of these networks represents its recognition of both the reality of new initiatives being undertaken by congregations and governing bodies, and the division's own need to shift from being a regulatory agency to being an enabling agency, a shift from control to facilitation.[34] "The network experiment has been a great success," said Will Browne, associate director for ecumenical partnerships. "Networks are here to stay to help the whole of the PC(USA) engage in international mission."[35] As of July of 2006, there were twenty-six country networks and eight people group networks recognized by the Worldwide Ministries Division. Other networks, not sponsored by the WMD, are also bringing Presbyterians together, such as the Sertão Network for Presbyterians working in northeastern Brazil. The mission networks provide an opportunity for congregations to learn from one another and to explore common standards for Presbyterian mission work with church partners and among unreached peoples.

ASSOCIATION OF PRESBYTERIAN MISSION PASTORS

The Association of Presbyterian Mission Pastors (APMP) was founded in 1989 as the Mission Pastor Network, the outcome of a conversation among Presbyterian mission pastors who met at the 1987 Urbana Conference sponsored by Inter-Varsity Christian Fellowship.[36] At a time when the number of pastors and church staff members focusing on mission as a specialized area of ministry was increasing, those who met at Urbana agreed that it would be helpful to share information about Presbyterian global mission and to encourage one another in ministry.

Representatives from the group met with staff of the Global Mission Ministry Unit of the General Assembly in May of 1989 to explore the possibility of forming a network of Presbyterian mission pastors and directors of local church mission. Rev. Bill Cunningham of La Canada Presbyterian Church in California placed an announcement in the magazine *Monday Morning*, inviting interested mission pastors and directors to meet in Louisville in December of 1989. Those who gathered were welcomed by the Director of the Global Mission Ministry Unit, Clifton Kirkpatrick, and other staff members, and one of the first actions of the group was to form a task force to prepare a display on PC(USA) mission for the next Urbana conference.

The APMP now includes both clergy and laypeople who facilitate the mission outreach of PC(USA) congregations, along with denominational staff, seminarians, and other mission leaders. The group's membership has continued to grow, and annual conferences typically have been held in Louisville to facilitate relationship-building between congregational leaders and denominational mission staff. The APMP officers have also sought to build open relationships with the PC(USA)'s validated mission support groups. Conference speakers are often drawn from the broader Presbyterian and ecumenical family, seeking to broaden and deepen participants' understanding of how the church is engaging in mission. Recent efforts of the organization include creating vehicles for sharing best practices and strategies for the missional renewal of congregations.

The APMP has made a significant contribution, planting seeds for a broader vision of Presbyterian mission, especially as leaders have encouraged denominational staff to recognize the validity of mission appointments through other sending agencies. This vision has been embodied by the APMP-related congregations such as University Presbyterian Church in Seattle, a congregation that has provided significant leadership in mission, deploying hundreds in mission service through many different agencies, and through its entrepreneurial leadership, connecting the PC(USA) in new ways to mission work in such places as the Balkans and Turkey. Another group contributing to this broader vision has been the Association of Presbyterian Mission Professors, which has regularly included denominational mission staff in its meetings. Formal and informal conversations have helped to shape shared missiological commitments.

MISSION CONFERENCES

At the General Assembly meeting in 1997, when it was learned that the PC(USA) would no longer sponsor the annual mission conference at the Montreat Conference Center in North Carolina (a decision protested by the APCCM), Bill Bryant of the Outreach Foundation initiated conversations with Harold Kurtz of Presbyterian Frontier Fellowship, Dan Force of Medical Benevolence Foundation, Brad Long of Presbyterian and Reformed Renewal Ministries, and Jeff Ritchie (then on the Worldwide Ministries Division staff). They discussed at length whether or not these organizations should accept the challenge of hosting a mission conference in order to keep the mission vision before the church, and several decided to move forward. In September of 1998, a major Presbyterian Global Evangelism Conference was held at Peachtree Presbyterian Church in Atlanta, sponsored by the Outreach Foundation and Presbyterian Frontier Fellowship, drawing over fifteen hundred people from around the globe. In 2005, the Outreach Foundation and Presbyterian Frontier Fellowship sponsored another conference at Peachtree with the theme "From Everywhere to Everyone: The New Global Mission," focusing on the growth of the church around the world and what Presbyterians could learn from the majority church.

The Worldwide Ministries Division did not abandon mission conferences altogether. A conference held in November of 1997 in St. Louis, with the theme

"Congregations in Global Mission: New Models for a New Century," lifted up a new vision for congregational participation in mission. That conference was followed by three regional conferences in 1999. In September of 2000, through its Office of International Evangelism, the PC(USA) sponsored a national conference on frontier mission, and two WMD conferences on the theme "Hospitality in the Household of God" were held in the fall of 2001. Another group that has sought to publicize and support the work of the WMD is the Witherspoon Society, which hosted a global mission conference in September of 2005 that focused on the ways that mission provides support for peace and justice in the United States and around the globe.

A century-old catalyst for renewal of the Presbyterian Church's mission vision has been the New Wilmington Missionary Conference, a conference begun in the United Presbyterian Church in North America (UPCNA) that celebrated its 100th anniversary in 2005. In 1904, the ecumenical Young People's Missionary Movement held its third conference at Silver Bay on Lake George, New York. Six members of the UPCNA were in attendance and decided to try their own "Silver Bay."[37] This was held the next year at Allegheny Theological Seminary (now Pittsburgh Theological Seminary). It was so successful that the new president of Westminster College offered the (New Wilmington, Pa.) campus for a week in August for the 1906 conference. The conference continues to meet at Westminster College, not as a denominational event but under the direction of an independent board of managers.

One of the conference's stated purposes has been to recruit and encourage young people to serve Christ on the mission field, and through the conference, hundreds of young people have accepted the challenge to mission service in the United States and abroad, some for short terms and others for career service. Since 1961, three hundred college-aged people have participated in the conference's summer service program, sharing in mission work in the United States, Puerto Rico, Alaska, Ethiopia, Tanzania, Ireland, Kenya, Pakistan, Thailand, Taiwan, Italy, Brazil, Russia, Turkey, Korea, Malawi, Egypt, and India.

In 1906, two hundred people registered for the first conference. The target group was young adults in high school and the early years of college. Recent conferences have gathered more than one thousand people to a program that serves all ages. During the 100th conference in 2005, a year when the General Assembly did not meet, PC(USA) missionaries were commissioned at the conference. For many, it was a welcome return to the past, for the UPCNA had traditionally commissioned its missionaries at the summer mission conference.

WORLD MISSION INITIATIVE

Pittsburgh Theological Seminary has a long history of involvement in preparing men and women for world mission. Recognizing that the changes sweeping the world and shaping the church necessitate innovative structures to continue the mission of Jesus Christ, pastors, missionaries, and church leaders met with denominational officials, seminary faculty, and administrators at Pittsburgh Theological Seminary in April of 1996 to discuss, pray, and strategize about ways to support the work of local congregations in world mission. From these initial meetings, promoted by Dr. Glendora Paul, the World Mission Initiative (WMI) was born.

The WMI has become a fellowship of Presbyterians dedicated to developing mission vision, nurturing missionary vocations, and cultivating missional congregations, seeking to unite the resources of key mission entities—local congregations, Pittsburgh Theological Seminary, New Wilmington Mission Conference, and the denominational mission offices—to advance the mission of Jesus Christ in the world. According to Rev. Dr. Scott Sunquist, professor at Pittsburgh Theological Seminary and one of WMI's cofounders, "Our goal is that every Presbyterian will be engaged by a vision of Jesus Christ sending his Church into the world—to the end that every person on the face of the earth hears the gospel."[38] The WMI staff members provide support to congregations seeking missional renewal, and the ministry also seeks to shape seminarians as missional leaders. Since its founding, WMI has facilitated cross-cultural mission experiences for scores of seminarians, and in 2005 it appointed its first long-term missionaries.

LITERACY AND EVANGELISM INTERNATIONAL

Literacy and Evangelism International (LEI) was founded in 1967 by Dr. Robert F. Rice, a former missionary to South Korea.[39] After serving for fifteen years in South Korea, he saw firsthand the need for adult literacy. Rice initially traveled around the United States and in Latin America, helping to create Bible-content adult literacy materials and helping to begin community literacy evangelism ministries. The ministry grew as Rice trained and mentored others in primer construction and tutor training. Today, LEI has assisted more than 140 churches and Christian groups in forty-two countries. Rice, who died in 2002, had been previously succeeded as executive director by Rev. John C. Taylor, who restructured the ministry into regions around the globe and delegated and empowered regional directors to oversee the work. The ministry is now led by Rice's son, Rev. Sid Rice.

The goal of LEI is that all the peoples of the earth would be able to read the Bible for themselves, in their own language. In pursuit of that goal, LEI provides consulting services to mission groups or churches for creating adult literacy materials in needed languages, offering materials for teaching English as a second language, and training leaders for literacy and/or English as a Second Language (ESL) ministry. Each summer, through an International Literacy Training Institute, LEI offers intensive training in literacy evangelism.

While its roots are in the Presbyterian Church and it continues to register as an affinity group of the General Assembly, LEI is an interdenominational, intermission fellowship. It seeks to cooperate with all Christian groups (churches, mission agencies, and parachurch organizations) by offering them training and assistance in creation of literacy materials. For nearly forty years, LEI has ministered to nonreaders of the world, seeking to bring them to Jesus Christ by enabling them to read the written Word of God.

OTHER ORGANIZATIONS

The organizations described above are not the only ones outside of the denomination's structure that have sought to advance the church's global mission work. While no longer active, Presbyterians United for Mission Advance worked in concert with the Presbyterian Center for Mission Studies in the 1980s, establishing regional mission promotion organizations in southern California, northern California, Oregon, and western New York. Led by elders serving on their church mission committees, PUMA held regional mission conferences and educational events. United Presbyterians for World Mission carried on similar advocacy for global mission among Presbyterians in western Pennsylvania and eastern Ohio from the mid-1970s until reunion in 1983.

The Knox Fellowship, which provides evangelism training to congregations and presbyteries, has for more than a decade also been engaged in mission work in Europe and South America, and more recently they have developed outreach ministries in the United States among Brazilian, Hispanic, and Nepalese immigrants. Presbyterian Reformed Ministries International, whose antecedents were the Presbyterian Charismatic Communion and Presbyterian Renewal Ministries, has undertaken work in Brazil, Taiwan, New Zealand, Uganda, the United Kingdom, the Philippines, and most recently, in China. At each General Assembly, continuing a practice begun by the Covenant Fellowship of Presbyterians, Presbyterians for Renewal lifts up the importance of mission service by awarding the Bell-Mackay Prize, named for Dr. L. Nelson Bell and Dr. John A. Mackay, both missionary statesmen.

CONCLUSION

During the 1995 General Assembly, the Worldwide Ministries Division hosted what was called "An Extended Family Gathering," which included representatives of thirty different Presbyterian-related mission groups. In describing the event, Dr. Clifton Kirkpatrick, then director of the WMD, said, "The heart of the concern is to focus not only what Worldwide Ministries Division does in mission, but [also] how we engage Presbyterians who are engaged in mission. We're gather[ing] the network of Presbyterians."[40] Yet for many Presbyterians, it must be admitted that staying engaged with the denomination has not been a high priority. Recent decades include not only the story of groups that have sought to stay connected to the denomination's mission work; it is also replete with examples of congregations that have largely, if not entirely, shifted their mission work outside the denomination.

Beyond the theological and social debates that rage within the church, the historic tension between modalities and sodalities helps to explain what has transpired. Bob Henderson observes that control has been one of the issues:

> The more rigidly we seek to impose our order on the church, the more we diminish its true Life, and the more likely we are to see some new missional movement erupt, or some end run emerge in some totally unexpected way. It will do this either inside that existing church institution, or outside in some new communal expression.[41]

Presbyterian groups have risen in response to the perception that the denominational offices were too regulatory, too focused on the church as an institution, and too focused on their own efforts. But that perception does not take into account the full reality. In this time of change, the denomination has highlighted important issues, including the holistic nature of the gospel, the incarnational character of Jesus' own mission, the need to honor the church in each place, and the need to be good stewards of resources and relationships.

During the last decade, the WMD leaders have affirmed the growing congregational initiatives in mission. The WMD's vision statement "Mission in the 1990s"[42] identified congregations as God's primary agent of mission in the world, a theme championed by Kirkpatrick during the years that he led the division. Dr. Marian McClure (whose tenure as WMD director ended in 2006 as part of denominational downsizing) observed that the 1997 conference, "Congregations in Global Mission," was a cathartic moment: "Congregational initiatives were truly acknowledged and honored. And national staff discovered that when we group people by the countries or regions they care about, they learn from each other very quickly and start to collaborate and coordinate their efforts with each other and with the denomination."[43] The subsequent conferences helped the movement to take off, and this new energy is a hopeful sign for Presbyterian mission.

Recent Presbyterian mission history includes many examples of missions within the mission, groups that have formed to advocate for and support global mission work. The continuing reduction in the size and scope of denominational mission efforts suggests that groups such as these may become even more important in the years ahead. New groups are forming and new initiatives are taking shape as organizations outside the denominational structure seek to be faithful in mission. In 2006, TOF and PFF announced a strategic initiative to send more Presbyterians in mission service, through the PC(USA), through other agencies, and under their own appointment, all using a faith-mission approach to missionary support. And a new group, the Presbyterian Global Fellowship (PGF), is taking shape, calling for a renewal of the church around its missional purpose. Nearly a thousand people gathered in August of 2006 for the inaugural PGF conference in response to an invitation to explore a new way to build relationships within the PC(USA) and to build partnerships with the majority church.

Darrell Guder helpfully argues that it is missiologically more correct to refer to such groups as paraparochial, not parachurch.[44] They are alongside the ecclesiastical structures of the church, but they are not apart from the church. During most of the last century, the denomination's tendency was to count what the denominational mission offices did as the real mission, with the efforts by others being viewed as something less. It is not a surprise, therefore, that in a time of diminishing denominational resources, some church leaders would feel threatened by others who are seeking new means by which to participate in mission. At the same time, it is easy, and often a mistake, for those outside of the denominational mission structure to ignore the experience, wisdom, and relationships that the denominational mission offices bring to Presbyterian participation in mission.

What is needed in this day is a true spirit of collaboration, not a spirit of competition. As Ralph Winter rightly asserts, both the modalities and sodalities have a role in God's redemptive purpose. They need each other. Yet how this pattern unfolds for Presbyterians in the years ahead may not be comfortable. Andrew Walls, in his wonderfully titled and insightful essay "Missionary Societies and the Fortunate Subversion of the Church," writes that the faith missions and voluntary mission societies have been just as revolutionary in their effect as the monasteries were in their spheres. He concludes, "The sodalities we now need may prove [to be] equally disturbing."[45]

Chapter 6

Missionaries Speak

CAROLINE N. BECKER

Christian mission is essentially about the life and work of missionaries. In the five preceding chapters we have addressed Presbyterian mission from a variety of other angles: ecumenical interactions, finance and statistics, denominational journeys, and changing mission structures. The work of Presbyterian mission has thus far been broadly described from the general vantage point of *what* and *how* Presbyterians were engaging in mission. It is important to reflect upon theological and structural changes in mission, but such reflection is incomplete if the implementation by individuals on "the field," where real lives are affected, is not also considered. Therefore, in this chapter we pause to focus on the Presbyterians *who* were sent around the globe to participate in God's mission: the missionaries.[1]

A qualitative analysis like this would not be possible without the generous sharing of written and oral stories, reflections, and detailed information from Presbyterian missionaries themselves.[2] Countless hours have been spent reading, charting, cataloging, and synthesizing both the survey data and interview manuscripts. The organization of this chapter flows out of the general order of interview and survey questions.[3] First, the various initial motives for serving as a missionary will be explored, along with what types of work were done, and how the missionaries understood their effectiveness, or lack thereof, and their main accomplishments. Second, their joys and difficulties as missionaries will be explored. Third, changes in their respective missions and mission work will be summarized. Here, special attention will be given to the development of Presbyterian mission theory and policy during their time of service and how these changes affected their work abroad. Finally, the missionaries will leave us with lessons that they would like to pass on to the denomination, local churches, and future missionaries.

MISSIONARY MOTIVES

Presbyterian missionaries who served long-term appointments[4] during our time period initially committed to overseas appointments because of particular personal motivations. Although individual past experiences, professional training, and missiological convictions resulted in a range of motivations, they can be grouped into six categories: to witness, in response to a call or commission, to help the local church, to serve people's basic needs, in response to influential past experiences, and to follow a spouse.

About one-third of the missionaries serving during this time period articulated a commitment to overseas service, which grew out of their desire to serve as Christ's witness. This motivation was expressed in a number of ways, such as "to serve Christ and his church," "to share the gospel of Jesus Christ" and "to share God's love/the love of Jesus Christ." Closely connected to the expressed motivation of being Christ's witnesses was another separately articulated motivation: "obedience to fulfilling the commands of Christ" or "to fulfill the Great Commission." Together, these calls (to witness to Christ, and to follow God's will in fulfilling the commands of Christ) accounted for the motivations of about half of all missionaries.

Presbyterians leaving for mission service also expressed a sense of call born out of their desire to help the local church overseas. For some, this was a general desire for serving the church, while for others it was a country-specific call.[5] Many who were called to help the local church expressed it in terms of vocational specificity, such as persons intending to serve in the areas of theological education, pastoral ministries, and rural evangelism. In whatever role(s) that they served, missionaries felt called to assist, support, encourage, prepare, strengthen, and work with the local church in their country of service.

While many missionaries felt called to service within and for the church overseas, some felt particular calls to serve people in general. Sometimes this call was articulated as a desire "to serve people in need," and other times it was a call to some type of medical assistance or other particular skill-based support they were trained to offer. A number of people specifically mentioned their call being related to their firsthand witness of the dire situation in many countries at the end of World War II. One person went because of his "experience of poverty in

China while serving in the marines," another went because he had "been encouraged in overseas mission by eight months' military service in the Philippines at the end of World War II," and another said that he considered a mission career after "experiences in Japan during military occupation."[6]

The experiences of a particular event, personal interaction, or life circumstance also played a role in calling missionaries overseas. Besides the military encounters above, a number of missionaries mentioned their calls to overseas service coming from participation in certain conferences (such as the Presbyterian Youth Convention, the "Youth Track" at Montreat's World Mission Conference, and the International Christian Endeavor conference in Atlantic City). Others referred to interactions, both personal and through literature, with missionaries or missionary kids whom they knew as influencing their decisions to become missionaries.[7] A fair number of missionaries grew up as missionary kids, citing that experience as being their motivation for overseas service. One man shared this call story: "I was born in Tsingtao, North China, of missionary parents, the youngest of five children [Tsingtao (Qingdao) was at that time a German colony]. All my siblings became missionaries to China, so I always felt I was headed for China, too. But with the communist takeover, [we] . . . were assigned to Korea."[8]

There were also people who, while not mentioning a particular reason or influence, nevertheless specifically referred to their call as occurring at a young age. Such persons felt a particular call to "foreign missionary service" or "evangelistic mission" around their teenage years or even before. The following quote is an example of a clear call to mission work that could be pinpointed to an early period in a missionary's life: "I felt the call of God as a child to be a missionary. I, therefore, prepared myself in education to be a missionary. I never wavered in my commitment to be a missionary in spite of trials during 1937–49."[9]

Finally, although an overall minority, a few people mentioned their call to mission work derived from their call to marrying a missionary or future missionary. In these cases, usually a wife mentioned going overseas to be married or because her husband was called.[10]

Over half of the missionaries expressed having no change to their initial mission motivation throughout their time of service. For those who did express a change in their motivation or general sense of call, a majority of the responses mentioned a particular shift of focus in their ministry from programs to people.[11] Many missionaries began their assignments focused on performing particular tasks, such as "preach to the unreached" or "to be a caregiver in my profession of nursing." Over time, however, missionaries grew to see the need for empowering the people where they served to continue the work that they were doing. In other words, as one missionary stated, "At first, I saw myself as 'doing something,' and increasingly I saw myself as one helping others to be engaged in ministry."[12] As they developed relationships with the people in their countries and grew to better understand their role, many missionaries' purpose changed to focus on strengthening the local church or hospital or school or other agency and developing local leadership and infrastructures that would sustain it.[13]

VARIOUS TYPES OF MISSION SERVICE

When sent overseas, most missionaries were assigned to serve in one of six general types of work: education, evangelism, health care, administration, development, and hospitality.[14] Educators made up the largest number of missionaries serving during this time period. People serving in the area of education focused on Christian education (mainly theological studies), the education of missionary children, English as a second language, college teaching, serving as school principals, adult education, grade school teaching, and curriculum and material development.

The second greatest number of missionaries served in the area of evangelism. Like education, this area included a broad range of functions (such as pastor, evangelist, chaplain, music ministry, campus ministry, and Christian radio development). About half of the missionaries categorized under evangelism served as pastors, evangelists, and church planters.

The third greatest area in which Presbyterians served was health care. Missionaries recorded themselves as having "practiced medicine" (such as general practice, surgery, anesthesiology, ophthalmology, dentistry, rehab, and nursing), having taught or trained other medical workers, performing hospital administration oversight, being involved in public health, and founding or setting up hospitals.[15] Many of those who initially began as hospital administrators stepped down to serve other roles after an indigenous person was trained to take their place.

The final three areas of service, administration, development, and hospitality had a combined number of persons serving that was less than the number of persons serving in any of the previous areas of service. Although people in education and health care served administrative roles, the specific category of administration mostly referred to missionary roles associated with the earlier operations of mission stations. These particular tasks, primarily field secretary, mission treasurer, and local presbytery work, were virtually eliminated when missions integrated into the local churches. Missionaries categorized under "development" were mostly involved in rural or village development, relief work, and construction, while those under "hospitality" usually opened their homes for students and visitors or served as coordinators for short-term mission guests from the United States.

Overall, the top ten categories of mission service performed by missionaries during this time period, from the greatest to the least, are Christian educators, medical practitioners, missionary children educators (including home schooling), pastors, evangelists, ESL teachers, college teachers, school directors, adult educators, and medical trainers and teachers.[16]

THE LEAST VALUABLE OR EFFECTIVE
ELEMENTS OF MISSION WORK

Reflection upon the least valuable or effective elements of their mission work exposes the self-effacing nature of many missionaries. Honest statements, such as

"There are a number of things that come to mind that I could have done better and are hard to enumerate" and "We had lots of mistakes, but God helped us," reveal the ease with which missionaries have critiqued their own life's work.[17] Many wished that they could have "done more" to be a more effective leader or teacher or better nurse, to convert more of their patients or medical students to Christ, or just to make decisions that would have led to more effective contributions on the whole. We have already demonstrated that the Presbyterian Church sent out very driven and passionate people, with specific calls to overseas mission service. Therefore, it was not for lack of motivation that missionaries felt ineffective in their work. In this case, the opposite is probably true; with great needs and limited resources, work becomes an ongoing and long-term process.[18]

When reflecting on specific hindrances to their work, missionaries' overwhelming responses regarded their limited language ability. Although many of the missionaries, especially career missionaries, received intensive language training, not all truly mastered the language. Understandably, missionaries had plenty of "regular" work, so language study could easily be put off because of pressing ministry needs. As one missionary wrote, "I was never able to learn sufficient Chinese and Thai languages. I was too busy trying to be a doctor."[19] Those who knew the language well felt quite comfortable in their local culture and cited the ways in which it blessed their ministry. The missionaries who never grasped the ability to directly communicate with others were hindered from truly understanding those with whom they worked, lived, shopped, and worshiped.

A second aspect of missionary life articulated as limiting effectiveness was "being so rich." Compared to their Indian, Congolese, Thai, or Brazilian neighbors and colleagues, the Presbyterian missionary salary was quite large. For many missionaries, their wealth was often a hindrance to their work. Generally, missionaries desired to adopt lifestyles similar to those with whom they worked, and thus they desired to receive similar wages. Moreover, just because they were from the West, missionaries symbolized wealth to many of the local people. In some instances, this led to people seeking friendships with missionaries in the hopes that they would connect them to overseas money. One missionary to India describes the predicament as follows: "Our income was too high for comfort in rural India. We wanted to get what our local doctors got and have the rest in the United States on furlough when we needed it. It was a barrier."[20]

After limited language ability and being (relatively) wealthy, the list of least effective elements of missionary work becomes scattered with a multiplicity of statements from many individuals. The reflections can be grouped into two general categories: missionary relations to the home board or board policies, and missionary life on the field. Regarding relations with the home board, a few people mentioned wasted time dealing with staff from the New York office (UPCUSA). One person thought that the first-world training (orientation at Stony Point, N.Y.) that they received was impractical for their service in the third world, while another expressed that the amount of stress relating to moving home for furloughs every five years was unhelpful. As for particular work overseas, missionaries believed that evangelism among the majority community was generally ineffective, as was itinerant preaching without adequate follow-up. Some felt restricted by having to keep American Presbyterian standards of church polity, and others even felt restricted by having to work under the local church leadership.[21] Others mentioned the lack of time with children, the ongoing problem of being too "culturally bound," and the struggle to nourish their own personal faith.

THE MOST VALUABLE OR EFFECTIVE ELEMENTS OF MISSION WORK

No matter how the pie of effectiveness in Presbyterian mission work is sliced, the largest piece is always the training or teaching of local leaders. Whether it be seminary professors, medical doctors or nurses, itinerant preachers, or community development workers, missionaries believe that their most valuable work was training leaders for the countries in which they served so that they would be strong leaders in their own countries and replace the need for missionaries to serve such roles. A missionary to Brazil succinctly states this feeling: "I feel the most valuable was at the Colégio [Presbyteriano] Quinze de Novembro. It prepared young people to become leaders. Some later held extremely important positions. It prepared many to enter Presbyterian seminary, and untold [numbers] became ministers. Our goal was to turn over leadership of the church to nationals."[22] Numerous missionaries joyfully referred to their many former students who had gone on to become leaders within their synods, running training conferences, in charge of former mission schools, and medical professionals. They were effective because they invested in training local leaders to lead their own indigenous ministries.

Missionaries also lifted up the relationships that they formed with students, patients, coworkers, and local leaders as highly valuable elements of their mission work. One might expect missionaries to view their relationships as a valuable part of their ministries, for mission is basically about relationships and communication. Yet we found that missionaries almost unanimously stressed the importance of the many long-term relationships that they developed with the people in their countries of service. For example:

> The most valuable elements in my mission work were the relationships with my coworkers in Kwangju and Seoul . . .
> Relationships were and are important to us. Being able to communicate with the people and to work with and become friends with many of our African colleagues. To know them and their families, to worship together and serve Jesus Christ side by side in kingdom building.[23]

Besides the relationships that they made, much of what missionaries believed was effective in their work was their particular work itself. Missionary professors cited their teaching as being most effective, while missionary medical professionals cited their medical work. Others referred to their evangelistic efforts, Bible teaching, work with children, rural work, and work with women. Just as some mentioned their lack of language as contributing to ineffectiveness in their work, a significant number of missionaries mentioned speaking the local language as being a valuable contribution in itself.

MAIN ACCOMPLISHMENTS
AS A PRESBYTERIAN MISSIONARY

As one may surmise, missionaries' sense of accomplishment was closely related to, and sometimes synonymous with, the most valuable part of their mission work. The striking chord of accomplishment for most missionaries was that they were able to work themselves out of a job. Although our Presbyterian missionaries used to depart for their respective countries of service committed to a lifetime of service, they did not go with the goal of starting projects for which they would always remain at the highest level of leadership. These missionaries went with the vision to train local leadership to replace them.[24] A missionary to Kenya worked to "empower [laypeople] to do leadership development," while a missionary to India succeeded at "passing on the leadership to local Indians at the hospital."[25] As earlier chapters have noted, mission integration was certainly the mission buzzword and goal of Presbyterian mission agencies in the late 1950s and early 1960s. Judging from our missionaries' responses, this purpose was brought to the field as, if not before, it was programmatically initiated from the denominational level. Nurses, pastors, doctors, and professors alike all felt fulfilled in their work when they were able to point to the indigenization of their work.

Correspondingly, such accomplishments were often articulated as successes within a missionary's particular specialty. For example, a missionary to Thailand who was involved in music ministry cited the establishment of music programs in particular Thai universities and the rewriting of the Thai hymnal to reflect Thai musical rhythms as her main accomplishments. Moreover, as the hymnal is being revised again, she is proud that the main players are students who were trained in those university music programs that she helped to establish.[26] Another missionary who started out as a rural evangelist soon turned to put his architectural training into practice. By the time of his retirement, he had completed over a hundred different projects in Thailand, and today he is introduced as "the one who designed the first church in Chiang Mai."[27]

The missionaries who went overseas at the beginning of our time period had the extra privilege of being a part of "firsts" on the field. Some were the first foreign seminary professors, and others were the first medical specialists at a particular hospital. A medical missionary who ended up in Thailand after the closing of China in the early 1950s reflected on his "first":

> There is no question in my mind that when we retired and left in 1972, I have felt that I had the privilege of accomplishing something that very few

missionaries could say that they could do: starting a new institution. Most of the time we went out where there were already these schools, churches, and hospitals, and this was an opportunity that came to me. When I left the country, I had seen a project get started; that was a personal accomplishment for me.[28]

For an evangelist in Japan, being able to start churches and see them grow brought him great satisfaction because of the joy that came from seeing something new come to life.[29] Overall, planting churches, founding institutions, and starting programs that would serve the local community for years to come gave missionaries a great sense of accomplishment.

In the midst of their particular assignments, missionaries' daily work often evolved into, or soon incorporated, other types of activities and ministry. A missionary's initial assignment was seldom synonymous with what one actually did on the field. Adaptations were based on perceived need, improved effectiveness, and cultural appropriateness. In a number of cases, this additional work often brought missionaries the greatest sense of accomplishment.

A striking example of this comes from a seminary professor who served in Syria/Lebanon. After his first year of teaching, he began taking one to two students with him each weekend to a group of villages where there was only a small Christian presence. Since there were not enough Christians in each village to form separate congregations, this missionary and his students developed a cooperative parish from the seven villages. This ministry continued for thirteen years, aiding in both the missionary's Arabic language improvement and the development of closer relations with the students. For this particular missionary it was "a beautiful experience, with God's rich blessings in bringing that about. I don't think this was anything I thought through, planned, or projected; I just fell into this pattern, and years later I came to realize that this was the great work of God."[30]

One missionary to Thailand commented on how her main accomplishment was mission interpretation when her family was back on home assignment/furlough in the United States. Although without a particular "success" on the field, she learned to exercise her gifts among American Presbyterians. While back in the United States, her family learned to think "like Americans again" and thus find helpful ways for U.S. Christians to understand their work in Thailand, as well as the particular situation of the church in Thailand.[31]

A final grouping of missionary accomplishments comes with the perspective of time. Many missionaries who served long-term in one or more countries have been able to return to those countries many years after retiring from mission service. Quite often, the depth of their impact is only revealed through the passage of time. For example, one missionary couple went back to where they used to live in Kinshasa, Congo, to find 183 different parishes where there used to be only seven and to see the school where the husband served for a few years as principal.[32] With time, other missionaries are now able to see the development of ministries that they began and students whom they trained.[33]

GREATEST DIFFICULTIES OR FRUSTRATIONS
IN MISSION WORK

Between 1944 and 2006, missionaries generally experienced difficulties in one of five general areas: their children's education, cultural adjustments, isolation, sensitive financial circumstances, and political unrest. Due to the lack of English-language schooling opportunities in places where Presbyterian missionaries served, especially during the first half of this period, most missionary children were sent away to boarding school. The separation of young children from their families during the school year was very difficult for missionary parents.[34] It was the most frequently mentioned difficulty.

The next area of difficulty for missionaries is a large general category related to typical cross-cultural adjustments. Simply put, they were "language, heat, and culture."[35] Missionaries spent much time devoted to language learning before serving overseas.[36] Although some had up to two years of training before going on the field, they still found it difficult. Languages are hard to learn in general and especially during adulthood. Thus, it is no surprise that so many missionaries had difficulties with languages. Some commented on how they learned the language with academic proficiency but had a harder time with daily fluency. Others were able to grasp general communication, but found the intimacy of "prayer language" more difficult to master.

As most North Americans are used to the change of seasons, serving in tropical climates was an initial difficulty for some. Over time, though, many missionaries grew accustomed to the heat and humidity, even to the point of preferring it over their native climates in the United States.

All missionaries had to undergo some degree of cultural adjustments to their new homes overseas. The degree of cross-cultural difficulty encountered by each missionary varied. Many people had to adjust to a new diet, which became a difficulty for some when it resulted in illness and/or extreme weight loss. Persons serving in Muslim contexts had to get used to working on Sundays, since the holy day in those countries is Friday. Missionaries in Asian contexts would often become frustrated with the concept of "face," because it often meant that they were never sure how honest people were really being with them. Those serving in Latin America had to learn to shed their quick and efficient American approach to life and adapt to the "slower" approach of their national colleagues and friends.

The cultural adjustment learning curve was initially very steep. As time passed and as missionaries learned from their experiences, they became more accustomed to and at home in their countries of service. Reflective of this change from cultural ignorance to cultural adaptation is the following story from a woman who served in Egypt:

> The first year and the last years were the hardest because of the terrible mistakes I made in the first year and how hard it was to leave the last year. I

remember one time I was trying to treat a driver/cook as you would a servant in America; I tried to treat him on more of an equal basis, and it turned into an embarrassing situation as he misunderstood me as wanting to share my bed with him! I got into all kinds of trouble over that one. Another time, I was to be hiring someone to work in our small library in our building, and I offered someone a salary of about three times what a teacher was being offered in a mission school, which she grasped immediately. It upset everyone else, and of course I had to rescind the offer immediately.[37]

In the days before faxes, e-mail, and FedEx, slow communication from friends and family back in the United States was trying for missionaries. When missionary children were young, they were unable to interact with their grandparents as frequently as they would have if they were living in the United States. When these children grew up and went away to college, their missionary parents were then less able to keep in touch with them.[38]

Besides isolation from home, some missionaries were also isolated from other missionaries in the countries where they served. This separation was emotionally difficult because even though they had local friends, cultural differences often inhibited deep friendships giving the emotional support that the missionaries desired.

Spiritual isolation was also an articulated difficulty that missionaries faced. Regarding this matter, a missionary to Japan stated his difficulty as "not having a regular group to pray with or be accountable to. The mission expected us to get all our emotional and spiritual needs filled by the Japanese church—and that doesn't work. For one thing, we couldn't be open with them about our own struggles, and we certainly couldn't be open with Louisville."[39] A missionary to Cameroon also felt the need for more spiritual support: "Sometimes we felt like we were hung out on a line to dry. We sometimes had an adversarial relation with the EPC [local denomination]; they did not want the missionaries to meet with each other and were paranoid about our intentions."[40]

The financial difficulties that missionaries faced were varied: making too much money (relative to their national coworkers), hyperinflation of the local currency, and the trend of financial cutbacks from their sending agencies. In most countries where Presbyterian missionaries served,[41] the cost of living was significantly lower than in the United States. While grateful for the reliable payments from the church every month, missionaries were often put in the awkward position of receiving far more money than necessary for daily living overseas. Frustration arose from them not being able to accept just a portion of their salaries on the field and having the remaining amount saved for them in the United States for their furloughs or ultimate relocation back home. One missionary to India described her financial frustration: "Income tax time was BAD. Louisville insisted [that] we had to take all our pay—couldn't keep it for us for use in the USA. We were taxed on all income. I remember one Bank Manager, in front of local villagers, yelling, 'My goodness, Sahib, you people earn more than the Prime Minister!' Not a happy experience."[42]

For persons trying to adapt to the local culture through ways such as using the same language and eating the same foods, the great financial divide between missionaries and indigenous persons was often a relational hindrance. In many poorer nations of service, hyperinflation contributed greatly to this financial frustration. A missionary to Congo described his experience:

> Dealing with hyperinflation, dealing with money: a constant problem for eighteen years in the Congo. The rates went crazy all the time. We were told in the offices back home never to use the black market, but that's what we called the true value market! But this was always a problem. It was a constant frustration. After I left the Congo, I got a letter from a man whose salary I had paid, and the stamps on the letter were more than his salary two years before![43]

The trend of decreased funding for mission during this time period posed great difficulties and frustrations for missionaries.[44] A number of missionaries mentioned that they themselves were "not sent back" to their countries of service "because there was not enough money" for them to stay. Others mentioned having friends on the field who later were not able to return to their countries of service after a furlough in the United States for the same reason. Many missionaries also mentioned the Angela Davis affair as specifically impacting the decrease in mission giving to the UPCUSA.[45] The missionaries were perplexed by the disconnect between the way churches in the United States would extravagantly spend money on their own property but were not willing to put forth much effort to raise the necessary funds for sustaining the denomination's mission work overseas. For example, one missionary couple was sent home because of a lack of funding and visited a Michigan church in the hometown of the inventor of Saran Wrap. They noted that this particular church replaced its drapes "at the cost of what would have supported us for three more years."[46] Sometimes missionaries would sacrifice some of their own income in order to keep another missionary on the field.

The final major difficulty for missionaries during this time period was the great political unrest in nations where they served. Although World War II was drawing to a close in the early years of this period, the collapse of colonialism resulted in national wars. Regarding political instability, wars, and rumors of war, the regions of Egypt, Syria/Lebanon, Congo, Cameroon, Sudan, Ethiopia, China, and India/Pakistan were more affected than others. A missionary to Egypt recalled never having a day that was not affected by politics. She said, "They [politics] affected everything we did. We were accused of saying things we didn't dare say (I went in 1951), and from the time Israel was created, it was like a black cloud that covered the entire Middle East. The government people assumed we were all there as spies. We were always under suspicion."[47] A missionary couple to Cameroon lived through three years of curfew when the Dasa tribe revolted against the French. They remembered the experience thus: "We had many close calls and lived in constant changes, from both the French and the rebels."[48] It was quite common for missionaries serving in those countries to speak of living through two, three, or even four different wars.

Although their personal safety was at stake during the difficult times of war and unrest, the circumstances generally did not faze the missionaries. Their commitment to fulfilling God's call to the people whom they were serving was stronger than any concern for their own personal well-being. Sometimes war was just a nuisance: "The war in Lebanon was frustrating, but we could carry on."[49] Other times, political unrest sent all foreigners but U.S. Presbyterian missionaries fleeing home for safety.[50]

Missionaries to North India remember well the wars along the border between India and Pakistan. They ironically refer to them as the "American and Russian Wars," since Pakistan and India were supported by the United States and Russia respectively. In 1971, one couple was working at a mission hospital five miles from the Pakistan border when the maternity ward was hit by shells. Besides the miracle of nobody being hurt, the commitment of the missionaries to stay with the people during the conflict brought them into better contact and relationships with the local people. Although the U.S. embassy called daily, trying to get them to flee for their safety, these missionaries were committed to the people whom they were serving in India. During one of the wars, even BBC news personnel drove up from Delhi to inform them that they were the only foreigners on the border during the war and that the U.S. embassy would remove them if that was what they wanted. The couple declined the offer because they knew that they would be "the worst witnesses" if they left.

GREATEST JOYS AS A MISSIONARY

Although Presbyterian missionaries served in a range of functions, in different cultural settings, and for various lengths of time, whenever asked to reflect upon their greatest joys as missionaries, the most frequent response was "getting to know the people." Virtually without hesitation, interviewed missionaries' eyes would light up with delight as they recalled the friends they made with their national coworkers, neighbors, and church members, as well as missionary colleagues. More than a general fascination with getting to know people of another culture, the missionaries' joy stemmed from the development of genuine friendships with people in the countries where they served.[51] Missionaries' personal investment in the lives of others, whether it was via training doctors, teaching women to read, or mentoring future pastors, were not artificial, one-sided investments but rather experiences of mutual investment and mutual return. A missionary doctor to India summarized this well: "I think I could say from the heart that the fellowship we had with nationals, as well as with fellow-missionaries, was one of the most inspiring things that brought joy to my own life. I do know that many of the nationals I worked with were real 'soul brothers.' It was a great inspiration to learn more from them spiritually than they learned from me."[52]

As one might expect, another area of greatest missionary joy stemmed from their specific work. Closely related to their greatest sense of accomplishment, missionaries found joy in doing what they were called to do overseas: developing new churches, developing local leadership (church, medical, or educational), watching formerly illiterate people read on their own, itinerating in villages with local pastors, teaching, and performing eye surgery, to name a few. Moreover, joy was particularly felt when the results of many years of service were tangibly witnessed. One example of this comes from an agricultural missionary to Cameroon:

> In agriculture, the development of a market for eggs and of getting people involved in agriculture in village situations was a great joy. Creating also a market for feed, to sell surpluses of food; and to create a market for eggs and see that expand. At the airport one time a plane took off 600 pounds overweight with eggs [from Cameroon] going to Chad.[53]

What started as a project to create an available source of protein that would be locally marketed and sustained became so successful that it turned into an exported good.

After these two greatest joys, other missionary joys varied from person to person. Some joys were particular to a unique experience in the country served. For example, one man mentioned the joy of being able to serve in China before World War II and the expulsion of missionaries, while another mentioned the "unrestrained joyful experience of worship that one sees in African congregations."[54] Other joys were more ubiquitous to the missionary experiences: the joy of serving overseas with one's family and the joy of having solid support from the denomination during periods of family crisis and/or illness.

MISSIONARIES REFLECTING ON CHANGING MISSION

As all previous chapters have described, this time period was filled with many changes in the context for, theories about, and approaches to mission. Many of the changes in Presbyterian mission were policy changes that flowed out of changes in mission theory. Some changes were dictated by the sending agency back in the United States for missionaries "on the field" to implement. Other changes grew out of missionary responses to their own changing cultural, religious, and political contexts in the countries where they served. Missionary reflections on these developments can be summarized into six areas of change: an increased emphasis on partnership, nomenclature for mission agencies and missionaries, the integration of missions into the local church, mission giving and funding, salary-related issues, and the duration of mission service.

Following the Lake Mohonk Consultation of 1956, the theme of partnership in mission became increasingly prominent in Presbyterian mission literature and discussions.[55] The church in the United States began to understand its overseas "daughter" churches as having grown up and matured into "sister" churches.

Thus, mission was no longer to be conducted as a one-way stream from the United States to other places abroad. Rather, the Presbyterian Church began to partner together with churches overseas in mission. Missionaries favored the official trend toward working in partnership because they, too, believed that the mission of the church was an activity in which the whole global church should be engaged. Many missionaries were already operating in some form of a partnership, and other missionaries, while maybe not engaged in a complete partnership, strove to eventually be working together in mission with the local church in the country where they served.

Ideas, however, are often easier to describe than implement. According to missionaries, partnership seems to be one idea that was harder to apply in a uniform manner. In some cases Presbyterian partnership has meant that the U.S. church left full responsibility for choosing the programs to be funded and the missionaries to be sent in the hands of the overseas church. The UPCUSA's role, then, was to implement the decisions that the local church or institution made.[56] This mode of partnership made the Presbyterian Church a passive partner, giving and taking as the local church dictated.

Translating "partnership" into local languages also led to difficulties in implementation. One missionary mentioned how "partnership" cannot be translated into African languages, for the core value where he served in Africa was "family," not "partnership." Where he served, people believed that their church and the Presbyterian Church in the United States should be "sharing just like they do in a family, because we are a part of that family."[57] Even translating partnership into today's PC(USA) is a difficult task. "I still question the concept of partnership as it is expressed," said another missionary; "that it is creating an illusion of a partnership that really does not exist. I like the idea, but I really don't see it happening."[58]

Flowing out of the Presbyterian Church's shift to participating in mission through partnership came linguistic changes in its terminology for the mission-sending agency and people sent in mission. Boards reasoned that the term "missionary" had many negative connotations, and so they chose to stress the equality that there was in mission by replacing "missionary" with "fraternal worker." Missionaries serving in Europe noted that local churches welcomed this change because "missionaries were thought of as bosses."[59] However, in other areas of the world, "fraternal worker" was difficult to translate into the local language. According to a missionary to Korea, "fraternal worker . . . could not be translated into Korean without it being an epithet, an insult. We were always 'missionaries.'"[60] In more recent history, PC(USA) missionaries are now called "mission coworkers." Such a title seems to be a type of middle ground between missionary and fraternal worker.[61]

Although they recognized the reasoning behind the name changes, most missionaries were indifferent to being called by different names, for their primary concern was their work, not their title. As one woman stated, "It [the name change] didn't make any difference to us, but I could understand their reason for trying to get this idea across—we are partners in mission, and so we should just be working on the same level."[62] Another woman reflected on how the name changes from the United States ultimately never mattered to the people with whom she served in Thailand because even while her title changed, her service to the church in Thailand remained the same. She commented,

> I think we have all been through missionary [and] fraternal worker, and now [we are] in the partnership era. The people in Thailand could care less about the new title; we were the first people they were to assign from the CCT. The Thai people were not clear that anything had really changed. Even today, forty or fifty years later, I am still called a missionary. Relationship hadn't changed, just a change in our name. The word *missionary* is engrained in us. And that is okay, but it still communicates what we do.[63]

The UPCUSA's new name for its mission-sending agency in 1958, the Commission on Ecumenical Mission and Relations (COEMAR), was another programmatic change in nomenclature designed to accurately describe and prescribe how the Presbyterian Church operated. As with other title changes, missionaries were generally indifferent, because it had little to no effect on their daily work overseas. Some missionaries questioned the change because the acronym COEMAR was hard to translate into the languages where they served, and it did not "inspire" people the way that "foreign missions" did. It was suggested that such a long description was better as the subheading of a denominational mission agency rather than the official title.[64]

The greatest change that most missionaries mentioned as occurring during their years of service was that of the integration of their mission-governed work into the local church. For many missionaries, this was not merely a new policy of the board that they were to implement, but rather a deep sense of call that they had already brought with them to the field. Missionaries of all professions believed that it was their responsibility to work themselves out of a job; they were to train local persons to do the tasks that they were performing and to manage the institutions that they had founded.

Given the varying contexts in which missionaries served, the timing of and process by which such integration occurred varied considerably. In some places, mission-church integration generally occurred smoothly; in others, the obstacles of finances, power struggles, and inappropriate timing inhibited such smooth transfers of authority. Missionaries who experienced smoother transitions thought that the key components were intentionality in training local leaders, their sensitivity to the local culture, and their partnering together with nationals in the transition process. For example, missionaries to Ethiopia working with the Anuak project had the goal of translating the Bible into the Anuak language, teaching people to read the Bible, and training Anuak pastors and evangelists to study the Bible in order to apply it to their own society and customs. From the beginning, these missionaries focused on training local leaders to lead their own people. As one missionary wrote, "We didn't build churches, we didn't pay pastors. The Anuak leadership was well established, and Anuaks now consider themselves a 'Christian' tribe."[65]

Presbyterian missionaries had been in Lebanon much longer and established more institutions than in Ethiopia. Missionaries there formed joint missionary-national committees, which jointly made decisions and planned for the transfer of authority to the local churches. Similarly in India, changing the top administrative and academic positions at institutions from being missionary-held to being held by Indian nationals was a welcomed change along the way to mission-church integration.

In places where integration occurred less smoothly, most missionaries cited the way in which the Presbyterian Church called for unilateral integration within a certain number of years, without taking the varying local church contexts into consideration. Missionaries working in Thailand stated clearly in our survey that the process was too rigid, too quick, culturally inappropriate, and imposed upon the ecumenical church: Church of Christ in Thailand.

In most countries where Presbyterians were serving, the local churches were all faced with the problem of maintaining the various hospitals, schools, and other institutions that missionaries founded with American dollars. Like Thailand, the Christian population in these countries was also a small minority and very poor. Missionaries believed that it was an unrealistic and even burdensome goal to expect the local church to suddenly manage and fund these institutions.

Finances and power struggles among local leadership also posed difficulties during the integration process. Many missionaries told of the "troubles" that local churches faced once they became solely responsible for the financial record-keeping, financial resources, and property that the mission had once managed.[66] In India, for example, Christians generally had few financial resources and had never been permitted to own their own land. This meant that they lacked the experience and wisdom necessary for successful maintenance of the church property and fiduciary responsibility associated with such care. In the Congo, missionaries created a joint-treasurer position as a way to help train Congolese Christians to do their own accounting. Sadly, although some of the local treasurers were "very strong Christians in the beginning," tribalism and other loyalties led to mishandling of funds and corruption within the church.

Although integration was one of the major changes that missionaries experienced during their years of service, not all missionaries had such an experience. In general, the missionaries who began their service after the early 1970s entered into contexts where the local church was already self-governing. Thus, from the beginning they worked for and were supervised by the local church. But in other countries (e.g., Japan and North India), the independence of the national church came decades earlier, and so "integration" meant something quite different. A missionary couple who was sent to work at a hospital in North India in the early 1960s recalled always working under the United Church of North India whose missionaries were not the head pastors of local churches.[67]

Closely affecting the missionary experience, especially for married women missionaries, were changes in salary structures. Most married women served with their husbands overseas, but they were excluded from Social Security and Pension Plan contributions because the family salaries were solely in the husband's name.[68] Many missionaries in the former UPCNA and PCUSA fondly recalled the time when missionaries were given a subsistence salary, to which allowances were added on for children, their education, help around the home, and other special needs. They appreciated the church's helping them to have "a lot saved up" for their children's college education and its provision for a whole month's allowance no matter when a child was born in that particular month. Without these financial worries, missionaries could fully invest themselves in their ministries.

When COEMAR formed in 1958, the Northern church changed its salary structure so that all missionaries, regardless of age or years of experience, were given the same salary. Married and single missionaries, however, were paid at different rates. Additionally, the salary for married couples was always in the husband's name, even if the wife was working. This was a point of frustration for many women who served overseas. One married missionary expressed extreme frustration at this aspect of the policy: she taught for twenty-five years overseas without any money going into her Social Security. It was not until the early 1980s that the Program Agency decided to implement a "fictitious" salary base for married women so that they would have both pension payments and some Social Security.

The universal salary of 1958 was set to be the same as the median salary of Presbyterian pastors in the United States. For many, this change meant an increase in salary. For others, it meant a decrease. For the denomination as a whole, however, it meant an overall increase in operating costs and therefore a decrease in the number of missionaries whom it could support. Some missionaries became vocally opposed to this change because it meant the removal of missionaries from the field.

Although funding changes during this time period were thoroughly addressed in chapter 2, numerous missionaries spoke of funding changes as being one of the significant changes during their years of service. Therefore, we revisit the issue again. Most comments regarding funding changes included mention of budget decreases in the 1970s and decreased funding for overseas mission-established institutions after the mission-church integration.

During the budget cutbacks of the 1970s, missionaries were most saddened that so many missionaries were cut: they were either not asked to return or were asked to leave.[69] In many instances, the leaders of the local church in the country where missionaries served were asked, as one missionary recalled, "Please send a list of missionaries to be returned home because of lack of finances."[70] Also during this time, the design for mission changed so that mission was promoted as being done at the lowest possible level, but always in light of the needs of the other governing bodies.[71] According to missionaries, once presbyteries began exercising more control over their funding, they began keeping larger percentages of their general contributions. Essentially, presbyteries allocated more money for their own presbytery needs, resulting in less money for overseas mission.[72]

The final change about which most missionaries spoke was the overall decrease in missionaries' years of service and the decrease in overall numbers of missionaries. Missionaries serving during the beginning of this period were commissioned as career missionaries and expected to serve overseas until their retirement. Over time, the terms of service were decreased while the frequency of return visits to the United States was increased. Missionaries referred to this trend of appointing short-term missionaries as "bad news" and having "a negative impact on the missionaries' understanding of the culture, the church, and for the continuity of the work."[73] Career missionaries found that short-termers were typically not expected to learn the local language and, as a result, were unable to effectively communicate or pick up extensive cultural knowledge where they served. Additionally, career missionaries also witnessed drastic decreases in the numbers of missionaries serving with them. For example, one career missionary began his service in the Middle East in 1955 alongside 140 career Arabic-speaking missionaries and ended it in 1995 with two others.[74]

Missionaries did acknowledge short-term missionaries as being helpful, for example, in teaching missionary children or working on specialized projects (such as construction) for which language was unnecessary and there was a defined time limit. However, the overwhelming cry regarding duration of mission service is one of distressed and troubled reflection: "We need longer-term service to prove that we want to understand their language and culture. . . . I wonder now, with people going out on short six-month terms or one year or three years, what effect has that had on the global mission of the church?"[75] For the many Presbyterian missionaries who have devoted their entire careers to serving the church overseas, the decline in overall numbers of missionaries and the years of service that those few missionaries are able to serve is a troubling change that they would prefer not continue.

RELATIONSHIPS WITH THE HOME BOARD OR SENDING AGENCY

An integral component of the missionary experience, if for no other reason than its enabling of one missionary call to become a living reality, has been the relationship between the missionary and the sending agency. As we know from earlier chapters, just as the various Presbyterian denominations underwent various unions, their respective mission boards also experienced a number of structural changes. Along with these changes came geographic relocations of the mission board offices.[76]

Missionaries' comments regarding relations with their home boards are generally positive, yet mixed. Most expressed great gratitude for the church's willingness not only to provide them with the opportunity to serve overseas, but also for its care, provision, and financial support throughout their terms of service.

Missionaries used words and phrases like "very supportive," "fine," "very good," "excellent," and "GREAT" to describe relations with their respective home board. One particular example highlights the much-appreciated expression of extreme care and concern that some missionaries received:

> Relations were the best. "New York" cared for our health (I got an infection that doctors there were only experimenting to cure. One day I got a telegram from New York offering to bring me to New York for treatment. Wow!) The Board kept touch on our health needs: economically we were adequately and comfortably cared for. Relationships were always open and supportive.[77]

The boards' dependable care and concern for missionaries as individuals and families were very important in sustaining missionaries as they served overseas.

When it existed, missionaries especially appreciated the pastoral support that they received from the designated "minister to missionaries." A number of PCUS missionaries specifically mentioned the pastoral care that they and their families received from the particular board person responsible for such a task. This intentionality of caring for missionary families fostered close relationships between the board and its missionaries. Of the former PCUS mission office in Nashville, one missionary wrote, "We knew all of the people in the office personally, and they cared for us, and they knew our children by name. We knew they would take care of our children when they came back to college."[78] Regrettably, not all missionaries experienced such personal investment and care from their respective boards. Moreover, many of those who did receive such care commented on the limited extent of the care over time.

Missionaries' negative comments regarding relations with their home boards mostly referred to the increased institutionalization, depersonalization, and general disconnect between the board and missionaries over time. Most of the comments regarding the increased institutionalization of the home board were directed at the changes that transpired after different boards unified.[79] Some missionaries succinctly stated their change in relationship as follows: New York: relations very good; Louisville: relations lukewarm to cool;[80] Nashville: personal and great; Atlanta: sometimes questionable; Louisville: cold.[81] Other missionaries explained the changing relationships in more detail: "Relations with the home board in Nashville were GREAT. As the church 'reorganized' several times, the relations definitely went down hill, . . . from warm and helpful and 'family' to institutionalized 'burden carrier.'"[82] Generally, missionaries from the PCUS who served long enough to relate to three different boards (Nashville, Atlanta, and Louisville) recalled the stark change from relating to the board like close family members early on to adjusting to the united board's "big business" mode of hierarchical layers of organization.

Moreover, the interim period between the formation of the PC(USA) and the complete joining of the PCUS's and UPCUSA's respective mission boards was hard on missionary relationships with the boards. Without the luxury of e-mail and faxing, it was hard for the missionaries to keep track of the many changes going on back home, let alone for the home board to keep the missionaries abreast of changes. One missionary recalled the many communication problems that she had during the transition period:

> They [the mission board] wouldn't answer telegrams or letters, and we felt very left out and unsupported. It was a very confusing time. There were two people in the same position—one was in New York and one was in Atlanta. The church leaders [overseas] were also confused; they didn't know whom to address for what. They thought they had the right person, but in many cases they didn't. Those years of combining the two boards were not easy.[83]

Another missionary expressed his frustration with a communication glitch between joining boards that resulted in the misallocation of funds that his family of six had specifically raised from U.S. churches. This missionary's family had raised money from their supporting churches for a family car. However, during the board's consolidation move from Atlanta to Louisville, the money was misdirected to a missionary in Africa. To recover the fund and buy their car, it took six more months beyond the time that it originally took to raise the money.[84]

Although missionary relations with the home board were especially strained during the boards' various transition periods, many missionaries also expressed feelings of general neglect and disinterest on the part of their board. One missionary expressed feeling like a "stepchild" because he never met the "home board," had few people from the mission board ever visit him overseas, and would only see national staff if he happened to be passing through New York or Louisville on his home leave.[85] Another missionary described his relations with the board as "extremely poor." His communication from the board in New York was usually information regarding changes in board office responsibilities, as opposed to queries into his or his family's life on the field. He described this neglect from the mission board thus:

> None of them, with the one sterling exception, . . . were interested in discovering who we were, what we were doing, what our problems were, or how we were surviving (this was felt keenly during high stress and civil war). The organizational structures left us in ecclesiastical limbo. We were neither consulted nor informed regarding the decisions made in New York, which controlled our lives. I survived by going underground, as it were.[86]

A number of missionaries expressed their disappointment in how the board would overlook its well-trained missionaries, never asking for their input, advice, or opinions regarding their work overseas. Instead, board officials would often deal directly with church leaders in their country of service. Some missionaries thought that such mission decision-making led to the type of paternalism that the board was trying to shed in its new day of ecumenical mission.[87] Missionaries wanted the board to listen to them when it came to matters that directly affected them and the country where they served. Their investments in learning the language, adapting to the culture, and building friendships were purposefully done so as to more effectively serve and more wisely make work-related decisions.[88]

Overall, relations with the mission boards can be summarized as mixed. On most levels, missionaries were grateful for the avenue for overseas service and the sustaining mechanisms that the board created for them; missionaries felt generally supported. However, it is also clear that missionaries bore the brunt of general, and surely unintended, board neglect during the decades of transitions. As the boards restructured, they seemed to grow increasingly pragmatic and decreasingly attuned to the particular nuances of mission work in the various countries and with various types of missionaries. Missionaries often had "fine" and "supportive" relations with their board until they made some type of decision that directly affected their work and appeared to be poorly thought through. In one case, a missionary couple had no complaints with their board until they were asked to leave the field just a few days before their pension would have been vested for ten years of service. Fortunately, the board listened to the couple's request and extended their termination date by one week so that they could have a pension.[89] In another case, a missionary expressed how much he, and the other missionaries with whom he worked, benefited from the "ideas and talk" from his board in New York, but how much the "rigid application" of policies across all mission fields hurt their work in particular.[90]

MISSIONARIES COMMENT ON THE FUTURE

When asked to comment on the future of Presbyterian mission, missionaries repeatedly raise two main areas of concern: the number of missionaries serving shorter terms of service, and the need for increased awareness of, and support for, mission in the Presbyterian Church. The invaluable perspective of decades of personal investment in the language, culture, and lives of others has given career missionaries great wisdom. Their experiences have taught them that time is needed to gain fluency in another language, to learn to how to appropriately relate with and gain the trust of people in another culture, to develop sustainable projects, to train local leaders and see the gospel transform others. A retired missionary said:

> One of the biggest problems of all is that the people are moving to only short-term service, and this does not allow for the learning of the language and culture. We must learn their language and culture to earn their respect and get to the heart of the people. I don't know if it is because of tight budgets or because people nowadays just don't want to stay for long periods of time.[91]

With drastically fewer missionaries serving long-term appointments overseas than sixty years ago, former missionaries long for the Presbyterian Church to regain its pioneering commitment to partnering with and investing in both churches and unreached peoples overseas.

Missionaries also believe that it is important to be telling the story of what we as a denomination are doing in mission. They see that local churches are disconnected with PC(USA) involvement overseas and desire for more mission awareness and involvement from Presbyterian congregations. One missionary expressed her disappointment at this lack of mission awareness as follows:

> Missions is not before our church today! We used to have mission conferences (I guess we still have the Westminster Conference in New Wilmington, Pa.); we had three thousand people every summer here in Montreat. The Presbyterian missionaries are needed to get back to our people, to let them be seen some way. The church cut back on bringing missionaries to Montreat years ago. We had the World Mission Building here, which housed conference offices and drew conferences in to purchase items from all of our mission fields in our international store.[92]

Some missionaries refer to the "minute for missions," a trite phrase symptomatic of a deeper general mission ignorance in the church. Retired missionaries joyfully recall their busy speaking schedules when they were on furlough back in the United States. They are thankful that the home boards so nicely arranged for them to speak at local churches when they were home. They enjoyed telling their stories and informing local churches about what "our church" was doing. Currently, however, missionaries regret not hearing about Presbyterian mission from their pulpits. One retired missionary at Westminster Gardens, a Presbyterian home for retired missionaries in Duarte, California, said that the only mission messages that he has heard are of non-Presbyterian missionaries. He believes that "people assume we are no longer in the missionary business. For the most part, they are not aware of Presbyterian missionary work. The average person in the pew is giving to mission causes, but not Presbyterian mission, because they do not know there are Presbyterian missions." Missionaries were glad to share their stories from overseas and found it a real joy to visit churches.

Today, missionaries still enjoy sharing their stories with others: stories of their call to overseas service, stories of their struggles to learn another language and adapt to another culture, stories of God's faithfulness, stories of their friends; stories of the miraculous works that they witnessed, and stories of people who changed their lives. Presbyterian missionaries are forever thankful to the Presbyterian Church for supporting them as they participated in God's mission to the world. They view their lives as being "a rare privilege" and "wouldn't have traded jobs with anyone in the world."[93] Their hope is that the stories continue to be told as the denomination continues to "empty itself" for the sake of God's global mission in a very needy world.

PART II
REGIONAL HISTORIES

Chapter 7

Latin America
and the Caribbean

FRANK L. ARNOLD

Latin America is a collection of nations, large and small, extending from the southern border of the United States to the southern tip of the continent of South America. The vast majority of its people are descendants of Spanish or Portuguese colonists who entered the region five centuries ago and of the indigenous people who inhabited the land before the colonists. A casual observer might conclude that the region was Christianized in the sixteenth century as a result of being colonized by devout Catholic nations, but legitimate doubts may be expressed as to how Christian it really was. After over a century of Presbyterian missionary involvement in Latin America, the international mission agency of the UPCUSA noted in its annual report: "A vast portion of the population of Latin America holds no real religious faith. The nominal creed is usually Roman Catholicism, but there are many millions who do not practice this or any other religious faith."[1]

Many in the region considered themselves to be Catholic simply because they were born in a Catholic country. However, a relatively small percentage of those who considered themselves to be members actually attended church. Protestantism made dramatic gains in the twentieth century. Although most of the adherents were from the ranks of the nominally Catholic, they were often more conscious of having come into a first-time relationship with Christ and his church than they were of having left one denomination to join another.

By the end of World War II, about 180 U.S. Presbyterian missionaries were at work in six countries in Latin America and the Caribbean, and the future seemed promising for indigenous churches in these and other countries in the region. The mission force had been depleted during the war years, but the cry for help was heard, and between 1945 and 1960, the missionary force doubled in size. The postwar task of these men and women was formidable: the reality they faced included an incredible gap in the distribution of wealth, with great majorities of the population of most countries impoverished. The UPCUSA's secretary for Latin America, Stanley Rycroft, pinpointed the challenge when he described Latin America as "a battlefield for men's minds in the midst of a social revolution."[2] The land was ripe for revolution, and it was no surprise that Latin America became the birthplace of what became known as "liberation theology," which stressed God's unique concern for the poor and downtrodden and counted both Catholic and Protestant theologians among its advocates.

The pioneer Presbyterians in Latin America aimed at establishing indigenous national churches. To do that, they followed the historic pattern of missions in the 1800s and established mission organizations that related directly to the home church mission agency.[3] After World War II, mission structures were dissolved to allow full sovereignty for the younger churches. Just how that happened is of considerable missiological importance and forms the common thread that runs through many of the individual stories that are the focus of this essay.

Presbyterian mission strategy shifted in the postwar years to that of improving the deplorable socioeconomic reality of many of the region's people. This led U.S. Presbyterian mission agencies to establish cooperative ministries in almost every country of the region, both with already-established denominations and with regional and international ecumenical organizations.

The Pentecostal movement entered the region in the early twentieth century, realized phenomenal growth, and triggered a renewal movement that significantly influenced more-traditional Protestants. In many Latin American countries today, Pentecostal believers account for over half of all non-Catholic Christians. In the postwar period, significant changes took place in the Catholic Church, including the rise of charismatic Catholic groups whose preaching and style of worship differed minimally from that of the Protestants. In most recent years, neo-Pentecostalism, with its prosperity gospel and a pragmatic approach toward attracting converts, has had great success.

We shall look at mission in Latin America and in the Caribbean wherever U.S. Presbyterians have been at work in the vast region, beginning with Mexico and going to the Caribbean, Central America, Brazil, and finally, Spanish-speaking South America. The amount of space dedicated to each country is roughly proportional to postwar Presbyterian mission investment in that country.

MEXICO

Mexico, the northern and westernmost country in Latin America, is the most populous Spanish-speaking country in the world. Colonized by the Spanish, it is predominantly Roman Catholic and has the world's second-largest Catholic population, although in recent decades, Protestant Christianity has experienced explosive growth. Presbyterians began work in Mexico in 1872, when the PCUSA began a ministry in Mexico City. They were followed by the PCUS in the following year. Each church set up its mission organization, but early on, they began to coordinate their work to minimize the complications of two American denominations working with one national church that was eventually named the "National Presbyterian Church of Mexico" (NPCM).

By the end of World War II, Presbyterian congregations were spread throughout the central and southern regions of the country, and the Mexican church had two synods with six presbyteries. It had its own seminary in Mexico City, plus four Bible schools. When the war ended, new missionaries began to arrive, and their force soon doubled.[4] The government, however, imposed serious restrictions upon the church and especially upon foreign missionaries. Foreigners were not permitted to perform duties peculiar to the clergy, such as baptizing.[5] They also were not permitted to be directors of schools or pastors of churches or even to celebrate Holy Communion in Mexican churches. There was considerable prejudice against Protestants in Mexico at the time, and missionary reports include documentation of acts of physical persecution.[6]

The Diamond Jubilee year of the National Presbyterian Church of Mexico was 1947, and it was celebrated with enthusiasm. The General Synod, at its 1941 meeting, launched a "Six Year Progressive Movement,"[7] culminating in the formation of the General Assembly in the jubilee year, when seventy-five years of Presbyterianism in Mexico was celebrated. The church was still not fully independent, however. This fact was recognized in the report of the PCUS Mission when it met the following month: "If the development is normal, the Missions, long before another seventy-five years have passed, will have withdrawn from Mexican church history."[8] In that same year, with the creation of the Mixed Committee of the Assembly, formed to study and make recommendations on the relationship between the church and the missions, another step was taken toward that eventual autonomy.

Centennial

In the decade before the 1972 centennial celebration, growth was slowed as problems arose with dissident elements in the church, and this lack of growth had to be dealt with.[9] Mission-church relationships were good, and progress was being made in passing control to the national church. Missionaries were involved in pioneering work, and although all regular schools were under Mexican leadership, missionaries provided direction for several Bible schools and participated in medical work at the following hospitals: Sanatorio la Luz in Morelia and Sanatorio de la Amistad in Ometepec.[10]

Along with the approach of the centennial of Mexican Presbyterianism came the realization among the cooperating agencies and the church itself that the nearly hundred-year-old NPCM was still not fully independent; included in the plans for the celebration was the termination of the old mission structures. Mexican church leaders, as well as the majority of the missionaries, thought that it was time for the church to be truly on its own and that the best way to bring that about was to call for a moratorium on North American help in the form of missionaries and financial subsidies. This action probably reflected the call for moratorium that came out of the Bangkok meeting of the International Missionary Council in 1975. No timetable was set for a return to cooperation; rather, it was thought that the Mexican church should make its own way and take the initiative that it believed was right.

A New Plan for Cooperation

Except for limited short-term projects conducted through ecumenical agencies, all grants from the U.S. churches were stopped beginning in 1973; the moratorium resulted in the Mexican church's financial independence and was deemed a "stewardship success."[11] In 1978, the General Assembly of the NPCM voted to reestablish a relationship with the American churches.[12] In the following year, a delegation from the Mexican church attended the joint General Assemblies of the Northern and Southern churches in Kansas City and presented a document that proposed a new mission relationship. The result was the formation of the International Joint Commission, which was to be a coordinating body for new mission partnerships. Its bylaws provided that all decisions would be made mutually and that neither church would make unilateral decisions regarding cooperative mission in the United States or Mexico. As a priority for the National Presbyterian Church of Mexico, the document highlights the planting of churches in growing cities along both sides of the U.S.–Mexican border, in state capitals, and in the centers of tourism. It acknowledged the work of Project Verdad (an already-established border ministry that was held up as an example of what could be done) and suggested that binational ministries expand wherever possible. Conspicuous by their absence were the old North American mission structures.

The Joint Commission immediately took action to implement projects of cooperation on the border between Mexico and the United States, which included the establishment of new congregations, principally in the Pacific region. Each program included both U.S. and Mexican codirectors, who were nominated by their respective churches and confirmed by the Joint Commission. Two missionary couples initially designated for work in the interior of Mexico were reassigned to begin border ministries. Some ten million Mexicans had immigrated to the border to work in newly established U.S. assembly plants, and new congregations quickly appeared.[13] The new form of cooperation was deemed a good approach to mission by all of the partners. Rev. Saul Tijerina of the NPCM wrote, "The National Presbyterian Church of Mexico dreams of having a very real presence on the border, with established and self-sustaining churches. It would like to see those established churches on the border, in partnership with the U.S. Presbyterian Church, respond to the pain the border causes, the damage it does to family, the vices it promotes: unemployment, illness, the exploitation of women in the twin plants, and lack of concern for the family's well-being. The constantly changing border population and the pain and sorrow of its people are, and will continue to be, a priority concern for the church—as they are to God and rightly so."[14] Tijerina's comments reflected the views of many Mexican leaders, although there were some others who wanted the cooperative projects to concentrate entirely on evangelism and the planting of new churches.

In the following years, several major border projects were founded. Among them were Puentes de Cristo (Bridges of Christ) in 1980 and Projecto Amistad (Project Friendship) in 1985. In 1986, the Presbyterian Border Ministry Corporation was formed and put in charge of fund-raising and fiscal oversight. The ministries became the recipients of a significant grant from the Birthday Offering of the Presbyterian Women of the Church, which was designated entirely for ministry along the borders. These ministries continue to be joint projects of the Presbyterian Churches of the United States and Mexico and seek to present a holistic gospel to those who live along the two-thousand-mile line between the two countries.

In 2000, the covenant between the Mexican and the American Presbyterian partner churches was reevaluated and, with minor changes, renewed for another twenty-year period, amid joyful worship and celebration.

THE CARIBBEAN

The island chain of the Caribbean, or West Indies, is the region of the Americas that lies to the east of Central America. The ethnically and religiously diverse region did not become a focus for Presbyterian mission concern until toward the end of the nineteenth century. Cuba presents the closest approximation to traditional Presbyterian mission work in the region, and today it has the region's strongest Presbyterian national church.

Cuba

Presbyterian work in Cuba began through the witness of Cuban Presbyterians and was supported in the late nineteenth century by the Foreign Mission Boards of the Northern and Southern branches of the North American church, which had sent missionaries to the island nation in the late nineteenth century. The Presbytery of Havana was organized in 1904 as part of the Synod of New Jersey, and in 1917, the work of the two U.S. boards was merged and came under the

PCUSA's Board of Home Missions. In 1930, the presbytery's name was changed to the Presbytery of Cuba.

By the end of the Second World War, the Presbyterian Church was a significant force in Cuba. It had some of the finest schools in the country, and the church included members of all classes of Cuban society.[15] When the Revolution under Castro came in 1959, it appeared to be too radical for many Presbyterians, and many left the island. It is estimated that by 1966, the church had lost half of its members and two-thirds of its clergy.[16] One mission worker, Ms. Lois Kroehler, remained in Cuba, supported by the national church. About her relationship as a North American with the Cuban people, she writes that they were "always friendly, even during U.S.–Cuba Government hostilities, . . . even during the Bay of Pigs invasion."[17]

The Presbyterian Board of National Missions decided to help and support both those who chose to leave and those who stayed. The presence of Cuban refugees in the United States presented a major challenge for U.S. Presbyterians and led the UPCUSA to organize a new department for Hispanic ministries. The UPCUSA and the PCUS worked together with other denominations through Church World Service to respond to the needs of the Cuban refugees.[18]

Although initially opposed by the Synod of New Jersey, the plan to form the Presbyterian-Reformed Church in Cuba (IPRC) was passed by the General Assembly of the UPCUSA in 1967, and the church gained complete autonomy. Responsibility for maintaining relations with the IPRC passed to COEMAR and later to the Program Agency of the UPCUSA. The relationship between the sister IPRC and the PC(USA) entered into a new phase with the advent of presbytery partnerships, the first one made in 1986 with the Presbytery of South Louisiana and the Presbytery of Matanzas. The IPRC has a General Assembly and eight presbyteries and continues to enjoy a close relationship with its North American sister church. It participates in the PC(USA)'s "Mission to the U.S.A." program and now has partnership relationships with eight presbyteries of that church.

Haiti

By government statistics, Haiti is the least developed country in the Western Hemisphere and one of the poorest in the world, with a turbulent history marked by numerous military dictatorships, political instability, and violence. For Christians with a compassion for the poor, Haiti is a field of opportunity, and it was just such compassion that brought Presbyterians to that country in the early 1970s, when a PCUS member on a visit was overwhelmed by the poverty that he saw and urged his church to do something about it. The PCUS Board of World Missions responded by sending Dr. and Mrs. Rion Dixon to work with a tiny medical clinic that had just been established by the Episcopal Diocese in Leogane, about twenty miles from Port-au-Prince. This was during the time of the moratorium in Mexico, and the Dixons, who had been serving there, were available. Other mission personnel followed, providing support for the Diocese's ministry in agriculture, medical care, and education. Later, the Birthday Offering from the Presbyterian Women of the Church was directed toward the building of the Hospital St. Croix on the site of the original clinic.

The medical work thrived, and the hospital began to send health-care teams out to the surrounding areas. Initially, staffing depended on visiting teams of physicians from the United States. These physicians would stay in Leogane for a week or two, coordinated by the Medical Benevolence Foundation of the PCUS, but over a period, changes brought in Haitians as hospital director and practically all of the staff. Agricultural training was begun, using specialized mission personnel, and the already-established trade school in Port-au-Prince was followed by another in Cap-Haitien on the Northern coast. Through a U.S. presbytery partnership with the Episcopal Diocese in Haiti, medical care, as well as schools and a goat husbandry project, were provided for some of the extremely poor inhabitants of the large island of La Gonave, just off the coast of Port-au-Prince.

The arrangement with the Episcopal Diocese has worked well for U.S. Presbyterians for about thirty years. The church-to-church relationship has been and is increasingly supplemented by the direct involvement of North American presbyteries and local church mission groups in that ministry.

Other Caribbean Countries

Many other Caribbean countries have Reformed churches today, including Trinidad, Tobago, Curaçao, Guyana, and Grenada. None of them are the result of missionary efforts of the UPCUSA or PCUS Boards of Foreign Missions working alone, however. In each case, as well as in several countries where there are no Reformed churches, the PC(USA) relates to national entities ecumenically through the Caribbean and North American Council for Mission (CANACOM).

CANACOM is a partnership made up of three North American denominations and nine Caribbean denominations that are committed to work together in mission in their regions. It purports to be both a facilitator and a collaborator in mission and has one staff person. CANACOM's mission statement commits the partners "to bear witness, to challenge and empower one another for creative involvement in mission."[19]

Of the older mission efforts in the Caribbean, Puerto Rico is in a class by itself with respect to North American Presbyterian involvement, since it has been a territory of the United States since 1898. The first missionaries arrived the following year, sent by the PCUSA's Home Missions Board. A few years later the Presbytery of Puerto Rico was organized as a part of the Synod of Iowa. Later it came under the Synod of New York, and by 2006 Puerto Rico had its own synod, with three presbyteries.

In addition to relating to Caribbean churches through CANACOM, U.S. presbyteries have become directly involved through partnership agreements. There are four such partnerships in effect with the United Church of Jamaica and

the Cayman Islands (UCJCI).[20] Many North American presbytery and congregational mission groups go to the islands every year at the invitation of local
churches there.

CENTRAL AMERICA

By the close of World War II, North American Presbyterians already had well over
a half-century of mission experience in Central America, all of it in Guatemala,
where the church established by early missionaries was about to organize itself
into a synod. Comity agreements made at the Congress on Christian Work in
Latin America, held in Panama in 1916, had restricted their efforts to that country. When attention returned to Central America in the 1970s, in part due to the
natural disasters that savaged the region in that decade, mission emphasis had
changed from the establishment of indigenous churches to ecumenical cooperation. One important ecumenical partner was the Latin American Evangelical
Center for Pastoral Studies (CELEP) and its Central American branch located in
Guatemala, known as CEDEPCA. CELEP incorporated a concern for the poor
and marginalized into its evangelical theological posture in harmony with concerns of postwar North American Presbyterian goals. It welcomed mission personnel into its ministry. Other avenues of ecumenical cooperation were made
through non-Presbyterian denominations and ecumenical agencies in Nicaragua,
Honduras, Costa Rica, and El Salvador.

Guatemala

Guatemala is the most populous country in Central America and is now its most
industrialized. It was at the center of the great Mayan civilization and still counts
over half of its population as indigenous. The Mission of the Presbyterian Church
dates to 1882, when John Clark Hill became the first Protestant missionary to
Guatemala. By 2006 the National Evangelical Presbyterian Church of Guatemala
(NEPCG) had a synod composed of six Spanish-speaking and twelve indigenous-
language presbyteries.[21] A major revolution in the country in the closing years of
World War II did not hinder, and in some ways furthered, the work of the growing
church.[22] In 1947, Presbyterians were involved in church planting, Christian education, theological education, and medical and agricultural work. Institutions that
they had founded included the La Patria High School and the La Patria school in
Quetzeltenango, plus a hospital in Guatemala City. The Maya Quiche Bible Institute was founded in 1941, to train indigenous leaders. Presbyterian mission workers were members of the PCUSA's Mission in Guatemala, and they worked closely
with and were voting members of the national church's presbyteries.

In 1950, the Synod of the National Evangelical Presbyterian Church of
Guatemala was established with five presbyteries.[23] The organization of the first
indigenous language presbytery in 1959 was a significant step in the church's life.[24]

Church growth continued at a rapid pace in the 1950s, and in 1954 the NEPCG constituted the third largest Presbyterian church in Latin America. Growth slowed somewhat in the mid-1960s, but it increased again after the earthquake of 1976. In 1957, the NEPCG celebrated the 75th year of the arrival of the first Presbyterian missionary to Guatemala. The report of the Board of World Missions of the PCUSA for 1957 noted that the church was still "Mission dominated." A major step toward changing that came in that same year with the setting up of a joint committee charged with the approval of budgets, the direction of the mission's institutions, and the assignment of mission personnel. That step soon led to the dissolution of the mission in May of 1962, after which mission personnel continued to work but now under the leadership of the national church.[25]

The little Presbyterian Church of Guatemala made a significant contribution to the world church when, in 1962, leaders observed that the residential seminary model for theological education was providing trained leadership for only a small portion of their growing congregations and preaching points throughout the country. Because few of these worshiping communities could provide adequate financial support for full-time pastors, they were utilizing homegrown, natural leaders. The NEPCG's seminary decided to create a new model, which they called "theological education by extension" (TEE). Faculty members distributed study materials to local lay leaders and then went out to meet with them in weekly seminars. The model worked and soon became known and was adapted for use throughout Latin America and then in other parts of the world.

In 1982, the Guatemalan church celebrated a hundred years of Presbyterianism, and by the end of that year, the last of the missionaries had gone, and the national church was in charge of its own destiny. The centennial celebration took place in the midst of ongoing internal tensions and in the context of a political scene marked by government oppression.[26] During this period of violence, Presbyterians were among the hundreds of thousands of Guatemalans who fled to the cities or across the Mexican border for refuge.

The Guatemalan church contributed a martyr to the cause of human rights in May of 1995, when an indigenous Presbyterian pastor and president of his presbytery's Human Rights Office was killed by a death squad. Because of continuing danger to his wife and family, a PC(USA)-sponsored team went to Guatemala to accompany them and the pastor who took his place. Most recently, besides the PC(USA)'s partnership relationship to the NEPCG, and in keeping with a general trend in the American church, twelve U.S. presbyteries are engaged in partnership pacts with presbyteries in the Guatemalan church.

Costa Rica

A Scottish Presbyterian has the distinction of starting the first Reformed ministry in Costa Rica when he arrived there in 1921. Rev. Henry Strachan founded churches that together formed a movement called the Association of Costa Rican Bible Churches (ACBC). Driven by the renewal movement in Latin America, seven of the churches in the Association left it in 1985 and formed the Fraternity of Costa Rican Evangelical Churches (FCEC). From its beginning, the FCEC has maintained close ties with other denominations and ecumenical entities in Latin America and throughout the world. In 2003, the FCEC voted to return to its origins and become the Costa Rican Presbyterian Church. Today, the Church has roughly nineteen congregations spread throughout five Costa Rican provinces.

American Presbyterians have cooperated with the Latin American Biblical Seminary in San Jose, especially in the formation of leaders. The institution began as a women's Bible school, but later it became a seminary, and today it is the widely respected Biblical University of Costa Rica. The university is known for its outreach program through theological education by extension and serves students in about nineteen countries in Latin America and the Caribbean, offering programs from lay training to master's degrees.

Other Central American Countries

The PC(USA) maintains partnership relationships in Nicaragua, El Salvador, and Honduras, despite the fact that there is no Presbyterian denomination in any of those countries that was founded as the result of PCUSA mission involvement. It was through disaster relief work that PCUSA cooperation was launched in both Nicaragua and Honduras, and more recently, in El Salvador.

The PC(USA) relates to Christians in Nicaragua, El Salvador, and Honduras with several partners and in a variety of ways. In Nicaragua and Honduras, where the Moravian Church has a strong presence, a relationship is maintained with that denomination, and mission personnel have been ceded to work with it. A Honduran partner is the Christian Commission for Development (CCD), an ecumenical group serving in the areas of development and emergency assistance, with headquarters in Tegucigalpa. The CCD also participates in the PC(USA)'s Reconciliation and Mission program, which invites partners from Central America to meet with U.S. Presbyterians, to listen to one another's stories and perceptions of the world and to reflect on them in the interest of reconciliation and the solidarity of the church.[27]

In Nicaragua, where the PCUSA responded to an earthquake disaster in 1972, the Council of Protestant Churches of Nicaragua is a major partner. Twenty-eight denominations are voting members of the Council, which acts as a voice for the evangelical community and promotes development and emergency relief work. It also coordinates the visits of Christians from around the world to share with and learn from Nicaraguan believers.

The PC(USA) partners with the Lutheran Church of El Salvador and, in community development work, with Alfalit.[28] It also relates to the small Calvinist Reformed Church in the country. The Self-Development of Peoples and the Presbyterian Hunger programs as well as the PC(USA)'s Reconciliation and Mission program all relate to Christians in El Salvador.

PORTUGUESE-SPEAKING SOUTH AMERICA

Brazil

The story of the involvement of North American Presbyterians in Brazil provides a classic example of how foreign mission from Western countries was done in the mid-nineteenth century. Early on, Presbyterian Foreign Mission Boards invested heavily in Brazil, and at the end of World War II, Brazil had, by a wide margin, more missionaries than any country in Latin America. Its mission history provides an excellent example of how the "younger churches" got their start, matured, and eventually became independent of the parallel work of the North American Missions. Just how that independence came about forms a major focus for the story of Presbyterians in Brazil since the Second World War.

Off-limits to Protestantism before 1810, the first North American Presbyterian missionaries disembarked in Rio in 1859, just a few years before the American Civil War. Ten years later they were joined by missionaries from the recently organized Presbyterian Church in the United States (PCUS), the "Southern Church." Although the missionaries coordinated their church-planting efforts, each denomination established its own mission. Through their efforts, the Presbyterian Church of Brazil (IPB) was soon established with the formation of the first presbytery in 1864, a synod in 1888, and a General Assembly in 1910.

In 1944, Presbyterianism in Brazil was stronger than in any other Latin American country, although it had suffered a major schism in 1903 when a group of leaders in São Paulo, unwilling to accept Freemasons as church members and concerned over missionary control of theological education, founded the Independent Presbyterian Church of Brazil (IPIB) with the intention of working apart from the North American missionaries.

By the end of World War II, the IPB was little more than a decade away from celebrating its centennial and was already planning for it in cooperation with the IPIB. There would be much to celebrate. The Presbyterian family numbered well over a hundred thousand communicant members scattered throughout each of the country's 26 states. In 1945, the 54 missionaries of the PCUSA belonged to the Central Brazil Mission, while the 52 that had been sent out by the PCUS were divided among the East, West, and North Brazil Missions. The working agreement then in effect between the missionaries and the national church was known as the Modus Operandi, or "Brazil Plan." Under its provisions, missionaries could not be members of presbyteries of the national church. They worked mostly in areas designated as "mission fields," with the understanding that the churches that they established would be turned over to the presbyteries as soon as they were self-sufficient. Missionaries were automatically members of the missions that were, in effect, parachurch organizations, composed entirely of foreigners.

The idea behind the Brazil Plan was that the Americans, with their access to financial resources from the United States, would reach out to the unevangelized areas in the South, West, and North of the country, while national church workers would work in the rapidly growing urban areas of the East. One problem with this arrangement was that it isolated the missionaries from their Brazilian counterparts, and they were thus only minimally aware of what was going on at the national church level. The arrangement also left big urban areas like Rio, Sao Paulo, and Belo Horizonte understaffed and unable to take full advantage of the opportunities to plant churches among the millions (many of whom were open to the gospel) now flocking to those burgeoning cities.

From the beginning, education had been a priority for the missionaries, and the "Protestant School" in Sao Paulo, founded in 1870 by PCUSA missionaries, became the Mackenzie University, the largest Protestant university in Latin America. At the time of World War II, theological education for pastors had long been under the control of the national church and was accomplished through the prestigious Presbyterian Seminary of the South in Campinas, and of the North in Recife. In 1946, the Bible Institute of the North in Garanhuns, Pernambuco, was inaugurated adjacent to the Fifteenth of November school, one of several large educational institutions founded by missionaries and still under their direct supervision. Already existing was the missionary-founded Edward Lane Bible Institute in Central Brazil; it had been furnishing lay leaders, who since 1932 were often employed as "evangelists."

The Integration Debate

In the postwar era, events in other parts of the world were having a profound effect on missionary-national church relations in Brazil. A strong push for "younger church" autonomy came out of the International Missionary Council meeting in Whitby, Ontario, in 1947. Foreign Mission structures were seen as obsolete, to be abandoned as soon as possible. This strategy was known as "integration," and it was adopted as the policy of the Board of Foreign Mission of the PCUSA. Integration ideology spread rapidly and soon became the subject of intense debate in Brazil. Many, however, including PCUS Board of World Missions officials, were not convinced by the arguments of the integrationists. The board opted to continue its policy of consulting with the missions in the fields, implying that those missions would be left intact. Integration was also opposed by many Brazilians, who feared that foreigners, operating inside their church courts, might exercise pressure to go in directions that were against their wishes.

Another issue affecting the IPB and its relationship with American Presbyterians and the worldwide church was the debate concerning the ecumenical movement. In 1945, the IPB elected to send delegates to the Amsterdam Assembly of the World Council of Churches.[29] Many in the church objected, and the resulting controversy led to a decision of the GA in 1950 to adopt the policy of "equidistance" between the WCC and the conservative International Council of Christian Churches, founded by maverick American Presbyterian Carl McIntire.

In Brazil, the controversy over integration soon focused on the Modus Operandi. The PCUS Board in Nashville defended its continuation, while the

PCUSA Board in New York pressed for radical change that would lead to the dismantling of the mission structures and the complete autonomy of the national church.[30] Most of the missionaries from both Northern and Southern streams were against integration. It appeared to them that the staff in New York had decided what was best for Brazil and was determined to put it into practice, whatever the cost. Many simply thought that the old mission structures were still needed to bolster a church that was not yet quite ready for full independence.

Pressured to produce a solution, the Modus Operandi committee, composed of missionaries and members of the national church, called for an inter-Presbyterian conference, with the participation of representatives of the IPB, both U.S. denominations, and selected missionaries. The conference, held in Campinas in 1954, decided to end the Modus Operandi and initiate a new kind of relationship among the partners that would be a transition toward the IPB's eventually having direct control over all cooperative work in Brazil. To this end, an Inter-Presbyterian Council (IPC) was created, with representation from each of the partners. Missionaries would not become members of IPB presbyteries, but the IPC would promote deeper cooperation between the Brazilians and the American missionaries and also serve as the agency to give direction to the work of the missions in Brazil. Though the New York Board's hopes for full integration were frustrated by this action, the IPC members clearly recognized that the future was going to be different from the past.

Everyone was agreed that the newly formed IPC faced an enormous challenge. Church growth had slowed, and a new strategy was needed. At its first meeting, the council approved a series of recommendations by the missionaries that was aimed at more closely coordinating their work and the work of the national church. Among the recommendations was the possibility that missionaries might be assigned to urban areas. Other actions, introduced by Brazilian members, directed that the churches in the fields under the missions send tithes of their income to the IPB's General Assembly, as did the churches under the presbyteries. The missions also had to submit their annual statistical reports to the national church. It was a modest beginning of what was to be the gradual relinquishing of the autonomy still held by the American Missions, although Nashville insisted on understanding the new relationship as a simple reaffirmation of the old Modus Operandi with modifications. The New York Board held tenaciously to its course. A major conference that was held at Lake Mohonk, New York, in the spring of 1956 called for full integration of all PCUSA missions within a period of five years.

A full ten years before the centennial celebration of Brazilian Presbyterianism, elaborate preparations were already under way, directed by a committee composed of members of the IPB and the IPIB. The occasion called for cooperation between the two churches, both of which considered their own beginnings as going all the way back to Ashbel Green Simonton, the first Presbyterian missionary. Ambitious goals were set, including that of doubling membership in the decade before the centennial. The missionaries contributed toward that goal when, in 1956, they turned over several churches that together formed the Presbytery of the Minas Triangle.

The Brazilian church had proved itself to be conservative, not only in missiological issues, such as its relations with the foreign missions, but also with respect to the great social issues of poverty and human need that were so prevalent in Brazil. Evangelism and church growth were given a high priority, and for some, they were the only priorities. However, the church soon engaged "liberation theology," which was beginning to take root in Latin America, in the controversy surrounding the work of a Presbyterian missionary named Richard Shaull, who was from the New York Board.

Shaull arrived in Brazil in 1952, after a period of service in Colombia, and began teaching at the seminary in Campinas. He questioned the idea that efforts at development could ever resolve the problems of Brazil's poor and suggested that only revolutionary changes could alter the unjust socioeconomic conditions under which they lived. Shaull gained admirers among the students and, not surprisingly, the displeasure of some leaders. He was asked to resign and left Brazil in 1962, just two years before the military takeover of the federal government imposed its own restrictions on those who, like Shaull, were perceived to be leaning too far to the left.

The postcentenary recognition that their church was now over a hundred years old was no doubt a confidence-builder for all of the members of the Brazilian Presbyterian churches. The IPB representatives on the Inter-Presbyterian Council were making even bolder proposals that were aimed at bringing the work of the North American missions more under the control of the national church. Some missionaries resented these steps as a growing intervention into what they considered to be their own sphere of responsibility, but the time for change had arrived, and its momentum was not to be stopped.

A major opportunity for Presbyterian mission outreach in Brazil presented itself in 1960 with the inauguration of the new capital: Brasilia. President Juscelino Kubitschek's bold initiative to move the center of the country's political activity from Rio to the high plains of central Brazil attracted an army of workers to build the modern city. They erected and lived in satellite cities surrounding the capital and were open to the message of the gospel. Growth was rapid when Presbyterian workers began a ministry there.

In 1963, the PCUS Women's Birthday Offering was dedicated to integrated ministry along the new highway that just opened between Brasilia and Belem, a large city at the mouth of the Amazon in northern Brazil. A number of missionaries moved to key areas around the southern and northern ends of the highway. They planted churches, opened schools and medical clinics, and initiated agricultural projects to minister to the tens of thousands of settlers moving into the virgin areas opened up by the highway.

In the meantime, changes were taking place back in the home churches. In 1958, the PCUSA phased out its Board of World Missions and placed both home and international mission under a new Commission on Ecumenical Mission and Relations (COEMAR). In 1963, after the lengthy and firm leadership of Dr.

C. Darby Fulton, the PCUS Board received a new chief in the person of Dr. T. Watson Street. As one of his first actions, Dr. Street called for a major consultation on partnership in mission and invited representatives from partner churches around the world. Its major conclusion concerning the relationship between the mother church in the United States and its daughter churches around the world was that "the structure of this relationship should be determined individually *by the national churches* in consultation with the PCUS."[31]

On March 31, 1964, an event took place that radically changed the political direction of Brazil and exerted a significant influence in the religious sphere. In a bloodless coup, the army overthrew the left-leaning government of President João Goulart and replaced it with a military junta headed by army general Humberto Castelo Branco. The new regime in 1968 instituted a series of draconian measures, including the infamous Institutional Act No. 5, against those who opposed it and those with real or perceived "progressive" political convictions (suspending civil rights such as habeas corpus). During this period the Catholic Church, traditionally aligned with the rich and powerful, became an adversary of the military government and, in some instances, found itself to be persecuted by the government. Also during this period, UPCUSA mission worker James Wright was invited by the influential archbishop of Sao Paulo, Cardinal Everisto Arns, to join a top-secret project of the archdiocese to document the abuses. This liaison resulted in the publication of the book *Torture in Brazil* in 1985,[32] the year that civilian rule was restored. Wright was personally motivated by the fact that his own brother, a former state congressman, had been abducted, tortured, and killed in 1973. The reaction of the Presbyterian Church of Brazil to the military rule was determined by the president of its General Assembly, Rev. Boanerges Ribeiro. Conservative both theologically and politically, Ribeiro set a narrow course for the church and took measures to eliminate his own opposition, especially in the seminaries.

Through its Monreat Consultation, the PCUS had opened the door for radical changes, and they were not long in coming. Many PCUS partner churches opted for a new relationship that eliminated the parallel structures of the American missions and integrated North American personnel into the national church. Although the Montreat conclusions applied to all PCUS partners overseas, the Brazilian Church made no move to eliminate the missions, although through its representation on the IPC, the church insisted on speeding up the process of transferring to its presbyteries the local churches considered to be under missionary control for too long.

The missions responded to their ever-lessening autonomy by restructuring. In 1965, the venerable North, East, and West Brazil Missions of the PCUS were replaced by a single organization called the Brazil Mission, covering all of the country. That was not enough to satisfy the PCUS Board, which was now questioning the legitimacy of a mission operating parallel to a national church. The missionaries could see the handwriting on the wall and pushed for the continuation of some form of missionary structure, but it was too late to stem the pressure now coming from both Brazil and the United States. The power and authority of the Brazilian church was increasing, while the mission's was diminishing. Without fanfare, integration, Brazilian style, was already happening.

Break with the New York Board

Within the PCUSA camp, changes were coming even more rapidly. In 1958, the PCUSA merged with the United Presbyterian Church of North America (UPCNA) to form the United Presbyterian Church U.S.A. (UPCUSA). The friction that had already existed between the PCUSA and the IPB was now intensified.[33] There had been serious differences between the IPB and its North American partners over the integration issue and the transfer to the IPB of educational institutions founded by the missionaries. But at the heart of the tensions were the basic issues of what should be the message, the mission, and the ecumenical stance of a church in the twentieth century.[34] The conservative Brazilian church saw itself as being much more interested in evangelism than its American counterpart, while the American church perceived the IPB as being much too complacent in the face of the crying social needs of Brazil's people. In addition, the IPB disapproved of what it perceived as the UPCUSA's too-cozy relationship with Catholics. The ongoing friction resulted in an almost total absence of mutual trust between the leaders of the two churches. A crisis seemed unavoidable.[35]

By the end of the 1960s, COEMAR had drastically reduced the number of its missionaries in Brazil, and in 1972 it dissolved the old Central Brazil Mission, setting up in its place the Brazil Advisory Committee. This meant, in effect, the end of the UPCUSA's mission structure in Brazil. The IPC questioned the new entity's eligibility to participate in the council, and the fragile relationship between the IPB and the UPCUSA was on the edge of collapse. In February of 1973, the executive committee of the IPB's General Assembly declared, in an article in the church's newspaper, that its relationship with the UPCUSA was terminated.

The PCUS Goes It Alone

The Inter-Presbyterian Council did not survive the break between the IPB and the UPCUSA. In the beginning of 1973, the IPB and the PCUS (its remaining North American partner) signed a bilateral cooperative agreement, to be supervised by a newly established Permanent Commission of Presbyterian Cooperation (PCPC), which was composed of members from both churches. While the IPB readily agreed to establish a bilateral relationship with the PCUS, it insisted on new rules, with important innovations. The bylaws defined the participation of the American church in cooperative projects in Brazil as "transitory" and that of the IPB as "permanent."[36] New was the right that the PCPC reserved for itself of initiating the process for the immediate transfer to the IPB of all remaining mission fields that were still under the control of the North American missions. The new bylaws prohibited missionaries who were members of North American presbyteries from becoming members of Brazilian presbyteries at the same time, and they also prohibited them from pastoring churches that belonged to IPB presbyteries. With the advent of the PCPC, what little freedom remaining with the missionaries became increasingly limited and quickly ended.

One of the provisions of the new agreement gave the missionaries special concern. The PCPB's bylaws contained a clause, placed there by the Brazilian delegation, that in the event of the union of either of the partner churches with another denomination, the agreement would automatically be rescinded. The Brazilians were quite aware that rapid progress was being made in the efforts to reunite the PCUS and UPCUSA and that the probability was high that a reunion would soon take place. In succeeding meetings of the PCPB, the changes leading in the direction toward total IPB control over PCUS missionary activities in Brazil became even more open and intentional.

By 1979, the General Assembly Mission Board (GAMB), which had replaced the PCUS Division of International Mission, was beginning to exercise its prerogative of choosing its own U.S.-based representatives to the meetings of the coordinating body in Brazil, rather than leaving that up to the missionaries in Brazil. The mission was now required to get GAMB approval for everything that it wanted to send to the IPB. The Brazilian delegates to the Permanent Commission were giving their attention to the last remaining areas of cooperation in which the national church did not have direct administrative control.

In 1980, the partner churches sponsored another consultation in Montreat, North Carolina. Delegates agreed that for cooperation to be truly mutual, it should include Brazilian participation in projects in the United States and give the church in the country in which the project existed full jurisdiction over every aspect of that project.

As the decade of the 1980s began, the Brazilian church was fairly satisfied with its relationship with the PCUS. There were no more missionary-controlled fields that were operating in parallel with the national church, and all mission personnel assigned to the IPB now worked with and under the direction of its agencies, although not within its presbyteries. The IPB exercised control over missionary assignments. All of the properties that once belonged to the missions or the U.S. church were in the process of being turned over to Brazilian ownership. For its part, the PCUS was disappointed that the IPB had shown little interest in developing a more holistic ministry to the poor and oppressed of their country. It cannot be known how this concern would have been addressed, because an unprecedented, though not unexpected, event was to abruptly end the relationship between North American Presbyterians and the Presbyterian Church of Brazil. That event was the 1983 reunion of the Southern and Northern branches of U.S. Presbyterianism.

1983 Reunion and the Camp Calvin Pronouncement

In the euphoria of the 1983 reunion of the two North American Presbyterian denominations that had been separated since the Civil War, few at the scene remembered—and probably few even knew—that at that same moment, the cooperative agreement between the former PCUS and the IPB had been revoked. In accordance with the PCPC bylaws, a meeting was called to be held at Camp Calvin in Atlanta to decide on the future relationship between the IPB and the newly formed PC(USA). The director of the Division of International Mission of the new church made it clear that he hoped for "an uninterrupted relationship with the IPB, with new goals and methods."[37] At that meeting, the Brazilian delegation's head, Rev. Boanerges Ribeiro, announced that the IPB did not wish to make a partnership agreement with the American church. The Brazilian leader spoke for himself, but he was unopposed by any of the other members of the delegation.

With one or two exceptions, the withdrawal of PC(USA) mission personnel from the PCB was completed in 1984, in accordance with the old agreement.[38] Some Brazilian leaders were upset by the break with the "mother church" and brought proposals for the reestablishment of the relationship to a vote at subsequent meetings of their General Assembly. A small but influential conservative group within the denomination opposed this, pointing out that the American church is a member of the WCC and claiming, inaccurately, that it ordained practicing homosexuals. Although PC(USA) officials have sought to maintain friendly relations with the IPB since the 1983 merger, the IPB's General Assembly has consistently opposed the restoration of a formal relationship.

New Partnerships Emerge

Though the relationship with the Presbyterian Church of Brazil was at an end, two newer Presbyterian denominations in Brazil arose to establish partnership agreements with the new American church. At the time of reunion, conversations were already being held with the smaller Independent Presbyterian Church of Brazil, and these soon resulted in formal church-to-church partnership relationships with the PC(USA). Another relationship was forged when a federation of churches that had left the IPB earlier decided to institutionalize themselves. They created the United Presbyterian Church of Brazil (IPU) in 1984. Its leadership expressed a desire to dialogue with the PC(USA), and a formal agreement came out of those talks. The IPIB and the IPU are today the PC(USA)'s two partner churches in Brazil.

A Mission Restored

As it turned out, the North American Presbyterian mission in Brazil had, after the rescinding of the agreement with the IPB, only a couple of years to live and was formally dissolved on December 31, 1985. The demise of the mission was not a direct consequence of the break between the IPB and the PC(USA), however. Rather, it was the entirely natural result of the intentional turning over of all its responsibilities to the national church. The PC(USA) General Assembly had approved the dissolution of the Brazil Mission before it knew that the IPB would choose not to continue in cooperation. The end of the mission came quite independently of the decision at Camp Calvin.

When representatives of the three partner churches met in 1989 to discuss strategy, a decision was made to resurrect the mission but with a slightly changed name and a different mandate. The mission's name was legally changed from the "Presbyterian Mission *in* Brazil" to the "Presbyterian Mission *of* Brazil" (PMB), and its members were not individuals, but the three partner churches along with "other Presbyterian or Reformed churches which come to associate with it."[39] It was hoped that the mission would be a vehicle for mutual mission in Brazil, although after a few years, the partners agreed that it was no longer necessary to their goals, and the PMB was formally dissolved in 2006.

Supported in recent years by the Outreach Foundation, which works directly with the IPIB in projects such as holistic evangelism in Brazil's Northeast and the Amazon, and bolstered by cooperative relationships with PC(USA) presbyteries, American Presbyterians continue to relate to the vibrant and independent Presbyterians in the land where their ministry dates back to the mid-nineteenth century.

SPANISH-SPEAKING SOUTH AMERICA

In Spanish-speaking South America, the PC(USA) continues to relate with partner Presbyterian Churches in Chile, Colombia, and Venezuela that its missionaries helped to establish in the nineteenth century.

Chile

Being a far southern country in Latin America did not prevent Chile from receiving the early attention of mission-minded American Presbyterians. Sent out by an independent board, Dr. David Trumbull arrived in Chile on Christmas day in 1845 and established a congregation in Santiago with a Presbyterian form of government. When the PCUSA Board sent its own missionaries in 1873, Trumbull's congregation became the first Presbyterian Church in the land. The Presbytery of Chile was formally established in 1889 and linked to the Synod of New York.[40] At World War II's end, the presbytery's work was focused on evangelism, education, and literature.[41] Twenty-four missionaries were working in Chile, mostly in churches that were planted in the North.

In 1944, the first of several divisions in Chilean Presbyterianism occurred when a number of young leaders, arguing that the presbytery had little interest in evangelism and was dominated by the foreign missionaries working with it, left to form the National Presbyterian Church of Chile.[42] Following modest growth in the postwar years, the Presbyterian Church of Chile was organized in 1964 with a synod and three presbyteries and became an independent, completely self-supporting denomination.[43]

Another split occurred in 1972, when the Evangelical Presbyterian Church in Chile (EPCC) was formed. It established a sister relationship with the UPCUSA. The Presbyterian Church in Renewal was formed in 1974,[44] taking with it nearly 70 percent of the membership of the Presbyterian Church of Chile. Since then, new denominations have been formed in Chile by Korean Presbyterians and by the Presbyterian Church in America. Presbyterianism has a myriad of expressions in Chile.

In recent decades, the Evangelical Presbyterian Church in Chile became a partner with five Chilean denominations in forming an ecumenical seminary, the Evangelical Theological Community of Chile. Although they built a seminary campus in the capital city of Santiago, theological education by extension was and remains an important feature of the project. The PC(USA) continues to cooperate as a sister church with both the Presbyterian Church of Chile and the EPCC in the seminary.[45]

Colombia

Located in the north of the continent of South America and with coasts on both oceans, Colombia is the continent's fourth-largest country. The PCUSA began its work in Latin America here in 1856 and became the first Protestant denomination to arrive in the country. The Presbyterian Church of Colombia (PCC) was a result of the early efforts of those pioneers, which included education and evangelism. In 1936, the Synod of the PCC was founded, and by the end of World War II, significant advances had been made. There were three presbyteries, and schools of distinction had been established in Bogotá, Barranquilla, and several smaller cities. At the end of World War II, the Presbyterian mission included forty mission personnel heavily involved in the education of the children of believers and the poor, literacy and literature work, agricultural ministry, and leadership training. A seminary had already been established.[46] The years immediately following the war also brought violent religious persecution to the Colombian church when the Conservative Party obtained control over the congress. Known today as *la violencia,* it was a time when churches were destroyed, leaders' homes were burned, Protestant schools were closed, and many were forced to flee for safety.[47] Lasting over ten years, the period also revealed the strong faith and courage of many Protestants. In one town, the local priest, jealous of the popularity of the Presbyterian school in the area, let it be known that every father who allowed his sons to attend that school was guilty of mortal sin, pardonable not even in death. Not a single student was withdrawn.[48] The period of extreme violence ended in 1957, when schools reopened and churches began to be rebuilt. Of this period, mission worker G. Lee Stewart writes enthusiastically about "seeing thousands of these people . . . finding a personal relationship with Jesus Christ through reading their Bibles and [hearing] my preaching."[49]

In 1950, the Evangelical Confederation of Colombia was formed and included Presbyterians, as well as other Protestant groups that had begun working in the country since 1856. The Presbyterian mission structure was still intact in 1955, but that year saw the "Plan of Integration," which gave jurisdictional responsibilities to the Synod. It also purposed to bring the mission's work entirely under the control of the national church within a few years. This was actually accomplished by 1959, and the mission was dissolved in July of that year, after over a hundred years of existence.

The centennial year of 1956 brought crowds to a big celebration, especially since it marked the beginning of Protestant work in Colombia, as well as the 100th anniversary of Presbyterian mission work in Latin America. Never a large church, in 1956, the Synod had some eighteen thousand members in twenty-three churches. In 1959, there were seventeen schools, the largest and most influential of them at that time being the Colegio Americano in Bogotá.[50]

The 1960s brought with them economic instability and political unrest, although the climate between Protestants and Catholics had improved.[51] A bold move was taken in 1982 when, following a regional consultation on theological education in Bogotá, the decision was made to create the Presbyterian Theological Seminary of the Gran Colombia in that city. The seminary was to provide theological education for candidates for the pastoral ministry, not only in Colombia but also in Venezuela and Ecuador.[52]

In the early 1990s, differences within the Colombian church threatened a schism, but it was narrowly averted with a 1993 decision to form two separate synods. The agreement commits each to respect the other and to cooperate in theological education, social service projects, and church celebrations. Today, the Presbyterian Church of Colombia has roughly fifty churches in its six presbyteries. Violence, in the form of reprisals against those whose lives are at risk because of their support for human rights, continues to plague the country, and a Presbyterian Accompaniment Program was established to demonstrate solidarity and to prevent harm to those at risk.

Venezuela

Of the major initiatives of the Presbyterian pioneer missionaries in planting churches in Latin America in the twentieth century, Venezuela was the last. It began in 1897 in Caracas, with the arrival of Rev. Theodore Pond and his wife. They had been transferred to Venezuela from the Colombia mission. While in Colombia, the Ponds had made contact with the newly converted Venezuelan family of Dr. Heraclio Osuna, who then returned to Venezuela and organized a small primary school before the Ponds' arrival. Today, that school is the Colegio Internacional de Caracas, a center of evangelical testimony as well as quality education.[53]

The El Redentor church was organized in 1900 in a location near the national capital in Caracas. However, educational work remained a major emphasis of the Venezuelan Mission, and only two other churches were established in the first decades of the twentieth century. It was not until the 1940s that mission activity moved out to the rural state of Miranda and in the 1960s to several states in western Venezuela. The production of petroleum for the United States during World War II made some observers believe that the prosperity that this brought was a contributing factor to making spiritual values of low priority among the people.[54]

Perhaps because church growth was slow, the missionaries in Venezuela were late in beginning to plan for the eventual autonomy of the church that they had helped to bring into existence.[55] In 1926, an effort was made by the mission to form a committee that included national evangelists to coordinate the work of the church, but reluctance on their part led to the postponement of the project.[56] It was not until the formation of the presbytery in 1946 that a start was made in the direction of national church autonomy. With the beginning of a national church structure, a Five Year Plan was put into effect in 1956, which included concrete steps toward the integration of the church and the mission. An "Integration Agreement" was approved in 1961, which included an affirmation of the autonomy of each partner church.[57] At that time it was agreed to implement a scaled reduction of support for pastors' salaries and other subsidies coming from the New York Board, with the expectation that financial aid would be ended by 1970.[58]

During its first half century of existence, the church's activity was limited to the capital of Caracas and the adjacent state of Miranda. In 1948, a missionary couple began an agricultural ministry in the Tuy Valley, forty miles south of Caracas, and a new phase in the national church's ministry was begun. Subsequently, new work was opened in Barquisimeto, Maracaibo, Punto Fijo, Valencia, Maracay, and Merida. In 1962, for the first time in its history, the presbytery met outside its traditional field of Caracas and the state of Miranda.[59]

In recent decades, the number of U.S. Presbyterian mission personnel assigned to Venezuela has declined, and no new personnel have been sent in the last decade. The Presbyterian Church of Venezuela now has two presbyteries, with about fifteen congregations. It is an active member and participant in the Association of Presbyterian and Reformed Churches in Latin America (AIPRAL).

Ecuador

There was never an attempt on the part of American Presbyterians to plant a Presbyterian denomination in Ecuador. Work in that country began in 1946 when Presbyterians from both Northern and Southern branches cooperated with the Evangelical and Reformed Church and the Evangelical United Brethren Church to form the United Andean Indian Mission (UAIM). Ecuador has one of the largest proportions of aboriginal peoples in South America, and the purpose of the mission was "to help the Indian enter upon his rightful inheritance, as a son of God, through an experience of the redeeming power of Christ."[60]

The work began with the purchase of a large farm in Picalqui, which was intended to be the focus of a holistic approach that would include agricultural demonstrations to help the poor farmers in the area, combined with education and medical ministries. Two missionary couples were working with UAIM in

1947. The first baptisms happened in 1953, and by 1960, there were four schools and eight medical stations, and the work had spread to other areas.[61] Growth was slow but steady, and in 1961, six missionary couples were assigned to the project. By 1963, the mission had recognized that the demonstration farm model was not the best approach and began selling plots of land at the Picalqui farm.

The following year, efforts began to establish a church among the converts. That was accomplished in 1965, when believers of the UAIM joined with the existing Church of the Brethren in Ecuador to form the United Evangelical Church of Ecuador (UECE). The church was recognized by the Ecuadorian government in 1967. It was unique in that the UECE was only the second church in Latin America and the Spanish-speaking Caribbean that was organized by more than one denomination. The church later reorganized itself as a Methodist denomination, and the PC(USA) presently relates to Ecuador through the Latin American Council of Churches.

Other Spanish-Speaking Latin American Countries

The PC(USA) also cooperates in mission with a number of South American churches that its missionaries had no part in founding. Presbyterian and Reformed beginnings in Argentina came through the efforts of Scottish Presbyterians, and in Guyana, Dutch settlers helped to found the Presbyterian Church. The PC(USA) has been a strong supporter of the multidenominational seminary in Argentina that is known as the University Institute of Higher Theological Studies (ISEDET). The university offers degrees in theology to students from many denominations in many Latin American countries. The PC(USA) partners with the Waldensian Evangelical Church of the River Plate (WECRP) in Argentina and Uruguay. For many years, the PC(USA) had a Young Adult Volunteer site in Argentina, which placed young U.S. Presbyterians with churches in Argentina and Uruguay, including the WECRP.[62] The Presbyterian presence in Paraguay is a result of Brazilian and Korean missionary efforts. In Peru, a PC(USA) partner is the Evangelical Presbyterian and Reformed Church of Peru, a union of two denominations with both Scotch and PC(USA) ancestry. The North American denomination relates to it through projects sponsored by the One Great Hour of Sharing, such as the Self-Development of Peoples and the Presbyterian Hunger Program, enhanced by the visits of many mission groups from PC(USA) congregations.

Since World War II, the PC(USA) has increasingly engaged in ecumenical cooperative programs and has assigned mission personnel to serve in several countries through organizations like the Alliance of Presbyterian and Reformed Churches in Latin America (AIPRAL) and the Latin American Council of Churches (CLAI). Through these organizations, it relates not only to the churches that its missionaries helped to found, but also to other denominations on the continent that are its partners today. In Guyana, where the Reformed presence dates back to Dutch settlers in the late sixteenth century, the PC(USA) relates to its three partners, all acquired since World War II, through CANACOM. Through

CANACOM, it also relates to Presbyterian Churches in Grenada, Trinidad, and Tobago and with the Protestant Church of Curaçao.[63]

The AIPRAL is a community of about thirty churches in eighteen countries, with a total membership of about 2.5 million. They are Congregational, Reformed, and United churches with roots in the Calvinist branch of the Protestant Reformation and include the Waldensian Church.

The CLAI is a broader ecumenical organization in Latin America, including in its membership not only churches of the Reformed persuasion but also Methodists, Pentecostals, and others. It was founded in 1982, inspired by the great gathering of evangelical churches that was held in Oaxtepec, Mexico, in 1978. CLAI has as its purpose promoting unity among Christians of the continent.

Bolivian Presbyterianism owes its origin to missionaries from Korea. The church in Bolivia has divided several times, and the PC(USA) partner has become the Independent Presbyterian Church in Bolivia, of more recent origin and unrelated to Korean Presbyterianism. The PC(USA) also partners with a network of churches and grassroots organizations known as Joining Hands with Peru.

Most of the ministry and programs that are sponsored by the PC(USA) through its partners in Latin America have been in the areas of theological education, higher education, human rights, and hunger-related issues. Evangelism and church planting have been carried out by the national churches for the past decades. The pattern of Presbyterian missionary partnership in Latin America is now one of working in specified areas of ministry as determined by national leadership, whether it be through one or more national churches or ecumenical partners.

Chapter 8

United States

God's Mission Field

PATRICIA LLOYD-SIDLE

In the decades following World War II, Presbyterians in the United States increasingly came to view Christians from Africa, Asia, and Latin America as equal colleagues in the body of Christ. "Mission on six continents" became a familiar phrase. Receiving and learning, as well as sending and teaching, were gradually accepted as key aspects of international mission. The Lake Mohonk Consultation in 1956 (PCUSA) and the 1962 Montreat consultation (PCUS) articulated and embodied this shift when leaders from the "national churches" met together with U.S. mission board leaders to make decisions together.[1]

In 1958 the Board of Foreign Missions reported that there had been nine "Fraternal Workers to the U.S.A." over the past five years, noting that the "Fraternal Workers to the United States program was proclaimed a priority at the Mohonk Conference." Serving in congregational, academic, or denominational staff positions for two or three years, these fraternal workers took "their places in regularly established patterns of work, living among the people and ministering to them." The report spoke of their impact:

> These men and their families who have come out of experience of spiritual encounter and suffering have brought a sharp understanding of the gospel for individuals and society today. They have laid bare the fallacy of our desire

for security and status. They have disturbed our relatively easy faith and comfortable existence, and have brought viability to the Biblical concept of confession and forgiveness, with all its personal and social implications.[2]

Developing leaders was a high priority for overseas national churches. Following World War II, the mission boards raised funds and developed programs to bring young leaders to the United States for education. In 1951, when Margaret Flory became staff for the newly created Office for Student Work of the Board of Foreign Missions, there were twenty-six international scholars from nine countries. While they were in the United States preparing for leadership in their home countries, they also participated in the life and ministry of U.S. churches. In the summer months they traveled extensively to camps and conferences, presbytery and synod meetings, General Assemblies, meetings of Presbyterian women, and ecumenical student conferences.[3] Both "Fraternal Workers to the U.S.A." and the presence of international scholars in church activities were precursors to the Mission to the U.S.A. program that came into being in the 1970s.

In 1968 the United Presbyterian Church responded to the national turmoil of racial tension and violence and the assassination of Martin Luther King Jr. by issuing a Macedonian call (Acts 16:9) to church leaders from other countries as well as to UPCUSA fraternal workers serving abroad. This cry, "Come over and help us!" was a clear statement of urgent need in the "mission field" of the United States.[4] Those who responded to the call were deployed around the country to put their specific skills and their international perspective at the service of the yearlong "Crisis in the Nation" program.[5]

MARGARET FLORY

Margaret Flory, an energetic, visionary leader in mission and ecumenism, served on the staffs of the Board of Foreign Mission, the Commission on Ecumenical Mission and Relations (COEMAR), and the Program Agency. Throughout her career she formed strong and lasting relationships and gave birth to numerous mission programs: Junior Year Abroad, International Study Fellowship for University Ministry,[6] Frontier Internship in Mission, Bi-National Service, Overseas Associates, and Mission to the U.S.A.

As Secretary for Student World Relations for COEMAR, Flory was deeply involved in the planning of the 18th Quadrennial Student Conference on Christian World Mission held in Athens, Ohio, in 1959. The conference theme, "Frontiers," reflected a growing consensus that mission frontiers were no longer primarily geographical. Large numbers of international students attended and made significant contributions to the conference. Flory played a key role in the subsequent quest to put the conference theme into practice, a quest that led to the birth of the Frontier Internship in Mission program (FIM). She developed and administered FIM from 1960 until 1974, when the program administration moved to Geneva, Switzerland.[7]

In the program's early years, most Frontier Interns were sent from and returned to the United States. The internships enabled them to experience the global dimensions of one or more social and political frontiers: crucial challenges facing the Christian community such as racism, militarization, human rights, displaced and uprooted peoples, modern secularism, and militant non-Christian religions.

BI-NATIONAL SERVICE

Bi-National Service emerged in part from a felt need of persons who returned to the United States after studying overseas or serving as Frontier Interns. During a 1968 sabbatical, Margaret Flory thought and prayed about "all those people coming back and wishing they could keep in touch with the place [where they had lived abroad], longing for community and ways to share what they had learned." She remembered: "One girl said to me: 'You prepared us very well to go away, Miss Flory; but you didn't prepare us to come home!'"[8] Flory returned from sabbatical to a newly created position in COEMAR, "Director of New Dimensions in Mission," and went to work on a proposal that was approved by the COEMAR board in June 1970, creating the Bi-National Service (BNS) Council.

Bi-National Service was a multilayered pattern of mission service that was often misunderstood. Bi-National Service was "a program for people who had lived and worked in a culture other than their own and are committed to the mission of the church in their promotion of global awareness, justice, and peace."[9] It provided an avenue of service for persons who were not, or no longer were, full-time mission workers and whose international experience and perspectives were not always welcome in their home church communities.

Clifton Kirkpatrick, director of the Global Mission Ministry Unit, recognized that "one of the great gifts of the Bi-National Service program has been to keep people who have global involvements and connections related to the Presbyterian Church (U.S.A.)." He believed: "This both allows the challenges and insights that come from their global involvement to shape the life of our church, and it allows our church to provide a supporting and nurturing network for people whose ministries are often on the 'cutting edge.'"[10]

During the first few years, Bi-National Servants were U.S. persons who had studied or served outside of the United States, many of them in ministries begun by Margaret Flory.[11] Bi-National Service decided to transform itself so that the community reflected its mission. Colleagues from around the world who had studied or served in mission outside their home countries were encouraged to apply. In 1981 there were 92 Servants from 39 countries.[12] In 2004 there were 136 Servants, 60 of whom were from countries other than the United States. Of those 60, some 45 were living in the United States and 15 outside the country.[13]

After twenty years, Bi-National Service began working intentionally to recruit or otherwise work with a younger generation. Several joint meetings were held with Global Mission Ministry Unit network of Diaconal Workers and returned Mission Volunteers during the 1990s. By 2004, a number of young adults had joined Bi-National Service.

Bi-National Servants made commitments to (1) maintain relationships with the persons and churches and institutions with which they had worked; (2) actively participate in faith and justice activities where they now lived; and (3) support the Bi-National community with time, talents and resources. Similar to a congregation, the service took place both when the community was gathered and when it was dispersed.

The decision to become a Bi-National Servant was not one taken lightly. There was an application process, a covenant, and a strong expectation that the commitments would be taken seriously: "Another unusual aspect was the covenant agreement made between the servant and the Council [on behalf of the Program Agency of the United Presbyterian Church U.S.A.]. The covenant may be for life, but usually it begins with a three-year commitment, renewed for five years, and so on."[14]

The first commitment, to maintain relationships with persons and communities in the other country/culture/region, involved various disciplines of communication, travel, and hosting traveling Servants and international visitors. One Servant couple disciplined themselves to live on one salary and save the second salary for giving away and for travel. Some Servants were professors, church leaders, or staff for organizations for whom these relationships were essential to their work. Others were ministers, artists, and activists for whom the ongoing global contacts brought important information and inspiration.

Second, all Servants were enriched and sustained by the international relationships and found a myriad of ways to share that with local faith communities and other grassroots organizations. "Participating in the life of a Christian community, preferably in and through a local congregation," was expected of all Servants. Third, Servants contributed to the Bi-National community by attending a Week of Work or a regional BNS gathering at least once every three years, submitting an annual report/reflection, and making an annual contribution based on one's financial circumstances.

There were also the annual gatherings of the BNS community. Called a "Week of Work," each gathering focused on a particular theme. Week of Work themes over the years reflected the urgent social and political concerns facing churches around the world: militarization, world hunger, interfaith dialogue, globalization, human rights, women in church and society, internationalization of mission, the environment, and many more. Approximately every third year, the Week of Work focused on a particular country or region outside the United States and was hosted by churches or church-related organizations in that location: (then) Czechoslovakia, Puerto Rico, Nicaragua, the Middle East, Geneva, India, and others.

Some years, the Week of Work resulted in a document or other global education resource, such as a paper on the "Globalization of Theological Education," a booklet on *Women in the Middle East*, and a resource for congregations observing the 500th anniversary of the arrival of Columbus, "Beyond the Columbus Myth: Indigenous Peoples, Justice, and a Sense of Place." On several occasions, the Week of Work was scheduled to coincide with a larger church conference— Global Village at Stony Point and Montreat's Global Mission Conference— enabling Servants to participate and provide conference leadership.

One year, the Week of Work was held in conjunction with General Assembly. On behalf of the BNS community, several U.S.-based Servants had worked through their respective presbyteries to send an overture to the 1997 General Assembly, proposing a three-way dialogue on social justice and the emerging global economy. The gathered Servants monitored the progress of the overture, which passed and led eventually to a three-country travel-study seminar and a publication, *Voices from Korea, U.S.A., and Brazil: The Reformed Faith and Global Economy.*[15]

MISSION TO THE U.S.A.

Margaret Flory credits the "hook and eye action of the Holy Spirit" with giving birth to the Mission to the U.S.A. program.[16] One day in 1973, two letters appeared on her desk. John Gatu, then general secretary of the Presbyterian Church of East Africa (PCEA), wrote to say that the PCEA wished to send a missionary to the United Presbyterian Church for two years. The second letter, from Hudson River Presbytery, requested help in locating an evangelist from an overseas church to work in the presbytery. Flory writes that she "was not only surprised but elated as [she] clipped the two letters together!"[17]

Mission to the U.S.A. assignments typically took place in a single congregation for a period of four to six weeks. Often they assumed the flavor of "mission interpretation," a time for learning about mission going on somewhere else in the world. Frequently, however, congregations moved to a deeper mode and experienced the joy of hearing the gospel message in fresh ways. Many U.S. Presbyterians found that their faith was renewed through prayer, Bible study, and interaction with a Christian colleague from abroad. Evaluation forms, articles, and reports on Mission to the U.S.A. are filled with enthusiastic comments similar to the one below, which reflects on a Kenyan pastor's presence in Wisconsin:

> Stephen Kariuki shared with us his faith. And that is beautiful! I'm not saying that we Pioneer Parish Presbyterians do not have a deep and lively spirituality. I am simply saying that we are not used to letting it show and we are too uptight to let it flow. . . . I believe that we could gain most from his visit if we remember his simple, free-flowing style in communicating his faith to others. For the Kingdom's sake—for Heaven's sake—let us no longer be embarrassed to express our faith.[18]

Some U.S. Presbyterians occasionally suggested that "third-world missionaries" could help "in new geographic and social settings in the United States,"[19] while Mission to the U.S.A. participants would express interest in having more contact with "the third world within the U.S.A."[20] On rare occasions Mission to the U.S.A. involved ministry with persons on the margins of U.S. society. For the most part, however, the locus of ministry was a particular Presbyterian congregation, its members and activities.

In a very real sense, Mission to the U.S.A. was a program of congregational transformation. It functioned best when the immersion methodology was followed and less well when the Mission to the U.S.A. participant divided his or her time between a number of congregations. Time spent together allowed relationships to develop, which in turn allowed for grace-filled encounters, according to a report on a 1980 Mission to the U.S.A. project that brought 16 "ecumenical ministers" from the Caribbean, the Middle East, India, and East Asia to the Pittsburgh Presbytery. Entitled "Our Learnings Come through Encounter," it reported that "the American Christians came to know and to cherish new special relationships across cultural barriers. [The program] was based on a giving-receiving ministry to enable sharing of life and faith across geographical boundaries through face-to-face encounter."[21]

The number of Mission to the U.S.A. assignments fluctuated from fewer than twenty to as many as seventy per year. Research for a 1992 program evaluation found that there had been a total of 513 Mission to the U.S.A. participants during 1980–91.[22] Other statistics for 1980–91[23] and for 1995–2001[24] tell more of the story:

1980–91 MUSA participants by gender	*1980–91 MUSA participants as clergy/lay*
Male: 351, or 68.5% of total	*Clergy*: 294, or 57.5% of total
Female: 162, or 31.5% of total	*Lay*: 42.5% of total
	(Most from churches with Presbyterian form of government were ordained elders.)

MUSA personnel by region	*1980–91*
Southern Africa	47
East-West Africa	45
East Asia/Pacific	78
Southeast Asia	36
Middle East/Southern Asia	91
Central America/Caribbean	79
South America/Mexico	42
Europe	82
China	7
Native America	2
USSR	4

MUSA assignment by synod	1980–91
Alaska/Northwest	18
Covenant	94
Lakes and Prairies	42
Lincoln Trails	7
Living Waters	16
Mid-America	8
Mid-Atlantic	25
Northeast	98
Pacific	23
Puerto Rico	0
Rocky Mountains	1
South Atlantic	5
Southern California/Hawaii	28
Southwest	12
Sun	11
Trinity	125

COUNTRY/REGION	1995–96	1996–97	1997–98	1998–99	1999–2000	2000–2001
Southern and East Africa	11	5	1	4	13	2
Central and West Africa	3	3	1	7	4	3
East Asia/Pacific	0	3	1	2	4	5
Middle East and Southern Asia	3	15	4	7	8	5
South America	2	13	9	6	2	2
Central America/Caribbean/Mexico	10	11	7	15	1	22
Europe	6	9	12	16	7	8
Congo	0	0	1	1	0	0

SYNOD	1995–96	1996–97	1997–98	1998–99	1999–2000	2000–2001
Alaska-Northwest	0	1	0	1	5	3
Covenant	7	12	12	14	12	10
Lakes and Prairies	5	17	4	15	1	12
Lincoln Trails	0	0	0	0	2	0

(continued)

SYNOD	1995–96	1996–97	1997–98	1998–99	1999– 2000	2000– 2001
Living Waters	1	3	0	1	0	1
Mid-America	2	0	0	2	2	0
Mid-Atlantic	2	3	2	4	4	3
Northeast	0	6	1	3	5	10
Pacific	3	1	1	1	0	2
Puerto Rico	0	0	0	0	0	1
Rocky Mountains	0	0	8	0	0	0
South Atlantic	4	3	0	5	3	2
Southern California/Hawaii	0	0	3	2	1	0
Southwest	6	4	1	0	0	1
Sun	5	3	1	8	6	2
Trinity	7	5	3	4	0	0
GA (Louisville)	2	1	1	1	3	2

	1995–96	1996–97	1997–98	1998–99	1999– 2000	2000– 2001
TOTAL MUSA PARTICIPANTS	35	59	36	58	39	47

Mission to the U.S.A. always involved a partnership between three entities: the General Assembly, the receiving congregation or other church entity, and the overseas partner church. During the 1970s and well into the 1980s, the role of General Assembly staff was essential for making contact with partner churches, maintaining communication, and handling international travel arrangements. Cultural and technological shifts changed that. By the 1990s, presbyteries and congregations were increasingly taking the initiative for planning and implementing the logistics of Mission to the U.S.A. (and other international mission endeavors). General Assembly staff focused more on education for mission, especially as it related to the third entity in the Mission to the U.S.A. program: the overseas partner church. For many congregations, this was their first experience of cross-cultural partnership in mission.

By the early 1990s there was sufficient mission-receiving activity in mainline denominations to warrant the formation of an "Ecumenical Working Group on Mission to the U.S.A. and Canada." The Working Group concentrated on the preparation and care of persons from other parts of the world who were living and working in North America. It published an orientation guide,[25] portions of which were translated into several languages. It also sponsored several ecumenical consultations for global partners engaged in ministry in the United States or Canada. The PC(USA)-sponsored participants in these consultations were not, for the most part, persons serving a typical six-week MUSA assignment. Rather, they were among the small number of MUSA participants who served one, two, or three years in language-specific New Church Development assignments, teaching positions, or adjunct staff positions in a presbytery, synod, or the General Assembly.

During the 1990s, the Mission to the U.S.A. office of the PC(USA) established a Mission Partner in Residence program through which an overseas partner church was invited to send someone to serve the PC(USA) for one year. The program concept was developed in conjunction with the United Church of Christ of the Philippines (UCCP), which had a well-articulated theology and policy of mission partnership, as well as significant experience in sending and receiving persons in mission.[26]

The first Mission Partner in Residence was sent by the UCCP in 1992–93. Subsequent Mission Partners came from the Presbyterian Church of Ghana, the Church of South India, the Myanmar Institute of Theology, the Independent Presbyterian Church of Brazil, the Evangelical Church of Czech Brethren, the Indonesian Christian Church of West Java, the Evangelical Presbyterian Church, Ghana, and the Evangelical Lutheran Church in Jordan and the Holy Land.

Mission Partners in Residence were based in the denominational offices in Louisville and provided leadership for mission personnel orientations and reentry events, for mission conferences and other churchwide conferences. They traveled to presbyteries, synods, and congregations to speak, preach, and teach. Depending on particular skills and interests, they became part of the staff team in one or more General Assembly offices. As with all Mission to the U.S.A. assignments, the details of the assignments were less important than the new perspectives gained, the love shared, and the bonds forged in Christ's name.

The Reverend Thomas John of the Church of South India used the term "reflective presence" to describe his role as a missionary to the United States and to the Presbyterian Church. "In a community where men and women are struggling to fulfill their public responsibilities, within a highly bureaucratic and technological system we need a reflective presence—a 'question-putter'—to probe large visions."[27]

Dr. Anna May Say Pa of Myanmar (Burma) told stories from her country and context as she preached and taught Bible.

> One of the evangelists sent to the Dhai people [by the Presbyterian Church of Myanmar] was a woman named Pi Liankimi. Deeply moved by the plight of the babies, she went from village to village teaching that as all babies are gifts of a gracious God who loves all people, a baby should never be abandoned. Many Dhais became Christian, and in Christian villages the custom is banned.[28]

These question-putters from around the world caused discomfort at times, and the storytellers often surprised their listeners. But hearts and minds opened more easily because the questions and the stories came from warm, gracious, deeply committed brothers and sisters in Christ.

LIVING LINKS

In a 2004 interview, Margaret Flory referred to Bi-National Servants as "living links between cultures and churches."[29] On another occasion she referred to the international students she had known early in her ministry as

> living links between their churches and ours, returning from time to time to participate in crucial projects and events, such as the Advisory Study and the Crisis in the Nation program, and renewing their ties at the General Assemblies when they later came as delegates of their churches. Now . . . they have been coming back under the Mission to the U.S.A. program as missionaries to us.[30]

Both Bi-National Service and Mission to the U.S.A. began at a time when many Presbyterian missionaries were ending their service as part of an effort to give national churches more opportunity to develop their own identity and leadership. Relationships between the churches in the United States with churches elsewhere in the world, always carried in significant ways by U.S. mission personnel, began to be carried in new ways as well. At the same time that there were losses in relationships with fewer missionaries in place, the increased number of overseas Christians visiting U.S. churches through Mission to the U.S.A. and the nurturing of community through Bi-National Service created many new opportunities for global connections.

Mission to the U.S.A. was designed to foster relationships. It was not to be "a visitation but a living-in-the-midst-of approach, which involves listening, learning, and receiving on the part of American Christians and their congregations."[31] Bi-National Service, too, was primarily about relationships between Christians on six continents. Each individual Bi-National Servant maintained relationships with Christian colleagues in the country or region where they had served. Further, the Bi-National Servant community itself was composed of Christians from various parts of the world.

Reconciliation and Mission (R&M), a mission personnel program founded in 1992, combined the two approaches: formation of a mission community and the "living-in-the-midst-of approach." Reconciliation and Mission was jointly designed and administered by a commission of persons from Central American churches (and later, the Presbyterian Church of Mexico) as well as the PC(USA). A one-year program, R&M brought together Central American and U.S. Christians for an initial period of cross-cultural learning, language study, and biblical reflection on reconciliation. The community formed during this four- to six-week period was maintained during the year by the sharing of monthly written reflections and a final gathering for debriefing. During the year each Central American joined in the ministry of a particular congregation, while each U.S. participant did the same in Central America or Mexico.

In a study paper that accompanied the 2003 policy statement, "Presbyterians Do Mission in Partnership," Philip Wickeri, Professor of Evangelism and Mission at San Francisco Theological Seminary, lifted up Thai theologian Koson Srisang's concepts of "incarnational solidarity" and "friendship."[32] This is not, Wickeri argues, "simply a new way of speaking about partnership in mission. It has a structural dimension for which a renewed commitment to the gospel message and new disciplines of thought and action are required."[33]

Through the living links forged by Bi-National Service, Mission to the U.S.A., and Reconciliation and Mission, thousands of U.S. Presbyterians formed deep cross-cultural friendships, received fresh insights and hope, and renewed their commitment to the community that is Christ's body in the world. Mission to six continents, as we can see, was also being forged in the North American context, through different programs.

Chapter 9

East Asia

Destructions, Divisions, and Abundance

SCOTT W. SUNQUIST

ASIA AWAKES

Few people writing about East Asia in the aftermath of Japanese aggression and then atomic destruction would ever have guessed that by the turn of the century, East Asia would be the place of greatest economic growth. It is also doubtful that any of our missionaries, imprisoned by the Maoists in China, or accused of embezzlement or spying (two of the most common accusations), would have predicted Christianity's present vitality and growth. For America, the Pacific War was a three-year war, but for Korea and parts of China, it was a half-century war of Japanese colonial expansion in East Asia. By the time Japan was defeated, most of East Asia had been humiliated by Japan, and rebuilding economies and societies seemed to be a nearly hopeless prospect. Colonial powers held on for a while, but the shock of Asian imperialism dislodged the British, Dutch, and French from most of their holdings. The rise of a new force, Asian communism, created new global relationships and new religious and political tensions. The transformation of East Asia was sudden. Within two decades of the close of the Pacific War, most Asian countries had become independent and communist, or were reasserting their religious heritage of Buddhism or Islam. As the chart at the end of this chapter indicates, most of these countries went through transitions of government, ideology, and economy within fifteen years of the defeat of Japan.

Although Presbyterian missionary work was not in every one of these countries, the regional changes had international consequences. For example, the Maoist "liberation," as it is called in China, created an international communist militant movement throughout southeast Asia. The communist threat was felt by governments in the Philippines, Vietnam, Korea, Cambodia, Laos, Malaysia, Indonesia, and Taiwan. Their responses had an impact upon missionary work and upon the development of Christianity in the region. In Indonesia, the communist-led aborted coup led to government regulations requiring all citizens to register as one of five "theistic" religions. Many Indonesians registered themselves as "Christian," finding this designation the most appealing in light of the communist attacks. In this context, the 1960s in Indonesia mark a period of rapid Christian growth. The presence and activities of the U.S. government and military both opened and closed doors for missionary work and ecumenical relationships. The long-term American military presence in the Philippines was a hindrance, but other countries (Malaysia, Singapore, Indonesia) recognized some of the importance of American presence in the region for political stability.

Our Presbyterian missions, from the PCUS (Southern) and the PCUSA (Northern), worked in China, Korea, the Philippines, Taiwan, Hong Kong, Japan, Thailand, and to a much-smaller extent, in Indonesia, Malaysia, and Singapore. The original "fields" were China, Korea, Japan, Thailand, and the Philippines. Compared to Presbyterian missionary work in Africa and Latin America, work in East Asia, except for Thailand, came relatively late in the modern missionary movement. Vietnam, Laos, and Cambodia were colonized by French Catholics, the Philippines were held by Spanish Catholics, the East Indies were colonized by the Dutch, and Malaya by the British. China, Korea, and Japan were the last countries to open up to Western commerce and missionaries. When these countries did sign treaties to open their ports for trade, it was often at the end of a rifle that they did so. British gunships opened treaty ports in China beginning in 1842, and Commodore Perry's imposing new steamship made quite an impression on the waning Tokugawa shogunate in 1853. The more resistant Koreans did not sign a treaty until 1882. Both Korea and Japan were opened to the West by treaties with the United States. Thus, the main work of Presbyterians in the region (except for Thailand) was from the 1860s until the 1960s: about one hundred years. In China, the main Presbyterian work was from the 1860s until the end of the War of Japanese Aggression, about eighty years.

One of the most striking patterns that shaped our missionary involvement in East Asia during this period was warfare. When we begin, in 1944, the Pacific War was coming to a close. But without any time to reimagine mission in the post-Japanese imperialist era, ongoing war boiled over in China. Korea turned into a country splashed with blood and refugees. The same ideology that was driving war in China and Korea was also creating conflict in Vietnam; in fact Communist insurgents were active throughout southeast Asia through the 1970s. As a result, Presbyterians both directly and through cooperative agencies became heavily involved in such ministries as food distribution, building quick housing, ministry to prisoners of war, and chaplaincy training. The Mission Board reports from 1944 through the 1950s always show much discussion of responding to the ravages of war.

In this chapter we will trace what we can of the lines of Presbyterian missional involvement in East Asia during this turbulent time. We have already seen something of the tremendous changes that were taking place in the ecumenical church, missional theology, and the structures of the Presbyterian Church(es). Here we will look at the development of Presbyterian mission thought and practice in East Asia. Our approach involves looking at the annual reports to the General Assemblies, (when possible) the statistics on missionaries and moneys spent, denominational magazines,[1] missionary books and pamphlets, and results from our missionary surveys and interviews. In general, these provide three angles of vision: denominational records, popular publications, and missionary voices. All records are somewhat incomplete (annual reports are not consistent in what they report), and yet we do trace a basic story line of Presbyterian missionary accomplishments and priorities.

SHIFTING PLACES, CHANGING PRIORITIES

Before looking at each of the countries, some general comments and observations may help to give a picture of the sixty years. This period saw a great reduction in the number of mission personnel working in East Asia, but also a diversification of these smaller numbers. In 1944 there were well over 600 Presbyterian missionaries working in East Asia, the largest number (about 330 for the PCUSA and 138 for the PCUS) still working in China. By 1954 there were about 333; none of these were now in China, but new areas of ministry opened up: Taiwan, Hong Kong, and Indonesia. In 1979 there were 100 missionaries in East Asia (with 2 each in Singapore and Malaysia), and this number remained unchanged for a decade. In 2007, the PC(USA) had 45 mission coworkers placed in East Asia, and 16 of these were in Japan, many teaching English. There are fewer than 6 missionaries working in each of the following countries: Singapore, Indonesia, Hong Kong, Taiwan, Philippines, and Korea. About 10 work in Thailand. In addition, there are many Presbyterians teaching at various universities and normal schools in China, through the Amity Foundation, bringing the total Presbyterian presence in East Asia to just under 70 in 2007. Thus, a smaller Presbyterian presence is more geographically diverse than in the past.

A second general shift is in the type of work being done. After the Pacific War and the Korean War, there was a great demand for medical doctors and nurses, as well as for architects, builders, evangelists, and educators. Presbyterians still sent some evangelists and church planters, but much of our work involved responding to the great human need in postcolonial East Asia. As local medical people were trained, largely through hospitals (established and redeveloped by people like Paul Crane, David Seel, and Howard Moffett in Korea and Marshall Welles in Thailand) there was less of a need for medical personnel from the West. In the aftermath of the December 26, 2004, Indian Ocean tsunami, for example, thousands of medical personnel from East Asian nations responded immediately, many of them trained in hospitals and schools established by missionaries. Presbyterians also provided help and relief for young abandoned girls who were caught up in prostitution in Korea. In the early 1960s, three houses were established (Grace, Hope, and then Faith) to take in, educate, and help to relocate these young prostitutes, often only eleven or twelve years old. The largest single occupation of Presbyterian missionaries in East Asia is teaching English. East Asia has been going through an economic miracle, and one important dimension to that economic development is access to knowledge, which requires language facility. Especially in China and Japan, but also in Thailand and the Philippines, there is a great demand for "native" English teachers. Presbyterians also respond to requests for theological educators and other specialty teachers (agriculture, music, and so forth).

A third major shift, reflected in all of the Presbyterian work during this period, was the movement, sometimes more carefully syncopated than at other times, of transferring all leadership to the national church. There is universal respect for the consistency with which the Presbyterian Church stood for this principle of indigenous leadership. Many of our missionaries, when asked what they learned from other missions and other churches in Asia, often remarked that they learned that they were glad they were working with a mission having a healthy regard for national leadership. This is not to say that the method and timing of this transfer of leadership and resources was universally agreed upon. Some of the major tensions in Presbyterian missions in East Asia revolved around the question of what new role, if any, there would be for Presbyterian missionaries. The tension was expressed well in a 1967 article on Thai leadership in *Presbyterian Life:*

> The American fraternal worker who is in charge of a congregation in Thailand is now the exception, and will continue to be so. . . . There are some in Asia who feel that "American mission boards should think twice before sending American church workers to Asia, and then think again. . . . Yet Thai Christians and American fraternal workers alike view with alarm what they see [as] the tendency of American Presbyterian Church officials to cut down on the number of fraternal workers available—and the concomitant tendency on the part of American church goers to limit their giving on the theory that missionaries are obsolete. [However] thus far, the national structure of the church is not self-supporting.[2]

On the one hand, many missionaries had a difficult time leaving after a large Presbyterian presence had been a historic part of the church. On the other hand, in many countries the local leadership was still very "thin," and the institutional development was very large, and so the transfer was much more complex. Still, the clear message was that national churches were in charge. They would decide on what missionaries were needed for their churches, hospitals, schools, and national church offices. By the middle of the 1970s, most of this transfer had taken place, but the path was not smooth. A number of missionaries, both out of a positive conviction and out of frustration and despair over what they saw as a misguided policy, decided not to return when on furlough during the 1960s and 1970s.

A fourth major shift that has taken place in our global mission but has been especially pronounced in East Asia is the move from long-term (career) missionaries to short-term service. Traditionally, before the end of the 1950s, all missionaries were expected to arrive overseas before they were thirty-five years old, so they could learn the language, learn the culture, and serve a number of decades. In the middle of the 1950s, it was recognized that many of the responsibilities that missionaries originally carried out could now be transferred to local church leaders. The understanding began to develop in the home boards that "mission on six continents," and mission in ecumenical partnership, meant a new pattern of "missionary as short-term specialist." The 1956 report to the General Assembly from the PCUSA Board of Foreign Missions reported: "The day is past when a Christian worker from a foreign country settles down into a certain location and spends his missionary life there. He goes instead where there is an urgent need for his particular capabilities, and after consultation and study with responsible . . . church leaders."[3] Many of our missionaries now come as short-term consultants—helping with library development, financial planning for large institutions, new medical procedures, linguistics—they do a job and then leave. This was meant to provide better coordination and planning with local church leaders, but it has also meant that Presbyterians seldom learn the local language and culture. Missionary work is less of a life's vocation and more of a hired adviser. Retired missionaries commented that we no longer have groups of people in different countries who have "taken on" or "entered into" the local cultures and become comfortable enough to both challenge and fully participate in the local ministry.

Finally, and this is no surprise to anyone who has traveled much in East Asia, the economic boom has meant that mission work is much more costly than it used to be. It has been difficult to consider placing missionaries in Japan unless they are teaching at a local university and receiving a salary from that university. Korea, Taiwan, Singapore, and Hong Kong are more expensive to live in than most cities of the United States. What does it now mean to do "mission" work in countries which are just as technologically advanced and more economically heated than most of America? Missionaries in Tokyo live like pastors in Atlanta or like professors in New York City, only it costs a lot more to live there. Patterns of support and patterns of service have changed with the changing economies and advancing technologies of East Asia. We turn now to look briefly at the major areas where Presbyterians have labored since the Pacific War.

CHINA

Presbyterian missionary work in China began with the conclusion of the First Opium War in 1842. Rev. Walter M. Lowrie arrived in Macau in 1842 and Rev. and Mrs. Thomas L. McBryde arrived the following year after burying their infant child in Singapore. The McBrydes left for health reasons soon after they arrived, but in 1844 Presbyterian work began in a great flurry with the arrival of eleven new missionaries and the opening up of mission stations in Xiamen (Amoy), Ningbo, and Guangzhou (Canton). China was soon to become the largest of the Presbyterian mission fields, with eight different missions throughout the country, a budget of over $700,000, and 350 missionaries at the time of Japanese invasions in 1937. Presbyterian work in China was like a major international corporation with 49 hospitals and 101 schools,[4] all of which were founded between 1861 and 1924.[5]

Although Presbyterian work in Korea[6] and Japan was much curtailed by the Japanese rule, work in China moved along apace until the Japanese turned their guns on China, beginning in 1937. Japanese bombed, invaded, and raped the land and women, beginning with the south; the invasion of Nanjing (Nanking) was the most famous, but not at all atypical of the Japanese destruction. Some missionaries served under "occupied China," using their neutrality and status as Americans to protect the Chinese, while others migrated to the West, over the mountains, where hundreds of factories and schools were relocated. The relocation was an effort to "keep on" producing and educating as a way to prepare to retake lands lost to the Japanese. Supplies were first brought in on the famous Burma Road, but when the Japanese invaded Burma, supplies had to be flown in over the Himalayas from India. In all places the missionaries, rather than being falsely identified with British colonialists who had been forcing China to buy opium, were now identified with Chinese peasants and nationalists, opposing the oppressive Japanese presence. Missionaries were now received as friends and protectors of Chinese women and children. And here is one of the great ironies of history, that just thirty-seven years earlier missionaries and Chinese Christians were being killed by Chinese nationalists in the Boxer Rebellion. Now they were perceived as friends of the oppressed Chinese.

The war years did not end Presbyterian mission work in China; it only redirected and ennobled their work. Dr. Nelson Bell spoke prophetically: "If missionaries stay out now, they will miss the grandest chance God ever gave them for winning the confidence and love of the people."[7] Bell was correct. China was in turmoil with its own Nationalist government, and communists were fighting against Japanese invasions. Meanwhile the missionaries provided medical care for soldiers and abused women and children, kept schools running, and carved out safety zones where refugees could flee for protection and food. In all of the missionary reports, there is both great angst and suffering, but there is also overwhelming response to the gospel message. Some of the missionaries were captured by the Japanese (once war was declared on Japan), and we read, for example, in the 1944 Minutes of the PCUS General Assembly[8] a word of thanksgiving for "the eleven missionaries who have been freed and returned to the U.S.A."

The Japanese surrender transformed East Asia. Presbyterians returned to pick up where they left off. In 1946 a deputation was sent to China to assess what should be done in this, our largest mission field. The report, printed in 1947, is amazing in its detailed description of what would be needed to rebuild churches, hospitals, and schools, and in revealing the new approach that should be taken in China. Chinese leaders should be directing the future work. "The Deputation presents this report under the deep conviction that we must promptly reestablish our work . . . in cooperation with a Church in China that is eager to go forward with us." All requests for missionaries should be made by a local church to their synod, and then "these requests should be transmitted to the General Assembly of the China Christian Council." Regarding property, the report said, it should "carry out the established policy of transferring the Board's equities and titles of church and chapel property to the General Assembly of the CCC."[9] In this post-colonial China, the PCUSA was clear that there should immediately be a three-self church.[10] The report, however, is not all about organization and finances. "The Primary task of the Church is evangelism. . . . We believe the time is ripe for an intensive nationwide evangelistic effort."[11]

Thus, there was a sense of urgency that the work and institutions should be quickly turned over to Chinese leadership. Either because of the advancing communists, or because of the experience of the war, both missionaries and executives in Nashville (PCUS) and New York (PCUSA) wrote much about the urgency of training Chinese leaders. Medical doctor Marshall Welles began work in Shandong in the 1930s, but within fifteen months after the war, he had to move hospitals four times because of the communist advance. The destruction in China by the Japanese and then during the civil war made it very difficult to "pick up where we left off." The first months of work under the Communists were a period of hopeful anticipation. Even after so many years of wars and relocation, missionary optimism and persistence were not easily stifled.

However, two documents from the China Christian Council (CCC) slowly unfolded the new situation in China. The December 1949 "Message from Chinese Christians to Mission Boards Abroad" seemed to be a mediating message: there is a radical new political reality in China now that imperialism has been overthrown, but "we wish to assert that missionary work in China never had any direct relationship with government policies."[12] Missionaries are not imperialists. Less than a year later, however, in July of 1950 the "Christian Manifesto," written by Y. T. Wu (Wu Yaozong) in consultation with the new government (Premier Zhou Enlai), made it clear that the day of Christian missions in China was over. A year later, Wu had organized the Three-Self Patriotic Movement (TSPM), a government-guided Chinese Church order that would serve the new China. Not all Christians agreed that Chinese Christians should cooperate so closely with the new communist government, and so divisions already present regarding theology and church and society deepened following 1950.[13] Missionaries who had not yet left China began to be interrogated, publicly shamed (often by their own students), detained, and expelled from the country. The charges were usually embezzlement of funds or treason. Exorbitant taxes, travel restrictions, and house arrests also made it impossible for missionaries to stay. One by one they left: Rev. & Mrs. Frank Price were the last PCUS missionaries to leave in 1952; the last PCUSA missionaries were Dr. and Mrs. Homer Bradshaw and Ms. Sarah Perkins, who left in the summer of 1955, after nearly five years in prison. For the first time in 113 years, there were no American missionaries in China. It was reported in the United States, though, that there was still a faithful Korean Presbyterian missionary serving in Shandong in 1956.[14]

A number of missionaries migrated from China to Hong Kong (under British control until 1997, when it was restored to China). The needs in Hong Kong were similar to the needs in South Korea: refugee issues. In this case, there was a massive influx of Chinese from the Mainland, and so the population of Hong Kong exploded from 800,000 to 2.5 million in just eight years. Poor housing, disease, and lack of social services were common to the landscape. The British colonial government encouraged mission societies to help out with matters that they could not handle. Presbyterian missionaries entered this new field to "assist with relief undertakings consisting of children's centers, family welfare projects, work relief projects, case work centers, hostels, nurseries, medical clinics, and tuberculosis sanatorium and refugee handcraft projects."[15]

Presbyterian involvement and support of the church in China began to reconnect after Richard Nixon's famed visit to China (1972), the subsequent normalizing of United States–China relations, and then the death of Mao Zedong (1976). Beginning in 1979, Philip Wickeri was appointed mission coworker in Hong Kong in large part to continue liaison work with the church in China. In 1985 he accepted the position with the newly organized Amity Foundation,[16] as Overseas Coordinator. Missionaries are no longer permitted to work in China, but through the Amity Foundation, the Presbyterian Church, in cooperation with the Outreach Foundation and Medical Benevolence Foundation, has contributed greatly toward producing Bibles in China, sending teachers, and building churches and hospitals during the last two decades of our period.

TAIWAN

After 1951, many of the missionaries scattered throughout East Asia, working among Chinese in other nations; some followed the great exodus of Mainland Chinese to Taiwan. This created a political dilemma that is still with us today. Taiwan was already a mixture of local tribal people and Chinese who had migrated over the centuries, but now there was a third group: government officials and other wealthy Chinese fleeing the new social order in Mao's China. Many longtime Taiwanese resented the influx of the Mainland Chinese, who brought both rule and riches from the Mainland, but it was not the first time.

Taiwan's history has been bound loosely with the history of China, mainly Fujian Province, since the conquest of the Dutch in Taiwan by Koxinga of Fujian in 1662. From that time onward, Chinese dominated the island, and in 1887 Taiwan became the twentieth province of China. This did not last long, however. The Japanese conquest in the First Sino-Japanese War of 1894–95 broke the hold of China on Taiwan, and Japan then treated Taiwan as an agricultural colony until the end of the Pacific War. When China, led by Chiang Kai-Shek, came as liberators, they were only briefly celebrated, because the Taiwanese quickly realized that they had merely exchanged one form of foreign rule for another.

It is into this history of colonialisms and struggle for independence that Presbyterian missionary work developed in Taiwan in the 1950s. Previously, Presbyterians working in Taiwan were from Canada or England. The PCUS and PCUSA work began with displaced missionaries from China working with Mainland Chinese and also with Aboriginals in Taiwan. One of the earlier couples to work in Taiwan remembered the political tensions with Mainland Chinese ruling in Taiwan, along with the joys of training Taiwanese leaders. He was teaching university students when some of the students were sent as spies from the government, and some of the church leaders were imprisoned because of the perceived threat of communism.[17] As a university professor, he reported, he had to carefully stick to his subject matter and avoid political conflicts.[18]

By 1957, Presbyterian missionaries had settled into a pattern of working with the Canadian Presbyterians in the north and the English Presbyterians in the southern end of the island. Missionaries were largely involved in teaching in colleges and seminaries (including the newly opened Tunghai University in Taichung) and doing evangelistic and church-planting work among the various Aboriginals. Presbyterian missionary presence grew in the 1960s, with about half of the missionaries as ordained pastors or medical people. Presbyterians were working among Aboriginals (including the Amis and Tyal, among others) and helping with the translation of the Bible into Bunun. Presbyterians also helped with literacy and translation work among the Amis, Paiwan, Yami, Bunun, Taroko, and Tyal. Many had to use Japanese as the common language with which to communicate. Literacy work often meant translating or writing simple books that would introduce the Christian faith.[19] Much of the aboriginal work is now well established, with churches built, local leaders trained, and Bibles and other basic material in local languages. Today Presbyterians have close ecumenical relations with Taiwan (in spite of the sensitivities of the China Christian Council) but only a few resident missionaries.

JAPAN

Japan was one of the last countries to allow missionary work in the modern world,[20] and it began to open up at the time of the rise of the United States as a world power. Commodore Matthew C. Perry, Father of the Steam Navy, entered Endo (Tokyo) Bay on July 8, 1853, with four ships; one was the pride of the navy, "a smoke-belching sail-and-steam side-wheeler."[21] Slowly the parochial shogunate dissolved, and Japan within a decade would again be ruled by an emperor. One of the first Protestant missionaries to take up residence in Japan was the Pennsylvania Presbyterian medical doctor James Curtis Hepburn, whose legacy is not only his medical work, but also his Japanese-English dictionary, his system of romanization of Japanese, and his important role in the first translation of the Bible into Japanese. Presbyterian work proceeded along the lines of education, church planting, and medical work, but the work became much more complex as the Japanese began to inflict their will on other nations in the region where Presbyterian missionaries were also laboring. Not only Japanese imperialism, but also Japanese nationalism, centered around the ancient Shinto worship, challenged missionary integrity. In both Japan and Korea, the schools were used to promote the extreme nationalism and devotion at Shinto shrines. Church attendance and even church membership began to decline, since Christianity was so much identified with the West in general and with America in particular. Earlier in the century, Japanese Christians identified Shinto devotion as religious worship by which they could not abide, but in 1936, under pressure from the government, the National Christian Council in Japan issued a declaration with the opposite (and convenient) interpretation: "Christians should recognize the national character and value of these shrines and as loyal citizens pay homage to those whose memories are enshrined there. Christians should accept the government's interpretation that these shrines are not religious."[22]

The missionary presence decreased, funds also declined as government restrictions increased, and missionaries, even before 1941, were often suspected as spies. The Religious Bodies Law of 1939 mandated that only one Protestant Church would be recognized by the government, and so what missionaries had begun with the Federation of Christian Missions (1925), and continued with the National Christian Council, finally and hurriedly became the Church of Christ in Japan (Nihon Kirisuto Kyodan) in June of 1941. Still, some prominent Japanese Christians were arrested, and the Presbyterian missionaries turned over the last accounts, property, and church work to Japanese before leaving by the end of the year.

Japan was a devastated country at the end of the Pacific War. It was not only Hiroshima and Nagasaki that were destroyed by what the best human minds could devise. Suddenly this proud nation had the American military moving about with ease, while the Japanese shuffled to and fro, looking for food, shelter, and work. In 1948 the periodical *Presbyterian Life* called for Presbyterians to respond, "to help in Christian and philanthropic work among the Japanese." The article was descriptive, but even more, it was a plea: an American and Presbyterian plea to come alongside the Japanese. "Missionaries are needed more than ever in Japan, . . . American influence and help are in such demand." What were American missionaries to do? "Christian evangelism is an integral part of the occupation, for there is a real danger in trying to give a people democracy apart from Christianity."[23] The conquering General Douglas MacArthur expressed a similar sentiment: "Due to the vacuum which events have left in the spiritual phase of Japanese life, there now exists an opportunity without counterpart since the birth of Christ for the spread of Christianity among the peoples of the Far East."[24] Possibly in light of the humiliation and rearmament of Germany after World War I, the United States was united in the common concern to "come over and help" the Japanese and especially the Christians of Japan.

With strong calls from the military and from the Presbyterian Church, and with the closing of the largest mission field of China, it is surprising that Presbyterians didn't respond in greater numbers and with greater sacrifice. The PCUSA/UPCUSA never had more than 74 missionaries in Japan, and by 1960 the numbers started to decline. The PCUS never had more than 72 missionaries, and then in 1961 their numbers also began to decline. At most, and this was only from about 1956 to 1962, there were about 140 Presbyterian missionaries in Japan. By 1972 there were 84, and the numbers continued to decline. There was great hope, expressed in missionary writings as well as in periodical and General Assembly Reports, that the Japanese would rapidly come to Christ. After all, the General Assembly reported in 1957 that 500,000 Japanese New Testaments were sold in Japan in one year. Christian radio broadcasting was beginning, Christian films were being produced, and even newspaper evangelism was taking off. Presbyterians were involved in all of these endeavors, as well as helping to start "industrial evangelism" in the new industrial zones. The PCUS had added five new mission stations (Kasugai, Zentsuji, Osaka, Ogaki, and Tajimi) by 1957. In that same year, however, it was reported that there was a dearth of Christian instructors for the Christian schools, and there is "no widespread movement toward Christianity."[25] Another strategy that was tried at the time involved sending teams of American pastors, who would come for about six weeks of "intensive services." These pastors did not speak Japanese, so their ministries would take some of the best career missionaries away from their work for extended periods of time to provide interpretation.

By 1966 the total Protestant missionary community in Japan had grown from 450 in 1957 to 543, but the Presbyterian presence was in decline. The Annual Report of the Board of World Foreign Missions (PCUS) for that year describes the problem as "religious indifference: a recent survey in Tokyo said that 75% of the people have no religious faith" (in any religion). Presbyterians were helping to develop prison chaplaincy, and the PCUS had three of its people doing full-time work in the prisons. Nearly every missionary, it was reported, was teaching English, mostly in their homes, since the Japanese were eager to learn English. The report then noted that the Japanese were more interested in the language of the Americans than in their religion. Presbyterian work in education was laudatory. Each year the various Board Reports discussed the need for more teachers for the work in high schools and colleges. The newly founded ecumenical Japan

International Christian University had over five hundred students by 1953, and although the PCUSA did not officially join the foundation, Presbyterians were involved in raising funds and providing teachers. In the past, education had been a tool whereby Christians could meet an important societal need and at the same time teach about the Christian faith. By the mid-1950s the government schools were getting much stronger and becoming well funded, so the role of the Christian school was not as clear, and its attraction not as great. Christian medical work, another of the important tools of earlier Protestant missions, only began for Presbyterians in Japan in 1955. Medical practice in Japan was fairly advanced, and so in the past there was not a need. However, the destruction of an estimated 20 percent of the medical facilities during the war created a great need. The first new Christian hospital was opened in the Yodogawa district of Osaka, and for the first time Presbyterians began a brief period of medical work in Japan.

Most of the Presbyterian missionaries who went to Japan in the 1950s and 1960s planned to plant churches and to be involved in evangelism. These were people who spent two years studying the language and who often planted a number of churches, both rural and urban. One missionary, Harriet Johnson, went to Japan and tried to avoid being an English teacher because she wanted to be an evangelist. She seemed to have been gifted in such work:

> A dear woman named Toki Sudoh who was about 15 years older than I (and a widow with two children) took me under her wing and shared her home with me. Because of her love and patience and after 10 years of training, I was able to work alone and be ordained. This dear woman was my friend all these years. We were both ordained (separately) and sent off in different directions to work in the same Presbytery.[26]

Many of those who were surveyed spoke of their greatest experiences as being the close relationships they developed with Japanese in starting new churches.

The financial problems that developed in the early 1970s came about as a result of controversies in the UPCUSA and the exchange rate: the yen was doing well, and it was becoming extremely expensive to support even a single missionary in Japan. The Japanese Church and its institutions did not want to lose the Presbyterian missionaries, and so a program of "shared support" developed, whereby the Japanese college (or hospital for chaplains) would pay most or part of the salary of the missionary, and the Americans would pay for travel, insurance, and retirement. This helped to keep missionaries in Japan, but it meant we had fewer missionaries relating to the Kyodan and fewer missionaries doing church planting. As one missionary said, still only about 1 percent of the Japanese population is Christian, thousands of villages have no church, and we soon will have no one planting churches at all. Today the PC(USA) has more missionaries in Japan than any other country in Asia, but the area of work has been narrowed, for the most part, to educational work, with an emphasis upon English teaching. Japan remains one of the least Christian nations in Asia.

KOREA

Of all of the Presbyterian missionary work in the world, Korea must be the most well-known: the jewel in the Presbyterian crown. Korea was given the title Hermit Kingdom because it was nearly completely cut off from the world until so late in modern history. The first residential missionary did not arrive until 1884, the Presbyterian medical doctor Horace N. Allen; with three long months of medical care, he fortuitously saved the life of Prince Min Yong-Ik. The door was thus opened for missionaries to enter the country. From the beginning, Presbyterian missionaries, especially in the North, were strongly committed to the Nevius Method, as it was called, planting "three-self churches." John L. Nevius, a Presbyterian missionary to Shandong, China, spoke at a missionary retreat in Korea in the summer of 1890. He did not exactly describe three principles, but he did make it clear that churches must be started that can be led and supported by the Koreans themselves. He also was clear that converts were not to be taken out of their environment and sent off to schools in big cities. Instead, the local converts should be kept and then trained in their villages, living with their families, where they could have the most direct and personal ministry. This pattern was followed, and Korea missionaries two and three generations later acknowledged that method with appreciation.[27] John Talmage,[28] who served in Korea both before and after the Korean War, was very clear when asked about the Nevius Method in our interview: "Yes, we all knew about it even before we went to Korea, and it was our common policy that a church couldn't have a pastor until they could pay for his support."[29]

New Christians in northern Korea, where the Presbyterian work was the strongest, would come two times a year for Bible training events: usually after harvest and before planting. By 1907, the time of the Great Korea Revival, there were over a thousand coming for these training events, then fanning out to hundreds of villages in the North. With the planting of the new churches came other institutions: schools, clinics, and hospitals.

However, Japanese occupation and restrictions (such as requiring Shinto worship in Christian schools) tested the young church, and eventually Presbyterian missionaries were unable to work in Japanese imperial Korea. By 1941 the number of missionaries still in Korea had sharply declined. Several suffered detention for periods of time, and Dr. John V. Talmage was imprisoned for 121 days. When he was released in 1942, he and the other three remaining PCUS missionaries were evacuated. In June of the same year, the first four members of Seoul Station (PCUSA) left the country following six months' internment.[30]

The first Presbyterian missionaries did not return to Korea until 1947, with the exception of Dr. Horace H. Underwood, who was called back as a Department of the Army Civilian (DAC) adviser to the interim government in 1945. Mr. Dexter Lutz came back, also as a DAC in January of 1946. Several missionary sons served in the U.S. army in Korea during and immediately after the end of the war. Mrs. Underwood made her way back to join her husband in 1946, and a few of the other men returned to the devastated country during that year.

Missionaries did not return at all to their stations in northern Korea because of the Russian refusal to allow general elections for the entire nation. The United Nations Command had allowed the Russians to accept the surrender of the Japanese north of the 38th parallel. The Communist occupation resulted in splitting the country in two and was a tragedy for the church equal to that of the Japanese, who had just been defeated.

In July of 1947, a deputation of five from the Board of Foreign Missions arrived and spent the whole month studying the situation. At that time the Presbyterians and Methodists were working closely together, and they requested permission for a delegation to visit North Korea; the request was flatly denied by the Soviet occupying forces. After much discussion, new priorities were set, and a plan was established to restart Presbyterian missionary work only in the South, at least for the moment, it was thought. Liberated Korea was to have free and open elections, but the Soviets refused this in the North, and eventually the Communist North, with the help of the Communist Chinese, invaded the South. After three years of warfare, Korea was divided at the 38th parallel, refugees had fled to the South, churches and other public buildings were destroyed, families were divided; yet in the midst of this tragedy, the church south of the Demilitarized Zone rapidly grew. "The result of three years of war (June 25, 1950, to July 10, 1953) was to make Korea the most devastated country in modern times."[31] Horace Underwood wrote that the city of Seoul, which had a population of 1.4 million, was reduced to maybe 20,000–40,000 people. There was an eerie silence in the midst of the shocking devastation. Youngnak Church, with a membership of over 3,000 members, began worship with only 40 people, led by its great pastor, Reverend Han Kyung Chik.

It soon became clear that two tragedies had befallen Korea: Japanese imperialism had left Korea impoverished and with inadequately trained professionals, and the Korean War brought further devastation to the infrastructure. The first wave of Korea's returning Protestant missionaries came as medical and educational people. Dr. Paul and Sophie Crane were sent to Chonju, a large region with no modern medical facility. It was Paul's assignment to help develop a modern hospital out of a small clinic,[32] and Sophie did what she could to help set up a medical lab. The PCUS changed its strategy from supporting five small hospitals, one in each of the mission stations, to an expanded response to medical needs that would include "training facilities in Chonju and a tuberculosis hospital and outreach in Kwangju, and a continuing leprosy hospital in Soonchon."[33] The development of the hospital was put on hold, as the Korean War unfolded, for many doctors (including Crane) served in the U.S. military during that war. The PCUSA also developed its medical work further in light of the overwhelming needs. Howard Moffett, son of the Pyengyang pioneer missionary Samuel Austin Moffett, turned a medical center in Tegu into a thousand-bed hospital and medical training center. Moffett required that all nurses and doctors be Christians with evangelistic zeal, since they were often sent out into villages to set up clinic during the day and then have preaching services in the evening.[34]

One of the biggest issues in the postwar period was refugees. Before the war and during the war, it is estimated that eight million Koreans migrated from the north to the south. The Presbyterian Church had a special responsibility to Korean pastors and their families, many of whom had fled the communists in the north, and others who had fled the advancing armies. As the missionaries returned, it was decided (even with no such item in the budget) to pay each pastor from the north an equivalent of one month's wages to help with basic necessities.

Immediately upon the heels of the war, and in part as a result of that war, the Presbyterian Church in Korea began to split. At first, divisions between Korean churches began to develop over the war, but soon American Presbyterian divisions from the 1920s and 1930s began to creep in. The 1956 Report to the PCUSA General Assembly was a little too optimistic: "The tensions due to the controversies that have been raging within the church since the end of World War II have almost disappeared."[35] In fact, divisions occurred based upon how or whether to cooperate ecumenically (the WCC was founded in 1948), how to respond to church leaders who cooperated with Shinto Shrine worship under the Japanese, how to start theological education, doctrinal issues, and as always, personalities. Presbyterian missionaries worked toward greater unity, when possible; but by the late 1960s, the UPCUSA ended up working with the Presbyterian Church in Korea (PCK), or Tonghap,[36] and the Presbyterian Church in the Republic of Korea (PROK), which separated mostly over biblical interpretation and theology in 1953.[37] The Hapdong Presbyterian Church[38] split off from the PCK in 1959 and is identified more with the scholastic Presbyterianism of Westminster Seminary in the United States. To make matters more complicated, there are actually over a hundred Presbyterian denominations in Korea, with the largest still being the PCK (Tonghap) and the Hapdong Presbyterian Church.

It was not always easy for the PCUS to honor the independence and self-governance principles, especially in the midst of these theological divisions. In the Board of World Missions Annual Report (PCUS) in 1954, concern was expressed about "the ten million displaced persons" and the "almost insuperable hardships and obstacles," but also about the "theology of the Korean Church," which was "much narrower, more literalistic and intolerant than that of our own church." The solution suggested was direct intervention. They need "a more forward-looking program of theological education and Christian education, such as we have in the PCUS." Koreans need to be "well informed on Biblical scholarship and forward looking in policies and methods." Apparently it would have been easier to control the theology of the Korean Presbyterians without "the Christian refugees from North Korea (especially Pyongyang) to South Korea, [who] are ultra conservative."[39]

However messy and embarrassing many of these divisions were, the fact was that Christianity was now growing at a faster rate than ever. Seminaries, Bible institutes, and colleges were springing up every year. Radio, Bible clubs,[40] correspondence courses, military chaplaincy, orphanage work, and hundreds of new churches were appearing all across the southern half of the peninsula. Korea had well-trained leaders before the wars, but now most of those leaders were dead; leadership training was crucial. Presbyterian missionaries returned in greater numbers to Korea than to Japan initially, but by the 1960s there were nearly identical numbers. Many more of the missionaries were medical doctors, nurses, and health-care workers, responding to the problems of leprosy, tuberculosis, amputations, and the tragedies of war. Presbyterians supported the important work of the Bible clubs, work with prostitutes (often trapped in hopeless economic despair), and work in the slums; they also helped to develop both college and theological education. Ruth Folta, for example, wrote an important textbook for training Christian health-care workers. Her two-hundred-page book, *Spiritual Care*, first written in Korean, has since become a standard and has been translated into fifteen languages. The work of Presbyterians in Korea is of such importance that the names of Underwood, Moffett, Clark, and Crane are well respected throughout Korea.

Both the decrease in funding for Presbyterian mission (which became dramatic at the end of the 1960s) and the changing policies of the UPCUSA in light of the Advisory Study[41] resulted in a sharp decline in the number of missionaries: 68 in 1969 to 32 in 1975. In 1983, with the reunion of the PCUS and the UPCUSA, the Korean Mission was dissolved, and from that point on, the initiative for missionary work resided in Korea. Today there are far more Koreans working as missionaries in the United States than American missionaries in Korea.

One of the major issues for the Korean Church today, and one for which the PC(USA) still has an important role to play, is reunification. Two of the area secretaries for the Presbyterian Church have been Koreans, Drs. Syngman Rhee and Insik Kim. As early as 1978, Dr. Syngman Rhee began visiting North Korea, trying to reestablish ties with the Christians in the North, including his own family members. He has been actively engaged in helping to bring food aid in the midst of famines in North Korea. He has appealed to the U.S. government to be more responsive, and he has helped with negotiations encouraging the reunification of North and South Korea.[42]

The PC(USA), with the support of various presbyteries and support groups, has raised money to help with famine relief and medical care in the North. After two visits of Billy Graham[43] to North Korea (1992 and 1994), former Presbyterian missionaries (and their children) who had worked in Korea organized two agencies: first the "Eugene Bell Centennial Foundation," and later also the "Christian Friends of Korea" (CFK). The latter group, though not now exclusively Presbyterian, is an independent agency established, for the most part, "to feed the hungry and heal the sick." Since its founding, the CFK has sent over $20 million worth of food and supplies to North Korea. By 2007 a Roman Catholic Church, two Protestant churches,[44] and a new Orthodox Church were reopened in North Korea. The first Presbyterian coworker in North Korea since the partition teaches in Pyongyang. The PC(USA) works closely with the PCK and the PROK on issues of reconciliation and reunion, as well as in global Christian witness. At present between 26 and 30 percent of South Korea is Christian, and Korea, which had been known as the Hermit Nation, is now one of the most outward-looking missionary nations in the world.

PHILIPPINES

All Protestant work in the Philippines began with the conclusion of the Spanish American War (1898), whereby the end of Spanish colonialism came about and the United States as a colonial power came center stage. Cuba, Puerto Rico, the Philippines, and Guam were all taken over by the United States, but only Cuba was given independence. Between 1898 and 1902 most of the major Protestant missions began their work in the Philippines, having earlier met in New York to decide upon regions or territories where the various missions would work. This cooperative ecumenical movement was later named the Evangelical Union of the Philippine Islands (1932), and it became the basis for what would become in 1948 the United Church of Christ of the Philippines (UCCP).

The PCUSA work[45] included Manila (an ecumenical region for missionary work) and the islands of Luzon, Negros, Leyte, Panay, and Samar. On Luzon, stations were established in Laguna (1902), Albay (1903), Tayabus (1905), Camarines (1911), and Batangas (1917). Presbyterian work in the Philippines, similar to the work in Latin America, involved working both in a former Spanish (Roman Catholic) colony and among the Philippines indigenous peoples, generally without written language, who were scattered on hundreds of islands. From the beginning there was a strong emphasis on medical and educational work. Clinics, dispensaries, and medical training facilities were established at Tacloban, Bohol, Albay, Iloilo, and Dumaguete. Educational work was focused on the first Protestant college, Silliman University in Dumaguete City, Negros (founded in 1901), and Ellinwood Bible School, which in 1907 joined with the Methodist school to form Union Theological Seminary. Because of the United Church of Christ of the Philippines (UCCP) union in 1948, Presbyterian work in the Philippines has been a partnership with this union church.

Missionary work in a country that was an American colony and then a Commonwealth (from 1935) was a unique situation for Americans. During the Pacific War the Japanese invaded the Philippines, and after 1945 the Philippines received their independence. Some Presbyterian missionaries, like Alexander Christie, were interned by the Japanese for the duration of the war (Pearl Harbor to VJ Day). American presence, both through the military bases and military advisers, was very strong through the 1980s. After the Pacific War, there were fifty-one PCUSA missionaries working in the Philippines; the numbers increased to seventy-two in 1950 and then began slowly declining until they reached (and maintained) single digits beginning in 1975. The intentional policy of downsizing missionary presence and handing over all initiative in mission to the national church had a dramatic affect on PC(USA) presence in the Philippines. There were four coworkers in the Philippines in 2007.

With Philippine independence came the possibility of the country moving away from providing raw materials for the colonial nations, to developing their own factories for refining and production. Slowly the Philippines began to develop its own industrial infrastructure, and with this development, the PCUSA sent missionaries to work as "industrial missionaries," often with the Urban-Industrial Mission.[46] Richard P. Poethig served from 1957 to 1972, organizing workers, advocating for basic human rights, and helping with education and the welfare of laborers. There was such a dominant U.S. military presence in the Philippines that the view of American missionaries by Filipinos deteriorated some, and a number of pastors and university students, especially in the late 1970s and 1980s, began to turn to a Marxist critique. This created a new dynamic for the number of missionaries working in educational settings. In this context the work of mission coworkers like the Elwoods at Silliman University is so important. Douglas Elwood published books like *Christ in Philippine Context* and *Asian Christian Theology*, and Bettie Elwood helped to establish a psychology department and women's study program at Silliman University. Other educational missionaries also wrote some of the earliest college and seminary textbooks for the UCCP.[47]

THAILAND

The first ongoing Presbyterian work in Siam began in 1844 with the arrival of Rev. and Mrs. Stephen Mattoon and Dr. Samuel R. House, MD. From the beginning, the work was evangelistic, educational, and medical.[48] Baptist and Congregational work preceded the work of the Northern Presbyterian mission, and in 1934 a union of all three ecclesiastical streams was formed as the Church of Christ in Thailand (CCT). Thus, before the Japanese occupation, our Presbyterian work was done in partnership with an independent and united national church. Presbyterian missionary work in Thailand became well-established and well-respected during the later part of the nineteenth through the twentieth centuries. Major secondary schools, hospitals, clinics, seminaries, and even the first Protestant University, Payap (in Chiang Mai), grew out of the institutional work of the Presbyterian Church in Thailand. For the size of the CCT today, Christianity has had a much larger impact upon society than its numbers would indicate. The present king's father (Prince Mahidol), for example, did his internship at the famous Presbyterian Hospital (McCormick) in Chiang Mai, and King Bhumibol himself honored the hospital at the royal opening of a new wing.

Medical work continued to be a priority in Thailand after the Second World War. One of the displaced China missionaries, Dr. Marshall P. Welles, while waiting for approval to go to the Philippines, received a telegram from New York stating that a doctor was immediately needed in Bangkok. With only forty-eight hours to decide, they made plans to go to Thailand. Thus, in 1949 Marshall began immediately doing surgery and receiving patients in a small clinic. He started a small hospital and began to train medical people. That now is Bangkok Christian

Hospital, one of the largest in Thailand, and it is run by the Church of Christ in Thailand. When he went home on his first furlough from Thailand, Welles asked that a Thai be put in charge of the hospital, and so from its third year of existence, the hospital was directed by local Thai Christian leadership. Welles told us in an interview, "Fifty years later, in 1999, a non-Christian doctor asked 'How did you feel when you were no longer in charge of everything?' I said it felt great because that is what we went there for in the first place—to train and hand over work to the national church."[49] It did not always happen so easily in Thailand.

During this time period, one of the central issues regarding Presbyterian work in all of East Asia was the complex issue of dissolving the various missions in the countries, in order to honor the indigenous leadership of the local church. From the late 1950s through the 1970s, missions were dissolved, and everything, including property and institutions, was handed over to national leadership. Part of this transfer of power meant the transfer of decision making concerning missionary partnerships. Local Asian churches would now take the initiative by making requests or appointment of new missionaries, and they would make decisions about continuing or terminating present missionaries. Initially, however, the change in policy was made in New York. The Thai Church, unlike the churches in Korea or Taiwan, was still quite light in terms of national trained leadership, and this made the transition especially rough. Missionaries were warned that there would be a downsizing of missionaries, and at one point representatives from COEMAR in New York came to Thailand to communicate that the number of mission personnel would have to be cut by half and the CCT would be given the opportunity to decide which missionaries and programs should stay. A number of missionaries, including a couple (trained medical doctors who had spent two years studying the Thai language), elected to return to the United States. It was a very difficult time for both missionaries and Thai Christian leaders. Still, there was unanimity (missionaries and administrators of COEMAR and then of the Program Agency) concerning the principle that more leadership and authority needed to be given to the national church. However, as one missionary put it in a group interview,

> I think we forced this situation much more than it should have been forced. We did the same thing in this country [Thailand], turning everything over to the national church when it was not ready. We had twenty-eight schools in Thailand and 150 churches, seven hospitals, and we turned it over to a Christian population of only about 30,000 to 35,000 people. In the United States, how many presbyteries would be willing to take on this responsibility? We did this precipitously, and we didn't do it well. But this was the new philosophy—turn everything over to the local church. When we were on furlough, we tried to analyze and interpret this. It was sort of like the way Americans do things with these types of transitions.[50]

The move to reduction of missionaries, as in the Philippines, happened quickly. In 1970 there were sixty-eight Presbyterian missionaries in Thailand, and five years later there were twenty-eight.

Thailand, like Japan, has had a strong missionary force for a long time, with a Christian population that never gets much beyond 1 percent of the total population. This has been an important issue when it comes to education because turning over the many schools, seminaries, and the university to local leadership requires that Thai Christians be found to teach at these Christian institutions. Except for the seminaries, there have never been enough Christians to teach at the CCT schools; often students will go to Christian schools in Thailand and be taught by Buddhist teachers, where Buddhism is a required part of the curriculum.

Two other important contributions made by Presbyterian missionaries were providing leadership in the modern translation of the Bible into Thai and the encouragement and development of literature and the arts. The Bible translation project was a twelve-year project that involved about thirty-five Thais and Americans. Providing project leadership were Presbyterian missionaries Herbert G. Grether, Kenneth Wells, and Francis M. Seely. The Thai Bible was published in 1966. Presbyterians have also encouraged the development and use of Thai music and art in Christian worship. Thai Drama teams were developed by Presbyterian missionaries in Chiang Mai beginning in 1978, using traditional Thai drama (*ligay*). This developed into the Christian Communications Institute of Payap University, which works in all areas of Christian communication today. Thai Christian music and choirs were encouraged at both the high school and college level. Carolyn Kingshill opened the first music department at Thailand Theological Seminary (McGilvary School of Theology), and she was the first head of the music department at Payap University. She worked with Thai musicians to rewrite the Thai hymnal, following the five-tonal system of the Thai language.

INDONESIA, MALAYSIA, AND SINGAPORE

Protestant missions that worked in the East Indies until after the defeat of the Japanese were mostly Continental groups from Holland, Germany, and Switzerland. Singapore was served mostly by British missions (London Missionary Society, Church Mission Society, and others), except for the American Methodists, who began in the later part of the nineteenth century as an extension of their work in India. Until after the Pacific War and the defeat of the Japanese, only British Presbyterians (both Scottish and English) worked in Singapore and Malaya. American Presbyterians had passed through Singapore on their way to Thailand, or had worked briefly in the region until after China opened up after the First Opium War (1842). Thus, most of the Presbyterian work in what was British Malaya and the Dutch East Indies developed after independence, and the missionaries came to work in specialized ministries of education, agriculture, and medicine.

The Presbyterian Church has never had more than twenty-five people at a time working in these three countries (never more than three in Malaysia and Singapore combined). The first Presbyterians arrived in Indonesia in 1952, and in 2007 there were only two couples working in the region: one couple each in

Singapore and Indonesia. Most of the missionaries have been seconded to local seminaries in Jakarta (Sekolah Tinggi Theologia), Bandung, Yogyakarta, or Singapore (Trinity Theological College).

PRESBYTERIANS IN EAST ASIA IN THE FUTURE?

In 1963 a report was done on Asia by COEMAR's Office for Research. The report was confidently called *A Factual Study of Asia*.[51] Over forty years later, we see how the evaluations of Asia have changed and also how our response and involvement have changed. The report is remarkable for its thoroughness in describing and giving factual information on agricultural imports, foreign aid, age composition, population growth, urban growth, development of education, resurgent religions, and even Christian radio broadcasting and audiovisual centers. There are no conclusions at the end, but the last section, on religions in Asia, serves as a way forward for the church. A few observations will help us see what has taken place in East Asia and how the Presbyterian Church has participated in these changes.

First, it is noteworthy that almost nothing is said about North Korea or the People's Republic of China. There are six paragraphs on China, which are somewhat optimistic about the Chinese Church now finally being completely independent. North Korea is only mentioned in passing. Now, forty-five years later, we can see that much has changed. The PC(USA) has been directly involved in relief efforts and conversations that have been part of a larger ecumenical effort to reopen churches in the North and to advocate reconciliation. In China, matters have changed dramatically. The PC(USA) has had a number of people working in China, mostly teaching English through the Amity Foundation. Every year groups of church leaders from the PC(USA) make visits and have cultural exchanges through the CCC/TSPM. Some of these exchanges are arranged through Worldwide Ministries, but now groups like the Outreach Foundation and Medical Benevolence Foundation are also involved in ministries and partnerships with the CCC/TSPM and the Amity Foundation. There have also been a few Presbyterian theological faculty members who have taught courses at Nanjing Theological Seminary. Thus, relationships are slowly being reestablished in these post-Maoist contexts.

Another interesting observation from the report is that Christianity struggles for acceptance in East Asia because of the resurgence of Asian religions and the Western nature of Christianity.[52] Some of the issues are still quite real today, for Buddhism, Islam, and Hinduism are enjoying some new resurgent expressions. However, what has changed is that Christianity today is much more Asian. Most of the missionary work being done in Asia is by Asians, not by Westerners. Thus, when American Presbyterians go to China to teach English and to be a Christian presence, we affirm the ecumenical nature of Christianity, but we are not the main representation of Christianity. In Taiwan and the Philippines where we have had some long-term involvement, there are far more Singaporeans, Malaysians, and Koreans serving as missionaries today.

A third observation made in this *Factual Study* has to do with the communications revolution in Asia. The authors were on target in focusing on dramatic changes taking place in communications, but even they had no idea of what DVDs, the computer, and the Internet would do to broaden and deepen this revolution. The revolution in communications did have a great impact upon our involvement in East Asia. Earlier, most of the specialists were in basic health needs—medicine, nursing, water purification, and food production—but now communications technologies are of central importance in delivering education in East Asia.

A fourth issue that is part of the conclusion of this *Factual Study* is the issue of "Unity for Mission."[53] When this study was done, the regional bodies such as the East Asia Christian Conference were in their nascent stages, and there was great energy and optimism about Asian Christians working with Western Christians in ecumenical partnership. However, all of those churches were Western divisions transplanted into Asia soil and were now working together as Asian partners. Sadly, Western divisions continue to be imported, or absorbed in the Asian churches, even as East Asian churches unite (China Christian Council) and divide (Korean Presbyterians), and start afresh (Presbyterian Church of Vietnam).

Finally, the *Factual Study* presents a chart on "Bible Distribution." For countries in East Asia, Japan has the largest distribution, according to the American Bible Society's 1962 report, with 2.5 million Bibles; Korea is number two, with a little over one million. No one would have dreamed that by 2007 Amity Press in Nanjing would have produced over 54 million Bibles and New Testaments for the Church in China.[54] In fact, who would have guessed that Christians in China would be exporting Bibles to other Chinese churches throughout the world? The Presbyterian Church (U.S.A.) has helped to see this vision come to reality.

In 1965, Presbyterian fraternal worker Herbert G. Grether wrote an interesting piece on the work of Presbyterians in the country of Thailand, caught between tradition and rapid modernization. This article was written as the UPCUSA was moving toward major and sudden changes in the relationship between mission and church. He comments that the common watchword in our work was "a self-governing, self-supporting, and self-propagating church in every place." He agrees that this has been our goal, and this watchword has helped us to build strong indigenous churches.

> But the church around the world is beginning to see in our day that at the heart of the gospel something else is called for in our world. We are called upon by God and by his Christ to a continuing partnership in every place, a partnership in which the strong will help the weak, and though each bears his own burden as he is able, we also bear one another's burdens. For no one is in himself able for everything, and no church in all the world can rightly claim to be fully "grown up" in every way.[55]

As we have seen, Presbyterians are still called in partnership in East Asia today, but now we are partners with churches that are quite grown up.

Independence from Colonial Powers (Japan, Holland, Britain, France, United States)

Korea	1945 from Japan (by 1953 divided)
Philippines	1946 from Japan (1945), then the United States
Indonesia	1949 from Holland
Taiwan	1949[56]
Cambodia	1953 from France
Laos	1954 from France
Vietnam	1954 from France
Malaysia	1957 from Great Britain
Singapore	1959 from Malaysia

"Liberation" by Communists

China	1949
North Korea	1953
Vietnam	1976[57] (partitioned in 1954)

Not Colonized

Thailand	(buffer state between French Indochina and British India)
China	
Japan	

Chapter 10

American Presbyterians and the Middle East

STANLEY H. SKRESLET

As a mission field, the Middle East attracted the attention of Presbyterians quite soon after American Protestants became involved in foreign missions.[1] At first, a primary aim was to convert the Jews of the Holy Land, an action thought to be required before the new age of the Messiah's reign could commence. High hopes were also held for the rapid evangelization of Muslims in the Middle East, although the complexities of that task were little understood. The ancient Christian communities of the region were a third object of evangelical missionary concern almost from the outset of the modern Protestant missionary movement.[2]

American Presbyterians initially channeled their enthusiasm for mission in the Middle East through the American Board of Commissioners for Foreign Missions (ABCFM), established in 1810 with significant Presbyterian involvement. Eventually, separate Presbyterian mission boards were created, and these assumed responsibility for a portion of the work begun by the ABCFM in the Middle East, while also expanding into new areas. Some cooperative arrangements with the Church of Scotland and other Reformed bodies were occasionally entered into but rarely sustained; each participating denomination usually concluded that autonomous structures could be more efficiently managed on the field and would be more generously supported at home.

On the eve of the Second World War, after more than a century of work in the Middle East, American Presbyterians had become by far the most active national Protestant missionary group in the region. Two major denominations had established extensive operations in different Middle Eastern countries, with the Presbyterian Church in the United States of America (PCUSA) focusing on Syria (from 1943 this field also encompassed the new country of Lebanon), Iran, and Iraq, while the United Presbyterian Church of North America (UPCNA) related to Egypt. The (Southern) Presbyterian Church in the United States (PCUS) would join the United Mission to Iraq in the 1950s but until then had not participated organizationally in mission efforts to the area. The UPCNA complemented its activities in Egypt with significant involvements in the Sudan, Ethiopia, and India (from 1947 also West Pakistan). All four UPCNA fields were contexts in which Muslims were numerous if not the majority religious tradition.

In keeping with the overall purpose of the present volume, what follows in this chapter is not primarily about beginnings or early experiments in American Presbyterian missions but more a matter of understanding how a group of relatively long-established missionary ventures evolved in recent times. A small number of key factors shaped this history to a great degree. Changes in mission theology among conciliarist Presbyterians, for example, prompted executives, missionaries, and national church leaders to reevaluate their goals and to scrutinize long-standing practices of missionary work. The complications of global politics likewise forced strategic decisions to be made that might otherwise have been avoided or postponed. In addition, local conditions regularly came into play in each of the countries where Presbyterians were active, such that a thoroughly uniform story of Presbyterian missions in the Middle East during this period cannot be expected.

Three distinctive phases seem to be discernible over the years 1944–2004 and so suggest an overall structure for the bulk of this chapter. The first of these stretches from the end of World War II to 1958, when the merger of the PCUSA and the UPCNA took place. This period is marked by an upsurge in mission activity in the Middle East by both denominations, undertaken along the lines of prewar patterns. A time of transition follows, which may be said to run through the 1970s. This is a period of thoroughgoing change during which many of the conventional structures of Presbyterian mission that participants assumed at the beginning of the twentieth century were effectively dismantled, not only in the Middle East but also globally. For the past quarter century or so, a concern for national church leadership in mission has dominated American Presbyterian thinking about mission work in the Middle East.

REBUILDING THE PRESBYTERIAN MISSION PROJECT

The prospect of an end to the Second World War raised hopes that an extended season of lean times for Presbyterian missions would finally come to a close. The financial exigencies of the 1930s had necessitated retrenchments in the Middle

East, as elsewhere. Wartime economies at home, restrictions on sea travel to foreign fields, and uncertain local conditions abroad during the war pushed mission boards to adopt cautious policies that aimed above all to keep existing mission institutions open, even if only barely. In some places missionaries were compelled by the needs of war-stressed communities to provide relief and military chaplaincy services, further stretching already-thin human and financial resources.

A dramatic decline in the number of missionaries deployed to the Middle East over the years 1929–44 illustrates on a regional scale demographic trends that held more generally for Presbyterian missions around the world during this period. In 1929, for example, one could count some 312 career missionaries and 111 short-termers at work in the four Middle Eastern fields to which the UPCNA and PCUSA were related.[3] By 1944 the number of career missionaries actually deployed in the region had shrunk to 154, with short-term service essentially suspended.[4] These numbers do not represent all those still considered to be under appointment by the sending churches. A growing number of missionaries had to be listed as furloughed or on "extended furlough" as the conflict wore on. Out of this group of "detained" workers, many were the spouses of male missionaries who had steadfastly remained at their posts for the duration of the war, despite the absence of family members.

Once military victory had been secured in Europe, the churches quickly moved to reinvigorate their missionary operations in the Middle East. The levels of the 1920s were not to be reached again, but a substantial increase in mission personnel assigned to the Middle East certainly was realized. Overall growth in numbers was not uniform through the 1950s. An early surge just after the war ended was followed by a drop in the totals of career Presbyterian missionaries appointed to the Middle East in the mid-1950s, probably the result of the high number of retirements that came due from among the unusually large group of those appointed in the 1920s.[5] The apogee of the churches' postwar drive to replenish their depleted missionary ranks in the Middle East appears to have been reached in 1958, just as the two major supporting denominations made final preparations to unite and become the United Presbyterian Church in the United States of America (UPCUSA). According to the first General Assembly report of the new denomination's combined mission agency (COEMAR), there were 261 career Presbyterian missionaries at work in the Middle East during 1958.[6]

Though numbers cannot tell the whole story of mission commitment and effectiveness, many Presbyterians at midcentury would have considered them a crucial indicator of the general health of a given mission field. A clue is provided by the prominence given to these statistics in the official reports of the responsible mission agencies and the frequent calls for more missionaries that issued not only from the fields but also from the headquarters of the two denominations during these years. Advocates for more missionaries pressed their cases for the different fields with such fervor that in the early 1950s the PCUSA was compelled to articulate a clear policy for assigning new personnel. The fairest approach, it was decided, would be to maintain the existing geographical distribution of forces.[7] While not discounting the importance of short-term service, these pleas for "reinforcements" focused almost exclusively on the number of new "career" missionaries felt to be needed for the future. Lifetime service was still taken to be the standard term of appointment, and the number of missionaries so designated remained a decisive marker by which many supporters and participants measured the progress of the missionary enterprise. The conceptual role played by statistics, the decision to maintain the status quo geographically while increasing the total number of missionaries deployed worldwide, and the widespread currency of career service nomenclature—these are three reasons in particular to characterize this period of American Presbyterian mission history in the Middle East as a time of "rebuilding" a model of mission that had been received from the past.

More missionaries were thought to be necessary after the war, especially because of the large number of well-established institutions for which the missions were still directly responsible. In Egypt, Iran, and Lebanon particularly, Presbyterians had been hard at work for over a century, creating a variety of educational, medical, and social service institutions to complement their church planting activities. Most of the congregations and a majority of the schools had already been turned over to local control, but many of the more specialized service institutions remained in the hands of the missions. Particular pride was taken in programs and organizations that had spearheaded notable innovations in their context (for example, education for women and girls), provided vital services of compassion otherwise still in short supply to local populations, or for some other reason enjoyed a high reputation at home and abroad, a factor that could bring prestige (and financial support) to the mission.

The leading institutions operated by the mission in Egypt in the early 1950s certainly included the hospitals in Tanta and Assiut, the American College for Girls in Cairo, the Schutz School in Alexandria, and Assiut College. The Theological Seminary in Cairo, although answering to the Synod of the Nile rather than the American Mission, was another high-profile institution that consistently included on its permanent faculty several missionary members.[8] In Iran, Presbyterian missionaries took care in their reports to highlight the work of the Alborz Foundation, the Bethel Community Center, and the Clinic of Hope (all located in Tehran), as well as five hospitals spread throughout the country and three associated nursing programs. Over this period a steady number of missionaries were also assigned to the Community School in Tehran, which offered its well-regarded educational program to a relatively few missionary children and a much larger and growing group of international expatriate students and children of the Iranian elite. Most of the ongoing Presbyterian institutional commitments in Syria-Lebanon were also educational, with the American School for Girls in Beirut, Beirut College for Women (begun as the American Junior College), and Aleppo College (operated together with the ABCFM) leading the list.[9] Also noteworthy in Lebanon was the Kennedy Memorial Hospital in Tripoli and the Near East School of Theology in Beirut, both still headed by American missionaries through most of this period. At the center of Presbyterian efforts in Iraq was the Baghdad Girls' School.

In each of the fields (Iraq was the exception, because it was so small), groups of Presbyterian personnel also tended to cluster around the missionary establishment itself. Some long-term people were needed to manage the complex business of the missions. Ongoing expenses and salaries (not only for missionaries but also for local employees and some church workers on the payroll of the mission) required the services of accountants, business managers, and mission treasurers. A steady stream of official correspondence with the church back home and the constant need to interact with local authorities and various national government agencies on a variety of issues also occupied the staff attached to the mission office, some of whom would have been career missionaries (spouses assumed many of these office duties, often without much recognition). Generally speaking, the mission organizations themselves had to secure work permits for missionaries in this period. With so many foreign workers involved in five different countries, the administrative demands on time could be substantial, especially when problems arose. Similarly long were the hours needed to keep track of property matters.[10] The head of the mission, generally chosen from among those missionaries with the most experience on the field, presided over the whole administrative structure.

Other missionaries were assigned to evangelistic work. Exactly what that designation might have meant during this period was not fixed, but often implied a close working partnership with one or more native pastors in a local setting. The opportunities for visiting, speaking at church gatherings, and working with youth were virtually limitless. Aside from technological advances in the medical field introduced through the mission hospitals and nursing programs, this is the area of mission service where new approaches were most likely to be tried in the 1950s. In Beirut, Cairo, and Tehran, for example, new attempts at outreach were begun that focused on university students. That this had become a primary emphasis of the Alborz Foundation by the late 1950s was signaled by the decision of the mission to move the activities of this program (centered on English language instruction) to a building located near the main gate of Tehran University. In Beirut, a new University Christian Center served a similar function for interested students attending the American University of Beirut, Beirut College for Women, and other colleges in the area.

Other new initiatives were begun in the area of audiovisuals. An early pioneer was Ewing M. Bailey in Cairo, whose vision in the 1950s for an expanded media ministry under the auspices of the mission eventually became the Christian Center for Audio-Visual Services in 1963. The Center lent filmstrips, reel recordings, projectors, and other equipment to borrowing churches located throughout Egypt. This project was a boon to the Christian Education programs of as many as a thousand different Protestant, Orthodox, and Catholic congregations spread throughout the country.[11] The Center also undertook to produce films, focusing on the life of Christ and episodes from the history of the early church. To the extent that these activities could (and did) reach beyond the walls of existing congregations and so tell the church's story to a broader audience, the mission's audiovisual ministries were also evangelistic endeavors. In the late 1950s, less extensive media programs were similarly developed in Beirut and Tehran.

The needs and special circumstances of rural Middle Easterners prompted some additional fresh thinking by the missions in this period. Again, the Presbyterian mission in Egypt may have been the most innovative of the four Presbyterian mission bodies, launching creative ventures in animal husbandry and literacy in particular.[12] The new work in literacy, begun in the late 1940s by Davida Finney, was remarkable in more than one respect. Not only did this program (following the methods of Frank Laubach) succeed as a means of enabling significant numbers of adults in Egyptian villages to read; it also became the starting point of a comprehensive approach to development and evangelical outreach that would eventually encompass a range of additional projects in agriculture, medical care, health education, home economics, book publishing, Bible study, leadership training, and even interfaith dialogue. A transitional element was supplied in 1957 by the creation of the Rural Church Service Team, a cooperative venture jointly sponsored by the mission and the Egyptian Evangelical Church. A few years later, the government demanded that the expanding assemblage of religious and social services offered by the team in the region of Middle Egypt (roughly, between Assiut and Minya) be officially registered with the Ministry of Social Affairs. To comply, a completely new administrative structure had to be devised. This was the Coptic Evangelical Organization for Social Services (CEOSS), created in 1960 under the direction of the Reverend Samuel Habib.[13] Thus, in the course of the 1950s, a rather modest set of programmatic beginnings guided primarily by missionaries evolved in just a decade to become a self-standing church-related development organization that was quite independent of the mission. Over the next four decades, CEOSS would be recognized repeatedly as a model indigenous nongovernmental organization (NGO) in service to the rural poor.

Up to 1958, most of the hundreds of Presbyterian missionaries sent to the Middle East were trained for their work on the field. Medical personnel aside, the vast majority of these missionaries had not acquired any specialized skills that would have qualified them for the jobs described above that they were about to assume.[14] A typical first-termer was a graduate of a church-related college who had not previously studied Arabic (or Persian, for service in Iran). Educators, to be sure, brought with them whatever teaching credentials were required by the authorities and ordained personnel would have been to seminary, but even these new missionaries were still generalists, by and large, since few if any had been trained specifically for ministry or teaching in cross-cultural settings. It was the rare candidate who had a deep knowledge of Islam before taking up residence as a Presbyterian missionary in the Middle East. For their part, the sending churches provided only the briefest of orientation programs before dispatching their new personnel abroad.

Within this larger group of new recruits are two subsets, whose backgrounds distinguished them from the rest. The first of these were children of serving missionaries, who had spent substantial parts of their childhoods in the region. While not necessarily fluent in the local language at the time of their appointment, these young missionaries often had a readiness to learn that enabled them to make progress more quickly than those who had never been exposed to a Middle Eastern cultural environment. The other subset comprised those new missionaries who had already completed three-year appointments in the region as "short-termers." These, too, had had an opportunity to be acculturated to the Middle East in ways that could not be duplicated at home. They were not expected necessarily to have acquired fluency in the local language, but their experience abroad gave them an invaluable basis on which to build as first-term career appointees. Some overlap is to be found with respect to these two subsets. The robust program of short-term service in effect at midcentury worked quite well as a mechanism for recruiting and screening would-be career candidates.

The mission organizations on the field took responsibility for training new arrivals. Since career service was still the expected norm, an extended period of full-time language learning could be built into the first term of service abroad. Formal programs in the study of Arabic and Persian for foreigners were not numerous at this time. One possibility was offered by the Near Eastern Institute of Languages located in Jerusalem. During this period a large contingent of Egypt missionaries received their instruction in Arabic through the School of Oriental Studies at the American University in Cairo (AUC).[15] Many of those assigned to evangelism or development work (as opposed to medical service or teaching English in one of the mission's schools) were then placed in villages for several years, which became a kind of postgraduate course in the language and culture of their new home country. Typically, in all of the fields, a language committee of the mission would evaluate the linguistic progress of the first-termers.[16]

A survey of the missions as they appeared around the year 1958 will close out this section. We begin with Iraq, which was by far the smallest of the Middle Eastern fields to which Presbyterians were assigned. The United Mission in Iraq was a joint venture, in which the PCUSA, PCUS, the Reformed Church in America, and the United Church of Christ participated together. Through the 1950s, missionaries worked in as many as five different stations (Baghdad, Mosul, Kirkuk, Basheeqa, and Hillah), but their numbers were so few that it was not possible to staff all of these locations on a continuous basis. The Presbyterian-related Protestant church in Iraq counted several hundred communicant members, worshiping in four congregations and a few other meeting points, served by one ordained pastor and two evangelists.

In contrast to the situation in Iraq, the Iran Mission of the PCUSA was a flourishing enterprise in 1958. Almost all of the Presbyterian missionaries were assigned to work in or near six cities located in the northern half of the country (Tabriz, Tehran, Resht, Meshed, Kermanshah, and Hamadan). By comity agreement, the Anglican Church Missionary Society focused its energies on the south, where the British government had had a military presence during the Second World War. The demographic composition of the Protestant community in Iran was complex, with separate church bodies formed along the lines of language (Persian, Armenian, and Syriac/Assyrian). The aggregate number of Protestants spread out among these three Christian communities was quite small, with the result that the size of the mission (79 long-term missionaries reported in 1958) dwarfed that of the native church leadership (8 ordained pastors and 13 unordained evangelists). Another distinguishing characteristic of the Iran mission was the relative freedom its members enjoyed within that country.[17] This was a time during which official relations between Iran and the United States were warming, and it appears that the mission benefited from a generally good reputation still held by America within many sectors of Iranian society. Most extraordinarily for the region, a small but steady number of converts in Iran were coming to Christian faith from Islam during this period, with a few even serving as pastors or evangelists in the Persian-speaking Iranian church.

The Presbyterian mission in Syria-Lebanon resembled its Iranian counterpart in that its missionary corps outnumbered the native pastors and evangelists by more than two to one (59 long-term missionaries compared to 15 ordained ministers and 11 evangelists, according to 1958 UPCUSA statistics). Additionally, the mission was still responsible for a large number of institutions, as already noted. For the most part, these institutions were located in Lebanon rather than Syria, with a high concentration of missionaries assigned to Beirut. Several other local factors defined the circumstances of the mission in Syria-Lebanon during these years. First, an influx of Palestinian refugees into Lebanon after 1948 presented the mission with a pressing humanitarian emergency, to which several missionaries attempted to respond. At the same time, this crisis raised uncomfortable questions about the American nationality of the missionaries, since the United States was widely perceived to be Israel's enabler.[18] The contrast here with the situation of Presbyterian missionaries in Iran is striking. Restrictions on missionary activity in Syria-Lebanon were to increase in the 1950s. And a new tone began to be sounded in the calls to Arab nationalism that rang out in this part of the Middle East. Although American Presbyterian missionaries had strongly resonated with many earlier expressions of Arab nationalism that had stood in opposition to Turkish rule or French colonial activity, in the post-1948 era America increasingly became the "other" that was seen to threaten the well-being of the Arab nation.[19] Not surprisingly, this is also a time during which a new round of polemical antimissionary literature began to appear in Beirut and elsewhere.[20]

In the context of Egypt, especially after the 1952 revolution, a rising tide of Arab nationalism, stoked by President Gamal Abdul Nasser for his own political purposes, likewise translated into new constraints on missionary activities, especially in the area of education. In the mid-1950s, for example, government-promulgated regulations prohibited missionaries from teaching Christianity to Muslim students in their schools as they had been doing for generations.[21] Subsequently, the government would require foreign administrators in the mission schools to relinquish their leadership posts to Egyptian nationals. Despite these restrictions, the American Mission in Egypt continued to expand its ranks through the 1950s, as noted above. Its contingent of long-term workers (114 in 1958) remained the largest collection of Presbyterian missionaries in the region. In this case, however, a century of Presbyterian mission efforts (beginning in

1854) had resulted in a Protestant community of such a size that it was able to support many more ordained ministers (170 reported in 1958) than there were missionaries. This church, too, had developed into a mission-sending body, able to sponsor its own evangelists in the Sudan and to pioneer new methods of outreach domestically through CEOSS, the independent but still church-related social service agency. In Egypt at least, the stage had been set for a more mature partnership to develop between the American Mission and the indigenous Protestant church founded in response to its efforts.

THE HINGE OF TRANSITION

What follows in the two decades after the merger of 1958 is largely due to adjustments in mission theology that increasingly took hold among American Presbyterians from the mid-1950s, which attempted to reconcile an abiding commitment to Christian mission with a world context undergoing rapid social change. The leading articulators of the new approach were not theologians or serving missionaries but church executives. To a significant degree their point of view was shaped by active participation in the ecumenical movement and by the waves of decolonization that were then transforming many of the old Presbyterian mission fields. In the particular case of the Middle East, the missions and those trying to chart their future also had to contend with recurrent episodes of instability in the region, whether due to revolution, civil war, or large-scale conflicts between states.

When the UPCNA and PCUSA united in 1958, the four Presbyterian mission fields in the Middle East would find themselves together for the first time under a single administrative structure, COEMAR. Since the practices and policies of the two churches were not exactly the same across the board, the run-up to the merger created a rare opportunity for mission executives to reassess inherited patterns and the theological principles underlying them. This they did with some enthusiasm and a high sense of purpose, according to the accounts given later by John Coventry Smith and Donald Black.[22]

Thus, with respect to policy changes, the year 1958 by itself does not represent a sharp break with the past. It is more like the midpoint in a process of reassessment and planning that had already begun several years earlier in anticipation of ecclesiastical merger. A key event was the Lake Mohonk consultation, convened by the PCUSA in 1956.[23] Here the aim of "integration" was adopted as a cardinal principle of Presbyterian mission strategy going forward. Integration meant dismantling the mission organizations and missionary associations abroad, the transfer of property and responsibility for mission institutions to national churches or other parties as quickly as possible, and an intention that missionaries would answer more directly to national church leaders rather than to fellow missionaries. At about the same time, the UPCNA was doing its part to prepare the way for the merger by making two major changes in its own organizational structures related to mission. One of these involved the elimination of overseas synods, a designation whereby mission-founded churches had been treated juris-dictionally as foreign branches of the American denomination. As part of this process, the Synod of the Nile formally requested and received its complete inde-pendence from the UPCNA by action of that denomination's General Assembly in 1957. A second action that also brought the UPCNA more closely into con-formity with the practices of the PCUSA was its decision to end the separate authority for mission appointments and foreign mission grant-making up to then enjoyed by the Women's General Missionary Society.[24] By action of the 1955 Gen-eral Assembly, a single Board of Foreign Missions, with representatives from the Women's Society included in its membership, was to have authority over all mis-sion funds and personnel appointments.[25]

Fully implementing the perspective on mission represented by Lake Mohonk, which had been institutionalized in the structures and operating principles of COEMAR, was to take some time and would not go forward at the same rate in every location where Presbyterian missionaries were active. An initial priority in the Middle East as elsewhere was to prepare for the transfer of mission proper-ties. For this to happen, the receiving churches had to have administrative struc-tures in place that could take responsibility for the properties and manage the programs associated with mission-owned land and buildings. They also needed to have trained administrators at hand, which sometimes implied an additional investment of time and resources for leadership development. Many of the insti-tutions to be transferred to church authorities were not self-sustaining, whether through tuition payments or fees remitted by those who used medical and other social services. Would the churches be expected to make up the difference in run-ning costs while also having to maintain an aging infrastructure? To ease the financial shock of this transition, a significant portion of the 50 Million Fund was designated for the capital needs of sister churches abroad.[26]

Many properties and programs were successfully transferred to responsible church bodies, which proved themselves to be quite able to manage what the mis-sions had begun. In the case of CEOSS, already mentioned, an innovative agency related to a national Presbyterian church not only kept existing work in literacy and rural evangelism viable but soon moved to expand into new areas of service not necessarily anticipated by the missionary founders of what had been more limited programs. A similar outcome was achieved in Egypt with respect to the dozen schools still under mission control in the late 1950s. Prompted by a gov-ernment law promulgated in 1962 that required all school principals to be Egypt-ian, the church decided to create a new Board of Management that would assume immediate responsibility for the mission schools. In the decades since that deci-sion was taken, the Evangelical Church in Egypt has actually doubled the num-ber of schools under its management.[27] Along the way a notable innovation was embodied in the development of New Ramses College, a pioneering program in children's coeducation begun in the 1990s on the grounds of the Ramses College for Girls in Cairo (formerly the American College for Girls).

Not all transfers proposed by COEMAR proceeded as smoothly as these did. In Iran and Syria-Lebanon especially, much smaller churches simply could not absorb or manage all the programs offered to them. Some of these programs therefore had to be discontinued and, whenever possible, the properties were sold in order to fund other activities considered to be a higher priority by the national church. In several instances, mission institutions were turned over to secular entities. Such was the case of the American Mission hospital in Assiut, Egypt, for example, which was rented to the local governorate for a nominal sum.[28] In Iran, similar arrangements were made to link mission hospitals in Tabriz and Meshed to local university training programs in medicine. Another approach explored the possibility of transferring to the Ministry of Health a social service outreach program located in one of the poorest sections of Tehran and a nursing program in Meshed.[29]

In some cases, it was preferable to transfer authority for a given institution to an autonomous board of directors, on which the local church and COEMAR might both be represented. This was the method by which the Community School in Tehran, the Schutz School in Alexandria, Beirut Women's College, and what became Damavand College (earlier known as Iran-Bethel School) all passed out of mission control.[30] The Near East School of Theology in Beirut, as an institution serving the ministry training needs of more than one Protestant church community, was also placed under the authority of an independent board of directors, to which COEMAR was invited to appoint its own representatives. Additionally, the Middle East Council of Churches (MECC) assumed responsibility for two ministries of the American Mission located in Cairo: the Christian Center for Audio-Visual Services already mentioned and a Library of Sacred Music program that provided both resources and training to local church musicians.

Even after decades of effort to transfer real estate to local authorities, many mission properties would continue to be held in the name of the American church or one of its related entities. In the tricky legal environment of the Middle East, churches could not always be sure of their ability to hold on to properties received from American hands, especially if those holdings were located in particularly desirable real estate markets. In these circumstances, it sometimes made more sense for local church authorities to be given a power of attorney that granted them effective control over mission holdings but did not entail transfer taxes or unwanted exposure to an unpredictable legal system.[31]

Not surprisingly, through this period of transition the number of Presbyterian missionaries serving in the Middle East dropped steadily. In the first decade after the merger, the decrease was gradual and was managed according to a coherent strategy of retrenchment in personnel that matched the church's determination to shrink its institutional presence around the world. Most of the "career" missionaries already on the field were allowed to continue in that capacity until retirement. A few remained at their posts but were supported by their host institutions instead of COEMAR. Some new missionaries were sent to the region, but now with the understanding that theirs was a limited term (or "special term") rather than a lifetime appointment. By the end of 1966 the effects of this policy shift were becoming evident with respect to the level of Presbyterian missionaries then serving in the Middle East. The total number of fraternal workers reported in the 1967 Minutes of the General Assembly had dropped from 261 in 1958 to 210, with 160 of these classified "career" missionaries and 50 "special term." These were distributed as follows: 78 in Iran, 69 in Egypt, 48 in Lebanon, 8 in Iraq, plus 7 classified as "Middle East—General." Additionally, there were 22 volunteers in mission serving in Iran, Egypt, and Lebanon.[32]

From 1967 to 1979 a series of crises in the Middle East further stimulated the decline in the number of personnel deployed in the region.[33] The first of these emergency situations was presented by the June War of 1967. In the context of this pivotal conflict, America's military, financial, and diplomatic patronage of Israel put the safety of U.S. citizens at risk in several Arab states. A short-term result in Iraq was that all Presbyterian mission personnel had to leave the country for safe haven in Iran. After a few weeks these missionaries returned, but when the government of Iraq in 1969 moved to seize two schools operated by the United Mission to Iraq and to expel the missionaries working at the schools, COEMAR decided to close the mission altogether. The nine missionaries still assigned to that country were reassigned to other posts in the region.

Egypt was the other location most profoundly affected by the events of 1967. As in 1956, the missionaries were evacuated out of the country by order of the American Embassy, but this time mission executives decided not to have them return to Egypt immediately after the war's conclusion. A one-year moratorium was observed instead, during which extensive consultations on the future of Presbyterian mission work in that country were conducted with the Egyptian Evangelical Church. First, an interim agreement on the mission to be shared by the two churches together was drawn up. In connection with these discussions, it was decided to dissolve the American Mission as an official organization of the UPCUSA and to transfer all remaining institutions to Synod control. On the basis of this agreement, a limited number of Presbyterian missionaries received invitations to return to Egypt in the fall of 1968. Some longtime workers previously classified as "career" missionaries were not included in this group, a break with the pattern of force reductions in effect up to that time. The 1970 Minutes of the UPCUSA show 30 long-term Presbyterian missionaries on the rolls in Egypt (compared to 69 in December 1966).[34]

Lebanon was also affected by the June War of 1967 but not to the same degree as Egypt. Mission personnel were evacuated for a time, but most returned quite soon after the conclusion of hostilities. Lebanon's deeper crisis began in the mid-1970s, with the eruption of a civil war that would drag on for more than fifteen years. Many Westerners were evacuated in the summer of 1976 as civil order broke down and the prospects for a negotiated settlement diminished. A few long-serving Presbyterians stayed and did their best to contribute to the hard-pressed ministries and institutions to which they were assigned.[35] The kidnapping of Ben Weir in 1984 made it clear that even these mission workers were in danger, despite many years of acculturation and their knowledge of Arabic, and so almost all ended their work in Lebanon at this time.[36]

The Presbyterian mission in Iran was to face its most critical turning point in the late 1970s, on the occasion of the Iranian revolution that swept the Ayatollah Khomeini into power. Of the four traditional Presbyterian mission fields in the Middle East, this was the one least affected by the June 1967 war. As late as 1969, the mission establishment still numbered more than seventy.[37] But by the mid-1970s, this group had been whittled down to just fourteen fraternal workers, mostly through attrition and the transfer of almost all the mission institutions to Iranian control.[38] Then, almost overnight, the revolution brought more than a century of American Presbyterian mission presence in Iran to an abrupt end.

ONE ERA CLOSES, ANOTHER BEGINS

The previous section at several points has anticipated a part of the discussion to follow regarding the most recent period of Presbyterian mission in the Middle East. As we have seen, the 1960s and 1970s became a time during which many established patterns were broken and a new approach to mission in the Middle East was undertaken. It would be a mistake, however, to conclude that geopolitical crises alone determined the course of Presbyterian involvements in the Middle East during this period. After all, earlier challenges such as the 1956 Suez Crisis and the 1958 revolution in Iraq had only temporarily disrupted the Presbyterian mission program in the region, although the former event may have prompted a quickening of the impulse felt within the missions to nationalize their institutions.[39] To a great degree during this time of transition, mission theology led the way by suggesting how the UPCUSA ought to react to the difficulties and political roadblocks that arose.

Since the Iranian revolution, two trends have dominated Presbyterian mission work connected to the Middle East. The first of these is a matter of denouement, as the last of the career missionaries commissioned in the 1950s retired in the 1980s and 1990s. Some of these workers finished out their mission service in quiet but competent fashion, often with concerted efforts made to train their successors before leaving. Others used their last years on the field to bring long-term projects to completion; a few contributions of this nature may be mentioned here.

An example is the new Arabic hymnal produced in Lebanon under the direction of career missionary Else Farr. This resource for worship replaced the hymnal used since 1965 by the National Evangelical Synod of Syria and Lebanon, whose stocks had been completely destroyed in the Lebanese civil war.[40] Farr's work, carried out under the auspices of the Fellowship of Middle Eastern Evangelical Churches and involving many Lebanese collaborators, is all the more remarkable for having been completed in the chaotic circumstances of the Lebanese civil war.

John Lorimer's five-volume History of Christianity is another missionary project that was taken up in response to an articulated need of a partner church. A generation of seminary students in Egypt and elsewhere in the region has already benefited from this Arabic-language survey of Christian history that highlights theological and historical issues of particular interest to Middle Eastern Christians, both Orthodox and Protestant.[41]

A long-standing interest in the liturgical traditions of the Coptic Orthodox Church lay at the bottom of Martha Roy's work in musicology. Her most notable publication, jointly written over a decade with Ragheb Moftah and Margit Toth, presents the liturgy of St. Basil (with all its known variations included) as it has been used in the daily and special worship services of the Coptic Orthodox Church.[42] Moftah, director of the music and hymns department at the Coptic Institute for Higher Studies in Cairo, compiled the music, while Toth provided transcriptions. Besides editing the English and Arabic translations of the Coptic hymns, Roy contributed an introduction to the volume and its indices. The significance of Roy's work over many years in Coptic musicology cannot be summed up by reference to a single book. Through her teaching at the Evangelical Theological Seminary in Cairo (up to her formal retirement in 1978 and then for another two decades), the subject of liturgy and the importance of Orthodox worship traditions were given an emphasis not at all common among Middle Eastern Protestants. At the same time, Roy's teaching of musicology in non-Protestant contexts (most notably in the Faculty of Music Education of Helwan University) demonstrated an ecumenical spirit on the part of American Presbyterians. On more than one occasion, the Egyptian state has recognized Martha Roy's service to the nation. Among her honors is the National Award for Coptic Studies, conferred by President Anwar el-Sadat.[43]

Similarly multilayered is the educational ministry of Kenneth E. Bailey, offered over forty years of mission service through the Presbyterian Church and well into retirement. Over the course of his career, Bailey has specialized in New Testament studies, based at various times in Egypt, Lebanon, Cyprus, and Jerusalem. A long résumé of books, articles, film projects, and invited lectures attests to a sustained life of research on the parables of Jesus, the results of which have been mediated to a variety of publics in both the Middle East (primarily in Arabic) and the West.[44] Bailey's passion has been to understand the Near Eastern cultural background of the New Testament, especially the Palestinian village context of Jesus' ministry, which is completely opaque to most modern readers of the Gospels. Along the way, one of Bailey's aims has been to help living communities of Middle Eastern Christians connect with their own heritage. He has done this especially by working with church partners to establish academic institutes for the study of Middle Eastern Christianity at the Near East School of Theology in Beirut and the Evangelical Theological Seminary in Cairo.

In the case of Kenneth Bailey, the link between his early missionary experience and later scholarly contributions is clearly evident. Intensive Arabic study for several years at the beginning of his career, assignments in village settings, and the opportunity to be immersed in the life of Middle Eastern Christians nurtured an extraordinary point of view on the cultural background of the Bible. The other three individuals highlighted above likewise benefited from an approach to missionary formation that no longer exists in conciliar Protestant circles.[45] To a great degree, the accomplishments of Roy, Lorimer, Bailey, and Farr in their later years (plus others not mentioned by name here because of space limitations) may be understood to be a result of the church's careful investment in their development as missionaries many decades beforehand.

A second set of trends is attached to the group of Presbyterian missionaries more recently sent to the Middle East, who were not career appointees. Besides resembling each other with respect to their shorter terms of service, this group as a whole is also marked by a greater degree of specialization than would have been the case before the 1960s. More and more, the demand has been for coworkers with special skills or professional experience that enables them to contribute a particular kind of assistance to the mission of partner churches as quickly as possible. Examples include academics with advanced degrees, librarians, teacher training specialists, peace and justice workers with backgrounds in international law, community health practitioners, management experts, and people with fund-raising or grant-writing skills. A few mission personnel appointed since the 1960s have been connected to certain limited-term projects to which the UPCUSA or its successor, the Presbyterian Church (U.S.A.), has committed itself as a denomination.[46] Some coworker appointees in recent years have been able to complete substantial scholarly writing projects in the course of their work on behalf of the PC(USA).[47]

A shift has also taken place with respect to the locations to which Presbyterian mission workers have been sent since the 1970s. As we have seen, almost all of the missionaries dispatched to the Middle East until the mid-1960s went to one of five countries: Egypt, Iran, Syria, Lebanon, or Iraq. In each of these settings, missionary-directed structures were in place to receive new personnel and to coordinate Presbyterian work with a national partner church. Part of the restructuring that took place after 1958 at the behest of COEMAR involved the dismantling of missionary associations and mission organizations in favor of church-to-church relationships effected through church executives rather than missionaries.[48] Further, when new agreements were drawn up in the late 1960s between the UPCUSA and its longtime partner churches in the region, it was no longer assumed that the churches would restrict their ecumenical involvements to exclusive bilateral relationships as in the past.[49] This latter provision in the agreements seems to have been meant especially to encourage Middle Eastern churches to expand their ecumenical networks in support of indigenous mission goals. It also made room for American Presbyterians to consider allocating personnel and resources in new ways.

Thus, we begin to find Presbyterian missionaries assigned to some quite untraditional places in the Middle East from the early 1970s. These new placements included the Gulf region, in countries such as Oman, Bahrain, and Kuwait. A small but steady stream of Presbyterian workers to the West Bank and East Jerusalem got under way later in the same decade. Many of these were teaching at Birzeit University, the first Palestinian institution of higher education on the West Bank. Cyprus became another destination for personnel (both new and relocated), with most associated in some way with the Middle East Council of Churches, which had moved some of its offices temporarily to the island from war-torn Beirut. From time to time, one or another of the Presbyterian denominations has also had overseas associates in Turkey. As of the 2006 meeting of the General Assembly, 18 mission coworkers or mission specialists were assigned to the Middle East: 8 in Egypt, 6 in Turkey, 3 in the West Bank and Jerusalem, 1 in Lebanon. Seven other individuals currently serve in shorter-term capacities.

Presbyterian mission in the Middle East has been further shaped by at least one more trend that has emerged since the late 1970s. This is the growing need for Presbyterian missionaries and their national hosts to operate as interpreters of the Christian mission in the region for interested groups that come visiting from abroad. In earlier decades, American Presbyterians back home usually got their eyewitness accounts from missionaries on furlough, when they came to visit their supporting congregations. Such interactions still take place, but easier travel in recent decades has made it possible for many more American Christians to come and see for themselves.[50] Some are members of official church delegations. Others join a travel group brought together by a local congregation, an advocacy organization, or a church-related educational institution. As these groups became more numerous, Presbyterian mission personnel were increasingly called on to help Middle Eastern churches interpret their mission in this part of the world. And since conflict and passion seem to have become permanently attached to the Middle East, the interpretive task to be undertaken remains exceedingly complex.

AN ABIDING ISSUE

Throughout the period under discussion in this chapter, the struggle of Jews and Arabs over the land of Israel/Palestine has been a constant factor shaping the environment within which Presbyterian missions have had to operate in the Middle East. But not always in the same way, since the nature of that conflict has changed over time, and the manner in which Presbyterian churches have engaged with the region and its problems has also shifted in major ways.

Before 1967, Lebanon was the primary location for contact between Presbyterian missionaries and people directly affected in negative ways by the conflict. Hundreds of thousands of Palestinian refugees settled in Lebanon after the battles of 1948–49. Sizable refugee camps were set up in the area of Sidon and on the outskirts of Beirut, both places where mission institutions were already functioning. For a time, Presbyterian missionary Harry G. Dorman Jr. was executive secretary of the Near East Christian Council, which coordinated much of the relief work provided to refugees in Lebanon from Palestine.[51] Additional work in southern Lebanon in connection with the Marjayoun cooperative parish put missionaries in a particularly sensitive area just north of the Lebanese-Israeli border. Presbyterian missionaries in Syria, Egypt, and Iraq were not as often in daily contact with Palestinian refugees as their colleagues in Lebanon, but the Arab societies in which they lived and worked were permeated by strong feelings against the creation of the State of Israel, feelings impossible for the missionaries to ignore. In Iran under Mohammad Reza Shah Pahlavi (1941–79), Palestine was a more remote issue, lacking the strong resonance it had for Arabs. Up to 1967, there was no permanent American Presbyterian mission presence in Israel, Jordan (including the West Bank), or the Gaza Strip (under Egyptian control since 1948).

After 1967, the refugee population in Lebanon grew as new arrivals fled or were driven from their homes in Palestine. The country also became a major center for planning and launching attacks against targets in Israel by a variety of Palestinian guerilla forces. Large-scale military incursions by Israeli troops into Lebanon took place in 1978 and 1982, after which southern Lebanon found itself occupied by Israel until the year 2000. Coupled with the effects of Lebanon's own civil war (itself affected by the activities of many non-Lebanese interests at work in the country), these conditions of unrest eventually made it impossible for Presbyterian missionaries to remain in Lebanon.

As noted above, Presbyterian mission personnel were appointed for service in the West Bank from the early 1970s. At the same time, program grants began to be made to Palestinian institutions such as Birzeit University. These new forms of Presbyterian mission activity in the region happened to coincide with the commencement and then the explosive growth of Israeli settlements in the Occupied Territories. Before long, what had been primarily a set of relief programs for displaced persons soon became focused more on peace and justice issues, as attentive Presbyterians sought ways to encourage the establishment of peaceful relations between Israeli Jews and Palestinian Muslims and Christians on the basis of a just resolution of the disputes between them. Eventually, the Occupation itself became the central issue for many Presbyterians concerned about the Middle East.

The formulation of Presbyterian policy statements on the Middle East was largely carried out at church headquarters by mission executives rather than on the field by serving missionaries. This is not to say that the experience of missionaries in the Middle East had no effect on these statements. Broadly speaking, before the dissolution of the region's mission organizations, mission executives back home looked first to their people on the ground for expert advice. As national church leaders began to interface more directly with their counterparts in the American church structures from the late 1960s, their voices became increasingly influential in these debates. Especially in times of crisis, the concerns of Middle East Christians have also been articulated effectively through the offices of the Middle East Council of Churches. Some other Presbyterian actors with influential points of view worked in New York in connection with the Presbyterian United Nations office or in Geneva, where ecumenical discussions on the Middle East were taking place on a regular basis.[52] Executives within the central structures of the church with responsibility for interfaith relations have also contributed invaluable expertise.[53] In addition, acknowledgment has to be given to the unique role played by Benjamin and Carol Weir in Presbyterian debates on the Middle East since the mid-1980s. During Ben Weir's captivity, Carol Weir became a public spokesperson whose critique of the Reagan administration's approach to the Middle East received high visibility.[54] After his release in 1985, Ben Weir was elected moderator of the Presbyterian Church (U.S.A.), which meant that he has often been asked to comment on developments in the region, both inside and beyond church circles. Similarly active on a national level has been Fahed Abu-Akel, a Palestinian-American pastor elected moderator in 2002.

Within the different Presbyterian church structures that existed between 1944 and 2004, a single person usually was positioned at the point where these different sources of advice and information most often intersected: the Middle East "desk." When formal statements of policy had to be prepared or interpreted, the Middle East area secretary was often the one called upon to draft the language to be used. Many capable individuals have served in this position over the years, including at least two with relevant mission experience: Margaret O. Thomas (Iran) and Byron Haines (Pakistan). The current incumbent, Victor E. Makari, is a native of Egypt, who previously had been a member of the Program Agency Board (and for a time its chair) before his appointment as Middle East area coordinator in 1990. In all, Makari has been an able and active force in shaping Presbyterian policy on the Middle East for more than twenty-five years.

The following points, based on the pronouncements of multiple General Assemblies, sum up the current stance of the PC(USA) on the Israeli-Palestinian conflict:

- The PC(USA) supports the resolutions of the United Nations, affirming the right of Israel to exist within secure borders and the right of Palestinians to self-determination, including the establishment of their own sovereign state and right of return for Palestinian refugees.
- Presbyterians call on Palestinians and Israelis to cease their acts of violence against each other.
- The General Assembly urges the Israeli government to end its expansionist policies of confiscating land and water resources, building and enlarging settlements, and collectively punishing Palestinians.
- The church calls on the Israeli government to end the occupation of the West Bank, Gaza Strip, and East Jerusalem.
- The PC(USA) also calls on the United States government to intervene actively with the government of Israel and the Palestinian Authority to broker a just, secure, and permanent peace.[55]

Less settled at the close of the period under review is the proposal adopted by the 2004 General Assembly, whereby the church would begin a process of phased, selective divestment from multinational corporations that enable and profit from the Israeli occupation of Palestinian lands. Some opponents of the move mischaracterized it as a total boycott of Israel. In the aftermath of the Assembly, other critics appealed for support by suggesting that this was another example of national church staff members going off on their own without regard for the views of the rank and file in Presbyterian pews.[56] The General Assembly of 2006 adopted a resolution calling on the church to employ its Mission Responsibility through Investment (MRTI) process to ensure that only investments in "peaceful pursuits" would be made with the corporate funds of the PC(USA). No single interpretation of this shift in language seems to have taken hold up to now. On the one hand, the terminology of divestment has been made less prominent in favor of wording that highlights positive outcomes. Yet the possibility of divestment in the future remains, and the church's condemnation of the Occupation has not been essentially modified.[57]

AN ONGOING STORY

Sustained interest on the part of many Presbyterians in the just resolution of the Israeli-Palestinian conflict means that the denomination is bound to remain engaged with the region. Implied in this interest is a willingness to enter into serious dialogue with a variety of people living in the area who represent many different faith perspectives. Equally imperative is the need to remain connected to established Christian communities that find themselves under enormous political and demographic pressure. In Israel/Palestine especially, accelerating levels of Christian emigration from the area are threatening the viability of more than one church communion.[58] Presbyterians are thus being challenged to act in ways that will make their Christian and ecumenical commitments visible and meaningful in what are sure to remain contentious social contexts. In the mid-twentieth century, as we have seen, the sending of missionaries to the Middle East for lifetimes of service and witness was still considered to be the most genuine possible expression of dedication to mission in this part of the world. Now, shorter terms of service predominate, and a permanent missionary establishment is no longer at the center of Presbyterian mission efforts in the Middle East.

In whatever ways Presbyterians may decide to relate to the Middle East in the future, their involvements will occur in a historical context shaped by more than 175 years of mission experience. A particularly important by-product of this history is the set of relationships that has been forged over time between American Presbyterians and Middle Eastern Christians. Long-standing ties with fellow Christians need not be taken as restrictive limits beyond which American Presbyterians must never go, but they do represent an invaluable resource for reflection on the next stage of what has become a shared mission of Christian witness and service in the Middle East.

Chapter 11

Africa

WILLIAM B. ANDERSON

Presbyterian missionary work began in Africa in 1833 in western regions such as Liberia, Corsico, Spanish Guinea, Gabon, and finally in 1889 in the Cameroon, and 1890 in the Congo. It was the work in the Congo and Cameroon that was lasting, and these became two of the main missions of the Presbyterian Church. Work began in the Sudan (from the Egypt station) in 1900, and then the Ethiopia mission commenced in 1919. During these early periods, Christianity developed under the colonial European powers of France, Great Britain, Germany, and briefly under the Spanish.[1] This chapter will discuss what happened in the key areas in which the Presbyterian Church has historically been present in Africa (Ethiopia, Cameroon, Congo, and Sudan). A few other regions will also be mentioned but not to the same degree as the four main countries above since the history of Presbyterian involvement in those regions is shorter.

ETHIOPIA

The Presbyterian mission in Ethiopia[2] was started by Dr. Tom Lambie in 1919. Tom was working at Nasir in Sudan, on the edge of Ethiopia. He felt fascinated by the call of Ethiopia's Western Plateau, overlooking Sudan. The flu epidemic in 1918 made the call of Ethiopians for a doctor insistent, and Dr. Lambie was eager to go. In 1919, his small mission party climbed three days up the plateau to Dembi Dollo, among the Oromo, and quickly decided Western Ethiopia was their call.

One young blind man, Gidada, heard the gospel from Lambie and was taught by a missionary, Fred Russell. Gidada showed such ability to learn that he was called to live at the mission and learn daily. Before leaving because of the Italian invasion, Russell made arrangements for Gidada's marriage and for his ministry. It was only the beginning of an Oromo church, but the mission could not stay because in 1935 Italians invaded the country and swept through the whole land by mid-1936. The missionaries left, with many being reassigned to nearby South Sudan. The relationship between the mission work in Ethiopia and Sudan would be an important one. The Italians pushed the few new believers out of their church at the Dembi Dollo Mission, but the flow of Ethiopian evangelism was not stemmed. Believers sprang up, gathering under trees or in homes. The blind man, Gidada, and other leaders spreading the good news heard that one Presbyterian missionary remained in Addis Ababa: Duncan Henry. They wrote to him about the growing groups of believers and pled for pastors to baptize the many new converts, organize the churches, and conduct Holy Communion. Henry was astonished: he wrote back to Dembi Dollo to choose the best evangelists, who knew the Word of God, and send them to him at Addis. The first to be sent was Mamo Chorqa, whom Henry trained for two months and then ordained. The second sent was Gidada, who arrived with a guide. Gidada also received two months' training and then was ordained. To lay their hands on these evangelists, Henry gathered an extraordinary "team" that included himself and a former Ethiopian Orthodox priest, who became an evangelist and pastored a Lutheran congregation in Addis. They were joined by a Waldensian (Italian Calvinists who predate the Reformation) Italian army chaplain, making it one of the most ecumenical of ordinations.

Gidada and his guide returned to Dembi Dollo, building and spreading the church. In 1942, the Italians surrendered, and Emperor Haile Selassie returned in triumph. Dr. Dougherty, a missionary doctor then serving in Sudan but previously in Ethiopia, visited and reported: the Ethiopian church was alive; the single fellowship they left behind had become seven churches and was spreading! So the Mission returned to find an independent, fully functioning church, the Ethiopian Evangelical Church, Bethel. This church was unique in our mission work in Africa because it had never been under missionary control. It began as an independent and self-supporting African Christian movement.

The Mission decided to concentrate on evangelism and ministry in the remote west and southwest areas of Ethiopia that had become the Presbyterians' responsibility. This meant that the Mission decided not to reopen the large Ras Teferi Hospital in Addis Ababa in favor of concentrating on the West. In Addis Ababa, they kept the mission headquarters, as required by government regulation, and reopened the American Mission Girls' School, the first educational institution for girls, which was founded in 1924. The decision not to reopen the hospital caused a major conflict with the government. Ras Teferi Hospital had been the first mission hospital in Addis Ababa and was named after the crown prince, now Emperor Haile Selassie. Even so, the mission remained firm in its decision to concentrate on the southwest, so it abandoned the hospital to the government and was given a new parcel of land to rebuild the mission headquarters.

As the Ethiopia work expanded, the Mission invited Don McClure to center his Anuak work in Ethiopia, at Pokwo. McClure developed a good relationship with Haile Selassie and even secured permission to use, publish, and distribute literature in Anuak rather than Amharic, the official language of Ethiopia. The mission opened two new stations, one at Maji in 1948 and another at Ghimeera in 1951.

The mission kept searching for the best direction as it expanded its work among many illiterate peoples. Glen Reed, who had been the mission area director, chaired the Advisory Study, which COEMAR commissioned to evaluate its mission strategy.[3] The Mission studied it carefully. The Study dealt with making the message of the gospel "contextualized," fitting the good news to the context of the local population. It also stressed the value of the Nevius Plan, used in Korea, which stressed that each new church must be self-supporting, self-propagating, and self-governing. This Nevius Plan so effective in Korea now became a guiding principle for Ethiopia.

In early 1959, the Ethiopian emperor asked Don McClure why the mission was neglecting the huge remote southwest corner of Ethiopia. McClure replied that the mission needed more people to expand its work and that it could not secure government permission for any new missionaries. His Majesty replied, in effect, "If you will expand your work among those needy people, I will personally make sure that permission is given for all the new missionaries you request." Southwestern Ethiopia was a huge area with at least a million people and was divided into multiple tribes with differing languages, none of which had been studied or even written down. Although the emperor opened the door for more missionaries to arrive, the mission received little help from the home base in the United States. Funding was in decline, and Presbyterian philosophy at the time discouraged missionary initiative.

Around this time, Harold Kurtz and his family went home for a year. Harold was invited to be an "advisory delegate" at the 1959 UPCUSA GA meeting. He noticed that that year's financial report showed additional funds allocated to International Mission. With "the privilege of the floor," Harold reported the challenge of Emperor Haile Selassie to enter southwest Ethiopia. A commissioner told the denomination that Harold was giving a "Macedonian call" (Acts 16:9) and moved to take a special offering. This Ethiopian "Unreached Peoples'" project was thus made the centerpiece of the 50 Million Fund. New funds were raised, new missionaries were recruited, and missionaries, newly expelled from South Sudan, joined the project.

Moving missionaries to the "Unreached Peoples" in a remote part of Ethiopia involved physical difficulties. Since the tribal groups were living in remote areas accessible only by foot and pack animals, Mission Aviation Fellowship was urgently requested to begin operations in Ethiopia. It agreed, and an additional plane was promised. But the question still remained, Could our missionaries effectively work among illiterate peoples living in such remote areas?

When Niles Reimer and Harold Kurtz were on furlough one year, they attended the newly established School of World Mission at Fuller Seminary, in Pasadena, California. The opening of this school was very timely, for it provided these field missionaries new insights and tools in the critical area of how to plant a contextualized, indigenous church, one that spoke the "language" of the people, was rooted and grounded in the mother culture, and met the people's needs and anxieties. The insights learned from these studies led the Ethiopia Mission to make a dramatic and significant change in its policy and missiology. Kurtz was asked to assume the position of mission secretary and in that capacity to facilitate the implementation of the church growth strategies gained at Fuller.[4]

A few years later the Hoekstra family followed a similar course. Hoekstra had been a translator in Sudan and had put the entire New Testament into Anuak. In Ethiopia, he committed himself to the mission's decision to focus on developing a preliterate church rather than lose at least two generations while waiting for an educated leadership. Instead of waiting for the final translation and printing of the New Testament, he began to use tapes with Bible messages in the local language. These tapes were used to develop a biblical oral tradition that would serve the new community well until education and Bible translation began to have their influence.

A deep and effective partnership was worked out with Bethel Church to support the work of opening up southwest Ethiopia. The first new mission stations included medical and educational institutions, whose expert and dedicated staff were commissioned by Bethel and worked alongside the missionaries in these unevangelized areas. The witness of Jesus and the kingdom was understood to be more authentic with this multinational, multiethnic contribution. Also, the hoped-for new believers were expected to immediately feel part of a recognized community, supported by Ethiopian brothers and sisters.

Church Relations and the Orthodox

The mission felt that it was imperative to develop good relations with other Christians, especially with the Orthodox.[5] This was not always the feeling of the Bethel Church, which was often roughly treated by the ruling Orthodox. Though work among the new communities of the southwest was usually connected with Bethel, in one tribal area the local people, who did not want to create any unnecessary tensions with the government, aligned themselves with the Orthodox, who had a church in the local government town. As a result the mission established a unique ecumenical working relationship with the mission department of the Orthodox Trinity Cathedral in Addis Ababa.

Tension between the Mission and COEMAR

During this very fruitful period of southwest expansion, tension grew between the Ethiopia Mission and COEMAR in New York. During this late 1950s and early 1960s period, the trend in UPCUSA mission was to combine ecumenical mission and church relations. However, the Ethiopia Mission perceived COEMAR's shifting policies as favoring ecumenical relations at the expense of its mission involvement. It may have made sense for the denomination to decrease its mission force during the peak of the antimissionary attitude found in some receiving countries in the early 1970s. This attitude resulted from the excessive paternalism practiced by many missionaries in the life of the local church. However, the Ethiopia Mission was an anomaly because it had never officially been connected to the Bethel Church. It had also become the largest mission in the UPCUSA, continually demanding more missionaries. The COEMAR office philosophically wanted (and financially needed) to pare all missions down. The Ethiopia Mission felt that COEMAR (and later the Program Agency) did not understand the great opportunities for pioneering work presented by Ethiopia as a relatively young mission field, with an emperor who encouraged greater work for the sake of his country. The mission felt, with some justification, that its voice was unheard and unheeded.

At one point COEMAR was ready to summarily dissolve the Ethiopia Mission. A piece of unofficial communication informed the Mission that they were on the docket for the next official COEMAR meeting. As a preemptive response, missionaries took up a collection and sent two representatives to that meeting to give voice to their concerns. The Mission felt it needed to maintain its role as a decision-making body on the field, as all missions had done during their early stages. The Ethiopian Mission did manage to keep its organizational structure and decision-making power, and yet the Mission continually felt that it was seldom understood and greatly unappreciated for its innovative missiology and church-planting methods.

Bethel: Mekene Yesus Unity

When the Bethel Church[6] came into being during the Italian occupation, fruits of Lutheran work in the same general area in western Ethiopia also blossomed into congregations. Those two communities took parallel names: the Lutheran community called itself Mekene Yesus, "the dwelling place of Jesus." The Mekene Yesus believers had no pastors, so the newly ordained Presbyterian pastors also served them. During this cooperative process, Mekene Yesus became acquainted with the Presbyterian form of government and organized itself accordingly. When missionaries returned, the two churches maintained their common Presbyterian Church structure and good working relationships. Talk of union was always in the air and finally became a reality in 1972. On this occasion the two churches adopted Mekene Yesus as their common name, with one synod called Bethel, which comprised the former Bethel Church.[7] The Presbyterian Mission's one big concern revolved around the three-self policy. The Lutheran Churches of Europe gave their churches money for missions through the government tax system, which meant that the Mekene Yesus Church had been heavily subsidized through this method. This produced some tension in the mission when it adopted the "three-self" policy: now their new churches were required to be self-governing, self-propagating, and self-supporting.

The Mission and the Marxists

By the early 1970s Emperor Haile Selassie's authority was disintegrating, and he had no functioning parliament and no clear successor. A creeping revolution began in 1974, during which Selassie was deposed and many of his highest officials massacred. In the next few years, one and a half million people would be killed. The large pictures of three Europeans—Marx, Lenin, and Stalin—on great signboards peered at the multitudes thronging in the center of Addis Ababa.

Christians in Ethiopia were trapped in a revolutionary and antireligious movement. The Presbyterian Mission survived, but its name was changed under government order to the "American Mission." The name "American" had been selected in the mid-nineteenth century, when the United States was a more modest power. Although "American" avoided denominational labels, during revolutionary times it became a politically charged target. All missionaries were accused of being CIA agents, and worse, the local Christians were called "the puppy dogs of the Imperialists." Once when Harold Kurtz was on furlough, the New York office ordered him, as director of the Mission, not to return to Ethiopia because they feared he would be taken hostage. Back in Ethiopia, the Revolutionary Council of Dembi Dollo demanded that the mission hospital be handed over, together with a two-year running budget of about a million dollars. All the mission workers and missionaries were being held hostage until the full turnover took place. The mission begged Kurtz to hurry back, and New York agreed to let him go.

Through long negotiations Kurtz was able to reduce the hospital budget demand to acceptable limits and to have workers and missionaries released. The anti-American drift of the revolution made the mission's presence a danger to Ethiopian Christians and the Bethel Church.[8] As a result, Kurtz officially turned over all mission assets and property to the Mekene Yesus Church, and he placed the few remaining missionaries under the authority of that Church. Outside of Addis, only three missionaries were left: a Reformed Church doctor and his wife, Harvey and Margaret Dorinbos; and Jo Ann Griffith, a teacher in the secondary school in Dembi Dollo. In Addis Ababa four other missionaries also remained to work as teachers and translators. None of the delicate negotiations, both in the countryside and in Addis Ababa, could have been accomplished without the wisdom and assistance of the Bethel Synod president, Gutema Rufo.

The communist regime of Mengistu Haile Mariam lasted from 1977 to 1991. Before it came, there had been a strong charismatic revival in Ethiopia.

This began at Gorei, an old mission station that through the years had been rather dry and fruitless. Revival spread and seemed to prepare the whole Mekene Yesus Church for the testing times ahead. Certainly the policies and missiology of the mission laid a good foundation for the believing communities to move underground and not lose their identity, self-reliance, or passion to continue to share the good news: the gospel was in their languages, songs, and lives. Faithful believers not only survived the years of oppression and imprisonment, but also thrived.

By 1987 things began to ease up to the point that new missionaries were appointed to Ethiopia. The Bethel Synod's Coordinating Office requested that they assist the now rapidly growing church in carrying out its work and vision. Staffing increased at the Girls' School in Addis Ababa and the secondary school in Dembi Dollo. John and Gwen Haspels were asked to take up the work among the remote Surma people again, and missionary couples were appointed to help with Bible school training in both Dembi Dollo in the west and Gatcheb in the southwest. The Presbyterian Frontier Fellowship, the Outreach Foundation, and many congregations and presbyteries in the PC(USA) are now partnering with different areas of the Bethel Synods' work.

The church has grown dramatically since the revolution. The total membership of the Mekene Yesus Church prior to the Mengistu revolution was around 450,000 members. By 2004 it had grown to about four million, a growth of over 800 percent in less than thirty years. At the time of union of the two denominations (1983), there was one Bethel Synod, but now there are four "Bethel Synods." Much of the present church has an indigenous character, with many languages used, new songs being written that arise from the local culture, and the drum taking over as the primary instrument in worship. It is an African Church, a tribute to creative pioneer missionaries and faithful Ethiopians who have worked together over the decades.

CAMEROON

The other two largest and the most historic Presbyterian missions were in West Africa, in Congo (Zaire) and Cameroon, the latter being the largest PCUSA work in Africa. Both of these started late in the nineteenth century and flourished after World War I.

World War I had a direct impact upon the Cameroon because it was a German colony that was overrun by the Allies in 1916. The British took over its high and mountainous northern side, ruling it as part of Nigeria and, thus, making it an English-speaking area. The rest, to the south and east, was put under the "trusteeship" of France. Following World War II, France had a powerful Communist Party that radiated Marxism throughout its empire. The French Communist Party linked with Cameroonian unionists, who were part of the Union des Populations de Cameroun (UPC), the most powerful political party in the land. In 1948 the colonial government officially recognized the UPC; but after labor agitation led to fighting and widespread disorder, it was banned in 1955. Nevertheless, its goals of unifying French and English Cameroon and achieving independence were soon realized. After elections in 1957 and the subsequent formation of a Cameroonian government under the astute leader Ahmadou Ahidju, Cameroon moved to full independence on January 1, 1960. The period in which Cameroon gained its independence was accompanied by guerrilla war, which took its toll on the churches. In perhaps as many as three-quarters of the Protestant schools, churches and pastors' homes were destroyed. Cameroon's independence enabled it to reunite with English-speaking North Cameroon, leaving the country mostly French-speaking, yet allowing English as an official language.

Early in these uncertain times, the integration of the Presbyterian Mission with the Cameroonian Church took place. Since missionaries had carefully taught and promoted three-self support of the African church, congregations and presbyteries had been running themselves for a long time. However, L. K. Anderson at this time reported the complaint of a Cameroonian pastor-friend: "We call ourselves a *Presbyterian* church, but actually we are an episcopacy: the missionaries are the bishops, and we are the priests." In fact, key measures passed by the presbytery or synod were always confirmed, negated, or modified by a senior missionary giving the final word.

Around this same time, mission integration into local churches was being discussed at the PCUSA's Lake Mohonk consultation in 1956. The Mission in Cameroon would have worked toward implementing integration, but the UPC rebellion had already broken out in 1955, disrupting the Presbyterian areas of central and south Cameroon. At Lake Mohonk, Cameroonian pastor Meye me Nkpwele urged the dissolution of the Mission and the placing of all missionaries and mission projects under the authority of the Cameroonian Church. Three months later, the Mission accepted the proposal and started to plan its implementation. In June 1957, the PCUSA GA gave its approval.

The mission-church integration was formalized on December 11, 1957, at a huge celebration in a large Elat church. Dr. Eugene Carson Blake, the General Secretary of the PCUSA, preached from Galatians 5:13, "You were called to FREEDOM, only do not use your freedom as an opportunity for self-indulgence." Every time Dr. Blake repeated the magic word "freedom," a roar burst out from the crowd, drowning out the translation into French. French officials present were upset by the rowdy reaction because they thought about the vicious jungle war being fought in the forested countryside all around Yaounde. Nevertheless, the sermon was hurriedly translated into French and circulated to officials as a serious call to true Christian freedom and responsibility.

Changes

The accomplishments of the Presbyterian missionaries in Cameroon were remarkable, but not unique. Missions aimed to create in Africa and the world a church that was self-propagating, self-governing, and self-supporting. In Cameroon, the missionaries were remarkably successful. By 1960, the mission had an impressive school system that began in the local language, then turned to French, the national language of Cameroon. The mission developed and administered 235 primary schools with 28,500 students. Additionally, it established four middle schools with 231 students and a Teachers' Training School (called a Normal School), preparing 187 prospective teachers. It had also launched a Junior College, called the Cameroon Christian College (1946), which grew to serve 291 students. All advanced education was done in French. The PCUSA missionaries joined with the Paris Mission of French "Presbyterians" to build and launch this college, the first and largest Protestant Christian college in French-speaking Africa at that time.

It was clear that academic training would not be appropriate for all Cameroonians. As early as 1908 the mission developed the Frank James Technical Training School, a four-year institution with several areas of practical skill training: carpentry, tailoring, shoemaking, furniture making, ivory, hats, mechanical drawing, and masonry.[9] The mission also engaged in rural training in Libamba. Here missionaries trained local farmers and agricultural students to produce chickens and eggs for the market. Missionaries also helped to create the market for eggs in Cameroon.[10] Finally, the mission developed a printing press. This and all the other educational training institutes were handed over to the Presbyterian Church of Cameroon at the time of integration (1957).

Greater than any other service developed by the mission was the establishment of medical services. An early policy of the mission was to establish a dispensary or hospital at every new mission station. Many dispensaries later developed into hospitals. At the time of transition, the mission handed to the church six hospitals and twelve dispensaries, with a combined total of 1,561 beds. The mission also handed over a leprosarium and a dental clinic.

After a long period of institutional learning, the Presbyterian Church in Cameroon today serves its people with seven hospitals. The sudden handover of everything related to the Church and Church-affiliated institutions (such as the mission-founded hospitals) gave the Cameroon Church more than it could properly administer. The cause of missions also suffered. In 1958 there were 123 missionaries; ten years later there were 62. By 1972 there were 30 missionaries, and seven years later only 6. The departure of missionary doctors did not close the hospitals because Cameroonian doctors were able to continue their work. It did, however, put an end to the important training programs run by doctors in the hospitals, making the "self-operation" of hospitals nearly impossible.

Theological Education

During these years there were other important developments in Cameroon. In the 1960s, a great opportunity appeared: the Theological Education Fund (TEF). The TEF's purpose, as a U.S. organization, was to help young churches overseas develop solid theological foundations through supporting strong seminaries and well-trained teachers to train their pastors. Cameroon was chosen as a site for university-level theological training in French. Ten denominational leaders from six West African countries (Ivory Coast, Togo, Benin, Cameroon, Gabon, and Congo) sat on the board of this new development. After securing a good campus in Yaounde in February 1962, they launched the seminary Faculté de Théologie Protestante de Yaounde (FTPY), with courses offered in French.

Academically, for at least ten years, the courses of the FTPY were related to the Faculty of Theology of the University of Geneva, "relative to curriculum, the defense of the M.Th. theses, and professorial appointments."[11] At the start a basic decision was to make African studies a key part of the theological course: the first teacher to set up that department was the Presbyterian missionary William D. Reyburn. The Government of Cameroon officially recognized the Faculty of Theology and granted Cameroonian students full scholarships. Although the FTPY struggled to keep high standards, it was able to build a good reputation and an annual student body of over a hundred. In the 1980s, FTPY added students from backgrounds outside the recognized circles, such as students from Madagascar, the South Pacific, and a special student from the Kimbanguists, the largest Africanist spiritual sect of Congo. Although the school can point to some remarkable success stories, in some cases university-level training in a country where most people only have basic education is a way for students to "escape" from poverty by securing a high government appointment. Turning over the Mission to the Cameroonian church was important, but the ending of the Mission turned out to be awkward. In 1992 Dr. Donald C. Mullen, a missionary surgeon, visited Cameroon. Reflecting upon his experience in traveling through the country and talking with its people, he wrote, "People in the grassroots of the EPC in all areas of Cameroon feel like we have deserted them. 'Where are all your people? We are your children. Why have you deserted us? Parents do not desert their children—ever!'" On the whole, Dr. Mullen commented, "It has not worked."[12] The Presbyterian work was so vast that the transition to an independent church needed a much-longer time to succeed; and missionaries are still much needed.

One seemingly "hopeless" place has not been deserted by Presbyterian missions. On the south border of Cameroon lies the tiny country of Equatorial Guinea. The country found oil and subsequent wealth in the modern day, but that wealth has been carefully hoarded by the ruling clique. Missionary work started in Equatorial Guinea almost 150 years ago and then shifted over to Cameroon. In the meantime, Spanish rule in Equatorial Guinea had been quite oppressive. Protestant believers in Equatorial Guinea include Presbyterians, Methodists, and World-wide Evangelistic Crusaders. In 1996, the PC(USA) had one missionary, Rev. Diana Wright, living there and working as an evangelist and church administrator.[13]

CONGO—MAYHEM AND MUSIC

Even more than Cameroon, Congo was a grand investment of the Presbyterian Church, in this case the PCUS. The mission in the Congo began with great promise. Among the early pioneers was William Sheppard, the "black Living-stone," a well-educated, ordained Presbyterian pastor, and the son of a slave.[14] His colleague, Samuel N. Lapsley, was an excellent scholar and deeply passionate about evangelizing the most neglected peoples. His father was a slaveholder and a Pres-byterian pastor. This pair opened the Presbyterian Mission to Congo, first plant-ing it in Kasai, a thousand miles upriver from the capital, Leopoldville. The mission built its extensive work around education, medical care, and evangelism.

Congo had a troubled colonial history. At one time it was held by the king of Belgium as a private fiefdom, and the country would endure extreme exploita-tion and violence. In 1954, one bold Belgian "planner" said Belgium was aiming for total Congolese independence . . . in *thirty years*. Three years later Congolese mayors were elected, and they immediately demanded complete independence for the entire country. Belgium could hardly resist the movement when African nations all around were moving toward independence, especially in the countries in neighboring French Africa. At a Round Table Conference in early 1960, national elections were set. After the vote on June 30, 1960, full independence was granted.

Politicians and civilians were overjoyed at their freedom, but the armed forces were furious. They would not be receiving any boosts in their low pay, and their Belgian officers were still in place. Catastrophic rebellions occurred, and the whole country spun out of control. With looting and disorder rampant, most for-eigners fled for safety. Political leaders divided the land, and twice the Congo descended into war. The United Nations intervened, trying to hold it together, but it took ten years before Congo stabilized again. Stability came in 1965, when the U.S.-backed commander Joseph-Désiré Mobutu came to power, but he quickly morphed into a wealthy emperor.

The American Presbyterian Congo Mission (APCM) had a great record of ser-vice after World War II, part of which was its push for more education. Excellent and widespread medical services were improved, and the training of Congolese leaders was stepped up. Parallel to the work in Cameroon, in 1959–60 the APCM prepared to hand over its work to the Congo Church. The handover was sub-stantial but not total. Belgian rule, being deeply paternalistic, had inhibited the work of transition. It also became clear that hospitals, highly technical projects, and advanced education had to be very carefully handed over, with solid plans, funding, training, and experience in place.

Independence and Chaos

When Congo's independence was granted in 1960, missionaries felt joyously relieved that independence had happened so peacefully. The transition and the joy, however, had sprung out too quickly, for the army was in revolt, and the country was filled with panic and rioting. The U.S. Embassy immediately advised all U.S. citizens, including the APCM, to leave Congo, and a plane was arranged to carry them out. All 102 of the missionaries left, except one in Leopoldville

(Kinshasa). While the distraught missionaries waited anxiously at Kananga airport (Luluabourg), a great number of Congolese Christian women, as an incredible expression of their love, came with fruit and cooked food for them. A month later a few missionaries, especially the medically trained ones, returned. By the end of the year, forty-five had returned. In retrospect, missionaries reflected on whether or not their evacuation was wise or even right. Kiantandu, a Congolese, wrote: "This leaving was a shock to the Africans. . . . All the missionaries who talked to me recognized that it was a mistake to leave."[15]

Despite the temporary hiatus of many missionaries in 1966, all did not retreat. Dr. William Rule, a very experienced mission doctor, started Operation Doctor. With the rebellion going on, medical services in Congo had virtually vanished. Over 700 regular doctors were reduced to only 250, and most of them were missionaries. In order to meet this gap in medical care, Dr. Rule rounded up 50 Protestant missionary doctors and moved them around the country through missionary air services. Dr. Rule also appealed for 100 more doctors to come over from the United States and asked for extensive medical supplies. Through these efforts, Operation Doctor succeeded in meeting much of the medical crisis produced by the fighting.

During this transition period, it also became clear that Africans needed more advanced training for the modern world. Remarkably, at the time of its independence, Congo only possessed eleven university graduates. In 1961, twelve students were sent out of the country to study abroad: five went to (French-speaking) Switzerland to study theology and education, while seven went to the United States to study theology, medicine, and general education. This was just the beginning.

Over time, the training of pastors was also improved. The establishment of École de Théologie, which was moved from Kankinda to Ndesha, greatly strengthened the preparation of pastors. The school attracted students from Christian churches all over French-speaking Africa. Individual success, however, was always problematic.

Many of those trained abroad, or those who went abroad for short courses, found the implementing of their newly gained knowledge to be difficult. As one missionary commented, "They were Christian, but they were very militant and couldn't fit into the church well again. They came back with wonderful ideas and knowledge, but after six months, they fell back into the despair and inaction of so many other Africans."[16] Others, on the other hand, achieved much success, such as one of the great evangelists of the 1960s, Mawaji Apollo. He knew and used French as well as Chiluba, the best-known language of Kasai. Converted while in prison, he later went to a Bible school in Luebo and then exercised a great ministry through his preaching and singing. His life was written in a small book, *The Black Samson*.[17]

The 1960s were a decade of much uncertainty in the Congo. Two rebellions, Simba (Lions) and Mulele, together for a time controlled two-thirds of Congo. These were deadly movements for Christian workers. Some 150 Catholic and 29 Protestant missionaries died at the hands of rebels. Ruling much of the nation, they took the name the People's Republic of Congo, and thirteen left-leaning nations recognized it as the true Congo government. It established its base in Stanleyville and gained a huge popular following. On April 24, 1964, U.S. military transports dropped Belgian paratroopers at the edge of the city. They fought their way in, but it was a bitter fight, with many Congolese and foreigners dying. The Congolese National Army drove the Simba rebels out into the vast forestland.

One African pastor, from the Africa Inland Church, was seized by the Simbas and tied to a post for execution. He said that first he must pray to the Lord before death. The young rebels agreed. The pastor closed his eyes. Praying loudly, he asked God to forgive his sins and the sins of all the witnesses, including the young men about to execute him. After that prayer, no executioner would even lift his gun; the pastor was immediately untied. In a similar fashion, this growing Simba Movement was first overpowering, but then it collapsed and disappeared. As the rebellion faded away, Congo had another election in March 1965. Amid the political chaos, the Commander Mobutu took charge, setting aside the politicians and the constitution on November 24, 1965.

Mobutu survived as the head of state for the next thirty years. His reign was marked by the neglect of the country's infrastructure and the slow ebbing of Congo's great wealth while Mobutu became one of the wealthiest men in the world. When he was finally driven from power in 1997, Congo's population sank even further into hunger, disease, and poverty. Another "scramble for Congo" took place, but this time it was not a scramble of European powers or huge mining interests, but of African "powers."

Mobutu's main national policy was called *Authenticité* (Authenticity). He called Africans to be Africans, not European imitations. This call for authenticity applied to many fields, such as clothing, music, and literature. It also had a specific church application. All Christians in Congo were divided into three groups: Roman Catholics, Protestants, and Kimbanguists. The latter group was a charismatic movement that developed during Belgian rule, led by Simon Kimbangu. Although he was imprisoned, Kimbanguism spread, even beyond Congo. Finally, Kimbanguists were allowed their freedom, and Kimbanguism became the largest, most intertribal religion in Congo. In 1970, Protestant churches were called together and pressured to become one Église du Christ en Zaire. Presbyterians, like others, were part of the collective whole but free to follow their own doctrine and church laws.

Presbyterians in Independent Congo

The church in Congo has gone through dreadful times, but the Presbyterian community there is still estimated to be two million members. Today the Presbyterians of Congo have four old mission hospitals; some are barely working and others are doing well. Mission workers Haejung and Simon Park write about Bulape hospital: "Bulape is another former missionary station. . . . The hospital has more than 90 percent occupancy in the midst of war and economic turmoil. (It) does not run like a North American institution, but it serves the people effectively. Praise God."[18]

One outstanding hospital is the Institut Médical Chrétien du Kasai (IMCK), called the Good Shepherd Hospital and located in Tshikaji, near Kananga (Luluabourg). Built in 1975, it was the PCUS women's Birthday Offering that finally put the necessary funds over the top. It is the best hospital in Kasai and includes departments of surgery, obstetrics, gynecology, pediatrics, ophthalmology, internal medicine, pathology, orthopedics, and community health. It also has an intern program for physicians in training and is one of the few clinics addressing the overwhelming AIDS pandemic. The IMCK also has a dentistry program, both in the hospital and in a number of outside clinics. The ophthalmology department was run by missionary Dr. Shannon; when he retired in 1997, he left three Congolese in charge.

Education was another great emphasis of the Presbyterian Mission in the Congo, which ran three university-preparation high schools at Katumbuo, Bibamba, and Kinshasa. Currently, all three send a stream of students yearly into the universities. There is also a Protestant university, started in 1964 in the Lovanium (Catholic) University. It has since moved to Kisangani (Stanleyville), where it offers courses ranging from law to medicine, and has a Faculty (School) of Theology. The university is helped significantly by European donors and now caters to four thousand students. Several years ago, the Presbyterians of Kasai established the University of Lapsley and Sheppard, named in honor of their two pioneer missionaries. Some Congolese PhD-holders are lecturing there now.

All over eastern, central, and southern Africa, Congo is famous for one thing: its music. The musician who made it so was Franco. He was a great popular singer, producing countless records and tapes. He was tremendously popular in East Africa and toured most of Africa and beyond. Franco lived a more than exciting life and paid for it in the end: he became sick with AIDS. Rather than holing up and dying as privately as possible, he produced the song "Attention par SIDA," or "Pay Attention to AIDS." He confessed to his wife, family, and society to having committed much adultery, which he denounced as destructive—a salutary message for a society now enduring one of the great plagues of history.

In the midst of so much poverty, disease, and hopelessness, Congolese Christians have produced a vibrant witness to the believers' hope through their music. Moving Christian hymns are great teachers and inspirers. Indeed, Congolese music spread and helped to transform much of South Sudan in the early 1980s. This came through the Africa Inland Church, which resonates with Christian singing in Congo and Uganda. Challenging and joyful revival songs keep brightening bleak situations with their transcendent message.

Congolese music has been an important and growing part of worship life. Up to the 1970s, many of the hymns sung in church were translations of Moody-Sankey revival songs, such as "What a Friend We Have in Jesus." One missionary who devoted herself to Congolese music was Elspeth Shannon, the wife of

Dr. Shannon. She worked with the choir at a Kananga church in an extraordinary way. At the beginning of the week, the pastor shared his text with the choir. The next night one or two of the choir members would receive a tune *in a dream*. Then the choir would compose the music and words so that it would be ready for Sunday worship. Hymn tunes revealed by dreams are actually common in Africa. The best of these "dream songs" have been recorded and distributed.[19]

SUDAN: "GOD HAS COME AMONG US . . . SLOWLY"

Sudan is the largest country in Africa: a million square miles, approximately the same size as the United States east of the Mississippi.[20] The river running through the Sudan is the Nile, the longest river in the world.

Sudan was conquered by Britain and Egypt in 1898 after they defeated the Arabic-speaking Muslims of the North in the battle of Omdurman. Presbyterian missionaries then began working with Egyptian Christians who came to North Sudan to work following the conquest. The churches were supplied by pastors and evangelists from the large Evangelical (i.e., Protestant) church in Egypt. North Sudan became a Synod of the UPCNA, the Synod of the Nile. Because these Christians needed schools and churches, the mission and the Egyptian Evangelical Church helped provide such services.

The vast South had at least sixty tribes and languages. Presbyterians began with two mission posts in the Upper Nile Province of South Sudan. The first post at Doleib Hill was established in 1902, and the second post was established in 1912 among the Nuer, at Nasir, near the Ethiopian border. Neither mission had early success: the total number of converts by the end of World War II hardly exceeded five hundred.[21] The mission needed a dynamic plan of expansion, and many workers would be needed to make this a reality.

In 1946, the Mission knew that it had made little progress. When World War II broke out, there were only two and a half missions in southern Sudan. Doleib Hill and Nasir still existed from the early days, and Akobo had been just started, and evacuated, before the war.

Lowrie Anderson knew that advancing into South Sudan in 1946 was extremely urgent. Eight more mission posts were added (five were totally new), and pioneer work was started among three tribes.[22] Don McClure started work with the Akobo, but later he had a new vision. He dreamed of an Anuak project that in fifteen years would have enough missionaries to translate the Bible, educate, heal, and train pastors sufficient for all the Anuak people, who were concentrated around the border of South Sudan and Ethiopia.

McClure went on furlough and laid out his Anuak vision to churches in the United States. He knew how to turn paper proposals into living realities, especially in UPCNA churches. At this time United Presbyterians were considering a union with the Reformed Church in America (RCA), and so he was invited to share his message with these churches as well. They were electrified. The RCA's missions in the Arab world and India had shown slow, pitiful results. To hear about "a church in fifteen years" was a marvellous thing. In the end, the RCA never joined with the United Presbyterians, but they did support the Anuak Project, the Sudan Mission, and even later the Ethiopia Mission.

Lowrie Anderson had spent his first twenty years of service in North Sudan. He knew Arabic and understood Egypt. In Egypt he shared his vision for the south, and the Evangelicals of that country sent a promising young man, the Reverend Swailem Sidhom, to work in the areas needing help. Sidhom remained a missionary in South Sudan and Kenya for some time. Others also came to teach Arabic in southern schools. The mission soon began fruitful relations with the Church Missionary Society (CMS), evangelical Anglicans from Britain. Cooperation included the use of buildings in their seminary, Bishop Gwynne College.

The district commissioner at Akobo-Pibor, Dick Lyth, had been a CMS missionary. He started a government center church at each center that he toured. He conducted worship services in Southern Arabic, a local pidgin now much used in churches. His British colleagues called him "the Commissionary." At one church in Boma, on the Ethiopian border, a translator called Lado came to the service. At the close of the service, Lyth found him bowed, weeping. He thought he was about to confess some sins. Instead, he said: "I have found Him." Some light had appeared to Lado years before, sending him on a search hundreds of miles from his original home. When he heard of Christ, he discovered that the "light" had come. This was the beginning of the evangelization of the Murlei.

Independent Sudan

Political developments advanced quickly in Sudan. On January 1, 1956, Sudan became the first colonial African nation to govern itself. At this time Sudan fell under the control of the Arabized "elite" of Khartoum, who have ruled Sudan ever since, in a variety of guises. Their main goal has been to advance the unity of Sudan through Arabization and Islamization. To this end the government opened little Qur'an schools in the south to introduce black southerners to Arabic and Islam. Soon education was limited to Arabic: English was forbidden.

Arabization and Islamization thoroughly angered "African" Sudanese. Rebel groups, calling themselves Anyanya, formed in Uganda and the Equatoria Province of the southernmost part of South Sudan. In 1963 rebellion broke out. In February 1964, the Sudanese government ordered the expulsion of all missionaries in Southern Sudan. The missionaries handed over the property and assets of the church to the Sudanese people and left. The expelled missionaries felt the church had little future prospects.

After the rains broke in April 1964, most of Southern Sudan fell into rebel hands. The Nuer, strong supporters of Anyanya, knelt beside the huge swamps before going into battle, singing a song in Nuer that the missionaries had taught them, based on Psalm 23, "Jehovah Jesus is my shepherd." For them the "green pastures and still waters" of the psalmist were the extensive swamps in their own beloved land. For nine years neither side could win, and so in 1972 peace was made. During this war there occurred the first large turning to Christ in Upper Nile.

Many fled the war to seek work in the cities of North Sudan. Southern Christians opened night schools, teaching reading, writing, and also teaching Christianity. The Evangelical Church and North Sudan missionaries opened a Bible school to prepare evangelists. When peace came in 1972, many of the new pastors and evangelists returned from "exile" to their homelands. The Giffen Bible School was opened in 1974 to train evangelists at Doleib Hill, the first Sudan mission.

Sadly, peace lasted only ten years. The agenda of Arabization and Islamization was soon revived. The concessions that had brought peace were quietly shelved. Then oil was discovered in South Sudan, and well-positioned Northerners were quietly grabbing it. Southerners in the national army rebelled; they were joined and then led by Dr. John Garang. The Sudan People's Liberation Army (SPLA) fought a long war, finally "settled" in January 2005.

The war had been devastating for the African people of Sudan. "Oil greed" was compounded with religious violence and fueled it. Around four million people were uprooted from their homes; two million fled the country; and two million lived as unwanted refugees, mostly in wretched camps all around Khartoum, in North Sudan. A conservative estimate is that two million Southerners were killed by violence and ensuing famine. In 1989, when peace negotiations threatened the oppressors' rule, Omar al Bashir led the Islamists in taking over the government of Sudan. Al Bashir's group dug themselves deeply into power, steadily advancing their policy of the complete Islamization of the Sudan.

Revival in Renk

Nevertheless, Christians displayed much resilience. Everywhere night schools and churches sprang up. Many were excellently run. One of the great movements was in Renk, in the Upper Nile area, a few hundred kilometers from Ethiopia. Presbyterians did not organize a church there until about 1984, just as the war started. Perhaps the person most responsible for the success of this movement was Dr. Stephen Oyol. Though born at Doleib Hill, Oyol was never really part of the church at all. He studied veterinary science in the University of Alexandria and was posted to Renk. He had psychological problems; he felt oppressed, dogged by evil spirits, and turned to drinking. A Christian worker visited one day and witnessed to him in his office. After several visits, Oyol accepted Christ and got rid of most of his magic things, even a wire ring on which he had depended for psychological help. He and his family were instructed in the basic Christian teachings and were then baptized. Hearing of a great revival meeting at Kosti, a city about 150 miles north, Oyol took one of the veterinary vehicles to ferry people to Kosti. When the Veterinary Service heard of this, he was removed from the Veterinary Service. He then started working as an evangelist for the church and became an active participant in the revival meetings in Renk.[23] He trained at St.

Paul's United Theological College, Kenya, to be a pastor. In 2004, he was elected General Secretary of the Presbyterian Church of Sudan (PCOS).

In 1996, the SPLA surprised the Sudanese government by capturing Kurmuk, a city about a hundred miles east of Renk. The government demanded that the large Catholic school grounds there be given to the Popular Defence Force. All the Christians of Renk, fearing that they would lose their school, crowded onto the grounds just before the Defence Force arrived. They filled the whole area, dancing and singing. Government officers were furious, but the Christians succeeded in keeping them out and retaining the school for themselves.

With the war, evangelism, when it occurs, happens in big servings. In about 1992, the National Sudan Council of Churches (NSCC) made its first contacts with the war-battered "church in the bush." Presbyterians had, at the most, left 40 to 50 little churches in 1984. Eight years later, they discovered just over 1,400 churches, each under a "volunteer evangelist" who had gone to night school in North Sudan years before.

During the war years, the Egyptians dominated the Sudan Presbyterian Evangelical Church (SPEC), which underwent a remarkable change. For years it had helped to train black Sudanese, and it had baptized thousands of them. Only three, however, had been ordained as pastors, none had been ordained as elders, and no new churches had been organized. The Egyptian leadership was keeping church control away from the black Sudanese. Around 1990, a breakthrough was achieved: the SPEC began to ordain blacks as pastors and elders. The church soon developed branches in the Nuba Mountains, at least 350 miles southwest of Khartoum. Congregations also sprang up all over northern Sudan, even in the western province of Darfur.

From a very early time, Sudanese converts to Christianity made worship songs in their own language and style. Other African Christians sang translated gospel hymns for decades without ever attempting to create their own music. Sudanese Christians were perhaps strongly influenced by the Christian music that came from Congo: singing African songs in a popular musical style. Sudanese young people adopted songs from East Africa and made new ones of their own in an African style. The Sudanese sang in Southern Arabic, which is quite popular in Juba and the far South. New choirs sprang up, and great "Overnight" worship sessions were full of these African gospel hymns using Juba Arabic.

In Sudan, as in much of Africa, Bible schools train evangelists. All over Africa the evangelist is the key low-level pastor. The war forced Giffen Bible School to relocate to Malakal. Two others were started in the liberated areas. All of these have had their problems. Many of the pastors have had additional training in Kenya, but they found it difficult to leave the safe, liveable places of Kenya, for there were no safe, liveable places in liberated areas of Sudan.

A great project of the Presbyterian churches during the war was the founding of the Nile Theological College (NTC). With more students completing secondary education, the two Presbyterian churches joined to found this theological college. Planning began in 1988, and at the end of 1991 the college was finally opened. Both Presbyterian and Reformed churches in the United States contributed books to get the library started. The Evangelical church used old dorms no longer needed for their Girls' School in Khartoum. Foreign volunteer workers helped in clearing and building, especially those from the presbyteries partnered with Sudan: Trinity in South Carolina connected with the Malakal Presbytery (PCOS), and Shenango in Pennsylvania connected with SPEC. During the college's first year, a large number of Christians living and working in the capital volunteered to teach special courses. Southern Sudanese, teaching in some of the universities around the capital, have been very fruitful teachers. Later, NTC added an Arabic stream. Education in Sudan under the Islamist regime, which seized power in 1989, has (except for the medical school) been turned into Arabic from top to bottom.[24]

Mary Alueel's hymn quoted earlier, "God has come . . . slowly," goes on to say, "We receive salvation slowly, slowly: all of us together, with no one left behind." This is how the gospel is penetrating Sudan. It moves slowly and gradually through the Dinka and other societies, which resisted it for decades. It speaks especially to the almost entirely unevangelized areas of central and western Nuer and Dinka land, extending hundreds of miles on both sides of the Nile. In nine years of war, these areas birthed 1,400 new churches, led by volunteer leaders who were all informally trained in the faith when working in North Sudan. Now these leaders are self-appointed evangelists. Large numbers of refugees have also swept into the church. The black Sudanese are flocking to become Christians, and "no one is being left behind."

PRESBYTERIANS IN NEW AFRICAN FRONTIERS

At least since the 1960s, Presbyterian missions has been understood as originating from, and being initiated by, the new or "younger churches" in mission lands. The missions' challenge was to empower them to speak out about their own needs and to listen, discuss, and cooperate with them regarding furthering the work of their church, even when the money and expertise came from the United States. This vision also meant that mission was everywhere, not just limited to the church's historic mission sites in Africa. After the 1970s it was time for the Presbyterian Church to move into other countries.

Nigeria

By far, the most populous nation in Africa is Nigeria. This had not been a mission field for U.S. Presbyterians. Dr. Donald Bobb, sent by the PCUSA, saw in Nigeria large Muslim and Christian communities with serious misunderstandings and tensions. As a response, Dr. Bobb started the Islam in Africa project, designed to help Christians and Muslims learn about each other and build mutual understanding. It was not intended as a program for evangelism, but to bring about *shalom* in a tense region of Africa. Later, a branch of Islam in Africa was launched in Kenya.

Ghana

Ghana in West Africa had two large Presbyterian denominations, one from the Basel Mission in Switzerland, the other from the Bremen Mission in Germany. These churches have been open to U.S. volunteers with teaching, medical, or other callings.

Malawi

One country attracting varied service was Malawi, along Lake Nyasa in Central Africa. The lake was first seen by a European when David Livingstone led a mission there in 1859. After his death, missions went there from Scotland. In 1875, the Free Church of Scotland went to northern Malawi. The Church of Scotland sent a mission to South Malawi in 1876. Two years later, in 1878, the Dutch Reformed Church of South Africa started its mission at Mkhoma, in central Malawi. In 1926, the churches from those missions formed the Church of Central Africa Presbyterian.

North Malawi caught the attention of U.S. Presbyterians in the late 1980s, especially a large neglected hospital that was serving the whole of the North, at Embangweni. Help started when Dr. Kenneth McCall and his wife took charge, after they served for twenty years in Congo. The hospital buildings were without light, so Otis Rowe, a missionary already working in Malawi, came and installed solar lights.[25] The Medical Benevolence Foundation next sent Jim McGill to oversee building construction. He expanded Embangweni Hospital's capacity, increasing its 77 beds to 155. He also added covered walks connecting all the buildings. By the 1980s, malnutrition had replaced malaria as the major killer of babies. Twenty-five percent of newborn children were dying by the age of five from the "disease" malnutrition. The staff began a strong educational drive through its scattered clinics. They taught about balanced diets, improving agriculture, and the spacing of children. McGill, overseeing the improvements, developed local wells and pumps to avoid waterborne diseases. He also dug out and stocked small fish farms to improve nutrition. In 1991 Pittsburgh Presbytery began a partnership with the Synod of Blantyre in Malawi, which has resulted in many exchanges and the sending of many medical supplies.[26]

Kenya

In Kenya the Presbyterian Church of East Africa (PCEA) became the focus of the UPCUSA. Bill and Lois Anderson had been teaching at a pastoral training institution in Sudan, but in 1959 the Muslim government expelled them. They were invited to St. Paul's United Theological College, where Presbyterians, Episcopalians, and Methodists cooperated to train pastors in Kenya.

In 1961, the Third World Council of Churches met at New Delhi, India. Many from the Presbyterian mission agency COEMAR attended, dropping in at Kenya on the way home. They discovered the 25,000 member PCEA and were immediately overwhelmed by what they experienced. Africans in Kenya had gone through a revival and civil war. Just after World War II, the East African Revival erupted in the region. Thousands who had been Christians for years repented, confessed their sins, and began to testify of the salvation they had found in Jesus. The revival swept through the PCEA. And then another new hope dawned. The Kikuyu from Central Province in Kenya (the "Presbyterian" tribe) led in the Mau-Mau rebellion against white rule, and white settlers suffered greatly. The fighting lasted from 1952 to 1956. In 1960, Britain decided to transfer rule to Kenyan Africans, not the white settlers who had dominated Kenya for decades. Freedom was coming. The COEMAR people saw an upbeat Kenya, with a revived and thriving church, and immediately became "keen on Keenya" (the British pronunciation of Kenya). This keenness produced many new openings: Kenyans found more and more study opportunities in the United States.

Through the years U.S. Presbyterians have taken on many tasks in Kenya, even though our partnership came relatively late. Some of this has come about because of the two civil wars that Sudan has suffered, wars against the black Africans in southern Sudan. Sudanese pastoral trainees escaped to Kenya or have been sent there and supported by U.S. Presbyterians. Many went to St. Paul's, and others to the Pastoral Institute in Kikuyu. At least one Sudanese Presbyterian pastor taught at St. Paul's.

Since St. Paul's could not train enough Presbyterian pastors, other teaching posts have been called for by American Presbyterians. The PCEA developed Presbyterian College, originally called the Pastoral Institute, for training lower-level pastors. It still trains pastors but does more. An American Mission Volunteer, the Reverend Edward Danks, was a professor and library assistant and helped the institution through this transition process during the 1990s. Daystar University, a recently established evangelical university in Kenya, has included several PC(USA) professors and workers on its teaching staff.

One of the best training places in Kenya is Christian Organizations Research Advisory Trust (CORAT), specifically established (in 1975) to instill sound, honest business practices into churches and subsidiary organizations. It has been used widely in English-speaking Africa. Presbyterian missionaries Gordon and Carolyn Brown of the PC(USA) worked for years with CORAT and are now retired in Kenya. This organization is meeting one of the most basic needs of African Christian organizations: accurate accounting.

Just as U.S. Presbyterians resurrected the great Embangweni Hospital in Malawi, they did as much at the first Presbyterian hospital in Kenya, at Kikuyu. Scottish doctors kept it going for years, but the hospital became old, dingy, and underfunded. Then in 1990, the Topples came to Kikuyu after twenty-two years of work among lepers in Korea. Stan Topple was an orthopedic surgeon. Mia, his wife, was a dermatologist. The Topples were able to convince the Medical Benevolence Foundation to send a steady stream of expert medical staff and to help with a large new building to supplement the old dingy hospital buildings. These were funded skillfully: the MBF raised $800,000, and the U.S. government provided additional funds so that, in the end, there was $2 million for a beautiful new rehab center. It opened on May 17, 1998, and then Stan and Mia flew home to retire. Kikuyu also now has an eye center that is considered the best in East Africa.

One of Kenya's great church leaders for years has been John Gatu. He had been deeply touched by revival and was general secretary of PCEA for many years. He was quite active in the All-Africa Conference of Churches (AACC), with its headquarters in Nairobi. John did his undergraduate work at St. Paul's. In the 1970s, he went to the United States, studied at Princeton Seminary, and was granted a doctor's degree. He came out with a new vision that he revealed in several U.S. churches and took back home with him to Kenya: the termination of "foreign mission help and presence," at least for a time. John did not propose this out of personal bitterness against missionaries. He believed that African churches and African governments should be self-sufficient and not constantly searching for foreign aid. He wanted to put an end to dependency and to emphasize long-term planning. He took his proposals to end all dependency on foreign missions to a 1973 meeting of the AACC. The proposal sounded great and was "accepted" but never put into effect anywhere. Gatu never persuaded his own church, the PCEA, to make the proposal their own, and he never persuaded U.S. Presbyterians not to be "keen about Keenya."

Gatu was both ahead of his time and behind the times. As we have seen in this chapter in Ethiopia, Sudan, and Cameroon, the independence and equality of ecumenical partners may arrive at different times and be due to different catalysts. In Brazil (chap. 7), such calls for independence came much earlier and for different reasons. What we have also recognized is that, at least for some, foreign support is a narcotic to which African churches can easily become addicted. This type of dependence never creates strong or healthy churches. Consequently, American Presbyterians today are hearing two often-conflicting voices from Africa. One is the older, loud "Macedonian call" to come over and help. The other is the call for a partial or complete "moratorium" on missions. Presbyterians must discern how best to answer each call as they participate in partnerships that help to build stronger churches in this vast continent.

Chapter 12

Europe

DUNCAN HANSON

The history of Presbyterian Church (U.S.A.) work in Europe and the former Soviet Union during 1944–2004 is too rich to be told in a single chapter[1] or even in a single book.[2] These pages can only present an overview of Presbyterian mission in Europe, beginning with brief comments on its pre-1944 origins and then covering the work in Europe from its beginnings in Italy and France during the last days of World War II through 2004. In conclusion, I will describe some of the missiological assumptions that guided PC(USA) mission during those years.

EUROPEAN CHURCHES BECAME PART OF THE PRESBYTERIAN MOSAIC

During the first 158 years of the history of the PC(USA), the church's relationships with European churches mainly served to facilitate a more or less orderly exchange of personnel between the Reformed and Presbyterian churches in Europe to the clergy-poor Presbyterian churches in North America.

By far, the largest number of European pastors and laypeople to join in the life of the PC(USA), as well as the earliest, came from Scotland and Northern Ireland. In practically every presbytery of the PC(USA), it is possible to find a Knox Presbyterian Church or a Scots' Presbyterian Church or an Old Scots' Presbyterian Church. Though in some congregations the members and clergy have forgotten or almost forgotten their British heritage, these names still bear witness to the contribution of the Scots and Northern Irish in the early years of those congregations. Still, today there are about a thousand PC(USA) congregations left from the approximately two thousand that were originally founded by Scottish and Northern Irish immigrants to the United States.

Hungarian immigrants came to the United States in four successive waves. Their first wave came during what, in Hungary, were the difficult years following an uprising against Austrian rule in 1848. Their second wave left Hungary primarily for economic reasons during 1890 to 1925. The third wave came to the United States following the end of World War II, and the failure of the Hungarian Revolution of 1956 caused a fourth wave of immigration.

Some of the first-wave Hungarian immigrants joined Presbyterian congregations. Others in the first wave of immigrants joined congregations of the Reformed Church in America or the Evangelical and Reformed Church (which later joined with the Congregational Christians to form the United Church of Christ). The second wave of immigrants founded about a hundred Hungarian-speaking congregations, six of which are now related to the PC(USA). Those in the third wave of immigrants who joined churches, joined the congregations that had been founded by the second wave of immigrants. The fourth wave of immigrants either joined existing Hungarian-speaking congregations or joined the PC(USA) or other mainline English-speaking congregations. Over the last 150 years, there has been a constant influx of theologically trained persons from Hungary, many of whom have served as pastors of English-speaking congregations or as professors in seminaries. Many others became pastors of Hungarian-speaking congregations.

Approximately forty still-existing PC(USA) congregations were founded by Czech immigrants during the years 1890–1910 and were served by Czech pastors during their first two or three decades of existence. When the Synodal Senior of the Evangelical Church of Czech Brethren visited many of these congregations in 1998, a good number of them still remembered their Czech roots. Some still had at least a few Czech-speaking members, even though none had regularly held worship services in the Czech language since about 1930.

About fifteen PC(USA) congregations were founded partly or largely by Italian Waldensians. Most of these congregations were located in the urban areas of New York City and Chicago and quickly developed close ties with neighboring old-stock American congregations. With time, as most urban congregations declined in numbers and merged with neighboring congregations, almost all of the Waldensian congregations united with other PC(USA) congregations. In

2007, just two PC(USA) congregations, one in North Carolina and one in Missouri, still considered themselves to have a strong Waldensian identity.

EUROPE BECOMES A PRESBYTERIAN MISSION FIELD

Beginning with the liberation of Paris in 1944, staff members of the Board of Foreign Missions of the Presbyterian Church in the U.S.A. began talking with leaders of the Reformed Church in France about how their church could help to minister to the millions who had been displaced throughout Europe.[3] Those discussions soon resulted in a commitment on the part of American Presbyterians to work with CIMADE, the Comité Inter-Mouvements auprès des Evacués.

The CIMADE had been the answer of leaders of the French Protestant youth movement, as well as of the French YWCA and YMCA, to the refugee crisis that faced Europe when World War II broke out. The first challenge for CIMADE was to find a way to offer shelter, meals, and welcome to refugees leaving Alsace and Lorraine for other places in France. Then, in June of 1940, France surrendered to Germany; Spaniards, who were suspected of "Republican," or antifascist, tendencies, along with foreign Jews, were herded into camps. Shortly thereafter, French Jews were arrested as well. The CIMADE staff, all women, found creative ways to enter these camps and minister to the detainees. Just before the end of the war, the World Council of Churches and the Swiss Reformed Churches offered twenty large barracks to CIMADE to assist in relief and rehabilitation in France and Germany. In twenty cities and ports from Caen to Le Havre, Saint-Dié to Osterheim, these barracks became known as the Foyer CIMADE.[4]

In May of 1945, as the war ended, Ray and Claire Teeuwissen and Gibson Lewis arrived in Paris as Presbyterian missionaries assigned to CIMADE. The Teeuwissens, and later Robert and Hedy Lodwick, directed the Foyer CIMADE in Dunkerque/Coudekerque. Jim and Sally Bean were responsible for the CIMADE Foyer in Boulogna-sur-Mer, and later in Le Chambon. Other missionaries seconded to CIMADE did varied work. Around this time, Charles and Eugenie Arbuthnot were sent to Grenoble for work among students. In 1947, Camille and Eva Chazeaud were asked to locate in Paris and open a center for orienting missionaries going to Africa. At the time, almost all of Africa was still under colonial rule, and most of western and central Africa was under French or Belgian administration. Beginning in 1949, David Romig also served under appointment by the Presbyterian Board of Foreign Missions.

Some leaders of the French Reformed Church were shocked at the idea of a "missionary" coming to one of Protestantism's oldest churches. "L'Europe devenue champ de mission, vous vous imaginez!? [Europe is becoming a mission field, can you imagine that?]" Partly in response to such comments, the Board of Foreign Missions changed the title of those whom it sent abroad from "missionary" to "fraternal worker," a title that became, for several decades, the standard nomenclature for all Presbyterian appointees serving outside the United States.

With the end of the war, the Board of Foreign Missions also sought opportunities for mission even in Germany and Italy, the two countries that had just been defeated. One opportunity was provided by CIMADE, which had also opened Foyers in Germany. The irony of this development was not lost on anyone, since CIMADE had been founded by French Christians in order to care for people who had become refugees because of a war of aggression waged by Nazi Germany. In 1949 John and Mary Kay Healy were sent to work at the Haus Villigst, which had been opened by CIMADE in the Villigst neighborhood of Schwerte in the Ruhr Valley. One of the Healys' coworkers was Klaus von Bismarck, a great-grandchild of the first chancellor of Germany, Otto von Bismarck, who himself later became a well-known figure in German public life.[5] Basil Kusiev also served with displaced persons in Germany through CIMADE.

Charles and Ruth West had been missionaries in China during 1947–50. When the communists took China in 1950 and Western missionaries had to leave, the Board of Foreign Missions asked the Wests if they would like to be reassigned to the Gossner Mission in Mainz-Kastel, near Frankfurt, Germany. There they worked with Horst Symanowski, who a few years later would become famous for his writings on missiology; but in 1950, he was best known for having been a pastor in the Confessing Church, the movement in the German Church that resisted the Nazis' efforts to co-opt Christianity for its own purposes.[6] In 1951, the Wests were reassigned to Berlin, where Charles West taught Christian education and ecumenics and joined in meetings of the Arche, a group of German church leaders from both West and East Germany who had known each other from the days when they had been part of the Confessing Church. Among the Wests' American Presbyterian colleagues were Margaret Barnes and Hilma Madelaire.

Beginning in 1949, Hollywood First Presbyterian Church, California, began to develop another and quite different kind of mission work in Europe. Young adults from the Hollywood First Presbyterian Church, along with Brethren young people and others from all over the United States, were sent to CIMADE and Brethren Youth Camps at several places in Western Europe. After taking part in a work camp in Italy, Louis Evans Jr., the son of the senior pastor of the Hollywood church and himself later the pastor of the same church, traveled north to visit work camps in Berlin. There Evans met a young German pastor named Alfred Schroeder. Two years later, in 1952, Schroeder visited the Hollywood Presbyterian Church. As a result of this exchange of visits, the mission committee of the Hollywood First Presbyterian Church asked Walter E. James, an associate pastor at their church, to take some young adults from the Hollywood Church to participate in the Brethren and CIMADE work camps in Germany. In 1953, building further on the exchange of visits, Otto Dibelius, the bishop of the Evangelical Church of Berlin-Brandenburg and one of the founding figures of the World Council of Churches, formally asked the Hollywood Presbyterian Church to send a "field worker" to care for "endangered and nonchurched" youth. In response to this request, the Hollywood Church sent Samuel and Yolanda Entz to work in a new youth center of the Youth Commission of the Evangelical

Church of Berlin-Brandenburg. Taken together, these early contacts built friendships that made possible more difficult work as the Cold War progressed.

In 1961, when the Berlin Wall went up and contacts between East Germans and Americans became much more difficult, Protestants on the east side of the Berlin Wall asked their American friends to do all that they could to keep communication open to the East German churches. In response to that call, a small group of pastors, elders, and members of Presbyterian congregations in Southern California organized themselves into what became known as the Berlin Fellowship, and they asked Walt James to be their leader.[7]

Within months, the first small group of pastors and laypeople from congregations that belonged to what would become the Berlin Fellowship went to East Berlin to meet with their counterparts from a number of congregations. In the following years, an ever-increasing number of American Christians of all ages and occupations would fly to West Berlin, undergo a week of careful orientation, and then journey as tourists in small teams to visit congregations in various parts of East Germany. Their goal was to continue the work of reconciliation that had begun a decade-and-a-half before, after the end of World War II, and in both nations to keep the vision alive of the church as a place where loyalty to Jesus Christ transcends ideology or nationality.

An American Presbyterian pastor, Theodore Schapp, and a West Berlin church worker, Baerbel Eccardt, coordinated these visits by working out of a congregation in the Tempelhof section of Berlin, where Schapp was the pastor and Eccardt was the parish worker. On the East German side, an "East Committee" (German: Ostkomitee) was organized, which planned the itineraries of each visiting team.[8] The visits continued for many years. In fact, every year during the twenty-eight years from 1961 to 1989 there was at least one visit from members of the Berlin Fellowship to at least one congregation on the eastern side of the Berlin Wall. Through informal gatherings in private homes, meetings with youth and children's groups, and in conversation following worship services, American Presbyterians and East German Protestants came to know and care for each other.

The fall of the Berlin Wall in November 1989 made the systematic visitation of East German congregations no longer necessary. Even so, exchange visits continued for another seven years with the facilitation of Jane Holslag, a PC(USA) mission coworker who, at this writing, is still serving in Germany. Over the years, through the work of Jane Holslag, Theodore Schapp, and Baerbel Eccardt, a number of congregation-to-congregation partnerships developed. The longest-lasting partnerships, and perhaps the partnerships that resulted in the most significant ministry, were those between Bel Air Presbyterian Church in Los Angeles and a congregation in Niederoderwitz, in the Oberlausitz in eastern East Germany; and between Trabuco Presbyterian Church, also in southern California, and a congregation in Plauen, which was just south of Leipzig, in Saxony.

Another Presbyterian mission worker, Charles Yerkes, was appointed soon after the fall of the Berlin Wall to serve in Rostock on the German North Sea coast.[9]

In Italy, the search for an appropriate ministry was much simplified by the pioneering ministry of the Waldensian pastor Tulio Vinay. In 1947, just three years after the death of the former dictator, Benito Mussolini, Vinay founded the Agape Community in Prali, in the Germanasca Valley, which was not far from Torre Pellice, a predominantly Waldensian village in the foothills of the Alps, just west of Turin.[10] Vinay intended the Agape Community to be a place where young Italians, French people, Germans, and others could come to do physical work during the days and spend their evenings and weekends dreaming about how the churches could reconcile with former enemies. As it turned out, large numbers of young Americans, many of whom were Presbyterians, were also attracted by Agape and volunteered to help build this new community in northern Italy.

Over the course of their service, most of the young American Presbyterians who served at Agape became inspired with a vision of the church—not just of Agape—as a community of reconciliation and transformation and carried that vision into later leadership positions.[11] The effects were felt elsewhere, as many volunteers at Agape ventured past the little town of Prali, just down the hill from Agape, and began to visit other parts of Italy.[12] On their return to the United States, many joined what was called the Waldensian Aid Society and was later renamed the American Waldensian Society.[13] For years many of them continued to contribute their "energy, intelligence, imagination, and love" as well as their money to support Waldensian ministry in Italy.

As reconciliation among war antagonists began to recede in importance, Waldensians began to refocus their attention on the widespread poverty and crime that could be seen nearly everywhere in southern Italy. Tullio Vinay left the historic Waldensian valleys in the foothills of the Alps for the small town of Riesi, in the center of Sicily. There in 1961, he founded a new community, the Servi-cio Cristiano, which was based partly on the very successful experiment with the Agape Community in Prali, but the Servicio Cristiano was even more on Vinay's and the Waldensian Tavola's vision of ministry, because it joined proclamation of the Word with a literal living out of Jesus' command to love neighbors. In Riesi in 1961, with its very high unemployment, rising crime rate, and lack of accessible health care, there was no shortage of work for the new Servicio Cristiano. For decades, a succession of Presbyterian mission staff members invited young Presbyterians and others to serve a year at Servicio Cristiano. When budgets were ample or generous, congregations stepped forward, and these staff members helped to direct grants to the Servicio. Young European people still volunteer at the Servicio Cristiano, even though it has been a number of years since volunteers have come from the PC(USA) or other North American churches.[14]

Beyond these partnerships, in 1948 the Board of Foreign Missions held its first work camp for college students in Europe, led by Ray Downs, youth secretary of the Board of Foreign Missions. The work camp brought together French, German, and American youth who were interested in working for reconciliation between their countries. The students worked first at the College Cevenol in Le Chambon sur Lignon, a Protestant village known for what some would later refer to as its uncommon "normal decency" in offering shelter to Jewish refugees.[15] From Le Chambon, they visited the Taizé community, which in following decades would come to symbolize ecumenical spirituality for many in Western Europe and North America. Then, they progressed over the Alps to Prali, Italy, where the Agape Center was in the beginning stages of being constructed. The fourth and final station was the island of Iona, located off the western coast of Scotland, where participants helped to restore a medieval abbey in which a Scottish pastor, George MacLeod, was organizing an ecumenical peace center. A number of the young European people who came into contact with Presbyterian mission in those days eventually received Presbyterian-funded scholarships so that they could study in the United States or elsewhere.

In 1953, the Board of Foreign Missions began inviting pastors and laypeople from Europe and elsewhere to serve as missionaries in the United States for one to two years. From Europe, Jacques Beaumont, who had been director of CIMADE, came to the Westminster Foundation at the University of Wisconsin at Madison to do student ministry. Franz von Hammerstein was recruited in Berlin to work in a blue-collar community in Perth Amboy, New Jersey. These appointments were the beginning of the Mission to the U.S.A. program. In later years, as it became difficult to find suitable candidates for a year's service, and as more congregations expressed interest in welcoming fraternal workers from outside the United States, the Mission to the U.S.A. program was redesigned so that the term of service was normally six weeks rather than a year or two. The Presbyterian Church (U.S.A.) is still thought of warmly in a number of European churches because of the work that was done or supported by Presbyterian mission in those early years after the end of World War II.

Also, during these years the Board of Foreign Missions established two programs to help young Presbyterians learn more about their counterparts in Europe. Beginning in 1953, the Presbyterian Church appointed Working Fellows in France, Italy, Spain, and Portugal. Working Fellows were seminary students who were taking a year out of their studies to serve in European churches. The other program designed to help young Presbyterians learn about church life in Europe and on other continents was the Frontier Intern program. Established in 1961, this program deployed young Presbyterians to sites on the eastern side of the Iron Curtain, as well as to programs for immigrants and refugees in various Western European cities.

In describing Presbyterian presence in postwar Europe, it is also important to mention the appointment of a succession of what were first executives, and then area representatives, and finally area associates. Benjamin Rush was sent to Geneva in 1945, shortly after the war's end, to supervise the Board of Foreign Missions' new work in Europe. He was soon appointed to a staff position in the newly organized World Council of Churches, leaving the field executive position vacant. His immediate successor was Charles Arbuthnot. Charles and his wife, Genie, had previously been serving in Grenoble, and along with Charles Tudor Leber, they shaped PCUSA and UPCUSA work in Europe during the first two decades after the end of World War II.[16]

PRESBYTERIAN MISSION IN EUROPE
ADAPTS TO NEW CHALLENGES

In 1953 the session of the Fourth Presbyterian Church in Chicago and the Board of Foreign Missions of the Presbyterian Church (PCUSA) decided together that inexpensive student housing was needed in Geneva, Switzerland. Thus students from all over the world could study in Geneva and, through contact with the recently founded World Council of Churches and the somewhat older World Alliance of Reformed Churches, learn to appreciate the ecumenical movement. Thanks to the generosity of many, but especially of Fourth Presbyterian Church, enough money was raised to buy a chalet in the Champel area of Geneva. The chalet was renovated, and a number of rooms were joined together to serve as an apartment for the first director of the John Knox Center, Presbyterian mission coworker Ray Teeuwissen, who served until 1958. Other rooms were offered to eleven international students. Rather soon, the John Knox Center was a place of meeting and fellowship where students and short-term visitors talked about their respective churches, their life journeys and worldviews, and often shared meals and studied the Bible together.

Under the direction of Presbyterian mission worker Paul Frelick, who served from 1958 to 1966, annual seminars were organized for students from Africa and Asia and later from Latin America as well. Gradually, the center in Champel proved to be too small for the need. In 1962, it was decided to follow the World Council of Churches and to relocate the center to Grand-Saconnex, just an eight-minute walk from the new Ecumenical Center. The seminars continued during the stewardship of Presbyterian mission worker Charles Harper, who served from 1967 to 1974. Then, in 1973, in the wake of what many remember as the Angela Davis controversy,[17] the Commission on Ecumenical Mission and Relations (COEMAR) of the UPCUSA faced the first of what became a series of funding crises, and the Presbyterian Church's financial support for the John Knox Center had to be drastically reduced. Through the intervention of Edmond Peret, general secretary of the World Alliance of Reformed Churches, the John Knox Center's existence was continued, even though its mission had to be reenvisioned. Today, the John Knox Center is still the site of many international and ecumenical gatherings.

As Western Europe began to recover from the privations of the postwar years, Presbyterians turned their attention to newer regions of Europe. In 1951 Margaret Shannon, the associate for women's work in the Board of Foreign Missions, and Ada Black, also a staff member of the Board of Foreign Missions, were joined by Lena Robinson, president of the Presbyterian Women's Synodical organization in Texas, on what was called a Fellowship Mission to Europe. Their itinerary took them to visit the tiny Reformed churches of Portugal and Spain, as well as the somewhat larger Reformed churches in France, Switzerland, Germany, and the Netherlands. They were joined by Charles Tudor Leber and Charles W. Arbuthnot for the visit to the Reformed Christian Church in Yugoslavia. The translator for the American delegation was a young theology student, Endre Langh, who was elected to be the first bishop of the Reformed Christian Church in Croatia forty years later.[18]

At least for Margaret Shannon, the visit was profoundly moving. Shannon later wrote, "On the last day of our visit in Yugoslavia, a knock came at the door, and there was Maria Agoston with a heartfelt concern. 'You have been very careful to find out what you could do for us while you were here, but the greatest thing you could do for us is to tell us something we could do for you. Don't your Navajos need something?' We gave her the current 'Mission Yearbook of Prayer,' since it contained many of the persons and projects through which we worked, and urged that they reinforce our work. We thought that prayer was all that could be sought, for we knew they would not be allowed to send money out of the country. But God [was] greater than Tito." From this encounter, Presbyterian women began to become involved in a number of imaginative mission projects with the women of Yugoslavia from 1944 onward.

During that 1951 visit to the former Yugoslavia, the bishop of the Reformed Christian Church in Yugoslavia, Sandor Agoston, asked Charles Leber if the PCUSA could send a missionary or a missionary couple to encourage the congregations of his church. On behalf of the Board of Foreign Missions, Leber promised to do what was possible. Part of the rationale for Leber's promise was that American Presbyterians had a special interest in Yugoslavia. At that time, Yugoslavia was the only communist country that was actively trying to develop good relationships with the United States. Moreover, in the McCarthy era, the Christians of Yugoslavia were perhaps the only Christians in any communist country with whom Presbyterians could develop a partnership without having someone question their underlying loyalty to the United States.

Accordingly, in September 1956, just weeks before the Hungarian Revolution, the Board of Foreign Missions appointed Charles and Marie Mercer to be its first missionaries in that socialist world. Partly because neither the Board nor the Yugoslav bishop wanted to risk a crackdown on the Yugoslav Reformed Church by formally appointing missionaries in Yugoslavia, the Mercers were asked to begin their service as students. They moved to Belgrade, enrolled in the University of Belgrade, and began to study Serbo-Croatian and Yugoslav history and art. During their free time, they traveled up and down Yugoslavia, looking for Reformed churches. In the course of their travels, they met Bishop Agoston, who lived in Feketic in Voivodina, in the northern part of Serbia. The bishop introduced them to a house church in Belgrade that was particularly oriented to students. Wherever they went, they introduced themselves as "Christian students from America." Of the approximately eighteen pastors in the Yugoslav Reformed Church, they told only three, one of whom was Endre Langh, the current bishop of the Reformed Church in Croatia, that they were under appointment by the Board of Foreign Missions. Yet as students, they took part in women's meetings, church celebrations, pastors' gatherings, and over the years of their work, they eventually visited every congregation of the Reformed Christian Church in

Yugoslavia. The Mercers served until 1959, when the Yugoslav authorities decided not to renew their student visas. The Mercers maintained a long-distance friendship with a number of Yugoslav pastors, returning for visits in 1978 and 1996. Typical of the ecumenical openness of the Board of Foreign Missions, the Mercers were American Baptists, even though Marie had grown up in a Presbyterian church. Years later, the Mercers served two different terms as chaplains at the Moscow Protestant Chaplaincy in Russia, an ecumenical work that was supported by the Presbyterian Church (U.S.A.), as well as by several other North American denominations.

After the departure of the Mercers from Yugoslavia in 1959, there was no further Presbyterian mission presence in the area of Europe that used to be Yugoslavia until 1994, when Steven and Michelle Kurtz went to Osijek in Eastern Slavonia, in the newly independent country of Croatia. The Kurtzes were assigned to teach at the Evangelical Theological Faculty in Osijek. In later years, Michelle founded a program called "Alternatives to Violence" with help from the American Friends Service Committee.

As the years went by, the relationship with the Reformed Christian Church in Croatia became an increasingly important part of Steven Kurtz's work; at one point, he was even asked if he would be willing to be elected as bishop of the Reformed Church. Steven Kurtz declined because he believed that it would be better for a person who had been born and raised in Croatia to be the bishop of the Croatian church. In 2004 the Kurtzes left Croatia, to the great regret of the Croatian bishop.

In the late 1990s, the PC(USA) appointed Brett McMichael to teach at the Evangelical Theological Faculty in Osijek, as well as to help faculty colleagues to establish play areas in local hospitals and to lead seminars for health-care professionals on the special needs of children in their care. McMichael moved from Osijek to Zagreb in 2002 in order to focus his work on the health-care system. Others joined work in Croatia, helping with theological education, health-care issues, and alleviating church conflicts. Ministries continued to multiply, including such projects as the translation and distribution of seven hundred kits for teachers and social workers in Bosnia and Croatia. These kits contained information about communication and conflict resolution skills with children. Other books, dealing with social problems such as alcoholism and post-traumatic stress syndrome, were translated with the help of Presbyterian support. After a visit by Susan Ryan, a staff member and later coordinator of Presbyterian Disaster Service, and myself, Presbyterian Disaster Service also gave one hundred thousand dollars to Agape for a livestock project, which enabled villagers to return home and have a hope of starting over after the war.

Two other successor states of the Federal Republic of Yugoslavia also became fields for Presbyterian mission. One was in Voivodina, the northernmost province of Serbia, where Bishop Agoston and the Presbyterian women's delegation had their transformative meeting in 1951. The other successor state that became a field for Presbyterian mission was Croatia. After the Mercers left Yugoslavia in

1959, there has been only sporadic Presbyterian contact with the Reformed people in Voivodina.

In 1995 the General Assembly moderator, Bob Bohl; his wife, Judy; Marj Carpenter, a future moderator; Eugene Turner, the associate stated clerk for ecumenical relations; Bertalan Tamas, the ecumenical officer of the Reformed Church in Hungary; and I crossed the border for an evening and a day to visit the Reformed people in Feketic. The service and coffee hour passed without any mention of political or other problems. It was striking how nonpolitical the discussion was. Then one man left the coffee hour, whom the Presbyterian visitors later guessed might have been a government informant, and the conversation took on a far more serious tone. The congregation members explained that several young men in their church had been arrested without cause. They also explained that a twenty-year-old had been attacked and beaten by neighbors of a different ethnic group while the police looked on. The visiting Presbyterians thanked the congregation for speaking so openly and promised that their congregation and the others in the Reformed Christian Church in Voivodina would be in the prayers of American Presbyterians. There were not many dry eyes when the coffee hour was over.

In early October of 2000, just two weeks after the fall of the Serbian dictator Slobodan Milosevic, I, Bertalan Tamas, as well as several others visited the same Reformed congregation in Feketic. That was a hopeful and festive time for the Reformed people in Voivodina. As a follow-up to that visit, and in response to the massive changes in Serbia and Voivodina, the PC(USA) made a number of small grants to the Reformed Christian Church in Voivodina. I was serving as the Europe coordinator at the time and regretted deeply that declining budgets in the Worldwide Ministries Division made it impossible to do more to help the church in Voivodina to get back on its feet. In 2005, Cliff Kirkpatrick, president of the World Alliance of Reformed Churches; Setri Nyomi, the general secretary of the World Alliance; Bertalan Tamas; and I made a return visit to Voivodina as part of a larger tour of Hungarian-speaking Reformed churches in Central Europe. There was no stop on that trip where the response of those who were visited was stronger.

CZECHOSLOVAKIA AND THE CZECH REPUBLIC

Presbyterian ties with the Evangelical Church of Czech Brethren[19] in the former Czechoslovakia began with the Nazi occupation of that country in the months before the beginning of World War II. Like many other Czech intellectuals, the preeminent Czech theologian Josef Hromadka had to flee his homeland to save his life. He became a guest professor at Princeton Theological Seminary. Hromadka's experiences with North American Presbyterians were reflected in much of his later writings. Hromadka returned to Prague in 1947, after the end of the war, to help rebuild civil society in the former Czechoslovakia.[20]

At the end of World War II, Jaroslav Paul Tatter and Stuart Pratt were appointed by the Board of Foreign Missions to help in the relief and reconstruction work of the Czechoslovak churches. After the communist takeover of Czechoslovakia in 1948, it became much more difficult, however, for American church people to maintain active relationships with Czechoslovak Christians. Nevertheless, even during the forty years following 1948, some relationships continued. First, there were the lasting friendships that Hromadka and his family, particularly his daughter, Elena, had formed with colleagues at Princeton Seminary and in the Presbyterian offices in New York. Second, there were relationships mediated by Czech and Slovak Christians who had come to the United States after the communist takeover. Third, there were the relationships that developed as American Presbyterians and Czech Christians met in committees and general councils and assemblies of the World Council of Churches and the World Alliance of Reformed Churches.

The greatest number of American and Czech Christians met each other, however, through their common participation in a long series of international conferences that would later be called the Prague Peace Conferences. The formal presentations of the East Bloc participants at these meetings necessarily reflected the political perspectives of their respective governments. Between the formal presentations, however, there was a lively and much-more authentic give-and-take of ideas that was not possible during much of the Cold War in any other setting. Indeed, after the end of the Cold War, most PC(USA) mission appointments in the former East Bloc were facilitated by Central and Eastern European church leaders who had come to know American Presbyterians through these meetings. Three current and future stated clerks, James A. Andrews, William P. Thompson, and James I. McCord, participated in these meetings. Many future PC(USA) mission partners in Central and Eastern Europe also participated in these meetings.

The first North American Presbyterian to serve as a PC(USA) mission worker in Czechoslovakia following the end of the Cold War was John Michael, a pastor from Pennsylvania whose father had been born in what is now the Slovak Republic. Beginning in 1992, he worked with two congregations in what was then eastern Czechoslovakia before he accepted a transfer to work in the ecumenical office of the Evangelical Church of Czech Brethren in Prague.

Presbyterian work in the Czech Republic was also strongly influenced by Presbyterians who were living and working outside of the Louisville structure. In 1994, David Murdoch, an elder at the Sewickley Presbyterian Church (near Pittsburgh) contacted me to ask if he could represent the PC(USA) at a meeting of the Synodal Council of the Evangelical Church of Czech Brethren. After consulting with colleagues in the Synod of the Trinity, I weighed the possibility of opening new work in the Czech Republic and agreed to Murdoch's request. When Murdoch returned from Prague, he reported on what he had experienced at the Synodal Council, addressing all of the key missiological issues that needed to be considered before Presbyterians could engage in new work in the Czech Republic.

Almost immediately after receiving Murdoch's report, I told Murdoch that a new group would soon be organized by the General Assembly Council with membership from across the denomination to assist in developing new work with the Evangelical Church of the Czech Republic. Would Murdoch be willing, I asked, to become the chair of the new group, assuming that the group members were willing to elect him? Soon, the new group met, constituted itself as the Czech Working Group, and elected Murdoch as its chair. In time, the Czech Working Group became the model for numerous additional mission networks that linked Presbyterians with partner churches around the world.

Under the guidance of the Czech Working Group, a series of pastoral exchanges were organized. One of the Czech pastors, Ondrej Stehlik, serving in Prague, was invited to come to Louisville for a year to serve as a "mission partner in residence." In time, the Czechs decided to establish their own working group, the American Working Group, to coordinate their churches' engagement with the American Presbyterians. At the invitation of the Czech church, and with the endorsement of the Czech Working Group of the PC(USA), the missionary John Michael, who had been serving in Slovakia, was reassigned to work in the ecumenical office of the Evangelical Church of Czech Brethren. Also, as a result of discussions between both working groups, Frank Beattie, who was on the staff of the General Assembly Council agency that was responsible for helping congregations grow in numbers and mission, was asked to do a series of lectures on evangelism in several places in the Czech Republic. Ultimately, Beattie became an unofficial member of the PC(USA)'s Czech Working Group.

PRESBYTERIANS ON THE IBERIAN PENINSULA

Another field for Presbyterian work in Europe during the Cold War years was in Portugal. The first congregation of the Evangelical Presbyterian Church in Portugal had been founded on the island of Madeira in 1845 by a Scottish physician, Dr. Robert Kalley. Soon the congregation had five thousand members, too many to be easily ignored either by the Catholic Church or by the Portuguese government. The members of the congregations were forced into exile through a combination of church-sanctioned social pressure and government-authorized violence. Some went to Jacksonville and Springfield, Illinois; others went to Trinidad and Brazil. A couple of decades later, when those first Portuguese Presbyterians were finally able to return to Portugal, they founded new congregations in Lisbon, as well as in several cities in northern Portugal. From the time of the first Portuguese Presbyterians' return to their homeland to the end of World War II, the Evangelical Presbyterian Church in Portugal continued to open new congregations and reach out to their Portuguese neighbors without appreciable help from Presbyterians from the outside world.

Then, beginning in 1946, a series of American Presbyterian mission personnel were appointed to work in Portugal. Manuel L. and Alda Beatriz Fabio da Coonceicao started work in 1946, Michael and Christine Testa began in 1948, and Paul and Rosemary Pierson and Fred and Marguerite Bronkema started in the early 1950s. Working together with a number of Portuguese pastors and laypeople, the Bronkemas helped to open a retreat and conference center, as well as a model agricultural station. Others, including the Piersons, taught in a small seminary at Carcavelos. Eventually, a number of the Presbyterian mission workers in Portugal moved on to other significant mission assignments. Michael and Christina Testa left Portugal when Michael Testa was asked to become the UPCUSA Area Associate for Europe. Paul Pierson later worked in Brazil and then taught at Fuller Theological Seminary. Fred Bronkema left Portugal to serve in a number of ecumenical mission assignments in Italy, New York, and many years later, Honduras.

Then, beginning around 1970, there was a long period during which there was little American Presbyterian presence in Portugal. Finally, around 1988, José Leite, a Portuguese Presbyterian pastor, was appointed to a staff position in the Conference of European Churches with an office down the hall from Robert Lodwick, who was the Europe Associate for the PC(USA). Around the same time, the PC(USA) began to make modest grants to help the Evangelical Presbyterian Church in Portugal in the development of some new ministries. During 1990–92, the PC(USA) also shared financially in the appointment of a Brazilian Presbyterian pastor who served briefly in the Madeiras.

In 2000 a Presbyterian travel study seminar visited Portugal and Spain. This visit had two results. The first was the establishment of an informal partnership between the women in the Presbytery of Yellowstone in the PC(USA) and the women in the Portuguese church. The other result was the decision of the PC(USA) to appoint regional facilitators for Spain and Portugal. Bryce and Phyllis Little were selected for this work.[21]

Presbyterian missionaries have served for most of the last half century in Spain. The first American Presbyterians to serve in Spain were Latham and Roberta Wright and Thomas Goslin. They formed the first link in a long chain of Presbyterian missionaries to serve at the United Evangelical Seminary in Madrid. When the Wrights and Goslin went to Madrid, Spain was still a semifascist dictatorship ruled by the Caudillo (Leader), Francisco Franco, whose policy was to prohibit any non–Roman Catholic religious activity that could bring ordinary Spanish citizens into contact with a religion other than Catholicism. As a result, Spanish Protestants could not worship in buildings that looked like churches, nor could they perform weddings for their own members.

When Franco died and Juan Carlos became king of Spain in November of 1975, Spanish culture and politics began to evolve. After the appointment of Adolfo Suarez as prime minister in July of 1976 and the failure of a coup attempt by disgruntled loyalists of the old quasi-fascist dictatorship in February of 1981, Protestant Christianity began to emerge in public life. The legal discrimination of the Franco dictatorship against Spanish Protestants was largely, but not completely, eliminated, and the Spanish Evangelical Church, which was the result of a union between Spanish Presbyterians and Spanish Methodists, began to thrive.

North American Presbyterians continued to serve during this period of transition at the Ecumenical Seminary in Madrid, and they continue to do so today.

NORTHERN IRELAND

Presbyterian work in Ireland, like Presbyterian work in Germany, began as a congregational youth initiative. In the summer of 1970, Doug Baker, a young Presbyterian who was living in Seattle, was assigned to Ireland as a mission volunteer from University Presbyterian Church. In 1972, Baker returned as volunteer assistant to the chaplain at Queens University, primarily to create an interchaplaincy program between Catholics and Presbyterians, with thirteen hours a week to support the Presbyterian Church in Ireland (PCI) youth office. Even then, he worked on specific reconciliation projects with the Corrymeela Community.[22] After completing seminary at Princeton and spending two-and-a-half years at Trinity Presbyterian Church in Berwyn, Pennsylvania, he returned to Northern Ireland in 1979 as a UPCUSA mission worker to serve the Corrymeela Community in Christian Education. In 1984, he married the daughter of a former moderator of the Presbyterian Church in Ireland and dedicated himself to reconciling Catholics and Protestants in that land, where ancient religious conflicts have defined much of modern political and cultural life. Since 1993, Northern Ireland has been a Young Adult Volunteer site in which about seventy American Presbyterian young adults have served, seventeen or eighteen of whom are now Presbyterian pastors.

Another American Presbyterian, the chairperson of the General Assembly Council, Joe Beeman, urged the General Assembly Council to establish the Northern Ireland Working Group. This group took a significant role in annual talks between Northern Irish and American Catholics and Northern Irish and American Presbyterians. The Northern Ireland Working Group also sponsored the Business Education Initiative, which over several years brought a large number of Protestant and Catholic Irish young people to Presbyterian and other colleges in the United States. The Northern Ireland Working Group is now called the Presbyterian Committee for Northern Ireland and still devotes itself to the work of Protestant-Catholic reconciliation in Northern Ireland.

RUSSIA AND THE SOVIET REPUBLICS

In cooperation with other mainline American denominations, Presbyterian work in Russia began in 1962 with the founding of an ecumenical chaplaincy intended to conduct English-language worship services for the embassy communities. With the opening up of public life in the Soviet Union in the late 1980s, another, less-privileged, group of expatriates, African students and ex-students who were stranded in Moscow by conflicts in their home countries, began to take part in the worship and fellowship life of the Moscow Protestant Chaplaincy. In the early

1990s, the members of the Moscow Protestant Chaplaincy opened a number of soup kitchens in the central area of Moscow. These soup kitchens were largely staffed by the chaplaincy's African participants and mostly served elderly Russian women, who were affectionately called "babushkas" by the members of the chaplaincy. Over the years, a number of chaplains at the Moscow Protestant Chaplaincy have come from the PC(USA), including Charles Jester, Clarence and Sylvia Guinn-Ammons, and Bob and Stacy Bronkema.[23]

Beginning in the early 1980s, large numbers of Presbyterians and members of other mainline denominations joined in ecumenically sponsored travel study seminars in the Soviet Union. These trips were organized by the Europe Committee of the National Council of Churches of Christ in the U.S.A. and were mostly planned and led by Bruce Rigdon, who in the early 1980s was a professor at McCormick Theological Seminary and later became pastor of the Grosse Pointe Presbyterian Church outside of Detroit, Michigan.[24] These trips motivated a large number of North American Presbyterian congregations to seek Russian congregations with which they could have a twinning relationship, even though the twinning relationships themselves did not actually become feasible until a bit later. Through these trips, a number of future mission workers and mission volunteers became interested in service in Russia.

At the end of the 1980s, the Europe Committee of the National Council of Churches set up a congregational twinning program. This program, which ultimately established about ninety congregational twinning relationships that linked mainline American congregations with Russian Orthodox and Russian Baptist congregations, proved to be hard to sustain. Often, neither congregation in a twinning relationship knew what to do to further develop their relationship. Moreover, many congregations simply needed someone who could translate the letters that they wanted to send to their sister congregation.

As the National Council of Churches–sponsored program came to an end, the Outreach Foundation of the Presbyterian Church (U.S.A.) set up its own twinning program. A distinctive ingredient of the Outreach Foundation's twinning program was its decision to twin only congregations that had a member or staff person fluent in both Russian and English. The Outreach Foundation also asked representatives of the North American congregations to join in an initial visit to Russia that was led by the Outreach Foundation's president, Bill Bryant, as well as myself, representing the Europe Office of the PC(USA). After two trips, it became evident that a mission worker on the ground was needed to support existing twinnings and to facilitate new ones. In August of 1997, Donald and Laurie Marsden were appointed to coordinate the twinning program and to help in the production of Christian education materials. By 2001, it had become evident that Donald Marsden was needed on a full-time basis in Christian education work, and Ellen and Alan Smith were appointed to take over the twinning program. The congregational twinnings resulted in a wide variety of new mission projects, including support for orphanages and summer camps. With help from the Outreach Foundation, a number of new church buildings were also erected.

Presbyterians in Yukon Presbytery and elsewhere in Alaska had long had an interest in the peoples who lived across the Bering Straits in Russia. They knew that some of the indigenous people on the Alaska side of the straits spoke the same languages as their relatives on the other side of the straits. Indeed, indigenous peoples in Alaska and in the Chuhotka Peninsula had maintained contact with each other up until the beginning of the Cold War. Since a number of Presbyterians in Alaska were indigenous people, it was a natural, if not easy, step for Alaskan Presbyterians to seek to do ministry on the Chuhotka Peninsula. With the help of Presbyterian Frontier Fellowship and David Dobler, the moderator of the Orlando General Assembly, a considerable amount of support was raised from across the PC(USA) for this project.

The first Presbyterian mission workers to serve in Russia, Garth and Lyuda Moller, were actually appointed by the Northminster Presbyterian Church in Diamond Bar, California, and the Presbytery of San Gabriel. In 1994 they were also appointed as PC(USA) mission workers. During most of their stay in Russia, the Mollers have served in St. Petersburg with the Kargel and Baedeker School and Sluzhenia, which is Russian for "The Ministry," or "Service." Presbyterian work in Russia included alcohol and drug rehabilitation work, seminary ministry, work with orphans, and even work with local congregations.

Since 2000, the Presbyterian Church has also supported a World Alliance of Reformed Churches–related initiative known as the Mission in Unity Project for Ukraine and Belarus.[25] One by-product of Presbyterian participation in this project was a decision of the PC(USA) to support the AIDS education and prevention work of an Orthodox ministry that was related to the Belarus Round Table of the World Council of Churches.

At the invitation of Russian Baptists, a delegation from the PC(USA) and the Church of Scotland attended a conference on ministry with indigenous peoples in Salehard, Russia. As a result of this conference, Presbyterians committed themselves to working with Baptists to plant new congregations in places in Russian Siberia where there were no Baptist or Orthodox churches. Harold Kurtz and Donald Marsden made several follow-up visits to Siberia to guide Presbyterian participation in this work.[26] This expanded PC(USA) work in Russia, Ukraine, and Belarus was possible only because of the appointment of Gary Payton in 2000 as regional liaison for the Slavic Former Soviet Union and Poland.[27] Payton's work has four components:

1. Assisting on the U.S. domestic side in developing congregational twinning relationships between Presbyterian and Russian, Belarusian, Ukrainian, and Polish congregations.
2. Supporting Garth Moller, Donald Marsden, and Joe and Hannah Kang in their Christian education and theological education work.
3. Coordinating efforts to help Russian denominations plant new congregations in the vast areas of Siberian Russia where there is no Christian church.

4. Consulting with Ellen Smith, Jeff Koning, and others who are working with children and orphanages, HIV/AIDS education and prevention, medical outreach, and so forth.

PRESBYTERIAN MISSION IN EUROPE
CONTINUES TO EVOLVE

In retrospect, the fall of the Iron Curtain marked a turning point in Presbyterian mission in Europe. With the end of the Cold War in 1989, Presbyterians who were working in Europe were far less likely to be seen as ideological representatives of the United States government. Soon it became evident that Presbyterian mission personnel could be assigned far more easily in Central and Eastern Europe than had been the case only a couple of years before. Similar changes in the context for Presbyterian mission occurred simultaneously on other continents as well. Presbyterians needed a new charter for their global mission. Cliff Kirkpatrick, the director of the Global Mission (Ministry) Unit, drafted that charter, known as "Mission in the 1990s." After much consultation with staff, missionaries, and mission partners, "Mission in the 1990s" mandated new work in "socialist and former socialist countries," a mandate that, during the next decade, was to dramatically increase the breadth and depth of Presbyterian mission work in Europe.

The first new Presbyterian mission initiative after the end of the Cold War concerned the Kurds.[28] As a result of a coup in Iraq and revolution in Iran, Presbyterian ministries were forced to leave the Kurdish regions of Iraq in 1969 and Iran in 1979.[29] In the early 1980s, the PC(USA)'s Associate for International Evangelism, Morton Taylor, who had worked among Kurds in Iraq for sixteen years, learned that, with half a million Kurds within its borders, Germany had become home to the largest number of Kurds living in exile. In 1986, Taylor and the area associate for Europe, Robert C. Lodwick, decided to approach the Berlin Mission Society of the Protestant Church of Berlin-Brandenburg about the possibility of common work on behalf of the fifty thousand predominantly Muslim Kurds in Berlin, most of whom had come from Turkey. Roughly one year later, in July 1987, the PC(USA) and the Berlin Mission Society agreed on the appointment of Christine Goodman, the first staff person in that ministry. Before starting work, Goodman spent a year researching the situation of Kurds in Berlin and then proposed how a ministry might be organized that would bring together proclamation of the gospel and humanitarian service. The PC(USA) and the Berlin Mission Society explicitly affirmed their hope that the Holy Spirit would give birth to a church of Kurdish believers. They also affirmed four means to that end that still guide the PC(USA)'s Kurdish work:

1. Educating Germans about Kurdish history, culture, and religious experience.

2. Promoting dialogue and friendship between Kurds and Germans as well as between Muslims and Christians.
3. Engaging in service ministry, including social work, English-language instruction, pastoral care, and helping Kurds to explain their needs to German government agencies.
4. Sharing Christian literature with Kurds in order to encourage discussions about personal faith.

Though Presbyterian work with the Kurds has not had a strong human rights advocacy component, the fact that a North American church would make the Kurds, who have no unitary national homeland, a focus of ministry was, in several practical ways, a continuing reminder to Europeans, Americans, and Kurds alike that the legitimate claims of the Kurdish people cannot be ignored forever.

ROMANIA AND ALBANIA

In response to a request from Bishop Kalman Csiha of the Cluj Diocese in Romania, a country that had just freed itself from one of Central and Eastern Europe's most oppressive dictatorships, Robert Lodwick recruited the first PC(USA) missionaries to serve in that country. Harry and Christina Caldwell had been working in Louisville as missionaries-in-residence after teaching English in Pakistan when they agreed to go first to Cluj and then to Tirgu Mures to design an English-as-a-Second-Language program. In the mid-1990s, Elaine Matthes also served in a children's ministry in Iasi, Romania.[30]

The first Presbyterian work in Albania was done by University Presbyterian Church in Seattle. University Church's mission pastor, Art Beals, who would play a major role in PC(USA) denominational work in Europe and the former Soviet Union, had first heard about Albania from an American Baptist missionary who had served in Albania before World War II.[31] Even while Albania was still one of the most closed dictatorships in the communist world, University Presbyterian Church appointed John and Lynne Quanrud in 1986 to go to Pristina, Kosovo, in the former Yugoslavia, to learn Albanian. John Quanrud was a dedicated language learner and scholar, and in four years he became so fluent in Albanian that even Albanians could not tell that he was not a native speaker. While living in Kosovo, Quanrud prepared and printed Bible study and worship materials that ended up being used in Albania as well as in Kosovo. When the Albanian dictatorship collapsed in February of 1991, University Presbyterian Church asked the Quanruds to move to Tirana, the capital and largest city of Albania. They also sent a series of young people as well as an older couple to Albania during 1991 and 1992 to develop a student ministry under the auspices of the International Fellowship of Evangelical Students.

Robert Lodwick and I were the first PC(USA) national staff people to visit Albania. We left Albania with three strong impressions: the first was that University Presbyterian Church was doing very good work in Albania, and any new PC(USA) work should build on the work that University Presbyterian Church was doing. Second, we were astonished to learn that the Orthodox were very open to working with Presbyterians. The Orthodox archbishop, Anastasios, was a good friend of Cliff Kirkpatrick, the director of the Worldwide Ministries Division and later PC(USA) stated clerk; and the priest who was the senior pastor at the Orthodox Cathedral in Tirana was a Fuller Seminary graduate and had written his doctoral dissertation on mission under the supervision of Paul Pierson, who had previously served as a missionary in Portugal. Third, they had the privilege of meeting in the southern Albanian city of Korce one of the five "old men" who had continued to meet each week for Christian worship even after Christianity had been made illegal in 1967, when the Albanian dictator Enver Hoxha declared his country to be the world's first legally "atheist" country. This "old man" had known the Baptist missionary, Dr. Edwin Jacques,[32] who had served in Albania before the Italian occupation of Albania at the beginning of World War II and directly or indirectly influenced many of the missionaries who went to Albania after 1991.[33]

Shortly after Lodwick and I returned from our visit to Albania, Cliff Kirkpatrick suggested that I approach Art Beals to see if he would be willing to work with the PC(USA) in developing Presbyterian mission in Albania and other places of Europe. Beals became an invaluable colleague to me in developing new mission initiatives in Europe and Central Asia throughout the following decade.

Beginning in 1994, all University Presbyterian Church members appointed to serve in Albania were jointly appointed with the PC(USA). Missionaries from congregations other than University Church were also appointed, including most notably Bob and Dalia Baker, who were members of Fourth Presbyterian Church in Chicago. Presbyterian work in Albania during the 1990s had five major foci:

1. Training and mentoring an emerging Albanian church leadership.
2. Supporting ecumenical structures in Albania, including the Interconfessional Bible Society of Albania,[34] the Albanian Evangelical Alliance, and most notably the Albanian Encouragement Project, whose director during some of its most critical years was Bob Baker from Fourth Presbyterian Church.
3. Developing a trusting relationship with the Autocephalous Orthodox Church in Albania, which allowed PC(USA) to work closely together with the Albanian Orthodox Church and ACT (Action by Churches Together, a World Council–related relief and development agency) during the refugee crisis of 1999, a result of the war in Kosovo.
4. A student ministry done in cooperation with International Fellowship of Evangelical Students in Europe.
5. Support for a mission school, the Gjersasim Quirasi School, which offered primary and secondary school education for missionary children as well as a few Albanian children. Presbyterian mission workers

have served from the school's inception both as administrators and teachers.

In 2001, the Presbyterian Church (U.S.A.) and the Reformed Church in America established a mission partnership for Albania, and Jack and Susannah Dabney were appointed to help mentor young Albanian church leaders.

TURKEY

Presbyterian mission work in Turkey began in the early 1980s, when a Presbyterian medical doctor and his wife went to a major city in western Turkey.[35] This Presbyterian physician had been trained in a specialty that was, at the time of his arrival in Turkey, simply not practiced in Turkey. This physician began to work in his specialty and simultaneously sought opportunities to introduce his specialty to the Turkish medical community. After learning Turkish nearly perfectly, he began to lecture widely about his specialty. Soon he was asked to become a professor of medicine at a major Turkish university. He views his work as a reflection of his Christian faith, and he hopes that his contributions to Turkish medicine will strengthen the witness of indigenous Turkish Christians. He and his wife attend one of the relatively few Protestant Christian congregations in the country, and in the context of his congregation, he shares gladly with others about Christian faith. But he prefers not to use the moniker "mission worker" because in Turkey the words "missionary" and "mission worker" connote someone who seeks to convert other people by trickery, bribery, or force.

In 1994 a member of University Presbyterian Church in Seattle began to make annual summer visits to Istanbul. There he formed friendships with a Turkish pastor, Engin Yilidrim, as well as with several Turkish Protestant congregations. Soon he had an invitation to teach at Bithynia Bible College, and through Bithynia, he began inviting short-term mission teams from the United States to participate in various projects in the Istanbul area. In 1999 he was appointed as a coworker by the Worldwide Ministries Division. In 2004 he returned to the United States.

In 1995 the Worldwide Ministries Division added Turkey to the list of countries for which I was asked to serve as area coordinator. The assignment was natural, given that many Turks believed and still believe that their land is or at least ought to be more closely related to Europe than to the Middle East. It was also a welcome assignment for me since I had visited Turkey numerous times already, at least partly because Istanbul was a convenient stopping point for trips between the United States and Central Asia. Within days of being assigned responsibility for Turkey, I asked Art Beals if he would be willing to collaborate with me in designing a new strategy for work in Turkey.

A few months later, I traveled to western Turkey with Beals, where we visited the physician and his wife and an appointee of the United Church of Christ who had been working there, with a couple of interruptions, since the early 1960s. We also visited Bartholomew, the Ecumenical patriarch. Together we devised a four-part strategy that continues to shape Presbyterian work in Turkey:

1. The PC(USA) would commit itself to helping to give birth to an indigenous Turkish church even as it would seek to befriend and possibly to support the non-Turkish churches that for millennia had already been present in Turkey.[36]
2. The PC(USA) could best assist in the birth of a Turkish church by supporting the theological education and leader development as well as the social service efforts of indigenous Turkish Christians. That support could take the form of personnel assignments or grants or both.
3. The PC(USA) would seek always to build interfaith understanding and would always be respectful toward Islam and individual Muslims.
4. The PC(USA) would offer travel/study experiences to help North American Christians better understand the challenges of Christian ministry in an Islamic religious and cultural environment.

In 2000, 2001, and 2004, additional workers were assigned to Turkey to assist in theological education, college student ministry, and ministry with developmentally challenged young people and adults. Since 1995, Beals has made at least two trips a year to Turkey to offer pastoral support to Presbyterian appointees in Turkey and to introduce visiting groups of Presbyterians to their church's work in Turkey.

"GYPSIES": THE ROMA AND THE SINTI

The most socially prophetic work that the PC(USA) did in Europe during the years after the fall of the Berlin Wall had to do with the Roma and the Sinti.[37] That work had its origin in the observations of two Presbyterians. The first chronologically was myself, who first heard about the Roma in the early 1960s and recognized even then that they were victims of massive popular misunderstanding. After I became the area coordinator for Europe, I made it my practice to ask European church leaders and opinion-shapers to tell me about the Roma. At some point in each of those conversations, I would express my personal concern for the oppression the Roma had to live with as well as my conviction that the church someday would have to make the suffering of the Roma a priority for its ministry. When the opportunity presented itself for work with the Roma, I helped Presbyterians respond.

The Presbyterian who first brought the need for Roma work to the attention of Presbyterian congregations was Kaeja Cho. Kaeja and her husband, Stephen, were serving in a Korean-language Presbyterian congregation in California when they decided to seek a mission appointment with the Presbyterian Church in the

Republic of Korea, or PROK. Kaeja Cho had visited India and wanted to return to India as a mission worker. The PROK instead asked the Chos to coordinate visits by Korean Presbyterians in Hungary, where the PROK had recently entered into a mission partnership with the Reformed Church in Hungary. Since the PROK was facing a severe budget shortfall at the time, they asked the PC(USA) if it could share in some of the costs of the position. Almost immediately after their appointment, the Chos became active members of the informal fellowship of PC(USA) mission workers in Europe, and I became their de facto area coordinator. Soon Kaeja Cho noticed numbers of dark-complected, obviously economically disadvantaged people on the streets of Budapest. She asked who these people were and was told that they were Roma.[38] She spoke with me about the Roma and affirmed her interest in them. I encouraged the Chos to seek ways to reach out to the Roma and, as they did, to ask their Hungarian supervisor, Bertalan Tamas, the ecumenical officer of the Reformed Church in Hungary, for his support.

The Chos soon started visiting Roma villages in the Hungarian countryside. They learned that Roma in small villages had an unemployment rate, at least when the Chos started their work, of 99 percent. They also learned that few Roma were literate in any language and that Roma in the countryside were sometimes victims of arbitrary violence from non-Roma neighbors. In about 2000, perhaps responding to a combination of the Chos' obvious interest in Roma and the increasing interest in the Roma on the part of a number of European Union entities, the Reformed Church in Hungary appointed its first coordinator for Roma mission.

In the spring of 1999, Burkhard Paetzold was appointed to be the PC(USA)'s overall facilitator for Roma work.[39] To orient Paetzold to his new work with Roma and to gain the counsel of others with extensive mission experience, I organized a group that later came to be called the Roma Traveling Seminar. The participants in this group included Kaeja and Stephen Cho; Art Beals, who by this time was consulting with me about nearly every new PC(USA) initiative in Europe and Central Asia; Harold Kurtz, the executive director of the Presbyterian Frontier Fellowship; Dan McNerney, the staff member who would be assigned to Roma work by the Presbyterian Frontier Fellowship; Peter Sulyok, then the coordinator of the Advisory Committee on Social Witness Policy; Bertalan Tamas, the ecumenical officer of the Reformed Church in Hungary; John Stringham of the European Diaconal Year program; Ruzena Cerna and Damaris Vejnarova from the Czech Ecumenical Council; as well as Paetzold and myself.

This group undertook a lengthy and winding journey through Hungary, Slovakia, and the Czech Republic, visiting en route many Roma villages as well as a number of pastors and laypeople who at that time were already involved in Roma work.[40] The Roma Traveling Seminar affirmed the appointment of Burkhard Paetzold and set three priorities for broader ecumenical work with the Roma.

First was to assist Roma and the indigenous Gadje (non-Roma) church in each place to develop indigenously led Roma congregations. Under the influence of Harold Kurtz, who had spent many years trying to help birth an indigenous church among tribal peoples in Ethiopia, the Roma Traveling Seminar affirmed the concept that Roma needed to be able to worship in their own languages,[41] using their own culture's symbols and music. The second priority for Roma work was supporting educational and economic development work. Harold Kurtz and Art Beals argued strongly that effective work with the Roma would have to be holistic. The third priority for Roma work adopted by the Roma Traveling Seminar had to do with human rights. It was agreed that external churches, like the PC(USA), could not take the lead in advocating human rights for Roma. But it was also agreed that PC(USA) and other external churches working with Roma should do what they could to help the Roma and the Reformed churches in each place to work together for human rights. For the next several years, the Human Rights Updates of the Presbyterian General Assembly always contained a significant amount of information about Roma human rights issues.

Presbyterian Roma work has expanded over the years, principally with the appointment of a number of young adult volunteers to work in a program called the Roma-Gadje Dialogue through Service.[42] In this program young Western European and North American volunteers are matched with Central and Eastern European volunteers, some of whom are Roma, and assigned to work in social service and educational projects in several Central and Eastern European countries. The result is that the Western European and North American volunteers quickly learn from their Roma and Central and Eastern European counterparts about the critical cultural issues they need to understand to do their work. For their part, the Roma as well as the Central and Eastern Europeans receive an unparalleled introduction to the broad European and North American world.

Grant Lovellette was one of the first PC(USA) volunteers to serve in the Roma-Gadje Dialogue and later became the deputy coordinator of the overall program. Since 2006 a Reformed Church in America missionary couple, Dick and Carolyn Otterness, have been assigned to work with these volunteers and have become an important part of the support network for PC(USA) volunteers serving in the Roma-Gadje Dialogue.

HUNGARY

During 1944–2004, PC(USA) work in Hungary was considerably broader than just Roma work. The PC(USA)–Reformed Church in Hungary relationship was based on five pillars. The first pillar was the commitment of both churches to participate whenever possible in larger ecumenical meetings. These meetings frequently brought together Reformed Hungarians and American Presbyterians. Before 1989 ecumenical meetings were often the only context in which representatives of the two churches could meet. The second was the commitment of individual Presbyterians—many of whom were members of the ecumenical group, Christians Associated for Relationships in Eastern Europe (CAREE)—to maintaining the relationship. In Hungary CAREE helped sponsor a major conference on "Christian Faith and Human Enmity," which took place shortly after the end of the Cold War. The third pillar was the willingness of Princeton, Louisville, Columbia, Union (in Virginia), and Austin theological seminaries to offer admission and scholarships to a steady stream of students from the Reformed Church in Hungary. Many of these students eventually took significant leadership roles in Hungarian church life.

The long-standing twinning relationships—between Missouri Union Presbytery and the Miskolc District of the Reformed Church in Hungary, the Twin Cities Presbytery in Minnesota and the Western District of the Reformed Church in Hungary, the "Great" Church in Debrecen and a congregation in Charlotte, North Carolina—were the fourth pillar in the relationship of the PC(USA) with the Hungarian church. Over the years, these three twinning relationships have shaped the perceptions and widened the perspectives of Reformed and Presbyterian people on both sides of the Atlantic. The fifth pillar was the ability of Bertalan Tamas, the ecumenical officer of the Reformed Church in Hungary for many of those years, to engender close working partnerships with English-speaking church people.

LONG-STANDING THEMES IN PRESBYTERIAN MISSION IN EUROPE

Depending on how you count them, about three hundred men and women have served as fraternal workers, mission coworkers, mission specialists, mission diaconal workers, mission volunteers, young adult volunteers, regional liaisons, area representatives, area associates, and area coordinators in Europe during the sixty years from 1944 to 2004. Certain unifying principles gave cohesion to PC(USA) work during these years. There seem to be eight such unifying principles. More than just an intellectual construct applied in retrospect, most of these principles actually guided conversations about Presbyterian mission in Europe among mission personnel and denominational staff.[43]

The Indispensability of Partnership

Even before "partnership" became a popular word in Reformed missiology, Presbyterian mission in Europe was based on working closely with partner churches. Every mission agency works with indigenous churches and church people; otherwise it would be difficult to make contacts in the local society, secure visas and work permits, or even learn about the local health-care system. Some mission workers say they have partners and mean only that they have local helpers. Partnership, as the word was understood by Presbyterians working in Europe during 1944–2004, almost always meant much more. It meant accepting the right of the partner to share in making key decisions about the mission one wanted to do. It meant taking guidance from the people one had come to help. Thus, for instance, when Presbyterians began work in Germany after the end of World War II, it meant sharing the decision making about that work with citizens of a nation that had just been in a total war against the United States. Many times such a commitment has come with great burdens and miscommunication. However, through the years this has been a fundamental principle of PC(USA) ministry in Europe.

The Priority of Relationships

For years PC(USA) mission has been under pressure to evaluate itself in terms of results achieved: How many lives are actually being improved? How many children have been inoculated against some deadly disease? How many lay leaders have received training in Christian education? Even so, as important as achieving results were to Presbyterian mission workers in Europe during the sixty years of mission history this chapter recounts, building relationships with European church people was even more important.

A Commitment to Long-Term Mission

One Presbyterian mission worker used to describe anyone who wanted to serve for less than six years in his mission field as ecclesiastical tourists. His description of persons seeking to serve for shorter periods of time was more than a little harsh, but his attitude was nevertheless a natural consequence of the Presbyterian tendency to put the priority on building relationships. It is possible to build the kind of relationships that a mission partnership requires only when everyone understands that the relationship one is building is for a lifetime. Presbyterian missionaries who have served in Europe often tell a similar story: They came to a new field, fell in love with a place and a church, built deep friendships, and then, in time, left. But if their service had been happy, they continued their relationships even from a distance, returning for weddings and funerals and other special occasions, letting only death end their ties to the people they once served beside.

A Willingness to Invest in Mission Personnel

Once one believes that relationships should have priority in mission, then it is important to invest in mission personnel so they are able to relate with people in the partner church. At the very least, a mission worker needs to learn the language of the people with whom one works. Over the sixty years covered in this history, the Presbyterian Church generally but not always expected its mission personnel serving in Europe to learn the language of the people among whom they served. A missionary who speaks the language of the people where he is serving is more likely to be regarded as a valued colleague, more likely to be seen as a trustworthy recipient of information rarely shared with outsiders but very helpful for one's work.

Mission That Reflects the Gospel's Bias for the Marginalized

In missionary letters back to Presbyterian congregations, Presbyterian mission workers serving in Europe during 1944–2004 frequently cited Matthew 25:40, "Whatever you did for the least of these . . . , you did for me" (NIV). For them, this verse described the people to whom they had been sent. Yet those whom Presbyterian missionaries regarded as the "least of these" changed during the years of this history. At the beginning of this period, Presbyterian mission workers saw their defeated and often-traumatized former enemies; few with enough to eat, and many of whom had been driven out of their former homes by the Nazis' former victims, as being among the least of these. They also regarded those who had suffered under the Nazis and fascists as being among the least of these. By the mid-1950s, the "least of these" included the Protestants of southern Europe, and later Christians in Russia, Lithuania, Belarus, Ukraine, Romania, Albania, Croatia, Voivodina (in Serbia), Hungary, Slovakia, the Czech Republic, and Poland; almost all of these had suffered in one way or another during forty to seventy years of Soviet hegemony. After 1987, Presbyterian work in Europe began increasingly to focus on immigrants in Europe.

Mission That Is Holistic

Even as the foci of Presbyterian work in Europe evolved during 1944–2004, it remained almost always holistic: wherever they went, Presbyterians supported the local church in the proclaiming of the gospel or in some places did it themselves. But nowhere in Europe during these sixty years did they limit their work to just proclamation of the gospel. The Roma work and, to an only slightly less extent, the Kurdish work of the PC(USA) embody the kind of holistic mission that addresses simultaneously evangelism and church planting, addressing the needs of the poor, and assisting marginalized people to advocate for their basic human rights.

A Willingness to Embrace Innovations

The history of Presbyterian work in Europe during 1944–2004 reflects the willingness of Presbyterians to try new methods, even if doing so entailed risks. Sending the Mercers as students to Yugoslavia in the mid-1950s was certainly an innovative way to do mission. It was also the only way a government not at all friendly toward churches would allow an outsider to live in Yugoslavia. If the Presbyterians had been able to expand their work in Yugoslavia during the late 1950s or early 1960s, as had seemed quite possible when the Mercers began their work, then the cultural understanding and language skills the Mercers had acquired through their studies would have been quite valuable. When they went to Yugoslavia, no one could know for sure that Yugoslavia would open itself to outside mission workers, which meant that their assignment entailed at least the risk that the learning they did would never be used. In fact, for the thirty years following their departure from Yugoslavia, no additional PC(USA) mission workers were able to go to Yugoslavia. But after the successor states of the former Yugoslavia did finally open their borders to missionaries, I was told by people in the various successor states that the Presbyterian Church had shown its genuine concern for the peoples of former Yugoslavia by having sent the Mercers thirty years before.

The Importance of Ecumenism in the Formation of Presbyterian Mission

Unlike in much of the rest of the world, where PC(USA) missionaries began work in places in which there was often no existing Christian church, PC(USA) mission in Europe during 1944–2004 was built mostly on partnerships with long-established Reformed and Presbyterian churches. In most cases, the PC(USA) already enjoyed a relationship with these churches through the World Alliance of Reformed Churches or the World Council of Churches.[44] Moreover, since the founding of the World Council of Churches in 1948, Presbyterians have regularly become partners in specific mission projects with Orthodox, Lutheran, and Anglican churches.

THE GENEVA MODEL

For many years, the PC(USA) enjoyed the advantage of having its Europe coordinator posted at the Ecumenical Center in Geneva. Because they were based in Geneva, Robert Lodwick and his predecessors were inevitably invited to serve on numerous task forces and committees of the World Alliance of Reformed Churches, the Conference of European Churches, and the World Council of Churches. As a result, Lodwick and his predecessors were often able to mediate helpful connections between the PC(USA) congregations and members of the various world Christian bodies.[45]

Even after the Europe coordinator's official base was returned to Louisville at the beginning of the 1990s, the Geneva model—at least as I understood it—of bringing together varied voices from several different national churches continued through the end of the period covered in this chapter to guide PC(USA) engagement in such key mission initiatives in Europe as the Roma ministry and the Mission in Unity Project's work in Ukraine and Belarus.[46]

THE NEXT CHALLENGE FOR PC(USA) WORK IN EUROPE

The next challenge for PC(USA) work in Europe is to develop trusting relationships with Muslims and Jews who can authentically represent their respective faith communities.[47] In 1944, Europe was predominantly Christian. What had just happened to the Jews led Christians and Jews to see their relationship in terms of prejudice reduction. Both Christians and Jews understood that they had not responded early enough or strongly enough to the pestilence of anti-Semitism.

In 1944, there were large Muslim populations in Albania, Kosovo, and Bosnia but nowhere else in Europe. Muslim-Christian relationships in the late 1940s and for many years thereafter could focus on theological dialogues about the nature of God, the role of Mohammad and of Jesus in the two religions, and the differences and similarities between the Qur'an and the Bible—all interesting questions concerning which the two sides would never be able to reach a common answer.

Beginning in the 1960s, however, large numbers of Muslims from Turkey, Algeria, Morocco, and India and later from Iran, Iraq, Pakistan, Bangladesh, and elsewhere in the Islamic world began to come to Europe. Europe had a shortage of workers, and many Middle Eastern, North African, and South Asian countries had a surplus. At first everyone believed that these new workers would just work for a few years and then return home. This did not happen. Guest workers, just like missionaries, inevitably form attachments and relationships in the countries in which they work and often end up staying far longer than they or anyone else would have expected. As a result there are now 16 million Muslims in the European Union.

Necessarily, however, both Muslims and Christians sometimes find it difficult to live so closely together. The problems are no longer just theological. Today Muslims and Christians disagree about the role of religion in public discourse, where and how Muslims should be allowed to erect mosques and sound the call to prayer, whether Muslim women should wear a *hijab* or other religious head covering in public places, not to mention whether it is morally legitimate for Western nations to intervene politically or militarily in conflicts in the Muslim world. These are not only theological disagreements; they also have the potential to become serious threats to civil society in the West. Such continuing disagreements also make it much more difficult for Christians to offer an effective witness to the gospel among Muslims.

The next challenge for Presbyterian mission in Europe is to design ministries that make it possible for Presbyterians and other Christians to build trusting relationships with people of other faiths. Only in this way will the gospel be offered in a credible way to a new generation in Europe.

Chapter 13

South Asia

JOHN C. B. WEBSTER

Until quite recently, American Presbyterian mission in South Asia has been confined to three regions of the subcontinent: the Punjab in the northwest, the United Provinces or Uttar Pradesh in north central India, and western India in the present state of Maharashtra. It all began in November 1834, when the Reverend John C. Lowrie of the Western Foreign Missionary Society arrived at Ludhiana in the Punjab to begin the work of what was later called the Lodiana Mission of the Presbyterian Church in the U.S.A. In August 1855 the Reverend Andrew Gordon of the Associate Presbyterian Synod of North America arrived at Sialkot, also in the Punjab, to begin the work of what was to become the Sialkot Mission of the United Presbyterian Church of North America. Over the next century these two missions, known in India as the AP (American Presbyterian) and UP (United Presbyterian) Missions respectively, and their related churches grew in number, size, and complexity. By 1939 at the outset of World War II, the APs had 216 missionaries at 36 mission stations connected to three missions (one in each region), while the UPs had 110 missionaries at 17 mission stations.[1] At that time the United Church of Northern India, to which the APs were related, had achieved a high degree of ecclesiastical independence from both the Presbyterian Church in the U.S.A. and its related missions in India. This, however, was not true of the United Presbyterian Church, which was still strongly tied to the United Presbyterian Church of North America and its Sialkot Mission.

Events in the subcontinent would soon not only shift the major overseas mission emphasis of these two Presbyterian churches (which in 1958 together formed the United Presbyterian Church U.S.A.) from "reaching out" and "building up" to "handing over" and then "letting go," but also changed their relationships from that of parents and children to that of partners. This shift, and the transition it required, which was by no means a simple, "natural," or easy one, is the primary subject of this chapter. We will begin with a summary of relevant background history, proceed to the major events and processes through which this transition occurred, and then conclude with some brief reflections on what has happened over these past sixty years.

BACKGROUND HISTORY

The mission itself was a very un-Presbyterian institution forced upon the AP Board of Foreign Missions by its missionaries in the field and replicated by the UPs once they had established themselves in India. The first manual of the AP Board of Foreign Missions stated that "the General Assembly of the Presbyterian Church have directed all their foreign missionaries, wherever it is practicable, to form themselves into Presbyteries."

> When a Presbytery is formed, every missionary question, within its limits, in which advice or information is required, will come properly before it for discussion. All their proposed measures, every plan for doing good, will receive the consideration and direction of the ministers and elders, assembled in the name of the Lord, and as a judicatory of his Church, taking the oversight of her interests among the heathen.[2]

While this arrangement was in conformity with the Old School Presbyterian view of mission, which was so integral to the church that it should be carried out through its judicatories, the seven missionaries of the Board in India in 1836 did not seem to find it practicable. They did form the first Presbytery of Northern India in December 1836,[3] but at their annual meeting in 1837 they took steps to form themselves into a mission that had all of the powers and responsibilities that the Board assigned to the presbytery.[4] In 1840, with the arrival of more missionaries and the creation of mission stations at a considerable distance in what was to become the United Provinces, this mission bifurcated into the Lodiana (later Punjab) and Farrukhabad (later North India) Missions. In 1852 the Reverend and Mrs. Royal Wilder, New School Presbyterian missionaries working under the American Board of Commissioners for Foreign Missions, began work in the Indian state of Kolhapur in western India. When the northern Old and New School Presbyterians reunited after the Civil War, the American Board handed over the work being done by its Presbyterian missionaries in that region to the Presbyterian Board of Foreign Missions, and the Kolhapur (later Western India) Mission came into being in 1870. The UPs' Sialkot Mission never bifurcated since its work was concentrated in just one region.

Thus the missions controlled the churches and presbyteries, not the other way around. The missions were accountable to their Board of Foreign Missions and decided which mission stations should be established or maintained; assigned missionaries as well as Indian workers to specific mission stations and responsibilities; hired, fired, and determined the salaries of Indian mission workers; made decisions about the purchase, maintenance, and sale of property; and allocated funds sent from the United States for the mission's work. During much of the nineteenth century, the main responsibility of the presbyteries was to simply ordain and discipline clergy. The annual mission meetings lasted for a week or more; the annual presbytery meeting was concluded in a couple hours, with a worship service and little or no business. Throughout the nineteenth century only male missionaries were members of the mission. Female missionaries became voting members only in the twentieth century, and Indians, though occasionally invited to mission meetings, were never voting members of the mission. Ordained Indian clergy and elders were, however, full and equal members of the presbytery. Thus, although a start was made in forming Indian ecclesiastical bodies, Presbyterian mission in India was carried out through pyramid-shaped power structures, with the Boards of Foreign Missions at the apex, the missions in India in the middle, and the Indian churches at the bottom. The missions in India were American, even if Indians did most of "the work."

From the outset through at least the end of World War I, the aim of these Presbyterian missions was primarily evangelistic. They carried out their evangelistic mission most directly through street preaching in towns, cities, and villages, as well as through such ancillary activities as translating Scriptures and writing tracts for distribution. They were also quick to establish schools in which Christian worship and Bible classes were mandatory. Medical dispensaries and hospitals came later, from the 1870s onward, to further augment that evangelistic mission. At about the same time an increasing number of single women missionaries began arriving, to carry out evangelistic, educational, and medical work among women and children, so that by the turn of the century there were more female than male missionaries.

The pattern of conversion in response to these evangelistic initiatives proved to be remarkably similar in the Lodiana, Farrukhabad, and Sialkot Missions. Initially converts were not only very few, entering as individuals or nuclear families, but also socially diverse, being drawn from quite different religious and caste community backgrounds. In its early stages, Indian Presbyterianism in that region looked very urban, literate, and socially progressive. In the 1870s, however, a large-scale conversion movement began among rural Chuhras, a Dalit[5] caste of sweepers and menials, within the bounds of the Sialkot Mission. By the end of the 1880s, it had spread into the mission fields of the Lodiana Mission. By 1900 a similar movement among the Bhangis (the Chuhras' caste counterparts in the neighboring United Provinces) was well under way in the areas of the Far-rukhabad Mission. In all three cases, these conversion movements transformed the Christian community, and the Presbyterian portion of it, into a much-larger, overwhelmingly illiterate, impoverished, rural Dalit community. The pattern of conversion within the bounds of the Kolhapur Mission was somewhat different in that it seems to have been an overwhelmingly Dalit church from the outset.[6] Moreover, converts there came from two Dalit castes, the Mangs and Mahars, who brought their caste rivalries with each other into the churches, whereas in the Punjab and United Provinces, where only one caste had converted in large num-bers, caste rivalries were relatively minor.

This pattern of conversion is important not only because it gave Indian Pres-byterianism a social profile that has stayed with it ever since, but also because it affected relations between the foreign missions and the Indian churches that those missions had brought into being. The urban congregations were generally socially diverse, with an Indian leadership that was educated, generally English speaking, and often employed by the missions either as church workers or as staff members of mission institutions. While the proportion of members economically indepen-dent of the missions was quite small, these congregations were the first to become self-supporting and hence free to call their own pastors. The rural congregations were scattered among the poorest and most stigmatized and oppressed in the pop-ulation, who were bound in patron-client relationships that made them totally dependent upon the village landlords for their livelihoods. It was the elite section of the urban AP churches in the north that, both prior to and parallel with the nationalist challenge to the British Raj, began demanding changes in the mission-church relations that would give them greater decision-making power. The rural congregations were too poor and too dependent upon the mission as a counter-patron to the village landlords to be interested in making such demands.[7] In 1904 the churches related to the AP missions joined in forming the Presbyterian Church in India, which was ecclesiastically independent of the Presbyterian Church in the U.S.A. The UPs chose not to join, and their presbyteries remained part of the United Presbyterian Church of North America.

This is where matters stood in August 1917, when the British government, in an effort to retain Indian support in the face of Home Rule movements during World War I, announced its commitment to "the progressive realization of responsible government in India as an integral part of the British Empire."[8] This marked an important turning point in Indo-British relations that had important implications for the churches. In June 1920, in the lull between two of Gandhi's major campaigns, four members of the Presbyterian Church in India wrote a public letter to Dr. Robert E. Speer of the Board of Foreign Missions, indicating that the mission-and-church polity, and the gradual transfer of power from the former to the latter, to which the Board had committed itself back in 1889, was no longer effective. It was creating tensions and resentments between missionar-ies and Indians as well as providing a public demonstration of the failure of "prac-tical Christianity" in the face of racial strife.[9] This provoked the AP Mission to take the first step toward a significant transfer of power. The Saharanpur Plan, which went into effect in 1923, created a set of joint committees of elected representatives of the missions and of the presbyteries, with an Intermediate Board of both missionaries and Indians to coordinate the committees. Then in 1935 the Joint Church Councils Plan transferred the work of those committees and of the Intermediate Board to Central Boards of the Church Councils of the United Church of Northern India (UCNI),[10] made up of Indian and missionary members elected by their church councils in no fixed proportion. The missions were left only with the specific work that was not transferred, plus the care of their own missionaries, and the property owned by the Board of Foreign Missions.[11] This transfer of power represented a shift of American Presbyterian mission emphasis from "reaching out" in evangelism to "building up" the Indian church into a self-governing, self-supporting, and self-propagating body that could survive as a viable church if India were to become independent.[12]

The Joint Church Councils Plan also marked a significant transition toward handing over because, while individual AP missionaries could continue to exercise personal influence upon decisions affecting evangelistic, educational, and medical work, as well as upon the allocation of finances, they had lost their collective power over the churches and were subject to the decisions of the Indian majority within the church councils. The UP case was different. They had their own Synod of the Punjab, with its constituent presbyteries in India, but these were still part of the United Presbyterian Church of North America. In 1930 the Sialkot Mission had offered to transfer responsibility for all evangelistic work, as well as all the funds allocated for it, to the Synod, but the Synod turned the offer down. The Sialkot Mission repeated the offer in 1935 and was again turned down. After that no significant steps toward a handover were taken until World War II was over, although there was a general recognition within the Mission that such steps were necessary.[13]

INDEPENDENCE, PARTITION, AND HANDING OVER

Soon after the end of World War II, it became apparent that the British government itself would have to hand over control, let go, and leave India. The great unresolved issue was who its successor would be. The Indian National Congress, which had led the nationalist struggle for decades, was the obvious heir, but the Muslim League was demanding a separate Muslim state. After much failed negotiation, it was decided to partition India, and so on August 15, 1947, the two successor states of India and Pakistan became independent of British rule. Millions of Muslims, Hindus, and Sikhs crossed the borders, and an estimated half million people lost their lives in the resulting religious violence. Presbyterians, like other Christians, were considered neutral and impartial enough to play a trusted role in the enormous relief operations that accompanied these mass migrations. Presbyterian hospitals and medical teams cared for refugees, and Presbyterian educational institutions served as refugee camps for up to six months following partition.

The partition of India also partitioned the church, although the process was much slower in the latter case. The AP-related Lahore Church Council of the UCNI was in Pakistan, while the other AP-related church councils were in India. The UP-related Gurdaspur Presbytery was in India, while all the other UP-related presbyteries were in Pakistan. In the first couple years following partition, crossing the border for church meetings was relatively easy, but soon such travel became difficult and then virtually impossible. By 1952, after some territorial adjustments, the two UCNI church councils in the West Punjab formed the Synod of Pakistan, while the three in East Punjab formed the Punjab Synod. In 1954 the Gurdaspur Presbytery of the United Presbyterian Church joined the UCNI as an additional church council. Formal ties between the Synod of Pakistan and the rest of the UCNI were not severed until November 1970, when in India the UCNI joined with five other denominations to form the Church of North India.[14]

The connection between independence for the churches and for their two host countries was not as close as that between the partitioning of the country and church had been. As noted earlier, in the 1935 Joint Church Councils Plan, the APs already had, in effect, handed over the missions' responsibilities for "the work" to the already ecclesiastically independent UCNI. Individual missionaries might have power under this plan only if the church councils gave it to them, which they continued to do, but the missions as such had little power left. In 1955 the Western India Mission voted itself out of existence. The Punjab Mission followed suit in 1956, followed by the North India Mission and Pakistan Mission (created from the Punjab Mission following Partition) in 1957. These actions completed the handover process for the Presbyterian Church in the U.S.A.

The UPs took longer to make this same transition. Only in 1946 did the Sialkot Mission invite the Synod of the Punjab "to assume the authority and responsibility still vested in the Mission," and the Synod accepted this invitation.[15] However, the negotiations over the details of this transfer of authority and responsibility bogged down to the point where the Synod four years later voted unanimously not to proceed with the transfer for the time being.[16] It took another six years before a three-year plan to place all activities of both the Mission and the Synod under an administrative board was put into motion.[17] In April 1961 the Synod became the United Presbyterian Church of Pakistan, which was ecclesiastically independent of what had been the United Presbyterian Church of North America. At that time "the work formerly administered by the [Sialkot] Mission [would] now be under an Administrative Council of about forty-five members, two-thirds of whom are Pakistanis."[18] The Sialkot Mission did not go out of existence, but it now confined its activity to the care of missionary personnel, the management of mission property, and being a missionary fellowship. Meanwhile, on the Indian side of the border, an India Mission was created out of the Sialkot Mission. This new mission quickly voted to hand over all its work to the Gurdaspur Church Council of the UCNI and then voted itself out of existence in March 1957.[19] Thus the handover process among UPs was slower and more uneven among the APs.

All of these aspects of the handover were voluntary. However, there was another aspect of handing over and letting go that was not. The Government of India began by following the British policy of routinely granting visas to missionaries approved by the National Christian Council of India. However, in 1952 it turned down a good number of such applications and, after much discussion in church and governmental circles, in 1955 stated as policy that missionaries "coming for the first time in augmentation of the existing strength of a mission or in replacement will be admitted to India, if they possess outstanding qualifications or specialized experience in their lines."[20] In short, the government was forcing the pace of total independence by limiting the number of missionaries, a practice that fell particularly hard on missionaries from countries (like the United States) outside the British Commonwealth. The Government of Pakistan did not restrict missionary visas in the same way that the Government of India did, but in September and October 1972 Pakistan nationalized all privately managed colleges and schools, including Christian colleges and schools, thus effectively undermining a key historical component of Presbyterian mission there.[21]

In 1958, when the United Presbyterian Church of North America joined with the Presbyterian Church in the U.S.A. to form the United Presbyterian Church U.S.A., and when the Commission on Ecumenical Mission and Relations replaced the two Boards of Foreign Missions,[22] this new church had a significant, although not a controlling, mission presence in both India and Pakistan. In India, that presence worked in partnership primarily with the United Church of Northern India and then the Church of North India, within the framework of a secular and relatively stable democratic state, which guaranteed religious liberty, including the right to propagate religion. In Pakistan, that presence worked in partnership with the Lahore Church Council of the United Church of Northern India as well as with the United Presbyterian Church of Pakistan, within the context of an Islamic state, which alternated between democracy and military dictatorship but did grant religious liberty to all its citizens. In both countries Presbyterian partner churches were part of very small Christian minorities with limited influence upon their countries' destinies. Following the demise of the missions, direct relations between the United Presbyterian Church U.S.A. and the leadership of these churches were carried on through area secretaries in New York, and representatives in India and Pakistan who functioned like national Board ambassadors.

LETTING GO

The process of handing over authority and responsibility to independent partner churches in India and Pakistan was largely complete in 1958. The only exception, which the new Commission on Ecumenical Mission and Relations (COEMAR) had to deal with, was the Synod of the Punjab of the United Presbyterian Church. Even so, in that year there were a total of 160 Presbyterian missionaries in India

and another 91 in Pakistan. Moreover, the budgets of the two uniting Boards of
Foreign Missions were allocating a combined $1,158,933 to India and $450,082
to Pakistan.[23] In addition to this significant missionary presence and financial out-
lay, the uniting Presbyterian churches in the United States held title to the mission property in both countries. It is therefore not surprising that concerns about
dependence upon overseas personnel and money as hindrances to the well-being
of the Indian and Pakistani churches had already been expressed in the annual
reports of the AP Board of Foreign Missions.[24] Similar concerns were also apparent in the reluctance of the UP Synod of the Punjab to assume responsibility for
the work of mission in Pakistan. Central to defining and implementing a policy
aimed at reducing and eliminating dependency by letting go was *An Advisory
Study*, which affected first the church structures and then the Christian institutions that the missions had established in India and Pakistan. Each of these will
be examined in turn.

The Churches

The churches in South Asia, which were becoming self-governing as Presbyterians in the United States handed over to them the authority and responsibility
previously vested in the missions, were mostly self-propagating but not self-
supporting. There were reasons for this. Converts from all but low-status backgrounds invariably lost whatever property, jobs, or social connections they had
once they were baptized, and so they had to make a fresh start economically, often
as mission employees. However, the vast majority of Presbyterians both in India
and in Pakistan were rural Dalit menial laborers, who were very poor, illiterate,
and totally dependent upon the village landlords for their livelihoods.[25] From
almost the very outset of the Chuhra conversion movement, the UPs had emphasized self-support, not just as a means of increasing pastoral support, but more
importantly as a crucial step toward self-respect and liberation from a life of total
dependency.[26] As a result, they had the reputation for being the mission with the
highest level of self-support of any in the Punjab. The three AP missions had done
less well in that regard, but unlike the UPs, they had a good number of well-
educated and well-paid Indian clergy who, from the mission's early years, had
assumed responsibilities equal to those of any missionary. During the 1920s and
1930s, all the missions placed special emphasis upon self-support by conducting
surveys, training village elders, getting pastors to raise their own support, and
making direct appeals to the village Christians' obligations to support their pastors.[27] Yet, given the overwhelming poverty and levels of debt among rural Christians, self-support was still a distant goal.[28] Rural or "district" work remained
subsidized and, in many cases, still under missionary supervision in 1958.

Soon after its first meeting in 1958, COEMAR appointed an international
committee of fifteen to advise it on policy. The committee began its work in January 1960 and submitted its report, *An Advisory Study*, in September 1961.[29] The

report focused first on the structures of an indigenous, charismatic, evangelizing as well as serving church, and then on patterns of interchurch relations in the context of rapid social change. A central prerequisite for mature interdependence between churches, it argued, was that each church attain "authentic selfhood." This was described minimally not only as being free from excessive dependence and outside domination, but also as assuming "care for its worship, its teaching and pastoral ministries, the basic training and support of its clergy, some form of outreach in evangelism and service, and a minimum of church administration."[30] As a later reflection on *An Advisory Study* put it, COEMAR was making "an attempt to 'disentangle' [itself] from the central life of another Church, in order that such a Church can really be free to determine its own life."[31]

Between November 1963 and January 1964, COEMAR representatives met with representatives of the UCNI church bodies to which COEMAR had been historically related. In these consultations the reality of financial dependence was acknowledged, as was the attractiveness of church offices that carried the authority to disperse funds from overseas.[32] A five-year plan was recommended during which decreasing levels of financial support were guaranteed so as to give the UCNI time to make the necessary adjustments.[33] Moreover, a pattern of joint action for mission, based on mutual consultation, was agreed upon.[34] Similar consultations were held in Pakistan.[35] Following these consultations, COEMAR adopted two position papers in March 1964, one in relation to the UCNI in India and Pakistan, and the other in relation to the United Presbyterian Church of Pakistan. With regard to the former, it decided upon a phased, five-year withdrawal (from what *An Advisory Study* had called essential activities of a church), beginning on January 1, 1965, coupled with an offer to help those adversely affected with retirement allowances, severance pay, the education of their children, and the like.[36] It also stated that it would not allow fraternal workers to hold administrative positions within the UCNI unless the UCNI was involved in financially supporting that position.[37] The latter position paper was less emphatic and decisive, outlining potential areas of future partnership, since the problem of self-support was not as severe within the United Presbyterian Church of Pakistan as within the UCNI.[38]

The decision to let go in this way was painful and difficult. Robert Alter has said that paying "terminal salaries to some sixty pastors and rural teachers early in 1966" on behalf of the North India Synod was "probably my most difficult, single assignment."[39] He also described it as "The Demise of a Church: A Dream That Failed," for everyone directly involved there knew that a self-supporting rural church was an impossible dream.[40] In that region the rural church seemed to have withered away. In the Punjab, the churches were able to raise the level of local support for rural pastors in the short run,[41] but they could not sustain it for long. The resulting breakdown of the familiar COEMAR-supported rural church system, which replicated in a more humane way the rural pattern of patron-client relationships, was perhaps more chaotic in the Punjab than in the North India Synod. In the 1970s, when not only Roman Catholic missionaries from South

India arrived in force, but also Pentecostal pastors from within and outside the Punjab began to make their impact felt, the UCNI lost a lot of its rural members and congregations.[42] The United Presbyterian Church of Pakistan proved to be equally vulnerable to outside "patrons" and was seriously split in 1967 when Carl McIntyre sought to win adherents there.[43] The price that the Indian and Pakistani churches paid for the possibility of "authentic selfhood" was thus very high.

Also, COEMAR's own missionaries were affected. According to the *1959 Mission Yearbook of Prayer,* there were nineteen missionaries in India and fifteen in Pakistan who were engaged in rural work in that year.[44] By 1967 that list had dwindled to six in India and ten in Pakistan.[45] In 1972 two couples were engaged in rural work in Pakistan and none in India.[46] The others had either retired, resigned, gotten their work designated as a "special project," or joined an institution or ecumenical project. Thus, throughout most of this period, direct American Presbyterian mission in India and Pakistan was carried out through its personnel in institutions and projects rather than in the churches.

What proved most difficult for COEMAR and its successors to let go of was the property owned by their former missions. They certainly tried to transfer it, but the question of who were to be its recipients proved to be quite contentious. The plan was to transfer the property in India to the UCNI Trust and the Sialkot Mission property in Pakistan to the Synod, or a trust set up by the Synod of the United Presbyterian Church of Pakistan.[47] In other words, COEMAR sought to transfer its property to the highest body of the church possible rather than to local congregations, and to sell unused property.[48] This, however, proved difficult to implement because of both the legal problems involved and the faction-fights within the churches over who would get the property. In the survey of former missionaries conducted in conjunction with this history project, the transfer of property was listed as one of the least rewarding, least effective, most unseemly and depressing aspects of mission in this period, especially for those directly involved. The process has dragged on and has still not been completed.

Institutions

In 1960 when *An Advisory Study* was launched, COEMAR reported having 9 hospitals, 54 primary schools, 22 secondary schools, and 3 colleges (excluding union institutions) in India. Among fraternal workers there, 33 were teachers, 18 were doctors, and 21 were nurses. In Pakistan were 5 hospitals, 125 primary schools, 13 secondary schools, and 3 colleges, with 57 fraternal workers serving as teachers, 7 as doctors, and 13 as nurses.[49] This represented a significant COEMAR investment in educational and medical mission.

An Advisory Study took a much-less radical stand on institutional work than it had on the churches. It treated educational and medical institutions as instruments through which the church witnessed to the wider society by serving some of its needs. The study recognized not only the contribution that these institutions had been making, but also the fact that in the process they had absorbed much of the church's and missions' human and financial resources. The study therefore urged first that there be a serious reexamination of how best these institutions might serve in the future with only limited resources and, second, that the churches hand over governance of these institutions to separate boards of directors so as both to relieve the churches of a great burden and to give greater autonomy to the institutions.[50] These same two issues came up repeatedly in the follow-up consultations with representatives of the churches[51] as well as in COEMAR's position papers in relation to both the UCNI[52] and the United Presbyterian Church of Pakistan.[53] Both recommendations were implemented in India and Pakistan.

What *An Advisory Study* devoted less attention to was the issue of nationalizing the top leadership positions within Christian institutions, in part because that process had been largely completed by the time the report was written. Virtually all the schools had Indian or Pakistani headmasters and headmistresses. The colleges also had Indian or Pakistani principals. The transition was slower in the case of the hospitals, most of which still had fraternal worker medical superintendents and even nursing superintendents. Thus, central to the fraternal workers' vocation throughout this period (apart from carrying out one's own assigned responsibilities with skill and imagination) was the task, on the one hand, of providing loyal and reliable support to the new Indian and Pakistani leaders one was working under, and on the other, working oneself out of a job by training Indians and Pakistanis to take over those responsibilities.

If "working oneself out of a job" were the sole criterion of missionary effectiveness, then Presbyterians have been extremely successful in the years since *An Advisory Study*. In 1965, when its recommendations were put into effect, there were 135 career missionaries in India, over one-third of whom were medical missionaries, and 89 in Pakistan, over one-third of whom were educational missionaries.[54] By 1970 the numbers had dropped from 47 to 25 medical missionaries in India and from 31 to 13 educational missionaries in Pakistan.[55] A decade later there were a total of 29 fraternal workers in India and 28 in Pakistan.[56] By 1990 there were only 15 in India and 24 in Pakistan.[57] In 2000 the *Mission Yearbook for Prayer and Study* mentioned only 8 (plus 3 interns) in India and 9 in Pakistan.[58]

However, successfully working oneself out of a job hardly sums up American Presbyterian mission in South Asia during this period. Two things stand out in the responses to the survey conducted in conjunction with this history project. One was that a lot of good work was done, which made a significant difference in people's lives. These missionaries healed countless patients of their afflictions and taught and trained many students for their future work. Beyond that, a small sample of things done which these missionaries felt were important and valuable would include "winning nominal 'Christians' to full commitment and faith in Jesus Christ, discipling them to become witnesses and servants of Christ";[59] helping to make a half million Pakistanis functionally literate;[60] seeing students in a special study group win four of the five top places in a national physics exam;[61] "helping mission medical institutions develop community health programs in their surrounding catchment areas";[62] "helping develop an indigenous Christian medical mission";[63] guiding Woodstock School through the transition "from being a school for Missionary Children in North India, to the Christian International School it is today";[64] writing, teaching, and preaching to help Dalits, and especially Christian Dalits, in their struggle for dignity, equality, justice, and respect.[65] The other thing that stands out even more emphatically among the women, but also among the men, was the value they placed on the relationships they developed with Indian and Pakistani friends and colleagues, Christian and non-Christian. Many spoke of lasting and life-changing friendships across the great divides of nationality, culture, and even religion.

NEW VENTURES AND RELATIONSHIPS

In addition to handing over and letting go of the work of earlier generations of its missionaries, Presbyterian missionaries in South Asia launched some new ventures in areas where Presbyterians had traditionally worked, and also moved outside those areas, entering into partnerships with new churches. Examples of the former would be James and Barbara Alter, who established the Christian Retreat and Study Centre in Rajpur, near Dehra Dun in India, as well as Byron and Barbara Haines, who helped create the Christian Study Centre in Rawalpindi, Pakistan. Paul Love and I are examples of the latter type. While teaching in the Punjab, I received an invitation to join the faculty of United Theological College in Bangalore, almost all of whose faculty and students were members of churches in South or Northeast India. Soon afterward, Paul Love, who had started a very innovative MA English program at Baring Union Christian College in the Punjab, accepted an invitation to do the same at American College in Madurai (Tamil Nadu), where he also helped create The Study Centre for Indian Literature in English and Translation. In Pakistan, Frederick and Margaret Stock did rural evangelistic work in the province of Sindh under the Karachi Diocese of the Church of Pakistan. In 1972 the Program Agency voted to establish relations with the Church of Bangladesh, which had been a diocese of the Church of Pakistan before Bangladeshi independence. It reported to the 1979 General Assembly that, along with the Presbyterian Church in the U.S.A., it was supporting a medical missionary couple there who were related to the Bangladesh Baptist Union.[66] Presbyterian self-development and hunger program offerings went not only through the usual ecumenical channels within India and Pakistan but also to nongovernmental organizations that were doing grassroots community organizing among Dalits and other poor people.

However, two new ventures deserve special mention because of their size and influence. In response to a 1953 invitation from the Government of Nepal, Presbyterians joined with American Methodists and the Church of Scotland to form the United Mission to Nepal. The initial five-year agreement between the government and the mission was that the mission confine itself to medical work. The first Presbyterian missionaries in Nepal were Dr. Carl and Mrs. Elizabeth Fredericks. The agreement was extended for another five years, and in 1960, to ten years. Moreover, the work of the mission was allowed to expand to include educational and rural extension work as well. Evangelism was strictly forbidden since it was against the law for a Nepali citizen to change religions. As a result, the mission grew and expanded its service projects in complete separation from a Nepali church, which was emerging ever so slowly despite the anticonversion law. By 1965 the mission had 94 missionaries working in ten different projects.[67] In 1980, when a fourth agreement was signed, it had some 260 missionaries from 16 countries working on 40 different projects; of these missionaries 12 were American Presbyterians.[68] The *2000 Mission Yearbook for Prayer and Study* also listed 12 Presbyterian missionaries in Nepal, which suggests that the Presbyterian missionary presence there, unlike in India and Pakistan, has grown and been sustained rather than diminished.[69]

The other major new venture was the Gramin Prachin Mandal (Rural Presbyterian Church) or Dalit Avatari (devotee of the Dalit incarnation of God—a reference to Jesus) movement in western and central Uttar Pradesh in India. This has emerged from the rural Presbyterian communities there that had withered away following the implementation of the Advisory Study recommendations. The instigator and leader of this movement has been the Reverend Philip Prasad, a product of that withering church, who attended Dubuque Theological Seminary, settled in the United States, and learned community organization by working with César Chávez among migrant farm workers in California. In 1984 Prasad convened a meeting of some four thousand neglected rural UCNI members, all of whom, like Prasad himself, belonged to the Dalit Bhangi caste. At that meeting they decided to revive the church, and the result has been a virtual resurrection of a church pronounced dead and buried, which in the power of that resurrection has spread to the point where it is by far the largest organization of any kind that the Bhangis have. In 1994, a decade after starting, when the Gramin Prachin Mandal was formally organized, it had 68,370 baptized members in 1,883 congregations within eleven presbyteries.[70] By July 1998 the number of believers had risen to 206,392,[71] and by July 2001 there were 461,504 believers in 10,894 congregations within 56 presbyteries.[72] Presbyterians in the United States have channeled their support for this movement through Witnessing Ministries of Christ, based in Fresno, California, not by sending evangelists but by donating money initially for the education of children and for development projects aimed at making presbyteries self-supporting within a five-year period. Today the Gramin Prachin Mandal has over a million adherents in 68 presbyteries and is completely self-supporting.[73]

CONCLUDING REFLECTIONS

The big picture of American Presbyterian mission in South Asia during the past sixty years as presented here is largely one of handing over and then letting go. Everything else occurred within that larger context. The former process had already begun before this period began. The decisive moment in the latter process, which set the course of the future, was COEMAR's decision to move their related churches toward "authentic selfhood" by withdrawing financial support from what it considered to be the essential activities of any church. This was accompanied by the more gradual withdrawal of missionary personnel, first from essential church activities and then from Christian institutions and projects as well. By the end of the period, the career missionary or fraternal worker in South Asia was largely a thing of the past, and even short-term volunteers were relatively few. In the process of letting go, however, relations between the Presbyterian Church (U.S.A.) and their partner churches in India and Pakistan became less intertwined and more distant.

How did the Presbyterian missionaries caught up in this process of change view being part of such a "big picture"? The thirty-one missionaries who responded to the survey seemed to be unanimous in the belief that the time they spent in India and Pakistan had been worthwhile. Not all commented on this big picture, but those who did were quite ambivalent about it. It was a good and even necessary thing in principle and on paper. Some expressed great satisfaction in handing over responsibilities to Indian and Pakistani colleagues. However, the devil was definitely in the details. One described the experience as "walking on eggs." The committee meetings and paperwork, the clearing of property titles, the coping with long-held expectations that were no longer valid, the attempts to figure out who was trustworthy and who was not—these were all part of the burden, at least for some missionaries. So too was the frustration over seeing the infighting between contending "heirs apparent," over the court cases, splits, loss of members to other churches, and even corruption involved. There were both victories won and losses incurred. If authentic selfhood for the churches was indeed either the main goal or the main means to attain other goals, it was not always a beautiful thing to observe, especially while still in the making.

Handing over and letting go in the interests of promoting authentic selfhood represent an American Presbyterian mission history perspective on the big picture of this period. The events described above look somewhat different when viewed from the perspective of the changing internal dynamics of the Indian and Pakistani churches over the same period. Knowingly or not, American Presbyterian mission in India and Pakistan has long been engaged in liberating oppressed Dalits from generations of socialization to enforced, degrading, caste-based patron-client relationships; the churches to which American Presbyterians have been related are overwhelmingly churches of partially liberated Dalits. This kind of socialization, as well as the rebellion against it, has long influenced the political culture of these churches.[74] When handing over and letting go took place in India and Pakistan, whether to members of the non-Dalit elite minority or Dalit majority in the churches, its consequences were deeply affected by the dynamics of patron-client relationships carried over into the churches, as well as by ongoing Dalit struggles for increased social mobility, less discrimination, and more justice in the public realm, greater acknowledgment of and respect for their basic dignity and fundamental human rights—in other words, for their own authentic selfhood and authentic liberation as persons and as a people. Did Presbyterian handing over and letting go simply replace a foreign with an indigenous "colonial regime" in the churches, or did it trigger a significant social revolution and a "healing of the psychological consequences of oppression"[75] within them, so that they were transformed not only socially and politically but spiritually as well? There is evidence to support both possibilities, but that story has yet to be told.

Chapter 14

An Epilogue and a Prologue

Wisdom Gained for the Future

SCOTT W. SUNQUIST

The demise of Christian mission, like the secularization of the world predicted in the 1960s, was a false prophecy. Christian mission has not died, and the Western form of Christianity has not been swallowed up by secular and material pursuits. Both the secularized church and Christian mission, however, have been dramatically reshaped by global trends. Nations, political leaders, and even anthropologists and sociologists are adjusting to these new realities. The story we have just told is one piece of the much-larger drama that was first broadly publicized through the pen of Walbert Bühlmann in his volume *Es kommt die dritte Kirche* in 1974 (translated as *The Coming of the Third Church* by Orbis Books in 1976).[1] Bühlmann saw that the first church (Orthodox) and the second church (Western) were now going to be overtaken by the third church, which is the non-Western church. In short, the history of Presbyterian missions in this period is one small part of the major shift that took place and is now in place. It is helpful to put all of these reflections in this larger and more hopeful context.

With the help of some outsiders, I will lift up some observations and implications of this radical transformation. Although it would be helpful to have comments from every nation and every ecclesial tradition, that is not practical. We have, however, invited a small group of people to comment on this story, and of those we invited, a group of five did take the time to read and comment on this Presbyterian mission history. With the help of these mission specialists,[2] what follows is a brief summary of some of the trends and implications.

First, the trend toward more complex mission participation can best be understood as a return to the earlier forms of Protestant mission. In our preoccupation with Protestant missions today, we often forget that Protestant missions did not become a significant part of the church until the middle of the nineteenth century. It was only 200 years ago that Robert Morrison began his work in China, and it was just 150 years ago that David Livingstone searched out the source of the Nile River. When Protestant missions were starting out, they were organized ecumenically,[3] according to special strategic concerns,[4] and even according to gender.[5] Presbyterians cooperated with groups like the China Inland Mission, YMCA, various Zenana missions,[6] and Bible Societies. It was only later, beginning in the 1920s, that missionary vocations became more divided, more rigidly denominational, and less ecumenical.[7] Today we are witnessing a return to more diverse patterns and creative types of cooperation, much like the earlier period. The whole theology of partnership described in this volume is built more upon relationships than upon denominations. The advent of *Paraclete* organizations—those organizations separate, yet working alongside the denominational sending agencies—makes missionary work more complex, but also more flexible. It may be that the newer partnerships between Presbyteries and overseas churches, along with other newer initiatives, signal a *movement* beginning in the Presbyterian Church. The next decade will tell if it is a movement or the last gasps of our missionary enterprise.

Second, because of this volume, we have become very aware of the need to take contexts quite seriously. Good policies built upon good theology still need to be applied contextually. Not only must policies be shaped around local contexts, but as we have seen with regional wars and the changes in governments, we must recognize that the local contexts are also in flux. Many of the missionaries we interviewed are concerned that we have too few missionaries now who know local languages and contexts well. Past patterns of long-term (even lifelong) service are nearly obsolete, but the need to have long-term committed Presbyterians involved in ministry in different contexts remains. Wilbert Shenk echoed what retired missionaries have said: "The basic rationale [today] is visiting another culture and meeting people in other churches. These are not bad things in themselves, but these cannot be deemed serious mission goals. Learning a culture and language and making long-term commitments to a people are not priorities [in such visiting]." However, the Presbyterian Church has been well respected for our missionary involvement: it has had cultural sensitivity and was very responsive to local contexts. We have found that Presbyterians have a very good reputation in most areas of the world, and it seems that our care to understand and honor local contexts is one of the reasons for this reputation. How this will happen in the future is not clear.

William Burrows identified this struggle regarding local contexts and national churches as a similar theme of center and periphery in the Roman Catholic Church:

> Although the words spoken at "headquarters" in both churches are the right
> ones, one senses a lack of deeper understanding of the challenge of "inter-
> culturation"—by which I mean truly serious intercultural dialogue. Both
> Catholics and Presbyterians, I fear, failed—not for lack of good will—to
> achieve that dialogue or to make it the central dynamic of the period in
> which a more organic, global form of world Presbyterianism and Catholi-
> cism might have emerged.

This type of "interculturation," as Burrows calls it, is not something that can be
managed or prompted. It has to be allowed; the church has to be released. Lest
we think that this has only been a Roman Catholic and Presbyterian problem,
Wilbert Shenk reminds us that such letting go is never easy. "We know from experience that missions have been much better at starting new churches than in
handing over leadership responsibility and moving on." These contextual issues,
expressed both as contextual theologies and as the interplay of periphery and center, will become more and more important as we continue in the mission drama
of God.

Third, a series of comments came from our readers related to initiative and
evangelism. For the most part, Presbyterians have withdrawn from taking initiative and from leading overseas churches, but will the Presbyterian Church continue to participate in the basic call to "make disciples of all nations"? It was good
and necessary that Presbyterians set as a clear priority to integrate the missions
into the local churches, but that did not necessarily mean abdicating all responsibility for initiative, especially initiative in the areas of evangelism and church
planting. Presbyterians are taking initiative today, but more as local churches and
presbyteries than as a denomination. How will Presbyterians continue to proclaim the kingdom of God in various contexts while honoring local churches and
regional missionary agencies? For example, most of the evangelism and missionary work being done in Latin America, Africa, and Asia today is being done by
neighbors from the same continent. Do we still have a place, a calling to take initiative for the missionary work in these contexts?

Tharwat Wahba represents other overseas partners when he describes a per-
mutation on this issue of initiative and evangelism. He stated that younger local
leaders who were educated in the United States returned with a dichotomized
theology that forced a choice of either ecumenical relations and social work, or
evangelism and outreach. This dichotomy was an export from America, and as a
result "the mission work in Sudan was closed and the proposal to create a foreign
mission board was rejected." We need to admit, probably, that simply refraining
from sending missionaries, or sending fewer missionaries, does not mean that we
have reneged on all leadership and influence. The long shadow of Presbyterian
influence may merely be reconfigured rather than removed by restructuring the
mission and removing some missionaries. Initiative, influence, and evangelism
are themes that require ongoing attention and respect. Honoring the "call" of
God and at the same time honoring the leadership of indigenous and other
regional churches is a present issue that requires great care.

Others have made similar observations about our involvement in global mission today. Bishop Solomon of the Methodist Church in Singapore noted that our history seems to "tell the story from the American perspective—in the context of a declining denomination, theological pluralism, and a changed world, and, perhaps, lost confidence." Writing from Asia, he finds this a great contrast, for the Asian churches are growing, reaching out with creativity and confidence even while they are, in some places, persecuted greatly. One of the keys for the future will be to find the theological and ecumenical resources to continue to take humble but definite initiative in mission. Again, from Bishop Solomon: "This 'flattening' of the mission landscape . . . must not excuse the church that is well-endowed (namely the Church in the West) from not continuing in missionary endeavor in a still needy world. Mission must continue as long as the Lord tarries." These issues are, we have seen, related to money and the continuing power of American Presbyterians, who still have great wealth.

As the missionary presence was reduced and funding was decreased for churches and church workers, some money continued to be sent for support of other, and even newer, institutions. Tharwat Wahba commented to us:

> In the 1960s and 1970s, the financial issue was under discussion when the Mission reduced its support to the Synod of the Nile's general budget and directed it to other projects inside and outside the Church. . . . In the first hundred years of mission work in Egypt, the money was directed to evangelistic work, education, hospitals, and Bible distribution. Later, evangelistic work and Muslim evangelism were not given priority either in the vision or in the monetary support of the Mission. In the last fifty years, the money was directed mainly to social work, ecumenical relationships, the Seminary, and audiovisual ministry.

It was natural to use the money more for institutions that the local churches could not support, and yet at times this created new tensions: institutions (some not even under the church) were given more money, but the ongoing work of evangelism and church development was dropped. Many of the institutions were not "of" or "from" the local synod. No one would say that we should have dropped all medical and educational work, but quite often local churches, even though independent, could never dream of running these large Western-initiated institutions.

Fourth, as we have seen here, Presbyterian mission has become less territorial. Before colonialism was dismantled, Presbyterians had missions in particular geographic regions (such as the Shantung Mission, Sialkot Mission). With the integration of our missions came a new way of envisioning our missionary presence. We began to relate to political divisions (national churches) rather than to a geographically placed "mission," which was often part of a country, a province, or a colony. Another wrinkle of this shift away from territorial mission is the new emphasis upon ethnic groups rather than national churches or nations. Presbyterians have been actively involved in the AD 2000 movement[8] that sought to reach out to people according to ethnic identity rather than to "countries." The formation of the Presbyterian Frontier Fellowship with the watchword "For every people an indigenous church; for every church a mission vision" illustrates this shift from nation as political entity to "nation" as people group. Witness to Kurds in Germany and witness to the Roma in Eastern Europe are examples of this shift. Presbyteries now are developing partnerships with some unreached groups of people, as well as with presbyteries and local churches, irrespective of past "missions."

Fifth, Wilbert Shenk reminded us that as our missionary force was "devolving," newer missions were evolving that attracted many of our own youth. Shank notes that,

> in effect, the PCUS was "outsourcing" mission—without intending to do so. One must ask: What was the message to which these Presbyterians were responding? The implicit distance—theological and ideological—between rank-and-file members and denominational leadership is not something that can be ignored indefinitely.

Shenk speaks as an outsider-insider since he was given hospitality from Presbyterians in Indonesia, and he developed friendships with at least two UPCUSA executives in New York. He reminds us that the outward movement of the church in mission cannot just be cut off and redirected to other projects. Theologically, we might say that God's church will or must go out in mission, though that "going" is ever changing. Burrows, again, gives us a much larger view of this issue:

> These forty years are the last chapter of the history of classical nineteenth- and first-half-of-the-twentieth-century missions. But we understand it better if we realize mission history is a brief entr'acte in a much larger drama of God wrestling with a people he wants to use to demonstrate and realize his desire for kingdom righteousness that will embrace all creation.

Thus, it would be good to take time to reflect on this "larger drama of God" and only then to ask how God may now use us "to demonstrate and realize his desire for kingdom righteousness." If we do not find ways (plural) to channel the call of God to our church members, they will go out still. God will providentially carry out his mission; we are invited to find ways to facilitate the involvement of our members.

Sixth, money still matters, but there is often something the matter with our money; there just does not seem to be enough. A number of times we have seen the problem of declining dollars for Presbyterian mission. It may be helpful to put this into perspective. Money has always been a "problem." It would be hard to find an annual report that did not bemoan the lack of money to carry out important missionary activities. Apparently there have often been many more missionaries ready to sail than dollars to float their boats. I recently was reading about Henry ("Harry") Winters Luce and his clear sense of calling to China.[9] He and his young bride were accepted by the mission board, but the director, Robert E. Speer, apologized and told them that there was not enough money to send them to China. A couple from Luce's home church in Scranton, Pennsylvania (Mr. and Mrs. James A. Linen), came through, providing all of their support, and so they sailed in 1896 for Shantung. A similar story is true of our author (chap. 7) William Anderson and his wife, Lois. They were approved to go to Africa, but there was not enough money, so personal support came through to free up the mission to send them. In this volume we have learned how sensitive money issues and church policy and church decisions can be. This has not changed. What needs to be remembered and discussed further is the need for multiple patterns and structures for funding. Along with other themes of diversification and localization of Presbyterian mission, it makes sense that the ways of funding and supporting mission in this "flat world"[10] must be more diverse and plural than unified and centralized.

Seventh, we were surprised to find that three of our respondents noted that some of our writing neglected much of the "pathos" and "pain" of this period. It is true that we did, at times, try to avoid some of the stronger language to avoid the impression that everyone was in much pain over this period of great transitions and great downsizing. That would be a false impression. One of our outside respondents specifically mentioned that all of the reorganization and downsizing described in chapter 3 seemed to whitewash the pain and pathos that must have been felt. This period of great transformation, reorganization, and decline was painful for many. People lost their jobs; missionaries were called home or were not reappointed though they often felt that they had much more to do. Burrows puts the issue as his first observation: "My first observation has to do with the *pain* and *incomprehension* felt on both the local church and foreign missionary side between 1944 and the present."[11] The incomprehension is what this volume is about: to try to make sense of this seismic shift in Christian mission. We found, though, that much of the pain had been soothed, healed, or overwhelmed by a deeper joy for what has been accomplished and for the ongoing relationships with overseas church partners. Christian mission always walks through the trail of suffering, and it will be good for us to remember this, even when some of the pain is self-inflicted.

A final observation needs to be made, and that concerns the question Who are your partners? *Partnership* is the operative word in Presbyterian mission today, but we need to ask, "Who is your partner?" Our partners are changing. If we are involved in the Philippines, we will be relating to more Korean, Singaporean, Malaysian, and Taiwanese missionaries than British, Canadian, and Australian. In the past this was fairly straightforward: your partners were the churches you helped to "plant," or that were part of your communion. But when we began to be involved in Europe in the aftermath of World War II, we were working with churches that were not so much founded by us but which founded us. Our work in some regions involves a number of Presbyterian Churches (such as Korea and Brazil), or no Presbyterian Church (such as Russia),[12] and yet we find local partners. Partnerships can now be from various ecclesial levels (a national church down to a local church or fellowship group), and it can be from various ecclesial bodies (we work with Anglicans, Lutherans, the Church of South India, but also with Baptists and Orthodox in places like Russia). This can be a sensitive issue when, for example, we try to work with partners who are not on the best of terms with each other.[13] Many of our original partners are now in partnership with newer missions, NGOs, and churches. All of this is further evidence of the "flat" rather than hierarchical world of mission referred to by Bishop Solomon. Presbyterians will not back down from involvement simply because partnerships are becoming more complex, but we must be aware that even partnerships within the same ecclesial body can be explosive today. The growing divisions within the worldwide Anglican communion are a warning to us to stay close, honor each other, and mutually submit to one another.

These are all trends or observations made by a small group of scholars after reflecting on this mission history. However, as Wilbert Shenk has noted in fairly strong words: "Without defending particular forms and methods of past generations, I grieve over the fact that I hear no one today asking the basic question: What is mission? Without giving the matter thought we have allowed it to be redefined and cheapened by cultural/economic forces that care not a whit about mission."[14] Burrows expresses this concern with a related concern for ecumenical awareness: "How can the global body of Christ carry on the kind of dialogue that will nurture not theological uniformity but conscious bonds of affection, understanding, and solidarity both within churches in families such as the Reformed movement and among the many parts of Christ's Body?" This issue of "conscious bonds of affection" will be important as the Presbyterian Church (U.S.A.) as well as other Western churches carefully and prayerfully navigate mission in partnership with both traditional and newer partners in the coming decades.

Moving forward in mission with both the integrity and the power of the gospel of Jesus Christ is more than any one denomination can handle. In a world that continues to baffle us by its ongoing violence and surprises us by its wonders of grace, we are often at a loss as to how to plan, act, and evaluate what mission might look like in the coming months, not to mention the coming years. The ongoing story of our participation in God's mission is, as Marian McClure said in the Foreword, a love story: God's love poured out for us, and that divine love now expressed through our steadfast commitment to God and God's mission in the world. And so, we move forward on our knees, praying for the strength and conviction to move on, the humility to stop to admit our errors, and the wisdom to know which is called for, in each place, at each moment.

Appendix 1

Chronology of Presbyterian Mission History

1945   End of World War II or Pacific War; Beginning of the end for colonialism in Africa and Asia

1946   Civil war in China begins

1947   India becomes independent nation (partition of India)

1948   World Council of Churches holds first Assembly in Amsterdam; State of Israel is proclaimed

1950–53   Korean War; evacuation of missionaries

1954   UPCNA's BFM assigns Glenn Reed as first Foreign Secretary, located in Eritrea. T. Donald Black elected Executive Secretary

1956   UPCNA's BFM and Foreign Missions Division of WGM Society merged; Lake Mohonk conference PCUSA

1958   Union of PCUSA & UPCNA into UPCUSA; COEMAR established; Charles T. Leber elected General Secretary; Division of Relations moves into new areas in Africa and Middle East

1959   Darby Fulton retires after 27 years with PCUS's BWM; Tribal warfare breaks out in Congo/Zaire; Charles T. Leber dies; John Coventry Smith elected General Secretary

1960	International Advisory Study Committee established by COEMAR
1961	T. Watson Street elected Secretary of PCUS's BWM
1962	Montreat I Consultation, PCUS's BWM; UPCUSA's *An Advisory Study* published 1962; Rebellion in Sudan
1963	Medical Benevolence Foundation established in Nashville
1970	John Coventry Smith retires; Donald Black elected General Secretary of COEMAR
1972	UPCUSA Mission structure reorganized; Program Agency includes World Mission; J. Oscar McCloud elected General Director
1973	Merger of PCUS General Assembly Boards and move to Atlanta; T. Watson Street retires; G. Thompson Brown elected Director of Division of International Mission
1974	Withdrawal of the Presbyterian Church of America (PCA) from the PCUS; Haile Selassie deposed in Ethiopia; Lausanne Committee on World Evangelization
1978	Montreat II Consultation, PCUS
1979	Outreach Foundation incorporated in Georgia
1981	G. Thompson Brown becomes seminary professor; Clifton Kirkpatrick elected Director of Division of International Mission; PFF founded
1983	Reunion of PCUS and UPCUSA into PC(USA); break in relations with Presbyterian Church of Brazil: "Mission and Evangelism: An Ecumenical Affirmation" adopted by General Assembly
1987	New Mission structure installed, Ministry Unit for World Mission: Clifton Kirkpatrick, Director
1988	General Assembly Council established Validated Mission Support Groups
1993	Mission structure revised: World Ministries Unit created; "Mission in the 1990s" adopted at the General Assembly
1996	Clifton Kirkpatrick elected Stated Clerk
1997	Marian McClure elected Director of World Ministries Unit
2003	"Gathering for God's Future" adopted at General Assembly
2006	Restructuring of PC(USA) mission
2007	Hunter Farrell appointed head of World Mission

Appendix 2

Survey of Presbyterians in Mission, 1944–2004

1. Country(ies) of service and years (e.g., Egypt 1952–63, Ethiopia 1970–76):
2. Your name, address, contact phone number, and e-mail address:
   a. Date and place of birth:
   b. Schools attended and degrees earned (college, seminary, medical, postgrad):
3. Name of spouse and contact phone number (if married):
   a. Date and place of birth:
   b. Schools attended and degrees earned (college, seminary, medical, postgrad):
4. Names of children (if any):
   a. Dates and places of birth:
5. What type and length of country-specific training and/or orientation did you have (either predeparture or in country)?
   —What type and length of general missionary training did you have?
6. Number and dates of furlough or home-assignment visits back to the United States during entire years of service:

7. How would you describe your motives when you first went to your country? Did these change with the passing of years?

8. Type of work (be as specific as possible, including names of institutions, presbyteries, etc. where you served):

9. To whom did you directly report during your time of service? Where were they located (i.e., in your country of service or back in the United States)? And how was your work evaluated?

10. Would you care to comment on relationships with missionary colleagues, national coworkers, government officials, American business or consular people?

11. What were the local attitudes toward you and other foreigners like during your term of service? Did they change over time? How so?

12. Any experiences that were especially unusual, difficult, or rewarding?

13. What elements in your mission work did you feel were most valuable (or effective)?

14. What elements were least valuable (or effective)?

15. Please comment on steps that were taken to build a self-governing, self-supporting, self-propagating national church. What advanced and what hindered the transfer of authority to national leaders?

16. What was the relationship between the Presbyterian mission and church leadership to the non-Christian religions? To Catholics? To other Protestant churches?

17. Did you learn any lessons from other missions or mission fields during your time of service?

18. Please comment on relations you had as a missionary with the home board in New York, Nashville, Atlanta, or Louisville [Ky.].

19. How did structural changes within the U.S. church impact the local church in your country of service and your work as a missionary (i.e., long-term to short-term appointments, changes from paid to volunteer workers, etc.)?

20. What type (if any) of ongoing training did you receive after serving for a number of years abroad?

21. List books, periodicals, articles, pamphlets, manuscripts you have written that describe your work or the work of your relations or institution. (Where can these be found? If possible, could you enclose a copy?)

22. Do you have any collected materials (photographs, letters, or other memorabilia) from your time of service that you would be willing to donate to an archive for preservation? If so, what?

23. Can you provide any names of leaders in your country of service whom you feel have a good understanding of the working of the Presbyterian church, and the Protestant church at large, in that country? How could we contact them to interview them?

24. Are there any other comments, suggestions, or criticisms that you would like to add to help us better understand your experience and your work?

25. Would you be willing to be contacted for a personal interview?
    YES   NO

26. Please provide us with the name(s) and contact information of any other PC(USA) missionaries you know who served at least five years in the field (between 1945–2000) and who did not officially retire as missionaries from the PC(USA). Thank you!

Notes

Introduction

1. Christianity's "Constantinian Revolution" was not exactly global in its impact, but it did affect Christianity on three continents: Europe, Asia, and Africa.
2. First published as the extended introduction to the 1970 edition of Kenneth Scott Latourette's *A History of the Expansion of Christianity*, 7 vols. (Grand Rapids: Zondervan).
3. See, for example, Lamin Sanneh's creative little book, *Whose Religion Is Christianity? The Gospel Beyond the West* (Grand Rapids: Wm. B. Eerdmans Publishing Co., 2003).
4. We say missions (in the plural) because what is now the Presbyterian Church (U.S.A.) started out in our time period as three denominations and three missions. This is explained in chapter 2.
5. It should be noted that 62 surveys were sent to people who were either too ill to complete the survey, had insufficient addresses, or were already deceased. Additionally, 44 of the uncompleted surveys were from persons whose spouse had already completed a survey. Missionary couples were both requested to complete their own surveys, yet not obligated to do so.
6. The name was changed to New Wilmington Mission Conference in 2006 to reflect the conference's primary concern with God's mission.
7. PCUS GA Minutes, 1951, 60.
8. UPCUSA COEMAR Report in the GA Minutes, 1964, 259.
9. PCUS GA Minutes, 1953, 95.

Chapter 1. Historical Context for Mission, 1944–2004

1. Kenneth S. Latourette, *A History of the Expansion of Christianity*, vol. 7, *Advance through Storm* (New York: Harper & Brothers, 1945), 504.
2. F. A. Iremonger, *William Temple, Archbishop of Canterbury: His Life and Letters* (Oxford: Oxford University Press, 1948); John Kent, *William Temple: Church, State, and Society in Britain, 1880–1950* (New York: Cambridge University Press, 1992).
3. Lesslie Newbigin, "Mission to Six Continents," in *A History of the Ecumenical Movement,* vol. 2, ed. Harold E. Fey (Philadelphia: Westminster Press, 1970), 178.
4. Susan Dicklitch and Heather Rice, "The Mennonite Central Committee (MCC) and Faith-based NGO Aid to Africa," *Development in Practice* 14, no. 4 (August 2004): 663–64.
5. John Coventry Smith, *From Colonialism to World Community: The Church's Pilgrimage* (Philadelphia: Geneva Press, 1982), 157, 167.

6. John A. Mackay, in a speech to the 1957 General Assembly of the Presbyterian Church in the U.S.A. Quoted by R. Pierce Beaver, *From Missions to Mission* (New York: Association Press, 1964), 39.

7. Thomas Stransky, "Missio Dei," *Dictionary of the Ecumenical Movement*, 2nd ed., Nicholas Lossky et al. (Geneva: WCC Publications, 2002), 780.

8. Stephen Neill, *Colonialism and Christian Missions* (New York: McGraw-Hill, 1966), 420.

9. From the "Message" of the IMC's 1946 Lausanne Conference, in *Toward Worldwide Christianity*, ed. O. Frederick Nolde (New York: Harper & Brothers, 1946), 232.

10. W. Richey Hogg, *New Day Dawning* (New York: World Horizons, 1957).

11. W. Stanley Rycroft, *The Ecumenical Witness of the United Presbyterian Church in the U.S.A.* (New York: COEMAR, 1968), 165.

12. Ibid., 166.

13. Donald Black, *Merging Mission and Unity* (Philadelphia: Geneva Press, 1986), 74–75.

14. G. Thompson Brown, "Overseas Mission Program and Policies of the Presbyterian Church in the U.S., 1861–1983," *American Presbyterians: Journal of Presbyterian History* 65, no. 2 (1987): 166.

15. Rodger C. Bassham, *Mission Theology, 1948–1975: Years of Worldwide Creative Tension, Ecumenical, Evangelical, and Roman Catholic* (Pasadena, CA: William Carey Library, 1979), 340f.

16. Hans Küng's introduction to changing theological paradigms, in Hans Küng and David Tracy, *Paradigm Change in Theology: A Symposium for the Future* (New York: Crossroad Press, 1989).

17. David J. Bosch, *Transforming Mission: Paradigm Shifts in Theology of Mission* (Maryknoll, NY: Orbis Books, 1991), 188.

18. Margrethe B. J. Brown, *Conversations with Roman Catholics on the Nature of the Church and on Ecumenism*, Resources for Ecumenical Encounter (New York: COEMAR, 1965).

19. *Common Witness: A Study Document of the Joint Working Group of the Roman Catholic Church and the World Council of Churches* (Geneva: WCC Publications, 1982), 28.

20. Thomas F. Stransky, "SODEPAX," *Dictionary of the Ecumenical Movement,* 2nd ed., 1055f.

21. R. Pierce Beaver, *American Missions in Bicentennial Perspective* (Pasadena, CA: William Carey Library, 1977), 276.

22. Harding Meyer and Lukas Vischer, eds., *Growth in Agreement: Reports and Agreed Statements of Ecumenical Conversations on a World Level* (New York: Paulist Press, 1984), 4, 277ff., 433ff.

23. George Vandervelde, "Evangelical Ecumenical Concerns," *Dictionary of the Ecumenical Movement,* 2nd ed., 437–38; Melanie A. May, "The Unity We Share, the Unity We Seek," in *A History of the Ecumenical Movement*, vol. 3, ed. John Briggs, Mercy Amba Oduyoye, and George Tsetsis (Geneva: WCC Publications, 2004), 94ff.

24. Odair Pedroso Mateus, *The World Alliance of Reformed Churches and the Modern Ecumenical Movement* (Geneva: WARC, 2005), 98–111.

25. Georges Tsetsis, "The Significance of Regional Ecumenism," *A History of the Ecumenical Movement*, 3:461.

26. Bert Hoedemaker, *Secularization and Mission: A Theological Essay* (Harrisburg, PA: Trinity Press International, 1998), 1–6.

27. Charles C. West, "Secularization," *Dictionary of the Ecumenical Movement,* 2nd ed., 1031ff.; two proponents of secularization as the wave of the future were

A. T. van Leeuwen, author of *Christianity in World History* (London: Edinburgh House, 1964); and Harvard professor Harvey Cox in his best-selling *The Secular City: Secularization and Urbanization in Theological Perspective* (London: SCM Press, 1965). By the 1980s, Cox reassessed his position based on signs of new life in the world's religions, in *Religion in the Secular City: Toward a Postmodern Theology* (New York: Simon & Schuster, 1985).

28. Dietrich Bonhoeffer, *Letters and Papers from Prison,* ET (London: SCM Press, 1953), 122.

29. Federico Pagura, "Missionary, Go Home . . . Or Stay," in *Christian Century* 90 (April 11, 1973); reprinted in *Mission Trends,* no. 1, ed. G. H. Anderson and T. F. Stransky (Grand Rapids: Wm. B. Eerdmans Publishing Co., 1974), 115–16; English translation by William J. Nottingham.

30. Quoted by David Bosch, op. cit., 518.

31. H. Richard Niebuhr, *Christ and Culture* (New York: Harper & Row, 1951).

32. Quotations in this paragraph are cited from Gerald H. Anderson, "A Moratorium on Missionaries?" *Mission Trends,* no. 1, 133ff.; Anderson's article originally appeared in *Christian Century* 91 (January 16, 1974): 43–45.

33. G. T. Brown, "Overseas Mission," 167.

34. John Nurser, *For All People and All Nations: The Ecumenical Church and Human Rights* (Washington, DC: Georgetown University Press, 2005), 179.

35. Nicolas Zernov, "The Eastern Churches and the Ecumenical Movement in the Twentieth Century," in *A History of the Ecumenical Movement,* vol. 1, ed. Ruth Rouse and Stephen Charles Neill (Philadelphia: Westminster Press, 1954), 667.

36. John Witte Jr. and Michael Bourdeaux, *Proselytism and Orthodoxy in Russia: The New War for Souls* (Maryknoll, NY: Orbis Books, 1999).

37. World Council of Churches, *Annual Report, 2004* (Geneva: WCC Publications, 2005), 27.

38. Black, *Merging Mission and Unity,* 16.

39. John A. Mackay, *Ecumenics: The Science of the Church Universal* (Englewood Cliffs, NJ: Prentice-Hall, 1964); T. Watson Street, *The Church and the Churches* (Richmond, VA: Covenant Life Curriculum, 1965).

40. Mackay, *Ecumenics,* 189.

41. G. T. Brown, "Overseas Mission," 166.

42. Timothy Yates, *Christian Mission in the Twentieth Century* (Cambridge: Cambridge University Press, 1994), 218.

43. J. Smith, *From Colonialism to World Community,* 281.

44. Quoted in M. M. Thomas and Paul Abrecht, eds., *World Conference on Church and Society: Christians in the Technical and Social Revolutions of Our Time* (Geneva: WCC Publications, 1967), 25.

45. Charles R. Harper, *O Acompanhamento: Ecumenical Action for Human Rights in Latin America, 1970–1990* (Geneva: WCC Publications, 2006).

46. Erskine Clarke, "Presbyterian Ecumenical Activity in the United States," in *The Diversity of Discipleship: The Presbyterians and Twentieth-Century Christian Witness,* ed. Milton J Coalter, John M. Mulder, and Louis B. Weeks (Louisville, KY: Westminster/John Knox Press, 1991), 167.

47. Baldwin Sjollema, "Combating Racism: A Chapter in Ecumenical History," *Ecumenical Review* 56, no. 4 (October 2004): 474.

48. A Catholic member of the commission who also spoke at Louvain was Professor Joseph Ratzinger of the University of Regensburg, later to become Pope Benedict XVI.

49. Eugene Carson Blake, "General Secretary's Louvain Address," *The Ecumenical Review* 29 (1972): 27.

50. Konrad Raiser, "Eugene Carson Blake: Acting on the Gift of Unity for Christ's Church," *Journal of Presbyterian History* 76, no. 4 (1998): 307.

51. Quoted by Willem A. Visser 't Hooft, *Has the Ecumenical Movement a Future?* (Atlanta: John Knox Press, 1974), 25.

52. Quoted in David L. Edwards, "Signs of Radicalism in the Ecumenical Movement," *A History of the Ecumenical Movement,* 2:406.

53. Bassham, *Mission Theology,* 76ff.

54. Ibid., 97.

55. Charles C. West, *Communism and the Theologians: Study of an Encounter* (Philadelphia: Westminster Press, 1958), 365ff.

56. Paul Abrecht, "Society," *Dictionary of the Ecumenical Movement,* 2nd ed., 1053.

57. John Waliggo, "Inculturation," *Dictionary of the Ecumenical Movement,* 2nd ed., 571–72.

58. Gustavo Gutiérrez, *A Theology of Liberation: History, Politics, and Salvation,* ET (New York: Orbis Books, 1973), 104.

59. Arthur F. Glasser and Donald A. McGavran, *Contemporary Theologies of Mission* (Grand Rapids: Baker Book House, 1983), 164.

60. Ibid., 93.

61. Michael Nazir Ali, "Directions in Mission: Christian Worship, Witness, and Work in Islamic Contexts," *International Review of Mission* 76 (1987): 34.

62. John R. W. Stott, "The Biblical Basis of Evangelism," in *Mission Trends,* no. 2, ed. Gerald H. Anderson and Thomas F. Stransky, CS (Grand Rapids: Wm. B. Eerdmans Publishing Co., 1975), 17–18.

63. Robert T. Coote, "Lausanne Covenant," *Dictionary of the Ecumenical Movement,* 2nd ed., 671–72.

64. Robert T. Coote, "Lausanne Committee for World Evangelization," *Dictionary of the Ecumenical Movement,* 2nd ed., 671; Edward R. Dayton and Samuel Wilson, eds., *The Future of World Evangelization: The Lausanne Movement* (Monrovia, CA: MARC, 1984).

65. See, for example, Harvey T. Hoekstra, *The World Council of Churches and the Demise of Evangelism* (Wheaton, IL: Tyndale House Publishers, 1979); cf. Robbins Strong's review of Hoekstra in *International Review of Mission* 70 (1981): 79–81.

66. Patricia M. Roach, "From San Antonio to Manila," *Monday Morning* 55 (January 22, 1990): 4.

67. WCC, *Mission and Evangelism: An Ecumenical Affirmation* (Geneva: WCC Publications, 1981), also in *International Review of Mission* 71 (1982): 192ff.

68. James A. Scherer, *Gospel, Church, and Kingdom: Comparative Studies in World Mission Theology* (Minneapolis: Augsburg, 1987), 40–44.

69. C. Rene Padilla, "Mission in the 1990s," *International Bulletin of Missionary Research* 13 (1989): 150ff.; Vinay Samuel and Christ Sugden, *The Church in Response to Human Need* (Grand Rapids: Wm. B. Eerdmans Publishing Co., 1987); Robert T. Coote, "Lausanne II and World Evangelization," *International Bulletin of Missionary Research* 14 (1990): 10ff.; and Bernard Thorogood, *Gales of Change: Responding to a Shifting Missionary Context* (Geneva: WCC Publications, 1994), 248ff.

70. Chung Hyun-Kyung, "Welcome the Spirit, Hear Her Cries," *Christianity and Crisis* 51 (1991): 220ff.; Alan Neely, *Christian Mission: A Case Study Approach* (Maryknoll, NY: Orbis Books, 1995), 204ff.; Mary Ann W. Lundy, "Departure under Fire," in *Re-Membering and Re-Imagining,* ed. Nancy J. Berneking and Pamela Carter Joern (Cleveland: Pilgrim Press, 1995), 121–23.

71. G. Thompson Brown, *Christianity in the People's Republic of China,* rev. ed. (Atlanta: John Knox Press, 1986), 163–64.

72. Feng Gao, "Church Leaders and Church Development in China," in *Protestant Church Development in China: How Did It Happen and Where Is It Leading?* ed. Tak-Ho Lam (Geneva and Hong Kong: Lutheran World Federation, 2003), 215–16.

73. Milton J Coalter, John M. Mulder, and Louis B. Weeks, *The Mainstream Protestant "Decline": The Presbyterian Pattern* (Louisville, KY: Westminster/John Knox Press, 1990), 17.

74. Ibid., statistical tables, 33ff.

75. John R. Fitzmier and Randall Balmer, "A Poultice for the Bite of the Cobra: The Hocking Report and Presbyterian Missions in the Middle Decades of the Twentieth Century," in Coalter et al., *Diversity of Discipleship*, 124–25.

76. Samuel Kobia, "Global Challenges to North American Christians: 23rd Peter Ainslie Lecture," *Call to Unity* 5 (December 2005): 4. For details on the demographic shift, see Todd M. Johnson and Sun Young Chung, "Tracking Global Christianity's Statistical Center of Gravity, AD 33–AD 2100," *International Review of Mission* 93 (2004): 166ff.

77. As one example, see Lesslie Newbigin, *Foolishness to the Greeks: The Gospel and Western Culture* (Geneva: WCC Publications, 1986).

78. Lesslie Newbigin, "The Dialogue of Gospel and Culture: Reflections on the Conference on World Mission and Evangelism, Salvador, Bahia, Brazil," *International Bulletin of Missionary Research* 21 (1997): 52.

79. Quoted by Marc Weitzman, "Intellectuels Américains," *Le Monde* 2, no. 157 (February 17, 2007): 22.

80. Erskine Clarke, "Presbyterian Ecumenical Activity in the United States," in Coalter, Mulder, and Weeks, *Diversity of Discipleship*, 167.

81. Paul A. Crow Jr., "North America," in *A History of the Ecumenical Movement*, 3:615. Writers related to the Institute on Religion and Democracy have continued to allege leftist tendencies and to employ the vocabulary of the Cold War in their critiques of the WCC; see Mark D. Tooley, "Lord, Have Mercy: The U.S. Delegation to the World Council of Churches Apologizes for America," posted March 1, 2006, on the Web site of *The Weekly Standard*, http://www.weekly standard.com/Content/Public/Articles/000/000/011/902soluo.asp.

82. Fukuyama's essay "The End of History?" appeared in the summer 1989 edition of *The National Interest* and is available online: http://www.wesjones.com/eoh.htm.

83. The issue of Orthodox resistance to proselytization came to the fore with the introduction of Western Protestant and Catholic projects of evangelism aimed at formerly communist nations. See Newbigin, "Dialogue of Gospel and Culture," 50–51; Witte and Bourdeaux, *Proselytism and Orthodoxy;* and commentaries on "The Final Report of the Special Commission on Orthodox Participation in the WCC," *Ecumenical Review* 55 (2003).

84. Huntington's essay "The Clash of Civilizations?" appeared in the summer 1993 issue of *Foreign Affairs* and is available online: http://www.foreign affairs.org/19930601faessay5188/samuel-p-huntington/the-clash-of-civilizations .html.

85. In the spring 2004 issue of *The National Interest*, Samuel Huntington published an essay, "Dead Souls: The De-nationalization of the American Elite," in which he argued that certain elites within the United States grow increasingly out of touch with most of the public because their cosmopolitan connections and perspectives distance them from nationalistic self-identity.

86. Kobia, "Global Challenges," 3.

87. For example, see Julio de Santa Ana, ed., *Religions Today: The Challenge to the Ecumenical Movement* (Geneva: WCC Publications, 2005).

88. World Council of Churches, *Reflections on Ecumenism in the 21st Century* (Geneva: WCC Publications, 2004).
89. Quoted in a WCC feature release of May 2005, http://cwme.wcc-coe.org/Kinnamon-on-mission-confe.1027.0.html.

Chapter 2. Counting the Cost

1. Before 1959 each denomination had always used its own Board of Foreign/World Missions as the mission governing and sending structure of the denomination. The impetus for major changes in this basic structure came with the mission conferences at Lake Mohonk (PCUSA, 1956) and Montreat (PCUS, 1962). Although there were major changes in mission following the Second World War, it was this period, and beginning with these conferences, that changes were set in motion into the twenty-first century.
2. PCUS GA Minutes, 1949, 137. Before this the PCUS had an Executive Committee of Foreign Missions. This was part of a pattern of rejecting the idea of "boards" as being unbiblical, based on the arguments of James Thornwell in the early 1830s.
3. J. Smith, *From Colonialism to World Community,* 173ff.
4. PCUS GA Minutes, 1973, 9, 78. The Board of World Missions ended November 1, 1973, and the Division of International Mission under the General Executive Board (later the GA Mission Board) commenced on January 1, 1974.
5. Research has been done mostly from Board Reports and GA Minutes, not in the archives of Board files. For our purposes, the data from annual Board Reports is adequate.
6. All data, unless otherwise noted, is from the annual report of the Board of Foreign Mission and its successor boards or the Minutes of the GA.
7. This marks the high point of mission personnel in the second half of the century at 1,849. The earlier high point was 1927 in the PCUSA, 1,606; UPCNA, 490; and 1964 in the PCUS, 569. The collective high point total was 1927, with 2,649 missionaries (PCUSA, 1,606; PCUS, 553; UPCNA, 490). See G. Thompson Brown, *Presbyterians in World Mission,* rev. ed. (Decatur, GA: Columbia Theological Seminary Press, 1995), 41. The Great Depression cut into foreign mission, and the recovery did not begin until the mid-1940s.
8. PC(USA) GA Minutes, 1990, 364. This represents the combined figures from the three predecessor denominations (merger of UPCUSA and PCUS in 1983). Thereafter the Minutes did not report a comparable number until 2006.
9. This represents the first net gain since 1927.
10. Older figures for the PCUSA: 1850, 74; 1900, 728; 1927, 1,606, highest point.
11. In 1944 almost half of the missionaries in the UPCNA were directly supported by the Women's General Mission Society, which survived until the 1958 merger. In fact, before 1923 all three denominations had women's boards for foreign mission. In that year, "without even consulting the women, the Presbyterian Church in the U.S.A. eliminated its national female mission organization." Dana L. Robert, ed., *Gospel Bearers, Gender Barriers* (Maryknoll, NY: Orbis Books, 2002), 10. The role of women in foreign mission is another very important dimension of the story that is worth a separate volume.
12. The high point in PCUS mission personnel came in 1964 with 569.
13. The official number presented at GA in June 2006 was 235, but the actual number of persons in the field that summer was 250. See *Presbyterians Today,* October 2006, 29.
14. This variation will be discussed in more detail under the heading "Categories of Mission Service."

15. The UPCNA records "short-termers" serving in Egyptian mission schools during these early years.

16. See chapter 6, on the missionary experience, for more detailed comments regarding language orientation.

17. UPCUSA, COEMAR, *Sharing Gifts of Grace* (New York: COEMAR, 1962), 14.

18. Ibid. These frontiers were specifically identified as technological upheaval, racial tension, new nationalisms, modern secularism, the university world, militant non-Christian faiths, communism, responsibility for statesmanship, and displaced, uprooted, rejected people.

19. By 1985 this number had declined to 86. PC(USA) GA Minutes, 1986, 595. The term used in the PCUS was "Mission Volunteer."

20. PC(USA) GA Minutes, 1987, 249.

21. Binational servants were U.S. and other personnel who had spent significant time in two or more cultures and continued their interest in the one where they were no longer residing. Sometimes this included returning missionaries. The focus of the group tended to be peace and justice concerns.

22. These persons would work, usually for a relatively short term, for subsistence wages, emulating as closely as possible the lifestyle of the people with whom they were serving.

23. These individuals were already working in another country in business, government, or other organizations and would intentionally affiliate themselves with Presbyterian work in that area.

24. As representatives of the UPCUSA, such individuals were seconded to ecumenical bodies, such as the NCC, WCC, and WARC.

25. These were persons from partner churches overseas who served in Presbyterian settings (congregation, presbytery, synod, or GA) generally for a few weeks. Many of these persons have participated in the program for more than 20 years. The MUSA program began in 1975 (UPCUSA GA Minutes, 1976, 544ff.; Minutes, 1975, 711ff.). One can see the roots of this forming in the thinking of J. Smith, *From Colonialism to World Community*, 106ff. A more recent version of this pattern has been the International Peacemakers, usually formed as a team (Jew, Christian, Muslim) to itinerate in the United States and supported by Peacemaking Offering funds.

26. These were persons from partner churches who served in a third country and were financially supported (at least in part) by Presbyterians in the United States. Sometimes these persons served in countries where U.S. citizens could not obtain visas.

27. PC(USA) GA Minutes, 1993, 979–89.

28. PC(USA) GA Minutes, 2004, 1119–31. For several years the Armed Forces Chaplains have been included in this list. For many years Presbyterian churches, colleges, seminaries, and other institutions had been sending many times this number of volunteers to work throughout the United States and overseas without any reference to the GA. The one category for which the GA expertise was most needed, "Mission Coworkers," continued to decline dramatically.

29. The other countries were Iran, Japan, Brazil, Chile, Colombia, Guatemala, Mexico, Venezuela, Philippines, Syria-Lebanon, Thailand, and Iraq.

30. PCUSA GA Minutes, 1957.

31. In 1944 more missionaries were in China alone than the total PC(USA) missionaries in the world in 2004. See chapter 9 for a discussion of China.

32. See chapters 3 and 4 for discussions on policy changes directed to reduce the number of missionaries.

33. It is difficult to count how many "missionaries" are actually working full-time outside of the United States, and then to compare that number with earlier

figures. Since the 1970s it has become quite complex. Counting missionaries is not an exact science; it may be a little like counting Christians in China.

34. This was confirmed in an e-mail from the World Mission Office, April 10, 2007. In addition, there are 35 Young Adult Volunteers working for one year, and five Amity teachers funded by Church World Service.

35. Beginning in 1956 the PCUSA began listing field representatives and their wives in both the missionary and staff statistics. These were field-based missionaries who served an administration role for the home board, on site at the mission. That number fluctuated between 14 and 24 until the formation of the Program Agency in 1972.

36. Furthermore, the head person was on a two-year trip to visit the UPCNA fields.

37. Don Black lists four executives in Philadelphia and one women's staff person for the UPCNA. He identifies 27 in New York plus eight in area offices across the US. Black, *Merging Mission and Unity*, 23.

38. See J. Smith, *From Colonialism to World Community,* 183ff; see also Black, *Merging Mission and Unity.* Regional offices had been part of the PCUSA interpretation program. In 1959 the newly merged church moved its offices to 475 Riverside Drive, New York.

39. UPCUSA Minutes, 1974, 684; UPCUSA Minutes, 1975, 702.

40. PC(USA) GA Minutes, 1988, 180.

41. Bill Simmons, personnal correspondence to author, November 7, 2006. "We might draw attention to 'Parkinson's Law' by C. Northcote Parkinson, who in the British Empire similarly observed that the number of employees in the Colonial Office continued to rise as the work itself decreased in importance. 'Work expands to fill the time available for its completion,' was his expression. We might add, 'Staff expand as the work (and number of missionaries) decreases.'"

42. Back in 1963, only 110 of the 400 overseas church missionary requests were filled. COEMAR, *A Single New Humanity,* Sixth Annual Report (New York: UPCUSA, 1964), 43. Even at the Lake Mohonk Consultation in 1956, the overseas delegates asked the PCUSA to increase its total missionary numbers by 300. The UPCUSA, again, found this to be true in a Program Agency series of consultations initiated in October 1974 (UPCUSA, GA Minutes, 1975, 549).

43. PCUS GA Minutes, 1956, 73.

44. PCUS GA Minutes, 1978, 442; Black, *Merging Mission and Unity,* 90.

45. UPCUSA GA Minutes, 1972, 883ff. A lot of mixed messages were being sent in the early 1970s. John Gatu of the Presbyterian Church of East Africa was calling for a moratorium on the sending of missionaries, even though he personally invited Timothy and Sue Anne Fairman to serve at St. Andrew's Church in Nairobi. At the same time, consultations with partner churches overseas resulted in requests for an increased number of missionaries.

46. Such committees existed much earlier in Presbyterian history, but the 1920s' reorganizations and unified budgets made them superfluous. The GA was essentially asking the presbyteries to more generously divide the unified mission dollar with the GA. However, 1972 also marked the national reorganization that called for presbyteries to take more responsibility for mission locally, so presbyteries were shifting more money to their budgets. (See parallel notes in the financial section.)

47. In 1973 the number actually went up to 402. There was no number reported in 1974, and the number reported in 1975 was 352. (See PCUS GA Minutes, 1972, 127; PCUS GA Minutes, 1974, 74; PCUS GA Minutes, 1976, 426; and PCUS GA Minutes, 1977, 442.)

48. UPCUSA GA Minutes, 1976, 99. Giving continued to decline relative to inflation.

49. UPCUSA GA Minutes, 1984, 250ff. This Mission Funding System was built on "interjudicatory consultations and mission funding goals." The approach was budget-focused, to supply "what is necessary to fund the mission of the church." Goals were based on the "needs of the church," less on the needs or concerns of the donor who would be supporting the work. Unified and centralized giving and budgeting were foundational to the plan.

50. Ibid. The regional staff for the new mission funding system did not begin until 1981. "Goal setting" was barely on the radar screen in 1983.

51. PC(USA) GA Minutes, 1986, 44, 88, 820. Page 820 indicates that a substitute overture was approved but does not indicate what it entailed. Apparently it was the recommendation of the GA Committee on Budget and Finance to refer it to the new Global Mission Ministry (88). The 1987 GA Minutes mention this (61, 196) as being in process of being considered in the new Global Mission Ministry Unit. See the 1988 and 1989 GA Minutes for further developments (194, 396ff).

52. PC(USA) GA Minutes, 1987, 94, 816.

53. PC(USA) GA Minutes, 1988, 194.

54. PC(USA) GA Minutes, 1989, 383, 396ff.

55. PC(USA) GA Minutes, 1994, 218.

56. In the last few years of that period, the report indicated totals for mission personnel in the 700–800 range. However, these were mostly short-term volunteers.

57. As defensible and reasonable as the name changes may have been, neither local congregations nor our overseas partners ever universally received them.

58. UPCUSA GA Minutes, 1975, 699–701.

59. Grassroots organizations emerged across the church, partly to counter what was perceived as a growing loss of mission nerve. Presbyterians United for Mission Advance (California) and United Presbyterians for World Mission (western Pennsylvania) are two examples.

60. One could argue that the roots go deeper, even into nineteenth-century liberalism, post–World War I disillusionment with Western democracy and religious hegemony, and views represented in the Hocking Report ("Re-Thinking Missions") of the 1930s.

61. Gerald H. Anderson, "A Moratorium on Missionaries?" *Christian Century* 91 (January 16, 1974): 43–45.

62. PCUS GA Minutes, 1974, 74.

63. UPCUSA GA Minutes, 1974, 687ff.

64. One problem with this policy was that a missionary working in education might be supervised by someone who knows nothing about education in the missionary's country of work.

65. Church partnerships in places like Korea and Brazil have been gently bruised by the PCUSA's commitment to ecumenical discussions and relationships through the WCC.

66. See also Kenneth E. Bailey, "Cross-cultural Mission: A Tale of Three Cities," W. Donald McClure Lectures, Pittsburgh Theological Seminary, 1984, where he makes the case that missionaries have been disenfranchised by this polity.

67. Black, *Merging Mission and Unity*, 89–90, addresses this by remarking that COEMAR tried to be open to other contacts.

68. UPCUSA GA Minutes, 1974, 693.

69. UPCUSA GA Minutes, 1974, part 1, 94. The Lausanne Congress of 1974 was a factor in raising this awareness in the Presbyterian churches.

70. UPCUSA GA Minutes, 1975, 543.

71. Information comes from each denomination's Web site: http://www.pcanet.org/general/history.htm and http://www.epc.org/about-epc/index.html.

72. It would be difficult to document this, but all knowledgeable observers would affirm that it is true. More than half of the typical congregation's mission giving is directed outside PC(USA) channels. This is certainly true of "local missions" and probably true for global mission support.

73. Inflation from 1944 to 2004 was 944 percent.

74. PCUSA Board of Foreign Mission Report, 1944, 139. The goal for women's organizations for the next year was $975,000, the same amount as for the Board of National Missions.

75. From this point giving for international mission dropped in the early 1960s until it recovered to $13,829,006 in 1976 and grew from there.

76. UPCNA GA Minutes, 1945, 513. Of this total amount, $502,140 was spent overseas, the remainder in the United States on cross-cultural home missions (UPCNA Minutes, 1944, 129, 187). The Women's General Missionary Society contributed $354,556 of the total. In 1957 WGMS gave $356,891.

77. PCUS GA Minutes, 1944, 80; PCUS GA Minutes, 1957, 148; and PCUS GA Minutes, 1982, 363.

78. Worldwide Ministries 2005 Budget supplied by Bill Simmons.

79. Ibid.

80. PCUSA GA Minutes 1945, 304ff; UPCNA GA Minutes, 1945, 481; PCUS GA Minutes, 1945, 91; the Thirty-third Annual Report of the GA's Committee for Woman's Work counted 207,775 members who gave $1,772,788 to Benevolence (18), but the numbers are difficult to reconcile. We assume "benevolence" means much more than foreign mission work. (The Executive Committee for Foreign Missions of the PCUS became the Board of World Mission in 1949 [PCUS GA Minutes, 1949, 137]).

81. Robert, *Gospel Bearers, Gender Barriers* has been most articulate in telling the story of women in mission. This story turns to the 1920s denominational reorganizations, which forced women's independent organizations into the centralized (and male-headed) system for foreign missions. There were a variety of resulting consequences, a decline in the vitality of women's work, and the subsequent move toward women's ordination.

82. From 1944 to 2005 personal income increased 57.66 times compared to the 9.44 times CPI increased, which means that giving for international mission has decreased much more dramatically than the −5.2 percent normally cited. However, this great difference is probably attributable to the rapidly widening gap between the rich and poor in America. The "average" has gone up so dramatically because the top-end incomes have gone up exponentially. Still, it is fair to say that the "average" Presbyterian is giving a far smaller part of one's income internationally. To view U.S. personal incomes, search the Bureau of Economic Analysis Web site at http://www.bea.gov/national/nipaweb/SelectTable.asp#S2.

83. See PC(USA) GA Minutes, 1988, 214, for one explanation of why this is happening.

84. Central Receiving Agency, *Comparative Statistics 2005* (Louisville, KY: PCUSA), table 12.

85. PCUS GA Minutes, 1971, 13, 16.

86. UPCUSA GA Minutes, 1976, 99.

87. Scott W. Sunquist and Caroline N. Becker, "Interviews with Retired Missionaries," Duarte, CA, March 2, 2006, 12ff.

88. See David G. Dawson, "Mission Philanthropy, Selected Giving and Presbyterians: Part I," *American Presbyterians* 68 (Summer 1990): 121–32; "Part 2," 69 (Fall 1991): 203–25.

89. Ibid., 209.

90. Within weeks, the declining support of Angela Davis even reached Alaska. First Presbyterian Church in Anchorage immediately cancelled its giving to National Missions. Most churches that dropped or reduced their support did not differentiate between national or international mission: http://yukonpresbytery.com/YukonPresbytery/Interviews/corbett.htm.

91. UPCUSA GA Minutes, 1975, 707. Records for 1974 actually report a temporary increase in GA General Mission giving and the One Great Hour of Sharing (a designated giving channel) reached a 25-year high.

92. PC(USA) GA Minutes, 1986, 309.

93. Dawson, "Mission Philanthropy," 219.

94. PC(USA) GA Minutes, 1983, 55.

95. PC(USA) GA Minutes, 1988, 322, 324. Although reunion came in 1983, it was not until 1988 that the first joint report under the new structure was produced.

96. PCUS GA Minutes, 1975, 309; 1977, 473.

97. Sunquist and Becker, "Interviews with Retired Missionaries," Duarte, CA, March 4, 2006, 8.

98. Sunquist and Becker, "Interviews with Retired Missionaries," Montreat, NC, March 7, 2006, 11–12. (Emphasis added. These were oral interviews.) A few missionaries, however, mentioned that they appreciated unified giving because they felt that it was more fair to those persons less gifted in public presentations and fund-raising.

99. Ibid., 11.

100. Meadville, Pennsylvania, was the site for missionary orientation for Presbyterians and other denominations in the 1950s until the merger in 1958, when ecumenical orientation began to be done at Stony Point, New York. Sunquist and Becker, "Interviews with Retired Missionaries," Duarte, CA, March 2, 2006, 18.

101. The 2005–2006 Worldwide Ministries Division Budget provided by Bill Simmons.

102. See chapter 8.

103. This story is told in more detail in chapter 11, on Africa.

104. UPCUSA GA Minutes, 1972, 884. Of the total (after expenses) produced by the Fifty Million Fund ($62,688,244), 27.4 percent went for international work. GA Minutes, 1973, 346ff.

105. UPCUSA GA Minutes, 1976, 295.

106. PCUS GA Minutes, 1970, 2.

107. PC(USA) GA Minutes, 1985, 261; 1986, 305; 1987, 242; 1988, 334.

108. PC(USA) GA Minutes, 1988, 197; 1988, 208–9.

109. UPCUSA GA Minutes, 1980, 249.

110. PCUS GA Minutes, 1971, 13, 16, 163.

111. PCUS GA Minutes, 1971, 163.

112. PCUSA Benevolence Report, 1951, Presbyterian Historical Society, Record Group #31, Box 188.

113. PCUS GA Minutes, 1977, 198, 310ff. Although not recorded, it would be interesting to know what persons in what positions in the PCUS were offering this "resistance to any change."

114. UPCUSA GA Minutes, 1978, 175.

115. Marian McClure, speech to the Association of Presbyterian Mission Pastors, December 3, 1999. As recorded by the author.

116. UPCUSA GA Minutes, 1976, 295; PCUS GA Minutes, 1950, 15–16. The PCUS per-member giving to foreign missions in 1927 was $3.74. In 1948–49 it was $3.00, including 82 cents from a special capital campaign; PCUS GA Minutes, 1969, 10ff., mentions an increasing portion being used for current expenses in local churches.

117. UPCUSA GA Minutes, 1979, 267ff.
118. Partners in Mission, the Financial Stewardship Plan for the GA of the Presbyterian Church (U.S.A.), January 28, 1992, lines 263–64. This was adopted by the 1992 GA; see Minutes, 56–57.
119. PC(USA) GA Minutes, 1998, 209–33.
120. Ibid.
121. Ibid.
122. PCUSA GA Minutes, 1944, 304.
123. PCUSA BFM Report, 1945, 140.
124. PCUSA GA Minutes, 1974, 718–19, 986. This may not have included One Great Hour of Sharing, some of which went overseas.
125. UPCUSA GA Minutes, 1973, 718ff.; 1974, 580ff.; 1975, 576ff.; 1976, 559ff.; 1977, 328ff.; 1978, 366ff.; 1979, 254ff.; 1980, 333ff.; 1981, 373ff.; 1982, 449ff.; 1983, 481ff.
126. In 2004 GA Council Director John Detterick admitted that the funding system was "dead." But as of this writing, nothing has been done to change it.
127. Presbyterian Historical Society, "A Manual for the Foreign Missions Conference" (Philadelphia, 1948), 24.
128. Lamin Sanneh, "Christian Missions and the Western Guilt Complex," *Christian Century* 104, no. 11 (April 6, 1987): 331.
129. Presbyterian News Service #06453, September 5, 2006.

Chapter 3. Structures for a Changing Church

1. Associate Reformed Synod and the Associate Synod of North America.
2. See chapters 7 through 13 for discussions of the national churches, how they developed, and how they related to the various Presbyterian Missions.
3. James Cogswell, *Until the Day Dawn* (Nashville: Board of World Missions, PCUS, 1957), 177.
4. See chapter 9 for a fuller discussion of East Asia in this period.
5. Cogswell, *Until the Day Dawn*, 180.
6. C. Darby Fulton, "Contemporary Problems in Mission," *Southern Presbyterian Journal* 17 (July 20, 1959): 5. Note, however, that the statistics do not include China, which was the largest PCUS field. All missionaries there had left, many to serve in other countries. See chapter 2 for a more-detailed analysis of missionary statistics between 1944 and 2004.
7. The compilers of this study decided to divide the time periods according to the tenure of the executive secretaries then in office. Although many took part in policy discussions and decisions, it was the Executive Secretary who was charged with this responsibility, and it is fitting to include a brief summary of each.
8. Fulton, "Contemporary Problems in Missions," 5.
9. PCUS Consultation Report to the General Assembly, October 13–19, 1962 (unanimously adopted).
10. Vernon Anderson, *Still Led in Triumph* (Nashville: Board of World Missions, PCUS, 1959).
11. See chapter 1 for a discussion of mission policy coming from Lake Mohonk as it related to the larger ecumenical stage and mission strategy.
12. In 1962, Richard Shaull, who was teaching at the Campinas Seminary, was asked to resign because of his theological views, which antagonized the more conservative Brazilian Presbyterians.
13. It should be noted that as the UPCUSA and the IPB were breaking relations, the UPCUSA had established relations and was sending personnel to work with the Independent Presbyterian Church and with the new United Presbyterian Church

of Brazil, a group that split from the IPB over many of the concerns that caused difficulty with the UPCUSA.

14. PCUS Report of Actions of the General Assembly on Restructuring Boards and Agencies, 1969, 18.

15. For a discussion of the decline in funds, see chapter 2.

16. The development of these latter two "validated" mission agencies is further discussed in chapter 5.

17. The church in Ethiopia was independent and known as the Ethiopian Evangelical Church, Bethel. See chapter 11 for a discussion of the Bethel Church.

18. The Thank Offering was often received in a fall worship service, giving the entire congregation an opportunity to support this important part of the church's mission activity. This tradition still continues in churches today.

19. These Bible schools were an especially important ministry geared toward women in Islamic societies. The hospitals later became general hospitals, though still supported by the Women's Board.

20. In 2006 the NWMC board voted to change the "Missionary" of its name to "Mission." This change reflects the conference's shift in emphasis on missionaries specifically to the more-general call of mission involvement and mission-mindedness of all Christians.

21. Hogg, *New Day Dawning*.

22. Mackay, *Ecumenics*, 33.

23. Lake Mohonk marked the first Board-sponsored conference where overseas guests comprised a majority of the participants. In attendance were also representatives of the UPCNA, PCUS, and other NCC-member churches. For many of these overseas church representatives, Lake Mohonk marked the first time that they had shared with each other about the situation of the church in their respective contexts.

24. Local church leaders were therefore often put in the awkward position of telling their former leaders that their services were no longer needed. They were also left with increased financial burdens because integration meant the cessation of Mission-given salaries.

25. Although some churches had already integrated before the clear call to do so in 1956, the integration process lasted until the early 1980s.

26. This was especially true in those areas, such as Europe, where there was no pioneering mission work, but rather an established church with whom Presbyterians could work alongside.

27. Both the UPCNA and the PCUS were also members of these ecumenical bodies.

28. Glenn Reed, the Commission Representative for Ethiopia and the Sudan, was given a leave to provide staff services for the Advisory Study Committee.

29. COEMAR's process of selecting a committee that represented a diversity of people (clergy and laity, men and women, and people from various countries) demonstrated both its desire to form a progressive committee and its struggle to let other national leaders actually have authority. After COEMAR decided upon potential committee members, it shared the names with local church leaders as to seek their approval. Although the Presbyterian Church of Brazil rejected COEMAR's selected names (Richard Shaull and Esdras Costa), COEMAR still kept them on the committee. This action insulted the Brazilian Church and resulted in many years of estrangement between the two denominations. See Black, *Merging Mission and Unity*, 74–76, for reflections on this episode.

30. COEMAR, Advisory Study Committee, *An Advisory Study* (New York: UPCUSA, 1962), 5.

31. J. Smith, *From World Colonialism to World Community*, 206.

32. This seemed to anticipate, or even pioneer, the present concept of the "missional church."

33. COEMAR, *An Advisory Study*, 78.

34. However, since this was a UPCUSA-produced and -focused document, the extent to which overseas churches engaged the material varied. It was hard, for example, to get overseas churches that had not been a part of developing the study to be concerned with a study that was not specifically about them. This same problem even occurred back home in the United States because many within the denomination viewed *An Advisory Study* as a document that only pertained to the church's mission program rather than to the church as a whole.

35. See more details on the Frontier Interns in chapter 8, page 283.

36. Black comments that during the time when COEMAR ran the intern program, interns increasingly lost concern for the churches with which they worked and focused more on the way that American power was being used abroad. Although they were COEMAR-supported, some developed their own projects without COEMAR approval. See Black, *Merging Mission and Unity*, 127.

37. See chapter 6 for missionary comments on this pension situation, especially as it related to working missionary wives.

38. As demonstrated in *An Advisory Study*, there also was a burgeoning shift in the mission philosophy of the "new era" (1960s) whereby shorter terms of service were upheld as the new trend. This shift was understood to be more suited for the context of integrated mission sites, where local churches were in charge and missionaries only served as the local churches requested.

39. See chapter 5 for a more detailed analysis of these groups.

40. See chapter 2's sections on "Numbers of Staff" and "Number of missionaries" and "Efforts to Reverse the Decline" for a more detailed discussion.

41. See chapter 2's section on "Numbers of Staff" for an analysis of the increasing national staff and continual decline of missionaries.

42. This present volume is much indebted to the studies that were done under this earlier WMD initiative.

Chapter 4. Faithfulness through the Storm

1. Milton J. Coalter, John M. Mulder, and Louis B. Weeks, *Vital Signs: The Promise of Mainstream Protestantism* (Grand Rapids: Wm. B. Eerdmans Publishing Co., 1996), 89–96.

2. Ibid.

3. Ibid., 96.

4. Daniel J. Adams, "From Colonialism to World Citizen: Changing Patterns of Presbyterian Mission," *American Presbyterians* 65 (Summer 1987): 147.

5. Ibid., 148.

6. The Nicene Creed is one of the most ecumenical creeds. *The Constitution of the Presbyterian Church (U.S.A.)*, Part 1, *Book of Confessions* (Louisville, KY: Office of the General Assembly, 1996), 1.3.

7. Mackay, *Ecumenics*, (1964), 9.

8. Ibid., 11–12.

9. J. Smith, *From Colonialism to World Community*, 151.

10. Harold E. Fey, "Confessional Families and the Ecumenical Movement," in Fey, *A History of the Ecumenical Movement*, 2:121.

11. The International Missionary Council had been integrated into the WCC and became the "Division of World Mission and Evangelism." This was the first conference of this new division.

12. Darrell L. Guder, ed., *Missional Church* (Grand Rapids: Wm. B. Eerdmans Publishing Co., 1998), 81.

13. Theo Gill, "American Presbyterians in the Global Ecumenical Movement," in Coalter, Mulder, and Weeks, *Diversity of Discipleship*, 144.

14. Ibid, 145.

15. Philip Jenkins, *The Next Christendom: The Coming of Global Christianity* (New York: Oxford University Press, 2002).

16. The statement from the *Presbyterian Survey*, September 1987, 12–15, is quoted in Milton J. Coalter, John M. Mulder, and Louis B. Weeks, *The Re-Forming Tradition: Presbyterians and Mainstream Protestantism* (Louisville, KY: Westminster/John Knox Press, 1992), 183.

17. See chapter 8, "The Presbyterian Predicament: A Case of Conflicting Allegiances," in Coalter, Mulder, and Weeks, *Re-Forming Tradition*, 225–44. This volume concludes the seven-volume research project titled The Presbyterian Presence: The Twentieth-Century Experience.

18. John Mackay was first a missionary to Peru before being elected president of Princeton Theological Seminary from 1936 to 1959. During his tenure at Princeton, he was also president of the PCUSA Board of Foreign Missions (1939–51), president of the WARC (1954–59), and a key leader of the IMC and WCC. Clifton Kirkpatrick was elected director of the Division of International Mission of the PCUS in 1981 and was the first director of Global Missions Ministry Unit and Worldwide Ministries Division of the reunited PC(USA) from 1983 to 1997. Since 1997, he has been the Stated Clerk of the Office of the General Assembly of the PC(USA). Kirkpatrick has served on the Central Committee of the WCC and from 2004 is the president of WARC. Marian McClure served as director of the Worldwide Ministries Division of the PC(USA) from 1997 until 2006. She has served on the Committee of World Mission and Evangelism of the WCC and has represented the PC(USA) in conversations at the Vatican. As an ordained woman in a top executive position, she further represents the advancement of women in leadership in mission in the PC(USA).

19. Approved by the 197th General Assembly (1985). Cited in Margaret O. Thomas, ed., *Being Ecumenical: A Compendium on Ecumenical and Interfaith Relations; Actions of the General Assembly of the Presbyterian Church (U.S.A.)* (Louisville, KY: Worldwide Ministries Division, 1994), 5–6.

20. Clifton Kirkpatrick, *Mission in the 1990s: A Strategic Direction in Worldwide Ministry for the Presbyterian Church (U.S.A.)*, adopted by the 205th General Assembly (1993) (Louisville, KY: Worldwide Ministries Division); *Gathering for God's Future: Witness, Discipleship, Community; A Renewed Call to Worldwide Mission*, adopted by the 215th General Assembly (2003) (Louisville, KY: Worldwide Ministries Division).

21. J. Smith, *From Colonialism to World Community*, 145–46.

22. Kwame Bediako, *Christianity in Africa* (Maryknoll, NY: Orbis Books, 1995), 131.

23. Adams in "From Colonialism to World Citizen" describes the move "toward an indigenous church" and elaborates on the changes that resulted from the Mohonk and Montreat Consultations and the 1982 event.

24. G. Brown, *Presbyterians in World Mission* (1995), 49–53.

25. In "The Empty Basket of Presbyterian Mission: Limits and Possibilities of Partnership," Stanley H. Skreslet criticizes this document and the strong emphasis on partnership and warns that when mission is reduced to partnership, we offer the world an "empty basket" and "lose sight of the core concerns of the gospel message," *International Bulletin of Missionary Research* 19, no. 3 (July 1995): 103. I

believe that our partner churches have helped the PC(USA) to keep our eyes focused on the truth of the gospel of Jesus Christ and the reign of God.

26. Romans 1:12.
27. Philip L. Wickeri, *Partnership, Solidarity, and Friendship: Transforming Structures in Mission,* A Study Paper for the Presbyterian Church (U.S.A.) (Louisville, KY: Worldwide Ministries Division, 2003), 3.
28. *Gathering for God's Future* and "Presbyterians Do Mission in Partnership" were both approved by the 215th General Assembly of the PC(USA) in 2003 and published by Worldwide Ministries Division.
29. Sherron Kay George, *Called as Partners in Christ's Service: The Practice of God's Mission* (Louisville, KY: Geneva Press, 2004).
30. Wickeri, *Partnership, Solidarity, and Friendship,* 3.
31. Ibid.
32. Ibid., 8.
33. Ibid., 10.
34. *Buscando salidas . . . caminando hacia adelante!* (Quito, Ecuador: Consejo Latinoamericano de Iglesias, 2003).
35. Robert McAfee Brown, *Unexpected News: Reading the Bible with Third World Eyes* (Philadelphia: Westminster Press, 1984).
36. Joerg Rieger, *God and the Excluded: Visions and Blindspots in Contemporary Theology* (Minneapolis: Fortress Press, 2001).
37. Thomas John, *A Strange Accent: The Reflections of a Missionary to the United States* (Louisville, KY: Worldwide Ministries Division, 1996).
38. *Gathering for God's Future,* 7.
39. *Leaders for a Global Church,* quarterly publication of the Office of Global Education and International Leadership Development in Worldwide Ministries Division, no date.
40. *Gathering for God's Future,* "Developing Leaders," 7.
41. Kenneth L. Woodward, "The Changing Face of the Church," *Newsweek,* April, 16, 2001, 49.
42. Black, *Merging Mission and Unity,* 101–2.
43. Ibid.
44. G. Brown, "Overseas Mission Program and Policies," 170.
45. Stephen Knisely, *Faith in Action: Understanding Development Ministries from a Christian Perspective* (Louisville, KY: Worldwide Ministries Division, 2000), 59.
46. Clifton Kirkpatrick, "The Unity of the Church in Mission," address given in St. Louis in November 1997, in *Congregations in Global Mission: New Models for a New Century; A Conference Report* (Louisville, KY: Worldwide Ministries Division, 1998), 5.
47. *Gathering for God's Future,* "Sharing People and Resources," 9.
48. Ibid.
49. Ibid.
50. Bruce Gannaway, *Mission: Commitment to God's Hopeful Vision* (Louisville, KY: Global Mission Ministry Unit, 1992), 30.
51. Ibid., 30–33.
52. Stephen Bevans, "Seeing Mission through Images," *Missiology* 10, no. 1 (January 1991): 45–57.
53. Sherron Kay George, "The Quest for Images of Missionaries in a 'Post-Missionary' Era," *Missiology* 30, no. 1 (January 2002): 51–65.
54. George, *Called as Partners in Christ's Service,* 63–82.
55. Coalter, Mulder, and Weeks, *Vital Signs,* 91.
56. Stephen Neill, *Salvation Tomorrow* (Nashville: Abingdon Press, 1976), 57.
57. Coalter, Mulder, and Weeks, *Re-forming Tradition,* 111.

58. Ibid., 107.
59. Ronald C. White Jr. has a very good discussion of this debate in his essay "Social Witness and Evangelism: Complementary or Competing Priorities?" in *How Shall We Witness?* ed. Milton J. Coalter and Virgil Cruz, 136–61 (Louisville, KY: Westminster John Knox Press, 1995).
60. Vera White, *Hand in Hand: Doing Evangelism and Doing Justice* (Louisville, KY: Presbyterian Peacemaking Program, 1991).
61. *Gathering for God's Future,* 1.
62. Ibid., 16.
63. Ibid., 13.
64. Ibid., 13, 15.
65. Ibid., 2–5.
66. *The Constitution of the Presbyterian Church (U.S.A.),* Part 2, *Book of Order.* For pedagogical reasons, all citations from the *Book of Order, Form of Government,* chapter 3, "The Church and Its Mission," and *Worship Directory,* chapter 7, "Worship and the Ministry of the Church in the World," will be indicated in the text as G-3 and W-7.
67. Presbyterian Church (USA), *Turn to the Living God: A Call to Evangelism in Jesus Christ's Way* (Louisville, KY: Office of the General Assembly), adopted by the 203rd General Assembly (1991).
68. *Gathering for God's Future,* 5.
69. Knisely, *Faith in Action,* 13.
70. "Local-Global Mission: The Cutting Edge" is the title of my article that was published in *Missiology: An International Review* 27, no. 2 (April 2000): 187–97. Figure 2 was a part of that article, as were many of the thoughts in this section.
71. Coalter, Mulder, and Weeks, *Re-forming Tradition,* 113.
72. Kirkpatrick, "Unity of the Church in Mission," 5.
73. Marian McClure, "Dichotomy Busters," address given in St. Louis in November 1997, in *Congregations in Global Mission,* 83–86.
74. Rick Ufford-Chase, "Beyond Business as Usual," *Presbyterians Today,* March 2006, 13–15.
75. Ibid.
76. Ibid.
77. Marian McClure, "The Cascading Effect in Mission," sermon preached on October 19, 2005, for mission conference in Atlanta, in "Speaking of Mission: A Collection of Sermons and Speeches," unpublished manuscript, 22–23.
78. Stanley H. Skreslet, "Networking, Civil Society, and the NGO: A New Model for Ecumenical Mission," *Missiology* 25, no. 3 (July 1997): 308–9.
79. Ibid.
80. *Gathering for God's Future,* 13.
81. Ibid., 14–15.
82. Ibid., 17.

Chapter 5. Missions within the Mission

1. Ralph D. Winter, "The Two Structures of God's Redemptive Mission," in *Perspectives on the World Christian Movement,* ed. Ralph D. Winter and Steven C. Hawthorne, 3rd ed., 220–29 (Pasadena, CA: William Carey Library Publishers, 1999).
2. Paul E. Pierson, *Transformation: A Unifying Vision of the Church's Mission,* Forum for World Evangelization (Bangkok, 2004), 8.
3. Ibid., 13.
4. Ibid., 16.

5. Andrew F. Walls, *The Missionary Movement in Christian History: Studies in the Transmission of the Faith* (Maryknoll, NY: Orbis Books, 1996), 246.

6. Pierson, *Transformation,* 16.

7. Coalter, Mulder, and Weeks, *Re-Forming Tradition,* 99.

8. These shifts are described in Milton J. Coalter, John M. Mulder, and Louis B. Weeks, eds., *The Organizational Revolution: Presbyterians and American Denominationalism* (Louisville, KY: Westminster/John Knox Press, 1992).

9. PCUS GA Minutes, 1960, 129, Annual Report of the Board of World Missions.

10. PCUS GA Minutes, 1980, 336–37, Program Audit of the Office of Review and Evaluation, "Trends in Overseas Mission."

11. PC(USA) GA Minutes, 1988, 826ff., "Is Christ Divided?" Report of the Task Force on Theological Pluralism within the Presbyterian Community of Faith.

12. "Is Christ Divided?" was named for the chapter in the Plan for Reunion approved by the PCUS and the UPCUSA, which provided for special organizations.

13. See Gary S. Eller's helpful "Special-Interest Groups and American Presbyterians," in Coalter, Mulder, and Weeks, *Organizational Revolution,* 254–78.

14. PC(USA) GA Minutes, 1992, 684.

15. Bailey, "Cross-Cultural Mission."

16. This trend can be traced through such parallel decisions as turning the International Missionary Council into a division of the WCC, merging the PCUSA and UPCNA mission boards into a new Commission on Ecumenical Mission and Relations (COEMAR) when those churches united in 1958, and later disbanding COEMAR in favor of a Program Agency in which mission became one program among many.

17. Black, *Merging Mission and Unity.*

18. Much of this section is taken from an unpublished history of the MBF by one of its presidents, R. Teryl Brooks Jr., MD, based upon archival documents, 2000. Available at the MBF offices.

19. Information in this section is taken from an unpublished history of The Outreach Foundation by Bette Bryant, which incorporated an earlier essay by Howard Chadwick. Available at the Outreach Foundation Office.

20. Much of the detail in this section is taken from an unpublished "Short History of Presbyterian Frontier Fellowship." Available at the PFF main office.

21. Interview with Ralph Winter at the 25th anniversary celebration of Presbyterian Frontier Fellowship, June 8, 2006.

22. The 50 Million Fund was a churchwide campaign, and its purpose included international mission, such as the outreach efforts in Ethiopia and expansion of hospitals in a dozen countries, along with domestic projects such as urban church renovation, campus ministries, and seminary improvements.

23. Ibid.

24. Interview with Harold Kurtz at the 25th anniversary celebration of Presbyterian Frontier Fellowship, June 8, 2006.

25. The "Commitment to Share Good News" was one of the recommendations in the resolution "Turn to the Living God."

26. Robert A. Blincoe, "The Strange Structure of Mission Agencies, Part III," *International Journal of Frontier Missions,* 19, no. 3 (Fall 2002): 45.

27. www.reconsecration.org. Accessed June 4, 2007.

28. This section draws heavily upon an article by G. Thompson Brown, "Twenty Years in Cross-Cultural Mission," *Cross Culture: A Newsletter of the Association of Presbyterians for Cross-Cultural Mission* 49 (October 2004): 1–3.

29. See G. Thompson Brown and Donald G. Black in this volume, chapter 3, "Structures for a Changing Church."

30. Pat Cole, "In Praise of Partnerships," *Presbyterians Today,* January/February 2005, 19.
31. Paternalism was not only expressed through former patterns of dominance but also in more-recent patterns of deference.
32. PC(USA) GA, 2003, policy statement, "Presbyterians Do Mission in Partnership."
33. Cole, "In Praise of Partnerships," 23.
34. Will Browne, WMD Associate Director, Mission Network Leaders meeting, Louisville, KY, July 12–14, 2006.
35. *PCUSA WORLDWIDE Newsletter,* August 14, 2006, www.pcusa.org/wmd/pdf/ august06newsletter.pdf. Accessed November 21, 2007.
36. The APMP describes its history on its Web site, http://www.missionpastor.org/ history.htm. Accessed November 21, 2007.
37. Parts of this history come from the New Wilmington Mission Conference Web site, http://www.nwmcmission.org. Accessed November 21, 2007.
38. Chris W. Erdman, "Pittsburgh Seminary Helps Launch World Mission Initiative," *Presbyterian Layman* 31, no. 3 (May/June 1998).
39. Literacy and Evangelism International, "About LEI," http://www.literacy evangelism.org/about. Accessed November 21, 2007.
40. Alexa Smith, "Meetings Are Planned to Strengthen Ties between Church and Other Mission Groups," Presbyterian News Service story, March 28, 1995.
41. Robert T. Henderson, *Enchanted Community* (Eugene, OR: Wipf & Stock, 2006), 15.
42. See Kirkpatrick, *Mission in the 1990s.*
43. Marian M. McClure, "Creative Changes in International Mission," *Presbyterian Outlook* (August 14, 2006): http://www.pres-outlook.com/tabid/1009/Article/ 2609/Default.aspx. Accessed November 21, 2007.
44. Darrell L. Guder, "Para-Parochial Movements: The Religious Order Revisited," unpublished manuscript, 1993. Manuscript held by author and at William Carey University library.
45. Walls, *Missionary Movement in Christian History,* 254.

Chapter 6. Missionaries Speak

1. This chapter in no way assumes that the missionary experience can be summed up in one brief chapter. However, the editors believe that it is vitally important, at least as a start, to listen and record some of what has been learned by these missionaries. Without them, there surely would be no mission history.
2. See the introduction for more details on how this information was gathered. Although our history covers missionaries sent out by various boards, they will usually be addressed as a general group. Particular comments regarding one's country of service or relation to the sending board may reveal differences between the various mission agencies of the PCUS, UPCNA, PCUSA, UPCUSA, and PC(USA).
3. See appendix 2 for the survey questions. In the following notes, "Q" represents Question (#); "R" represents the Respondent (#).
4. For the purposes of this project, "long-term" missionaries are those who served for a minimum of five years.
5. For example, one person wrote, "To serve the Church in India," and another wrote, "To assist the Korean church in their evangelistic task."
6. PMHP Survey, Q7: R149, R485, R386.
7. A couple of people mentioned being challenged by missionaries, current and former, who visited or were members of their church. Moreover, many of these

conference experiences or personal encounters occurred during a missionary's childhood. For example, one person stated a call as being "inspired by a Sunday school teacher and Albert Schweitzer at 11 yrs. of age." Ibid. Q7: R38. There were also many people who, while not mentioning a particular reason or influence, nevertheless specifically referred to their call as occurring at a young age.

8. Sunquist and Becker, "Interviews with Retired Missionaries," Montreat, NC, March 7, 2006, 2.

9. PMHP Survey, Q7: R588.

10. Although some husbands may have gone overseas because their wives were called, none of the missionaries whom we interviewed or surveyed gave such a reason. One husband, however, mentioned the guidance and stability that his wife, a former missionary kid, provided him when they set sail for Korea in 1954. It was his first overseas experience. Sunquist and Becker, "Interviews with Retired Missionaries," Montreat, NC, March 7, 2006, 14.

11. The response that best summarizes this shift is as follows: "Motive also changed from 'developing programs' to 'developing people to continue the programs and to start new ones.'" PMHP Survey, Q7: R82.

12. Ibid., Q7: R439.

13. "Looking back," wrote one missionary, "I can see [that] I had a lot of 'glamour' ideas about the mission field. My motives definitely changed as time went on. I really saw us involved in strengthening the Church and developing leadership for it." Ibid., Q7: R415.

14. These categories were taken from the PC(USA)'s method of classifying the services of retired missionaries. This list follows the order of greatest to least numbers of persons serving in those areas.

15. These roles are listed in order from greatest to least involvement.

16. Keep in mind that even though this list may seem reasonably accurate, it comes from surveys and so is not an official list.

17. PMHP Survey, Q14: R548, R615.

18. As one missionary put it, "Everything seemed valuable; we never had enough time to do all that was necessary or desired, it seemed." Ibid., Q14: R442.

19. Ibid., Q14: R588.

20. Ibid., Q14: R468.

21. This particular feeling came from a missionary to Sudan who wrote, "The necessity of working under the leadership of the Evangelical Church of Sudan was restricting and hampered my desire, my calling, to work with Muslims. The local church folk did not believe a Muslim could convert, and hence the atmosphere in the church was unfriendly and unwelcoming to any Seeker." PMHP Survey, Q14: R383.

22. Ibid., Q13: R509.

23. Ibid., Q13: R640, R580.

24. The following quotation from a missionary succinctly states this goal: "The principle that we went out with was to work ourselves out of a job; to find local people who were capable and train them and then leave." Sunquist and Becker, "Interviews with Retired Missionaries," Duarte, CA, March 3, 2006, 14.

25. Ibid.

26. Another missionary to the Middle East mentioned the satisfaction of seeing an ongoing project to produce an Arabic hymnal come to completion in 1990. Ibid., March 4, 2006, 3.

27. Ibid., 19.

28. Ibid., March 3, 2006, 33.

29. Ibid., March 4, 2006, 27.

30. Ibid.

31. Ibid., 17.
32. Sunquist and Becker, "Interviews with Retired Missionaries," Montreat, NC, March 7, 2006, 15.
33. A former medical missionary to Korea has been able to, as he wrote, "see my dental grads develop the Korea Dental mission for Christ, now with 30 dental missionaries in 10 countries." PMHP Survey, Q12: R384.
34. Some children began going away to school as early as six years old, while others were homeschooled up until middle school/junior high. In at least one instance, a missionary mother had a nervous breakdown from having to send her young children to school so far away from home.
35. Sunquist and Becker, "Interviews with Retired Missionaries," Duarte, CA, March 4, 2006, 11.
36. This statement is more true for those serving in the first one-half to two-thirds of this time period.
37. Sunquist and Becker, "Interviews with Retired Missionaries," Duarte, CA, March 4, 2006, 11.
38. This lack of communication between overseas and the United States diminished greatly during the latter fourth of this time period as both the frequency of furloughs/home assignments and the number of technological communication advances increased.
39. PMHP Survey, Q12: R466.
40. Ibid., Q24: R787.
41. Exceptions would be later years in Japan, Hong Kong, Singapore, and even Korea.
42. PMHP Survey, Q12: R468.
43. Sunquist and Becker, "Interviews with Retired Missionaries," Montreat, NC, March 7, 2006, 19.
44. See chapter 2 for greater detail on the many causes playing into this downward trend of mission support.
45. See chapter 2 (48f.) for a discussion of Angela Davis. One missionary mentioned the extent to which the Angela Davis affair permanently affected financial giving to the denomination in this personal anecdote: "10–15 years later, after Angela Davis, we went to a wealthy Presbyterian in Orange County, but he would not support the PC(USA) because of the church support for radical causes. It was used as an excuse by many." Sunquist and Becker, "Interviews with Retired Missionaries," Duarte, CA, March 3, 2006, 13.
46. Ibid.
47. Ibid.
48. PMHP Survey, Q12: R446.
49. Ibid., Q12: R544.
50. One missionary shared his experience in Lesotho: "In 1998 in Lesotho there was a big political uprising (mostly Protestants vs. Catholic; 78/80 seats in Parliament). We figured we had to stay with our students. The capital was burned out, and we were the only Americans left in Lesotho."
51. A number of people mentioned the correlation between learning the local language well and developing deep friendships with the people where they served. One missionary even mentioned that his language ability was probably the reason that he is treated as "one of the old-timers" when he returns to visit his former country.
52. Ibid., 2.
53. Ibid.
54. Sunquist and Becker, "Interviews with Retired Missionaries," Duarte, CA, March 3, 2006, 30.
55. See chapters 1 (7f.) for more details regarding the Lake Mohonk Consultation.

56. This was often the Presbyterian Church telling missionaries that they would not be returning to their country of service because the local church or institution did not deem their work necessary. Such cases were mentioned in the earlier section on difficult parts of mission service.

57. Sunquist and Becker, "Interviews with Retired Missionaries," Montreat, NC, March 7, 2006, 8.

58. Ibid., 11. This person went on to describe the danger that he sees in mission trends in partnership today: "In the PC(USA) now there is much emphasis on congregations becoming little mission bodies, but it does create a new type of paternalism; and this can revert to an older type of view of what mission is all about. A congregation working in partnership can become very dominating and especially since they are sending money; and they don't have the experience to know what this means and what can and should be done. I am always a little worried when I hear this. Even though it is our money, we may have to go about it in a different way."

59. Ibid., 8. Since the term "missionary" has historically been associated with Christians sent to share the gospel to places for the first time, Christians in Europe preferred "fraternal worker."

60. Ibid.

61. Some missionaries, however, have not liked this title. One missionary's survey response read as follows: "We were called 'coworkers,' but there was no question that we would be fired if we disagreed with them [the sending agency]. We were employees, not coworkers." PMHP Survey, Q19: R466.

62. Sunquist and Becker, "Interviews with Retired Missionaries," Duarte, CA, March 2, 2006, 7.

63. Ibid., March 3, 2006, 12.

64. Before the formation of the UPCUSA in 1958, the PCUSA's BFM actually began including such a subheading on its stationery as a way to better express its involvement in ecumenical mission and relations.

65. PMHP Survey, Q15: R787.

66. This example from a missionary to Guatemala elucidates one problematic financial issue related to mission-church integration: the difference between U.S. church design and local church expectation. This missionary wrote, "The United Presbyterian Church decided that it was time to turn the mission work and church ministry over to the leadership of the Synod of Guatemala. Synod representatives were invited to hear a proposal, and they were thrilled. Once transfer began, Guatemalans thought they were to receive homes and cars [that the] missionaries were using. When they learned that those were not under their authority, some were disappointed." Ibid., Q15: R555.

67. Sunquist and Becker, "Interviews with Retired Missionaries," Duarte, CA, March 2, 2006, 4.

68. Single women missionaries earned their own salaries and, therefore, also earned Social Security and pension contributions.

69. It should not be ignored that missionaries have also referred to this situation as being a problem today. Second-generation Presbyterian missionaries are being cut from overseas service today because of funding problems.

70. Sunquist and Becker, "Interviews with Retired Missionaries," Duarte, CA, March 3, 2006, 35.

71. This is a paraphrase of what two missionaries said during separate interviews.

72. One missionary spoke of his personal experience in witnessing such allocation trends: "I was in a lot of presbyteries where final decisions were made about the distribution of the general mission dollar. Never once did I hear [that] the decisions were made to increase the presbyteries' percentage of the mission dollars in the light of the needs of the other governing bodies. The Overseas Missions

received decreasing amounts of general mission monies while Presbyteries grabbed what they said they needed for their own budgets." Ibid., 36.

73. Sunquist, "Interviews with Retired Missionaries," New Wilmington, PA, July 25, 2005; PMHP Survey, Q19: R493. This particular response further noted that decision making was more and more removed from those on the field who knew what was going on.

74. He noted, "The missionary presence and witness which we [PC(USA) missionaries] represented was taken over by independent evangelical missions who filled the void." PMHP Survey, Q19: R14.

75. Ibid., Q19: R485; Sunquist and Becker, "Interviews with Retired Missionaries," Duarte, CA, March 3, 2006, 28.

76. The PCUS mission offices were first in Nashville, TN, and then in Atlanta, GA. The UPCNA offices were in Pittsburgh and Philadelphia, PA, until they moved to New York, NY, joining the PCUSA's offices when they united to become the UPCUSA in 1958. Initially, after the union of the PC(USA), in 1983 mission offices continued being operated out of Atlanta and New York until they all consolidated and relocated to Louisville, KY. Missionary responses regarding relations to their home board often used the city's name of where the board was located to refer to the board itself.

77. PMHP Survey, Q18: R521.

78. Sunquist and Becker, "Interviews with Retired Missionaries," Montreat, NC, March 7, 2006, 7.

79. Such comments referred to the UPCNA and PCUSA merger in 1958, as well as to that of the UPCUSA and PCUS in 1983. However, most of the comments specifically discussed the stark change between the PCUS mission board and the resulting PC(USA) board after the northern and southern churches united.

80. PMHP Survey, Q18: R570.

81. Ibid., Q18: R405.

82. Ibid., Q18: R354.

83. Sunquist and Becker, "Interviews with Retired Missionaries," Montreat, NC, March 7, 2006, 6.

84. Ibid., Q18: R645.

85. Ibid., Q18: R382.

86. Ibid., Q18: R14.

87. "After our field missions were destroyed, the authority over funds and personnel that had been lodged in field missions was returned to the staff in N.Y. There was no public recognition of the fact that the N.Y. staff was gradually becoming more and more powerful, and their bureaucracies were becoming larger and larger. We, as career missionaries, had absolutely no voice in either funding or placement of personnel. On the other hand (inevitably), we were foreigners in the countries where we served. Regardless of how deep the inculturation or how well Arabic had been mastered, at the end of the day, we were still foreigners. This meant that 'partnership in mission' translated into a mating of bureaucracies, with all career missionaries left out of the equation. The sad part is that no one noticed the loss of authenticity and realism that resulted from this equation." Ibid., Q24: R14.

88. "The most disappointing aspect of our whole missionary service was that our worst relations (as a project) were with our Mission Board in N.Y., who sent a representative out once a year who listened to the wrong people (the opportunists who spoke English), made promises that couldn't be kept, and inaccurately reported to N.Y." Ibid., Q18: R787.

89. Ibid., Q18: R758.

90. Sunquist, "Interviews with Retired Missionaries," New Wilmington, PA, July 25, 2005, 2.

91. Sunquist and Becker, "Interviews with Retired Missionaries," Duarte, CA, March 4, 2006, 30.
92. Sunquist and Becker, "Interviews with Retired Missionaries," Montreat, NC, March 7, 2006, 12.
93. PMHP Survey, Q24: R581, R467.

Chapter 7. Latin America and the Caribbean

1. UPCUSA GA Minutes, 1959, 109, Report of the Board of Foreign Missions.
2. W. Stanley Rycroft, *Religion and Faith in Latin America* (Philadelphia: Westminster Press, 1958), 9.
3. To distinguish between mission (as in the mission of the church) and a Mission (as referring to a North American missionary organization) when the latter is meant, the word Mission will be capitalized.
4. PCUSA GA Minutes, 1945, 82, Report of the Board of Foreign Missions.
5. PCUS GA Minutes, 1944, 49, Report of the Executive Committee of Foreign Missions.
6. PCUSA GA Minutes, 1947, 98, Board of Foreign Missions.
7. Alice J. McClelland, *Mission to Mexico* (Nashville: Board of World Missions, 1960), 69.
8. Ibid., 72.
9. PCUS GA Minutes, 1954, 120, Report of the Board of World Missions.
10. Correspondence with Robert L. Armistead, former PCUS missionary to Mexico.
11. PCUS GA Minutes, 1976, 421, Report of the Division of International Mission.
12. UPCUSA GA Minutes, 1979, 346, COEMAR.
13. Correspondence with Robert L. Armistead.
14. Article on National Presbyterian Church of Mexico Web site, www.binational ministry.org/INPMHistory.htm. Accessed November 21, 2007.
15. Karla Ann Koll, "Volcanic Revolution of the Home Mission Fields: Response of the United Presbyterian Church in the United States of America to the Revolution in Cuba," *Journal of Presbyterian History* 82, no. 3 (Fall 2004): 154.
16. Ibid., 162.
17. From a written survey completed by Ms. Lois Kroehler, former mission worker in Cuba.
18. Koll, "Volcanic Revolution," 160.
19. From the Web site of the PC(USA), www.pcusa.org/worldwide. Accessed November 21, 2007.
20. Ibid.
21. Ibid.
22. Correspondence with Karla Ann Koll.
23. PCUSA GA Minutes, 1951, 117, Board of Foreign Missions.
24. Correspondence with Karla Ann Koll.
25. PCUSA GA Minutes, 1963, 40, COEMAR.
26. Correspondence with Karla Ann Koll.
27. PC(USA) Web site.
28. Alfalit International, Inc., is a faith-based nonprofit organization, founded in 1961, that provides programs to the most needy of the world in literacy, basic education, preschool, health, nutrition, and community development in Latin America, the Caribbean, Africa, Portugal, and the United States.
29. Paul E. Pierson, *A Younger Church in Search of Maturity* (San Antonio, TX: Trinity University Press, 1974), 202.
30. Much of the material that follows relates to the changes in structures in Brazil and is taken from the author's essay "From Sending Church to Partner Church:

The Brazil Experience," *Journal of Presbyterian History* 81, no. 3 (Fall 2003), as well as from his personal experience as a missionary of the PCUS and PC(USA) to Brazil from 1963 through 1996.

31. T. Watson Street, *On the Growing Edge of the Church* (Richmond, VA: John Knox Press, 1965), 60; emphasis added by author.

32. The Archdiocese of São Paulo secretly prepared the book and originally published it in Brazil under the title *Brasil nunca mais* [literally, *Brazil Never Again*] (Petrópolis, Brazil: Editoria Vozes, 1985); ET, *Torture in Brazil*, trans. Jaime Wright, ed. Joan Dassin (Austin: Institute of Latin American Studies, University of Texas, 1998).

33. *Brazil Notes* (published by the Central Brazil Mission of the UPCUSA), March 30, 1974 (no. 4), 2.

34. Ibid., No. 6 (April 27, 1973).

35. Tensions were only raised when Richard Shaull was selected on the important "Advisory Study" as the representative from Brazil. See chapter 3 on the "Advisory Study" of COEMAR.

36. Bylaws of the PCPC, 1973, article 2, first paragraph, 2. Copy in author's possession.

37. Letter from Clifton Kirkpatrick, Director of the Division of International Mission, July 12, 1983. Copy in author's possession.

38. American Presbyterian missionary presence was declining much more, as might be expected, from the Northern church (UPCUSA) than from the Southern church (PCUS). The Northern Presbyterian Church numbers went from 53 (1945) to 80 (1955) to 71 (1965) to 14 (1975) to 11 (1982). The PCUS was much larger through the 1970s, although it started out almost identically after World War II: 52 (1945), 110 (1955), 169 (1965), 125 (estimated in 1975), and 72 (1982). Thus, the loss of this Brazilian connection was much greater to the PCUS than to the UPCUSA.

39. Minutes of the Presbyterian Mission of Brazil, July 1989.

40. Web site of the PC(USA), www.pcusa.org/worldwide/chile/international.htm.

41. Roberto E. Seel, *Breve historia de Presbiterianos* (Brief History of Presbyterians) (Monterrey, Ca: published privately, 1994), 83.

42. PCUSA GA Minutes, 1946, 79, BFM.

43. Web site of the PC(USA), www.pcusa.org/worldwide/chile/international.htm.

44. UPCUSA GA Minutes, 1975, 561, Report of The Program Agency.

45. Correspondence with Robert L. Armistead, former PCUS missionary to Chile.

46. PCUSA GA Minutes, 1946, 84, BFM.

47. Ibid., 1957, 79, BFM.

48. Ibid., 1944, 79, BFM.

49. From a written survey completed by the Reverend G. Lee Stewart, former mission worker in Colombia.

50. PCUSA GA Minutes, 1959, 110, COEMAR.

51. Ibid., 1965, 97, COEMAR.

52. UPCUSA GA Minutes, 1981, 323, Report of the Program Agency.

53. Correspondence with Rev. John H. Sinclair, former Area Secretary for Latin America with COEMAR, and Rev. Robert E. Seel, former Presbyterian missionary to Venezuela.

54. Ibid.

55. John H. Sinclair, in *La historia general de la iglesia Cristiana en la América Latina* [The General History of the Christian Church in Latin America], vol. 7 (Salamanca, Spain: CEHILA-Ediciones, Sígueme, 1981), 630–41, has written about this subject. He points to several factors: the lack of a strong theological seminary in the country (pastors had been trained outside the country until very recently),

the large number of nonconciliar (faith-based) missionary groups working in the country, the inability of the Presbyterian Church of Venezuela to retain newly ordained pastors (either they left the ministry for secular work or went to work in other countries, including the United States), and the lack of ecumenical connections outside of Venezuela by the national church.

56. Robert E. Seel, "Venezuelan Sojourn" (unpublished manuscript, 1995), 12.
57. Ibid., 80.
58. Ibid., 89.
59. Ibid., 75.
60. PCUS GA Minutes, 1964, 120, BWM.
61. Ibid., 1960, 15, BWM.
62. Correspondence with Maria Arroyo, PC(USA) Area Associate for Latin America.
63. Ibid.

Chapter 8. United States: God's Mission Field

1. G. Brown, *Presbyterians in World Mission* (1995), 43.
2. "Fraternal Workers to the U.S.A.," Board of Foreign Mission, Presbyterian Church U.S.A. (MRT, 4–22-58), located in Mission to the U.S.A. program files in Louisville, Ky.
3. Margaret Flory, "Walking in One Company," in "More Than They Know: The Presbyterian Mission Effort and the Advancement of Human Liberties," *Church and Society* 78, nos. 2–3 (November/December 1986–January/February 1987): 31–32.
4. John C. Moyer, "Crisis in the Nation," in "More Than They Know," 76–80.
5. A 2005 letter from PC(USA) mission coworker Donna Laubach Moros suggests, "We should put into place once again the great CRISIS IN THE NATION program done by the northern stream in the sixties. We brought in church leaders from other countries to look at ourselves, and to help us see ourselves inside out. This helped us to define a new approach to urban ministry, and to help our presbyteries and synods to structure meaningful ways to communicate and to rearrange ourselves, so we could respond to God's call to us in the midst of our problems of racial injustice and the war in Vietnam." Witherspoon Society Web site, Archives 2005, http://www.witherspoonsociety.org/2005/oct 2005.htm.
6. A program of leadership development, the first International Study Fellowship took place in 1963–64 and was sponsored by the World Student Christian Federation and COEMAR. The 23 participants from 19 countries lived together in Christian community in Princeton, N.J., for five months, served in university ministries around the world for four months, and gathered for a final consultation in Geneva. The ISF model was replicated in other regions of the world, particularly in Asia. Margaret Flory, *From Past to Future: Experiments in Global Bridging* (New York: World Christian Student Federation History Project, 1977), 73–86.
7. Frontier Internship in Mission was to be an ecumenical program, but only the Presbyterians had the combination of vision, finances, and administrative will to launch and sustain FIM during the first decade of its life. Black, *Merging Mission and Unity*, 127.
8. Videotaped interview with Margaret Flory, 2004 (Louisville, KY: Office of Communications).
9. Margaret Flory, *Dear House, Mission Becomes You* (Louisville, KY: Bridge Resources, 2000), 44.
10. Clifton Kirkpatrick's memo to Lew Lancaster, August 25, 1992 (Louisville, KY: Bi-National Service files, Worldwide Ministries Division).

11. In 1981, 33 percent of Bi-National Servants had previously studied or served in programs Margaret Flory initiated and administered. Barbara Roche, "Initiating and Sustaining Ecumenical Ministries: A Study of the Ministry of Margaret Flory, 1951–1980" (DMin diss., San Francisco Theological Seminary, 1983), 147.

12. Ibid.

13. Bi-National Servants address list, 2003–4 (Louisville, KY: Bi-National Service files, Worldwide Ministries Division).

14. Roche, "Initiating and Sustaining Ecumenical Ministries," 146.

15. Jean S. Stoner, ed., *Voices from Korea, U.S.A., and Brazil: The Reformed Faith and Global Economy* (Louisville, KY: Worldwide Ministries Division, 2001).

16. Mission to the U.S.A. (MUSA) began as a pattern of missionary service in the People in Mission Office of the Program Agency, United Presbyterian Church (U.S.A.). In 1988 it became a part of the Mutual Mission Office of the Global Mission Ministry Unit of the reunited Presbyterian Church (U.S.A.). The 1993 restructuring lodged MUSA in the People in Mutual Mission program area of the Worldwide Ministries Division. In 2001 MUSA moved to the Ecumenical Partnership program area of Worldwide Ministries.

17. Margaret Flory, *Moments in Time: One Woman's Ecumenical Journey* (New York: Friendship Press, 1995), 88–89.

18. Lynn S. Larson, "Our Guest Served Us as a Missionary," *Mission to the U.S.A. Occasional Bulletin*, February 1978, The Program Agency, United Presbyterian Church, 16.

19. "One Mission under God (A Report Approved by the 119th General Assembly), with Mission Direction Statements (Adopted as Expressions of the Report)," Mission Direction Statements, 5. "Partnership, #2," in *God's Claims, Our Mission*, ed. Marvin Simmers (Atlanta: General Assembly Mission Board, Presbyterian Church, U.S., 1983), 110.

20. Patricia Lloyd-Sidle, Memo RE: Mission to the U.S.A. Consultations, January 12, 1993 (Louisville, KY: Mission to the U.S.A. files, Worldwide Ministries Division).

21. "Our Learnings Come Through Encounter," *Mission to the U.S.A. Occasional Bulletin*, Summer 1981, 3.

22. "Mission to the U.S.A. Personnel: 1980–1991," two-page statistical report (Louisville, KY: Mission to the U.S.A. files, Worldwide Ministries Division).

23. Ibid.

24. MUSA Participants by Country/Region and by Synod (Louisville, KY: Mission to the U.S.A. files, Worldwide Ministries Division).

25. Ecumenical Working Group on Mission to the U.S.A., Affiliated with Church World Service and Witness of the NCCC/USA, *Reaching Out to You: An Orientation Guide for Visitors to the U.S.A*, 1993; revised, 1998.

26. United Church of Christ in the Philippines, *Partnership in Mission*, 1989.

27. Thomas John, *A Strange Accent*, vi.

28. Anna May Say Pa, *Dancing in Winter: Reflections of a Missionary to the United States* (Louisville, KY: Presbyterian Church (U.S.A.), Worldwide Ministries Division, 2000), 42.

29. Videotaped interview with Margaret Flory, 2004.

30. Flory, "Walking in One Company," 35.

31. *Mission to the U.S.A.: Occasional Bulletin*, Summer 1981, 1.

32. Wickeri, *Partnership, Solidarity, and Friendship*, 11.

33. Ibid., 15.

Chapter 9. East Asia: Destructions, Divisions, and Abundance

1. *Presbyterian Outlook* (which came from *The Presbyterian of the South, Southwestern Presbyterian*, and *The Presbyterian Standard*), *Presbyterian Survey, Presbyterians*

Today, A.D., Southern Presbyterian Journal, Christian Observer, and *Presbyterian Life.*

2. Janet Harbison Penfield, "Presbyterians' Thai Tie," *Presbyterian Life,* January 15, 1971, 26.
3. PCUSA BFM Report, 1956, 13.
4. This includes high schools, Bible institutes, and colleges.
5. From the excellent list of hospitals and schools in G. Thompson Brown's *Earthen Vessels and Transcendent Power: American Presbyterians in China, 1837–1952* (Maryknoll, NY: Orbis Books, 1997), 223–30.
6. In Korea, the church still grew at a rapid rate throughout the Japanese occupation.
7. Quoted from G. Brown, *Earthen Vessels and Transcendent Power,* 272.
8. Ibid., 64.
9. PCUSA BFM, *Report of the Deputation . . . to China* (1947), 2–24.
10. Self-propagating, self-supporting, and self-governing.
11. At the time there were about 700,000 to 800,000 Protestant Christians in China. Today there are between 30 and 80 million, which represents the largest growth of a national church in the history of Christianity.
12. See Wallace C. Merwin and Francis P. Jones, eds., *Documents of the Three-Self Movement* (New York: Far Eastern Office of Division of Foreign Missions, NCC, 1963), 15.
13. For a discussion of the deep theological divisions among missionaries and Chinese Christians that surfaced in the 1920s, see Kevin Xiyi Yao's *The Fundamentalist Movement among Protestant Missionaries in China, 1920–1937* (Lanham, MD: University Press of America, 2003).
14. Pang Chi-Il is mentioned in the PCUSA GA Minutes, 1956, 19.
15. PCUSA GA Minutes, 1957, 23–24, part 2, Board Reports.
16. From the Amity Foundation Web site: "The Amity Foundation, an independent Chinese voluntary organization, was created in 1985 on the initiative of Chinese Christians to promote education, social services, health, and rural development from China's coastal provinces in the east to the minority areas of the west." http://www.amityfoundation.org/page.php?page=5. Accessed November 21, 2007.
17. From 1948 to 1987 the country was under martial law, with one party ruling the country. The special situation was called "Temporary Provisions Effective during the Period of Communist Rebellion."
18. Sunquist and Becker, "Interviews with Retired Missionaries," Montreat, NC, March 7, 2006.
19. Blake and Faith Bradley, for example, produced four booklets (1. Christian and Non-Christian in Dialog; 2. The Life of Christ; 3. Catechism; 4. The Ten Commandments) in Bunun and then helped to teach the people to read their own language. From Faith Bradley, PMHP Survey, March 2005.
20. Japan had been remarkably "open" to trade and missionary work in the late sixteenth and early seventeenth centuries, but had suddenly closed itself off to the world with the rise of the Tokugawa Shogunate and the unification of Japan beginning in 1603.
21. Samuel H. Moffett, *A History of Christianity in Asia,* vol. 2 (Maryknoll, NY: Orbis Books, 2005), 502.
22. Cogswell, *Until the Day Dawn,* 144.
23. Grace K. Kerr, "Report From Tokyo," *Presbyterian Life,* June 19, 1948, 16–18.
24. Cogswell, *Until the Day Dawn,* 176.
25. PCUSA GA Minutes, 1957, 10–15.
26. Sunquist and Becker, "Interviews with Retired Missionaries," Duarte, CA, March 2, 2006, 1.

27. Most of the retired missionaries who had worked in Korea specifically mentioned that the "Nevius Method" was the standard in Korea (see question #15 in appendix 2).
28. As this chapter was being edited, John Edward Talmage passed away on February 24, 2007, at the age of 94.
29. Sunquist and Becker, "Interviews with Retired Missionaries," Montreat, NC, March 7, 2006, 25–26.
30. One of those interned, Mr. R. O. Reiner, suffered the "water cure" (water torture: water is forced down the throat and into the stomach).
31. Harry A. Rhodes and Archibald Campbell, eds., *History of the Korea Mission, Presbyterian Church U.S.A.*, vol. 2, *1935–1959* (New York: COEMAR; Seoul: Chosen Mission Presbyterian Church U.S.A., 1964), 38.
32. The clinic was one of the first in Korea, started in 1897 by Mattie Ingold, later Mattie Tate. See George Thompson Brown, *Mission to Korea* (Nashville: Board of World Missions, 1962), 41.
33. Paul Shields Crane, PMHP survey filled out for this project.
34. Howard Moffett kept a framed picture of the province in his office with a light marking every village where a converted patient had planted a church. Over 140 lights were last seen on the unique map.
35. PCUSA GA Minutes, 1956, 15–19.
36. The PCK has membership in the WCC and over two million members.
37. According to the PROK Web site, they split off to retain freedom of interpretation of the Bible, opposing the "conservative, fundamentalists' theology propounded by the missionaries." Their Chosun Theological Seminary (now the graduate department of Hanshin University) made more use of higher criticism, Minjung theology, and other contextual theologies. Presently the PROK has about 323,000 members in 1,442 congregations.
38. A member of a newer global family known as the International Reformed Fellowship, the Hapdong runs the Chongsin University and Seminary in Seoul and has about two million members.
39. PCUS GA Minutes, 1954, 160–61.
40. Bible Clubs were started by PCUSA missionary Francis Kinsler in 1930 to provide basic, well-rounded education as well as leadership skills for the poor and disenfranchised young people. After the war over 50,000 children enrolled in this unique program.
41. See chapters 3 and 4 for a discussion of *An Advisory Study.*
42. Rhee was Moderator of the PC(USA) in 2000 and was President of the National Council of Churches in 1992–93.
43. Billy Graham's wife, Ruth Bell Graham, attended the famous school for missionary children in Pyongyang. Her father, L. Nelson Bell, was a Presbyterian medical missionary to China.
44. The second Protestant church opened was the rebuilt church where Kim Il Sung's mother, Kang Pan Sok, served as a deaconess.
45. The PCUS did not work in the Philippines.
46. Presbyterian Henry D. Jones pioneered this type of mission in Shanghai in 1947.
47. Alexander Christie, for example, wrote *The Old Testament Survey, How to Study the Bible* (translated and used in East Pakistan [Bangladesh], *The Church in the Book of Acts and in the Philippines,* and others.
48. Even though we assume that missionary service involves medical work, it was only in the 1840s that medical skill in the West had enough to offer that it began to be one of the standard tools in the missionary toolbox. Previously literacy, education, and agricultural work were the basic ministries alongside evangelism, church planting, and leadership development.

49. Sunquist and Becker, "Interviews with Retired Missionaries," Duarte, CA, March 2, 2006, 30.
50. Ibid., March 4, 2006, 14.
51. W. Stanley Rycroft and Myrtle M. Clemmer, *A Factual Study of Asia* (New York: Commission on Ecumenical Mission and Relations, 1963).
52. Quoting Rajah H. Manikam, the report accurately notes that the arrival of Christianity in Asia consistently serves to challenge and bring some revival to the major religions in the region. "Whenever Christianity is proclaimed in the East, the resurgence of ancient religions takes place: Hinduism, Buddhism or Islam is aroused to new life." Ibid., 152, citing Manikam's *Christianity and the Asian Revolution* (New York: Friendship Press, 1954), 169.
53. Rycroft and Clemmer, *Factual Study of Asia*, 159–60.
54. Amity Foundation Web site, http://www.amityprinting.com/englishweb/efirst.htm. Accessed March 25, 2007.
55. Herbert G. Grether, "God's Work in 'The Land of the Free,'" *Presbyterian Life*, June 15, 1965, 30.
56. Taiwan had been ruled by Japan until the Japanese defeat in 1945. For a four-year period the Taiwanese viewed the Chinese as liberators, but the Chinese briefly reasserted their authority over the island, and then their Republic of China government in exile came to rule Taiwan directly.
57. The official date when Vietnam was reunited as a communist country.

Chapter 10. American Presbyterians and the Middle East

1. Syngman Rhee, Marian McClure, Jack Lorimer, Victor Makari, Heather Sharkey, Tharwat Wahba, and Paula Skreslet were all kind enough to read earlier drafts of this chapter. I am grateful to these colleagues for the questions, challenges, observations, and suggestions they so thoughtfully raised in response to what I had written.
2. Perhaps the first to champion the notion of Protestant outreach to Orthodox Christians in the Middle East was the British Anglican chaplain Claudius Buchanan, who suggested this strategy in *Christian Researches in Asia* (Boston: Samuel T. Armstrong, 1811) as a way to begin evangelizing Muslims and Jews in the region. That his idea had gained traction among American Protestants even before the first American missionaries had been sent to the Middle East (Pliny Fisk and Levi Parsons in 1819) is proved by the example of William Goodell. Among Goodell's unpublished papers now held in the archives of Andover Newton Theological Seminary is a student essay that outlines the prospects for missions to Armenians in the Middle East. According to a note in these materials, Goodell delivered an address on this subject to Andover's Society of Inquiry Respecting Missions in September 1817. By December 1818 he had transcribed his essay (with quotes from Buchanan included) into the collected papers of the Society under the title "Brief History and Present State of Armenia as a Missionary Field." After some years of residence in Beirut, Goodell settled in Constantinople by 1831, where he concentrated his efforts among Armenians living in the Ottoman capital.
3. For Egypt, the UPCNA GA Minutes, 1930, 690, show a total of 144 career missionaries and 92 short-termers at work in that country during 1929. In the same year, the Board of Foreign Missions (BFM) indicated in its report to the PCUSA General Assembly (on a foldout statistical table) that it was supporting 117 career missionaries in Persia (Iran), 45 in Syria, and 6 in Mesopotamia (Iraq). The BFM of the PCUSA also reported a total of 19 "special term and affiliated" missionaries under appointment in the Middle East (13 in Persia, 6 in Syria).

4. The country totals for 1944 are as follows: 54 in Egypt, 68 in Iran, 30 in Syria-Lebanon, 2 in Iraq.

5. The 1950 roster of single women missionaries in Egypt supported by the Women's General Missionary Society of the UPCNA provides a vivid illustration of the early postwar demographic situation of Presbyterian missions in the Middle East. Out of a group of 59 missionaries, 10 were first appointed before 1920, 18 in the 1920s, 5 in the 1930s, and 26 had been added since 1944. For these data, see UPCNA GA Minutes, 1950, 1148.

6. The full name of the new mission agency, created at the time of the 1958 merger not only for the purpose of supervising the work of all the missions but also for managing the denomination's ecumenical commitments, was the Commission on Ecumenical Mission and Relations. The country totals reported for 1958 were 114 career missionaries in Egypt, 79 in Iran, 59 in Syria-Lebanon, and 7 in Iraq. Two other individuals also residing in the Middle East were designated as representatives of COEMAR and so were counted separately. The exact number of short-term missionaries is not possible to determine exactly, based on the records to which I have had access so far, but seems to have been not less than 70 for 1958, with about half assigned to Egypt.

7. This policy is referred to in the BFM Report of the PCUSA GA Minutes, 1951, 158, part 2.

8. Synod of the Nile is but one name that continues to be used to refer to the largest Protestant denomination in Egypt. Other official names in our period have been the Coptic Evangelical Church and the Evangelical Presbyterian Church of Egypt (since 2004). Within Egypt the church is often referred to simply as the Evangelical Church. To distinguish this body from several of its Middle Eastern sister churches that travel under similar names, I will usually refer to it as the Egyptian Evangelical Church.

9. In 1958 the Syria-Lebanon mission of the PCUSA was still managing 11 schools in the two countries. At the same time, the national Synod was responsible for operating another 16 schools. See the PCUSA BFM Report for 1957, which was published in the 1958 Minutes of the newly formed UPCUSA, part 2, 134–35.

10. Good record keeping could pay dividends in the end, however. This was demonstrated in the case of the American Mission in Egypt, which successfully recovered compensation from the government of Egypt for land and buildings expropriated by various means in the two decades after the revolution in 1952. In the context of improving relations with the United States after 1973, Egypt was prompted to settle outstanding claims lodged against it by American corporate entities and citizens. An original award of two million dollars (doubled a decade later, when an unexpected payment of "interest" on the first sum was determined also to be owed to validated claimants) was disbursed through the Mission to the Synod of the Nile and various ministries related to it. Commission representative Willis A. McGill coordinated the complex and tedious effort to collect all the documents needed to sustain the Mission's claim; the success of the case he presented depended in large part on the habit of the organization to be held accountable in the smallest detail to its many supporters back home through the BFM. This, too, was a value carried forward into the second half of the twentieth century from an earlier era.

11. For this detail, I am indebted to an account of the Cairo Center written by one of its past directors, Richard Gibson, whose historical summary has appeared in Jack [John G.] Lorimer, *The Presbyterian Experience in Egypt 1950–2000* (Denver, CO: Outskirts Press, 2007), 47–49 [hereafter, Lorimer].

12. On the contributions of the mission through Assiut College to dairy farming and other animal husbandry projects in the 1950s, see Lorimer, 97–102.

13. The story of CEOSS is told biographically by David Virtue in *A Vision of Hope: The Story of Samuel Habib* (Oxford: Regnum Books, 1996). See also Marjorie J. Dye, *The CEOSS Story* (Cairo: Dar al-Thaqafa, 1979), and Lorimer, 55–95.

14. What follows in the next three paragraphs is based partly on survey data collected through the Presbyterian Mission History Project. Also relevant is the chapter on "missionary lives" in Lorimer, 217–26.

15. From its inception in 1921 (as a continuation of the missionary-run Cairo Study Center) up through the mid-1950s, the School of Oriental Studies at AUC had an indirect relationship with the American Mission in Egypt. New missionaries were regularly sent to the institution for instruction in Arabic. Several members of the Mission served as faculty members, including Samuel Zwemer, C. C. Adams, and E. E. Elder. Subsequently, the School of Oriental Studies would be succeeded by the Center for Arabic Study Abroad (CASA), perhaps the leading program in the world for advanced training in Arabic for non-native speakers.

16. As the mission organizations were dissolved one by one after 1958, other arrangements were devised to compensate for the loss of their orientation function, including the creation of an Ecumenical Study Center at Stony Point, New York. Although probably successful in inculcating a new approach to mission theology, longer programs of orientation run by headquarters before the departure of missionaries could not begin to substitute for the cultural learning that used to take place on the field.

17. This is a recurrent theme in the BFM reports on Iran prepared during this period for inclusion in the PCUSA General Assembly Minutes, beginning with the 1944 report: "Never was there a time when the doors of evangelistic work were so wide open as now" (1945 Minutes, part 2, 66). The lifting of restrictions on the movement of foreigners in the country is noted in the 1950 report: "There is great freedom for evangelization and proclamation of the Gospel" (PCUSA 1951 Minutes, part 2, 72).

18. An extended discussion of the position(s) taken by Presbyterians on the Arab-Israeli conflict since 1944 will follow below.

19. On the affinity of Presbyterian missionaries in Lebanon with expressions of Arab nationalism between the two world wars, see Ellen Fleischmann, "The Impact of American Protestant Missions in Lebanon on the Construction of Female Identity, c. 1860–1950," *Islam and Christian-Muslim Relations* 13 (2002): 420–22. Also relevant more generally is Joseph L. Grabill, "Protestant Diplomacy and Arab Nationalism," *American Presbyterians* 64 (1986): 113–24.

20. In a recent review of this literature, historian Heather J. Sharkey draws attention to the "pathbreaking" role played by one book in particular, published in 1953 in Beirut: Mustafa Khalidi and 'Umar Farrukh, *Al-tabshir wa-al-isti'mar fi al-balad al-'arabiyya* [Evangelism and Imperialism in the Arab World]. For Sharkey's analysis, see her "Arabic Antimissionary Treatises: Muslim Responses to Christian Evangelism in the Modern Middle East," *International Bulletin of Missionary Research* 28 (2004): 98–104. In an essay soon to be published, Sharkey puts an earlier generation of Muslim responses to Protestant missionary activity into the broader context of interwar Arab nationalist attitudes and an emerging human rights discourse to which Protestant missionaries were actively contributing: "Muslim Apostasy, Christian Conversion and Religious Freedom in Egypt: A Study of American Missionaries, Western Imperialism, and Human Rights Agendas," in *Proselytization Revisited: Rights Talk, Free Markets, and Culture Wars*, ed. Rosalind I. J. Hackett (London: Equinox, forthcoming 2008). In Mahmoud Haddad, "Syrian Muslims' Attitudes toward Foreign Missionaries in the Late Nineteenth and Twentieth Centuries," in *Altruism and Imperialism: Western Cultural and Religious Missions in the Middle East*, ed. Eleanor H. Tejirian

and Reeva Spector Simon (New York: Middle East Institute, Columbia University, 2002), 253–74, several Muslim evaluations of Protestant mission activities at the turn of the twentieth century are described, including the position taken by Rashid Rida (1865–1935), editor of the influential early Salafist journal *al-Manar*. Rida expresses appreciation for the educational efforts of American missionaries in Syria, urges tolerance in the face of Christian proselytizing activities, while advising Muslim students in the Syrian Protestant College to emulate the methods of the missionaries as they seek to defend Islam.

21. Lorimer discusses this issue in his chapter on mission schools (1–17).

22. Black was executive secretary of the UPCNA's BFM before the merger. At the same time, J. Smith was a mission executive with the BFM of the PCUSA. Each would eventually have a chance to lead COEMAR. Both credit Charles Leber, COEMAR's first executive head, as the driving force behind the vision that brought COEMAR and its new approach to mission into being. Cf. J. Smith, *From Colonialism to World Community*; and Black, *Merging Mission and Unity*.

23. For a description of this consultation, see Hogg, *New Day Dawning*.

24. Just how important this women's organization was to the UPCNA mission in Egypt is indicated by the statistics reported for the mid-1950s. According to the UPCNA Minutes, 1955, 1688–94, the WGMS supported 36 long-term women missionaries in Egypt and 21 short-termers in 1954, while the BFM listed 37 career missionaries on its rolls. Earl E. Elder, *Vindicating a Vision: The Story of the American Mission in Egypt, 1854–1954* (Philadelphia: United Presbyterian Board of Foreign Missions, 1958), 317–18, supplies the names of six male short-termers on the field in 1954, all presumably supported by the BFM.

25. This move replicated within the UPCNA what the PCUSA had already done in the early 1920s, when its women's mission organizations were absorbed into a centralized mission structure. On the PCUSA's earlier reorganization of its mission bureaucracy, see Richard W. Reifsnyder, "Managing the Mission: Church Restructuring in the Twentieth Century," in Coalter, Mulder, and Weeks, *The Organizational Revolution: Presbyterians and American Denominationalism*, (Louisville, KY: Westminster/John Knox Press, 1992), esp. 55–63.

26. The first part of these funds became available in 1966, according to the COEMAR report submitted to the 1967 UPCUSA General Assembly (see Minutes, part 2, 3, 91–92). The report indicates an intention to allocate some $16 million, in such grants to meet these capital needs in the course of the campaign.

27. Lorimer (16) reports a total of 25 schools in the church's educational system as of 2003.

28. Discussed in Lorimer (20–24), where the continuing chagrin of the local Christian community at the loss of "their" hospital is noted.

29. These examples from Iran are briefly described in Black, *Merging Mission and Unity*, 122–24. Black alludes to a certain eagerness widely shared among the executives back home for seeking ways to work cooperatively with secular authorities abroad at this time (the 1960s), but admits that few of these arrangements so carefully negotiated over many years were successful in the end. As Black observes, the executives eventually learned through their experience that "working with secular institutions to accomplish the goals of the Christian mission is not easy" (*Merging Mission and Unity*, 125).

30. Initially (1968–76), the Schutz School was linked to Tarkio College in Missouri, one of the colleges historically connected to the UPCNA.

31. Lorimer (209) discusses the advantages of such an arrangement in the context of Egypt.

32. See the 1967 Minutes, part 2, 112, on the COEMAR report. Commission representatives are included in the totals given for fraternal workers. In addition, 19

missionaries in the Middle East (3 career and 16 special term) were reported to be receiving their support from sources other than COEMAR.

33. Church officials also cited financial exigencies at home as a reason for cutting further the number of missionaries on the field. In a review of its activities between 1972 and 1987, the Program Agency put the situation in these terms: "The Program Agency inherited a declining level of missionary personnel. This decline had originally been strategic, but by the early 1970s had become increasingly driven by limits on available resources in the face of worldwide inflation." Cf. Minutes of the 1988 General Assembly (part 1, 764). One former missionary in Lebanon, in her response to the PMHP Survey form, reported having been told that the reason for her termination in 1972 was "the church's financial crunch engendered by the Angela Davis affair."

34. See COEMAR report in the 1970 Minutes, part 2, 43. Lorimer (243–46) discusses this episode in some detail and provides the names of 25 individuals invited back to Egypt after the moratorium. He recalls COEMAR initially proposing that the WCC conduct these negotiations on behalf of the UPCUSA, but the Evangelical Church insisted that its longtime American church partner also be directly involved. According to Black (*Merging Mission and Unity*, 116–17), the idea behind this strategy was to encourage the Egyptian church to invite non-American churches to contribute some of the needed personnel and so initiate a new set of ecumenical relations through shared mission service. "Career" nomenclature is not used in the 1970 Minutes. In the statistical table presented as part of COEMAR's report, all personnel are considered "term" appointees (from two to 10 years). As before, COEMAR representatives and their spouses were technically understood to be members of the Commission's executive staff deployed abroad.

35. Ten fraternal workers appointed to Lebanon are listed in the "1979 Mission Yearbook for Prayer and Study": Benjamin and Carol Weir, Kenneth and Ethel Bailey, Else Farr, Dorathea Teeter, Edwin and Arpine Hanna, plus Hans and Anna Schellenberg. Except for the Schellenbergs (first sent to Lebanon in 1969), all of these Presbyterian workers began their mission service in the Middle East no later than the mid-1950s.

36. The exception is Else Farr, who stayed in Lebanon until 1987.

37. See the COEMAR Report in the 1970 Minutes, part 2, 43, where 71 fraternal workers and Commission representatives are counted, plus 4 other missionaries with other support. In addition, the statistics list 17 volunteers in mission in Iran, compared to 5 each in Lebanon and Egypt.

38. This is the number given in the 1976 Program Agency Report, in UPCUSA Minutes, part 1, 572). A spike in the number of "overseas associates" listed in these statistics for Iran (10) likely indicates that additional Presbyterian mission personnel had managed to secure other support while remaining in their positions.

39. Ewing Bailey, then head of the American Mission in Egypt, seems to have drawn this conclusion after the events of 1956. See Lorimer, 237–38.

40. Farr reported on the beginning of this project in the "1980 Mission Yearbook for Prayer and Study." The new hymnal was finally published in Cyprus in 1990. Again, see her interview with Sunquist and Becker, "Interviews with Retired Missionaries," Duarte, CA, March 3, 2006.

41. John Lorimer, *Tarikh al-kanisa*, 5 vols. (Cairo: Dar al-Thaqafa, 1982–91).

42. Ragheb Moftah, Margit Toth, and Martha Roy, *The Coptic Orthodox Liturgy of St. Basil: With Complete Musical Transcription* (Cairo: American University in Cairo Press, 1998).

43. For more on Martha Roy's career and accomplishments, see Lorimer, 131–33. A measure of Roy's influence is also reflected in the special prominence given to her

work in the commemorative history volume issued by the Evangelical Presbyterian Church of Egypt on the occasion of its 150th anniversary. See Emil Zaki, *Al-kanisa al-injiliyya al-mashikhiyya bi-misr: Mi'at wa khamsun sana* (Cairo: Dar al-Thaqafa, 2005), 86.

44. Kenneth E. Bailey, *Poet and Peasant: A Literary-Cultural Approach to the Parables in Luke* (Grand Rapids: Eerdmans, 1976); idem, *Finding the Lost: Cultural Keys to Luke 15* (St. Louis: Concordia Publishing House, 1992); these are perhaps the best known of Bailey's print publications. Based on this research is a feature-length film (*Finding the Lost*), produced in Egypt with professional actors, for which Bailey wrote the Arabic screenplay.

45. It may be added that Roy, Lorimer, and Bailey were all children of UPCNA missionaries in Egypt; and that Roy, Lorimer, and Farr served as short-termers before their appointments as career missionaries.

46. An early example is Norman Horner's appointment in 1968. According to his own account, he was asked to do research and consultation on interchurch relationships, especially with Orthodox and Eastern-rite Catholic Churches. Cf. Horner, "My Pilgrimage in Mission," *International Bulletin of Missionary Research* 14 (1990): 36.

47. Examples include a long list of publications from Mark N. Swanson on the Arabic Christian theological tradition. For part of Swanson's period of service at the Evangelical Theological Seminary in Cairo, the Presbyterian Church (U.S.A.) shared in his support with the Evangelical Lutheran Church in America. Also at the Evangelical Theological Seminary in Cairo was Stephen J. Davis, among whose most recent publications on Coptic Christianity is *The Early Coptic Papacy: The Egyptian Church and Its Leadership in Late Antiquity* (Cairo: American University in Cairo Press, 2004). Stanley H. Skreslet has contributed a Greek New Testament grammar in Arabic, entitled *Usul al-lugha al-yunaniyya lil-'ahd al-jadid* (Cairo: Bible Society of Egypt, 1995).

48. The Presbyterian Mission in Syria-Lebanon was dissolved in 1959. The Iran Mission followed suit in 1965. In Egypt, the missionary association held its last meeting in 1966; the American Mission in Egypt ceased to be an active administrative structure in 1968. Presbyterian activities in Iraq were administered on the field through the joint structure of the United Mission in Iraq, until it disbanded in the late 1960s.

49. This was one of the reasons why COEMAR wanted to negotiate the return of its missionaries to Egypt after the 1967 moratorium through the WCC. From the perspective of COEMAR's executives, a good outcome for these negotiations would have seen the Egyptian Evangelical Church establishing new relationships with a variety of overseas church partners in order to meet any ongoing needs they had for mission coworkers from abroad. On this idea and a related push by COEMAR at about the same time to step up its promotion of "three-way mission," see Black (*Merging Mission and Unity*, 92–94, 116–17) and Lorimer. As Black admits, the logistical difficulties posed by "three-way mission" (i.e., one denominational mission board paying the costs of missionaries from a second nation who serve in a third country) have prevented it from being widely adopted in the Middle East or anywhere else.

50. A turning point may have been reached in the late 1970s in this regard. In the "1980 Mission Yearbook for Prayer and Study" (161), an insert quote from John G. Lorimer indicates that welcoming and introducing visiting American groups to the work of the church in Egypt had become part of what Presbyterian missionaries in that country were expected to do. More generally, at a 1986 Presbyterian Church (U.S.A.) consultation event in Larnaca, Cyprus, with the Synod of the Nile and the Synod of Syria and Lebanon, this same interpretive task was

identified as a priority for all three church bodies. The report from this consultation is cited in David Dawson, "Presbyterian Missionaries in the Middle East" (STM thesis, Yale Divinity School, 1987), 68.

51. Founded in 1929, the Near East Christian Council for Missionary Cooperation became the Near East Council of Churches (NECC) in 1964. A decade later, three groups of churches (Oriental Orthodox, Eastern Orthodox, and Protestant/Episcopal) joined together to create the Middle East Council of Churches. The MECC was further expanded in 1990, when seven Catholic bodies in the region joined the organization as its fourth "family" of churches, a development that has made this regional council the most ecumenical in the world. Presbyterians, initially missionaries and then representatives of the churches they founded, have been very active participants in the work of the NECC/MECC.

52. Paul A. Hopkins draws attention to the important role played by Clifford Earle in the 1950s and 1960s during his period of service in New York in a variety of capacities. Cf. Hopkins, "Presbyterians and the Middle East Conflict," *American Presbyterians* 68 (1990): 143–65. Hopkins is particularly informative with respect to the internal dynamic then at work within the Presbyterian national offices, where some national mission and Christian education specialists pushed a hard-line Israeli position at the behest of Jewish colleagues with whom they had worked closely in the civil rights movement or on related social issues (for Hopkins, Earle is a prime example of this tendency), while the foreign mission executives were generally more sympathetic to the concerns of Arab Christian partner churches. Another New York–based Presbyterian executive who took an active interest in Middle East policy issues was Robert F. Smylie, who headed the Presbyterian United Nations office between 1975 and 2002.

53. Most recently, Margaret O. Thomas and Jay Rock have been deeply involved in Middle East issues from the perspective of interfaith relations.

54. Carol Weir's emergence as a public figure is half of the story told in Ben and Carol Weir (with Dennis Benson), *Hostage Bound, Hostage Free* (Philadelphia: Westminster Press, 1987). For her forthrightness, she has had to contend with many hostile critics. Neoconservative Robert D. Kaplan, for example, in *The Arabists: The Romance of an American Elite* (New York: Free Press, 1993), 189–91, dismisses her willingness to criticize American foreign policy in the Middle East as a sign of "estrangement" from her national background, based on a "missionary version of reality" that he predicted was about to disappear along with the "Arabist old guard" in the State Department that his book attempts to identify and discredit.

55. These points are drawn from a resolution affirmed by the 2003 General Assembly of the Presbyterian Church (U.S.A.), which to a large degree reiterated positions and wording adopted by many previous General Assemblies. Cf. 2003 Minutes, part 1, 636.

56. Both arguments are made in an op-ed piece published in the *Pittsburgh Post-Gazette* (March 30, 2005, A-17), which may be cited as an example of the vigorous campaign against divestment that was waged through local newspapers and educational events held around the country in the months after the Assembly: "The Presbyterian Divestment Train: Why Does the National Church Continue to Support Economic Sanctions against Israel?" The author of this article is a Jewish activist, but many concerned Presbyterians and other Christians accepted the validity of the charges made and on that basis were disposed to support a reversal of the policy at the church's next General Assembly in 2006. On a national level, some members of Congress also expressed their disagreement with the church's position. Cf. "Israel Divestment Blasted: Presbyterian Stance Draws Bipartisan Fire," in *Rollcall*, September 20, 2004.

57. In a recent review of this controversy, Ronald R. Stockton has outlined thirteen different interpretations of what took place at and between the 2004 and 2006 General Assemblies, concluding that all of these readings are true to some extent. Cf. Stockton, "Presbyterians, Jews and Divestment: The Church Steps Back," *Middle East Policy* 13, no. 4 (2006): 102–24. See also Stockton, "The Presbyterian Divestiture Vote and the Jewish Response," *Middle East Policy* 12, no. 4 (2005): 98–117.

58. Broad trends in Arab Christian emigration from the Middle East as well as the specific case of Palestinian out-migration are discussed in Bernard Sabella, "The Emigration of Christian Arabs: Dimensions and Causes of the Problem," in *Christian Communities in the Arab Middle East: The Challenge of the Future*, ed. Andrea Pacini (Oxford: Clarendon Press, 1988), 127–54.

Chapter 11. Africa

1. Ethiopia was one of the few African regions that resisted colonial rule. The Spanish, from Eritrea, briefly ruled in Ethiopia in 1936–1941.

2. I am much indebted to longtime missionary Harold Kurtz for his contribution to the Ethiopia section of this chapter.

3. See chapter 3 for further detail regarding *An Advisory Study*.

4. Some of the key scholars from the School of World Missions also visited the mission, studying what was occurring and advising accordingly. These included the anthropologist Alan Tippett, who made many key observations and gave advice. Even the founder of the School, Donald McGavran, visited and studied this work in southwest Ethiopia.

5. Since earliest times the Ethiopian Orthodox Church had been The Church in Ethiopia.

6. "Bethel" in Hebrew means "House of God."

7. Today there are four Bethel synods.

8. On March 27, 1977, missionary W. Donald McClure was shot and killed by Somali Marxist guerillas while he continued his work in the Ogaden Desert.

9. Efesoa Mokosso, Henry Teddy. "The United Presbyterian Mission Enterprise in Cameroun, 1879–1957." PhD diss., Howard University, 1987, 47.

10. Missionaries knew the market had expanded when on one occasion a Cameroonian plane took off 600 pounds overweight with eggs going to Chad. Sunquist and Becker, "Interviews with Retired Missionaries," Montreat, NC, March 7, 2006, 2.

11. E-mail correspondence to author, October 16, 2006.

12. James A. Cogswell, *No Turning Back: A History of American Presbyterian Mission Involvement in Sub-Saharan Africa, 1833–2000* (manuscript, 2006), 254 (cf. Philadelphia: Xlibris Corp. [distributor], 2007).

13. Ibid., manuscript, 257–58.

14. See William E. Phipps, *William Sheppard: Congo's African-American Livingstone* (Louisville, KY: Geneva Press, 2002).

15. Mavumi-sa Masakumunwa Kiantandu, "A Study of the Contribution of American Presbyterians to the Formation of the Church of Christ in Zaire with Special Reference to Indigenization, 1891–1960" (ThD diss., Union Theological Seminary in Virginia, 1978), 524.

16. D. Miller, interview with author, July 5, 2006, 5–6.

17. Authored by Levi Keidel, Mennonite Missionary to Zaire/Congo, and now available online, esp. for "prisoners": http://www.misslink.org/samson1.html.

18. Haejung and Simon Park, letter of May 13, 2001.

19. Telephone conversation with Elsbeth Shannon, October 14, 2006.

20. Congo is only slightly smaller than Sudan.
21. Mary Alueel, a Dinka woman converted in 1984, years later composed this hymn: "God has come among us *slowly*, and we didn't realize it." Although some peoples in Sudan responded quickly to the gospel, others responded very slowly.
22. This was the first foreign missionary work ever among the Murlei people.
23. The revivals in Renk united people from all churches. They were mostly seminars with various lectures and discussions on crucial aspects of the Christian life, like marriage. These bound all Christians together powerfully.
24. The Southern Sudan and rebels from the Nuba Mountains have kept an English-based education system.
25. The first lights were installed in the birthing room. On that day of installation, a child was born. Otis gave her the appropriate name of "De-light!" The whole hospital was soon solar-lighted.
26. To date, over 1,000 Malawian Presbyterians and U.S. Presbyterians have visited one another's countries on exchange trips: http://www.malawipartnership.org/about/about.shtml.

Chapter 12. Europe

1. The author of this chapter would like to thank a number of people for helping him with details relating to their areas of specialty. Art Beals made critical contributions to this chapter's treatment of Presbyterian work in Albania and Turkey. Gary Payton provided details about and reviewed the sections on Russia. Bob Lodwick helped with many details about the years before my time in the Europe office. Jane Holslag assisted with the early work in Berlin as did Bryce Little for Spain. Greg and Chris Callison assisted with information regarding the Kurds; Doug Baker filled in details about Ireland, and Burkhard Paetzold provided assistance with the Roma section. Finally Bryan Reiff, a former colleague from the Europe office, provided helpful editorial review of the whole chapter.
2. For the sake of brevity, this chapter describes Presbyterian mission without distinguishing between the three major Presbyterian churches that, over the course of the years covered in this history, united to become the Presbyterian Church (U.S.A.). Each body had its own mission board and, at least until each merged with the other Presbyterian bodies, its own mission history. For the sake of readers who may not know the history, the Presbyterian Church in the United States of America (PCUSA) and the United Presbyterian Church in North America (UPCNA) joined in 1958 to become the United Presbyterian Church in the United States of America (UPCUSA). The UPCUSA reunited with the Presbyterian Church U.S. in 1983 to become the Presbyterian Church (U.S.A.), or PC(USA).
3. Robert C. Lodwick and Bryan Reiff, who for about five years worked with author in the PC(USA) Europe office, provided critical information for this chapter about Presbyterian work in Europe.
4. For more information about CIMADE, see their Web site, http://www.cimade.org/, or the book edited by Jeanne Merle d'Aubigné, Violette Mouchon, and Émile C. Fabre, *Les clandestins de Dieu: C.I.M.A.D.E. 1939–1945* (Geneva: Labor et Fides, 1989).
5. Von Bismarck later became a professor of theology as well as president of the German public broadcasting system. In 1977 he was elected president of the Kirchentag movement in the German churches. As a church representative, von Bismarck contributed significantly to developing a dialogue between German employees and employers. Later in life, he also served as president of the Goethe Institute in Munich, a position that he held during the collapse of the East Bloc and which he used to reach out to Eastern Europeans after the fall of the Iron Curtain.

6. See A. C. Cochrane, *The Church's Confession under Hitler* (Philadelphia: Westminster Press, 1962).

7. The book *Tumbling Walls* (translated into German as *Wenn Mauern fallen* [Berlin: Wichern Verlag, 1993]) written by Rev. Walter E. James and Kristy Zatkin (La Jolla, CA: Diaspora Foundation, 1990), details the early history of these partnerships and the experiences of a large number of American and German Christians in postwar, prewall Berlin and other parts of the former East Germany.

8. The Ostkomitee understandably kept no written records and had no formal membership. Jane Holslag, a PC(USA) mission worker, is now trying to reconstruct that history.

9. Charles Yerkes died in January 1994 while still under appointment.

10. See the history of Agape written by its founder. Tullio Vinay, *Love Never Fails: The Agape Story* (Turin, Italy: Claudiana, 1996).

11. Some of the volunteers who worked at Agape during the late 1940s and 1950s eventually became very well known in the Presbyterian Church. They included Louis Evans Jr., Colleen Townsend Evans, Frank Gibson, Robert Lodwick, and Francis Rivers. Many others who served at Agape went on to be Presbyterian pastors, General Assembly staff members, or members and officers of the American Waldensian Society.

12. To learn more about Waldensians, see Giorgio Tourn, *The Waldensians: The First 800 Years (1174–1974)*, trans. Camillo P. Merlino, ed. Charles W. Arbuthnot (Turin, Italy: Claudiana; New York: America Waldensian Aid Society, 1980; distributed by Friendship Press).

13. The American Waldensian Society, or the "Society," as it is still affectionately called, was founded in 1906 by an ecumenically mixed group of large-church pastors in New York City in order to support Waldensian ministries in Italy. In 2007, the Society celebrated its one hundredth anniversary with a major conference on "The Role of Religious Minorities in Pluralistic Societies" at the Rutgers Presbyterian Church in New York City. Today the Society continues to play a pivotal role in connecting Presbyterians, Methodists, and Reformed Church members in North America with Waldensians in Italy (as well as in Uruguay and Argentina since the early 1980s). For more inforamtion on the Society, see the American Waldensian Society Web site, www.waldensian.org.

14. Although the last PC(USA) mission workers left Italy in January 2006, there are now United Methodist and Reformed Church in America mission workers in Italy, appointments that would not have been made had not Presbyterians in earlier generations pioneered the work in Italy.

15. See Philip Hallie, *Lest Innocent Blood Be Shed: The Story of Le Chambon and How Goodness Happened There* (New York: Harper & Row, 1979).

16. Charles Tudor Leber, Charles Arbuthnot, Michael Testa, Robert Lodwick, Duncan Hanson, Victor Makari, and Jon Chapman all served later as PC(USA) staff people with a Europe portfolio.

17. See chapter 2 for discussions on the Angela Davis affair and mission funding.

18. Both Ada Black and Endre Langh described the visit as a turning point in their lives. After the trip, Endre and his wife, Olga, and Ada Black began a correspondence relationship that was to last until Ada's death in 2006.

19. The Evangelical Church of Czech Brethren is institutionally the result of a merger in 1919 of the Czech Reformed Church and the somewhat smaller Czech Lutheran Church. The Evangelical Church of Czech Brethren traces its spiritual heritage, however, to John (Jon) Hus (ca. 1370–1415).

20. Josef Hromadka, who had been an implacable critic of the Nazis and had viewed resistance to Nazi sovereignty over the church and cultural life as a gospel imperative, saw the communist dictatorship that took over his country in 1948

as somewhat more benign. In Hromadka's opinion, Czech and Slovak Christians were bound to treat their communist government in accordance with the stricture in 1 Peter 2:17, "Fear God. Honor the emperor." After the Soviet-led invasion of Czechoslovakia in August 1968 in response to the so-called Prague Spring or political opening that had unfolded earlier in 1968, Hromadka became much more critical of his communist government. Some critics did not understand Hromadka's highly principled, biblical stand in regard to his government and instead saw him as simply a collaborator with an evil system.

21. Bryce and Phyllis Little had served earlier as mission workers in Thailand, and Bryce later served as an associate pastor at Hollywood First Presbyterian Church and as the executive presbyter for San Gabriel presbytery.

22. The Corrymeela Community, founded by an Irish Presbyterian elder, Ray Davies, brings Catholics and Protestants together to work on difficult social and political issues in Northern Ireland.

23. Charles and Marie Mercer, an American Baptist couple, who had previously served as PC(USA) missionaries in the former Yugoslavia, also served twice as chaplains at the Moscow Protestant Chaplaincy. I also served for many years as the chair of the so-called New York Committee of denominational representatives for the Moscow Protestant Chaplaincy. Another Presbyterian, Gary Payton, is now the chair of the New York Committee.

24. Bruce Rigdon was also for many years a Presbyterian representative on the Europe Committee of the National Council of Churches.

25. Gary Payton has served as a member of the steering committee of the Mission in Unity initiative for Ukraine and Belarus since the program was started. I was the organizer and from 1999 to 2006 served as chair of this project.

26. Participants in the Siberia trip included Harold Kurtz (of the Presbyterian Frontier Fellowship), Donald Marsden, Gary Payton, Ian Alexander (the Europe secretary of the Church of Scotland), Norman Hutchinson (of the Church of Scotland), and Duncan Hanson.

27. Gary Payton is an elder in the First Presbyterian Church in Sandpoint, Idaho, where his wife, Nancy Copeland-Payton, is the pastor. He had previously served in Louisville, Kentucky, from 1996 to 1999 as the coordinator of the Presbyterian Peacemaking Program. When he resigned from the Peacemaking Program (his wife accepted the invitation of the Sandpoint congregation to be their pastor), I invited Payton to become the regional liaison for Russia, Belarus, and Ukraine, since I had previously worked with him on issues related to Kosovo and elsewhere in Central and Eastern Europe. In 2004 Payton's assignment was expanded to include Poland.

28. The Kurds are a people with their own language as well as their own centuries-old culture and literature. Their geographical homeland lies in the mountainous border region in southeastern Turkey, northern Iraq, northwestern Iran, and northern Syria, with additional tiny Kurdish populations in Armenia, Georgia, and Jordan. Before 1919, the Kurds lived almost entirely within the borders of the Ottoman Empire. When the Ottoman Empire was dissolved in the aftermath of World War I, a number of ethnic groups received their own states; other states were created (for example, Iraq) whose borders did not correspond to ethnic or linguistic divisions; and one people, the Kurds, were arbitrarily divided among a number of states. There are approximately 25,000,000 Kurds altogether, of which about 600,000 now live in Europe.

29. To learn more about Presbyterian work among Kurds, see Robert Blincoe, *Ethnic Realities and the Church: Lessons from Kurdistan; A History of Mission Work 1668–1990* (Pasadena, CA: Presbyterian Center for Mission Studies, 1998).

30. In 2002 Elaine Matthes was appointed to work on the Worldwide Ministries Division staff in Louisville, Kentucky, in the office responsible for supporting mission workers with their personnel concerns.

31. Before being recruited by Earl Palmer, the pastor of University Presbyterian Church in Seattle, Washington, to be that congregation's mission pastor, Art Beals had been the founding president and chief executive officer of World Concern, a major mission relief and development agency then based in Seattle. When Beals retired as a pastor at University Church in 1999, he continued to work with me as the Area Liaison for Albania and Turkey, with additional responsibility to serve as a kind of consulting missiologist for Presbyterian workers in Southeastern Europe as a whole as well as in Central Asia. Art Beals is the author of *When the Saints Go Marching Out: Mobilizing the Church for Mission* (Louisville, KY: Geneva Press, 2001).

32. Edwin E. Jacques later wrote a history of Albania, *The Albanians: An Ethnic History from Prehistoric Times to the Present* (Jefferson, NC: McFarland, 1995).

33. With the help of Edwin Jacques, this "old man," Gligor Cilka, had helped organize a federation of Albanian Protestants during the 1930s. When the Albanian Evangelical Alliance was reorganized in the mid-1990s with help from the PC(USA), this same "old man" was elected its first president.

34. The Interconfessional Bible Society of Albania produced the first modern translation of the Bible in Albanian, which was also the first translation of the Bible ever to be accepted by Orthodox, Roman Catholics, and Protestants together.

35. Even though Presbyterian appointees in Turkey do not engage in religious proselytism, many Turks look with suspicion at all foreigners in their country. The suspicion that some Presbyterian personnel regularly experience could turn into outright hostility if it became known that they had been sent to Turkey by a Christian church. For this reason, the names of Presbyterian appointees in Turkey are not given in this chapter.

36. There are about two thousand Greeks in the Istanbul area, almost all of whom are at least nominally Orthodox. Before a mass exodus in the early 1920s, there were many more Greeks in Turkey. The ecumenical patriarch, who is the nominal leader of all the world's Orthodox, has his seat in Istanbul. There are about 60,000 Armenians in Turkey, almost all of whom live in the Istanbul area. Armenians in Turkey, as in most other countries, generally belong to one of three Christian bodies: the Armenian Apostolic Church (an Oriental Orthodox [non-Chalcedonian] Church), the Armenian Catholic Church (in liturgy and organization almost identical to the Apostolic Church, differing from that church only by being in communion with the pope in Rome); and the Armenian Evangelicals (who cover the Protestant spectrum from conservative evangelical to mainline). There are also perhaps 10,000 Syrian Orthodox, almost all of whom live in southeastern Turkey. There are also French- and Italian-speaking Roman Catholics along Turkey's west and southern coasts.

37. The most common popular name for the Roma and Sinti, at least in English, is Gypsy. Although many Roma use this name to describe themselves, the name has the unfortunate connotation of "gyp" as in "to gyp someone." The title Gypsy also is based on a false etymology. Before modern times most Europeans believed that the Roma and Sinti came from Egypt and therefore called them Gypsies. In fact, the Roma are genetically closely related with some modern Indians, and the indigenous Roma languages are related to several modern Indian languages, which makes it seem more likely that the Roma really came from India. Most contemporary community leaders in this ethnic group use the names Roma and Sinti to name their ethnic membership. For more information on the Roma and

Sinti, see Ian Hancock, *We Are the Romani People* (Hatfield, UK: University of Hertfordshire Press, 2002).

38. There are about 30 million Roma worldwide. About 8 million of these 30 million live in Central and Eastern Europe, another million live in Spain, and another million elsewhere in Western and Southern Europe. It is not clear whether the Roma were first a separate tribal group, genetically related to some north Indians, or whether they were composed from one or more Hindu castes. In any case, the first Roma left their north Indian homelands in the fifth century. Probably as a result of a Muslim invasion of India in the eleventh century, the number of Roma leaving India vastly increased. They passed through what is now Iran and Turkey into areas of what is now Turkey in which Greek was then spoken. As a result, there are a large number of Iranian, Turkish, and Greek words in all of the Roma languages. The Roma began entering Europe in the fifteenth century.

39. Burkhard Paetzold was not Presbyterian, but a German Lutheran who had been trained as an engineer and had served as the mayor of Petershagen in the former German Democratic Republic.

40. At the same time the "Roma Traveling Seminar" was taking place, the Conference of European Churches organized a meeting on Roma in Bratislava, the capital of Slovakia. The recommendations of the Bratislava conference closely paralleled the recommendations of the Roma Traveling Seminar.

41. Most Roma in Central Europe speak the language of the country in which they live. Some also speak a Roma dialect, the most widespread of which is the Vlach Roma language. All of the seven Roma language groups or dialect groups trace descent to a protolanguage in India. (The Roma languages are just dissimilar enough that they can be described either as belonging to closely related language families or starkly dissimilar dialects descending from a common protolanguage. It is not always possible for the Roma from different places to understand each other.)

42. The word "Gadje" means "non-Roma."

43. The past tense is used because this is a history of Presbyterian mission in Europe from 1944 to 2006. In fact, most or all of these values still guide Presbyterian work in Europe.

44. The Hungarian, Czech, German Reformed, Waldensian, Swiss Protestant, and many other European churches along with the PC(USA) had all been members of the World Alliance of Reformed Churches since that organization's founding in 1875. Presbyterians have met with representatives of those churches and others during meetings of the General Council of the World Alliance on a more or less regular basis since 1975. Similarly, over many years, beginning with the Edinburgh Missionary Conference (1910) and continuing to the present day through its membership in the WCC (founded August 1948), Presbyterians have met representatives of European churches in broader ecumenical settings.

45. The decision not to post Duncan Hanson in Geneva was intended to save the PC(USA) the expense of renting offices in the ecumenical center as well as paying the salary of an administrative assistant in Geneva, both of which would have cost considerably more in Geneva than they did in Louisville, Kentucky. One unexpected positive benefit of that decision was that it made it necessary for me to visit partners almost exclusively in their home countries rather than sometimes also in Geneva. Nothing communicates the interest of one church for another or of a sending church for its mission personnel like a personal visit.

46. Today both initiatives continue to enjoy the participation of individual Presbyterian mission workers and have been significantly strengthened by the participation of new mission workers from a sister North American Reformed church, the Reformed Church in America.

47. According to Zentral-Institut Islam-Archiv-Deutschland, in 2006, of the 494.7 million EU citizens, 224.5 million are Roman Catholic, 115 million are atheist, 57.8 million are Protestant, 39 million are Orthodox, 15.9 million are Muslim, and 1.5 million are Jewish. The Muslim birth rate is almost exactly three times the European birth rate of 1.4 per woman.

Chapter 13. South Asia

1. PCUSA BFM Annual Report, 1939, 110–14; UPCNA GA Minutes, 1939, 1014, 1195, 1198–99.
2. *A Manual Prepared for the Use of Missionaries and Missionary Candidates in Connection with the Board of Foreign Missions of the Presbyterian Church* (New York, 1840), 6. The 1873 Manual was the first to recognize the existence of missions, but still preferred that missionaries work through presbyteries as originally stated. *A Manual for the Use of Missionary Candidates and Missionaries in Connection with the Board of Foreign Missions of the Presbyterian Church* (New York: Mission House, 1873), 7–8.
3. This was done somewhat irregularly since one of the Presbyterian Church in the U.S.A. ministers was unable to attend the meeting, and so the Reformed Presbyterian minister was used as the third minister required to form a presbytery.
4. For a fuller discussion of this, see John C. B. Webster, *The Christian Community and Change in Nineteenth-Century North India* (Delhi: Macmillan, 1976), 208–9; "Introduction," *Journal of Presbyterian History* 62, no. 3 (Fall 1984): 191–93.
5. "Dalit" is best translated as "beaten down," "broken," or "oppressed." It is a somewhat controversial label, which those formerly called "untouchables" have given themselves. The use of this name has gained general acceptance over the past one or two decades.
6. "In view of the strong anti-Brahman feeling that characterizes the Marathas one might have hoped that Christianity could long before this have won converts from some other communities besides the outcaste Mahars and Mangs. Almost without exception the Christians have come from these depressed communities." Robert E. Speer and Russell Carter, *Report on India and Persia of the Deputation sent by the Board of Foreign Missions of the Presbyterian Church in the U.S.A. to Visit These Fields in 1921–22* (New York: Board of Foreign Missions of the Presbyterian Church in the U.S.A., 1922), 73.
7. The details are provided in Webster, *Christian Community and Change*, 208–23.
8. The Announcement of the Secretary of State for India of August 20, 1917, is given in C. H. Philips, H. L. Singh, and B. N. Pandey, eds., *The Evolution of India and Pakistan 1858 to 1947: Select Documents* (London: Oxford University Press, 1962), 264–65.
9. This letter, originally published in *The Indian Standard* of September 1920 (259–64) and Dr. Speer's reply are reprinted in "Laying and Challenging the Foundations of Presbyterian Work in India: Three Letters," *Journal of Presbyterian History*, 62, no. 3 (Fall 1984): 266–81.
10. In 1924, between the adoption of the Saharanpur and the Joint Church Councils Plans, the Presbyterian Church in India joined with the General Aikya (or Congregational Unions) of the Congregational Churches of Western India to form the United Church of Northern India. In the UCNI, presbyteries were renamed church councils. For a history of the formation of the UCNI, see Kenneth Lawrence Parker, "The Development of the United Church of Northern India," *Journal of the Department of History of the Presbyterian Church in the U.S.A.* 17, nos. 3–4 (September–December 1936): 113–204.

11. For a more detailed account of the development of the Saharanpur and Joint Church Councils Plans, see John C. B. Webster, "American Presbyterian Missionaries and Nationalist Politics in the Punjab, 1919–1935," *Indian Church History Review* 32, no. 1 (June 2000): 59–63, 69–72.

12. One can see this shift most clearly in two key aspects of mission during the interwar period. Rural missionaries now spent more of their touring time in the villages, visiting groups of baptized believers in an effort to build them up in the Christian faith and life, than in preaching to the unbaptized. In like manner, Christian schools now gave greater priority to building up educated leadership for the church than to the earlier aim of evangelizing those who were not Christians.

13. UPCUSA, *A Century for Christ in India and Pakistan, 1855–1955* (Lahore: The United Presbyterian Church in the U.S.A., 1955), 37, 40, 41, 43.

14. However, the UCNI's Synod of Pakistan chose not to join with the Anglicans and Methodists in forming the Church of Pakistan.

15. UPCNA GA Minutes, 1947, 1248.

16. Ibid., 1950, 952.

17. Ibid., 1956, part 1, 61–62; ibid., 1957, part 1, 598.

18. *1962 Mission Yearbook of Prayer,* 224.

19. Leonard A. McCulloch, "What Befell Gurdaspur Presbytery?" *Missionary Horizons*, April 1958, 471–72; J. Morgan McKelvey, "Integration of Mission and Church," *Missionary Horizons,* April 1958, 473–74.

20. Cited by Korula Jacob, "The Government of India and the Entry of Missionaries," *International Review of Missions* 47 (1958): 413.

21. Annual Narrative for Pakistan—1972 (G. LeRoy Selby). R. Park Johnson Papers RC291. Presbyterian Historical Society, Philadelphia. These institutions were "returned" only in 2003.

22. See chapter 3 for a fuller discussion of these changes.

23. UPCUSA GA Minutes, 1958, 140, 186, 248, 257–58.

24. PCUSA BFM Annual Report, 1953, 39; 1958, 44.

25. A survey conducted in 1937–38, which included twelve villages around the UP mission station of Pasrur, found that 81.9 percent of the Christians there were in debt for an average equivalent of nineteen months' labor. E. D. Lucas and F. Thakur Das, *The Rural Church in the Punjab: A Study of Social, Economic, Educational and Religious Conditions Prevailing amongst Certain Village Christian Communities in the Sialkot District* (Lahore: Northern India Printing and Publishing Co., 1938), 17.

26. Andrew Gordon, *Our India Mission: A Thirty Years' History of the India Mission of the United Presbyterian Church of North America Together with Personal Reminiscences* (Philadelphia: Andrew Gordon, 1886), 438, 445.

27. See, e.g., "The Editor to His Readers: Hoshiarpur Conference Summons Christians to Advance," *The Indian Standard,* June 1925, 178; and C. H. Loehlin, "Self-Support in Village Churches: A Report of a Survey," ibid., April 1929, 89–93; W. H. Wiser, "A Study in Potential Giving," ibid., 159–66; J. G. Campbell, "Self-Support in Village Churches in India: 3, The Synod of the Punjab—The United Presbyterian Church," ibid., July–August 1929, 193–97; W. H. Wiser, "The Rural Church in the United Provinces," *United Church Review,* October 1938, 234–39.

28. Lucas and Thakur Das (*Rural Church in the Punjab*, 46–51) accepted the estimate that it took between 100 and 150 rural Christian families to support a pastor. Thus self-support was closely linked to the demographics of the Christian community. If there were that many Christian families concentrated in several adjacent villages, they could support a pastor; if Christian families were widely dispersed over a large area, they could not.

29. *An Advisory Study* (New York: COEMAR, 1962), 1. One committee member, W. S. Theophilus, was an Indian. See also chapter 3 in this volume.

30. Ibid., 71; see 66–73.

31. *An Advisory Study, 1961–1966: A Report on the Study Process* (New York: COEMAR, 1966), 4. COEMAR insisted throughout that the study was advisory and not policy, but at least with regard to India, COEMAR took that advice very seriously.

32. "The Church and Its Mission: Reports of United Church of Northern India Consultations Held in India November 1963 and January 1964" (Dehra Dun, 1964), 10–111.

33. Ibid., 20, 35.

34. Ibid., 5, 26.

35. During these consultations, Donald Black felt obliged to challenge the "mother-daughter" metaphor commonly used to describe relations between the UPCUSA and the churches there by preparing an address titled "Don't Call Me Mother." Black, *Merging Mission and Unity*, 86. His description of these consultations covers pages 84–88.

36. "Position Paper of the United Presbyterian Church in the United States of America as a Partner in Mission with the United Church of Northern India/Pakistan" (typed manuscript), Commission Action #64–149, March 17, 1964, 5–6.

37. Ibid., 9.

38. "A Position Paper of the United Presbyterian Church in the United States of America as a Partner in Mission with the United Presbyterian Church of Pakistan" (typed manuscript), Commission Action # 64–150, March 17, 1964. Back in 1939, the United Presbyterians reported that 118 of their 129 congregations were self-supporting. UPCNA GA Minutes, 1939, 1005.

39. Robert C. Alter, Survey of Presbyterians in Mission, 1945–2000.

40. Robert C. Alter, *The Demise of a Church: A Dream That Failed* (Louisville, KY: Worldwide Ministries Division and the Presbyterian Historical Society, 1999), 1–11.

41. COEMAR Annual Report, 1965, 66; COEMAR Annual Report, 1966, 23.

42. This is spelled out in some detail in John C. B. Webster, *A Social History of Christianity: North-west India since 1800* (New Delhi and Oxford: Oxford University Press, 2007).

43. UPCUSA GA Minutes, 1969, part 1, Journal, 594.

44. *1959 Mission Yearbook of Prayer* (Board of National Missions and COEMAR of the UPCUSA), 188–240.

45. *1967 Mission Yearbook,* 210–58.

46. *1972 Mission Yearbook,* 103, 107.

47. COEMAR Annual Report, 1960, 56; Minutes of the 101st Annual Meeting (104th Year), Sialkot, April 21–25, 1959, Including Minutes to Date of the Executive Committee for 1958–59 of the Sialkot Mission of the UPCUSA, 20.

48. The principle is enunciated in The India Council (Punjab and North India Synods and Kolhapur Church Council of the United Church of Northern India and the COEMAR of the UPCUSA), Fiftieth Annual Meeting, 1964, Held at "Lowriston," Dehra Dun, U.P., India, November 28–December 4, 1964, 82.

49. COEMAR, "Preliminary Reports of the Major Program Agencies to the 172nd General Assembly of the UPCUSA, Cleveland, Ohio, May 18, 1960," 53, 210–11. The number of hospitals in Pakistan is drawn from a later report.

50. *An Advisory Study,* 55–60, 68–69.

51. "The Church and Its Mission: Reports" (1964), 6, 12–13, 25, 30–31.

52. "Position Paper of the UPCUSA as a Partner with UCNI/Pakistan," 7–8.

53. "Position Paper of the UPCUSA as a Partner with the UP Church of Pakistan," 3.

54. UPCUSA GA Minutes, 1965, part 2, Annual Reports of the Major Program Agencies, 124–25.
55. UPCUSA GA Minutes, 1970, part 2, Annual Reports of the Major Program Agencies, 41–42.
56. UPCUSA GA Minutes, 1980, part 1, Journal, 251.
57. *1990 Mission Yearbook for Prayer and Study,* 334–47, 350–56.
58. *2000 Mission Yearbook for Prayer and Study,* 144, 149.
59. Alfred A. Schlorholtz, Survey of Presbyterians in Mission, 1945–2000.
60. Edwin C. Carlson, ibid.
61. James D. Harvey, ibid.
62. Ronald S. Seaton, ibid.
63. Symon Satow, ibid.
64. Robert C. Alter, ibid.
65. I add my own personal testimony here.
66. UPCUSA GA Minutes, 1972, part 1, Journal, 876; UPCUSA GA Minutes, 1979, part 1, Journal, 348.
67. COEMAR Annual Report, 1960, 56; 1961, 51–52; 1965, 67; 1966, 31; 1967, 26.
68. *1981 Mission Yearbook for Prayer and Study,* 212–13.
69. *2000 Mission Yearbook for Prayer and Study,* 146.
70. Witnessing Ministries of Christ, "Annual Performance Report, July 1, 1994, to June 30, 1995," 3, 36.
71. "The Annual Performance Report of Witnessing Ministries of Christ, July 1, 1997, to June 30, 1998," 8.
72. Ibid., "July 1, 2000, to June 30, 2001," 1.
73. Telephone conversation with the Reverend Philip Prasad, November 20, 2006. Two analyses of differing aspects of this movement may be found in John C. B. Webster, *Religion and Dalit Liberation: An Examination of Perspectives,* 2nd ed. (New Delhi: Manohar, 2002), 96–98, 144; idem, "Whither Dalit Theology: An Historian's Assessment," in *Dalit Issue in Today's Theological Debate,* ed. James Massey and S. Lourduswamy (New Delhi: Centre for Dalit/Subaltern Studies [Theology], 2003), 30–32, 36–38.
74. See J. C. Heinrich, *The Psychology of a Suppressed People* (London: George Allen & Unwin, 1937).
75. Heinrich raised this issue, but a more recent analysis is in Webster, *Religion and Dalit Liberation,* 119–47.

An Epilogue and a Prologue

1. Bühlmann was a Roman Catholic, OFM (Cap.), theologian from Switzerland (August 6, 1916–May 16, 2007).
2. In preparation for writing this chapter, large sections of the book were sent to "outsiders" for their comments on our Presbyterian history. We wanted to hear observations from church leaders and theologians from other church traditions (in this case Roman Catholic, Methodist, and Mennonite) as well as from different areas of the world (Singapore, Egypt, Zambia, Indonesia, and Papua New Guinea). The respondents whose comments are included in this chapter are Methodist Bishop Robert Solomon from the Republic of Singapore; William Burrows, an Orbis Books editor; Tharwat Wahba, mission and evangelism lecturer in the Evangelical Theological Seminary in Cairo; Wilbert Shenk, Senior Professor of Mission History and Contemporary Culture at Fuller Seminary; and Amon Kasambala, formerly professor at Justo Mwale Theological College,

Lusaka Zambia. Except where marked otherwise, all quotations are taken from their written responses.

3. Presbyterians actively participated with the "undenominational" American Board of Commissioners for Foreign Missions (ABCFM, 1810) until about 1870.

4. The YMCA and YWCA sent out missionaries throughout the world to reach university students. Presbyterians were among the most active in the YMCA and the later World Christian Student Federation. Among many other societies, we also think of the American Bible Society.

5. Women's missionary societies were so important in Protestant missions that the largest article in the 1891 *Encyclopedia of Missions*, edited by Edwin Munsell Bliss (New York: Funk & Wagnalls) is on "Women's Work for Women" (44 pages). This article describes over 50 women's missionary societies. Of these, fifteen were "undenominational" or Presbyterian/Reformed.

6. Mission societies established for women to reach women who lived in zenanas or harems.

7. We are using the word *ecumenical* here in its more general Christian usage: the whole church in the whole world. We should also remember that Presbyterians started out in mission by participating with the ABCFM, but then a "Presbyterian missionary society" was formed. The Presbyterian mission society was not a national board; it was a local synod mission board. Although the convivial folks of the Synod of Pittsburgh invited other Presbyterians to be involved in their "Western Foreign Missions Society," it was their synodical society.

8. The goal of reaching out to 200 unreached people groups was accepted at the 1996 General Assembly of the PC(USA).

9. B. A. Garside, *One Increasing Purpose: The Life of Henry Winters Luce* (New York: Fleming H. Revell Co., 1958), 60–61.

10. From Thomas L. Friedman's *The World Is Flat* (New York: Farrar, Strauss & Giroux, 2005).

11. Italics have been added.

12. Although after the Iron Curtain fell in Russia, Korean Presbyterians established a Presbyterian Church in Russia.

13. The China Christian Council is clear that the Presbyterian Church of Taiwan, like the island of Taiwan, is part of China. It can be quite delicate to stay in fellowship and work in partnership in such a context.

14. Wilbert Shenk, personal correspondence with the author, May 29, 2007.

Bibliography

Abrecht, Paul A. "Society." In *Dictionary of the Ecumenical Movement*, edited by Nicolas Lossky et al. 1049–53. 2nd ed. Geneva: WCC Publications, 2002.

Adams, Daniel J. "From Colonialism to World Citizen: Changing Patterns of Presbyterian Mission." *American Presbyterians* 65 (Summer 1987): 147–56.

Ali, Michael Nazir. "Directions in Mission: Christian Worship, Witness, and Work in Islamic Contexts." *International Review of Mission* 76 (January 1987): 33–37.

Alter, Martha Payne. *Letters from India to America, 1916–1951*. Edited by Ellen and Bob Alter. Mussoorie, 2006.

Alter, Robert C. *The Demise of a Church: A Dream That Failed*. Louisville, KY: Worldwide Ministries Division and the Presbyterian Historical Society, 1999.

Amity Foundation. "About The Amity Foundation." http://www.amityfoundation.org/page.php?page=5 (accessed November 19, 2007).

Anderson, Emma Dean, and Mary Jane Campbell. *In the Shadow of the Himalayas: A Historical Narrative of the Missions of the United Presbyterian Church of North America as conducted in the Punjab, India, 1855–1940*. Philadelphia: The United Presbyterian Board of Foreign Missions, 1942.

Anderson, Gerald H. "A Moratorium on Missionaries?" *Christian Century* 91 (January 16, 1974): 43–45.

———, ed. *Asian Voices in Christian Theology*. Maryknoll, NY: Orbis Books, 1976.

Anderson, Gerald H., and Thomas F. Stransky, eds. *Mission Trends*, nos. 1–5. Grand Rapids: Wm. B. Eerdmans Publishing Co., 1974–81.

Anderson, Vernon A. *Still Led in Triumph*. Nashville: Board of World Missions, PCUS, 1959.

Anderson, William and Lois, et al. *The Rock from Which We Were Quarried: Memories of John Lowrie and Margaret Anderson*. 1999.

Anderson, William B., and Charles R. Watson. *Far North in India: A Survey of the Mission Field and Work of the United Presbyterian Church in the Punjab*. Rev. ed. Philadelphia: Board of Foreign Missions, 1911.

Archdiocese of São Paulo. *Brasil, nunca mais*. Petropólis, Brazil: Editora Vozes, 1985. ET, *Torture in Brazil*. Translated by Jaime Wright. Edited by Joan Dassin. Austin: Instute of Latin American Studies, University of Texas, 1998.

Arnold, Frank L. "From Sending Church to Partner Church: The Brazil Experience." *Journal of Presbyterian History* 81, no. 3 (Fall 2003): 178–92.

Ash, Timothy Garton. *The Uses of Adversity: Essays on the Fate of Central Europe.* New York: Random House, 1990.

Association of Presbyterian Mission Pastors. http://www.missionpastor.org/history/htm.

Badr, Habib. *Christianity: A History of the Middle East.* Beirut: Middle East Council of Churches, 2005.

Bailey, Kenneth E. "Cross-cultural Mission: A Tale of Three Cities." In "The W. Donald McClure Lectures." 3 sound cassettes. Pittsburgh: Pittsburgh Theological Seminary, 1984.

———. *Finding the Lost: Cultural Keys to Luke 15.* St. Louis: Concordia Publishing House, 1992.

———. *Poet and Peasant: A Literary-Cultural Approach to the Parables in Luke.* Grand Rapids: Wm. B. Eerdmans Publishing Co., 1976.

Barber, Benjamin. *Jihad vs. McWorld: How Globalism and Tribalism Are Reshaping the World.* New ed. London: Corgi, 2003.

Barrett, David B., George Thomas Kurian, and Todd M. Johnson, eds. *The World Christian Encyclopedia.* 2nd rev. ed. Oxford: Oxford University Press, 2001.

Bassham, Rodger C. *Mission Theology, 1948–1975: Years of Worldwide Creative Tension, Ecumenical, Evangelical, and Roman Catholic.* Pasadena, CA: William Carey Library, 1979.

Beals, Arthur. *When the Saints Go Marching Out: Mobilizing the Church for Mission.* Louisville, KY: Geneva Press, 2001.

Bear, James E. Nashville: Board of World Missions, PCUS, 1971.

Beaver, R. Pierce, ed. *American Missions in Bicentennial Perspective.* Pasadena, CA: William Carey Library, 1977.

———. *From Missions to Mission.* New York: Association Press, 1964.

Bediako, Kwame. *Christianity in Africa.* Maryknoll, NY: Orbis Books, 1995.

Bevans, Stephen. "Seeing Mission through Images." *Missiology* 10, no. 1 (January 1991): 45–57.

Beversluis, Joel, ed. *A Source Book for the Community of Religions.* Chicago: Council for a Parliament of the World's Religions, 1993.

Black, Donald. *Captives in Christ's Triumphal Procession: A Commentary on "An Advisory Study."* New York: PCUSA, 1962.

———. *Challenge to Presbyterians in the 1990s: Can This Mainline Denomination Be Responsive to God's Call to Mission?* 4 audio cassettes. 1986.

———. *An Historical View of Developing Missionary Policy.* New York: Presbyterian Distribution Service, PC(USA), 1986.

———. *Merging Mission and Unity: A History of the Commission on Ecumenical Mission and Relations.* Presbyterian Historical Society Publications, no. 24. Philadelphia: Geneva Press, 1986.

Blake, Eugene Carson. *The Church in the Next Decade.* New York: Macmillan, 1966.

———. "General Secretary's Louvain Address." *The Ecumenical Review* 29 (1972): 26–29.

Blanford, Carl E. *Chinese Churches in Thailand.* Bangkok: Suriyaban Publishers, 1975.

Blincoe, Robert A. *Ethnic Realities and the Church: Lessons from Kurdistan: A History of Mission Work, 1668–1990.* Pasadena, CA: Presbyterian Center for Mission Studies, 1998.

———. "The Strange Structure of Mission Agencies, Part III." *International Journal of Frontier Missions* 19, no. 3 (Fall 2002): 43–46.

Board of Foreign Missions of the Presbyterian Church in the U.S.A. *The Hundredth Year: Between Two Centuries.* New York: Board of Foreign Missions, Presbyterian Church in the U.S.A., 1937.

Board of Foreign Missions of the United Presbyterian Church of North America. *Handbook on Foreign Missions of the UPC, USA, 1953*. Philadelphia: Board of Foreign Missions and the Board of Directors of the Women's General Missionary Society, 1953.

Bonhoeffer, Dietrich. *Letters and Papers from Prison*. ET. London: SCM Press, 1953.

Bosch, David J. *Transforming Mission: Paradigm Shifts in Theology of Mission*. Maryknoll, NY: Orbis Books, 1991.

Boyd, Robin. *The Witness of the Student Christian Movement: Church Ahead of the Church*. London: SPCK, 2007.

Brackenridge, R. Douglas. *Eugene Carson Blake: Prophet with Portfolio*. New York: Seabury Press, 1978.

Brazil Notes. Central Brazil Mission of the UPCUSA. No. 4 (March 30, 1974).

Brereton, Virginia Lieson. "United but Slighted: Women as Subordinated Leaders." In *Between the Times: The Travail of Protestant Establishment in America*, edited by William Hutchison, 143–67. New York: Cambridge University Press, 1989.

Briggs, John, Mercy Amba Oduyoye, and Georges Tsetsis, eds. *A History of the Ecumenical Movement*. Vol. 3, *1968–2000*. Geneva: WCC Publications, 2004.

Brown, Arthur Judson. *One Hundred Years: A History of the Foreign Missionary Work of the Presbyterian Church in the U.S.A., with Some Account of Countries, Peoples and the Policies and Problems of Modern Missions*. New York: Fleming H. Revell Co., 1936.

Brown, G. Thompson. *Christianity in the People's Republic of China*. Rev. ed. Atlanta: John Knox Press, 1986.

———. *Earthen Vessels and Transcendent Power: American Presbyterians in China, 1837–1952*. Maryknoll, NY: Orbis Books, 1997.

———. *Mission to Korea*. Nashville: Board of World Missions, 1962.

———. "Overseas Mission Program and Policies of the Presbyterian Church in the U.S., 1861–1983." *American Presbyterians: Journal of Presbyterian History* 65, no. 2 (Summer 1987): 157–70.

———. *Presbyterians in World Mission: A Handbook for Congregations*. Decatur, GA: Columbia Theological Seminary Press, 1988. Rev. ed. 1995.

———. "Twenty Years in Cross-Cultural Mission." *Cross Culture: A Newsletter of the Association of Presbyterians for Cross-Cultural Mission*, no. 49 (October 2004): 1–3.

Brown, Margrethe B. J. *Conversations with Roman Catholics on the Nature of the Church and on Ecumenism*. Resources for Ecumenical Encounter. New York: Commission on Ecumenical Mission and Relations, 1965.

Brown, Robert McAfee. *Unexpected News: Reading the Bible with Third World Eyes*. Philadelphia: Westminster Press, 1984.

Brush, Stanley Elwood. "Protestants in the Punjab: Religion and Social Change in an Indian Province in the Nineteenth Century." PhD diss., University of California, Berkeley, 1971.

Buchanan, Claudius. *Christian Researches in Asia: With Notices on the Translation of the Scriptures into the Oriental Languages*. Boston: Samuel T. Armstrong, 1811.

Buscando salidas . . . caminando hacia adelante: Las iglesias evangélicas dicen basta! Quito, Ecuador: Consejo Latinoamericano de Iglesias, 2003.

Campbell, E. Y. *The Church in the Punjab: Some Aspects of Its Life and Growth*. Lucknow: National Christian Council of India, 1961.

Campbell, J. G. "Self-Support in Village Churches in India: 3, The Synod of the Punjab—The United Presbyterian Church." *The Indian Standard* (July–August 1929): 193–97.

Castro, Emilio. *Sent Free: Mission and Unity in the Perspective of the Kingdom*. Grand Rapids: Wm. B. Eerdmans Publishing Co., 1985.

Chung Hyun-Kyung. "Welcome the Spirit, Hear Her Cries." *Christianity and Crisis* 51 (1991): 220–23.

Clarke, Erskine. "Presbyterian Ecumenical Activity in the U.S." In *The Diversity of Discipleship*, edited by Milton J. Coalter, John M. Mulder, and Louis B. Weeks, 149–69. Louisville, KY: Westminster/John Knox Press, 1991.

Coalter, Milton J., John M. Mulder, and Louis B. Weeks, eds. *The Diversity of Discipleship: The Presbyterians and Twentieth-Century Christian Witness.* Louisville, KY: Westminster/John Knox Press, 1991.

———, eds. *The Mainstream Protestant "Decline": The Presbyterian Pattern.* Louisville, KY: Westminster/John Knox Press, 1990.

———, eds. *The Organizational Revolution: Presbyterians and American Denominationalism.* Louisville, KY: Westminster/John Knox Press, 1992.

———. *The Re-Forming Tradition: Presbyterians and Mainstream Protestantism.* Louisville, KY: Westminster/John Knox Press, 1992.

———. *Vital Signs: The Promise of Mainstream Protestantism.* Grand Rapids, MI / Cambridge, UK: William B. Eerdmans, 1996.

Cochrane, A. C. *The Church's Confession under Hitler.* Philadelphia: Westminster Press, 1962.

Cogswell, James A. *No Turning Back: A History of American Presbyterian Mission Involvement in Sub-Saharan Africa, 1833–2000.* Manuscript, 2003. Philadelphia: Xlibris Corp. [distributor], 2007.

———. *Until the Day Dawn.* Nashville: Board of World Missions, PCUS, 1957.

Cole, Pat. "In Praise of Partnerships." *Presbyterians Today* 95 (January–February 2005): 19–23.

Commission of the Churches on International Affairs. *Armenia: The Continuing Tragedy.* Geneva: World Council of Churches, 1984.

Coote, Robert T. "Lausanne Committee for World Evangelization." In *Dictionary of the Ecumenical Movement*, edited by Nicolas Lossky et al., 673. 2nd ed. Geneva: WCC Publications, 2002.

———. "Lausanne Covenant." In *Dictionary of the Ecumenical Movement*, edited by Nicolas Lossky et al., 673–74. 2nd ed. Geneva: WCC Publications, 2002.

———. "Lausanne II and World Evangelization." *International Bulletin of Missionary Research* 14 (January 1990): 10, 12–17.

Cox, Harvey. *Religion in the Secular City: Toward a Postmodern Theology.* New York: Simon & Schuster, 1985.

———. *The Secular City: Secularization and Urbanization in Theological Perspective.* London: SCM Press, 1965.

Cox, Jeffrey. *Imperial Fault Lines: Christianity and Colonial Power in India, 1818–1940.* Stanford, CA: Stanford University Press, 2002.

Crane, Sophie Montgomery. *A Legacy Remembered: A Century of Medical Missions.* Franklin, TN: Providence House Publishers, 1998.

Crow, Paul A., Jr. "Eugene Carson Blake: Apostle of Christian Unity." *Ecumenical Review* 38, no. 2 (April 1986): 228–36.

———. "North America." In *A History of the Ecumenical Movement*, vol. 3, edited by John Briggs, Mercy Amba Oduyoye, and Georges Tsetsis, 609–41. Geneva: WCC Publications, 2004.

Davey, Ray, and Cole, John. *A Channel of Peace: The Story of the Corrymeela Community.* Grand Rapids: Zondervan Press, 1993.

Davis, Stephen J. *The Early Coptic Papacy: The Egyptian Church and Its Leadership in Late Antiquity.* Cairo: American University in Cairo Press, 2004.

Dawson, David G. "Mission Philanthropy, Selected Giving and Presbyterians: Part 1." *American Presbyterians* 68 (Summer 1990): 121–32. "Part 2." 69 (Fall 1991): 203–25.

———. "Presbyterian Missionaries in the Middle East." STM thesis, Yale Divinity School, 1987.

Dayton, Edward R., and Samuel Wilson, eds. *The Future of World Evangelization: The Lausanne Movement*. Monrovia, CA: MARC, 1984.

Dicklitch, Susan, and Heather Rice. "The Mennonite Central Committee (MCC) and Faith-Based NGO Aid to Africa." *Development in Practice* 14, no. 4 (August 2004): 660–72.

Driskill, J. Lawrence. *Japan Diary of Cross-cultural Mission*. Pasadena, CA: Hope Publishing House, 1993.

Dye, Marjorie J. *The CEOSS Story*. Cairo: Dar al-Thaqafa, 1979.

Edwards, David L. "Signs of Radicalism in the Ecumenical Movement." In *A History of the Ecumenical Movement*, vol. 2, *1948–1968*, edited by Harold E. Fey, 373–409. Philadelphia: Westminster Press, 1970.

Eggleston, Forrest C. *Where Is God Not? An American Surgeon in India*. Franklin, TN: Providence House Publishers, 1999.

Elder, Earl E. *Vindicating a Vision: The Story of the American Mission in Egypt, 1854–1954*. Philadelphia: United Presbyterian Board of Foreign Missions, 1958.

Eller, Gary S. "Special-Interest Groups and American Presbyterians." In *The Organizational Revolution: Presbyterians and American Denominationalism*, edited by Milton J. Coalter, John M. Mulder, and Louis B. Weeks, 254–78. The Presbyterian Presence: The Twentieth-Century Experience. Louisville, KY: Westminster/John Knox Press, 1992.

Erdman, Chris W. "Pittsburgh Seminary Helps Launch World Mission Initiative." *The Presbyterian Layman* 31, no. 3 (May/June 1998).

Evangelical Presbyterian Church. "About the Evangelical Presbyterian Church." http://www.epc.org/about-epc/index.html.

Feng Gao. "Church Leaders and Church Development in China." In *Protestant Church Development in China: How Did It Happen and Where Is It Leading?* edited by Tak-Ho Lam. Geneva and Hong Kong: Lutheran World Federation, 2003.

Fey, Harold E. "Confessional Families and the Ecumenical Movement." In *A History of the Ecumenical Movement*, vol. 2, *1948–1968*, edited by Harold E. Fey, 115–42. Philadelphia: Westminster Press, 1970.

———, ed. *A History of the Ecumenical Movement*. vol. 2, *The Ecumenical Advance, 1948–1968*. Philadelphia: Westminster Press, 1970.

Fleischmann, Ellen. "The Impact of American Protestant Missions in Lebanon on the Construction of Female Identity, c. 1860–1950." *Islam and Christian-Muslim Relations* 13, no. 4 (October 2002): 411–26.

Fletcher, Archibald G. *To India and Beyond: Memoirs of a Missionary Surgeon*. Philadelphia: Xlibris Corp. [distributor], 2005.

Flory, Margaret. *Dear House, Mission Becomes You*. Louisville, KY: Bridge Resources, 2000.

———. *From Past to Future: Experiments in Global Bridging*. New York: The History Project, World Student Christian Federation, 1997.

———. *Moments in Time: One Woman's Ecumenical Journey*. New York: Friendship Press, 1995.

———. "Walking in One Company." In "More Than They Know: The Presbyterian Mission Effort and the Advancement of Human Liberties." *Church and Society* 78, nos. 2–3 (November/December 1986–January/February 1987).

Fonseca, Isabel. *Bury Me Standing: The Gypsies and Their Journey*. New York: Random House, 1995.

Fukuyama, Francis. "The End of History." *The National Interest*, Summer 1989.

Fulton, C. Darby. "Contemporary Problems in Mission." *The Southern Presbyterian Journal* 17 (July 29, 1959): 5.

Gannaway, Bruce. *Mission: Commitment to God's Hopeful Vision*. Louisville, KY: Global Mission Ministry Unit, 1992.

George, Sherron Kay. *Called as Partners in Christ's Service: The Practice of God's Mission*. Louisville, KY: Geneva Press, 2004.

———. "Local-Global Mission: The Cutting Edge." *Missiology: An International Review* 27, no. 2 (April 2000): 187–97.

———. "Presbyterian Participation in God's Mission." In *Congregations in Global Mission: Stepping into God's Future; A Conference Report.* Address given in Houston in October 1999. Louisville, KY: Worldwide Ministries Division, 2001.

———. "The Quest for Images of Missionaries in a 'Post-Missionary' Era." *Missiology: An International Review* 30, no. 1 (January 2002): 51–65.

Gill, Theodore A., Jr. "American Presbyterians in the Global Ecumenical Movement." In *The Diversity of Discipleship,* ed. Milton J. Coalter, John M. Mulder, and Louis B. Weeks, 126–48. Louisville, KY: Westminster/John Knox Press, 1991.

———. "Journey of the WCC and PC(USA): A Drama with a Cast of Thousands." *Journal of Presbyterian History* 84, no. 2 (2006): 139–51.

———. "Michael Kinnamon Welcomes, Reflects on Expanded Participation in Mission Conference," May 2005. World Council of Churches: http://cwme.wcc-coe.org/kinnamon-on-mission-confe.1027.0.htm.

Gilly, William Stephen. *Waldensian Researches during a Second Visit to the Vaudois of Piemont.* London: Rivington Press, 1831.

Glasser, Arthur F., and Donald A. McGavran. *Contemporary Theologies of Mission.* Grand Rapids: Baker Book House, 1983.

Glenny, Misha. *The Fall of Yugoslavia. The Third Balkan War.* London: Penguin Publishing, 1992.

González, Justo L. *The Story of Christianity.* Vol. 2, *The Reformation to the Present Day.* San Francisco: Harper & Row, 1985.

Goodall, Norman, ed. *Missions under the Cross.* London: Edinburgh House, 1953.

Gordon, Andrew. *Our India Mission: A Thirty Years' History of the India Mission of the United Presbyterian Church of North America together with Personal Reminiscences.* Philadelphia: Andrew Gordon, 1886.

Grabill, Joseph L. "Protestant Diplomacy and Arab Nationalism." *American Presbyterians* 64, no. 2 (Summer 1986): 113–24.

Grether, Herbert G. "God's Work in the Land of the Free." *Presbyterian Life,* June 15, 1965.

Guder, Darrell L. "From Mission and Theology to Missional Theology." *The Princeton Seminary Bulletin* 24, no. 1 (2003): 36–54.

———, ed. *Missional Church.* Grand Rapids: Wm. B. Eerdmans Publishing Co., 1998.

———. "Para-Parochial Movements: The Religious Order Revisited." Unpublished manuscript. 1993.

Gutiérrez, Gustavo. *A Theology of Liberation: History, Politics, and Salvation.* New York: Orbis Books, 1973.

Haddad, Mahmoud. "Syrian Muslims' Attitudes toward Foreign Missionaries in the Late Nineteenth and Twentieth Centuries." In *Altruism and Imperialism: Western Cultural and Religious Missions in the Middle East,* edited by Eleanor H. Tejirian and Reeva Spector Simon, 253–74. New York: Middle East Institute, Columbia University, 2002.

Hallie, Philip. *Lest Innocent Blood Be Shed: The Story of Le Chambon and How Goodness Happened There.* New York: Harper & Row, 1979.

Hancock, Ian. *We Are the Romani People.* Hatfield, UK: University of Hertfordshire Press, 2002.

Harper, Charles R. *O Acompanhamento: Ecumenical Action for Human Rights in Latin America, 1970–1990.* Geneva: WCC Publications, 2006.

Heinrich, J. C. *The Psychology of a Suppressed People.* London: George Allen & Unwin, 1937.

Held, Heinz Joachim. "A Remarkable Document: Reflections on the Final Report of the Special Commission on Orthodox Participation in the WCC." *Ecumenical Review* 55, no. 1 (January 2003): 56–66.

Henderson, Robert T. *Enchanted Community*. Eugene, OR: Wipf & Stock, 2006.

Hill, Toya Richards. "Mission Uncertain." *Presbyterians Today* 96 (October 2006): 28–29.

Historical Sketches of the India Missions of the Presbyterian Church in the United States of America, Known as the Lodiana, the Farrukhabad, and the Kolhapur Missions: From the Beginning of the Work, in 1834, to the Time of Its Fiftieth Anniversary, in 1884. Allahabad: Allahabad Mission Press, 1886.

Hocking, William Ernest. *Re-thinking Mission, a Layman's Inquiry after 100 Years*. New York: Harper and Bros., 1932.

Hoedemaker, Bert. *Secularization and Mission: A Theological Essay*. Harrisburg, PA: Trinity Press International, 1998.

Hoekstra, Harvey T. *The World Council of Churches and the Demise of Evangelism*. Wheaton, IL: Tyndale House Publishers, 1979.

Hogg, W. Richey. *New Day Dawning*. New York: World Horizons, 1957.

Hopkins, Paul A. "Presbyterians and the Middle East Conflict." *American Presbyterians* 68 (Fall 1990): 143–65.

Horner, Norman A. "My Pilgrimage in Mission." *International Bulletin of Missionary Research* 14 (January 1990): 35–37.

Hutchison, William R. *Errand to the World: American Protestant Thought and Foreign Missions*. Chicago: University of Chicago Press, 1987.

Huntington, Samuel P. "The Clash of Civilizations." *Foreign Affairs* 72 (Summer 1993): 22–49.

———. "Dead Souls: The Denationalization of the American Elite." *The National Interest* 75 (Spring 2004): 5–19.

Iremonger, F. A. *William Temple, Archbishop of Canterbury: His Life and Letters*. Oxford: Oxford University Press, 1948.

Jacob, Korula. "The Government of India and the Entry of Missionaries." *International Review of Missions* 47, no. 4 (October 1958): 410–14.

Jacques, Edwin E. *The Albanians: An Ethnic History from Prehistoric Times to the Present*. Jefferson, NC: McFarland, 1995.

James, Walter E., with Christy H. Zatkin. *Tumbling Walls: A True Story of Ordinary People Bringing Reconciliation in Extraordinary Ways to an Alienated World*. La Jolla, CA: Diaspora Foundation, 1990.

Jenkins, Philip. *The Next Christendom: The Coming of Global Christianity*. New York: Oxford University Press, 2002.

John, Thomas. *A Strange Accent: The Reflections of a Missionary to the United States*. Louisville, KY: Worldwide Ministries Division, 1996.

Johnson, Todd M., and Sun Young Chung. "Tracking Global Christianity's Statistical Center of Gravity, AD 33–AD 2100." *International Review of Mission* 93, no. 369 (2004): 166–81.

Judt, Tony. *Postwar: A History of Europe since 1945*. London: Penguin Books, 2005.

Kaplan, Robert D. *The Arabists: The Romance of an American Elite*. New York: Free Press, 1993.

Keidel, Levi. *The Black Samson*. The Missing Link, Inc.: http://www.misslink.org/blacksam.html.

Kelley, Arleon L., ed. *A Tapestry of Justice, Service, and Unity: Local Ecumenism in the United States, 1950–2000*. Tacoma, WA: National Association of Ecumenical and Interreligious Staff, 2004.

Kent, John. *William Temple: Church, State, and Society in Britain, 1880–1950*. New York: Cambridge University Press, 1992.

Kerr, Grace. "Report from Tokyo." *Presbyterian Life*, June 19, 1948.

Kinnamon, Michael, and Brian E. Cope, eds. *The Ecumenical Movement: An Anthology of Key Texts and Voices*. Grand Rapids: Wm. B. Erdmans Publishing Co., 1997.

————. *The Vision of the Ecumenical Movement and How It Has Been Impoverished by Its Friends*. St. Louis: Chalice Press, 2003.

Kirkpatrick, Clifton. *Mission in the 1990s: A Strategic Direction in Worldwide Ministry for the Presbyterian Church (U.S.A.)*. Adopted by the 205th General Assembly. Louisville, KY: Worldwide Ministries Division, 1993.

————. "The Unity of the Church in Mission." In *Congregations in Global Mission: New Models for a New Century; A Conference Report*. Address given in St. Louis in November 1997. Louisville, KY: Worldwide Ministries Division, 1998.

Knisely, Stephen. *Faith in Action: Understanding Development Ministries from a Christian Perspective*. Louisville, KY: Worldwide Ministries Division, 2000.

Kobia, Samuel. *Called to the One Hope: A New Ecumenical Epoch*. Geneva: WCC Publications, 2006.

————. "Global Challenges to North American Christians." 23rd Peter Ainslie Lecture. *Call to Unity* 5 (December 2005): 4.

Koll, Karla Ann. "Presbyterians, the United States, and Central America: Background of the 1980s Debate." *Journal of Presbyterian History* 78, no. 1 (Spring 2000): 87–102.

————. "Struggling for Solidarity: Changing Mission Relationships between the PC(USA) and Christian Organizations in Central America during the 1980s." PhD diss., Princeton Theological Seminary, 2003.

————. "Volcanic Revolution of the Home Mission Fields: Response of the United Presbyterian Church in the United States of America to the Revolution in Cuba." *Journal of Presbyterian History* 82, no. 3 (Fall 2004): 149–68.

Korea Mission of the United Presbyterian Church in the USA. "Minutes and Reports of the Annual Meeting."

Küng, Hans, and David Tracy. *Paradigm Change in Theology: A Symposium for the Future*. New York: Crossroad Press, 1989.

Laquer, Walter. *Europe since Hitler: The Rebirth of Europe*. London: Penguin, 1970.

Larson, Lynn S. "Our Guest Served Us as a Missionary." *Mission to the U.S.A. Occasional Bulletin*, February 1978.

Latourette, Kenneth Scott. *A History of Christianity*. Vol. 2, *Reformation to the Present*. San Francisco: Harper, 1975.

————. *A History of the Expansion of Christianity*. Vol. 7, *Advance through the Storm*. New York: Harper & Brothers, 1945.

Les clandestins de Dieu: C.I.M.A.D.E., 1939–1945. Edited by Jeanne Merle d'Aubigné, Violette Mouchon, and Émile C. Fabre. Geneva: Labor et Fides, 1989. "About CIMADE." http://www.cimade.org/.

Literacy and Evangelism International. "About LEI." http://www.literacyevangelism.org/about.

Loehlin, C. H. "Self-Support in Village Churches: A Report of a Survey." *The Indian Standard*, April 1929, 89–93.

Lorimer, Jack [John G.]. *The Presbyterian Experience in Egypt, 1950–2000*. Denver, CO: Outskirts Press, 2007.

————. *Tarikh al-kanisa*. 5 vols. Cairo: Dar al-Thaqafa, 1982–91.

Lossky, Nicolas, et al., eds. *Dictionary of the Ecumenical Movement*. 2nd ed. Geneva: WCC Publications, 2002.

Lucas, E. D., and F. Thakur Das. *The Rural Church in the Punjab: A Study of Social, Economic, Educational and Religious Conditions Prevailing amongst Certain Village Christian Communities in the Sialkot District*. Lahore: Northern India Printing & Publishing Co., 1938.

Lundy, Mary Ann W. "Departure under Fire." In *Re-Membering and Re-Imagining*, edited by Nancy J. Berneking and Pamela Carter Joern, 121–23. Cleveland: Pilgrim Press, 1995.

Mackay, John A. *Ecumenics: The Science of the Church Universal*. Englewood Cliffs, NJ: Prentice-Hall, 1964.

Mateus, Odair Pedroso. *The World Alliance of Reformed Churches and the Modern Ecumenical Movement*. Geneva: WARC, 2005.

May, Melanie A. "The Unity We Share, The Unity We Seek." In *A History of the Ecumenical Movement*, vol. 3, edited by John Briggs, Mercy Amba Oduyoye, and George Tsetsis, 83–102. Geneva: WCC Publications, 2004.

McClelland, Alice J. *Mission to Mexico*. Nashville: Board of World Missions, 1960.

McClure, Marian. "The Cascading Effect in Mission." Sermon preached on October 19, 2005, for mission conference in Atlanta. In "Speaking of Mission: A Collection of Sermons and Speeches." Unpublished manuscript, 22–23.

———. "Creative Changes in International Mission." *The Presbyterian Outlook* 188, no. 27 (August 14, 2006): 11, 13.

———. "Dichotomy Busters." *Congregations in Global Mission: New Models for a New Century; A Conference Report*. Address given in St. Louis in November 1997. Louisville, KY: Worldwide Ministries Division, 1998.

McCulloch, Leonard A. "What Befell Gurdaspur Presbytery?" *Missionary Horizons*, April 1958, 471–72.

McKelvey, J. Morgan. "Integration of Mission and Church." *Missionary Horizons*, April 1958, 473–74.

McKim, Donald K., ed. *Encyclopedia of the Reformed Faith*. Louisville, KY: Westminster/John Knox Press, 1992.

McMullen, Clarence O., John C. B. Webster, and Maqbul Caleb. *The Amritsar Diocese: A Preliminary Survey*. Batala: Christian Institute of Sikh Studies, 1973.

Merwin, Wallace C., and Francis Jones, eds. *Documents of the Three-Self Movement*. New York: National Council of the Churches of Christ, Far Eastern Office, Division of Foreign Missions, 1963.

Meyer, Harding, and Lukas Vischer, eds. *Growth in Agreement: Reports and Agreed Statements of Ecumenical Conversations on a World Level*. New York: Paulist Press, 1984.

Miller, Donald G. *The Nature and Mission of the Church*. Richmond: John Knox Press, 1957.

Mission to the U.S.A. "Our Learnings Come through Encounter." *Mission to the U.S.A. Occasional Bulletin*, Summer 1981, 3.

Moffett, Samuel H. *A History of Christianity in Asia*. Vol. 2. Maryknoll, NY: Orbis Books, 2005.

Moftah, Ragheb, Margit Toth, and Martha Roy. *The Coptic Orthodox Liturgy of St. Basil: With Complete Musical Transcription*. Cairo: American University in Cairo Press, 1998.

Morse, Hermann N. *From Frontier to Frontier: An Interpretation of 150 Years of Presbyterian National Missions*. Philadelphia: Board of Christian Education, Presbyterian Church in the U.S.A., 1952.

Moyer, John C. "Crisis in the Nation." In "More Than They Know: The Presbyterian Mission Effort and the Advancement of Human Liberties." *Church and Society* 78, nos. 2–3 (November/December 1986–January/February 1987): 76–80.

Mutshi, Morrisine Flennaugh. *African Americans in Mission: Serving the Presbyterian Church from 1833 to the Present*. Office of Global Awareness & Involvement, PC(USA), 2000.

Nansen, Fridtjof. *Armenia and the Near East*. New York: Duffield & Co., 1928.

Neely, Alan. *Christian Mission: A Case Study Approach*. Maryknoll, NY: Orbis Books, 1995.

Neill, Stephen. *Colonialism and Christian Missions*. New York: McGraw-Hill, 1966.

———. *A History of Christian Missions*. Revised by Owen Chadwick. 2nd ed. London: Penguin, 1986.

———. *Salvation Tomorrow*. Nashville: Abingdon Press, 1976.

New Wilmington Mission Conference. http://www.nwmcmission.org.

Newbigin, Lesslie. "The Dialogue of Gospel and Culture: Reflections on the Conference on World Mission and Evangelism, Salvador, Bahia, Brazil." *International Bulletin of Missionary Research* 21 (April 1997): 50–52.

———. *Foolishness to the Greeks: The Gospel and Western Culture.* Geneva: WCC Publications, 1986.

———. "Mission to Six Continents." In *A History of the Ecumenical Movement,* vol. 2, edited by Harold E. Fey, 178. Philadelphia: Westminster Press, 1970.

Niebuhr, H. Richard. *Christ and Culture.* New York: Harper & Row, 1951.

Nolde, O. Frederick, ed. *Toward World-wide Christianity.* New York: Harper & Brothers, 1946.

Nurser, John. *For All People and All Nations: The Ecumenical Church and Human Rights.* Washington, DC: Georgetown University Press, 2005.

Padilla, C. Rene. "Mission in the 1990s." *International Bulletin of Missionary Research* 13 (October 1989): 146–50, 152.

Pagura, Federico. "Missionary, Go Home . . . Or Stay." ET by William J. Nottingham. *Christian Century* 90 (April 11, 1973): 420.

Parker, Kenneth Lawrence. "The Development of the United Church of Northern India." *Journal of the Department of History of the Presbyterian Church in the U.S.A.* 17, nos. 3–4 (September–December 1936): 113–204.

Partee, Charles. *Adventure in Africa: The Story of Don McClure from Khartoum to Addis Ababa in Five Decades.* Lanham, MD: University Press of America, 2000.

Paterson, Thomas G., J. Garry Clifford, and Kenneth J. Hagan. *American Foreign Policy: A History since 1900.* Lexington, MA: D. C. Heath, 1983.

Penfield, Janet Harbison. "Presbyterians' Thai Tie." *Presbyterian Life,* January 15, 1971, 24–27.

Phillips, C. H., H. L. Singh, B. N. Pandey, eds. *The Evolution of India and Pakistan 1848 to 1947: Select Documents.* London: Oxford University Press, 1962.

Phipps, William E. *William Sheppard: Congo's African-American Livingstone.* Louisville, KY: Geneva Press, 2002.

Pierson, Paul E. *Transformation: A Unifying Vision of the Church's Mission.* Bangkok: Forum for World Evangelization, 2004.

———. *A Younger Church in Search of Maturity.* San Antonio, TX: Trinity University Press, 1974.

Piper, John F., Jr. *Robert E. Speer: Prophet of the American Church.* Louisville, KY: Geneva Press, 2000.

Potter, Philip, and Thomas Wieser. *Seeking and Serving the Truth: The First Hundred Years of the World Student Christian Federation.* Geneva: WCC Publications, 1997.

Presbyterian Church. "A Manual Prepared for the Use of Missionaries and Missionary Candidates in Connection with the Board of Foreign Missions of the Presbyterian Church." New York. 1840. (Subsequent editions under slightly altered titles appeared in 1862, 1873, 1881, 1882, 1889, 1894, 1904, 1906, 1910, 1912, 1915, etc.)

———. "Mission Yearbook for Prayer and Study" or "Mission Yearbook of Prayer." 1959, 1962, 1967, 1972, 1979, 1980, 1981, 1990, and 2000.

Presbyterian Church, Board of Foreign Missions. "Annual Reports." 1945–58.

Presbyterian Church in America. "Brief History of the PCA." www.pcanet.org/general/history.htm.

Presbyterian Church of the United States. "General Assembly Minutes and Reports." 1944, 1945, 1949, 1950, 1954, 1956, 1957, 1960, 1962, 1964, 1969–78, 1980, and 1982.

Presbyterian Church (U.S.A.). "The Annual Performance Report of Witnessing Ministries of Christ." July 1, 1997–June 30, 1998.

———. "The Annual Performance Report of Witnessing Ministries of Christ." July 1, 2000, to June 30, 2001.

Presbyterian Church (USA), Board of Foreign Mission. "Fraternal Workers to the U.S.A.," Louisville, KY: PC(USA), MUSA, 1958.

Presbyterian Church (U.S.A.), Central Receiving Agency. *Comparative Statistics 2005*, table 12. Louisville, KY: PC(USA), 2005.

———. *The Constitution of the Presbyterian Church (U.S.A.).* Part 1, *Book of Confessions.* Louisville, KY: Office of the General Assembly, 1996.

———. *The Constitution of the Presbyterian Church (U.S.A.).* Part 2, *Book of Order,* chap. 3, "The Church and Its Mission" and *Worship Directory;* chap. 7, "Worship and the Ministry of the Church in the World." Louisville, KY: Office of the General Assembly, 2002.

———. *Gathering for God's Future: Witness, Discipleship, Community; A Renewed Call to Worldwide Mission.* Adopted by the 215th General Assembly. Louisville, KY: Worldwide Ministries Division, 2003.

———. "General Assembly Minutes and Reports." 1939, 1944–47, 1951, 1953, 1956, 1957, 1959, 1963, 1965, 1974, 1983, 1985–90, 1992, 1993, 1994, 1998, 2003, and 2004.

———, Global Mission Unit. "Annual Reports." 1988–92.

———. "Presbyterians Do Mission in Partnership." Policy Statement adopted by the 215th General Assembly. Louisville, KY: Worldwide Ministries Division, 2003.

———. *Turn to the Living God: A Call to Evangelism in Jesus Christ's Way.* Adopted by the 203rd General Assembly. Louisville, KY: Office of the General Assembly, 1991.

———. *PC(USA) WORLDWIDE Newsletter,* August 14, 2006. http://www.pcusa .org/wmd/pdf/august06 newsletter.pdf.

———, World Ministries Division. "Annual Reports." 1993–2004.

———. "Worldwide: Involvement of the Presbyterian Church (U.S.A.) in Countries around the World." http://www.pcusa.org/worldwide.

Presbyterian Historical Society. "Benevolence Report." 1951.

———. "A Manual for the Foreign Missions Conference." Philadelphia, 1948.

Presbyterian Mission of Brazil. "July 1989 Minutes."

Raiser, Konrad. "Eugene Carson Blake: Acting on the Gift of Unity for Christ's Church," *Journal of Presbyterian History* 76, no. 4 (1998): 251–316.

———. *For a Culture of Life: Transforming Globalization and Violence.* Geneva: WCC Publications, 2002.

Reifsnyder, Richard W. "Managing the Mission: Church Restructuring in the Twentieth Century." In *The Organizational Revolution: Presbyterians and American Denominationalism,* edited by Milton J. Coalter, John M. Mulder, and Louis B. Weeks, 55–95. Louisville, KY: Westminster/John Knox Press, 1992.

Rhodes, Harry A., ed. *History of the Korea Mission, Presbyterian Church U.S.A., 1884–1934.* 2 vols. Seoul: Chosen Mission Presbyterian Church U.S.A., 1934–64.

Rieger, Joerg. *God and the Excluded: Visions and Blindspots in Contemporary Theology.* Minneapolis: Fortress Press, 2001.

Roach, Patricia M. "From San Antonio to Manila." *Monday Morning* 55 (January 22, 1990): 4–5.

Robert, Dana L., ed. *Gospel Bearers, Gender Barriers: Missionary Women in the Twentieth Century.* Maryknoll, NY: Orbis Books, 2002.

Roche, Barbara Anne. "Initiating and Sustaining Ecumenical Ministries: A Study of the Ministry of Margaret Flory, 1951–1980." DMin diss., San Francisco Theological Seminary, 1983.

Rouse, Ruth, and Stephen Charles Neill, eds. *A History of the Ecumenical Movement.* vol. 1, *1517–1948.* Philadelphia: Westminster Press, 1954.

Rycroft, W. Stanley. *The Ecumenical Witness of the United Presbyterian Church in the U.S.A.* Philadelphia: Published for COEMAR by the Board of Christian Education of the United Presbyterian Church in the U.S.A., 1968.

————. *Religion and Faith in Latin America*. Philadelphia: Westminster Press, 1958.

Rycroft, W. Stanley, and Myrtle M. Clemmer. *A Factual Study of Asia*. New York: Commission on Ecumenical Mission and Relations, 1963.

Sabella, Bernard. "The Emigration of Christian Arabs: Dimensions and Causes of the Problem." In *Christian Communities in the Arab Middle East: The Challenge of the Future*, edited by Andrea Pacini, 127–54. Oxford: Clarendon Press, 1998.

Samuel, Vinay, and Christ Sugden. *The Church in Response to Human Need*. Grand Rapids: Wm. B. Eerdmans Publishing Co., 1987.

Sanneh, Lamin. "Christian Missions and the Western Guilt Complex." *Christian Century* 104, no. 11 (April 6, 1987): 330–34.

————. *Whose Religion Is Christianity? The Gospel beyond the West*. Grand Rapids: Wm. B. Eerdmans Publishing Co., 2003.

Santa Ana, Julio de, ed. *Religions Today: The Challenge to the Ecumenical Movement*. Geneva: WCC Publications, 2005.

Say Pa, Anna May. *Dancing in Winter: Reflections of a Missionary to the United States*. Louisville, KY: Worldwide Ministries Division, PC(USA), 2000.

Scherer, James A. *Gospel, Church, and Kingdom: Comparative Studies in World Mission Theology*. Minneapolis: Augsburg Publishing House, 1987.

Scott, Kenneth M. *Around the World in Eighty Years*. Franklin, TN: Providence House Publishers, 1998.

Seel, Roberto [Robert] E. *Breve historia de Presbiterianos* [Brief History of Presbyterians]. Monterey, CA: published privately, 1994.

————. "Venezuelan Sojourn." Unpublished manuscript, 1995.

Sharkey, Heather J. "Arabic Antimissionary Treatises: Muslim Responses to Christian Evangelism in the Modern Middle East." *International Bulletin of Missionary Research* 28, no. 3 (July 2004): 98–104.

————. "Empire and Muslim Conversion: Historical Reflections on Christian Missions in Egypt." *Islam and Christian-Muslim Relations* 16, no. 1 (January 2005): 43–60.

————. "Missionary Legacies: Muslim-Christian Encounters in Egypt and the Sudan during the Colonial and Postcolonial Periods." In *Muslim-Christian Encounters in Africa*, edited by Benjamin F. Soares, 57–88. Leiden and Boston: Brill, 2006.

————. "Muslim Apostasy, Christian Conversion and Religious Freedom in Egypt: A Study of American Missionaries, Western Imperialism, and Human Rights Agendas." In *Proselytization Revisited: Rights Talk, Free Markets and Culture Wars*, edited by Rosalind I. J. Hackett. London: Equinox, forthcoming 2008.

Shtulman, David. "The Presbyterian Divestment Train: Why Does the National Church Continue to Support Economic Sanctions Against Israel?" *Pittsburgh Post-Gazette*, March 30, 2005, A-17.

Sialkot Mission of the United Presbyterian Church in the United States of America. "Minutes of the 101st Annual Meeting (104th Year)," including minutes to date of the Executive Committee for 1958–59. Sialkot, April 21–25, 1959.

Sinclair, John H. *La historia general de la iglesia Cristiana en la América Latina* [The General History of the Christian Church in Latin America]. Vol. 7, *Colombia y Venezuela*. Salamanca, Spain: CEHILA-Ediciones Sígueme, 1981.

Sjollema, Baldwin. "Combating Racism: A Chapter in Ecumenical History." *Ecumenical Review* 56, no. 4 (October 2004): 470–79.

Skreslet, Stanley H. "The American Presbyterian Mission in Egypt: Significant Factors in Its Establishment." *American Presbyterians* 64, no. 2 (Summer 1986): 83–95.

————. "The Empty Basket of Presbyterian Mission: Limits and Possibilities of Partnership." *International Bulletin of Missionary Research* 19, no. 3 (July 1995): 98–103.

————. "Networking, Civil Society, and the NGO: A New Model for Ecumenical Mission." *Missiology* 25, no. 3 (July 1997): 307–19.

————. *Usul al-lugha al-yunaniyya lil-ʿahd al jadid*. Cairo: Bible Society of Egypt, 1995.

Smith, Alexa. "Meetings Are Planned to Strengthen Ties between Church and Other Mission Groups." *Presbyterian News Service.* March 28, 1995.

Smith, John Coventry. *From Colonialism to World Community: The Church's Pilgrimage.* Philadelphia: Geneva Press, 1982.

Smylie, James H., Dean K. Thompson, and Cary Patrick. *Go, Therefore: 150 Years of Presbyterians in Global Mission.* Atlanta: General Assembly Mission Board, 1987.

Speer, Robert E. "Laying and Challenging the Foundations of Presbyterian Work in India: Three Letters." *Journal of Presbyterian History* 62, no. 3 (Fall 1984): 266–81.

Speer, Robert E., and Russell Carter. *Report on India and Persia of the Deputation Sent by the Board of Foreign Missions of the Presbyterian Church in the U.S.A. to Visit These Fields in 1921–22.* New York: Board of Foreign Missions of the Presbyterian Church in the U.S.A., 1922.

Stephens, Prescot. *The Waldensian Story: A Study in Faith, Intolerance and Survival.* Lewes, UK: Book Guild, 1998.

Stewart, Robert. *Life and Work in India: An Account of the Conditions, Methods, Difficulties, Future Prospects and Reflex Influence of Missionary Labor in India, Especially in the Punjab Mission of the United Presbyterian Church of North America.* New ed. Philadelphia: Pearl Publishing Co., 1899.

Stock, Frederick and Margaret. *People Movements in the Punjab, with Special Reference to the United Presbyterian Church.* Pasadena, CA: William Carey Library, 1975.

Stockton, Ronald R. "The Presbyterian Divestiture Vote and the Jewish Response." *Middle East Policy* 12, no. 4 (2005): 98–117.

———. "Presbyterians, Jews and Divestment: The Church Steps Back." *Middle East Policy* 13, no. 4 (2006): 102–24.

Stoner, Jean S., ed. *Voices from Korea, U.S.A., and Brazil: The Reformed Faith and Global Economy.* Louisville, KY: Worldwide Ministries Division, PC(USA), 2001.

Stott, John R. W. "The Biblical Basis of Evangelism." In *Mission Trends, no. 2, Evangelization,* edited by Gerald H. Anderson and Thomas F. Stransky, 423. New York: Paulist Press, 1975.

Stransky, Thomas F. "SODEPAX." In *Dictionary of the Ecumenical Movement,* edited by Nicolas Lossky et al., 1055–56. 2nd ed. Geneva: WCC Publications, 2002.

Street, T. Watson. *The Church and the Churches.* Richmond: Covenant Life Curriculum, 1965.

———. *On the Growing Edge of the Church.* Richmond: John Knox Press, 1965.

Sunquist, Scott W. "Interviews with Retired Missionaries." New Wilmington, PA: July 25 and 27, 2005.

Sunquist, Scott W., and Caroline N. Becker. "Interviews with Retired Missionaries." Duarte, CA: March 2–4, 2006. Montreat, NC: March 7, 2006.

Thomas, M. M., and Paul Abrecht, eds. *World Conference on Church and Society: Christians in the Technical and Social Revolutions of Our Time.* Geneva: WCC Publications, 1967.

Thomas, Margaret O., ed. *Being Ecumenical: A Compendium on Ecumenical and Interfaith Relations: Actions of the General Assembly of the Presbyterian Church (U.S.A.).* Louisville, KY: Worldwide Ministries Division, 1994.

Thorogood, Bernard. *Gales of Change: Responding to a Shifting Missionary Context.* Geneva: WCC Publications, 1994.

Tijerina, Saul. "National Presbyterian Church of Mexico: Presbyterian Border Ministry." http://www.binationalministry.org/INPMHistory.htm.

Ting, K. H. *No Longer Strangers.* Maryknoll, NY: Orbis Books, 1982.

Tooley, Mark D. "Lord, Have Mercy: The U.S. Delegation to the World Council of Churches." *Weekly Standard,* March 1, 2006. http://www.weeklystandard.com/content/public/articles/000/000/011/902soluo.asp.

Toulouse, Mark. *The Transformation of John Foster Dulles.* Macon, GA: Mercer University Press, 1985.

Tourn, Giorgio. The *Waldensians: The First 800 Years (1174–1974)*. Translated by Camillo P. Merlino. Edited by Charles W. Arbuthnot. Turin: Claudiana; New York: American Waldensian Aid Society, 1980.

———. *You Are My Witnesses: The Waldensians across 800 Years*. With the collaboration of Giorgio Bouchard, Roger Geymonat, and Giorgio Spini. Edited by Frank G. Gibson Jr. Turin: Claudiana Editrice, 1989.

Tsetsis, George. "The Significance of Regional Ecumenism." In A *History of the Ecumenical Movement*, vol. 3, edited by John Briggs, Mercy Amba Oduyoye, and George Tsetsis, 461–68. Geneva: WCC Publications, 2004.

Ufford-Chase, Rick. "Beyond Business as Usual." *Presbyterians Today*, March 2006, 13–15.

United Church of Christ in the Philippines. *Partnership in Mission*. 1989.

United Presbyterian Church of North America. "General Assembly Minutes and Reports." 1930, 1939, 1944, 1945, 1947, 1950, 1955, 1956, and 1957.

———, Women's General Missionary Society. "Annual Reports." 1945–55.

United Presbyterian Church in the United States of America. *A Century for Christ in India and Pakistan, 1855–1955*. Lahore: The United Presbyterian Church in the U.S.A., 1955.

———. *Introductory Information on the Commission on Ecumenical Mission and Relations*. New York: The United Presbyterian Church in the U.S.A., 1958.

———. "General Assembly Minutes and Reports." 1958, 1959, 1965, 1967, 1969, 1970, and 1972–84.

———. "Program Agency Annual Reports." 1972–82.

———. *Report of Survey Evaluation of Twenty-Eight Schools and Colleges Related to the United Church of Northern India August 9–November 22, 1962*. New York: The United Presbyterian Church in the U.S.A., 1963.

United Presbyterian Church in the United States of America, Commission on Ecumenical Mission and Relations. *An Advisory Study, 1961–1966: A Report on the Study Process*. New York: COEMAR of The United Presbyterian Church in the U.S.A., 1966.

———. *Conversations with Roman Catholics on the Nature of the Church and on Ecumenism*. Resources for Ecumenical Encounter, no. 1. New York: COEMAR of The United Presbyterian Church in the U.S.A., 1965.

———. *Sharing Gifts of Grace*. Fourth Annual Report. New York: COEMAR, 1962.

United Presbyterian Church in the United States of America, Commission on Ecumenical Mission and Relations, Advisory Study Committee. *An Advisory Study*. New York: COEMAR, 1962.

United Presbyterian Church in the United States of America, Commission on Ecumenical Mission and Relations. "Annual Reports." 1958–72.

United Presbyterian Church of the United States of America. The India Council (Punjab and North India Synods and Kolhapur Church Council of the United Church of Northern India and the Commission on Ecumenical Mission and Relations of the UPCUSA). "Fiftieth Annual Meeting." "Lowriston," Dehra Dun, U.P., India, November 28 to December 4, 1964.

United Presbyterian Mission. *A Century for Christ in India and Pakistan, 1855–1955*. Lahore, Pakistan: United Presbyterian Church, 1955.

Vandervelde, George. "Evangelical Ecumenical Concerns." In *Dictionary of the Ecumenical Movement*, edited by Nicolas Lossky et al., 437–40. 2nd ed. Geneva: WCC Publications, 2002.

Van Leeuwen, A. T. *Christianity in World History*. London: Edinburgh House, 1964.

Vardy, Stephen Bela. *The Hungarian Americans*. Boston: Twayne Publishers, 1985.

Verkuyl, Johannes. *Contemporary Missiology: An Introduction*. Translated by Dale Cooper. Grand Rapids: Wm. B. Eerdmans Publishing Co., 1978.

Vinay, Tullio. *Love Never Fails: The Agape Story*. Turin: Claudiana, 1996.

Virtue, David. *A Vision of Hope: The Story of Samuel Habib.* Oxford: Regnum Books, 1996.

Visser 't Hooft, Willem A. *Has the Ecumenical Movement a Future?* Atlanta: John Knox Press, 1974.

———. *Memoirs.* Philadelphia: Westminster Press, 1973.

Waliggo, John. "Inculturation." In *Dictionary of the Ecumenical Movement,* edited by Nicolas Lossky et al., 571–72. 2nd ed. Geneva: WCC Publications, 2002.

Walker, Martin. *The Cold War.* New York: Henry Holt, 1993.

Wallison, Ethan. "Israel Divestment Blasted: Presbyterian Stance Draws Bipartisan Fire." *Roll Call,* September 20, 2004.

Walls, Andrew F. *The Missionary Movement in Christian History: Studies in the Transmission of Faith.* Maryknoll, NY: Orbis Books, 1996.

Webb, Pauline, ed. *A Long Struggle: The Involvement of the World Council of Churches in South Africa.* Geneva: WCC Publications, 1994.

Weber, Hans-Ruedi. *A Laboratory for Ecumenical Life: The Story of Bossey, 1946–1996.* Geneva: WCC Publications, 1996.

Webster, John C. B., ed. "American Presbyterians in India/Pakistan: 150 Years." *Journal of Presbyterian History* 62, no. 3 (Fall 1984): 189–282.

———. "American Presbyterian Missionaries and Nationalist Politics in the Punjab, 1919–1935." *Indian Church History Review* 34, no. 1 (June 2000): 51–73.

———. *The Christian Community and Change in Nineteenth-Century North India.* Delhi: Macmillan, 1976.

———. *Religion and Dalit Liberation: An Examination of Perspectives.* 2nd ed. New Delhi: Manohar, 2002.

———. *A Social History of Christianity: North-west India since 1800.* New Delhi and Odford: Oxford University Press, 2007.

———. "Whither Dalit Theology: An Historian's Assessment." In *Dalit Issue in Today's Theological Debate,* ed. James Massey and S. Lourduswamy, 14–38. New Delhi: Centre for Dalit/Subaltern Studies [Theology], 2003.

Weir, Ben and Carol, with Dennis Benson. *Hostage Bound, Hostage Free.* Philadelphia: Westminster Press, 1987.

Weir, John Barr. "Presbyterian Church and Mission Cooperation Studied Historically." PhD diss., University of Chicago, 1934.

Weitzman, Marc. "Intellectuels Américains." *Le Monde 2,* no. 157 (February 17, 2007): 18–25.

West, Charles C. *Communism and the Theologians: Study of an Encounter.* Philadelphia: Westminster Press, 1958.

Wharton, Ethel Taylor. *Led in Triumph.* Nashville: Board of World Missions, PCUS, 1952.

Wheeler, W. Reginald, ed. *The Crisis Decade: A History of the Foreign Missionary Work of the Presbyterian Church, 1937–1947.* New York: Foreign Missions and Overseas Interchurch Service, 1950.

Wherry, E. Morris. *Our Missions in India, 1834–1924.* Boston: Stratford Co., 1926.

White, Ronald C., Jr. "Social Witness and Evangelism: Complementary or Competing Priorities?" In *How Shall We Witness?* edited by Milton J. Coalter and Virgil Cruz, 136–61. Louisville, KY: Westminster John Knox Press, 1995.

White, Vera. *Hand in Hand: Doing Evangelism and Doing Justice.* Louisville, KY: Presbyterian Peacemaking Program, 1991.

Wickeri, Philip L. *Partnership, Solidarity, and Friendship: Transforming Structures in Mission.* A Study Paper for the Presbyterian Church (U.S.A.). Louisville, KY: Worldwide Ministries Division, 2003.

Williamson, C. J., ed. *March On! With the United Presbyterian Church of North America.* Pittsburgh: Board of Administration, United Presbyterian Church, 1933.

Winter, Ralph D. "The Two Structures of God's Redemptive Mission." In *Perspectives on the World Christian Movement*, ed. Ralph D. Winter and Steven C. Hawthorne, 220–29. 3rd ed. Pasadena, CA: William Carey Library Publishers, 1999.

Wiser, W. H. "The Rural Church in the United Provinces." *United Church Review* (October 1938): 234–39.

———. "A Study in Potential Giving." *The Indian Standard*, April 1929, 159–66.

Witherspoon Society. Letter from Missionary Donna Laubach Moros Regarding the Crisis in the Nation Program. October 4, 2005. http://www.witherspoonsociety .org/2005/oct 2005.htm.

Witte, John, Jr., and Michael Bourdeaux. *Proselytism and Orthodoxy in Russia: The New War for Souls*. Maryknoll, NY: Orbis Books, 1999.

World Council of Churches. *Annual Report, 2004*. Geneva: WCC Publications, 2005.

———. *Common Witness: A Study Document of the Joint Working Group of the Roman Catholic Church and the World Council of Churches*. Geneva: WCC Publications, 1982.

———. *From Harare to Porto Alegre, 1998–2006*. Geneva: WCC Publications, 2005.

———. *A Handbook of Churches and Councils: Profiles of Ecumenical Relationships*. Geneva: WCC Publications, 2006.

———. *Mission and Evangelism: An Ecumenical Affirmation*. Geneva: WCC Publications, 1981.

———. *Reflections on Ecumenism in the 21st Century*. Geneva: WCC Publications, 2004.

Worldwide Ministries Division and Presbyterian Historical Society of the PC (USA). "Overseas Mission History Project: Papers from a Conference Held May 10–12, 1999."

Woodward, Kenneth L. "The Changing Face of the Church." *Newsweek*, April 16, 2001.

Yao, Kevin Xiyi. *The Fundamentalist Movement among Protestant Missionaries in China, 1920–1937*. Lanham, MD: University Press of America, 2003.

Yates, Timothy. *Christian Mission in the Twentieth Century*. Cambridge: Cambridge University Press, 1994.

Zaki, Emil. *Al-kanisa al-injiliyya al-mashikhiyya bi-misr: Mi'at wa khamsun sana*. Cairo: Dar al-Thaqafa, 2005.

Zernov, Nicholas. "The Eastern Churches and the Ecumenical Movement in the Twentieth Century." In *A History of the Ecumenical Movement*, vol. 1, edited by Ruth Rouse and Stephen Charles Neill, 645–76. Philadelphia: Westminster Press, 1954.

List of Contributors

William B. Anderson and his wife, Lois Anderson, served forty-nine years as Presbyterian missionaries in Africa. Their first and largest ministry was in Sudan, training aspiring Sudanese pastors, Episcopal and Presbyterian. Anderson then spent twelve years in Kenya, working mostly at the St. Paul's United Theological College, doing theological training. In 1972–73 he was offered a post at Makerere University, teaching and researching African church history, particularly that of East Africa. Bill was commissioned to write a history of Christianity in East Africa, which he researched and wrote in 1973 (published in 1975). In 1973 they returned to Sudan, where they started two Bible schools, and he helped to organize Nile Theological College, launched in 1991. In their last years, Bill joined with a British colleague, Andrew Wheeler, and a German—Dr. Roland Werner—to write *Day of Devastation, Day of Contentment,* a history of the Sudanese Church across two thousand years. This was completed and launched in June 2000, and then he and Lois returned to the United States to retire.

Frank Arnold is a former metallurgical engineer turned pastor who spent thirty-three years, along with his wife, Hope, and their five children, serving the PCUS and PC(USA) in Brazil. His work was mainly in the area of new church development, community development, and theological education. During that period Frank for two years was Area Secretary for Latin America and the Caribbean for the Division of International Mission of the former PCUS. He helped to start our partner church's new seminary in the Northeast of Brazil and was its first dean. Upon retirement in 1996, the Arnolds went to Atlanta where Frank is involved as a volunteer helping start immigrant churches in the tri-presbytery area.

Caroline N. Becker is a 2006 graduate of Pittsburgh Theological Seminary and now resides in New York City with her husband. Before enrolling in seminary, she served as a volunteer English teacher in Shanxi, China, through a partnership between the PC(USA) and the Amity Foundation in China. Her undergraduate studies were done at the University of Pennsylvania, where she majored in East Asian studies. Much of her childhood was spent as a missionary kid in the Republic of Singapore (1987–95).

T. Donald Black is a graduate of Grove City College, Pittsburgh-Xenia Seminary, and Conwell School of Theology (Temple University). Ordained in the United Presbyterian Church of North America, he has served pastorates in Oklahoma City, Philadelphia, and London. His career in church administration includes Executive Secretary, Board of Foreign Missions (UPCNA); General Secretary, Commission on Ecumenical Mission and Relations (UPCUSA); Associate General Director, Program Agency (UPCUSA); Executive Director, General Assembly Council of PC(USA), and interim staff positions with the National Council of Churches and the World Council of Churches. He is the author of *Merging Mission and Unity* (Geneva Press, 1986). He and Fran have three sons, seven grandchildren, five great-grandchildren.

G. Thompson Brown was born in China of missionary parents. He is a graduate of Davidson College, served in the U.S. Army during World War II, and then graduated with a PhD from Union Seminary (Richmond). He was a pastor in Gastonia, North Carolina, and then served twenty years with his wife, Mardia, in Korea, where he was President of the Ho Nam Theological Seminary, Kwangju, Korea. Upon his return to the States, he served as Asia Secretary for the Board of World Missions, was later elected to the position of Director of Division of International Mission, and then selected for the Faculty of Columbia Theological Seminary until retirement in 1989. Brown has five children and is author of *Face to Face* (Geneva Press), *Christianity in the People's Republic of China* (Westminster Press), and *Earthen Vessels and Transcendent Power* (Orbis Books).

David Dawson is a graduate of Westminster College and Pittsburgh Theological Seminary. He is the Executive Presbyter of Shenango Presbytery in western Pennsylvania. He has a master's degree in missiology from Yale Divinity School and does research and writing on mission administration and funding.

Sherron George served as a Presbyterian mission coworker in Brazil from 1972 to 1995, teaching in seminaries of two Presbyterian denominations. She served as Associate Professor of Evangelism and Mission at Austin Presbyterian Theological Seminary from 1996 to 2001. At present she is Theological Education Consultant and Regional Liaison for South America. Sherron's publication *Called as Partners in Christ's Service: The Practice of God's Mission* (Geneva Press, 2004) has recently been translated into both Spanish and Portuguese. Other English publications include "From Missionary to Missiologist at the Margins: Three Decades of Transforming Mission," in *Teaching Mission in a Global Context* (Geneva Press, 2001) and *Meeting Your Neighbor: Multiculturalism in Luke and Acts* (PC(USA), 2000—PDS 72305-00-001). She is an ordained minister of the PC(USA) and resides in Curitiba in south Brazil.

Theodore A. Gill Jr. is a Presbyterian minister serving as senior editor of the World Council of Churches in Geneva, Switzerland, and managing editor of the WCC's quarterly journal *The Ecumenical Review*. A former member of the ecumenical relations staff in the Office of the General Assembly, he has also edited such periodicals of the Presbyterian Church (U.S.A.) as *Monday Morning, Reformed Liturgy and Music,* and *Call to Worship.* He is a graduate of the University of Wisconsin–Madison, Princeton Seminary, and Oxford University, and he has pursued additional graduate courses in education, ecumenics, and modern history. He has reported on interchurch conferences and assemblies for *Presbyterian Survey, Presbyterian Outlook,* and the news services of the PC(USA) and the WCC.

Duncan Hanson since 2002 has been the area supervisor for Europe, the Middle East, and South Asia for the Reformed Church in America. For many years before beginning work with the RCA, Hanson served the Presbyterian Church (U.S.A.) as area coordinator for Europe and Central Asia. Hanson is a member of the Presbytery of San Jose and served as pastor in three congregations in Lakeview, Oregon; Seattle, Washington; and Aptos, California. Hanson is best known in the PC(USA) mission community for helping Presbyterian mission respond to the challenges of the new post–Cold War era in Central and East Europe and Russia as well as in the five Central Asian republics.

Patricia Lloyd-Sidle, a mission co-worker for the Presbyterian Church (U.S.A.), serves as the Regional Liaison for the Caribbean, with special attention to Cuba and the Caribbean and North American Council for Mission (CANACOM). She previously served as a coworker in Uruguay. From 1993 to 2001, Tricia was the coordinator of the Global Awareness and Involvement unit of the Worldwide Ministries Division. In this capacity she was the principal organizer of the series of global mission conferences held in 1997, 1999, and 2001. Tricia holds a bachelor of arts degree from Maryville College in Maryville, Tennessee, and a master of divinity degree from Union Theological Seminary in New York.

Marian McClure was the Director of the Worldwide Ministries Division of the PC(USA)'s General Assembly Council from 1997 to 2006, during which time the General Assembly vision paper *Gathering for God's Future* was produced under her leadership. Marian was also an adviser to the Planning Commission of Church World Service, and a member of the WCC's Commission on World Mission and Evangelism. She represented the PC(USA) at two worldwide meetings of the World Alliance of Reformed Churches and at one General Assembly of the World Council of Churches. Marian earned a PhD in political science at Harvard University, focusing on the role of the Catholic Church in bringing more participation and empowerment to Haitian peasants during the Duvalier dictatorship in Haiti. She then served for five years as a program officer for the Ford Foundation in its Mexico City office. She graduated from Louisville Presbyterian Seminary in 1995 and was ordained to the Ministry of Word and Sacrament in 1996.

Stanley H. Skreslet is F. S. Royster Professor of Christian Mission at Union Theological Seminary (Richmond) and Presbyterian School of Christian Education. Skreslet's interests include the history and theology of Christian mission, Islam, and Middle Eastern Orthodox Christianity. An ordained Presbyterian minister, he was a PC(USA) mission coworker, teaching at the Evangelical Theological Seminary in Cairo, Egypt, for ten years. He is the author of *Picturing Christian Mission: New Testament Images of Disciples in Mission* (Eerdmans, 2006) and of an introduction to New Testament Greek, written in Arabic and published by the Bible Society. Skreslet is a graduate of Lewis and Clark College and of Union Theological Seminary (Richmond); his PhD is from Yale University.

Scott W. Sunquist is the W. Don McClure Associate Professor of World Mission and Evangelism at Pittsburgh Theological Seminary. Before teaching at Pittsburgh, Sunquist and his wife, Nancy, were mission coworkers in Singapore, where he taught Asian Church History and ecumenics at Trinity Theological College in Singapore. His theological studies were done at Gordon-Conwell Theological Seminary and at Princeton Theological Seminary. Sunquist is the coauthor, with Dale Irvin, of *History of the World Christian Movement,* volumes 1 and 2 (Orbis Books), and he is the editor of *A Dictionary of Asian Christianity* (Eerdmans).

John C. B. Webster received degrees from Amherst College (BA), Union Theological Seminary (New York, BD), Lucknow University (MA), and the University of Pennsylvania (PhD). He went to India in 1960 to study at Lucknow University, and from 1963 to 1976 he taught history at Baring Union Christian College, Batala, Punjab. From 1971 to 1976 he was also Director of the Christian Institute of Sikh Studies and taught history at Guru Nanak University. He then became Assistant Professor of History of Christianity at United Theological College, Bangalore, 1977–81. Upon returning to the United States in 1981, he was Visiting Professor of Church History and World Mission at Pittsburgh Theological Seminary (1981–83), he served as Pastor of Crossroads Presbyterian Church in Waterford, Connecticut (1984–94) and since 1985 has taught at Union Theological Seminary in New York City as an occasional part-time Lecturer in Ecumenics. From 1994 until his retirement in July 2001, he was a Diaconal Worker of the Worldwide Ministries Division of the PC(USA). He was editor of the *Dalit International Newsletter* from its inception in 1996 to its close in 2006 and was Moderator of the Presbytery of Southern New England in 2004–5. He has published widely in the field of Indian history and especially in the history of Christianity in India. Among his many publications in the areas of Indian Christian history and Dalit Christian issues are *The Dalit Christians: A History* (ISPCK, 1992), *The Pastor to Dalits* (ISPCK, 1995), and *Studying History* (Macmillan, 1997).

Robert J. Weingartner is executive director of the Outreach Foundation, a validated mission support group of the PC(USA). He pastored congregations in Indiana and Ohio and has served on the PC(USA)'s General Assembly Council and Worldwide Ministries Division committee. He has also served on the boards of Pittsburgh Theological Seminary, the New Wilmington Missionary Conference, and Presbyterians for Renewal.

Index